70°N
40°E
50°E
60°E
70°E
60°N
80°E
N
RUSSIA
Lake Ladoga
St. Petersburg
Volga R.
Moscow
Volga R.
Astana
50°N
KAZAKHSTAN
Minsk
BELARUS
Kiev
Kharkov
Dnieper R.
Don R.
UKRAINE
Dnepropetrovsk
Donetsk
Aral Sea
UZBEKISTAN
40°N
MOLDOVA
Chisinau
Odessa
Caspian Sea
TURKMENISTAN
Ashgabat
Bucharest
GEORGIA
Tbilisi
Baku
Black Sea
AZERBAIJAN
ARMENIA
Yerevan
BULGARIA
AZER.
Istanbul
Ankara
Tehran
IRAN
TURKEY
SYRIA
Nicosia
Baghdad
CYPRUS
Beirut
IRAQ
30°N
LEBANON
Damascus

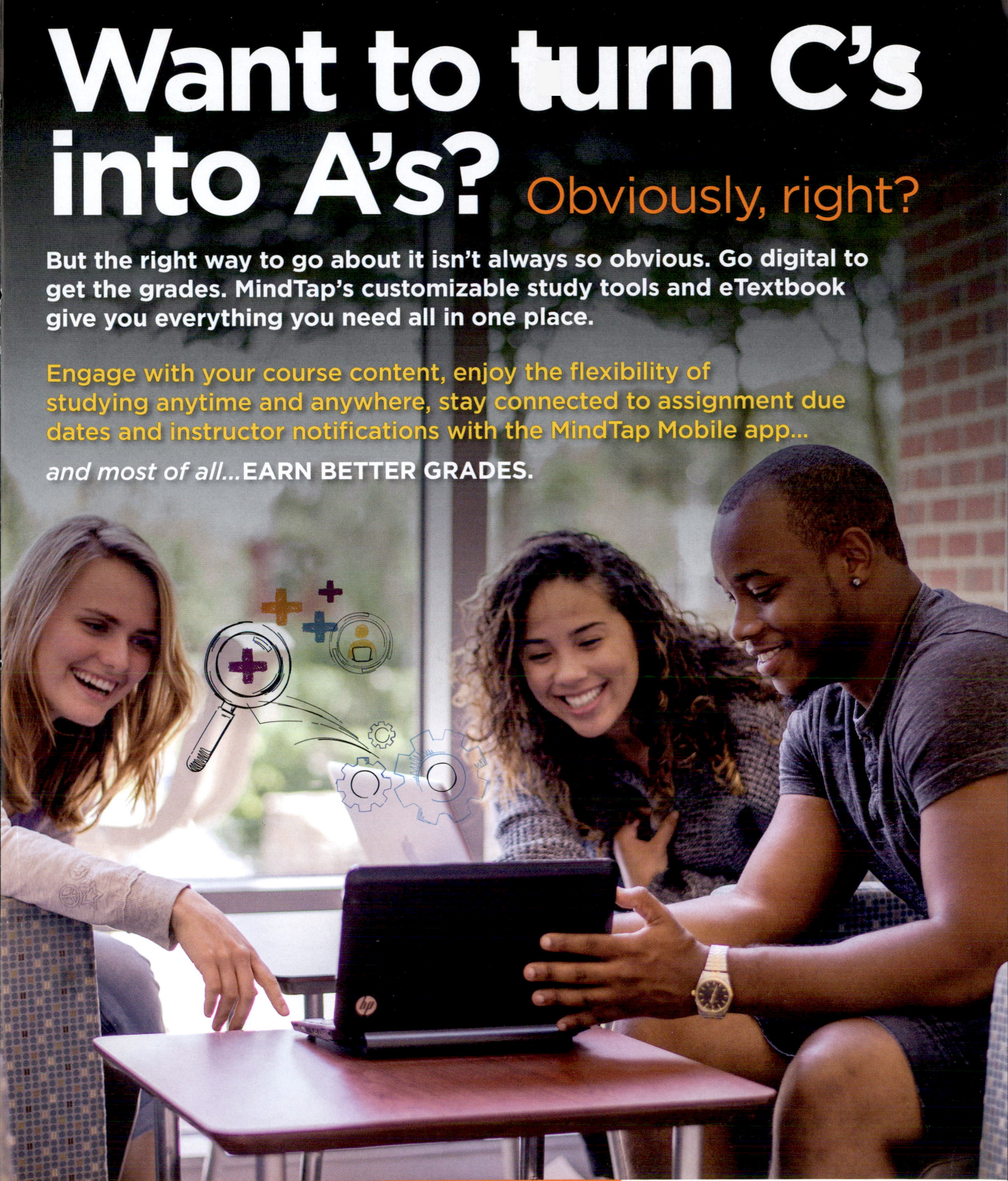
Want to turn C's into A's? Obviously, right?
But the right way to go about it isn't always so obvious. Go digital to get the grades. MindTap's customizable study tools and eTextbook give you everything you need all in one place.
Engage with your course content, enjoy the flexibility of studying anytime and anywhere, stay connected to assignment due dates and instructor notifications with the MindTap Mobile app...
and most of all...EARN BETTER GRADES.

WESTERN CIVILIZATION

TENTH EDITION

WESTERN CIVILIZATION

VOLUME B: 1300–1815

Jackson J. Spielvogel

The Pennsylvania State University

CENGAGE Learning®

Australia • Brazil • Mexico • Singapore • United Kingdom • United States

CENGAGE Learning®

Western Civilization, Tenth Edition, Volume B: 1300–1815
Jackson J. Spielvogel

Product Director: Paul Banks
Product Manager: Scott Greenan
Senior Content Developer: Margaret Beasley
Associate Content Developer: Andrew Newton
Product Assistant: Emma Guiton
Media Developer: Kate McLean
Senior Marketing Manager: Valerie Hartman
Senior Content Project Manager: Carol Newman
Senior Art Director: Cate Rickard Barr
Manufacturing Planner: Fola Orekoya
IP Analyst: Betsy Hathaway
IP Project Manager: Alex Ricciardi
Production Service/Compositor: Thistle Hill Publishing Services/ Cenveo® Publisher Services
Text and Cover Designer: Deborah Dutton/ Dutton & Sherman Design
Cover Image: Jacques-Louis David (1748–1825), "Portrait of Antoine Laurent Lavoisier," French chemist with his wife, 1788. DEA/E. Lessing/Getty Images

Library of Congress Control Number: 2016945331

Student Edition:
ISBN: 978-1-305-95282-9

Cengage Learning
20 Channel Center Street
Boston, MA 02210
USA

Printed in the United States of America
Print Number: 01 Print Year: 2016

ABOUT THE AUTHOR

JACKSON J. SPIELVOGEL is associate professor emeritus of history at The Pennsylvania State University. He received his Ph.D. from The Ohio State University, where he specialized in Reformation history under Harold J. Grimm. His articles and reviews have appeared in such journals as *Moreana*, *Journal of General Education*, *Catholic Historical Review*, *Archiv für Reformationsgeschichte*, and *American Historical Review*. He has also contributed chapters or articles to *The Social History of the Reformation*, *The Holy Roman Empire: A Dictionary Handbook*, the *Simon Wiesenthal Center Annual of Holocaust Studies*, and *Utopian Studies*. His work has been supported by fellowships from the Fulbright Foundation and the Foundation for Reformation Research. At Penn State, he helped inaugurate the Western civilization courses as well as a popular course on Nazi Germany. His book *Hitler and Nazi Germany* was published in 1987 (seventh edition, 2014). He is the coauthor (with William Duiker) of *World History*, first published in 1998 (eighth edition, 2016), and *The Essential World History* (eighth edition, 2017). Professor Spielvogel has won five major university-wide teaching awards. In 1988–1989, he held the Penn State Teaching Fellowship, the university's most prestigious teaching award. He won the Dean Arthur Ray Warnock Award for Outstanding Faculty Member in 1996 and the Schreyer Honors College Excellence in Teaching Award in 2000.

TO DIANE,
WHOSE LOVE AND SUPPORT MADE IT ALL POSSIBLE
J.J.S.

BRIEF CONTENTS

CONTENTS

DOCUMENTS

CHAPTER 15

CHAPTER 16

CHAPTER 17

CHAPTER 18

CHAPTER 19

MAPS

FEATURES

OPPOSING VIEWPOINTS

IMAGES OF EVERYDAY LIFE

FILM & HISTORY

GLOBAL PERSPECTIVES

PREFACE

DURING A VISIT to Great Britain, where he studied as a young man, Mohandas Gandhi, the leader of the effort to liberate India from British colonial rule, was asked what he thought of Western civilization. "I think it would be a good idea," he replied. Gandhi's response was as correct as it was clever. Western civilization has led to great problems as well as great accomplishments, but it remains a good idea. And any complete understanding of today's world must take into account the meaning of Western civilization and the role Western civilization has played in history. Despite modern progress, we still greatly reflect our religious traditions, our political systems and theories, our economic and social structures, and our cultural heritage. I have written this history of Western civilization to assist a new generation of students in learning more about the past that has helped create them and the world in which they live.

At the same time, for the tenth edition, as in the ninth, I have added new material on world history to show the impact other parts of the world have made on the West. Certainly, the ongoing struggle with terrorists since 2001 has made clear the intricate relationship between the West and the rest of the world. It is important then to show not only how Western civilization has affected the rest of the world but also how it has been influenced and even defined since its beginnings by contacts with other peoples around the world.

Another of my goals was to write a well-balanced work in which the political, economic, social, religious, intellectual, cultural, and military aspects of Western civilization have been integrated into a chronologically ordered synthesis. I have been especially aware of the need to integrate the latest research on social history and women's history into each chapter of the book rather than isolating it either in lengthy topical chapters, which confuse the student by interrupting the chronological narrative, or in separate sections that appear at periodic intervals between chapters.

Another purpose in writing this history of Western civilization has been to put the *story* back in history. That story is an exciting one, yet many textbooks fail to capture the imagination of their readers. Narrative history effectively transmits the knowledge of the past and is the form that best aids remembrance. At the same time, I have not overlooked the need for the kind of historical analysis that makes students aware that historians often disagree on their interpretations of the past.

Features of the Text

To enliven the past and to let readers see for themselves the materials that historians use to create their pictures of the past, I have included in each chapter **primary sources** (boxed documents) that are keyed to the discussion in the text. The documents include examples of the religious, artistic, intellectual, social, economic, and political aspects of Western life. Such varied sources as a Renaissance banquet menu, letters exchanged between a woman and her fiancé on the battle front in World War I, the Declaration of the Rights of Woman and the Female Citizen in the French Revolution, and a debate in the Reformation era all reveal in vivid fashion what Western civilization meant to the individual men and women who shaped it by their activities. I have added questions at the end of each source to help students in analyzing the documents.

To help students examine how and why historians differ in their interpretation of specific topics, new historiographical sections were introduced in the ninth edition. Examples include "Was There a United Kingdom of Israel?"; "Was There a Renaissance for Women?"; "Was There an Agricultural Revolution?"; "The Retreat from Democracy: Did Europe Have Totalitarian States?"; and "Why Did the Soviet Union Collapse?" Each of these sections is now preceded by the heading **Historians Debate** to make students more aware of the interpretive nature of history.

An additional feature that began in the seventh edition was **Images of Everyday Life**, which combines two or more illustrations with a lengthy caption to provide insight into various aspects of social life and includes such topics as "Children in the Roman World," "Family and Marriage in Renaissance Italy," "Women and the Enlightenment Salon," and "Political Cartoons: Attacks on the King." **Film & History**, which now appears in a new, brief format, can be found in eighteen chapters; the features reference twenty films, including the new additions of *Suffragette* and *The Imitation Game*.

Each chapter has an introduction and illustrated chapter summary to help maintain the continuity of the narrative and to provide a synthesis of important themes. Anecdotes in the chapter introductions dramatically convey the major theme or themes of each chapter. Detailed chronologies reinforce the events discussed in the text, and a **Chapter Timeline** at the end of each chapter enables students to review at a glance the chief developments of an era. Some of the timelines also show parallel developments in different cultures or nations. Beginning with the eighth edition, a new format was added at the end of each chapter. The **Chapter Summary** is illustrated with thumbnail images of chapter illustrations and combined with the **Chapter Timeline**. A **Chapter Review** assists students in studying the chapter. This review includes **Upon Reflection** essay questions and a list of **Key Terms** from the chapter. The **Suggestions for Further Reading** at the end of each chapter has been thoroughly updated and is organized under subheadings to make it more useful.

Updated maps and extensive illustrations serve to deepen the reader's understanding of the text. Detailed map captions are designed to enrich students' awareness of the importance of geography to history, and numerous spot maps enable readers to see at a glance the region or subject being discussed in the text. Map captions also include a map question to guide students' reading of the map. To facilitate understanding of cultural movements, illustrations of artistic works discussed in the text are placed near the discussions. Throughout the text, illustration captions have been revised and expanded to further students' understanding of the past. Chapter outlines and focus questions, including critical thinking questions, at the beginning of each chapter give students a useful overview and guide them to the main subjects of each chapter. The section **Connections to Today** is intended to help students appreciate the relevance of history by asking them to draw connections between the past and present.

The focus questions are then repeated at the beginning of each major section in the chapter. A glossary of important terms (boldfaced in the text when they are introduced and defined) is provided at the back of the book to maximize reader comprehension. A guide to pronunciation is provided in the text in parentheses following the first mention of a complex name or term, and **Chapter Notes** is now at the end of each chapter.

New to This Edition

While preparing the revision of *Western Civilization*, I reexamined the entire book and analyzed the comments and reviews of many colleagues who have found the book to be a useful instrument for introducing their students to the history of Western civilization. In making revisions to the tenth edition, I sought to build on the strengths of the first nine editions and, above all, to maintain the balance, synthesis, and narrative qualities that characterized those editions. To keep up with the ever-growing body of historical scholarship, new or revised material has been added throughout the book on the following topics:

Chapter 1 new Historians Debate feature, "Why Did Early Civilizations Develop?"; discovery of new hominids in Indonesia; Neanderthals and modern humans; the Lascaux cave; Enheduanna as chief priestess in Sumer; new feature, Global Perspectives: "The Stele in the Ancient World"; Hatshepsut.

Chapter 2 the Hebrew Bible, including the Documentary Hypothesis; the role of rabbis; the Ten Commandments; Assyrian society; Assyrian women; new document, "The Code of Assura"; new section, "Assyrian Culture."

Chapter 3 Minoan Crete; Mycenaean Greece; the so-called "Dark Age" in Greece; the polis; Greek cultural identity; new document, "The Teaching of Tyranny"; new feature, Global Perspectives: "The Influence of the East on the Greeks"; new Film & History format for *300*; the role of the Persian threat for a growing sense of Greek cultural identity; the decline of the Greek states and the Sacred Band of Thebes; Euripides and a new section, "The Themes of Greek Tragedies"; growing sense of Greek cultural identity due to athletic games.

Chapter 4 new Film & History format for *Alexander*; new document, "The Character of Alexander"; the Ptolemaic kingdom of Egypt; the Greco-Bactrian kingdom; the Indo-Greek kingdom; political and military institutions; new feature, Global Perspectives: "The Influence of the Greeks on India"; new section, "The Appeal of Epicureanism and Stoicism"; the mystery religions; Judas Maccabeus.

Chapter 5 new Historians Debate feature, "Who Were the Etruscans?"; Aeneas and Romulus and Remus and the legendary founding of Rome; Brutus and the founding of the Roman Republic; citizenship policy and the Roman army; new feature, Global Perspectives: "Roman and Chinese Roads"; Roman imperialism; edited coverage of Roman slavery; new Film & History format for *Spartacus*.

Chapter 6 comparison of Augustus and Julius Caesar; revolts against Roman rule during the *Pax Romana*; new Historians Debate feature, "What Was Romanization?"; the provinces; contacts with Han China; trade with India; new Film & History format for *Gladiator*; revolts against Roman rule in Judaea; new feature, Global Perspectives: "Women in the Roman and Han Empires."

Chapter 7 Diocletian's religious policy and persecution of Christians; the emperor Constantine; the early Germans; the Ostrogothic Kingdom of Italy; the Visigothic Kingdom of Spain; Pope Leo I; new document, "Pope Leo I and Attila the Hun."

Chapter 8 new feature, Global Perspectives: "Lords, Vassals, and Samurai in Europe and Japan"; new document, "A Manor House"; Empress Irene; new section, "Women in the Islamic World"; Islamic women.

Chapter 9 the role of agriculture in the development of trade in the High Middle Ages; the Commercial Revolution of the High Middle Ages; new feature, Global Perspectives: "Medieval Cities in West and East"; universities and the introduction of Aristotle's works in the West.

Chapter 10 new Film & History format for *The Lion in Winter*; Bernard of Clairvaux; new Film & History format for *Vision*; monasticism; new feature, Global Perspectives: "Medieval Monastic Life in West and East"; new document, "The Miraculous Power of the Sacraments"; new Historians Debate feature, "What Motivated the Crusaders?"; the Fourth Crusade; the effects of the crusades.

Chapter 11 the longbow; the battles of the Hundred Years' War; new document, "The Hundred Years' War"; new Film & History format for *Joan of Arc* and *The Messenger*; the Babylonian Captivity of the church; the Great Schism and popular religion; new feature, Global Perspectives: "Religious Imagery in the Medieval World"; new directions in medicine.

Chapter 12 the Hanseatic League and the city of Lübeck; Florence in the Renaissance; the spiritual perspective of Italian Renaissance humanism; new document, "The Genius of Michelangelo"; Albrecht Dürer.

Chapter 13 Erasmus; new Film & History format for *Luther*; the spread of Luther's ideas; new document, "Calvin's Rules for the Church in Geneva"; Calvin's view of female rulers; new Film & History format for *Elizabeth*.

Chapter 14 the Aztecs; Spanish cities in the New World; new feature, "Global Perspectives: West Meets East: An Exchange of Royal Letters"; Mughal India; British India; new Film & History format for *The Mission*; the Columbian Exchange.

Chapter 15 new material on women and witchcraft; new document, "The Destruction of Magdeburg in the Thirty Years' War"; new feature, Global Perspectives: "Sun Kings: West and East"; Peter the Great.

Chapter 16 technological innovations; academic institutions; Hermetic magic and the Scientific Revolution; Tycho Brahe; medical practice; new Images of Everyday Life feature: "The Science of Collecting."

Chapter 17 John Locke; Rococo art; new Film & History format for *Amadeus*; popular culture and the coffee house; new feature, Global Perspectives: "Popular Culture in West and East"; toleration and religion.

Chapter 18 new Film & History format for *Marie Antoinette*; Frederick II of Prussia; Joseph II of Austria; Spain; Portugal; the agricultural revolution; the consumer revolution.

Chapter 19 the Three Estates; French finances; new feature, Global Perspectives: "Revolution and Revolt in France and China"; the formation of political factions; new document, "Response to the King's Flight to Varennes"; the flight to Varennes; the French émigrés; the Terror.

Chapter 20 new document, "The Steam Engine and Cotton"; early railroads; the Industrial Revolution on the continent; British policies in India; cheap cotton; new feature, Global Perspectives: "Attitudes of the Industrial Middle Class in Britain and Japan".

Chapter 21 the French Revolution of 1830; the Revolutions of 1848; Romanticism; new document, "Beethoven's Instrumental Music."

Chapter 22 the Ottoman Empire; the Crimean War; the Franco-Prussian War; reforms in Russia; political life in Russia; Realism in art.

Chapter 23 economic growth; new feature, Global Perspectives: "West and East: Textile Factory Work"; the social classes; mass tourism; new document, "Women's Soccer, 1881."

Chapter 24 new document, "Dostovesky: An Attack on Reason"; new feature, Global Perspectives: "Impressionist Painting: West and East"; modernism and the arts; new Film & History feature on *Suffragette*; the United States; imperialism.

Chapter 25 new material in the Introduction; new Film & History format for *Paths of Glory*; new document, "The Reality of War: The Views of British Poets"; life in the trenches; new feature, Global Perspectives, "Soldiers from Around the World"; the November armistice; the Treaty of Versailles.

Chapter 26 the colonial empires; new document, "Spain in Turmoil: A View from Barcelona"; arts, film, and culture; new Film & History format for *Triumph of the Will*; new section, "The Culture of Nazism."

Chapter 27 naval battles, including the Battle of North Atlantic and Battle of Leyte Gulf; resistance movements; new Film & History format for *Europa, Europa*; new feature, Global Perspectives: "The Impact of Total War in West and East"; new section, "The Impact of Technology"; new Film & History feature on *The Imitation Game*.

Chapter 28 new Film & History format for *The Third Man*; decolonization in Africa; decolonization in the Middle East; new feature, Global Perspectives: "The Rise of the Supermarket in West and East."

Chapter 29 the European economy; new Film & History format for *The Iron Lady*; new document, "Margaret Thatcher: 'Thatcherism' and the Free Market"; Italy; the United States economy.

Chapter 30 Russia; Eastern Europe; Germany; Great Britain; France; Italy; the United States; Canada; new Film & History format for *The Lives of Others*; new document, "The West and Islam"; new sections, "Terrorism as a Global War," "Migration Crisis," "The New Urban Environment," "The Digital Age," "Art in the Contemporary World," and "Music Since 1985"; technology; religion; new feature, Global Perspectives: "The New Global Economy: Fast Fashion."

The enthusiastic response to the primary sources (boxed documents) led me to evaluate the content of each document carefully and add new documents throughout the text. The feature **Opposing Viewpoints**, which was introduced in the seventh edition, presents a comparison of two or three primary sources in order to facilitate student analysis of historical documents. This feature now appears in almost every chapter and includes such topics as "The Great Flood: Two Versions," "The Black Death: Contemporary Views," "A New Heaven: Faith Versus Reason," "The Response to Revolution," and "Czechoslovakia, 1968: Two Faces of Communism." Focus questions are included to help students evaluate the documents.

New to the tenth edition is a feature entitled **Global Perspectives**, which reinforces the relationship between the West and other parts of the world. This new feature, which is found in twenty chapters, includes such topics as "The Stele in the Ancient World," "Women in the Roman and Han Empires," "Medieval Monastic Life in West and East," "Revolution and Revolt in France and China," "West and East: Textile Factory Work," and "The New Global Economy: Fast Fashion."

Because courses in Western civilization at American and Canadian colleges and universities follow different chronological divisions, a one-volume edition, two two-volume editions, a three-volume edition, and a volume covering events since 1300 are being made available to fit the needs of instructors. Teaching and learning ancillaries include the following.

Supplements

MindTap Instant Access Code (full volume): ISBN–9781305952362
MindTap Instant Access Code (Volume 1): ISBN–9781305953239
MindTap Instant Access Code (Volume 2): ISBN–9781305953369

MindTap Printed Access Card (Full Volume): ISBN–9781305952379
MindTap Printed Access Card (Volume 1): ISBN–9781305953246
MindTap Printed Access Card (Volume 2): ISBN–9781305953376

MindTap for *Western Civilization*, 10e, is a personalized online learning platform that provides students with an immersive learning experience to build and foster critical thinking skills. Through a carefully designed chapter-based learning path, MindTap allows students to easily identify learning objectives; draw connections and improve writing skills by completing unit-level essay assignments; read short, manageable sections from the e-book; and test their content knowledge with map- and timeline-based critical thinking questions.

MindTap allows instructors to customize their content, providing tools that seamlessly integrate YouTube clips, outside websites, and personal content directly into the learning path. Instructors can assign additional primary source content through the Instructor Resource Center and Questia primary and secondary source databases that house thousands of peer-reviewed journals, newspapers, magazines, and full-length books.

The additional content available in MindTap mirrors and complements the authors' narrative but also includes primary source content and assessments not found in the printed text. To learn more, ask your Cengage Learning sales representative to demo it for you—or go to *www.Cengage.com/MindTap*.

Instructor's Companion Website The Instructor's Companion Website, accessed through the Instructor Resource Center (*login.cengage.com*), houses all of the supplemental materials you can use for your course. This includes a test bank, instructor's manual, and PowerPoint lecture presentations. The test bank, offered in Microsoft Word and Cognero formats, contains multiple-choice, identification, true or false, and essay questions for each chapter. Cognero is a flexible online system that allows you to author, edit, and manage test bank content for *Western Civilization*, 10e. Create multiple test versions instantly and deliver through your learning management system from your classroom or wherever you may be, with no special installs or downloads required. The instructor's resource manual includes chapter summaries, suggested lecture topics, map exercises, discussion questions for the primary sources, topics for student research, relevant websites, suggestions for additional videos, and online resources for information on historical sites. Finally, the PowerPoint Lectures are ADA-compliant slides that collate the key takeaways from the chapter in concise visual formats perfect for in-class presentations or for student review.

Cengagebrain.com Save your students time and money. Direct them to *www.cengagebrain.com* for a choice in formats and savings and a better chance to succeed in your class. *Cengagebrain .com*, Cengage Learning's online store, is a single destination for more than 10,000 new textbooks, e-textbooks, e-chapters, study tools, and audio supplements. Students have the freedom to purchase à la carte exactly what they need and when they need it. Students can save 50 percent on the electronic textbook and can purchase an individual e-chapter for as little as $1.99.

Doing History: Research and Writing in the Digital Age, 2e ISBN: 9781133587880 Prepared by Michael J. Galgano, J. Chris Arndt, and Raymond M. Hyser of James Madison University. Whether you're starting down the path as a history major or simply looking for a straightforward, systematic guide to writing a successful paper, this text's "soup to nuts" approach to researching and writing about history addresses every step of the process: locating your sources, gathering information, writing and citing according to various style guides, and avoiding plagiarism.

Writing for College History, 1e ISBN: 9780618306039 Prepared by Robert M. Frakes of Clarion University. This brief handbook for survey courses in American, western, and world history guides students through the various types of writing assignments they may encounter in a history class. Providing examples of student writing and candid assessments of student work, this text focuses on the rules and conventions of writing for the college history course.

The Modern Researcher, 6e ISBN: 9780495318705 Prepared by Jacques Barzun and Henry F. Graff of Columbia University. This classic introduction to the techniques of research and the art of expression thoroughly covers every aspect of research, from the selection of a topic through the gathering of materials, analysis, writing, revision, and publication of findings. The authors present the process not as a set of rules but through actual cases that put the subtleties of research in a useful context. Part One covers the principles and methods of research; Part Two covers writing, speaking, and getting one's work published.

Reader Program Cengage Learning publishes a number of readers. Some contain exclusively primary sources, others are devoted to essays and secondary sources, and still others provide a combination of primary and secondary sources. All of these readers are designed to guide students through the process of historical inquiry. Visit *www.cengage.com/history* for a complete list of readers.

Custom Options Nobody knows your students like you, so why not give them a text that tailor-fits their needs? Cengage Learning offers custom solutions for your course—whether it's making a small modification to *Western Civilization*, 10e, to match your syllabus or combining multiple sources to create something truly unique. Contact your Cengage Learning representative to explore custom solutions for your course.

ACKNOWLEDGMENTS

I BEGAN TO TEACH at age five in my family's grape arbor. By the age of ten, I wanted to know and understand everything in the world, so I set out to memorize our entire set of encyclopedia volumes. At seventeen, as editor of the high school yearbook, I chose "patterns" as its theme. With that as my early history, followed by many rich years of teaching, writing, and family nurturing, it seemed quite natural to accept the challenge of writing a history of Western civilization as I approached that period in life often described as the age of wisdom. Although I see this writing adventure as part of the natural unfolding of my life, I gratefully acknowledge that without the generosity of many others, it would not have been possible.

David Redles gave generously of his time and ideas, especially for Chapters 28, 29, and 30. Chris Colin provided research on the history of music, while Laurie Batitto, Alex Spencer, Stephen Maloney, Shaun Mason, Peter Angelos, and Fred Schooley offered valuable editorial assistance. I deeply appreciate the valuable technical assistance provided by Dayton Coles. I am deeply grateful to John Soares for his assistance in preparing the map captions and to Charmarie Blaisdell of Northeastern University for her detailed suggestions on women's history. Daniel Haxall of Kutztown University provided valuable assistance with materials on postwar art, popular culture, postmodern art and thought, and the Digital Age. I am especially grateful to Kathryn Spielvogel for her work as editorial associate for Chapters 15–30. I am also thankful to the thousands of students whose questions and responses have caused me to see many aspects of Western civilization in new ways.

My ability to undertake a project of this magnitude was in part due to the outstanding European history teachers that I had as both an undergraduate and graduate student. These included Kent Forster (modern Europe) and Robert W. Green (early modern Europe) at The Pennsylvania State University and Franklin Pegues (medieval), Andreas Dorpalen (modern Germany), William MacDonald (ancient), and Harold J. Grimm (Renaissance and Reformation) at The Ohio State University. These teachers provided me with profound insights into Western civilization and also taught me by their examples that learning only becomes true understanding when it is accompanied by compassion, humility, and open-mindedness.

I would like to thank the many teachers and students who have used the first nine editions. Their enthusiastic response to a textbook that was intended to put the story back in history and capture the imagination of the reader has been very gratifying. I especially thank the many teachers and students who made the effort to contact me personally to share their enthusiasm. Thanks to Cengage's comprehensive review process, many historians were asked to evaluate my manuscript and review each edition. I am grateful to the following people for their innumerable suggestions over the course of the first nine editions, which have greatly improved my work:

Anne J. Aby
Minnesota West Community and Technical College, Worthington Campus

Paul Allen
University of Utah

Randall Allen
Bay de Noc Community College

Gerald Anderson
North Dakota State University

Susan L. H. Anderson
Campbell University

Letizia Argenteri
University of San Diego

Roy A. Austensen
Illinois State University

James A. Baer
Northern Virginia Community College—Alexandria

James T. Baker
Western Kentucky University

Patrick Bass
Morningside College

John F. Battick
University of Maine

Frederic J. Baumgartner
Virginia Polytechnic Institute

Phillip N. Bebb
Ohio University

Anthony Bedford
Modesto Junior College

F. E. Beemon
Middle Tennessee State University

Leonard R. Berlanstein
University of Virginia

Cyriaque Beurtheret
Salt Lake Community College

Douglas T. Bisson
Belmont University

Charmarie Blaisdell
Northeastern University

Benay Blend
Central New Mexico Community College

Stephen H. Blumm
Montgomery County Community College

John Bohstedt
University of Tennessee—Knoxville

Hugh S. Bonar
California State University

Werner Braatz
University of Wisconsin—Oshkosh

Alfred S. Bradford
University of Missouri

Owen Bradley
Columbia College at Coast Guard Island

Janet Brantley
Texarkana College

Maryann E. Brink
College of William & Mary

Jerry Brookshire
Middle Tennessee State University

Daniel Patrick Brown
Moorpark College

Gregory S. Brown
University of Nevada—Las Vegas

Blaine T. Browne
Broward Community College

Daniel Bubb
Gonzaga University

Kevin W. Caldwell
Blue Ridge Community College

J. Holden Camp Jr.
Hillyer College, University of Hartford

Jack Cargill
Rutgers University

Martha Carlin
University of Wisconsin—Milwaukee

Elizabeth Carney
Clemson University

Susan Carrafiello
Wright State University

Jane Laurel Carrington
St. Olaf College

Joseph J. Casino
St. Joseph's University

Eric H. Cline
Xavier University

Robert G. Clouse
Indiana State University

Robert Cole
Utah State University

Elizabeth Collins
Triton College

William J. Connell
Rutgers University

Nancy Conradt
College of DuPage

Marc Cooper
Southwest Missouri State

Richard A. Cosgrove
University of Arizona

David A. Crain
South Dakota State University

Michael A. Crane Jr. (student)
Everett Community College

Luanne Dagley
Pellissippi State Technical Community College

John Davies
University of Delaware

Michael Dolski
Ball State University

Michael F. Doyle
Ocean County College

Hugh Dubrulle
Saint Anselm College

Joseph J. Eble
Burlington County College

James W. Ermatinger
University of Nebraska—Kearney

Porter Ewing
Los Angeles City College

Carla Falkner
Northeast Mississippi Community College

Steven Fanning
University of Illinois—Chicago

Ellsworth Faris
California State University—Chico

Gary B. Ferngren
Oregon State University

Mary Helen Finnerty
Westchester Community College

Jennifer Foray
Purdue University

Amy Forbes
Millsaps College

Jennifer E. Forster
Lakeland Community College

Patricia Frank
St. Clair County Community College

A. Z. Freeman
Robinson College

Marsha Frey
Kansas State University

Frank J. Frost
University of California—Santa Barbara

Frank Garosi
California State University—Sacramento

Laura Gellott
University of Wisconsin—Parkside

Richard M. Golden
University of North Texas

Manuel G. Gonzales
Diablo Valley College

Amy G. Gordon
Denison University

Richard J. Grace
Providence College

Charlotte M. Gradie
Sacred Heart University

Candace Gregory
California State University—Sacramento

Katherine Gribble
Highline Community College

Hanns Gross
Loyola University

John F. Guilmartin
Ohio State University

Paul Hagenloh
The University of Alabama

Jeffrey S. Hamilton
Gustavus Adolphus College

J. Drew Harrington
Western Kentucky University

James Harrison
Siena College

Doina Pasca Harsanyi
Central Michigan University

Jay Hatheway
Edgewood College

A. J. Heisserer
University of Oklahoma

Carol Herringer
Wright State University

Betsey Hertzler
Mesa Community College

Robert Herzstein
University of South Carolina

Michael C. Hickey
Bloomsburg University

Shirley Hickson
North Greenville College

Martha L. Hildreth
University of Nevada

Boyd H. Hill Jr.
University of Colorado—Boulder

Michael Hofstetter
Bethany College

Donald C. Holsinger
Seattle Pacific University

Frank L. Holt
University of Houston

W. Robert Houston
University of South Alabama

Michael W. Howell
College of the Ozarks

Anne Huebel
Franklin Pierce University

David Hudson
California State University—Fresno

Paul J. L. Hughes
Sussex County Community College

Richard A. Jackson
University of Houston

Fred Jewell
Harding University

Nicole Jobin
University of Colorado

Jenny M. Jochens
Towson State University

William M. Johnston
University of Massachusetts

George Kaloudis
Rivier College

Jeffrey A. Kaufmann
Muscatine Community College

David O. Kieft
University of Minnesota

Patricia Killen
Pacific Lutheran University

Jay Kilroy
Mesa Community College

William E. Kinsella Jr.
Northern Virginia Community College—Annandale

James M. Kittelson
Ohio State University

Doug Klepper
Santa Fe Community College

Cynthia Kosso
Northern Arizona University

Ed Krzemienski
The Citadel

Paul E. Lambert
Nichols College

Clayton Miles Lehmann
University of South Dakota

Diana Chen Lin
Indiana University, Northwest

Paul Douglas Lockhart
Wright State University

Ursula W. MacAffer
Hudson Valley Community College

Harold Marcuse
University of California—Santa Barbara

Mike Markowski
Westminster College

Michael Martin
Fort Lewis College

Mavis Mate
University of Oregon

Derek Maxfield
Genesee Community College

Priscilla McArthur
Troy State University—Dothan

T. Ronald Melton
Brewton Parker College

Martin Menke
Rivier College

Jack Allen Meyer
University of South Carolina

Eugene W. Miller Jr.
The Pennsylvania State University—Hazleton

David B. Mock
Tallahassee Community College

John Patrick Montano
University of Delaware

Rex Morrow
Trident Technical College

Wyatt S. Moulds
Jones County Junior College

Kenneth Mouré
University of California—Santa Barbara

Thomas M. Mulhern
University of North Dakota

Pierce Mullen
Montana State University

Cliona Murphy
California State University—Bakersfield

Frederick I. Murphy
Western Kentucky University

William M. Murray
University of South Florida

Otto M. Nelson
Texas Tech University

Sam Nelson
Willmar Community College

John A. Nichols
Slippery Rock University

Lisa Nofzinger
Albuquerque Technical Vocational Institute

Chris Oldstone-Moore
Augustana College

Donald Ostrowski
Harvard University

James O. Overfield
University of Vermont

Matthew L. Panczyk
Bergen Community College

Kathleen A. Parrow
Black Hills State University

Kathleen Paul
University of South Florida

Jody Peterson
Centralia College

Ted Petro
New England College

Carla Rahn Phillips
University of Minnesota

Keith Pickus
Wichita State University

Linda J. Piper
University of Georgia

Jeff Plaks
University of Central Oklahoma

Marjorie Plummer
Western Kentucky University

Janet Polasky
University of New Hampshire

Ann Pond
Bishop State Community College

Thomas W. Porter
Randolph-Macon College

Charles A. Povlovich
California State University—Fullerton

Penne L. Prigge
Rockingham Community College

Timothy Pytell
California State University—San Bernardino

Nancy Rachels
Hillsborough Community College

Norman G. Raiford
Greenville Technical College

Charles Rearick
University of Massachusetts—Amherst

Jerome V. Reel Jr.
Clemson University

Roger Reese
Texas A&M University

William Roba
Scott Community College

Kevin Robbins
Indiana University Purdue University—Indianapolis

Eric C. Roberson
Wake Technical Community College

Joseph Robertson
Gadsden State Community College

Jonathan Roth
San Jose State University

Constance M. Rousseau
Providence College

Beverly J. Rowe
Texarkana College

Matthew Ruane
Florida Institute of Technology

Julius R. Ruff
Marquette University

Mark Edward Ruff
Saint Louis University

David L. Ruffley
Pikes Peak Community College

Geraldine Ryder
Ocean County College

Richard Saller
University of Chicago

Magdalena Sanchez
Texas Christian University

Thomas J. Schaeper
St. Bonaventure University

Jack Schanfield
Suffolk County Community College

Roger Schlesinger
Washington State University

Joanne Schneider
Rhode Island College

Thomas C. Schunk
University of Wisconsin—Oshkosh

Kyle C. Sessions
Illinois State University

Linda Simmons
Northern Virginia Community College—Manassas

Donald V. Sippel
Rhode Island College

Stuart Smyth
University at SUNY—Albany

Glen Spann
Asbury College

Heath A. Spencer
Seattle University

John W. Steinberg
Georgia Southern University

Barbara Stengel
Yuba College

Robert P. Stephens
Virginia Tech

Paul W. Strait
Florida State University

James E. Straukamp
California State University—Sacramento

Brian E. Strayer
Andrews University

Fred Suppe
Ball State University

Roger Tate
Somerset Community College

Tom Taylor
Seattle University

Emily Teipe
Fullerton College

David Tengewall
Anne Arundel Community College

Jack W. Thacker
Western Kentucky University

Thomas Turley
Santa Clara University

John G. Tuthill
University of Guam

Maarten Ultee
University of Alabama

Donna L. Van Raaphorst
Cuyahoga Community College

J. Barry Vaughn
University of Alabama

Allen M. Ward
University of Connecticut

Richard D. Weigel
Western Kentucky University

Michael Weiss
Linn-Benton Community College

Alison Williams
Saint Joseph's University

Arthur H. Williamson
California State University—Sacramento

Daniel Woods
Ferrum College

Katherine Workman
Wright State University

Judith T. Wozniak
Cleveland State University

Walter J. Wussow
University of Wisconsin—Eau Claire

Edwin M. Yamauchi
Miami University

Robert W. Young
Carroll Community College

Sergei Zhuk
Ball State University

The following individuals contributed suggestions for the tenth edition:

Betsy Anderson
East Central Community College

Patrick Brennan
Gulf Coast State College

Matt Brent
Rappahannock Community College

Robert Brown
SUNY—Finger Lakes Community College

Claire Cage
University of South Alabama

Christine Eubank
Bergen Community College

Eric Fournier
West Chester University of Pennsylvania

Stella Gomezdelcampo
Roane State Community College

Awad Halabi
Wright State University

Sarah Jurenka
Bishop State

Thomas Mockaitis
DePaul University

Steven J. Williams
New Mexico Highlands University

Julianna Wilson
Pima Community College

The editors at Cengage Wadsworth have been both helpful and congenial at all times. I especially wish to thank Clark Baxter, who originally asked me to do this project, and whose clever wit, wisdom, gentle prodding, and good friendship added great depth to our working relationship. Margaret Beasley thoughtfully, wisely, efficiently, and pleasantly guided the overall development of the tenth edition. I also thank Scott Greenan for his suggestions and valuable editorial assistance. I also want to express my gratitude to Angela Urquhart, whose well-advised suggestions and generous support made the production process easier. Above all, I thank my family for their support. The gifts of love, laughter, and patience from my daughters, Jennifer and Kathryn; my sons, Eric and Christian; my daughters-in-law, Liz and Laurie; and my sons-in-law, Daniel and Eddie, were enormously appreciated. I also wish to acknowledge my grandchildren, Devyn, Bryn, Drew, Elena, Sean, Emma, and Jackson, who bring great joy to my life. My wife and best friend, Diane, contributed editorial assistance, wise counsel, good humor, and the loving support that made it possible for me to accomplish a project of this magnitude. I could not have written the book without her.

INTRODUCTION TO STUDENTS OF WESTERN CIVILIZATION

CIVILIZATION, AS HISTORIANS define it, first emerged between five and six thousand years ago when people in different parts of the world began to live in organized communities with distinct political, military, economic, and social structures. Religious, intellectual, and artistic activities assumed important roles in these early societies. The focus of this book is on Western civilization, a civilization that many people identify with the continent of Europe.

Defining Western Civilization

Western civilization itself has evolved considerably over the centuries. Although the concept of the West did not yet exist at the time of the Mesopotamians and Egyptians, their development of writing, law codes, and different roles based on gender all eventually influenced what became Western civilization. Although the Greeks did not conceive of Western civilization as a cultural entity, their artistic, intellectual, and political contributions were crucial to the foundations of Western civilization. The Romans produced a remarkable series of accomplishments that were fundamental to the development of Western civilization, a civilization that came to consist largely of lands in Europe conquered by the Romans, in which Roman cultural and political ideals were gradually spread. Nevertheless, people in these early civilizations viewed themselves as subjects of states or empires, not as members of Western civilization.

With the rise of Christianity during the Late Roman Empire, however, peoples in Europe began to identify themselves as part of a civilization different from others, such as that of Islam, leading to a concept of a Western civilization different from other civilizations. In the fifteenth century, Renaissance intellectuals began to identify this civilization not only with Christianity but also with the intellectual and political achievements of the ancient Greeks and Romans.

Important to the development of the idea of a distinct Western civilization were encounters with other peoples. Between 700 and 1500, encounters with the world of Islam helped define the West. After 1500, however, as European ships began to move into other parts of the world, encounters with peoples in Asia, Africa, and the Americas not only had an impact on the civilizations found there but also affected how people in the West defined themselves. At the same time, as they set up colonies, Europeans began to transplant a sense of Western identity to other areas of the world, especially North America and parts of Latin America, that have come to be considered part of Western civilization.

As the concept of Western civilization has evolved over the centuries, so have the values and unique features associated with that civilization. Science played a crucial role in the development of modern Western civilization. The societies of the Greeks, Romans, and medieval Europeans were based largely on a belief in the existence of a spiritual order; a dramatic departure to a natural or material view of the universe occurred in the seventeenth-century Scientific Revolution. Science and technology have been important in the growth of today's modern and largely secular Western civilization, although antecedents to scientific development also existed in Greek and medieval thought and practice, and religion remains an important component of the Western world today.

Many historians have viewed the concept of political liberty, belief in the fundamental value of every individual, and a rational outlook based on a system of logical, analytical thought as unique aspects of Western civilization. Of course, the West has also witnessed horrendous negations of liberty, individualism, and reason. Racism, slavery, violence, world wars, totalitarian regimes—these too form part of the complex story of what constitutes Western civilization.

The Dating of Time

In our examination of Western civilization, we also need to be aware of the dating of time. In recording the past, historians try to determine the exact time when events occurred. World War II in Europe, for example, began on September 1, 1939, when Hitler sent German troops into Poland, and ended on May 7, 1945, when Germany surrendered. By using dates, historians can place events in order and try to determine the development of patterns over periods of time.

If someone asked you when you were born, you would reply with a number, such as 1999. In the United States, we would all accept that number without question because it is part of the dating system followed in the Western world (Europe and the Western Hemisphere). In this system, events are dated by counting backward or forward from the year 1. When the system was first devised, the year 1 was assumed to be the year of the birth of Jesus, and the abbreviations B.C. (before Christ) and A.D. (for the Latin *anno Domini,* meaning "in the year of the Lord") were used to refer to the periods before and after the birth of Jesus, respectively. Historians now generally prefer to refer to the year 1 in nonreligious terms as the beginning of the "common era." The abbreviations B.C.E. (before the common era) and C.E. (common era) are used instead of B.C. and A.D., although the years are the same. Thus, an event that took place four hundred years before the year 1 would be dated 400 B.C.E. (before the common era)—or the date could be expressed as 400 B.C. Dates after the year 1 are labeled C.E. Thus, an event that took place two hundred years after the year 1 would be dated 200 C.E. (common era), or the date could be written as A.D. 200. It can also be written simply as 200, just as you would not give your birth year as 1999 C.E., but simply as 1999. In keeping with the current usage by most historians, this book will use the abbreviations B.C.E. and C.E.

Historians also make use of other terms to refer to time. A *decade* is ten years, a *century* is one hundred years, and a *millennium* is one thousand years. Thus, "the fourth century B.C.E." refers to the fourth period of one hundred years counting backward from the year 1, the beginning of the common era. Since the first century B.C.E. would be the years 100 B.C.E. to 1 C.E., the fourth century B.C.E. would be the years 400 B.C.E. to 301 B.C.E. We could say, then, that an event in 350 B.C.E. took place in the fourth century B.C.E.

Similarly, "the fourth century C.E." refers to the fourth period of one hundred years after the beginning of the common era. Since the first period of one hundred years would be the years 1 to 100, the fourth period or fourth century would be the years 301 to 400. We could say, then, that an event in 350 took place in the fourth century. Likewise, the first millennium B.C.E. refers to the years 1000 B.C.E. to 1 C.E.; the second millennium C.E. refers to the years 1001 to 2000.

The dating of events can also vary from people to people. Most people in the Western world use the Western calendar, also known as the Gregorian calendar after Pope Gregory XIII, who refined it in 1582. The Hebrew calendar uses a different system in which the year 1 is the equivalent of the Western year 3760 B.C.E., considered to be the date of the creation of the world according to the Bible. Thus, the Western year 2017 is the year 5777 on the Hebrew calendar. The Islamic calendar begins year 1 on the day Muhammad fled Mecca, which is the year 622 on the Western calendar.

WESTERN CIVILIZATION TO 1300

ALTHOUGH EARLY CIVILIZATIONS emerged in different parts of the world, we begin our story of Western civilization with the Mesopotamians and Egyptians, who developed cities and struggled with the problems of organized states. They developed writing to keep records and created literature. They constructed monumental architecture to please their gods, symbolize their power, and preserve their culture. They developed political, military, social, and religious structures to deal with the basic problems of human existence and organization. These first literate civilizations left detailed records that allow us to view how they grappled with three of the fundamental problems that humans have pondered: the nature of human relationships, the nature of the universe, and the role of divine forces in the cosmos. Although later peoples in Western civilization would provide different answers from those of the Mesopotamians and Egyptians, it was they who first posed the questions, gave answers, and wrote them down. Human memory begins with these two civilizations.

By 1500 B.C.E., much of the creative impulse of the Mesopotamian and Egyptian civilizations was beginning to wane. The entry of new peoples known as Indo-Europeans who moved into Asia Minor and Anatolia (modern Turkey) led to the creation of a Hittite kingdom that entered into conflict with the Egyptians. The invasion of the Sea Peoples around 1200 B.C.E., however, destroyed the Hittites, severely weakened the Egyptians, and created a power vacuum that allowed a patchwork of petty kingdoms and city-states to emerge, especially in the area of Syria and Palestine. All of them were eventually overshadowed by the rise of the great empires of the Assyrians, Chaldeans, and Persians. The Assyrian Empire was the first to unite almost all of the ancient Near East. Far larger was the empire of the Great Kings of Persia. Although it owed much to the administrative organization developed by the Assyrians, the Persian Empire had its own peculiar strengths. Persian rule was tolerant as well as efficient. Conquered peoples were allowed to keep their own religions, customs, and methods of doing business. The many years of peace that the Persian Empire brought to the Near East facilitated trade and the general well-being of its peoples. Many Near Eastern peoples expressed gratitude for being subjects of the Great Kings of Persia.

The Israelites were one of these peoples. Never numerous, they created no empire and were dominated by the Assyrians, Chaldeans, and Persians. Nevertheless, they left a spiritual legacy that influenced much of the later development of Western civilization. The evolution of Hebrew monotheism (belief in a single god) created in Judaism one of the world's great religions; it influenced the development of both Christianity and Islam. When we speak of the Judeo-Christian heritage of Western civilization, we refer not only to the concept of monotheism but also to ideas of law, morality, and social justice that have become important parts of Western culture.

On the western fringes of the Persian Empire, another relatively small group of people, the Greeks, were creating cultural and political ideals that would also have an important impact on Western civilization. The first Greek civilization, known as the Mycenaean, took shape around 1600 B.C.E. and fell to new Greek-speaking invaders five hundred years later. By the eighth century B.C.E., the polis or city-state had become the chief focus of Greek life. Loyalty to the polis created a close-knit community but also divided Greece into a host of independent states, two of which, Sparta and Athens, became the most important. They were very different, however. Sparta created a closed, highly disciplined society, whereas Athens moved toward an open, democratic civilization.

The classical age in Greece (ca. 500–338 B.C.E.) began with a mighty confrontation between the Greeks and the Persian Empire. After their victory over the Persians, the Greeks began to divide into two large alliances, one headed by Sparta and the other by Athens. Athens created a naval empire and flourished during the age of Pericles, but fear of Athens led to the Great Peloponnesian War between Sparta and Athens and their allies. For all of their brilliant accomplishments, the Greeks were unable to rise above the divisions and rivalries that caused them to fight each other and undermine their own civilization.

The accomplishments of the Greeks formed the fountainhead of Western culture. Socrates, Plato, and Aristotle established the foundations of Western philosophy. Our literary forms are largely derived from Greek poetry and drama. Greek notions of harmony, proportion, and beauty have remained the touchstones for all subsequent Western art. A rational method of inquiry, so important to modern science, was conceived in ancient Greece. Many of our political terms are Greek in origin, as are our concepts of the rights and duties of citizenship, especially as they were conceived in Athens, the first great democracy. Especially during their classical period, the Greeks raised and debated fundamental questions about the purpose of human existence, the structure of human society, and the nature of the universe that have concerned Western thinkers ever since.

While the Greek city-states were pursuing their squabbles, to their north a new and powerful kingdom—Macedonia—emerged. Under King Philip II, the Macedonians defeated a Greek allied army in 338 B.C.E. and then consolidated their control over the Greek peninsula. Although the independent Greek city-states lost their freedom when they were conquered by the Macedonians, Greek culture did not die. Under the leadership of Alexander the Great, son of Philip II, both the Macedonians and Greeks invaded and conquered the Persian Empire. In the conquered lands, Greeks and non-Greeks established a series of kingdoms (known as the Hellenistic kingdoms) and inaugurated the Hellenistic era.

The Hellenistic period was, in its own way, a vibrant one. New cities arose and flourished. New philosophical ideas captured the minds of many. Significant achievements occurred in art, literature, and science. Greek culture spread throughout the Near East and made an impact wherever it was carried. In some areas of the Hellenistic world, queens played an active role in political life, and many upper-class women found new avenues for expressing themselves. Although the Hellenistic era achieved a degree of political stability, by the late third century B.C.E., signs of decline were beginning to multiply, and the growing power of Rome eventually endangered the Hellenistic world.

Sometime in the eighth century B.C.E., a group of Latin-speaking people built a small community called Rome on the Tiber River in Italy. Between 509 and 264 B.C.E., this city expanded and united almost all of Italy under its control. Even more dramatically, between 264 and 133 B.C.E., Rome expanded to the west and east and became master of the Mediterranean Sea.

After 133 B.C.E., however, Rome's republican institutions proved inadequate for the task of ruling an empire. In the breakdown that ensued, ambitious individuals saw opportunities for power unparalleled in Roman history and succumbed to the temptations. After a series of bloody civil wars, peace was finally achieved when Octavian defeated Antony and Cleopatra. Octavian, who came to be known by the title of Augustus, created a new system of government that seemed to preserve the Republic while establishing the basis for a new system that would rule the empire in an orderly fashion.

After a century of internal upheaval, Augustus established a new order that began the Roman Empire, which experienced peace and prosperity between 14 and 180. During this era trade flourished and the provinces were governed efficiently. In the course of the third century, however, the Roman Empire almost collapsed because of invasions, civil wars, and economic decline. Although the emperors Diocletian and Constantine brought new life to the so-called Late Empire at the beginning of the fourth century, their efforts shored up the empire only temporarily. In the course of the fifth century, the empire divided into western and eastern parts.

The Roman Empire was the largest empire in antiquity. Using their practical skills, the Romans produced achievements in language, law, engineering, and government that were bequeathed to the future. The Romance languages of today (French, Italian, Spanish, Portuguese, and Romanian) are based on Latin. Western practices of impartial justice and trial by jury owe much to Roman law. As great builders, the Romans left monuments to their skills throughout Europe, some of which, such as aqueducts and roads, are still in use today. Aspects of Roman administrative practices survived in the Western world for centuries. The Romans also preserved the intellectual heritage of the ancient world.

During its last two hundred years, the Roman world underwent a slow transformation with the spread of Christianity. The rise of Christianity marked an important break with the dominant values of the Roman world. Christianity began as a small Jewish sect, but under the guidance of Paul of Tarsus it became a world religion that appealed to both Jews and non-Jews. Despite persecution by Roman authorities, Christianity grew and became widely accepted by the fourth century. At the end of that century, it was made the official state religion of the Roman Empire.

The period of late antiquity that saw the disintegration of the western part of the Roman Empire also witnessed the emergence of a new European civilization in the Early Middle Ages. This early medieval civilization was formed by the coalescence of three major elements: the Germanic peoples who moved into the western part of the empire and established new kingdoms, the continuing attraction of the Greco- Roman cultural legacy, and the Christian church. Politically, a new series of Germanic kingdoms emerged in western Europe. Each fused Roman and Germanic elements to create a new society. The Christian church (or Roman Catholic Church, as it came to be called in the west) played a crucial role in the growth of the new European civilization. The church developed an organized government under the leadership of the pope. It also assimilated the classical tradition and through its clergy brought Christianized civilization to the Germanic tribes. Especially important were the monks and nuns who led the way in converting the Germanic peoples in Europe to Christianity.

At the end of the eighth century, a new kingdom—the Carolingian Empire—came to control much of western and central Europe, especially during the reign of Charlemagne. In the long run, the creation of a western empire fostered the idea of a distinct European identity and marked a shift of power from the south to the north. Italy and the Mediterranean had been the center of the Roman Empire. The lands north of the Alps now became the political center of Europe, and increasingly, Europe emerged as the focus and center of Western civilization.

Building on a fusion of Germanic, classical, and Christian elements, the Carolingian Empire was well governed but held together primarily by personal loyalty to the strong king. The economy of the eighth and ninth centuries was based almost entirely on farming, which proved inadequate for maintaining a large monarchical system. As a result, a new political and military order—known as

fief-holding—subsequently evolved to become an integral part of the political world of the Middle Ages. Fief-holding was characterized by a decentralization of political power, in which lords exercised legal, administrative, and military power. This transferred public power into many private hands and seemed to provide security that the weak central government could not provide.

The new European civilization that had emerged in the ninth and tenth centuries began to come into its own in the eleventh and twelfth centuries, and Europeans established new patterns that reached their high point in the thirteenth century. The High Middle Ages (1000–1300) was a period of recovery and growth for Western civilization, characterized by a greater sense of security and a burst of energy and enthusiasm. Climatic improvements that produced better growing conditions, an expansion of cultivated land, and technological changes combined to enable Europe's food supply to increase significantly after 1000. This increase in agricultural production helped sustain a dramatic rise in population that was physically apparent in the expansion of towns and cities.

The development of trade and the rise of cities added a dynamic new element to the civilization of the High Middle Ages. Trading activities flourished first in northern Italy and Flanders and then spread outward from these centers. In the late tenth and eleventh centuries, this renewal of commercial life led to a revival of cities. Old Roman sites came back to life, and new towns arose at major crossroads or natural harbors favorable to trading activities. By the twelfth and thirteenth centuries, both the urban centers and the urban population of Europe were experiencing a dramatic expansion. The revival of trade, the expansion of towns and cities, and the development of a money economy did not mean the end of a predominantly rural European society, but they did open the door to new ways to make a living and new opportunities for people to expand and enrich their lives. Eventually, they created the foundations for the development of a predominantly urban industrial society.

During the High Middle Ages, a landed aristocracy whose primary function was to fight dominated European society. These nobles built innumerable castles that gave a distinctive look to the countryside. Although lords and vassals seemed forever mired in endless petty conflicts, over time medieval kings began to exert a centralizing authority and inaugurated the process of developing new kinds of monarchical states. By the thirteenth century, European monarchs were solidifying their governmental institutions in pursuit of greater power. The nobles, who rationalized their warlike attitudes by calling themselves the defenders of Christian society, continued to dominate the medieval world politically, economically, and socially. But quietly and surely, within this world of castles and private power, kings gradually began to extend their public powers and developed the machinery of government that would enable them to become the centers of political authority in Europe. The actions of these medieval monarchs laid the foundation for the European kingdoms that in one form or another have dominated the European political scene ever since.

During the High Middle Ages, the power of both nobles and kings was often overshadowed by the authority of the Catholic Church, perhaps the dominant institution of the High Middle Ages. In the Early Middle Ages, the Catholic Church had shared in the challenge of new growth by reforming itself and striking out on a path toward greater papal power, both within the church and over European society. The High Middle Ages witnessed a spiritual renewal that led to numerous and even divergent paths: revived papal leadership, the development of centralized administrative machinery that buttressed papal authority, and new dimensions to the religious life of the clergy and laity. A wave of religious enthusiasm in the twelfth and thirteenth centuries led to the formation of new religious orders that worked to provide for the needs of the people, especially their concern for achieving salvation.

The economic, political, and religious growth of the High Middle Ages also gave European society a new confidence that enabled it to look beyond its borders to the lands and empires of the east. Only a confident Europe could have undertaken the crusades, a concerted military effort to recover the Holy Land of the Near East from the Muslims.

Western assurance and energy, so crucial to the crusades, were also evident in a burst of intellectual and artistic activity. New educational institutions known as universities came into being in the twelfth century. New literature, written in the vernacular language, appealed to the growing number of people in cities or at courts who could read. The study of theology, "queen of the sciences," reached a high point in the work of Thomas Aquinas. At the same time, a religious building spree—especially evident in the great Romanesque and Gothic cathedrals of the age—left the landscape bedecked with churches that were the visible symbols of Christian Europe's vitality.

Growth and optimism seemed to characterize the High Middle Ages, but underneath the calm exterior lay seeds of discontent and change. Dissent from church teaching and practices grew in the thirteenth century, leading to a climate of fear and intolerance as the church responded with inquisitorial instruments to enforce conformity to its teachings. The breakdown of the old agricultural system and the creation of new relationships between lords and peasants led to local peasant uprisings in the late thirteenth century. The crusades ended ignominiously with the fall of the last crusading foothold in the east in 1291. By that time, more and more signs of ominous troubles were appearing. The fourteenth century would prove to be a time of crisis for European civilization.

WESTERN CIVILIZATION

CHAPTER

11

THE LATER MIDDLE AGES: CRISIS AND DISINTEGRATION IN THE FOURTEENTH CENTURY

AAAC/TopFoto/The Image Works

A medieval illustration of Death as a reaper during the Black Death

CHAPTER OUTLINE AND FOCUS QUESTIONS

A Time of Troubles: Black Death and Social Crisis

Q What impact did the Black Death have on the society and economy of Europe?

War and Political Instability

Q What major problems did European states face in the fourteenth century?

The Decline of the Church

Q How and why did the authority and prestige of the papacy decline in the fourteenth century?

The Cultural World of the Fourteenth Century

Q What were the major developments in literature and art in the fourteenth century?

Society in an Age of Adversity

Q How did the adversities of the fourteenth century affect urban life and medical practices?

Critical Thinking

Q *Make an argument either for or against the idea that climate and disease played a major role in producing social, economic, and political changes in the fourteenth century.*

Connections to Today

Q *What similarities and differences do you see in the responses to natural disasters in the fourteenth and twenty-first centuries?*

AS A RESULT OF THEIR CONQUESTS in the thirteenth and fourteenth centuries, the Mongols created a vast empire stretching from Russia in the west to China in the east. Mongol rule brought stability to the Eurasian trade routes; increased trade brought prosperity but also avenues for the spread of flea-infested rats that carried bubonic plague to both East Asia and Europe. The mid-fourteenth century witnessed one of the most destructive natural disasters in history—the Black Death. One contemporary observer named Henry Knighton, a canon of Saint Mary of the Meadow Abbey in Leicester, England, was simply overwhelmed by the magnitude of the catastrophe. Knighton began his account of the great plague with these words: "In this year [1348] and in the following one there was a general mortality of people throughout the whole world." Few were left untouched; the plague struck even isolated monasteries: "At Montpellier, there remained out of a hundred and forty friars only seven." Animals, too, were devastated: "During this same year, there was a great mortality of sheep everywhere in the kingdom; in one place and in one pasture, more than five thousand sheep died and became so putrefied that neither beast nor bird wanted to touch them." Knighton was also stunned by the economic and social consequences of the Black Death. Prices dropped: "And the price of everything was cheap, because of the fear of death; there were very few who took any care for their wealth, or for anything else." Meanwhile laborers were scarce, so their wages increased: "In the following autumn, one could not hire a reaper at a lower wage than eight pence with food, or a mower at less than twelve pence with food. Because of this, much grain rotted in the fields for lack of harvesting." So many people died that some towns were deserted and some villages disappeared altogether: "Many small villages and hamlets were completely deserted; there was not one house left in them, but all those who had lived in them were dead."[1] Some people thought the end of the world was at hand.

Plague was not the only disaster in the fourteenth century. Signs of disintegration were everywhere: famine, economic depression, war, social upheaval, a rise in crime and violence, and a decline in the power of the universal Catholic Church. Periods of disintegration, however, are often fertile ground for change and new developments. Out of the dissolution of medieval civilization came a rebirth of culture that many historians have labeled the Renaissance.

A Time of Troubles: Black Death and Social Crisis

FOCUS QUESTION: What impact did the Black Death have on the society and economy of Europe?

Well into the thirteenth century, Europe had experienced good harvests and an expanding population. By the end of the century, however, a period of disastrous changes had begun.

Famine and Population

For one thing, there were noticeable changes in weather patterns as Europe entered a "little ice age." Shortened growing seasons and disastrous weather conditions, including severe storms and constant rain, led to widespread famine and hunger. The great famine of 1315–1317 in northern Europe resulted in extreme hunger and starvation. The great famine expanded to other parts of Europe in an all-too-familiar pattern, as is evident in this scene described by a contemporary chronicler:

> We saw a large number of both sexes, not only from nearby places but from as much as five leagues away, barefooted and maybe even, except for women, in a completely nude state, together with their priests coming in procession at the Church of the Holy Martyrs, their bones bulging out, devoutly carrying bodies of saints and other relics to be adorned hoping to get relief.[2]

Some historians estimate that famine killed 10 percent of the European population in the first half of the fourteenth century.

Europe had experienced a great increase in population in the High Middle Ages. By 1300, however, indications are that Europe had reached the upper limit in the number of people who could be supported by existing agricultural production and technology. Virtually all productive land was being farmed, including many marginal lands that needed intensive cultivation and proved easily susceptible to changing weather patterns.

There was also a movement from overpopulated rural areas to urban locations. Eighteen percent of the people in the village of Broughton in England, for example, migrated between 1288 and 1340. There is no certainty that these migrants found better economic opportunities in urban areas. We might in fact conclude the opposite, based on the reports of increasing numbers of poor people in the cities. In 1330, for example, one chronicler estimated that of the 100,000 inhabitants of Florence, 17,000 were paupers. Moreover, evidence suggests that because of the growing population, by 1300 individual peasant holdings were shrinking in size to an acreage that could no longer support a peasant family. Europe seemed to have reached an upper limit to population growth, and the number of poor appeared to have increased noticeably.

Some historians have pointed out that famine may have led to chronic malnutrition, which in turn contributed to increased infant mortality, lower birthrates, and higher susceptibility to disease because malnourished people are less able to resist infection. This, they argue, helps explain the high mortality of the great plague known as the Black Death.

The Black Death: From Asia to Europe

In the mid-fourteenth century, the disaster known as the **Black Death** struck Asia, North Africa, and Europe. Although there were several types of plague, the most common and most important form in the diffusion of the Black Death was bubonic plague, which was spread by black rats infested with fleas who were host to the deadly bacterium *Yersinia pestis*.

ROLE OF THE MONGOLS This great plague originated in Asia. After disappearing from Europe and the Middle East in the Middle Ages, bubonic plague continued to haunt areas of southwestern China. In the early 1300s, rats accompanying Mongol troops spread the plague into central China and by 1331 to northeastern China. In one province near Beijing, it was reported that 90 percent of the population died. Overall, China's population may have declined from 120 million in the mid-fourteenth century to 80 million by 1400.

In the thirteenth century, the Mongols had brought much of the Eurasian landmass under a single rule, which in turn facilitated long-distance trade, particularly along the Silk Road (see Chapter 6), now dominated by Muslim merchants from Central Asia. The movement of people and goods throughout this Eurasian landmass also facilitated the spread of the plague.

In the 1330s, there were outbreaks of plague in Central Asia; by 1339, it had reached Samarkand, a caravan stop on the Silk Road. From Central Asia, trading caravans carried the plague westward, to Caffa, on the Black Sea, in 1346, and Constantinople by 1347. Its arrival in the Byzantine Empire was noted by Emperor John VI, who lost a son: "Upon arrival in Constantinople she [the empress] found Andronikos, the youngest born, dead from the invading plague, which . . . attacked almost all the seacoasts of the world and killed most of their people."[3] By 1348, the plague had spread to Egypt, Mecca, and Damascus as well as to other parts of the Middle East.

The Black Death in Europe

The Black Death of the mid-fourteenth century was the most devastating natural disaster in European history, ravaging

OPPOSING VIEWPOINTS

Causes of the Black Death: Contemporary Views

THE BLACK DEATH WAS THE MOST terrifying natural calamity of the Middle Ages and affected wide areas of Europe, North Africa, and Asia. People were often baffled by the plague, especially its causes, and gave widely different explanations. The first selection is taken from the preface to the *Decameron* by the fourteenth-century Italian writer Giovanni Boccaccio. The other selections are from contemporary treatises that offered widely different explanations for the great plague.

Giovanni Boccaccio, *Decameron*

In the year of Our Lord 1348 the deadly plague broke out in the great city of Florence, most beautiful of Italian cities. Whether through the operation of the heavenly bodies or because of our own iniquities which the just wrath of God sought to correct, the plague had arisen in the East some years before, causing the death of countless human beings. It spread without stop from one place to another, until, unfortunately, it swept over the West. Neither knowledge nor human foresight availed against it, though the city was cleansed of much filth by chosen officers in charge and sick persons were forbidden to enter it, while advice was broadcast for the preservation of health. Nor did humble supplications serve. Not once but many times they were ordained in the form of processions and other ways for the propitiation of God by the faithful, but, in spite of everything, toward the spring of the year the plague began to show its ravages.

On Earthquakes as the Cause of Plague

There is a fourth opinion, which I consider more likely than the others, which is that insofar as the mortality arose from natural causes its immediate cause was a corrupt and poisonous earthy exhalation, which infected the air in various parts of the world and, when breathed in by people, suffocated them and suddenly snuffed them out....

It is a matter of scientific fact that earthquakes are caused by the exhalation of fumes enclosed in the bowels of the earth. When the fumes batter against the sides of the earth, and cannot get out, the earth is shaken and moves. I say that it is the vapor and corrupted air which has been vented—or so to speak purged—in the earthquake which occurred on St. Paul's day, 1347, along with the corrupted air vented in other earthquakes and eruptions, which has infected the air above the earth and killed people in various parts of the world; and I can bring various reasons in support of this conclusion.

Herman Gigas on Well Poisoning

In 1347 there was such a great pestilence and mortality throughout almost the whole world that in the opinion of well-informed men scarcely a tenth of mankind survived.... Some say that it was brought about by the corruption of the air; others that the Jews planned to wipe out all the Christians with poison and had poisoned wells and springs everywhere. And many Jews confessed as much under torture: that they had bred spiders and toads in pots and pans, and had obtained poison from overseas; and that not every Jew knew about this wickedness, only the more powerful ones, so that it would not be betrayed. As evidence of this heinous crime, men say that the bags full of poison were found in many wells and springs, and as a result, in cities, towns and villages throughout Germany, and in fields and woods too, almost all the wells and springs have been blocked up or built over, so that no one can drink from them or use the water for cooking, and men have to use rain or river water instead. God, the lord of vengeance, has not suffered the malice of the Jews to go unpunished. Throughout Germany, in all but a few places, they were burnt. For fear of that punishment many accepted baptism and their lives were spared. This action was taken against the Jews in 1349, and it still continues unabated, for in a number of regions many people, noble and humble alike, have laid plans against them and their defenders which they will never abandon until the whole Jewish race has been destroyed.

Q *What were the different explanations for the causes of the Black Death? How do you explain the differences, and what do these explanations tell you about the level of scientific knowledge in the later Middle Ages? Why do you think Jews became scapegoats?*

Sources: Giovanni Boccaccio, *Decameron*, trans. F. Winwar (New York: Limited Editions, 1930), pp. xxii–xxiv, xxviii–xxix; "On Earthquakes as the Cause of Plague" and "Herman Gigas on Well Poisoning," in *The Black Death*, R. Horrox, ed., trans. (Manchester, U.K.: Manchester University Press).

Europe's population and causing economic, social, political, and cultural upheaval (see the box above). Contemporary chroniclers lamented that parents attempted to flee, abandoning their children; one related the words of a child left behind: "Oh father, why have you abandoned me?... Mother where have you gone?"[4] People were horrified by an evil force they could not understand and by the subsequent breakdown of all normal human relations.

Symptoms of bubonic plague included high fever, aching joints, swelling of the lymph nodes, and dark blotches caused by bleeding beneath the skin. Bubonic plague was actually the least toxic form of plague but nevertheless killed 50 to

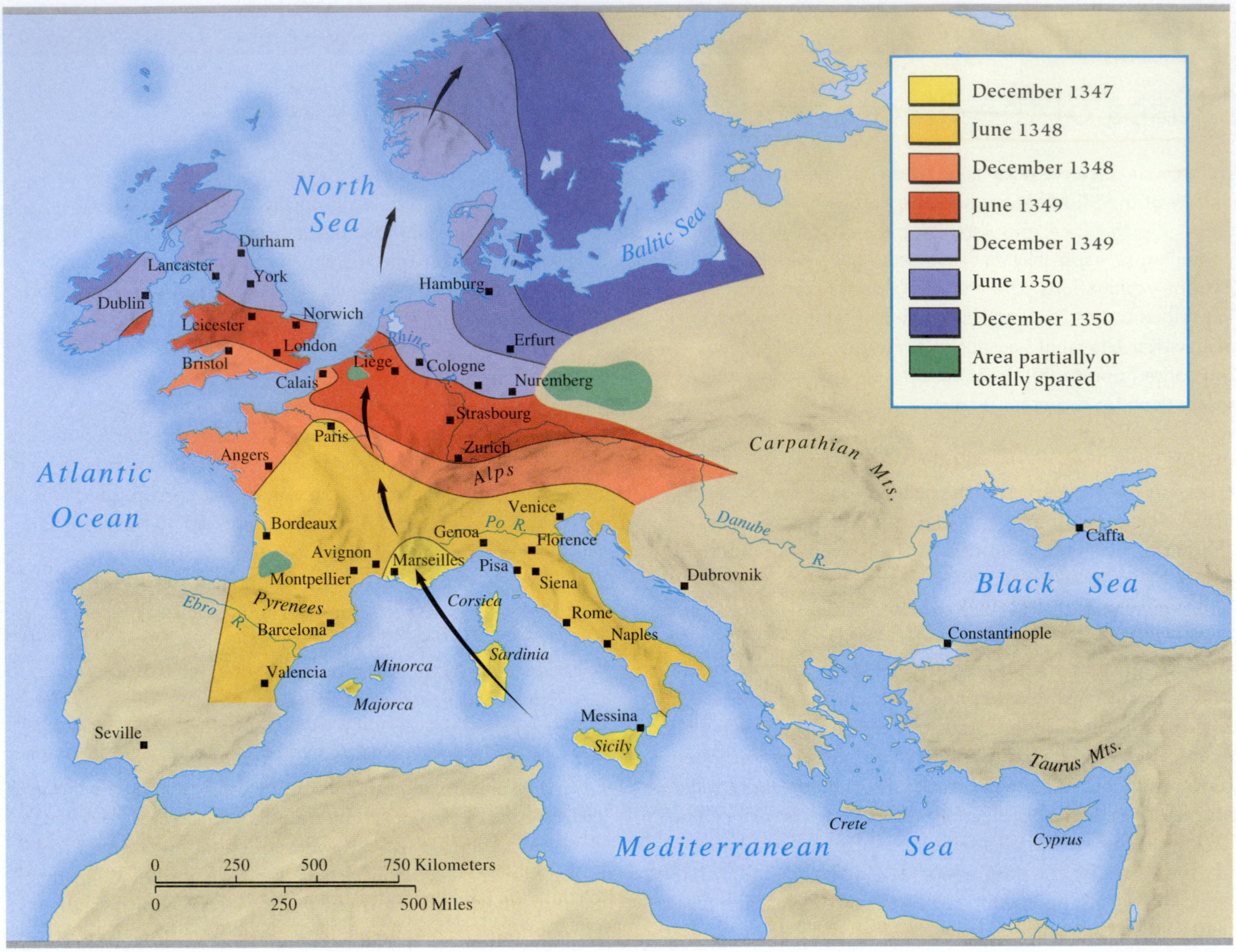

MAP 11.1 **Spread of the Black Death.** The plague entered Europe by way of Sicily in 1347 and within three years had killed between one-quarter and one-half of the population. Outbreaks continued into the early eighteenth century, and the European population took two hundred years to return to the level it had reached before the Black Death.

Q *Is there a general pattern between distance from Sicily and the elapsed time before a region was infected with the plague?*

60 percent of its victims. In pneumonic plague, the bacterial infection spread to the lungs, resulting in severe coughing, bloody sputum, and the relatively easy spread of the bacillus from human to human by coughing.

The plague reached Europe in October 1347 when Genoese merchants brought it from Caffa to the island of Sicily off the coast of Italy. One contemporary wrote: "As it happened, among those who escaped from Caffa by boat, there were a few sailors who had been infected with the poisonous disease. Some boats were bound for Genoa, others went to Venice and other Christian areas. When the sailors reached these places and mixed with the people there, it was as if they had brought evil spirits with them."[5] The plague spread quickly, reaching southern Italy and southern France and Spain by the end of 1347 (see Map 11.1). Usually, the diffusion of the Black Death followed commercial trade routes. In 1348, the plague spread through France and the Low Countries and into Germany. By the end of that year, it had moved to England, ravaging it in 1349. By the end of 1349, the plague had expanded to northern Europe and Scandinavia. Eastern Europe and Russia were affected by 1351, although mortality rates were never as high in eastern Europe as they were in western and central Europe.

Mortality figures for the Black Death were incredibly high. Italy was hit especially hard. As the commercial center of the Mediterranean, Italy possessed scores of ports where the plague could be introduced. Italy's crowded cities, whether large, such as Florence, Genoa, and Venice, with populations near 100,000, or small, such as Orvieto and Pistoia, suffered losses of 50 to 60 percent. France and England were also particularly devastated. In northern France, farming villages suffered mortality rates of 30 percent, while cities such as Rouen were more

Mass Burial of Plague Victims. The Black Death had spread to northern Europe by the end of 1348. Shown here is a mass burial of victims of the plague in Tournai, located in modern Belgium. As is evident in the illustration, at this stage of the plague, there was still time to make coffins for the victims' burial. Later, as the plague intensified, the dead were thrown into open pits.

severely affected and experienced losses as high as 40 percent. In England and Germany, entire villages simply disappeared. In Germany, of approximately 170,000 inhabited locations, only 130,000 were left by the end of the fourteenth century.

It has been estimated that the European population declined by 25 to 50 percent between 1347 and 1351. If we accept the recent scholarly assessment of a European population of 75 million in the early fourteenth century, this means a death toll of 19 to 38 million people in four years. And the plague did not end in 1351. There were major outbreaks again in 1361–1362 and 1369 and then recurrences every five or six to ten or twelve years, depending on climatic and ecological conditions, until the end of the fifteenth century. The European population thus did not begin to recover until around 1500 and took several generations after that to reattain thirteenth-century levels.

LIFE AND DEATH: REACTIONS TO THE PLAGUE Natural disasters of the magnitude of the great plague produce extreme psychological reactions. Knowing they could be dead in a matter of days, people began to live for the moment; some threw themselves with abandon into sexual and alcoholic orgies. The fourteenth-century Italian writer Giovanni Boccaccio (joe-VAH-nee boh-KAH-choh) gave a classic description of this kind of reaction to the plague in Florence in the preface to his famous *Decameron:*

> [Some people] held that plenty of drinking and enjoyment, singing and free living and the gratification of the appetite in every possible way, letting the devil take the hindmost, was the best preventative . . . and as far as they could, they suited the action to the word. Day and night they went from one tavern to another drinking and carousing unrestrainedly. At the least inkling of something that suited them, they ran wild in other people's houses, and there was no one to prevent them, for everyone had abandoned all responsibility for his belongings as well as for himself, considering his days numbered.[6]

Wealthy and powerful people fled to their country estates, as Boccaccio recounted: "Still others . . . maintained that no remedy against plagues was better than to leave them miles behind. Men and women without number . . . caring for nobody but themselves, abandoned the city, their houses and estates, their own flesh and blood even, and their effects, in search of a country place."[7]

The attempt to explain the Black Death and mitigate its harshness led to extreme sorts of behavior. To many people, the plague had either been sent by God as a punishment for humans' sins or been caused by the devil. Some resorted to extreme asceticism to cleanse themselves of sin and gain God's forgiveness. Such were the flagellants (FLAJ-uh-lunts), whose movement became popular in 1348, especially in Germany. Groups of flagellants, both men and women, wandered from town to town, flogging themselves with whips to win the forgiveness of God, whom they believed had sent the plague to punish humans for their sinful ways. One contemporary chronicler described a flagellant procession:

> The penitents went about, coming first out of Germany. They were men who did public penance and scourged themselves with whips of hard knotted leather with little iron spikes. Some made themselves bleed very badly between the shoulder blades and some foolish women had cloths ready to catch the blood and smear it on their eyes, saying it was miraculous blood. While they were doing penance, they sang very mournful songs about the nativity and the passion of Our Lord. The object of this penance was to put a stop to the mortality.[8]

The flagellants attracted attention and created mass hysteria wherever they went. The Catholic Church, however, became alarmed when flagellant groups began to kill Jews and attack clergy who opposed them. Some groups also developed a millenarian aspect, anticipating the imminent end of the world, the return of Jesus, and the establishment of a thousand-year kingdom under his governance. Pope Clement VI condemned the flagellants in October 1349 and urged the public authorities to crush them. By the end of 1350, most of the flagellant movement had been destroyed.

An outbreak of virulent anti-Semitism also accompanied the Black Death. Jews were accused of causing the plague by

THE CREMATION OF THE STRASBOURG JEWS

IN THEIR ATTEMPT TO EXPLAIN THE widespread horrors of the Black Death, medieval Christian communities looked for scapegoats. As at the time of the Crusades, the Jews were blamed for poisoning wells and thereby spreading the plague. This selection by a contemporary chronicler, written in 1349, gives an account of how Christians in the town of Strasbourg in the Holy Roman Empire dealt with their Jewish community. It is apparent that financial gain was also an important motive in killing the Jews.

Jacob von Konigshofen, "The Cremation of the Strasbourg Jews"

In the year 1349 there occurred the greatest epidemic that ever happened. Death went from one end of the earth to the other.... And from what this epidemic came, all wise teachers and physicians could only say that it was God's will.... This epidemic also came to Strasbourg in the summer of the above-mentioned year, and it is estimated that about sixteen thousand people died.

In the matter of this plague the Jews throughout the world were reviled and accused in all lands of having caused it through the poison which they are said to have put into the water and the wells—that is what they were accused of—and for this reason the Jews were burnt all the way from the Mediterranean into Germany....

[The account then goes on to discuss the situation of the Jews in the city of Strasbourg.]

On Saturday... they burnt the Jews on a wooden platform in their cemetery. There were about two thousand people of them. Those who wanted to baptize themselves were spared. [About one thousand accepted baptism.] Many small children were taken out of the fire and baptized against the will of their fathers and mothers. And everything that was owed to the Jews was canceled, and the Jews had to surrender all pledges and notes that they had taken for debts. The council, however, took the cash that the Jews possessed and divided it among the working-men proportionately. The money was indeed the thing that killed the Jews. If they had been poor and if the lords had not been in debt to them, they would not have been burnt....

Thus were the Jews burnt at Strasbourg, and in the same year in all the cities of the Rhine, whether Free Cities or Imperial Cities or cities belonging to the lords. In some towns they burnt the Jews after a trial, in others, without a trial. In some cities the Jews themselves set fire to their houses and cremated themselves.

It was decided in Strasbourg that no Jew should enter the city for 100 years, but before 20 years had passed, the council and magistrates agreed that they ought to admit the Jews again into the city for 20 years. And so the Jews came back again to Strasbourg in the year 1368 after the birth of our Lord.

Q *What charges were made against the Jews in regard to the Black Death? Can it be said that these charges were economically motivated? Why or why not?*

Source: J. R. Marcus, *The Jew in the Medieval World* (Pittsburgh: The Hebrew Union College Press, 1972).

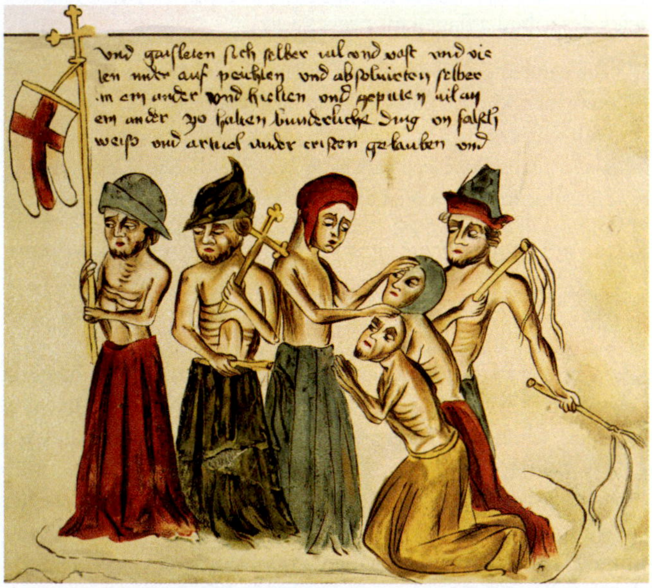

The Flagellants. Reactions to the plague were extreme at times. Believing that asceticism could atone for humanity's sins and win God's forgiveness, flagellants wandered from town to town flogging themselves and each other with whips as in this illustration from a fifteenth-century German manuscript.

poisoning town wells. Although Jews were persecuted in Spain, the worst organized massacres, or **pogroms** (POH-grums), against this helpless minority were carried out in Germany; more than sixty major Jewish communities in Germany had been exterminated by 1351 (see the box above). Many Jews fled eastward to Russia and especially to Poland, where the king offered them protection. Eastern Europe became home to large Jewish communities.

The prevalence of death because of the plague and its recurrences affected people in profound ways. Some survivors apparently came to treat life as something cheap and transient. Violence and violent death appeared to be more common after the plague than before. Post-plague Europe also demonstrated a morbid preoccupation with death. In their sermons, priests reminded parishioners that each night's sleep might be their last. Tombstones were decorated with macabre scenes of naked corpses in various stages of decomposition with snakes entwined in their bones and their innards filled with worms.

ART AND THE BLACK DEATH The Black Death made a visible impact on art. For one thing, it wiped out entire guilds of artists. At the same time, survivors, including the newly rich who patronized artists, were no longer so optimistic. Some

Francesco Traini, *The Triumph of Death.* The plague led to a morbid fascination with death that is visible in the art of the period. Shown here is the left side of Francesco Traini's fresco, which depicts a group of young aristocrats on a hunt encountering three decaying corpses in coffins. One of the nobles is shown gagging at the smell of the decomposing bodies.

were more guilty about enjoying life and more concerned about gaining salvation. Post-plague art began to concentrate on pain and death. A fairly large number of artistic works came to be based on the *ars moriendi* (AHRS moh-ree-EN-dee), the art of dying. A morbid concern with death is especially evident in the fresco *The Triumph of Death* by Francesco Traini (frahn-CHES-koh TRAY-nee) in Pisa. On the left side of the fresco, several young nobles encounter three coffins containing decomposing bodies, while on the right young aristocrats engage in pleasant pursuits but are threatened by a grim figure of Death in the form of a witch flying through the air swinging a large scythe. Beneath her lie piles of dead citizens and clergy cut down in the prime of life.

Economic Dislocation and Social Upheaval

The population collapse of the fourteenth century had dire economic and social consequences. Economic dislocation was accompanied by social upheaval. Between 1000 and 1300, Europe had been relatively stable. The division of society into the three estates of clergy (those who pray), nobility (those who fight), and laborers (those who work) had already begun to disintegrate in the thirteenth century, however. In the fourteenth century, a series of urban and rural revolts rocked European society.

NOBLE LANDLORDS AND PEASANTS Both peasants and noble landlords were affected by the demographic crisis of the fourteenth century. Most noticeably, Europe experienced a serious labor shortage that caused a dramatic rise in the price of labor. At Cuxham manor in England, for example, a farm laborer who had received two shillings a week in 1347 was paid seven in 1349 and almost eleven by 1350. At the same time, the decline in population depressed or held stable the demand for agricultural produce, resulting in stable or falling prices for output (although in England prices remained high until the 1380s). The chronicler Henry Knighton observed: "And the price of everything was cheap. . . . A man could buy a horse for half a mark [six shillings], which before was worth forty shillings."[9] Because landlords were having to pay more for labor at the same time that their rents or incomes were declining, they began to experience considerable adversity and lower standards of living. In England, aristocratic incomes dropped more than 20 percent between 1347 and 1353.

Landed aristocrats responded by seeking to lower the wage rate. The English Parliament passed the Statute of Laborers (1351), which attempted to limit wages to pre-plague levels and forbid the mobility of peasants as well. Although such laws proved largely unworkable, they did keep wages from rising as high as they might have in a free market. Overall, the position of landlords continued to deteriorate during the late fourteenth and early fifteenth centuries. At the same time, conditions for peasants improved, though not uniformly throughout Europe.

The decline in the number of peasants after the Black Death accelerated the process of converting labor services to rents, freeing peasants from the obligations of servile tenure and weakening the system of manorialism. But there were limits to how much the peasants could advance. Not only did they face the same economic hurdles as the lords, but the latter attempted to impose wage restrictions and reinstate old forms of labor service. New governmental taxes also hurt. Peasant complaints became widespread and soon gave rise to rural revolts.

PEASANT REVOLT IN FRANCE In 1358, a peasant revolt, known as the *Jacquerie* (zhahk-REE), broke out in northern France. The destruction of normal order by the Black Death and the subsequent economic dislocation were important factors in causing the revolt, but the ravages created by the Hundred Years' War also affected the French peasantry (see "War and Political Instability" later in this chapter). Both the French and English forces followed a deliberate policy of laying waste to peasants' fields while bands of mercenaries lived off the land by taking peasants' produce as well.

Growing class tensions also exacerbated peasant anger. Landed nobles were eager to hold on to their politically privileged position and felt increasingly threatened in the new post-plague world of higher wages and lower prices. Many aristocrats looked on peasants with utter contempt. A French tale told to upper-class audiences contained this remarkable passage:

> Tell me, Lord, if you please, by what right or title does a villein [peasant] eat beef? . . . Should they eat fish? Rather let them eat thistles and briars, thorns and straw and hay on Sunday and peapods on weekdays. They should keep watch without sleep and have trouble always; that is how villeins should live. Yet each day they are full and drunk on the best wines, and in fine clothes. The great expenditures of villeins come as a high cost, for it is this that destroys and ruins the world. It is they who spoil the common welfare. From the villein comes all unhappiness. Should they eat meat? Rather should they chew grass on the heath with the horned cattle and go naked on all fours.[10]

The peasants reciprocated this contempt for their so-called social superiors.

The outburst of peasant anger led to savage confrontations. Castles were burned and nobles murdered (see the box on p. 307). Such atrocities did not go unanswered, however. The *Jacquerie* soon failed as the privileged classes closed ranks, savagely massacred the rebels, and ended the revolt.

AN ENGLISH PEASANT REVOLT The English Peasants' Revolt of 1381 was the most prominent of all. It was a product not of desperation but of rising expectations. After the Black Death, the condition of the English peasants had improved as they enjoyed greater freedom and higher wages or lower rents. Aristocratic landlords had fought back with legislation to depress wages and attempted to reimpose old feudal dues. The most immediate cause of the revolt, however, was the monarchy's attempt to raise revenues by imposing a poll tax or a flat charge on each adult member of the population. Peasants in eastern England, the wealthiest part of the country, refused to pay the tax and expelled the collectors forcibly from their villages.

This action sparked a widespread rebellion of both peasants and townspeople led by a well-to-do peasant called Wat Tyler and a preacher named John Ball. The latter preached an effective message against the noble class, as recounted by the French chronicler Jean Froissart (ZHAHNH frwah-SAR):

> Good people, things cannot go right in England and never will, until goods are held in common and there are no more villeins and gentlefolk, but we are all one and the same. . . . If we all spring from a single father and mother, Adam and Eve, how can they claim or prove that they are lords more than us, except by making us produce and grow the wealth which they spend?[11]

The revolt was initially successful as the rebels burned down the manor houses of aristocrats, lawyers, and government officials and murdered several important officials, including the archbishop of Canterbury. After the peasants marched on London, the young King Richard II, age fifteen, promised to accept the rebels' demands if they returned to their homes. They accepted the king's word and dispersed, but the king reneged and with the assistance of the aristocrats arrested hundreds of the rebels. The poll tax was eliminated, however, and in the end most of the rebels were pardoned.

REVOLTS IN THE CITIES Revolts also erupted in the cities. Commercial and industrial activity suffered almost immediately

Peasant Rebellion. The fourteenth century witnessed a number of revolts of the peasantry against noble landowners. Although the revolts often met with initial success, they were soon crushed. This fifteenth-century illustration shows nobles during the French *Jacquerie* of 1358 massacring the rebels in the town of Meaux, in northern France.

A REVOLT OF FRENCH PEASANTS

IN 1358, FRENCH PEASANTS ROSE UP in a revolt known as the *Jacquerie*. The relationship between aristocrats and peasants had degenerated as a result of the social upheavals and privations caused by the Black Death and the Hundred Years' War. This excerpt from the chronicle of an aristocrat paints a horrifying picture of the barbarities that occurred during the revolt.

Jean Froissart, *Chronicles*

There were very strange and terrible happenings in several parts of the kingdom of France. . . . They began when some of the men from the country towns came together in the Beauvais region. They had no leaders and at first they numbered scarcely 100. One of them got up and said that the nobility of France, knights and squires, were disgracing and betraying the realm, and that it would be a good thing if they were all destroyed. . . .

They banded together and went off, without further deliberation and unarmed except for pikes and knives, to the house of a knight who lived nearby. They broke in and killed the knight, with his lady and his children, big and small, and set fire to the house. . . .

They did similar things in a number of castles and big houses, and their ranks swelled until there were a good 6,000 of them. Wherever they went their numbers grew, for all the men of the same sort joined them. The knights and squires fled before them with their families. They took their wives and daughters many miles away to put them in safety, leaving their houses open with their possessions inside. And those evil men, who had come together without leaders or arms, pillaged and burned everything and violated and killed all the ladies and girls without mercy, like mad dogs. . . . Never did men commit such vile deeds. They were such that no living creature ought to see, and the men who committed the most were admired and had the highest places among them. I could never bring myself to write down the horrible and shameful things which they did to the ladies. But, among other brutal excesses, they killed a knight, put him on a spit, and turned him at the fire and roasted him before the lady and her children. After about a dozen of them had violated the lady, they tried to force her and the children to eat the knight's flesh before putting them cruelly to death.

Q *Why did the peasants react so strongly against their aristocratic lords? Do you think this is an unbiased account? Why or why not?*

Source: Froissart, *Chronicles*, trans. G. Brereton (London: Penguin Classics, 1968; revised 1978).

from the Black Death. An oversupply of goods and an immediate drop in demand led to a decline in trade after 1350. Some industries suffered greatly. Florence's woolen industry, one of the giants, produced 70,000 to 80,000 pieces of cloth in 1338; in 1378, it was yielding only 24,000 pieces. Bourgeois merchants and manufacturers responded to the decline in trade and production by attempting to restrict competition and resist the demands of the lower classes.

In urban areas, where capitalist industrialists paid low wages and managed to prevent workers from forming organizations to help themselves, industrial revolts broke out throughout Europe. Ghent experienced one in 1381, Rouen in 1382. Most famous, however, was the revolt of the *ciompi* (CHAHM-pee) in Florence in 1378. The *ciompi* were wool workers in Florence's most prominent industry. In the 1370s, not only was the woolen industry depressed, but the wool workers saw their real wages decline when the coinage in which they were paid was debased. Their revolt won them some concessions from the municipal government, including the right to form guilds and be represented in the government. But their newly won rights were short-lived; authorities ended *ciompi* participation in the government by 1382.

Although the peasant and urban revolts sometimes resulted in short-term gains for the participants, the uprisings were quickly crushed and their gains lost. Accustomed to ruling, the established classes easily formed a united front and quashed dissent. Nevertheless, the rural and urban revolts of the fourteenth century ushered in an age of social conflict that characterized much of later European history.

War and Political Instability

Q **FOCUS QUESTION:** What major problems did European states face in the fourteenth century?

Famine, plague, economic turmoil, social upheaval, and violence were not the only problems of the fourteenth century. War and political instability must also be added to the list. Of all the struggles that ensued in the fourteenth century, the Hundred Years' War was the most famous and the most violent.

Causes of the Hundred Years' War

In 1259, the English king, Henry III, had relinquished his claims to all the French territories previously held by the English monarchy except for one relatively small possession known as the duchy of Gascony. As duke of Gascony, the English king pledged loyalty as a vassal to the French king. But this territory gave rise to numerous disputes between the kings of England and France. By the thirteenth century, the Capetian monarchs had greatly increased their power over their more important vassals, the great lords of France. Royal officials interfered regularly in the affairs of the vassals' fiefs, especially in matters of justice. Although this policy irritated all the vassals, it especially annoyed the king of England, who considered himself the peer of the French king.

A dispute over the right of succession to the French throne also complicated relations between the French and the English. In the fourteenth century, the Capetian dynasty failed to produce a male heir for the first time in almost four hundred years. In 1328, the last son of King Philip IV died without a male heir. The closest male relative in line to the throne was King Edward III of England (1327–1377), whose mother was Isabella, the daughter of Philip IV (see Chart 11.1). Known for her strong personality (she was nicknamed the "she-wolf of France"), Isabella, with the assistance of her lover, led a revolt against her husband, King Edward II, overthrew him, and ruled England until her teenage son, Edward III, took sole control of the throne in 1330. As the son of the daughter of King Philip IV, King Edward III of England had a claim to the French throne, but the French nobles argued that the inheritance of the monarchy could not pass through the female line and chose a cousin of the Capetians, Philip, duke of Valois (val-WAH), as King Philip VI (1328–1350).

Conduct and Course of the War

The Hundred Years' War began in a burst of knightly enthusiasm. Trained to be warriors, knights viewed the clash of battle as the ultimate opportunity to demonstrate their fighting abilities. But this struggle would change the nature of warfare, for as it dragged on, it was not knights but peasant foot soldiers who increasingly determined the outcomes of battles. The French army of 1337, with its heavily armed noble cavalry, resembled its twelfth- and thirteenth-century forebears. The noble cavalrymen considered themselves the fighting elite and looked with contempt on the foot soldiers and crossbowmen, their social inferiors.

The English army, however, had evolved differently and had included peasants as paid foot soldiers since at least Anglo-Saxon times. Armed with pikes, many of these foot soldiers had also adopted the longbow. The longbow was first used by the Welsh, but the English, recognizing the power of the longbow used against them, soon adopted its use. English archery laws in the thirteenth and fourteenth centuries also decreed that all English men should possess a bow and arrow and practice on Sundays and holidays. A well-trained longbowman could shoot ten to twelve arrows per minute, a more rapid speed of fire than the more powerful crossbow. And the arrows could pierce the armor of a knight at ranges of more than 250 yards. Although the English made use of heavily armed cavalry, they relied even more on large numbers of foot soldiers.

EARLY PHASES OF THE WAR Edward III's early campaigns in France achieved little. When Edward renewed his efforts in 1346 with an invasion of Normandy, Philip responded by raising a large force to crush the English army and met Edward's forces at Crécy (kray-SEE), just south of Flanders. Recent estimates are a French army of 30,000 warriors meeting an English army of 15,000 men. The larger French army followed no battle plan but simply attacked the English lines in a disorderly fashion. The arrows of the English archers devastated the French cavalry. It was a stunning victory for the English. The Battle of Crécy determined that the six-foot longbow would become a dominant battlefield weapon at the time. Edward followed up by capturing the French port of Calais (ka-LAY) to serve as a staging ground for future invasions.

The Battle of Crécy was not decisive, however. The English simply did not possess the resources to subjugate all of France. Truces, small-scale hostilities, and some major operations were combined in an orgy of seemingly incessant struggle. The English campaigns were waged by Edward III and his son Edward, the prince of Wales, known as the Black Prince. The Black Prince's campaigns in France were devastating. Avoiding pitched battles, his forces deliberately ravaged the land,

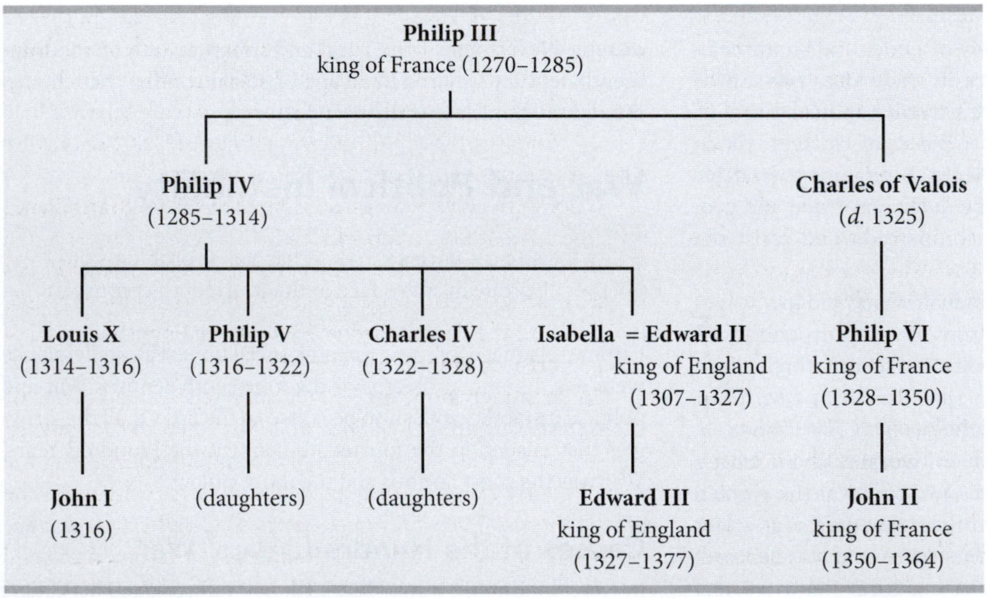

Chart 11.1 Background to the Hundred Years' War: Kings of France and England. The immediate cause of the war between France and England was yet another quarrel over Gascony. In 1337, when Edward III, the king of England and duke of Gascony, refused to do homage to Philip VI for Gascony, the French king seized the duchy. Edward responded by declaring war on Philip, the "so-called king of France." There is no doubt that the personalities of the two monarchs also had much to do with the outbreak of the Hundred Years' War. Both Edward and Philip loved luxury and shared a desire for the glory and prestige that came from military engagements. Both were only too willing to use their respective nation's resources to satisfy their own desires. Moreover, for many nobles, the promise of plunder and territorial gain was an incentive to follow the disruptive path of their rulers.

Fr 2643 f.165v Battle of Crecy from the Hundred Years War, from 'Froissart's Chronicle', 24th August 1346 (vellum), French School, (15th century)/Bibliotheque Nationale, Paris, France/Bridgeman Images

Battle of Crécy. This fifteenth-century manuscript illustration depicts the Battle of Crécy, the first of several military disasters suffered by the French in the Hundred Years' War, and shows why the English preferred the longbow to the crossbow. At left, the French crossbowmen have to stop shooting and prime their weapons by cranking the handle, while the English archers continue to shoot their longbows (a skilled archer could launch ten to twelve arrows a minute).

burning crops and entire unfortified villages and towns and stealing anything of value. For the English, such campaigns were profitable; for the French people, they meant hunger, deprivation, and death.

The army of the Black Prince was finally forced to do battle near Poitiers. Although the opposing forces were smaller than those at the Battle of Crécy, the results were again similar. French casualties included two thousand killed and two thousand captured, including their king, John II (1350–1364). This Battle of Poitiers (pwah-TYAY) (1356) ended the first phase of the Hundred Years' War. Under the Peace of Brétigny (bray-tee-NYEE) (1359), the French agreed to pay a large ransom for King John, the English territories in Gascony were enlarged, and Edward renounced his claims to the throne of France in return for John's promise to give up control over English lands in France. This first phase of the war made it clear that despite their victories, the English were not really strong enough to subdue all of France and make Edward III's claim to the French monarchy a reality.

Monarchs, however, could be slow learners. The Treaty of Brétigny was never really enforced. In the next phase of the war, in the capable hands of John's son Charles V (1364–1380), the French recovered what they had previously lost. The English returned to plundering the French countryside and avoiding pitched battles. That pleased Charles, who did not want to engage in set battles, preferring to use armed bands to reduce the English fortresses systematically.

By 1374, the French had recovered their lost lands, although France itself continued to be plagued by "free companies" of mercenaries who, no longer paid by the English, simply lived off the land by plunder and ransom. Nevertheless, for the time being, the war seemed over, especially when a twenty-year truce was negotiated in 1396.

RENEWAL OF THE WAR In 1415, however, the English king, Henry V (1413–1422), renewed the war at a time when the French were enduring civil war as the dukes of Burgundy and Orléans (or-lay-AHN) competed to control the weak French king, Charles VI (1380–1422). In the summer of 1413, Paris exploded with bloody encounters. Taking advantage of the chaos, Henry V invaded France in 1415. At the Battle of Agincourt (AH-zhen-koor) (1415), the French suffered a disastrous defeat, and 1,500 French nobles died when the heavy, armor-plated French knights attempted to attack across a field turned to mud by heavy rain. Altogether, French losses were 6,000 dead; the English lost only three hundred men.

Henry went on to reconquer Normandy and forge an alliance with the duke of Burgundy, which led Charles VI to agree to the Treaty of Troyes (TRWAH) in 1420. By this treaty, Henry V was married to Catherine, daughter of Charles VI, and recognized as the heir to the French throne. By 1420, the English were masters of northern France (see Map 11.2).

The seemingly hopeless French cause fell into the hands of Charles the dauphin (DAH-fin *or* doh-FAN) (heir to the throne), the son of Charles VI, who, despite being disinherited by the Treaty of Troyes, still considered himself the real heir to the French throne. The dauphin governed the southern two-thirds of French lands from Bourges. Charles was weak and timid and was unable to rally the French against the English, who in 1428 had turned south and were besieging the city of Orléans to gain access to the valley of the Loire. The French monarch was saved, quite unexpectedly, by a French peasant woman.

JOAN OF ARC Joan of Arc was born in 1412 to well-to-do peasants from the village of Domrémy in Champagne. Deeply religious, Joan experienced visions and came to believe that her favorite saints had commanded her to free France and have

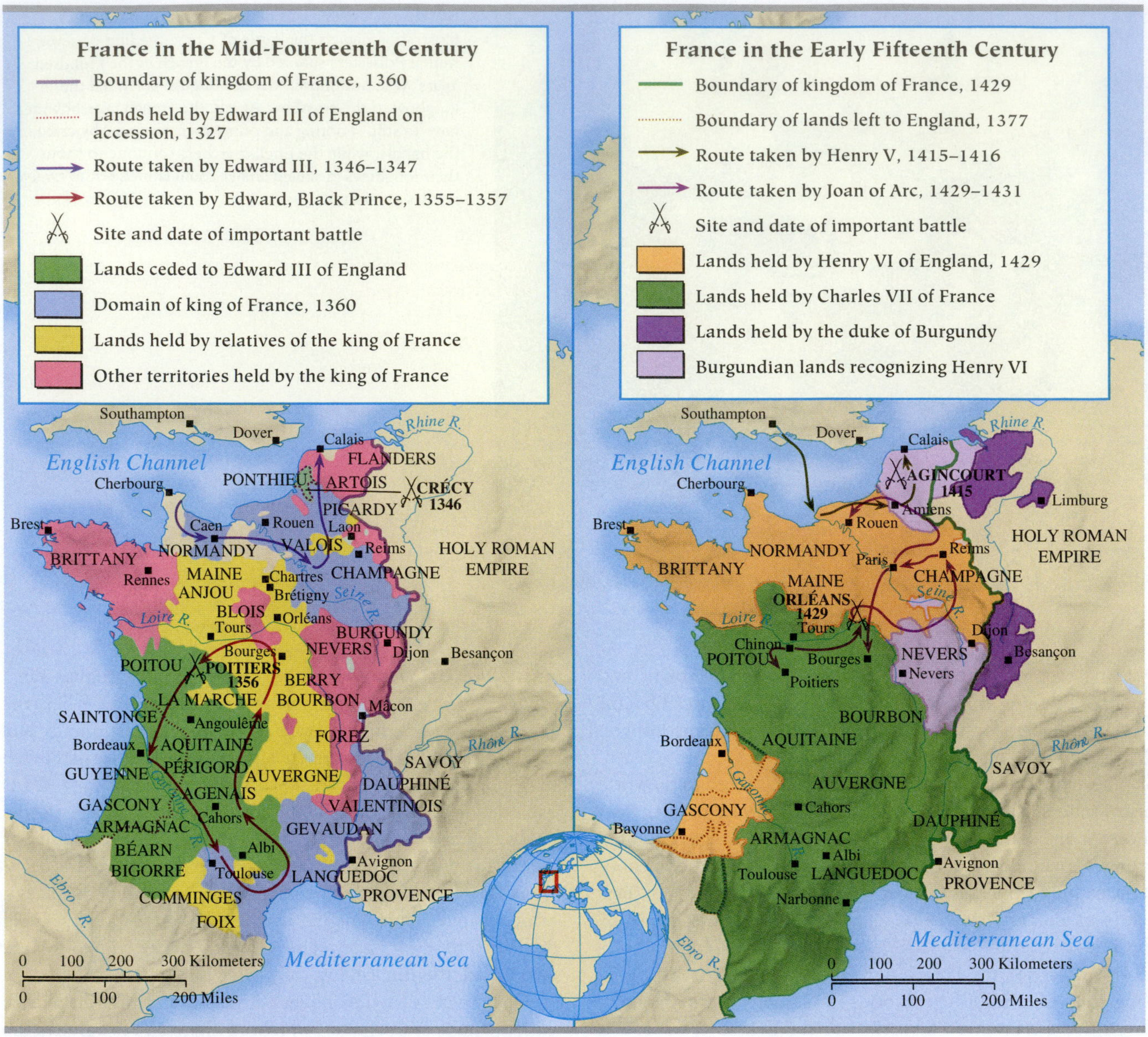

MAP 11.2 The Hundred Years' War. This long, exhausting struggle began in 1337 and dragged on until 1453. The English initially gained substantial French territory, but in the later phases of the war, France turned the tide, eventually expelling the English from all Continental lands except the port of Calais.

Q *What gains had the English made by 1429, and how do they correlate to proximity to England and the ocean?*

the dauphin crowned as king. In February 1429, Joan made her way to the dauphin's court, where her sincerity and simplicity persuaded Charles to allow her to accompany a French army to Orléans. Apparently inspired by the faith of the peasant girl, the French armies found new confidence in themselves and liberated Orléans, changing the course of the war. Within a few weeks, the entire Loire valley had been freed of the English. In July 1429, fulfilling Joan's other task, the dauphin was crowned king of France and became Charles VII (1422–1461). In accomplishing the two commands of her angelic voices, Joan had brought the war to a decisive turning point.

Joan did not live to see the war concluded, however. She was captured by the Burgundian allies of the English in 1430. Wishing to eliminate the "Maid of Orléans" for obvious political reasons, the English turned Joan over to the Inquisition on charges of witchcraft. In the fifteenth century, spiritual visions were thought to be inspired by either God or the devil. Because Joan dressed in men's clothing, it was easy for her enemies to believe that she was in league with the "prince of darkness." She was condemned to death as a heretic and burned at the stake in 1431, at the age of nineteen. To the end, as the flames rose up around her, she declared that her voices came from

Dea/G. Dagli Orti/De Agostini Picture Library/Getty Images

Joan of Arc. Pictured here in a fifteenth-century design for a window for the cathedral of Orléans, Joan of Arc is seen in a suit of armor entering the city. There are no known portraits of Joan made from life.

FILM & HISTORY

Watch ***Joan of Arc*** (1948) and ***The Messenger: The Story of Joan of Arc*** (1999), two films on one of history's best-known figures. The 1948 film version of Joan's story follows the main historical facts that are known about Joan. Joan's voices are accepted as an important part of a spiritually determined young woman. *The Messenger* presents a more contemporary and fictionalized approach to Joan. The brutality of war is rendered in realistically bloody detail, and the movie introduces revenge as a possible motive by having Joan witness the rape and murder of her sister by an English mercenary—she must kill the English to avenge her sister's death. After this traumatic incident, her voices become more strident.

Sierra Pictures/The Kobal Collection at Art Resource, NY

Gaumont/The Kobal collection at Art Resource, NY/English, Jack

Q *What are the significant differences in the approaches of these two films? What impact does the years in which the films were made have on these approaches? Which one is a more accurate rendering of Joan's life?*

God and had not deceived her (see "Film & History" above). Twenty-five years later, a church court exonerated her of these charges. To a contemporary French writer, Christine de Pizan (kris-TEEN duh pee-ZAHN), Joan was a feminist heroine (see the box on p. 312). In 1920, she was made a saint of the Roman Catholic Church.

END OF THE WAR Joan of Arc's accomplishments proved decisive. The war dragged on for another two decades, during which time the devastation of France continued (see the box on p. 313). However, defeats of English armies in Normandy and Aquitaine ultimately led to French victory. Important to the French success was the use of the cannon, a new weapon made possible by the invention of gunpowder. The Chinese had invented gunpowder in the eleventh century and devised a simple cannon by the thirteenth century. The Mongols greatly improved this technology, developing more accurate cannons and cannonballs; both spread to the Middle East and Europe by the thirteenth century.

The deaths of England's best commanders and the instability of the English government under King Henry VI (1422–1471) also contributed to England's defeat. By 1453, the only part of France that was left in English hands was the coastal town of Calais, which remained English for another century.

CHRONOLOGY	The Hundred Years' War
Outbreak of hostilities	1337
Battle of Crécy	1346
Battle of Poitiers	1356
Peace of Brétigny	1359
Death of Edward III	1377
Twenty-year truce declared	1396
Henry V (1413–1422) renews the war	1415
Battle of Agincourt	1415
Treaty of Troyes	1420
French recovery under Joan of Arc	1429–1431
End of the war	1453

Political Instability

The fourteenth century was a period of adversity for the internal political stability of European governments. Although government bureaucracies grew ever larger, at the same time the question of who should control the bureaucracies led to

A FEMINIST HEROINE: CHRISTINE DE PIZAN ON JOAN OF ARC

CHRISTINE DE PIZAN, FRANCE'S "first woman of letters," was witness to the rescue of France from the hands of the English by the efforts of Joan of Arc and was also present at the coronation of Charles VII as king of France. Christine believed that a turning point had arrived in French history and that Joan—a woman—had been responsible for France's salvation. She wrote a poem to honor this great occasion. The following stanzas are taken from her poem.

Christine de Pizan, *The Poem of Joan of Arc*, July 31, 1429

The year of fourteen twenty-nine
The sun came out to shine again.
It brings the season new and good,
Which we had not directly seen
Too long a time, while many passed
Their lives in sorrow; I am one.
But now, no longer do I grieve
Because I see what pleases me. . . .

And you, the King of France, King Charles,
The seventh of that noble name,
Who fought a mighty war before
Good fortune came at all to you:
Do, now, observe your dignity
Exalted by the Maid, who bent
Your enemies beneath your flag
In record time (that's something new!)

And people thought that it would be
Impossible indeed for you
To ever have your country back,
For it was nearly lost; but now,
It's clearly yours; no matter who
Has done you wrong, it's yours once more,
And through the clever Maid who did
Her part therein—thanks be to God! . . .

When I reflect upon your state,
The youthful maiden that you are,
To whom God gives the force and strength
To be the champion and the one
To suckle France upon her milk
Of peace, the sweetest nourishment,
To overthrow the rebel host:
The wonder passes Nature's work! . . .

But as for us, we've never heard
About a marvel quite so great
For all the heroes who have lived
In history can't measure up
In bravery against the Maid,
Who strives to rout our enemies.

It's God does that, who's guiding her
Whose courage passes that of men . . .
By miracle has she appeared,
Divine commandment sent her here.
God's angel led her in before
The king, to bring her help to him.
There's no illusion in her case
Because it's been indeed borne out
In council (in conclusion, then,
A thing is proved by its effect). . . .

What honor for the female sex!
God's love for it appears quite clear,
Because the kingdom laid to waste
By all those wretched people now
Stands safe, a woman rescued it
(A hundred thousand men could not
Do that) and killed the hostile foe!
A thing beyond belief before! . . .

While ridding France of enemies,
Retaking town and castle both
No force was ever quite so great,
If hundreds or if thousands strong!
Among our men so brave and apt
She's captain over all; such strength
No Hector or Achilles had.
All this God does, who's guiding her. . . .

The English will be crushed through her,
And never will they rise again
For God who wills it hears the voice
Of guiltless folk they tried to harm!
The blood of those they've killed, who'll walk
No more, cries out. God wants an end
To this; instead He has resolved
To chastise them as evil men.

Q *In Christine de Pizan's view, what had Joan accomplished? Why did Christine consider those accomplishments so unusual? What does Joan's career as a soldier tell you about the culture of late medieval France?*

Source: C. Cannon Willard, ed., *The Writings of Christine de Pizan* (New York: Persa Books, 1994).

THE HUNDRED YEARS' WAR

THE FOLLOWING EXCERPTS are taken from a collection of letters and other sources from the Hundred Years' War. They provide an excellent account of how noncombatants fared during the war. Included in the destruction were numerous churches and monasteries.

Accounts of the Hundred Years' War

The count of Arundel, John Fitz-Alain, attacked Millé and its church with fire. The women, boys, and old men took refuge in the tower of the church, but were soon surrounded by flames. The lead of the roof melted and fell in burning drops on the miserable folk below, and even the molten metal of the bells ran down upon all. All but two perished. The fire not only destroyed the church, but all the houses within a wide circuit to the number of more than seven hundred. The wretched inhabitants and the cultivators of the soil were ordered to be hung.

Out of one thousand churches in the region of Quercy, when the war with the English was done there were scarce three or four hundred left in which services could be held, so completely was everything devastated and consumed. Certain parishes . . . were entirely deserted by their former inhabitants, so that the bishop of Bourges was forced to give the lands belonging to his temporalities as fiefs to those living at a distance.

Charles VI, being dead, Charles VII succeeded to his father in the kingdom, in the year of our Lord 1422, when he was about twenty-two years of age. In his time, owing to the long wars which had raged within and without, the lethargy and cowardliness of the officers and commanders who were under him, the destruction of all military disciple and order, the rapacity of the troopers, and general dissolution into which all things has fallen, such destruction had been wrought that from the river Loire to the Seine—even to the Somme—the farmers were dead or had fled, and almost all the fields had for many years lain without cultivation or any one to cultivate them. A few districts might indeed be excepted, where if any agriculture remained, it was because they were far from cities, towns, or castles, and in consequence the constant excursions of the despoilers could not be extended to them. . . .

We have ourselves beheld vast regions . . . well-nigh deserted, untilled, without husbandmen, grown up to weeds and briers. In many places where fruit trees could flourish these had grown up into dense forests. The vestiges of such ruin, unless the divine clemency shall aid mere human endeavor, will, it is to be feared, last for long years to come.

Q *What do these accounts reveal about the nature of late medieval warfare and its impact on civilian populations?*

Source: J. H. Robinson, *Readings in European History*, vol. 1 (Boston: Ginn & Company, 1904), pp. 474–475.

internal conflict and instability. Like the lord-serf relationship, the lord-vassal relationship based on land and military service was being replaced by a contract based on money. Especially after the Black Death, money payments called **scutage** (SKYOO-tij) were increasingly substituted for military service. Monarchs welcomed this development because they could now hire professional soldiers, who tended to be more reliable anyway. As lord-vassal relationships became less personal and less important, new relationships based on political advantage began to be formed, creating new avenues for political influence—and for corruption as well. Especially noticeable as the landed aristocrats suffered declining rents and social uncertainties with the new relationships was the formation of factions of nobles who looked for opportunities to advance their power and wealth at the expense of other noble factions and of their monarchs as well. Other nobles went to the royal courts, offering to serve the kings.

The kings had their own problems, however. By the mid-fifteenth century, reigning monarchs in many European countries were not the direct descendants of the rulers of 1300. The founders of these new dynasties had to struggle for position as factions of nobles vied to gain material advantages for themselves. As the fifteenth century began, there were two claimants to the throne of France, two aristocratic factions fighting for control of England, and three German princes struggling to be recognized as Holy Roman Emperor.

Fourteenth-century monarchs of old dynasties and new ones faced financial problems as well. The shift to using mercenary soldiers left monarchs perennially short of cash. Traditional revenues, especially rents from property, increasingly proved insufficient to meet their needs. Monarchs attempted to generate new sources of revenues, especially through taxes, which often meant going through parliaments. This opened the door for parliamentary bodies to gain more power by asking for favors first. Although unsuccessful in most cases, the parliaments simply added another element of uncertainty and confusion to fourteenth-century politics. Turning now to a survey of western and central European states (eastern Europe will be examined in Chapter 12), we can see how these disruptive factors worked.

The Growth of England's Political Institutions

The fifty-year reign of Edward III (1327–1377) was important for the evolution of English political institutions in the fourteenth century. Parliament increased in prominence and developed its basic structure and functions during Edward's reign. Due to his constant need for money to fight the Hundred Years' War, Edward came to rely on Parliament to levy new taxes. In return for regular grants, Edward made several concessions, including a commitment to levy no direct tax without Parliament's consent and to allow Parliament to examine the government accounts to ensure that the money was being spent properly. By the end of Edward's reign, Parliament had become an important component of the English governmental system.

During this same period, Parliament began to assume the organizational structure it has retained to this day. The Great Council of barons became the House of Lords and evolved into a body composed of the chief bishops and abbots of the realm and aristocratic peers whose position in Parliament was hereditary. The representatives of the shires and boroughs, who were considered less important than the lay and ecclesiastical lords, held collective meetings and soon came to be regarded as the House of Commons. Together, the House of Lords and House of Commons constituted Parliament. Although the House of Commons did little beyond approving measures proposed by the Lords, during Edward's reign the Commons did begin the practice of drawing up petitions, which, if accepted by the king, became law.

After Edward III's death, England began to experience the internal instability of aristocratic factionalism that was racking other European countries. The early years of the reign of Edward's grandson, Richard II (1377–1399), began inauspiciously with the peasant revolt that ended only when the king made concessions. Richard's reign was troubled by competing groups of nobles who sought to pursue their own interests. One faction, led by Henry of Lancaster, defeated the king's forces and then deposed and killed him. Henry of Lancaster became King Henry IV (1399–1413). In the fifteenth century, factional conflict would lead to a devastating series of civil wars.

The Problems of the French Kings

At the beginning of the fourteenth century, France was the most prosperous monarchy in Europe. By the end of the century, much of its wealth had been dissipated, and rival factions of aristocrats had made effective monarchical rule virtually impossible.

The French monarchical state had always had an underlying inherent weakness that proved its undoing in difficult times. Although the Capetian monarchs had found ways to enlarge their royal domain and extend their control by developing a large and effective bureaucracy, the various territories that made up France still maintained their own princes, customs, and laws. The parliamentary institutions of France provide a good example of France's basic lack of unity. The French parliament, known as the Estates-General and composed of representatives of the clergy, the nobility, and the **Third Estate** (everyone else), usually represented only the north of France, not the entire kingdom. The southern provinces had their own estates, and local estates existed in other parts of France. Unlike the English Parliament, which was evolving into a crucial part of the English government, the French Estates-General was simply one of many such institutions.

When Philip VI (1328–1350) became involved in the Hundred Years' War with England, he found it necessary to devise new sources of revenue, including a tax on salt known as the *gabelle* (gah-BELL) and a hearth tax eventually called the *taille* (TY). These taxes weighed heavily on the French peasantry and middle class. Consequently, when additional taxes were needed to pay for the ransom of King John II after his capture at the Battle of Poitiers, the middle-class inhabitants of the towns tried to use the Estates-General to reform the French government and tax structure.

At the meeting of the Estates-General in 1357, under the leadership of the Parisian provost Étienne Marcel (ay-TYEN mahr-SEL), representatives of the Third Estate granted taxes in exchange for a promise from King John's son, the dauphin Charles, not to tax without the Estates-General's permission and to allow the Estates-General to meet on a regular basis and participate in important political decisions. After Marcel's movement was crushed in 1358, this attempt to make the Estates-General a functioning part of the French government collapsed. The dauphin became King Charles V (1364–1380) and went on to recover much of the land lost to the English. His military successes underscored his efforts to reestablish strong monarchical powers. He undermined the role of the Estates-General by getting it to grant him taxes with no fixed time limit. Charles's death in 1380 soon led to a new time of troubles for the French monarchy, however.

The insanity of Charles VI (1380–1422), which first became apparent in 1392, opened the door to rival factions of French nobles aspiring to power and wealth. The dukes of Burgundy and Orléans competed to control Charles and the French monarchy. Their struggles created chaos for the French government and the French people. Many nobles supported the Orléanist faction, while Paris and other towns favored the Burgundians. By the beginning of the fifteenth century, France seemed hopelessly mired in a civil war. When the English renewed the Hundred Years' War in 1415, the Burgundians supported the English cause and the English monarch's claim to the throne of France.

The German Monarchy

England and France had developed strong national monarchies in the High Middle Ages. Nevertheless, by the end of the fourteenth century, they seemed in danger of disintegrating due to dynastic problems and the pressures generated by the Hundred Years' War. In contrast, the Holy Roman Empire, whose core consisted of the lands of Germany, had already begun to fall apart in the High Middle Ages. Northern Italy, which the German emperors had tried to include in their medieval empire, had been free from any real imperial control since the end of the Hohenstaufen dynasty in the thirteenth century. In Germany itself, the failure of the Hohenstaufens ended any chance of centralized monarchical authority, and Germany became a land of hundreds of states that varied in size and power. These included princely states, such as the duchies of Bavaria and Saxony; free imperial city-states (self-governing cities directly under the control of the Holy Roman Emperor rather than a German territorial prince), such as Nuremberg; modest territories of petty imperial knights; and ecclesiastical states, such as the archbishopric of Cologne, in which an ecclesiastical official, such as a bishop, archbishop, or abbot, served in a dual capacity as an administrative official of the Catholic Church and as secular lord over the territories of the state. Although all of the rulers of these different states had some obligations to the German king and Holy Roman Emperor, more and more they acted independently.

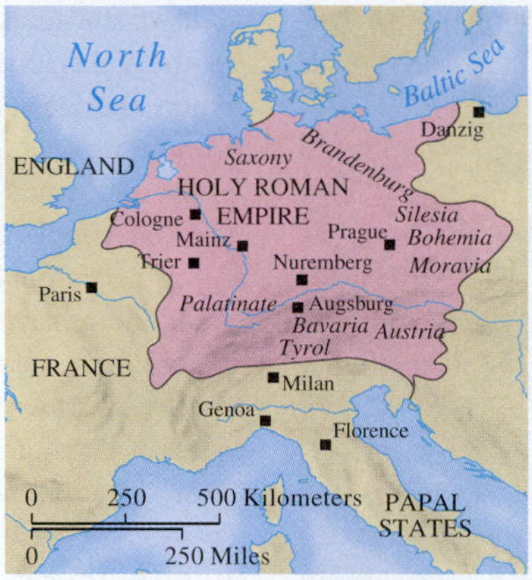

The Holy Roman Empire in the Fourteenth Century

ELECTORAL NATURE OF THE GERMAN MONARCHY Because of its unique pattern of development in the High Middle Ages, the German monarchy had become established on an elective rather than a hereditary basis. The Golden Bull issued in 1356 by Emperor Charles IV (1346–1378) standardized this principle of election. This document stated that four lay princes (the count palatine of the Rhine, the duke of Saxony, the margrave of Brandenburg, and the king of Bohemia) and three ecclesiastical rulers (the archbishops of Mainz, Trier, and Cologne) would serve as electors with the legal power to elect the "king of the Romans and future emperor, to be ruler of the world and of the Christian people."[12] "King of the Romans" was the official title of the German king; after his imperial coronation, he would also have the title of emperor.

In the fourteenth century, the electoral principle further ensured that kings of Germany were generally weak. Their ability to exercise effective power depended on the extent of their own family possessions. At the beginning of the fifteenth century, three emperors claimed the throne. Although the dispute was quickly settled, Germany entered the fifteenth century in a condition that verged on anarchy. Princes fought princes and leagues of cities. The emperors were virtually powerless to control any of them.

The States of Italy in the Fourteenth Century

The States of Italy

Italy, too, had failed to develop a centralized monarchical state by the fourteenth century. Papal opposition to the rule of the Hohenstaufen emperors in northern Italy had virtually guaranteed that. Moreover, southern Italy was divided into the kingdom of Naples, ruled by the French house of Anjou, and Sicily, whose kings came from the Spanish house of Aragon. The center of the peninsula remained under the rather shaky control of the papacy. Lack of centralized authority had enabled numerous city-states in northern Italy to remain independent of any political authority.

In fourteenth-century Italy, two general tendencies can be discerned: the replacement of republican governments by tyrants and the expansion of the larger city-states at the expense of the less powerful ones. Nearly all the cities of northern Italy began their existence as free communes with republican governments. But in the fourteenth century, intense internal strife led city-states to resort to temporary expedients, allowing rule by one man with dictatorial powers. Limited rule, however, soon became long-term despotism as tyrants proved willing to use force to maintain themselves in power. Eventually, such tyrants tried to legitimize their power by purchasing titles from the emperor (still nominally the ruler of northern Italy as Holy Roman Emperor). In this fashion, the Visconti became the dukes of Milan and the d'Este, the dukes of Ferrara.

The other change of great significance was the development of larger, regional states as the larger states conquered the smaller ones. To fight their battles, city-states came to rely on mercenary soldiers, whose leaders, called **condottieri** (kahn-duh-TYAY-ree), sold the services of their bands to the highest bidder. These mercenaries wreaked havoc on the countryside, living by blackmail and looting when they were not actively engaged in battles. Many were foreigners who flocked to Italy during the periods of truce in the Hundred Years' War. By the end of the fourteenth century, three major states came to dominate northern Italy: the despotic state of Milan and the republican states of Florence and Venice.

DUCHY OF MILAN Located in the fertile Po valley, at the intersection of the chief trade routes from Italian coastal cities to the Alpine passes, Milan was one of the richest city-states in Italy. Politically, it was also one of the most agitated until the Visconti family established themselves as the hereditary despots of Milan in 1322. Giangaleazzo Visconti (jahn-gah-lay-AH-tsoh vees-KOHN-tee), who ruled from 1385 to 1402, transformed this despotism into a hereditary duchy by purchasing the title of duke from the emperor in 1395. Under Giangaleazzo's direction, the duchy of Milan extended its power over all of Lombardy and even threatened to conquer much of northern Italy until the duke's untimely death before the gates of Florence in 1402.

REPUBLIC OF FLORENCE Florence, like the other Italian towns, was initially a free commune dominated by a patrician class of nobles known as the *grandi* (GRAHN-dee). But the rapid

Dea/G. Nimatallah/De Agostini Picture Library/Getty Images

A Famous *Condottiere*. Many of the *condottieri* who fought in Italy were foreigners. One of the most prominent was Sir John Hawkwood, who went to Italy after fighting on the English side in the Hundred Years' War. There he led a band of mercenary soldiers in many battles and was known for his brutality—he murdered the entire population of Cesena. Hawkwood, known to the Italians as Giovanni Acuto, ended his career in the early 1390s fighting for the city of Florence. To honor him, the city commissioned this fresco by Paolo Uccello (PAH-oh-loh oo-CHELL-oh), which can still be seen today in the cathedral of Florence.

expansion of Florence's economy made possible the development of a wealthy merchant-industrialist class known as the *popólo grasso* (PAWP-oo-loh GRAH-soh)—literally the "fat people." In 1293, the popólo grasso assumed a dominant role in government by establishing a new constitution known as the Ordinances of Justice. It provided for a republican government controlled by the seven major guilds of the city, which represented the interests of the wealthier classes. Executive power was vested in the hands of a council of elected priors. Around the mid-fourteenth century, revolutionary activity by the *popólo minuto*, the small shopkeepers and artisans, won them a share in the government. Even greater expansion occurred briefly when the *ciompi*, or industrial wool workers, were allowed to be represented in the government after their revolt in 1378. Only four years later, however, a counterrevolution brought the "fat people" back into virtual control of the government. After 1382, the Florentine government was controlled by a small merchant oligarchy that manipulated the supposedly republican government. By that time, Florence had also been successful in a series of wars against its neighbors. It had conquered most of Tuscany and established itself as a major territorial state in northern Italy.

REPUBLIC OF VENICE The other major northern Italian state was the republic of Venice, which had grown rich from commercial activity throughout the eastern Mediterranean and into northern Europe. A large number of merchant families became extremely wealthy. In the constitution of 1297, these patricians took control of the republic. In this year, the Great Council, the source of all political power, was closed to all but the members of about two hundred families. Since all other magistrates of the city were chosen either from or by this council, these families now formed a hereditary patriciate that completely dominated the city. Although the doge (DOHJ) (or duke) had been the executive head of the republic since the early Middle Ages, by 1300 he had become largely a figurehead. Actual power was vested in the hands of the Great

CHRONOLOGY	The States of Western and Central Europe
England	
Edward III	1327–1377
Richard II	1377–1399
Henry IV	1399–1413
France	
Philip IV	1328–1350
John II	1350–1364
Capture at Poitiers	1356
Charles V	1364–1380
Charles VI	1380–1422
German Monarchy	
Golden Bull	1356
Italy	
Florence	
Ordinances of Justice	1293
Venice	
Closing of Great Council	1297
Milan	
Visconti establish themselves as rulers of Milan	1322

Council and the legislative body known as the Senate, while an extraordinary body known as the Council of Ten, first formed in 1310, came to be the real executive power of the state. Contemporaries respected the Venetian government for its stability. A sixteenth-century Italian historian noted that Venice had "the best government of any city not only in our own times but also in the classical world."[13]

In the fourteenth century, Venice also embarked on a policy of expansion. By the end of the century, it had created a commercial empire by establishing colonies and trading posts in the eastern Mediterranean and Black Sea as well as continuing its commercial monopolies in the Byzantine Empire. At the same time, Venice began to conquer the territory adjoining it in northern Italy.

The Decline of the Church

> **FOCUS QUESTION:** How and why did the authority and prestige of the papacy decline in the fourteenth century?

The papacy of the Roman Catholic Church reached the height of its power in the thirteenth century. Theories of papal supremacy included a doctrine of "fullness of power" as the spiritual head of Christendom and claims to universal temporal authority over all secular rulers. But papal claims of temporal supremacy were increasingly out of step with the growing secular monarchies of Europe and ultimately brought the papacy into a conflict with the territorial states that it was unable to win.

Boniface VIII and the Conflict with the State

The struggle between the papacy and the monarchies began during the pontificate of Pope Boniface VIII (1294–1303). One major issue appeared to be at stake between the pope and King Philip IV (1285–1314) of France. In his desire to acquire new revenues, Philip claimed the right to tax the French clergy. Boniface VIII responded that the clergy of any state could not pay taxes to their secular ruler without the pope's consent. Underlying this issue, however, was a basic conflict between the claims of the papacy to universal authority over both church and state, which necessitated complete control over the clergy, and the claims of the king that all subjects, including the clergy, were under the jurisdiction of the crown and subject to the king's authority on matters of taxation and justice. In short, the fundamental issue was the universal sovereignty of the papacy versus the royal sovereignty of the monarch.

Boniface VIII asserted his position in a series of papal bulls or letters, the most important of which was *Unam Sanctam* (OO-nam SAHNK-tahm), issued in 1302. It was the strongest statement ever made by a pope on the supremacy of the spiritual authority over the temporal authority (see the box on p. 318). When it became apparent that the pope had decided to act on his principles by excommunicating Philip IV, the latter sent a small contingent of French forces to capture Boniface and bring him back to France for trial. The pope was captured in Anagni, although Italian nobles from the surrounding countryside soon rescued him. The shock of this experience, however, soon led to the pope's death. Philip's strong-arm tactics had produced a clear victory for the national monarchy over the papacy, and no later pope has dared renew the extravagant claims of Boniface VIII.

To ensure his position and avoid any future papal threat, Philip IV brought enough pressure to bear on the college of cardinals to achieve the election of a Frenchman as pope in 1305. Using the excuse of turbulence in the city of Rome, the new pope, Clement V (1305–1314), took up residence in Avignon (ah-veen-YOHN) on the east bank of the Rhône River. Although Avignon was located in the Holy Roman Empire and was not a French possession, it lay just across the river from the territory

Dea/A. Dagli Orti/De Agostini Picture Library/Getty Images

Pope Boniface VIII. The conflict between church and state in the Middle Ages reached its height in the struggle between Pope Boniface VIII and Philip IV of France. This fourteenth-century manuscript miniature depicts Boniface VIII promulgating his decrees.

BONIFACE VIII'S DEFENSE OF PAPAL SUPREMACY

ONE OF THE MOST REMARKABLE DOCUMENTS of the fourteenth century was the exaggerated statement of papal supremacy issued by Pope Boniface VIII in 1302 in the heat of his conflict with the French king Philip IV. Ironically, this strongest statement ever made of papal supremacy was issued at a time when the rising power of the monarchies made it increasingly difficult for the premises to be accepted.

Pope Boniface VIII, *Unam Sanctam*

We are compelled, our faith urging us, to believe and to hold—and we do firmly believe and simply confess—that there is one holy catholic and apostolic church, outside of which there is neither salvation nor remission of sins. . . . In this church there is one Lord, one faith and one baptism. . . . Therefore, of this one and only church there is one body and one head . . . Christ, namely, and the vicar of Christ, St. Peter, and the successor of Peter. For the Lord himself said to Peter, feed my sheep. . . .

We are told by the word of the gospel that in this His fold there are two swords—a spiritual, namely, and a temporal. . . . Both swords, the spiritual and the material, therefore, are in the power of the church; the one, indeed, to be wielded for the church, the other by the church; the one by the hand of the priest, the other by the hand of kings and knights, but at the will and sufferance of the priest. One sword, moreover, ought to be under the other, and the temporal authority to be subjected to the spiritual. . . .

Therefore if the earthly power err it shall be judged by the spiritual power; but if the lesser spiritual power err, by the greater. But if the greatest, it can be judged by God alone, not by man, the apostle bearing witness. A spiritual man judges all things, but he himself is judged by no one. This authority, moreover, even though it is given to man and exercised through man, is not human but rather divine, being given by divine lips to Peter and founded on a rock for him and his successors through Christ himself whom he has confessed; the Lord himself saying to Peter: "Whatsoever you shall bind, etc." Whoever, therefore, resists this power thus ordained by God, resists the ordination of God. . . .

Indeed, we declare, announce and define, that it is altogether necessary to salvation for every human creature to be subject to the Roman pontiff.

Q *What claims did Boniface VIII make in* Unam Sanctam*? To what extent were these claims a logical continuation of the development of the papacy in the Middle Ages? If you were a monarch, why would you object to this papal bull?*

Source: E. F. Henderson, *Select Historical Documents of the Middle Ages* (London: George Bell & Sons, 1896).

of King Philip IV. Clement may have intended to return to Rome, but he and his successors remained in Avignon for the next seventy-two years, thereby creating yet another crisis for the church.

The Papacy at Avignon (1305–1377)

The residency of the popes in Avignon for most of the fourteenth century led to a decline in papal prestige and growing antipapal sentiment. The city of Rome was the traditional capital of the universal church. The pope was the bishop of Rome, and his position was based on being the successor to the Apostle Peter, traditionally considered the first bishop of Rome. It was unseemly that the head of the Catholic Church should reside elsewhere. In the 1330s, the popes began to construct a stately palace in Avignon, a clear indication that they intended to stay for some time.

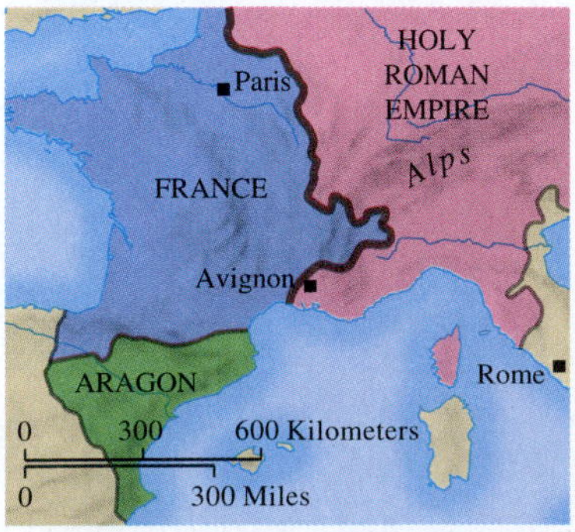

Avignon

Other factors also contributed to the decline in papal prestige during the Avignonese residency. It was widely believed that the popes at Avignon were captives of the French monarchy. Although questionable, since Avignon did not belong to the French monarchy, it was easy to believe in view of Avignon's proximity to French lands. The Italian scholar Petrarch (see "The Development of Vernacular Literature" later in this chapter) labeled this period as the Babylonian Captivity of the church, comparing the French holding the church in captivity to the exile of the Jews into captivity in Babylon in the sixth century B.C.E. (see Chapter 2). Moreover, during the seventy-two years of the Avignonese papacy, of the 134 new cardinals created by the popes, 113 were French. The papal residency at Avignon was also an important turning point in the church's attempt to adapt to the changing economic and political conditions of Europe. Like the growing monarchical states, the popes centralized their administration by developing a specialized bureaucracy. In fact, the papal bureaucracy in the fourteenth century under the leadership of the pope and college of cardinals became the most sophisticated administrative system in the medieval world.

At the same time, the popes attempted to find new sources of revenue to compensate for their loss of income from the Papal States and began to impose new taxes on the clergy.

Furthermore, the splendor in which the pope and cardinals were living in Avignon led to highly vocal criticism of both clergy and papacy in the fourteenth century. Avignon had become a powerful symbol of abuses within the church, and many people began to call for the pope's return to Rome.

One of the most prominent calls came from Catherine of Siena (ca. 1347–1380), whose saintly demeanor and claims of visions from God led the city of Florence to send her on a mission to Pope Gregory XI (1370–1378) in Avignon. She told the pope, "Because God has given you authority and because you have accepted it, you ought to use your virtue and power; if you do not wish to use it, it might be better for you to resign what you have accepted; it would give more honor to God and health to your soul."[14]

The Great Schism

Catherine of Siena's admonition seemed to be heeded in 1377, when at long last Pope Gregory XI, perceiving the disastrous decline in papal prestige, returned to Rome. He died soon afterward, however, in the spring of 1378. When the college of cardinals met in conclave to elect a new pope, the citizens of Rome, fearful that the French majority would choose another Frenchman who would return the papacy to Avignon, threatened that the cardinals would not leave Rome alive unless they elected a Roman or at least an Italian as pope. Indeed, the guards of the conclave warned the cardinals that they "ran the risk of being torn in pieces" if they did not choose an Italian. Wisely, the terrified cardinals duly elected the Italian archbishop of Bari, who was subsequently crowned as Pope Urban VI (1378–1389) on Easter Sunday. Following his election, Urban VI made clear his plans to reform the papal curia and even to swamp the college of cardinals with enough new Italian cardinals to eliminate the French majority. After many of the cardinals (the French ones) withdrew from Rome in late summer and were finally free of the Roman mob, they issued a manifesto, saying that they had been coerced by the mob and that Urban's election was therefore null and void. The dissenting cardinals thereupon chose one of their number, a Frenchman, who took the title of Clement VII and promptly returned to Avignon. Since Urban remained in Rome, there were now two popes, initiating what has been called the **Great Schism** of the church.

Europe's loyalties soon became divided: France, Spain, Scotland, and southern Italy supported Clement, while England, Germany, Scandinavia, and most of Italy supported Urban. These divisions generally followed political lines and reflected the bitter division between the English and the French in the Hundred Years' War. Because the French supported the Avignonese pope, so did their allies; their enemies, particularly England and its allies, supported the Roman pope. The need for political support caused both popes to subordinate their policies to the policies of these states.

The Great Schism lasted for nearly forty years and had a baleful effect on the Catholic Church and Christendom in general. The schism greatly aggravated the financial abuses that had developed within the church during the Avignonese papacy. Two papal administrative systems (with only half the accustomed revenues) worked to increase taxation. At the same time, the schism badly damaged the faith of Christian believers in the institution of the Catholic Church as its leader. The pope was widely believed to be the leader of Christendom and, as Boniface VIII had pointed out, held the keys to the kingdom of heaven. Since each line of popes denounced the other as the Antichrist, such a spectacle could not help but undermine the institution that had become the very foundation of the church.

New Thoughts on Church and State and the Rise of Conciliarism

As dissatisfaction with the papacy grew, so did the calls for a revolutionary approach to solving the church's institutional problems. One of the most systematic was provided by Marsiglio of Padua (mar-SIL-yoh of PAD-juh-wuh) (ca. 1270–1342), rector of the University of Paris and author of a remarkable book, *Defender of the Peace*. Marsiglio denied that the temporal authority was subject to the spiritual authority, as many popes had maintained. Instead, he argued that the church was only one element of society and must confine itself solely to spiritual functions. Furthermore, Marsiglio argued, the church is a community of the faithful in which all authority is ultimately derived from the entire community. The clergy hold no special authority from God but serve only to administer the affairs of the church on behalf of all Christians. Thus, final authority in spiritual matters must reside not with the pope but with a general church council representing all members.

THE CONCILIAR MOVEMENT The Great Schism led large numbers of churchmen to take up this theory, known as **conciliarism**, in the belief that only a general council of the church could end the schism and bring reform to the church in its "head and members." The only serious issue left to be decided was who should call the council. Church law held that only a pope could convene a council. Professors of theology argued, however, that since the competing popes would not

CHRONOLOGY	The Decline of the Church
Pope Boniface VII	1294–1303
Unam Sanctam	1302
Papacy at Avignon	1305–1377
Pope Gregory XI returns to Rome	1377
Great Schism begins	1378
Pope Urban VI	1378–1389
Failure of Council of Pisa to end schism; election of Alexander V	1409
Council of Constance	1414–1418
End of schism; election of Martin V	1417

do so, either members of the church hierarchy or even secular princes, especially the Holy Roman Emperor, could convene a council to settle all relevant issues.

In desperation, a group of cardinals from both camps finally convened a general council on their own. This Council of Pisa, which met in 1409, deposed the two popes and elected a new one, Alexander V. The council's action proved disastrous, however, when the two deposed popes refused to step down. There were now three popes, and the church seemed more hopelessly divided than ever.

Leadership in convening a new council now passed to the Holy Roman Emperor, Sigismund. As a result of his efforts, a new ecumenical church council met at Constance from 1414 to 1418. Ending the schism proved a surprisingly easy task: after the three competing popes either resigned or were deposed, a new conclave elected Cardinal Oddone Colonna, a member of a prominent Roman family, as Pope Martin V (1417–1431). The Great Schism had finally been ended.

Popular Religion in an Age of Adversity

The seeming preoccupation of the popes and leading clerics with finances and power during the struggles of Boniface VIII, the Avignonese papacy, and the Great Schism could not help but lead to a decline in prestige and respect for the institutional church, especially the papacy. At the same time, in the fourteenth century, the Black Death and its recurrences made an important impact on the religious life of ordinary Christians by heightening their preoccupation with death and salvation. The church often failed to provide sufficient spiritual comfort as many parish priests fled from the plague.

Christians responded in different ways to the adversities of the fourteenth century. First of all, there was a tendency to stress the performance of good works, including acts of charity, as a means of ensuring salvation. Bequests to hospitals and other charitable foundations increased. Family chapels were established, served by priests whose primary responsibility was to say Mass for the good of the souls of deceased family members. These chapels became even more significant as the importance of purgatory rose. Purgatory was defined by the church as the place where souls went after death to be purged of punishment for sins committed in life. In effect, the soul was purified in purgatory before it ascended into heaven. It was believed that like indulgences, prayers and private Masses for the dead could shorten the amount of time souls spent in purgatory.

Chalking up good deeds to ensure salvation was done in numerous ways but was nowhere more evident than in the growing emphasis on indulgences. We should also note that pilgrimages, which became increasingly popular, and charitable contributions were good works that could be accomplished without the involvement of clerics, a reflection of the loss of faith in the institutional church and its clergy and another noticeable feature of popular religious life. At the same time, interest in Christian faith itself did not decline; if anything, it increased (see "Global Perspectives" on p. 321). Indeed, people sought to play a more active role in their own salvation. This is particularly evident in the popularity of mysticism and lay piety in the fourteenth century.

MYSTICISM AND LAY PIETY The mysticism of the fourteenth century was certainly not new, for Christians throughout the Middle Ages had claimed to have had mystical experiences. Simply defined, **mysticism** is the immediate experience of oneness with God. It is this experience that characterized the teaching of Meister Eckhart (MY-stur EK-hart) (1260–1327), who sparked a mystical movement in western Germany. Eckhart was a well-educated Dominican theologian who wrote learned Latin works on theology, but he was also a popular preacher whose message on the union of the soul with God was typical of mysticism. According to Eckhart, such a union was attainable by all who pursued it wholeheartedly.

Eckhart's movement spread from Germany into the Low Countries, where it took on a new form, called the **Modern Devotion**, founded by Gerard Groote (GROH-tuh) (1340–1384). After a religious conversion, Groote entered a monastery for several years of contemplation before reentering the world. His messages were typical of a practical mysticism. To achieve true spiritual communion with God, people must imitate Jesus and lead lives dedicated to serving the needs of their fellow human beings. Groote emphasized a simple inner piety and morality based on Scripture and an avoidance of the complexities of theology.

Eventually, Groote attracted a group of followers who came to be known as the Brothers of the Common Life. From this small beginning, a movement developed that spread through the Netherlands and back into Germany. Houses of the Brothers, as well as separate houses for women (Sisters of the Common Life), were founded in one city after another. The Sisters and Brothers of the Common Life did not constitute regular religious orders. They were laypeople who took no formal monastic vows but were nevertheless regulated by rules that they imposed on their own communities. They also established schools throughout Germany and the Netherlands in which they stressed their message of imitating the life of Jesus by serving others. The Brothers and Sisters of the Common Life attest to the vitality of spiritual life among lay Christians in the fourteenth century.

UNIQUE FEMALE MYSTICAL EXPERIENCES A number of female mystics had their own unique spiritual experiences. For them, fasting and receiving the Eucharist (the communion wafer that, according to Roman Catholic doctrine, contains the body of Jesus) became the mainstay of their religious practices. Catherine of Siena, for example, gave up eating any solid food at the age of twenty-three and thereafter lived only on cold water and herbs that she sucked and then spat out. Her primary nourishment, however, came from the Eucharist. She wrote: "The immaculate lamb [Christ] is food, table, and servant. . . . And we who eat at that table become like the food [that is, Christ], acting not for our own utility but for the honor of God and the salvation of neighbor."[15] For Catherine and a number of other female mystics, reception of the Eucharist

Religious Imagery in the Medieval World

THE MIDDLE AGES WAS A GOLDEN AGE of religious art, reflecting the important role of religion itself in medieval society. These three illustrations show different aspects of medieval religious imagery. In Europe, much Christian art appeared in illuminated manuscripts. The illustration at the bottom left shows a page depicting the figure of Jesus from *The Book of Kells*, a richly decorated manuscript of the Christian gospels produced by the monks of Iona in the British Isles. Byzantine art was also deeply religious, as was especially evident in icons. At the top right is an icon of the Virgin and Child (Mary and Jesus) from the monastery of Saint Catherine at Mount Sinai in Egypt dating to around the year 600. Painted on wood, this icon shows the enthroned Virgin and Child between Saints Theodore and George with two angels behind them looking upward to a beam of light containing the hand of God. The figures are not realistic; the goal of the icon was to bridge the gap between the divine and the outer material world. Artists in the Muslim world faced a different challenge—Muslims warned against imitating God by creating pictures of living beings, thus effectively prohibiting the representation of humans, especially Muhammad. Islamic religious artists therefore used decorative motifs based on geometric patterns and the Arabic script. The scriptural panel in the lower illustration is an artistic presentation of a verse from the Qur'an, thus blending the spiritual and artistic spheres.

Q *How is the importance of religious imagery in the Middle Ages evident in these three illustrations?*

Erich Lessing/Art Resource, NY

Art Resource, NY

Vanni Archive/Art Resource, NY

was their primary instrument in achieving a mystical union with God.

Changes in Theology

The fourteenth century presented challenges not only to the institutional church but also to its theological framework, especially evident in the questioning of the grand synthesis attempted by Thomas Aquinas. In the thirteenth century, differences with Aquinas were kept within a framework of commonly accepted scholastic thought. In the fourteenth century, however, the philosopher William of Occam (1285–1329) posed a severe challenge to the scholastic achievements of the High Middle Ages.

Occam posited a radical interpretation of nominalism. He asserted that all universals or general concepts were simply names and that only individual objects perceived by the senses were real. Although the mind was capable of analyzing individual objects, it could not establish any truths about the nature of external, higher reality. Reason could not be used to substantiate spiritual truths. It could not, for example, prove the statement "God exists." For William of Occam as a Christian believer, this did not mean that God did not exist, however. It simply indicated that the truths of religion could only be known by an act of faith and were not demonstrable by reason. The acceptance of Occam's nominalist philosophy at the University of Paris brought an element of uncertainty to late medieval theology by seriously weakening the synthesis of faith and reason that had characterized the theological thought of the High Middle Ages. Nevertheless, Occam's emphasis on using reason to analyze the observable phenomena of the world had an important impact on the development of physical science by creating support for rational and scientific analysis. Some late medieval theologians came to accept the compatibility of rational analysis of the material world with mystical acceptance of spiritual truths.

The Cultural World of the Fourteenth Century

Q **FOCUS QUESTION:** What were the major developments in literature and art in the fourteenth century?

The cultural life of the fourteenth century was also characterized by ferment. In literature, several writers used their vernacular languages to produce notable works. In art, in addition to the morbid themes inspired by the Black Death and other problems of the century, the period also produced Giotto, whose paintings expressed a new realism that would be developed further by the artists of the next century.

The Development of Vernacular Literature

Although Latin remained the language of the church liturgy and the official documents of both church and state throughout Europe, the fourteenth century witnessed the rapid growth of vernacular literature, especially in Italy. The development of an Italian vernacular literature was mostly the result of the efforts of three writers in the fourteenth century: Dante, Petrarch (PEE-trark *or* PET-trark), and Boccaccio. Their use of the Tuscan dialect common in Florence and its surrounding countryside ensured that it would prevail as the basis of the modern Italian language.

DANTE Dante Alighieri (DAHN-tay al-lih-GAIR-ee) (1265–1321) came from an old Florentine noble family that had fallen on hard times. Although he had held high political office in republican Florence, factional conflict led to his exile from the city in 1302. Until the end of his life, Dante hoped to return to his beloved Florence, but his wish remained unfulfilled.

Dante's masterpiece in the Italian vernacular was the *Divine Comedy*, written between 1313 and 1321. Cast in a typical medieval framework, the *Divine Comedy* is basically the story of the soul's progression to salvation, a fundamental medieval preoccupation. The lengthy poem was divided into three major sections corresponding to the realms of the afterworld: hell, purgatory, and heaven or paradise. In the "Inferno" (see the box on p. 323), Dante is led by his guide, the classical author Virgil, who is a symbol of human reason. But Virgil (or reason) can lead the poet only so far on his journey. At the end of "Purgatory," Beatrice (the true love of Dante's life), who represents revelation—which alone can explain the mysteries of heaven—becomes his guide into "Paradise." Here Beatrice presents Dante to Saint Bernard, a symbol of mystical contemplation. The saint turns Dante over to the Virgin Mary, since grace is necessary to achieve the final step of entering the presence of God, where one beholds "the love that moves the sun and the other stars."[16]

PETRARCH Like Dante, Francesco Petrarca, known as Petrarch (1304–1374), was a Florentine who spent much of his life outside his native city. Petrarch's role in the revival of the classics made him a seminal figure in the literary Italian Renaissance (see Chapter 12). His primary contribution to the development of the Italian vernacular was made in his sonnets. He is considered one of the greatest European lyric poets. His sonnets were inspired by his love for a married lady named Laura, whom he had met in 1327. Though honoring an idealized female figure was a long-standing medieval tradition, Laura was very human and not just an ideal. She was a real woman with whom Petrarch was involved for a long time. He poured forth his lamentations in sonnet after sonnet:

> *I weary me alway with questions keen*
> *How, why my thoughts ne'er turn from you away,*
> *Wherefore in life they still prefer to stay,*
> *When they might flee this sad and painful scene,*
> *And how of the fine hair, the lovely mien,*
> *Of the bright eyes which all my feelings sway,*
> *Calling on your dear name by night and day,*
> *My tongue ne'er silent in their praise has been,*
> *And how my feet not tender are, nor tired,*
> *Pursuing still with many a useless pace*
> *Of your fair footsteps the elastic trace;*
> *And whence the ink, the paper whence acquired,*
> *Fill'd with your memories: if in this I err,*
> *Not art's defect but Love's own fault it were.*[17]

DANTE'S VISION OF HELL

THE *DIVINE COMEDY* OF DANTE ALIGHIERI is regarded as one of the greatest literary works of all time. Many consider it the supreme summary of medieval thought. It combines allegory with a remarkable amount of contemporary history. Indeed, forty-three of the seventy-nine people consigned to hell in the "Inferno" were Florentines. This excerpt is taken from canto 18 of the "Inferno," in which Dante and Virgil visit the eighth circle of hell, which is divided into ten trenches containing the souls of people who had committed malicious frauds on their fellow human beings.

Dante, "Inferno," *Divine Comedy*

Now as we were standing where the narrow path
Crosses the second mound, and of it makes
Support to bear it to the other arch.

Here, then, we felt the woeful groans of those
In the other gorge, sputtering with nose and mouth,
And themselves striking with their open palms.

The banks were crusted with a moldy paste,
Born of the breath below, and here it stuck,
Causing to eyes and nostrils rank offense.

So deep the depth, it needed we should mount,
If we would see the place, upon the arch,
Where to the highest point the rock rose up;

And there we came, and looking there, we saw
A crowd below in a dung pool immersed,
From human privies seemingly derived.

And while I looked beneath with searching eye,
There I saw one with head so foul with filth,
Cleric or lay person, which one I could not say

He cried to me, "Wherefore so eager you
Me more than the other filthy ones to scan?"
I answered him, "Because if memory holds,

Already have I seen you with dry hair,
[You are] Alessio Interminelli da Lucca.
Therefore I mark you more than all the rest."

Then, while he struck his head, again he spoke,
"Those flatteries have plunged me here below,
Of which my tongue no [excess] never knew."

Soon after this, my leader spoke, and said,
"A little further thrust you forth your face,
That with its eyes it may the features note

Of that disheveled [whore] foul and vile,
Who tears her body with her filthy nails;
Now lounging low, now on her feet upright.

Thais it is—the harlot who, when asked
Once by her lover, 'Do you give me great thanks?'
Answered him thus, 'Thanks marvelous indeed.'"

And now our eyes enough of this had seen.

Q *How does Dante's vision of hell reflect medieval religious thought? Why were there Florentines in hell? What lessons do you think this work was intended to teach its readers?*

Source: David Johnston, *A Translation of Dante's Inferno* (Bath, U.K.: Chronicle Office, 1867), pp. 104–105.

In analyzing every aspect of the unrequited lover's feelings, Petrarch appeared less concerned to sing his lady's praise than to immortalize his own thoughts. This interest in his own personality reveals a sense of individuality stronger than in any previous medieval literature.

BOCCACCIO Although he too wrote poetry, Giovanni Boccaccio (1313–1375) is known primarily for his prose. Another Florentine, he also used the Tuscan dialect. While working for the Bardi banking house in Naples, he fell in love with a noble lady, and under her inspiration, he began to write prose romances. His best-known work, the *Decameron*, however, was not written until after he had returned to Florence. The *Decameron* is set at the time of the Black Death. Ten young people flee to a villa outside Florence to escape the plague and decide to while away the time by telling stories. Although the stories are not new and still reflect the acceptance of basic Christian values, Boccaccio does present the society of his time from a secular point of view. It is the seducer of women, not the knight or philosopher or pious monk, who is the real hero. Perhaps, as some historians have argued, the *Decameron* reflects the immediate easygoing, cynical post-plague values. Boccaccio's later work certainly became gloomier and more pessimistic; as he grew older, he even rejected his earlier work as irrelevant. He commented in a 1373 letter, "I am certainly not pleased that you have allowed the illustrious women in your house to read my trifles. . . . You know how much in them is less than decent and opposed to modesty, how much stimulation to wanton lust, how many things that drive to lust even those most fortified against it."[18]

CHAUCER Another leading vernacular author was Geoffrey Chaucer (ca. 1340–1400), who brought a new level of sophistication to the English vernacular language in his famous *Canterbury Tales.* His beauty of expression and clear, forceful language were important in transforming his East Midland dialect into the chief ancestor of the modern English language. *The Canterbury Tales* is a collection of stories told by a group of twenty-nine pilgrims journeying from the London suburb of Southwark to the tomb of Saint Thomas à Becket at

Canterbury. This format gave Chaucer the chance to portray an entire range of English society, both high- and low-born. Among others, he presented the Knight, the Yeoman, the Prioress, the Monk, the Merchant, the Student, the Lawyer, the Carpenter, the Cook, the Doctor, the Plowman, and, "A Good Wife was there from beside the city of Bath—a little deaf, which was a pity." The stories these pilgrims told to while away the time on the journey were just as varied as the storytellers themselves: knightly romances, fairy tales, saints' lives, sophisticated satires, and crude anecdotes.

Chaucer also used some of his characters to criticize the corruption of the church in the late medieval period. His portrayal of the Friar leaves no doubt of Chaucer's disdain for the corrupt practices of clerics. Of the Friar, he says:

> *He knew the taverns well in every town.*
> *The barmaids and innkeepers pleased his mind*
> *Better than beggars and lepers and their kind.*[19]

And yet Chaucer was still a pious Christian, never doubting basic Christian doctrines and remaining optimistic that the church could be reformed.

CHRISTINE DE PIZAN One of the extraordinary vernacular writers of the age was Christine de Pizan (ca. 1364–1430). Because of her father's position at the court of Charles V of France, she received a good education. Her husband died when she was only twenty-five (they had been married for ten years), leaving her with little income and three small children and her mother to support. Christine took the unusual step of becoming a writer in order to earn her living (see the box on p. 312). Her poems were soon in demand, and by 1400 she had achieved financial security.

Christine de Pizan is best known, however, for her French prose works written in defense of women. In *The Book of the City of Ladies*, written in 1404, she denounced the many male writers who had argued that women needed to be controlled by men because women by their very nature were prone to evil, unable to learn, and easily swayed. With the help of Reason, Righteousness, and Justice, who appear to her in a vision, Christine refutes these antifeminist attacks. Women, she argues, are not evil by nature, and they could learn as well as men if they were permitted to attend the same schools: "Should I also tell you whether a woman's nature is clever and quick enough to learn speculative sciences as well as to discover them, and likewise the manual arts. I assure you that women are equally well-suited and skilled to carry them out and to put them to sophisticated use once they have learned them."[20] Much of the book includes a detailed discussion of women from the past and present who have distinguished themselves as leaders, warriors, wives, mothers, and martyrs for their religious faith. She ends by encouraging women to defend themselves against the attacks of men, who are incapable of understanding them.

A New Art: Giotto

The fourteenth century produced an artistic outburst in new directions as well as a large body of morbid work influenced by the Black Death and the recurrences of the plague.

Science Source

Christine de Pizan. Christine de Pizan was one of the extraordinary vernacular writers of the late fourteenth and early fifteenth centuries. In this fifteenth-century French illustration from the *Works of Christine de Pizan*, she is shown giving instructions to an assistant.

The city of Florence witnessed the first dramatic break with medieval tradition in the work of Giotto (JOH-toh) (1266–1337), often considered a forerunner of Italian Renaissance painting. Born into a peasant family, Giotto acquired his painting skills in a workshop in Florence. Although he worked throughout Italy, his most famous works were done in Padua and Florence.

Coming out of the formal Byzantine school, Giotto transcended it with a new kind of realism, a desire to imitate nature that Renaissance artists later identified as the basic component of classical art. Giotto's figures were solid and rounded; placed realistically in relationship to each other and their background, they conveyed three-dimensional depth. The expressive faces and physically realistic bodies gave his sacred figures human qualities with which spectators could identify. Although Giotto had no direct successors, Florentine painting in the early fifteenth century pursued even more dramatically the new direction his work represents.

Society in an Age of Adversity

FOCUS QUESTION: How did the adversities of the fourteenth century affect urban life and medical practices?

In the midst of disaster, the fourteenth century proved creative in its own way. New inventions made an impact on daily life at the same time that the effects of the plague were felt in many areas of medieval urban life.

Scala/Art Resource, NY

Giotto, *Lamentation.* The work of Giotto marked the first clear innovation in fourteenth-century painting, making him a forerunner of the early Renaissance. This fresco was part of a series done on the walls of the Arena Chapel in Padua begun in 1305. Giotto painted thirty-eight scenes on three levels: the lives of Mary, the mother of Jesus, and her parents (top panel); the life and work of Jesus (middle panel); and his passion, crucifixion, and resurrection (bottom panel). Shown here from the bottom panel is the *Lamentation*. A group of Jesus's followers, including his mother and Mary Magdalene, mourn over the body of Jesus before it is placed in its tomb. The solidity of Giotto's human figures gives them a three-dimensional sense. He also captured the grief and despair felt by the mourners.

Changes in Urban Life

One immediate by-product of the Black Death was greater regulation of urban activities by town governments. Authorities tried to keep cities cleaner by enacting new ordinances against waste products in the streets. Viewed as unhealthy places, bathhouses were closed down, leading to a noticeable decline in personal cleanliness. Efforts at regulation also affected the practice of female prostitution.

Medieval society had tolerated prostitution as a lesser evil: it was better for males to frequent prostitutes than to seduce virgins or married women. Since many males in medieval towns married late, the demand for prostitutes was high and was met by a regular supply, derived no doubt from the need of many poor girls and women to survive. The recession of the fourteenth century probably increased the supply of prostitutes, while the new hedonism prevalent after the Black Death also increased demand. As a result, cities intensified their regulation of prostitution.

By organizing brothels, city authorities could supervise as well as tax prostitutes. Officials granted charters to citizens who were allowed to set up brothels, provided they were located only in certain areas of town. Prostitutes were also expected to wear special items of clothing—such as red hats—to distinguish them from other women. It was assumed that the regulation of prostitution made it easier to supervise and hence maintained public order.

FAMILY LIFE AND GENDER ROLES IN LATE MEDIEVAL CITIES The basic unit of the late medieval town was the nuclear family of husband, wife, and children. Especially in wealthier families, there might also be servants, apprentices, and other relatives, including widowed mothers and the husband's illegitimate children.

Before the Black Death, late marriages were common for urban couples. It was not unusual for husbands to be in their late thirties or forties and wives in their early twenties. The expense of setting up a household probably necessitated the delay in marriage. But the situation changed dramatically after the plague, reflecting new economic opportunities for the survivors and a new reluctance to postpone living in the presence of so much death.

The economic difficulties of the fourteenth century also tended to strengthen the development of gender roles. Based on the authority of Aristotle, Thomas Aquinas and other scholastic theologians had advanced the belief that according to the natural order, men were active and domineering while women were passive and submissive. As more and more lawyers, doctors, and priests, who had been trained in universities where these notions were taught, entered society, these ideas about the different natures of men and women became widely accepted. This was evident in legal systems, many of which limited the legal capacity of women. Increasingly, women were expected to give up any active functions in society and remain subject to direction from males (see the box on p. 326). A fourteenth-century Parisian provost commented that among glass cutters, "no master's widow who keeps working at his craft after her husband's death may take on apprentices, for the men of the craft do not believe that a woman can master it well enough to teach a child to master it, for the craft is a very delicate one."[21] Although this statement suggests that some women were, in fact, running businesses, it also reveals that they were viewed as incapable of undertaking all of men's activities. Europeans in the fourteenth century imposed a division of labor roles between men and women that persisted until the Industrial Revolution.

In practice, however, some women in the fourteenth century benefited from the effects of the Black Death. The deaths of many male workers in cities opened up new jobs for women, such as metalworkers and stevedores. In cloth making, women were allowed to assume better-paying jobs as weavers. Brewing became an all-female profession by 1450.

A LIBERATED WOMAN IN THE FOURTEENTH CENTURY

DURING THE HIGH AND LATER MIDDLE AGES, women were increasingly viewed as weak beings who were unable to play independent roles. One exception in the fourteenth century was Grazida Lizier, a peasant woman of Cathar background who lived in the village of Montaillou in France. She expressed some radical views on religion and sexuality, as recorded by a Catholic inquisitor who was questioning her about her potentially heretical views.

The Testimony of Grazida Lizier

When I was married and made love with the priest Pierre, it did not seem more proper to make love with my husband—all the same it seemed to me, and I still believe, it was as little sin with Pierre as with my husband. Did I have any qualms at the time, or think that such deeds might displease God? No, I had none, and did not think my lying with Pierre should displease any living being, since it gave joy to us both.

If my husband had forbidden it? Supposing he had—even though he never did—I still would not have thought it a sin, because of the shared joy of love. If any man whatever lies with any women (unless she is related to him by blood), whether she's a virgin or has been seduced, whether in marriage or outside it—all such coupling of men and women gives displeasure to God, and yet I still do not think the partners sin, insofar as their joy is mutual. . . .

I don't know but I've heard it said there is a paradise, and I believe it; I've also heard there is a hell, but that I don't believe, though I won't urge it is untrue. I believe there is a paradise, for it is something good, as I've heard tell; I don't believe in hell (though I don't argue against it), for that is something evil, as people say. I've often heard that we shall rise again after death—I don't believe that, though I don't discredit it.

I still believe it is no sin when love-making brings joy to both partners. I have believed that ever since Pierre first knew me. No one taught me these ideas except myself. I haven't taught them to others—no one has ever asked me about them.

Q *Why were the views of Grazida Lizier on religion and sexuality so unusual? Did her Cathar background have any impact on her views?*

Source: E. Delamotte, N. Meeker, and J. O'Barr, *Women Imagine Change* (New York: Routledge, 1977), p. 53.

Widows also occasionally carried on their husbands' shops or businesses.

MEDIEVAL CHILDREN Parents in the High and later Middle Ages invested considerable resources and affection in rearing their children. The dramatic increase in specialized roles that accompanied the spread of commerce and the growth of cities demanded a commitment to educating children in the marketable skills needed for the new occupations. Philip of Navarre noted in the twelfth century that boys ought to be taught a trade "as soon as possible. Those who early become and long remain apprentices ought to be the best masters."[22] Some cities provided schools to educate the young. A chronicler in Florence related that between 8,000 and 10,000 boys and girls between the ages of six and twelve attended the city's grammar schools, a figure that probably represented half of all school-aged children. Although grammar school completed education for girls, some 1,100 boys went on to six secondary schools that prepared them for business careers, while another 600 studied Latin and logic in four other schools that readied them for university training and a career in medicine, law, or the church. In the High Middle Ages, then, urban communities demonstrated a commitment to training the young.

As a result of the devastating effects of the plague and its recurrences, these same communities became concerned about investing in the survival and health of children. A number of hospitals existed in both Florence and Rome in the fourteenth century, and in the 1420s and 1430s, hospitals were established that catered only to the needs of foundlings, supporting them until boys could be taught a trade and girls could marry.

New Directions in Medicine

The medical community comprised a number of functionaries. At the top of the medical hierarchy were the physicians, who received their education in the universities, where they studied ancient authorities, such as Hippocrates and Galen. As a result, physicians were highly trained in theory but had little or no clinical practice. By the fourteenth century, they were educated in six chief medical schools—Salerno, Montpellier, Bologna, Oxford, Padua, and Paris. Bologna and Padua were regarded as the most prestigious.

The pre-plague medicine of university-trained physicians was theoretically grounded in the classical Greek theory of the "four humors," each connected to a particular organ: blood (from the heart), phlegm (from the brain), yellow bile (from the liver), and black bile (from the spleen). Because the four humors corresponded in turn to the four elemental qualities of the universe—air (blood), water (phlegm), fire (yellow bile), and earth (black bile)—a human being was considered a microcosm of the cosmos. Good health resulted from a perfect balance of the four humors; sickness meant that the humors were out of balance. The task of the medieval physician was to restore proper order through a number of remedies, such as rest, diet, herbal medicines, or bloodletting.

Beneath the physicians in the hierarchy of the medical profession stood the surgeons, whose activities included performing operations, setting broken bones, and bleeding patients. Their knowledge was based largely on practical experience. Below surgeons were midwives, who delivered babies, and barber-surgeons, who were less trained than surgeons and performed menial tasks such as bloodletting and setting simple bone fractures. Barber-surgeons supplemented their income by shaving and cutting hair and pulling teeth. Apothecaries also constituted part of the medical establishment. They filled herbal prescriptions recommended by physicians and also prescribed drugs on their own authority.

All of these medical practitioners proved unable to deal with the plague. When King Philip VI of France requested the opinion of the medical faculty of the University of Paris on the plague, their advice proved worthless. This failure to understand the Black Death, however, produced a crisis in medieval medicine that resulted in some new approaches to health care.

Photo 12/Universal Images Group/Getty Images

A Medical Textbook. This illustration is taken from a fourteenth-century surgical textbook that stressed a how-to approach to surgical problems. *Top left*, a surgeon shows how to remove an arrow from a patient; *top right*, how to open a patient's chest; *bottom left*, how to deal with an injury to the intestines; and *bottom right*, how to diagnose an abscess.

One result was the rise of surgeons to greater prominence because of their practical knowledge. Surgeons were now recruited by universities, which placed them on an equal level with physicians and introduced a greater emphasis on practical anatomy into the university curriculum. Connected to this was a burgeoning of medical textbooks, often written in the vernacular and stressing practical, how-to approaches to medical and surgical problems.

Finally, as a result of the plague, cities, especially in Italy, gave increased attention to public health and sanitation. Public health laws were instituted, and municipal boards of health came into being. The primary concern of the latter was to prevent plague, but gradually they came to control almost every aspect of health and sanitation. Boards of public health, consisting of medical practitioners and public officials, were empowered to enforce sanitary conditions, report on and attempt to isolate epidemics by quarantine (rarely successful), and regulate the activities of doctors.

Inventions and New Patterns

Despite its problems, the fourteenth century witnessed a continuation of the technological innovations that had characterized the High Middle Ages.

THE CLOCK The most extraordinary of these inventions, and one that made a visible impact on European cities, was the clock. The mechanical clock was invented at the end of the thirteenth century but not perfected until the fourteenth. The time-telling clock was actually a by-product of a larger astronomical clock. The best-designed one was constructed by Giovanni di Dondi in the mid-fourteenth century. Dondi's clock contained the signs of the zodiac but also struck on the hour. Since clocks were expensive, they were usually installed only in the towers of churches or municipal buildings. The first clock striking equal hours was in a church in Milan; in 1335, a chronicler described it as "a wonderful clock, with a very large clapper which strikes a bell twenty-four times according to the twenty-four hours of the day and night and thus at the first hour of the night gives one sound, at the second two strikes . . . and so distinguishes one hour from another, which is of greatest use to men of every degree."[23]

Clocks revolutionized how people thought about and used time. Throughout most of the Middle Ages, time was determined by natural rhythms (daybreak and nightfall) or church bells that were rung at more or less regular three-hour intervals, corresponding to the ecclesiastical offices of the church. Clocks made it possible for people to plan their day and organize activities around the regular striking of bells. This brought a new regularity into the lives of workers and merchants, defining urban existence and enabling merchants and bankers to see the value of time in a new way.

EYEGLASSES AND PAPER Like clocks, eyeglasses were introduced in the thirteenth century but not refined until the fourteenth. Even then they were not particularly effective by modern standards and were still extremely expensive. The high cost of parchment forced people to write in extremely small script; eyeglasses made it more readable. At the same time, a significant change in writing materials occurred in the fourteenth century when parchment was supplemented by much cheaper paper made from cotton rags. Although it was more subject to insect and water damage than parchment, medieval paper was actually superior to modern papers made of high-acid wood pulp.

GUNPOWDER AND CANNONS Invented earlier by the Chinese, gunpowder also made its appearance in the West in the thirteenth century. The use of gunpowder eventually brought drastic changes to European warfare. Its primary use was in cannons, although early cannons were prone to blow up, making them as dangerous to the people firing them as to the enemy. Even as late as 1460, an attack on a castle using an enormous Flemish cannon called the "Lion" proved disastrous for the Scottish king James II when the "Lion" blew up, killing the king and a number of his retainers. Continued improvement in the construction of cannons, however, soon made them extremely valuable in reducing both castles and city walls. Gunpowder made castles, city walls, and armored knights obsolete.

CHAPTER SUMMARY

In the eleventh, twelfth, and thirteenth centuries, European civilization developed many of its fundamental features. Territorial states, parliaments, capitalist trade and industry, banks, cities, and vernacular literature were all products of that fertile period. During the same time, the Catholic Church under the direction of the papacy reached its apogee.

Fourteenth-century European society, however, was challenged by an overwhelming number of crises that led to the disintegration of medieval civilization. At mid-century, one of the most destructive natural disasters in history erupted—the Black Death, a devastating plague that wiped out at least one-third of the European population, with even higher mortality rates in urban areas. Reactions varied. Some people escaped into alcohol, sex, and crime. Others, such as the flagellants, believing the Black Death to be a punishment from God, attempted to atone for people's sins through self-inflicted pain. In many areas, the Jews became scapegoats. Economic crises and social upheavals, including a decline in trade and industry, bank failures, and peasant revolts pitting the lower classes against the upper classes, followed in the wake of the Black Death.

Political stability also declined, especially during the Hundred Years' War, a long, drawn-out conflict between the English and the French. Armored knights on horseback formed the backbone of medieval armies, but English peasants using the longbow began to change the face of war. After numerous defeats, the French cause was saved by Joan of Arc, a young peasant woman whose leadership inspired the French, who also began to rely on cannon and were victorious by 1453.

The Catholic Church, too, experienced a crisis. The confrontation between Pope Boniface VIII and Philip IV of France led to a loss of papal power and the removal of the papacy to Avignon on France's border in 1305. The absence of the popes from Rome created a new crisis, but the return of the papacy to Rome in 1377 only led to new problems with the Great Schism, which witnessed the spectacle of two competing popes condemning each other as the Antichrist. A new conciliar movement based on the belief that church councils, not popes, should rule the church finally ended the Great Schism in 1417.

All of these crises seemed to overpower Europeans in this calamitous fourteenth century. Not surprisingly, much of the art of the period depicted the Four Horsemen of the Apocalypse described in the New Testament Book of Revelation: Death, Famine, Pestilence, and War. No doubt, to some people, the last days of the world appeared to be at hand. European society, however, proved remarkably resilient. Already in the fourteenth century new ideas and practices were beginning to emerge, as often happens in periods of crisis. As we shall see in the next chapter, the pace of change began to quicken as Europe experienced a rebirth of classical culture that some historians have called the Renaissance.

CHAPTER TIMELINE

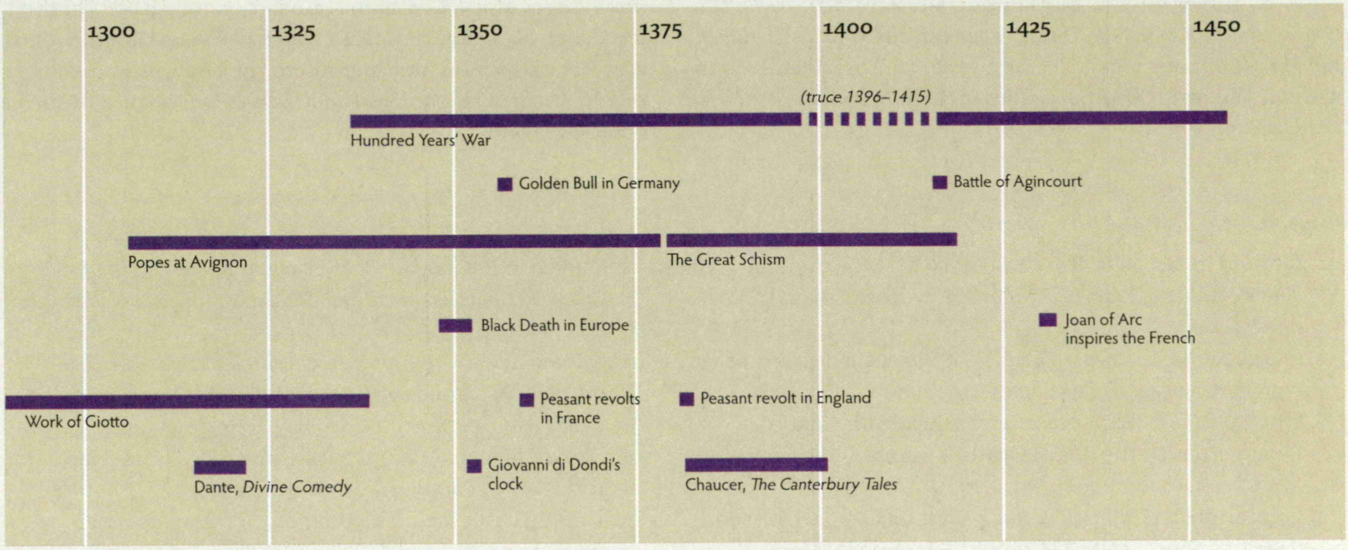

CHAPTER REVIEW

Upon Reflection

Q What were the chief factors that led to the urban and rural revolts of the fourteenth century?

Q What were the causes of the Hundred Years' War, and what were the results of the war in the fourteenth century for France and England?

Q What impact did the adversities of the fourteenth century have on Christian practices?

Key Terms

Black Death (p. 300)
pogroms (p. 304)
scutage (p. 313)
Third Estate (p. 314)
condottieri (p. 315)
Great Schism (p. 319)
conciliarism (p. 319)
mysticism (p. 320)
Modern Devotion (p. 320)

Suggestions for Further Reading

GENERAL WORKS For a general introduction to the fourteenth century, see **D. P. Waley** and **P. Denley**, ***Later Medieval Europe***, 3rd ed. (London, 2001), and **J. Aberth**, ***From the Brink of the Apocalypse: Confronting Famine, War, Plague, and Death in the Later Middle Ages*** (London, 2001).

THE BLACK DEATH On the Black Death, see **O. J. Benedictow**, ***The Black Death: The Complete History*** (Suffolk, 2008), and **J. Kelly**, ***The Great Mortality*** (New York, 2005).

HUNDRED YEARS' WAR Good accounts of the Hundred Years' War include **A. Curry**, ***The Hundred Years' War***, 2nd ed. (New York, 2004), and **R. H. Neillands**, ***The Hundred Years' War***, 2nd ed. (New York, 2001). On Joan of Arc, see **H. Carter**, ***Joan of Arc*** (New York, 2015).

POLITICAL HISTORY On the political history of the period, see **B. Guenee**, ***States and Rulers in Later Medieval Europe***, trans. **J. Vale** (Oxford, 1985). On medieval mercenaries, see **W. Urban**, ***Medieval Mercenaries*** (London, 2006). On the social revolts of the period, see **S. K. Cohn**, ***Lust for Liberty: The Politics of Social Revolt in Medieval Europe, 1200–1425*** (Cambridge, Mass., 2008).

CATHOLIC CHURCH A good general study of the church in the fourteenth century can be found in **F. P. Oakley**, ***The Western Church in the Later Middle Ages*** (Ithaca, N.Y., 1980). On female mystics in the later Middle Ages, see **D. Elliott**, ***Proving Woman: A Female Spirituality and Inquisitorial Culture in the Later Middle Ages*** (Princeton, N.J., 2004). On late medieval religious practices, see **R. N. Swanson**, ***Religion and Devotion in Europe, c. 1215–1515*** (Cambridge, 1995).

CULTURE A classic work on the life and thought of the later Middle Ages is **J. Huizinga, *The Autumn of the Middle Ages***, trans. **R. J. Payton** and **U. Mammitzsch** (Chicago, 1996). On Dante, see **B. Reynolds, *Dante: The Poet, the Political Thinker, the Man*** (London, 2006). The best work on Christine de Pizan is **C. C. Willard, *Christine de Pizan: Her Life and Works*** (New York, 1984).

SOCIAL HISTORY On women in the later Middle Ages, see **S. Shahar, *The Fourth Estate: A History of Women in the Middle Ages***, trans. **C. Galai**, rev. ed. (London, 2003). On childhood, see **N. Orme,** *Medieval Children* (New Haven, Conn., 2001). For a general introduction to the changes in medicine, see **N. G. Siraisi, *Medieval and Early Renaissance Medicine*** (Chicago, 1990).

Notes

1. Quoted in James B. Ross and Mary M. McLaughlin, *The Portable Medieval Reader* (New York, 1949), pp. 216–221.
2. Quoted in H. S. Lucas, "The Great European Famine of 1315, 1316, and 1317," *Speculum* 5 (1930): 359.
3. Quoted in C. S. Bartsocas, "Two Fourteenth-Century Descriptions of the 'Black Death,'" *Journal of the History of Medicine* (October 1966): 395.
4. Quoted in D. Herlihy, *The Black Death and the Transformation of the West*, ed. S. K. Cohn Jr. (Cambridge, Mass., 1997), p. 9.
5. Quoted in R. Horrox, ed., *The Black Death* (Manchester, U.K., 1994), pp. 18–19.
6. Giovanni Boccaccio, *Decameron*, trans. F. Winwar (New York, 1955), p. xxv.
7. Ibid., p. xxvi.
8. Jean Froissart, *Chronicles*, Geoffrey Brereton, ed., trans. (Harmondsworth, U.K., 1968), p. 111.
9. Quoted in J. B. Ross and M. M. McLaughlin, *The Portable Medieval Reader* (New York, 1949), pp. 218–219.
10. Quoted in B. W. Tuchman, *A Distant Mirror* (New York, 1978), p. 175.
11. Froissart, *Chronicles*, p. 212.
12. O. J. Thatcher and E. H. McNeal, eds., *A Source Book for Medieval History* (New York, 1905), p. 288.
13. Quoted in D. S. Chambers, *The Imperial Age of Venice, 1380–1580* (London, 1970), p. 30.
14. Quoted in R. Coogan, *Babylon on the Rhône: A Translation of Letters by Dante, Petrarch, and Catherine of Siena* (Washington, D.C., 1983), p. 115.
15. Quoted in C. W. Bynum, *Holy Feast and Holy Fast: The Religious Significance of Food to Medieval Women* (Berkeley, Calif., 1987), p. 180.
16. Dante Alighieri, *Divine Comedy*, trans. D. Sayers (New York, 1962), "Paradise," canto 33, line 145.
17. Sonnet LIV from *The Sonnets, Triumphs, and Other Poems of Petrarch*, edited by Thomas Campbell (London: George Bell and Sons, 1879), p. 78. Accessed at: http://www.gutenberg.org/files/17650/17650-h/17650-h.htm.
18. Quoted in M. Meiss, *Painting in Florence and Siena After the Black Death* (Princeton, N.J., 1951), p. 161.
19. Geoffrey Chaucer, *The Canterbury Tales*, in T. Morrison, ed., *The Portable Chaucer* (New York, 1949), p. 67.
20. Christine de Pizan, *The Book of the City of Ladies*, trans. E. J. Richards (New York, 1982), pp. 83–84.
21. Quoted in S. M. Stuard, "The Dominion of Gender, or How Women Fared in the High Middle Ages," in R. Bridenthal, C. Koonz, and S. Stuard, eds., *Becoming Visible: Women in European History*, 3rd ed. (Boston, 1998), p. 147.
22. Quoted in D. Herlihy, "Medieval Children," in B. K. Lackner and K. R. Philp, eds., *Essays on Medieval Civilization* (Austin, Tex., 1978), p. 121.
23. Quoted in J. Gimpel, *The Medieval Machine* (New York, 1976), p. 168.

CHAPTER

12

RECOVERY AND REBIRTH: THE AGE OF THE RENAISSANCE

Michelangelo's Creation of Adam *on the Sistine Chapel ceiling*

CHAPTER OUTLINE AND FOCUS QUESTIONS

Meaning and Characteristics of the Italian Renaissance

Q What characteristics distinguish the Renaissance from the Middle Ages?

The Making of Renaissance Society

Q What major social changes occurred during the Renaissance?

The Italian States in the Renaissance

Q How did Machiavelli's works reflect the political realities of Renaissance Italy?

The Intellectual Renaissance in Italy

Q What was humanism, and what effect did it have on philosophy, education, attitudes toward politics, and the writing of history?

The Artistic Renaissance

Q What were the chief characteristics of Renaissance art, and how did it differ in Italy and northern Europe?

The European State in the Renaissance

Q Why do historians sometimes refer to the monarchies of the late fifteenth century as "new monarchies" or "Renaissance states"?

The Church in the Renaissance

Q What were the policies of the Renaissance popes, and what impact did those policies have on the Catholic Church?

Critical Thinking

Q *How did Renaissance art and the humanist movement reflect the political, economic, and social developments of the period?*

Connections to Today

Q *How does the concept of the Renaissance have relevance to the early twenty-first century?*

WERE THE FOURTEENTH and fifteenth centuries a continuation of the Middle Ages or the beginning of a new era? Both positions can be defended. Although the disintegrative patterns of the fourteenth century continued into the fifteenth, at the same time there were elements of recovery that made the fifteenth century a period of significant political, economic, artistic, and intellectual change. The humanists or intellectuals of the age called their period (from the mid-fourteenth to the mid-sixteenth century) an age of rebirth, believing that they had restored arts and letters to new glory after they had been "neglected" or "dead" for centuries. The humanists also saw their age as one of accomplished individuals who dominated the landscape of their time.

Michelangelo, the great Italian artist of the early sixteenth century, and Pope Julius II, the "warrior pope," were two such titans. The artist's temperament and the pope's temper led to many lengthy and often loud quarrels between the two. The pope had hired Michelangelo to paint the ceiling of the Sistine Chapel in Rome, a difficult task for a man long accustomed to being a sculptor. Michelangelo undertook the project but refused for a long time to allow anyone, including the pope, to see his work. Julius grew anxious, pestering Michelangelo on a regular basis about when the ceiling would be finished. Exasperated by the pope's requests, Michelangelo once replied, according to Giorgio Vasari, his contemporary biographer, that the ceiling would be completed when it satisfied him "as an artist." The pope responded by threatening Michelangelo that if he did not finish the ceiling quickly, the pope would have him thrown down from the scaffolding. Fearing the pope's anger, Michelangelo began doing "all that was wanted" and quickly completed the ceiling, one of the great masterpieces in the history of Western art.

The humanists' view of their age as a rebirth of the classical civilization of the Greeks and Romans ultimately led historians to use the French word *Renaissance* to identify this age. Although recent historians have emphasized the many elements of continuity between the Middle Ages and the Renaissance, the latter age was also distinguished by its own unique characteristics.

Meaning and Characteristics of the Italian Renaissance

FOCUS QUESTION: What characteristics distinguish the Renaissance from the Middle Ages?

Renaissance means "rebirth." Many people who lived in Italy between 1350 and 1550 believed that they had witnessed a rebirth of antiquity or Greco-Roman civilization, marking a new age. To them, the thousand or so years between the end of the Roman Empire and their own era constituted a middle period (the "Middle Ages"), characterized by darkness because of its lack of classical culture. Historians of the nineteenth century later used similar terminology to describe this period in Italy. The Swiss historian and art critic Jacob Burckhardt (YAK-ub BOORK-hart) created the modern concept of the **Renaissance** in his celebrated book *The Civilization of the Renaissance in Italy*, published in 1860. He portrayed Italy in the fourteenth and fifteenth centuries as the birthplace of the modern world (the Italians were "the firstborn among the sons of modern Europe") and saw the revival of antiquity, the "perfecting of the individual," and secularism ("worldliness of the Italians") as its distinguishing features. Burckhardt exaggerated the individuality and secularism of the Renaissance and failed to recognize the depths of its religious sentiment; nevertheless, he established the framework for all modern interpretations of the period. Although contemporary scholars do not believe that the Renaissance represents a sudden or dramatic cultural break with the Middle Ages, as Burckhardt argued—there was, after all, much continuity in economic, political, and social life—the Renaissance can still be viewed as a distinct period of European history that manifested itself first in Italy and then spread to the rest of Europe.

Renaissance Italy was largely an urban society. As a result of its commercial preeminence and political evolution, northern Italy by the mid-fourteenth century was mostly a land of independent cities that dominated the country districts around them. These city-states became the centers of Italian political, economic, social, and cultural life. Within this new urban society, a secular spirit emerged as increasing wealth created new possibilities for the enjoyment of worldly things (see the box on p. 333).

Above all, the Renaissance was an age of recovery from the calamitous fourteenth century, a time for the slow process of recuperating from the effects of the Black Death, political disorder, and economic recession. This recovery was accompanied by a rediscovery of the culture of classical antiquity. Increasingly aware of their own historical past, Italian intellectuals became intensely interested in the Greek and Roman culture of the ancient Mediterranean world. This revival of classical antiquity (the Middle Ages had in fact preserved much of ancient Latin culture) affected activities as diverse as politics and art and led to new attempts to reconcile the pagan philosophy of the Greco-Roman world with Christian thought, as well as new ways of viewing human beings.

A revived emphasis on individual ability became a characteristic of the Italian Renaissance. As the fifteenth-century Florentine architect Leon Battista Alberti (LAY-un buh-TEESS-tuh al-BAYR-tee) expressed it, "Men can do all things if they will."[1] A high regard for human dignity and worth and a realization of individual potentiality created a new social ideal of the well-rounded personality or universal person—*l'uomo universale* (LWOH-moh OO-nee-ver-SAH-lay)—who was capable of achievements in many areas of life.

These general features of the Italian Renaissance were not characteristic of all Italians but were primarily the preserve of the wealthy upper classes, who constituted a small percentage of the total population. The achievements of the Italian Renaissance were the product of an elite, rather than a mass, movement. Nevertheless, indirectly it did have some impact on ordinary people, especially in the cities, where so many of the intellectual and artistic accomplishments of the period were most visible.

The Making of Renaissance Society

FOCUS QUESTION: What major social changes occurred during the Renaissance?

After the severe economic reversals and social upheavals of the fourteenth century, the European economy gradually recovered as the volume of manufacturing and trade increased.

Economic Recovery

By the fourteenth century, Italian merchants were carrying on a flourishing commerce throughout the Mediterranean and had also expanded their lines of trade north along the Atlantic seaboard. The great galleys of the Venetian Flanders Fleet maintained a direct sea route from Venice to England and the Netherlands, where Italian merchants came into contact with the increasingly powerful Hanseatic League of merchants. Hard hit by the plague, the Italians lost their commercial preeminence while the Hanseatic League continued to prosper.

A RENAISSANCE BANQUET

AS IN GREEK AND ROMAN SOCIETY, a banquet during the Renaissance was an occasion for good food, interesting conversation, music, and dancing. In Renaissance society, it was also a symbol of status and an opportunity to impress people with the power and wealth of one's family. Banquets were held to celebrate public and religious festivals, official visits, anniversaries, and weddings. The following menu lists the foods served at a grand banquet given by Pope Pius V in the sixteenth century.

A Sixteenth-Century Banquet

First Course
Cold Delicacies from the Sideboard

Pieces of marzipan and marzipan balls
Neapolitan spice cakes
Malaga wine and Pisan biscuits
Fresh grapes
Prosciutto cooked in wine, served with capers and grape pulp
Salted pork tongues cooked in wine, sliced
Spit-roasted songbirds, cold, with their tongues sliced over them
Sweet mustard

Second Course
Cold Hot Foods from the Kitchen, Roasts

Fried veal sweetbreads and liver
Spit-roasted skylarks with lemon sauce
Spit-roasted quails with sliced eggplants
Stuffed spit-roasted pigeons with capers sprinkled over them
Spit-roasted rabbits, with sauce and crushed pine nuts
Partridges larded and spit-roasted, served with lemon
Heavily seasoned poultry with lemon slices
Slices of veal, spit-roasted, with a sauce made from the juices
Leg of goat, spit-roasted, with a sauce made from the juices
Soup of almond paste, with the flesh of three pigeons to each serving

Third Course
Hot Foods from the Kitchen, Boiled Meats and Stews

Stuffed fat geese, boiled Lombard style and covered with sliced almonds
Stuffed breast of veal, boiled, garnished with flowers
Very young calf, boiled, garnished with parsley
Almonds in garlic sauce
Turkish-style rice with milk, sprinkled with cinnamon
Stewed pigeons with mortadella sausage and whole onions
Cabbage soup with sausages
Poultry pie, two chickens to each pie
Fricasseed breast of goat dressed with fried onions
Pies filled with custard cream
Boiled calves' feet with cheese and egg

Fourth Course
Delicacies from the Sideboard

Bean tarts
Quince pastries
Pear tarts, the pears wrapped in marzipan
Parmesan cheese and Riviera cheese
Fresh almonds on vine leaves
Chestnuts roasted over the coals and served with salt and pepper
Milk curds
Ring-shaped cakes
Wafers made from ground grain

Source: R. Tannahill, *Food in History* (New York: Broadway Books, 1973).

Q *What kinds of people would be present at a banquet where these foods would be served? What does this menu tell you about the material culture of the Renaissance and the association of food with social status?*

EXPANSION OF TRADE As early as the thirteenth century, a number of North German coastal towns had formed a commercial and military association known as the Hansa, or Hanseatic League. The city of Lübeck took the lead and became a major trading center for northern Europe and the chief city of the Hanseatic League. By 1500, more than eighty cities belonged to the League, which created its own armies for mutual protection and established settlements and commercial bases in many cities in England and northern Europe, including the chief towns of Denmark, Norway, and Sweden. For almost two hundred years, the Hansa had a monopoly on northern European trade in timber, fish, grain, metals, honey, and wines. Its southern outlet in Flanders, the port city of Bruges, became the economic crossroads of Europe in the fourteenth century, serving as the meeting place between Hanseatic merchants and the Flanders Fleet of Venice. In the fifteenth century, however, silting of the port caused Bruges to enter a slow decline. So did the Hanseatic League, which was increasingly unable to compete with the developing larger territorial states.

Overall, trade recovered dramatically from the economic contraction of the fourteenth century. The Italians and especially the Venetians, despite new restrictive pressures on their eastern Mediterranean trade from the Ottoman Turks (see

Interfoto/History/Alamy Stock Photo

Lübeck and the Hanseatic League. The Hanseatic League or Hansa was an economic and military alliance of northern European trading cities that established a monopoly on trade from the Baltic to the North Sea. The city of Lübeck in northern Germany played a major role in the founding of the Hanseatic League and became known as the "Queen of the Hansa." This colored woodcut by Michael Wohlgemut in Hartmann Schedel's *Chronicle of the World* presents a panoramic view of this prosperous German city.

"The Ottoman Turks and the End of the Byzantine Empire" later in this chapter), continued to maintain a wealthy commercial empire. Not until the sixteenth century, when transatlantic discoveries gave new importance to the states along the ocean, did the petty Italian city-states begin to suffer from the competitive advantages of the ever-growing and more powerful national territorial states.

INDUSTRIES OLD AND NEW The economic depression of the fourteenth century also affected patterns of manufacturing. The woolen industries of Flanders and the northern Italian cities had been particularly devastated. By the beginning of the fifteenth century, however, the Florentine woolen industry had begun to recover. At the same time, the Italian cities began to develop and expand luxury industries, especially silk, glassware, and handworked items in metal and precious stones.

Other new industries, especially printing, mining, and metallurgy, began to rival the textile industry in importance in the fifteenth century. New machinery and techniques for digging deeper mines and for separating metals from ore and purifying them were devised, and entrepreneurs quickly developed large mining operations to produce copper, iron, and silver. Especially valuable were the rich mineral deposits in central Europe. Expanding iron production and new skills in metalworking in turn contributed to the development of firearms that were more effective than the crude weapons of the fourteenth century.

BANKING AND THE MEDICI The city of Florence regained its preeminence in banking in the fifteenth century, due primarily to the Medici (MED-ih-chee) family. The Medici had expanded from cloth production into commerce, real estate, and banking. In its best days (in the fifteenth century), the House of Medici was the greatest bank in Europe, with branches in Venice, Milan, Rome, Avignon, Bruges, London, and Lyons. Moreover, the family had controlling interests in industrial enterprises for wool, silk, and the mining of alum, used in the dyeing of textiles. Except for a brief period, the Medici were also the principal bankers for the papacy, a position that produced big profits and influence at the papal court. Despite its great success in the early and middle part of the fifteenth century, the Medici bank suffered a rather sudden decline at the end of the century due to poor leadership and a series of bad loans, especially uncollectible loans to rulers. In 1494, when the French expelled the Medici from Florence and confiscated their property, the Medici financial edifice collapsed.

Social Changes in the Renaissance

The Renaissance inherited its social structure from the Middle Ages. Society remained fundamentally divided into three **estates**: the First Estate, the clergy, whose preeminence was grounded in the belief that people should be guided to spiritual ends; the Second Estate, the nobility, whose privileges were based on the principle that the nobles provided security and justice for society; and the Third Estate, which consisted of the peasants and inhabitants of the towns and cities. This social order experienced certain adaptations in the Renaissance, which we can see by examining the Second and Third Estates (the clergy will be examined in Chapter 13).

THE NOBILITY Throughout much of Europe, the landholding nobles faced declining real incomes during the greater part of the fourteenth and fifteenth centuries. Nevertheless, many members of the old nobility survived, and new blood infused their ranks. A reconstruction of the aristocracy was well under way by 1500. As a result of this reconstruction, the nobles, old and new, who constituted between 2 and 3 percent of the population in most countries, managed to dominate society as they had done in the Middle Ages, serving as military officers and holding important political posts as well as advising the king. In the sixteenth century, members of the aristocracy increasingly pursued education as the means to maintain their role in government.

By 1500, certain ideals came to be expected of the noble or aristocrat. These ideals were best expressed in *The Book of the Courtier* by the Italian Baldassare Castiglione (bal-duh-SAH-ray ka-steel-YOH-nay) (1478–1529). First published in 1528, Castiglione's work soon became popular throughout Europe and remained a fundamental handbook for European aristocrats for centuries.

In his book, Castiglione described the three basic attributes of the perfect courtier. First, nobles should possess fundamental native endowments, such as impeccable character, grace, talents, and noble birth. The perfect courtier must also cultivate certain achievements. Primarily, he should participate in military and bodily exercises, because the principal profession of a courtier was bearing arms. But unlike the medieval knight, who had been required only to have military skill, the Renaissance courtier was also expected to have a classical education and to adorn his life with the arts by playing a musical instrument, drawing, and painting. In Castiglione's hands, the Renaissance ideal of the well-developed personality became a social ideal of the aristocracy. Finally, the aristocrat was expected to follow a certain standard of conduct. Nobles were to make a good impression; while remaining modest, they should not hide their accomplishments but show them with grace.

What was the purpose of these courtly standards? Castiglione wrote:

> I think that the aim of the perfect Courtier, which we have not spoken of up to now, is so to win for himself, by means of the accomplishments ascribed to him by these gentlemen, the favor and mind of the prince whom he serves that he may be able to tell him, and always will tell him, the truth about everything he needs to know, without fear or risk of displeasing him; and that when he sees the mind of his prince inclined to a wrong action, he may dare to oppose him . . . so as to dissuade him of every evil intent and bring him to the path of virtue.[2]

The aim of the perfect noble, then, was to serve his prince in an effective and honest way. Nobles would adhere to these principles for hundreds of years while they continued to dominate European life socially and politically.

PEASANTS AND TOWNSPEOPLE Peasants made up the overwhelming mass of the Third Estate and continued to constitute 85 to 90 percent of the European population, except in the highly urbanized areas of northern Italy and Flanders. The most noticeable trend produced by the economic crisis of the fourteenth century was the decline of the manorial system and the continuing elimination of serfdom. This process had already begun in the twelfth century when the introduction of a money economy made possible the conversion of servile labor dues into rents paid in money, although they also continued to be paid in kind or labor. The contraction of the peasantry after the Black Death simply accelerated this process, since lords found it convenient to deal with the peasants by granting freedom and accepting rents. The lords' lands were then tilled by hired workers or rented out. By the end of the fifteenth century, serfdom was declining in western Europe, and more and more peasants were becoming legally free.

The remainder of the Third Estate centered around the inhabitants of towns and cities, originally the merchants and artisans who formed the bourgeoisie. The Renaissance town or city of the fifteenth century actually was home to a multitude of townspeople widely separated socially and economically.

At the top of urban society were the patricians, whose wealth from capitalistic enterprises in trade, industry, and banking enabled them to dominate their urban communities economically, socially, and politically. Below them were the petty burghers—the shopkeepers, artisans, guildmasters, and guild members, who were largely concerned with providing goods and services for local consumption. Below these two groups were the propertyless workers earning pitiful wages and the unemployed, living squalid and miserable lives; these people constituted 30 to 40 percent of the population living in cities. In many places in Europe in the late fourteenth and fifteenth centuries, urban poverty increased dramatically. One rich merchant of Florence wrote:

> Those that are lazy and indolent in a way that does harm to the city, and who can offer no just reason for their condition, should either be forced to work or expelled from the Commune. The city would thus rid itself of that most harmful part of the poorest class. . . . If the lowest order of society earn enough food to keep them going from day to day, then they have enough.[3]

But even this large group was not at the bottom of the social scale; beneath them were the slaves, especially in the Italian cities.

SLAVERY IN THE RENAISSANCE Agricultural slavery existed in the early Middle Ages but had declined for economic reasons and been replaced by serfdom by the ninth century. Although some domestic slaves remained, slavery in European society had largely disappeared by the eleventh century. It reappeared first in Spain, where both Christians and Muslims used captured prisoners as slaves during the lengthy *Reconquista*. In the second half of the fourteenth century, the shortage of workers after the Black Death led Italians to introduce slavery on a fairly large scale.

In the Italian cities, slaves were used as skilled workers, making handcrafted goods for their masters, or as household workers. Girls served as nursemaids and boys as playmates. Fiammetta Adimari wrote to her husband in 1469: "I must remind you that when Alfonso is weaned we ought to get a little slave-girl to look after him, or else one of the black boys to keep him company."[4] Most slaves, though, were females, many of them young girls. In Florence, wealthy merchants might own two or three slaves. Often men of the household took slaves as concubines, which sometimes led to the birth of illegitimate children. In 1392, the wealthy merchant Francesco Datini fathered an illegitimate daughter by Lucia, his twenty-year-old slave. His wife, Margherita, who was unable to bear any children, reluctantly agreed to raise the girl as their own daughter. Many illegitimate children were not as fortunate.

Slaves for the Italian market were obtained primarily from the eastern Mediterranean and the Black Sea region and included Tartars, Russians, Albanians, and Dalmatians. There were also slaves from Africa, either Moors or Ethiopians, and Muslims from Spain. Because of the lucrative nature of the slave trade, Italian merchants became involved in the transportation of slaves. Between 1414 and 1423, ten thousand slaves were sold on the Venetian market.

By the end of the fifteenth century, slavery had declined dramatically in the Italian cities. Many slaves had been freed by their owners for humanitarian reasons, and the major source of slaves dried up as the Black Sea slave markets were closed to Italian traders after the Turks conquered the Byzantine Empire. Moreover, a general feeling had arisen that slaves—the "domestic enemy," as they were called—were dangerous and not worth the effort. By the sixteenth century, slaves were in evidence only at princely courts, where they were kept as curiosities; this was especially true of black slaves.

In the fifteenth century, the Portuguese had imported increasing numbers of African slaves for southern European markets. It has been estimated that between 1444 and 1505, some 140,000 slaves were shipped from Africa. The presence of blacks in European society was not entirely new. Saint Maurice, a Christian martyr of the fourth century, was portrayed by medieval artists as a black knight and became the center of a popular cult in the twelfth and thirteenth centuries. The number of blacks in Europe was small, however, until their importation as slaves.

The Family in Renaissance Italy

The family played an important role in Renaissance Italy (see "Images of Everyday Life" on p. 337). Family meant, first of all, the extended household of parents, children, and servants (if the family was wealthy) and could also include grandparents, widowed mothers, and even unmarried sisters. Families that were related and bore the same surname often lived near each other and might dominate an entire urban district. Old family names—Strozzi (STRAWT-see), Rucellai (roo-CHELL-eye), Medici—conferred great status and prestige. The family bond was a source of great security in a dangerous and violent world, and its importance helps explain the vendetta in the Italian Renaissance. A crime committed by one family member fell on the entire family, ensuring that retaliation by the offended family would be a bloody affair involving large numbers of people.

MARRIAGE To maintain the family, parents gave careful attention to arranging marriages, often to strengthen business or family ties. Details were worked out well in advance, sometimes when children were only two or three years old, and reinforced by a legally binding marriage contract (see the box on p. 338). The important aspect of the contract was the amount of the dowry, money presented by the wife's family to the husband upon marriage. The dowry could involve large sums and was expected of all families. The size of the dowry was an indication of whether the bride was moving upward or downward in society. With a large dowry, a daughter could marry a man of higher social status, thereby enabling her family to move up in society; if the daughter married a man of lower social status, however, her dowry would be smaller because the reputation of her family would raise the status of her husband's family.

The father-husband was the center of the Italian family. He gave it his name, was responsible for it in all legal matters, managed all finances (his wife had no share in his wealth), and made the crucial decisions that determined his children's lives. A father's authority over his children was absolute until he died or formally freed his children. In Renaissance Italy, children did not become adults on reaching a certain age; adulthood came only when the father went before a judge and formally emancipated them. The age of emancipation varied from early teens to late twenties.

CHILDREN The wife managed the household, a position that gave women a certain degree of autonomy in their daily lives. Women of the upper and middle classes, however, were expected to remain at home, under the supervision of their father or husband. Moreover, most wives knew that their primary function was to bear children. Upper-class wives were frequently pregnant; Alessandra Strozzi of Florence, for example, who had been married at the age of sixteen, bore eight children in ten years. Poor women did not conceive at the same rate because they nursed their own babies. Wealthy women gave their infants out to wet nurses, which enabled them to become pregnant more quickly after the birth of a child.

For women in the Renaissance, childbirth was a fearful occasion. Not only was it painful, but it could be deadly; as many as 10 percent of mothers died in childbirth. In his memoirs, the Florentine merchant Gregorio Dati recalled that three of his four wives had died in childbirth. His third wife, after bearing eleven children in fifteen years, "died in childbirth after lengthy suffering, which she bore with remarkable strength and patience."[5] Nor did the tragedies end with childbirth. Surviving mothers often faced the death of their children. In Florence in the fifteenth century, for example, almost 50 percent of the children born to merchant families died before the age of twenty. Given these mortality rates, many upper-class families sought to have as many children as possible to ensure that there would be a surviving male heir to the family fortune. This concern is evident in the Florentine humanist Leon Battista Alberti's treatise *On the Family*, where one of the characters remarks, "How many families do we see today in decadence and ruin! . . . Of all these families not only the magnificence and greatness but the very men, not only the men but the very names are shrunk away and gone. Their memory . . . is wiped out and obliterated."[6]

SEXUAL NORMS Considering that marriages were arranged, marital relationships ran the gamut from deep emotional attachments to purely formal ties. The lack of emotional

IMAGES OF EVERYDAY LIFE

Family and Marriage in Renaissance Italy

THE FAMILY WAS AN IMPORTANT UNIT in Renaissance Italy. For the upper classes, family meant an extended household of parents, children, and servants, as is evident in the portrait of the Gonzaga family by Andrea Mantegna (ahn-DRAY-uh mahn-TEN-yah) at the left below. Ludovico Gonzaga, marquis of Mantua, is shown at the left listening to a messenger. To his right are his wife Barbara, two sons, and two daughters, as well as servants. In the lower right corner is a dwarf. Dwarfs were common at Italian Renaissance courts, where they were kept as a source of entertainment.

In the upper classes, parents arranged marriages to reinforce business or family connections. As seen in the painting at the right, the marriage ceremony involved an exchange of vows and the placing of a ring (see the inset) by the bridegroom on the bride's hand. The ring was a sign of affection and a symbol of the union of the two families. The church encouraged the presence of a priest, but it was not necessary. The wedding was then recorded in a marriage contract that was considered a crucial part of the marital arrangements. So was a wedding feast, as seen in the painting by Sandro Botticelli at the bottom. It shows the wedding banquet that celebrated the marriage of Nastagio degli Onesti and the daughter of Paulo Traversaro in Florence. After the feast, the couple retired to a bedroom, usually in the house of the bride, where they physically consummated their marriage. Later, the husband introduced his bride to his household, usually on Sunday, in order to make it public knowledge that the marriage had been consummated.

Scala/Art Resource, NY

Museum of London, London/The Art Archive at Art Resource, NY

Dagli Orti/The Art Archive at Art Resource, NY

Private Collection/Bridgeman Images

MARRIAGE NEGOTIATIONS

MARRIAGES WERE SO IMPORTANT in maintaining families in Renaissance Italy that much energy was put into arranging them. Parents made the choices for their children, most often for considerations that had little to do with the modern notion of love. This selection is taken from the letters of a Florentine matron of the illustrious Strozzi family to her son Filippo in Naples. The family's considerations were complicated by the fact that the son was in exile.

Alessandra Strozzi to Her Son Filippo in Naples

[April 20, 1464]... Concerning the matter of a wife [for you], it appears to me that if Francesco di Messer Tanagli wishes to give his daughter, that it would be a fine marriage.... Francesco Tanagli has a good reputation, and he has held office, not the highest, but still he has been in office.

[July 26, 1465]... Francesco is a good friend of Marco [Parenti, Alessandra's son-in-law] and he trusts him. On S. Jacopo's day, he spoke to him discreetly and persuasively, saying that for several months he had heard that we were interested in the girl and... that when we had made up our minds, she will come to us willingly. [He said that] you were a worthy man, and that his family had always made good marriages, but that he had only a small dowry to give her, and so he would prefer to send her out of Florence to someone of worth, rather than to give her to someone here, from among those who were available, with little money.... We have information that she is affable and competent. She is responsible for a large family (there are twelve children, six boys and six girls), and the mother is always pregnant and isn't very competent....

[August 31, 1465]... I have recently received some very favorable information [about the Tanagli girl] from two individuals.... They are in agreement that whoever gets her will be content.... Concerning her beauty, they told me what I had already seen, that she is attractive and well-proportioned. Her face is long, but I couldn't look directly into her face, since she appeared to be aware that I was examining her... and so she turned away from me like the wind.... She reads quite well... and she can dance and sing....

So yesterday I sent for Marco and told him what I had learned. And we talked about the matter for a while, and decided that he should say something to the father and give him a little hope, but not so much that we couldn't withdraw, and find out from him the amount of the dowry.... May God help us to choose what will contribute to our tranquility and to the consolation of us all.

[September 13, 1465]... Marco came to me and said that he had met with Francesco Tanagli, who had spoken very coldly, so that I understand that he had changed his mind.

[Filippo Strozzi eventually married Fiametta di Donato Adimari in 1466.]

Q *What were the most important considerations in marriage negotiations? Why were they so important?*

Source: G. Brucker, ed., *The Society of Renaissance Florence* (Toronto: University of Toronto Press, 1971).

attachment in arranged marriages did encourage extramarital relationships, especially among groups whose lifestyle offered special temptations. Although sexual license for males was the norm for princes and their courts, women were supposed to follow different guidelines. The first wife of Duke Filippo Maria Visconti of Milan had an affair with the court musician and was executed for it.

The great age difference between husbands and wives in Italian Renaissance marriage patterns also encouraged the tendency to seek sexual outlets outside marriage. In Florence in 1427–1428, the average difference was thirteen years. Though females married between the ages of sixteen and eighteen, factors of environment, wealth, and demographic trends favored relatively late ages for the first marriages of males, who were usually in their thirties or even early forties. The existence of large numbers of young, unmarried males encouraged extramarital sex as well as prostitution. Prostitution was viewed as a necessary vice; since it could not be eliminated, it should be regulated. In Florence in 1415, the city fathers established communal brothels:

> Desiring to eliminate a worse evil by means of a lesser one, the lord priors... have decreed that the priors... may authorize the establishment of two public brothels in the city of Florence, in addition to the one which already exists.... [They are to be located] in suitable places or in places where the exercise of such scandalous activity can best be concealed, for the honor of the city.[7]

A prostitute in Florence was required to wear a traditional garb of "gloves on her hands and a bell on her head."

The Italian States in the Renaissance

Q **FOCUS QUESTION:** How did Machiavelli's works reflect the political realities of Renaissance Italy?

By the fifteenth century, five major powers dominated the Italian peninsula: Milan, Venice, Florence, the Papal States, and Naples (see Map 12.1).

The Five Major States

Northern Italy was divided between the duchy of Milan and the republic of Venice. After the death of the last Visconti ruler of Milan in 1447, Francesco Sforza (frahn-CHESS-koh SFORT-sah), one of the leading *condottieri* of the time (see Chapter 11), turned on his Milanese employers, conquered the city, and became its new duke. Both the Visconti and the Sforza rulers worked to create a highly centralized territorial state. They were especially successful in devising systems of taxation that generated enormous revenues for the government. The maritime republic of Venice remained an extremely stable political entity governed by a small oligarchy of merchant-aristocrats. Its commercial empire brought in enormous revenues and gave it the status of an international power. At the end of the fourteenth century, Venice embarked on the conquest of a territorial state in northern Italy to protect its food supply and its overland trade routes. Although expansion on the mainland made sense to the Venetians, it frightened Milan and Florence, which worked to curb what they perceived as the expansionary designs of the Venetians.

The republic of Florence dominated the region of Tuscany. By the beginning of the fifteenth century, Florence was governed by a small merchant oligarchy that manipulated the apparently republican government. In 1434, Cosimo de' Medici took control of this oligarchy. Although the wealthy Medici family maintained republican forms of government for appearances' sake, it ran the government from behind the scenes. Through lavish patronage and careful courting of political allies, Cosimo (1434–1464) and later his grandson, Lorenzo the Magnificent (1469–1492), were successful in dominating the city at a time when Florence was the center of the cultural Renaissance.

To some Florentines, Florence was the ideal city. One city official at the beginning of the fifteenth century exclaimed:

> What city not merely in Italy, but in all the world, is more securely placed within its walls, more proud in its palazzi, more bedecked with churches, more beautiful in its architecture, more imposing in its gates, richer in piazzas, happier in its wide streets, greater in its people, more glorious in its citizenry, more inexhaustible in wealth, more fertile in its fields?[8]

But as one historian has recently noted, official praise of the city failed to note the ugly side of Renaissance Florence: the gross inequality between rich and poor; poverty that was common to a majority of Florentines, begging that was widespread, and both crime and disease that were rampant.

The Papal States lay in central Italy. Although these lands were nominally under the political control of the popes, papal residence in Avignon and the Great Schism had enabled individual cities and territories, such as Urbino (ur-BEE-noh), Bologna (buh-LOHN-yuh), and Ferrara, to become independent of papal authority. The Renaissance popes of the fifteenth century directed much of their energy toward reestablishing their control over the Papal States (see "The Renaissance Papacy" later in this chapter).

MAP 12.1 Renaissance Italy. Italy in the late fourteenth century was a land of five major states and numerous independent city-states. Increased prosperity and a supportive intellectual climate helped create the atmosphere for the middle and upper classes to "rediscover" Greco-Roman culture. Modern diplomacy was also a product of Renaissance Italy.

Could the presence of several other powers within easy marching distance make it more likely that a ruler would recognize the importance of diplomacy?

The kingdom of Naples, which encompassed most of southern Italy and usually the island of Sicily, was fought over by the French and the Aragonese until the latter established their domination in the mid-fifteenth century. Throughout the Renaissance, the kingdom of Naples remained a backward monarchy with a population consisting largely of poverty-stricken peasants dominated by unruly nobles. It shared little in the cultural glories of the Renaissance.

Independent City-States

Besides the five major states, there were a number of independent city-states under the control of powerful ruling families that became brilliant centers of Renaissance culture in the fifteenth century. These included Mantua (MAN-choo-uh), under the enlightened rule of the Gonzaga (gun-DZAH-gah) lords; Ferrara, governed by the flamboyant d'Este (DESS-tay) family; and perhaps the most famous, Urbino, ruled by the Montefeltro dynasty.

URBINO Federigo da Montefeltro (fay-day-REE-goh dah mahn-tuh-FELL-troh), who ruled Urbino from 1444 to 1482, received a classical education typical of the famous humanist school in Mantua run by Vittorino da Feltre (vee-tor-EE-noh dah FELL-tray) (1378–1446) (see "Education in the Renaissance" later in this chapter). He also learned the skills of fighting, since the Montefeltro family compensated for the poverty of Urbino by hiring themselves out as condottieri. Federigo was not only a good ruler but also a rather unusual condottiere by fifteenth-century standards. Although not a brilliant general, he was reliable and honest. He did not break his promises, even when urged to do so by a papal legate. At the same time, Duke Federigo was one of the greatest patrons of Renaissance culture. Under his direction, Urbino became a well-known cultural and intellectual center. Though a despot, Federigo was also benevolent. It was said of him that he could walk safely through the streets of Urbino unaccompanied by a bodyguard, a feat few Renaissance rulers dared to emulate.

THE ROLE OF WOMEN A noticeable feature of these smaller Renaissance courts was the important role played by women. Battista Sforza (buh-TEESS-tuh SFORT-sah), niece of the ruler of Milan, was the wife of Federigo da Montefeltro. The duke called his wife "the delight of both my public and my private hours." An intelligent woman, she was well versed in both Greek and Latin and did much to foster art and letters in Urbino. As a prominent condottiere, Federigo was frequently absent, and like the wives of medieval lords, Battista Sforza was respected for governing the state "with firmness and good sense."

Perhaps the most famous of the Renaissance ruling women was Isabella d'Este (1474–1539), daughter of the duke of Ferrara, who married Francesco Gonzaga, marquis of Mantua. Their court was another important center of art and learning in the Renaissance. Educated at the brilliant court of Ferrara, Isabella was known for her intelligence and political wisdom. Called the "first lady of the world," she attracted artists and intellectuals to the Mantuan court and was responsible for amassing one of the finest libraries in all of Italy. Her numerous letters to friends, family, princes, and artists all over Europe reveal her political acumen as well as her good sense of humor (see the box on p. 341). Both before and after the death of her husband, she effectively ruled Mantua and won a reputation as a clever negotiator.

Warfare in Italy

The fragmented world of the Italian territorial states gave rise to a political practice that was later used on a larger scale by competing European states. This was the concept of a balance

Alinari/Art Resource, NY

Piero della Francesca, *Duke and Duchess of Urbino.* Federigo da Montefeltro and his wife, Battista Sforza, ruled the small central Italian principality of Urbino. These profile portraits by Piero della Francesca gave a realistic rendering of the two figures. Visible in the background are the hills and valleys of Urbino.

THE LETTERS OF ISABELLA D'ESTE

MANY ITALIAN AND EUROPEAN RULERS at the beginning of the sixteenth century regarded Isabella d'Este as an important political figure. These excerpts from her letters reveal Isabella's political skills and her fierce determination. After her husband was taken prisoner by the Venetians in 1509, she refused to accept the condition for his release—namely, that her son Federico be kept as a hostage by the Venetians or the Holy Roman Emperor. She wrote to both the emperor and her husband, refusing to do as they asked.

Letter of Isabella d'Este to the Imperial Envoy

As to the demand for our dearest first-born son Federico, besides being a cruel and almost inhuman thing for any one who knows the meaning of a mother's love, there are many reasons which render it difficult and impossible. Although we are quite sure that his person would be well cared for and protected by His Majesty [the Holy Roman Emperor], how could we wish him to run the risk of this long and difficult journey, considering the child's tender and delicate age? And you must know what comfort and solace, in his father's present unhappy condition, we find in the presence of this dear son, the hope and joy of all our people and subjects. To deprive us of him, would be to deprive us of life itself, and of all we count good and precious. If you take Federico away you might as well take away our life and state.... Once [and] for all, we will suffer any loss rather than part from our son, and this you may take to be our deliberate and unchanging resolution.

Letter of Isabella d'Este to Her Husband, Who Had Ordered Her to Send the Boy to Venice

If in this matter Your Excellency were to despise me and deprive me of your love and grace, I would rather endure such harsh treatment, I would rather lose our State, than deprive us of our children. I am hoping that in time your own prudence and kindness will make you understand that I have acted more lovingly toward you than you have to yourself.

Have patience! You can be sure that I think continuously of your liberation and when the time comes I will not fail you, as I have not relaxed my efforts. As witness I cite the Pope, the Emperor, the King of France, and all the other reigning heads and potentates of Christendom. Yes, and the infidels as well [she had written to the Turkish sultan for help]. If it were *really* the only means of setting you free, I would not only send Federico but all the other children as well. I will do everything imaginable. Some day I hope I can make you understand....

Pardon me if this letter is badly written and worse composed, but I do not know if I am dead or alive.

Isabella, who desires the best for Your Excellency,
written with her own hand

[Isabella's husband was not pleased with her response and exclaimed angrily: "That whore of my wife is the cause of it all. Send me into battle alone, do what you like with me. I have lost in one blow my state, my honor and my freedom. If she does not obey, I'll cut her vocal cords."]

Q *What do these letters reveal about Isabella's character and about the attributes and strategies of expression on which noble women had to rely in order to participate effectively in high politics?*

Source: The Letters of Isabella d'Este, *The Bed and the Throne*, ed. G. R. Marek (New York: HarperCollins, 1976).

of power, designed to prevent the aggrandizement of any one state at the expense of the others. This system was especially evident after 1454 when the Italian states signed the Peace of Lodi (LAH-dee), which ended almost a half-century of war and inaugurated a relatively peaceful forty-year era in Italy. An alliance system (Milan, Florence, and Naples versus Venice and the papacy) was created that led to a workable balance of power within Italy. It failed, however, to establish lasting cooperation among the major powers.

The growth of powerful monarchical states (see "The European State in the Renaissance" later in this chapter) led to trouble for the Italians. Italy soon became a battlefield for the great power struggle between the French and Spanish monarchies. Italian wealth and splendor would probably have been inviting to its northern neighbors under any circumstances, but it was actually the breakdown of the Italian balance of power that encouraged the invasions and began the Italian wars. Feeling isolated, Ludovico Sforza, the duke of Milan, foolishly invited the French to intervene in Italian politics. The French king Charles VIII (1483–1498) was eager to do so, and in 1494, with an army of 30,000 men, he advanced through Italy and occupied the kingdom of Naples. Other Italian states turned to the Spanish for help, and Ferdinand of Aragon indicated his willingness to intervene. For the next fifteen years, the French and Spanish competed to dominate Italy. After 1510, the war was continued by a new generation of rulers, Francis I of France and Charles I of Spain (see Chapter 13). This war was part of a long struggle for power throughout Europe between the Valois and Habsburg dynasties. Italy was only a pawn for the two great powers, a convenient arena for fighting battles. The terrible sack of Rome in 1527 by the armies of the Spanish king Charles I brought a temporary end to the Italian wars. Thereafter, the Spaniards dominated Italy.

CHRONOLOGY	The Italian States in the Renaissance
Duchy of Milan	
The Viscontis	1311–1447
The Sforzas	1450–1494
Florence	
Cosimo de' Medici	1434–1464
Lorenzo de' Medici	1469–1492
Peace of Lodi	1454
Beginning of Italian wars; French invasion of Italy	1494
Sack of Rome	1527

Although some Italians had differentiated between Italians and "barbarians" (all foreigners), few Italians conceived of creating an alliance or confederation of states that could repel foreign invaders. Italians remained fiercely loyal to their own petty states, making invasion a fact of life in Italian history for all too long. Italy would not achieve unification and nationhood until 1870.

The Birth of Modern Diplomacy

The modern diplomatic system was a product of the Italian Renaissance. There were ambassadors in the Middle Ages, but they were used only on a temporary basis. Moreover, an ambassador, regardless of whose subject he was, regarded himself as the servant of all Christendom, not just of his particular employer. As a treatise on diplomacy stated, "An ambassador is sacred because he acts for the general welfare." Since he was the servant of all Christendom, "the business of an ambassador is peace.[9]

This concept of an ambassador changed during the Italian Renaissance because of the political situation in Italy. A large number of states existed, many so small that their neighbors easily threatened their security. To survive, the Italian states began to send resident diplomatic agents to each other to ferret out useful information. During the Italian wars, the practice of resident diplomats spread to the rest of Europe, and in the course of the sixteenth and seventeenth centuries, Europeans developed the diplomatic machinery still in use today, such as the rights of ambassadors in host countries and the proper procedures for conducting diplomatic business.

With the use of permanent resident agents or ambassadors, the conception of the purpose of an ambassador also changed. A Venetian diplomat attempted to define an ambassador's function in a treatise written at the end of the fifteenth century. He wrote, "The first duty of an ambassador is exactly the same as that of any other servant of a government, that is, to do, say, advise, and think whatever may best serve the preservation and aggrandizement of his own state."[10] An ambassador was now an agent only of the territorial state that sent him, not the larger body of Christendom. He could use any methods that were beneficial to the political interests of his own state. We are at the beginning of modern politics when the interests of the state supersede all other considerations.

Machiavelli and the New Statecraft

No one gave better expression to the Renaissance preoccupation with political power than Niccolò Machiavelli (nee-koh-LOH mahk-ee-uh-VEL-ee) (1469–1527). He entered the service of the Florentine republic in 1498, four years after the Medici family had been expelled from the city. As a secretary to the Florentine Council of Ten, he made numerous diplomatic missions, including trips to France and Germany, and saw the workings of statecraft at first hand. Machiavelli's political activity occurred during the period of tribulation and devastation for Italy that followed the French invasion in 1494. In 1512, French defeat and Spanish victory led to the reestablishment of Medici power in Florence. Staunch republicans, including Machiavelli, were sent into exile. Forced to give up politics, the great love of his life, Machiavelli now reflected on political power and wrote books, including *The Prince* (1513), one of the most famous treatises on political power in the Western world.

THE PRINCE Machiavelli's ideas on politics stemmed from two major sources, his knowledge of ancient Rome and his preoccupation with Italy's political problems. As a result of his experiences, Machiavelli fully realized that the small Italian states were no match for the larger monarchical states outside Italy's borders and that Italy itself had become merely a battleground for the armies of foreign states. His major concerns in *The Prince* were

AKG/Photo Researchers, Inc.

Niccolò Machiavelli. In *The Prince*, Machiavelli gave concrete expression to the Renaissance preoccupation with political power. This slender volume remains one of the most famous and most widely read Western treatises on politics. Machiavelli is seen here in a portrait by Santi di Tito.

the acquisition and expansion of political power as the means to restore and maintain order in his time. In the Middle Ages, many political theorists stressed the ethical side of a prince's activity—how a ruler ought to behave based on Christian moral principles. Machiavelli bluntly contradicted this approach:

> But since my intention is to say something that will prove of practical use to the inquirer, I have thought it proper to represent things as they are in real truth, rather than as they are imagined. . . . [For] the gulf between how one should live and how one does live is so wide that a man who neglects what is actually done with what should be done learns the way to self-destruction rather [than] self-preservation.[11]

Machiavelli considered his approach far more realistic than that of his medieval forebears.

In Machiavelli's view, a prince's attitude toward power must be based on an understanding of human nature, which he perceived as basically self-centered: "One can make this generalization about men: they are ungrateful, fickle, liars, and deceivers, they shun danger and are greedy for profit." Political activity, therefore, could not be restricted by moral considerations. The prince acts on behalf of the state and for the sake of the state must be willing to let his conscience sleep. As Machiavelli put it:

> You must realize this: that a prince, and especially a new prince, cannot observe all those things which give men a reputation for virtue, because in order to maintain his state he is often forced to act in defiance of good faith, of charity, of kindness, of religion. And so he should have a flexible disposition, varying as fortune and circumstances dictate. As I said above, he should not deviate from what is good if that is possible, but he should know how to do evil, if that is necessary.[12]

Machiavelli found a good example of the new Italian ruler in Cesare Borgia (CHAY-zah-ray BOR-juh), the son of Pope Alexander VI, who used ruthless measures to achieve his goal of carving out a new state in central Italy. As Machiavelli said: "So a new prince cannot find more recent examples than those set by the duke, if he thinks it necessary to secure himself against his enemies, win friends, conquer either by force or by stratagem, make himself both loved and feared by his subjects."[13] Machiavelli was among the first to abandon morality as the basis for the analysis of political activity (see the box on p. 344).

The Intellectual Renaissance in Italy

> **FOCUS QUESTION:** What was humanism, and what effect did it have on philosophy, education, attitudes toward politics, and the writing of history?

Individualism and **secularism**—two characteristics of the Italian Renaissance—were most noticeable in the intellectual and artistic realms. Italian culture had matured by the fourteenth century. For the next two centuries, Italy was the cultural leader of Europe. This new Italian culture was primarily the product of a relatively wealthy, urban lay society. The most important literary movement associated with the Renaissance was **humanism**.

Italian Renaissance Humanism

Renaissance humanism was an intellectual movement based on the study of the classical literary works of Greece and Rome. Humanists examined the *studia humanitatis* ("the studies of humanity")—grammar, rhetoric, poetry, moral philosophy or ethics, and history—all based on the writings of ancient Greek and Roman authors. These are the subjects we call the humanities.

The central importance of literary preoccupations in Renaissance humanism is evident in the professional status or occupations of the humanists. Some of them were teachers of the humanities in secondary schools and universities, where they either gave occasional lectures or held permanent positions, often as professors of rhetoric. Others served as secretaries in the chancelleries of Italian city-states or at the courts of princes or popes. All of these occupations were largely secular, and most humanists were laymen rather than members of the clergy.

THE EMERGENCE OF HUMANISM Petrarch (1304–1374) has often been called the father of Italian Renaissance humanism (see Chapter 11 on his use of the Italian vernacular). Petrarch rejected his father's desire that he become a lawyer and took up a literary career instead. Although he lived in Avignon for a time, most of his last decades were spent in Italy as the guest of various princes and city governments. With his usual lack of modesty, Petrarch once exclaimed, "Some of the greatest kings of our time have loved me and cultivated my friendship. . . . When I was their guest it was more as if they were mine."[14]

Petrarch did more than any other individual in the fourteenth century to foster the development of Renaissance humanism. He was the first intellectual to characterize the Middle Ages as a period of darkness, promoting the mistaken belief that medieval culture was ignorant of classical antiquity. Petrarch's interest in the classics led him on a quest for forgotten Latin manuscripts and set in motion a ransacking of monastic libraries throughout Europe. In his preoccupation with the classics and their secular content, Petrarch worried at times that he might not be sufficiently attentive to spiritual ideals (see the box on p. 345). His qualms, however, did not prevent him from inaugurating the humanist emphasis on the use of pure classical Latin, making it fashionable for humanists to use Cicero as a model for prose and Virgil for poetry. As Petrarch said, "Christ is my God; Cicero is the prince of the language."

HUMANISM IN FIFTEENTH-CENTURY ITALY In Florence, the humanist movement took a new direction at the beginning of the fifteenth century when it became closely tied to Florentine civic spirit and pride, giving rise to what one modern scholar has labeled **civic humanism**. Fourteenth-century humanists such as Petrarch had described the intellectual life as one of solitude. They rejected family and a life of action in the community. In the busy civic world of Florence, however, intellectuals began to take a new view of their role as intellectuals. The classical Roman statesman and intellectual Cicero became their model. Leonardo Bruni (leh-ah-NAHR-doh BROO-nee) (1370–1444), a humanist, Florentine patriot, and chancellor of

The Renaissance Prince: The Views of Machiavelli and Erasmus

AT THE BEGINNING OF THE SIXTEENTH CENTURY, two writers produced very different views of political power and how a ruler should conduct affairs of state. In 1513, Niccolò Machiavelli wrote a short treatise on political power that, justly or unjustly, has given him a reputation as a political opportunist. In this selection from Chapter 17 of *The Prince*, Machiavelli analyzes whether it is better for a ruler to be loved than to be feared. Three years later the Dutch intellectual Erasmus, leader of the Christian humanists (see Chapter 13), also wrote a treatise on political power, entitled *Education of a Christian Prince*. As is evident in this excerpt from his treatise, Erasmus followed in the footsteps of medieval theorists on power by insisting that a true prince should think only of his moral obligations to the people he rules.

Machiavelli, *The Prince* (1513)

This leads us to a question that is in dispute: Is it better to be loved than feared, or vice versa? My reply is one ought to be both loved and feared; but, since it is difficult to accomplish both at the same time, I maintain it is much safer to be feared than loved, if you have to do without one of the two. For of men one can, in general, say this: They are ungrateful, fickle, deceptive and deceiving, avoiders of danger, eager to gain. As long as you serve their interests, they are devoted to you. They promise you their blood, their possessions, their lives, and their children, as I said before, so long as you seem to have no need of them. But as soon as you need help, they turn against you. Any ruler who relies simply on their promises and makes no other preparations, will be destroyed. For you will find that those whose support you buy, who do not rally to you because they admire your strength of character and nobility of soul, these are people you pay for, but they are never yours, and in the end you cannot get the benefit of your investment. Men are less nervous of offending someone who makes himself lovable, than someone who makes himself frightening. For love attaches men by ties of obligation, which, since men are wicked, they break whenever their interests are at stake. But fear restrains men because they are afraid of punishment, and this fear never leaves them. Still, a ruler should make himself feared in such a way that, if he does not inspire love, at least he does not provoke hatred. For it is perfectly possible to be feared and not hated. You will only be hated if you seize the property or the women of your subjects and citizens. Whenever you have to kill someone, make sure that you have a suitable excuse and an obvious reason; but, above all else, keep your hands off other people's property; for men are quicker to forget the death of their father than the loss of their inheritance. Moreover, there are always reasons why you might want to seize people's property; and he who begins to live by plundering others will always find an excuse for seizing other people's possessions; but there are fewer reasons for killing people, and one killing need not lead to another.

When a ruler is at the head of his army and has a vast number of soldiers under his command, then it is absolutely essential to be prepared to be thought cruel; for it is impossible to keep an army united and ready for action without acquiring a reputation for cruelty.

Erasmus, *Education of a Christian Prince* (1516)

Follow the right, do violence to no one, plunder no one, sell no public office, be corrupted by no bribes.... As you would rather stand for an injury than avenge it at great loss to the state, perchance you will lose a little something of your empire. Bear that; consider that you have gained a great deal because you have brought hurt to fewer than you would otherwise have done.... If you cannot defend... your realm without violating justice, without wanton loss of human life, without great loss to religion, give up and yield to the importunities of the age!...

A good prince... is a living likeness of God, who is at once good and powerful. His goodness makes him want to help all; his power makes him able to do so. On the other hand, an evil prince, who is like a plague to his country, is the incarnation of the devil, who has great power joined with his wickedness. All his resources to the very last, he uses for the undoing of the human race....

[A good prince is one] who holds the life of each individual dearer than his own; who works and strives night and day for just one end—to be the best he can for everyone; with whom rewards are ready for all good men... for so much does he want to be of real help to his people, without thought of recompense, that if necessary he would not hesitate to look out for their welfare at great risk to himself; who considers his wealth to lie in the advantage of his country; who is ever on the watch so that everyone else may sleep deeply; who grants no leisure to himself so that he may spend his life in the peace of his country; who worries himself with continual cares so that his subjects may have peace and quiet.... He does everything and allows everything that will bring everlasting peace to his country, for he realizes that war is the source of all misfortunes to the state.

Q *What does Machiavelli have to say about being loved rather than feared? How does this view contrast with that of Erasmus on the characteristics of a good ruler? Which viewpoint do you consider more modern? Why? Which viewpoint do you think is correct? Why?*

Sources: Machiavelli, *The Prince* (1513), trans. D. Wootton (Indianapolis: Hackett Publishing Company, 1995), pp. 51–52; Erasmus, *Education of a Christian Prince* (1516), trans. L. K. Born (New York: Columbia University Press, 1936).

PETRARCH: MOUNTAIN CLIMBING AND THE SEARCH FOR SPIRITUAL CONTENTMENT

PETRARCH HAS LONG BEEN REGARDED as the father of Italian Renaissance humanism. One of his literary masterpieces was *The Ascent of Mount Ventoux*, a colorful description of his attempt to climb a mountain in Provence in southern France and survey the world from its top. Petrarch's primary interest is in presenting an allegory of his own soul's struggle to achieve a higher spiritual state. The work is addressed to a professor of theology in Paris who had initially encouraged Petrarch to read Augustine. The latter had experienced a dramatic conversion to Christianity almost a thousand years earlier.

Petrarch, *The Ascent of Mount Ventoux*

Today I ascended the highest mountain in this region, which, not without cause, they call the Windy Peak. Nothing but the desire to see its conspicuous height was the reason for this undertaking. For many years I have been intending to make this expedition. You know that since my early childhood, as fate tossed around human affairs, I have been tossed around in these parts, and this mountain, visible far and wide from everywhere, is always in your view. So I was at last seized by the impulse to accomplish what I had always wanted to do....

[After some false starts, Petrarch finally achieves his goal and arrives at the top of Mount Ventoux.]

I was glad of the progress I had made, but I wept over my imperfection and was grieved by the fickleness of all that men do. In this manner I seemed to have somehow forgotten the place I had come to and why, until I was warned to throw off such sorrows, for which another place would be more appropriate. I had better look around and see what I had intended to see in coming here.... Like a man aroused from sleep, I turned back and looked toward the west.... One could see most distinctly the mountains of the province of Lyons to the right and, to the left, the sea near Marseilles as well as the waves that break against Aigues-Mortes.... The Rhône River was directly under our eyes.

I admired every detail, now relishing earthly enjoyment, now lifting up my mind to higher spheres after the example of my body, and I thought it fit to look in the volume of Augustine's *Confessions* which I owe to your loving kindness and preserve carefully, keeping it always in my hands.... I opened it with the intention of reading whatever might occur to me first... I happened to hit upon the tenth book of the work.... Where I fixed my eyes first, it was written: "And men go to admire the high mountains, the vast floods of the sea, the huge streams of the rivers, the circumference of the ocean, and the revolutions of the stars—and desert themselves." I was stunned, I confess. I bade my brother [who had accompanied him], who wanted to hear more, not to molest me, and closed the book, angry with myself that I still admired earthly things. Long since I ought to have learned, even from pagan philosophers, that "nothing is admirable besides the soul; compared to its greatness nothing is great."

I was completely satisfied with what I had seen of the mountain and turned my inner eye toward myself. From this hour nobody heard me say a word until we arrived at the bottom. These words occupied me sufficiently. I could not imagine that this had happened to me by chance: I was convinced that whatever I had read there was said to me and to nobody else. I remembered that Augustine once suspected the same regarding himself, when, while he was reading the Apostolic Epistles, the first passage that occurred to him was, as he himself relates: "Not in banqueting and drunkenness, not in chambering and wantonness, not in strife and envying; but put you on the Lord Jesus Christ, and make no provision for the flesh to fulfill your lusts."

Q *What about his own intellectual pursuits troubled Petrarch? How does the conflict within Petrarch reflect the historical debate about the nature of the Renaissance?*

Source: E. Cassirer, P. Kristeller, and J. Randall Jr., *The Renaissance Philosophy of Man* (Chicago: University of Chicago Press, 1948).

the city, wrote a biography of Cicero titled *The New Cicero*, in which he waxed enthusiastic about the fusion of political action and literary creation in Cicero's life. From Bruni's time on, Cicero served as the inspiration for the Renaissance ideal that intellectuals had a duty to live an active life for their state. An individual only "grows to maturity—both intellectually and morally—through participation" in the life of the state. Civic humanism reflected the values of the urban society of the Italian Renaissance. Humanists came to believe that their study of the humanities should be put to the service of the state. It is no accident that humanists served the state as chancellors, councillors, and advisers.

Also evident in the humanism of the first half of the fifteenth century was a growing interest in classical Greek civilization. Bruni was one of the first Italian humanists to gain a thorough knowledge of Greek. He became an enthusiastic pupil of the Byzantine scholar Manuel Chrysoloras (man-WEL kris-uh-LAHR-uss), who taught in Florence from 1396 to 1400. Humanists eagerly perused the works of Plato as well as those of Greek poets, dramatists, historians, and orators, such as Euripides, Sophocles, and Thucydides, all of whom had been ignored by the scholastics of the High Middle Ages as irrelevant to the theological questions they were examining.

By the fifteenth century, a consciousness of being humanists had emerged. This was especially evident in the career of Lorenzo Valla (1407–1457). Valla was brought up in Rome and educated in both Latin and Greek. Eventually, he achieved his chief ambition of becoming a papal secretary. Valla's major work, *The Elegances of the Latin Language*, was an effort to purify medieval Latin and restore Latin to its proper position over the vernacular. The treatise examined the proper use of classical Latin and created a new literary standard. Early humanists had tended to take as classical models any author (including Christians) who had written before the seventh century C.E. Valla identified different stages in the development of the Latin language and accepted only the Latin of the last century of the Roman Republic and the first century of the empire.

HUMANISM AND PHILOSOPHY In the second half of the fifteenth century, a dramatic upsurge of interest in the works of Plato occurred, especially evident among the members of an informal discussion group known as the Florentine Platonic Academy. Cosimo de' Medici, the de facto ruler of Florence, encouraged this development by commissioning a translation of Plato's dialogues by Marsilio Ficino (mar-SIL-yoh fee-CHEE-noh) (1433–1499), one of the academy's leaders. Ficino dedicated his life to the translation of Plato and the exposition of the Platonic philosophy known as **Neoplatonism**.

In two major works, Ficino undertook the synthesis of Christianity and Platonism into a single system. His Neoplatonism was based on two primary ideas, the Neoplatonic hierarchy of substances and a theory of spiritual love. The former postulated the idea of a hierarchy of substances, or great chain of being, from the lowest form of physical matter (plants) to the purest spirit (God), in which humans occupied a central or middle position. They were the link between the material world (through the body) and the spiritual world (through the soul), and their highest duty was to ascend toward that union with God that was the true end of human existence. Ficino's theory of spiritual or Platonic love maintained that just as all people are bound together in their common humanity by love, so too are all parts of the universe held together by bonds of sympathetic love.

RENAISSANCE HERMETICISM **Hermeticism** was another product of the Florentine intellectual environment of the late fifteenth century. At the request of Cosimo de' Medici, Ficino translated into Latin a Greek work titled *Corpus Hermeticum* (KOR-pus hur-MET-i-koom). The Hermetic manuscripts contained two kinds of writings. One type stressed the occult sciences, with an emphasis on astrology, alchemy, and magic; the other focused on theological and philosophical beliefs and speculations. Some Hermetic writings espoused **pantheism**, seeing divinity embodied in all aspects of nature and in the heavenly bodies as well as in earthly objects. As Giordano Bruno (jor-DAHN-oh BROO-noh), one of the most prominent sixteenth-century Hermeticists, stated, "God as a whole is in all things."[15]

For Renaissance intellectuals, the Hermetic revival offered a new view of humankind. They believed that human beings had been created as divine beings endowed with divine creative power but had freely chosen to enter the material world (nature). Humans could recover their divinity, however, through a regenerative experience or purification of the soul. Thus regenerated, they became true sages or magi, as the Renaissance called them, who had knowledge of God and of truth. In regaining their original divinity, they reacquired an intimate knowledge of nature and the ability to employ the powers of nature for beneficial purposes.

In Italy, the most prominent magi in the late fifteenth century were Ficino and his friend and pupil, Giovanni Pico della Mirandola (PEE-koh DELL-uh mee-RAN-doh-lah) (1463–1494). Pico produced one of the most famous pieces of writing of the Renaissance, the *Oration on the Dignity of Man*. Pico combed diligently through the works of many philosophers of different backgrounds for the common "nuggets of universal truth" that he believed were all part of God's revelation to humanity. In the *Oration* (see the box on p. 347), Pico offered a ringing statement of unlimited human potential: "To him it is granted to have whatever he chooses, to be whatever he wills."[16] Like Ficino, Pico took an avid interest in Hermetic philosophy, accepting it as the "science of the Divine," which "embraces the deepest contemplation of the most secret things, and at last the knowledge of all nature."[17]

The works of Ficino and Pico show that Italian Renaissance humanism was not just a secular movement but also had a strong spiritual component. In the treatises of Ficino and Pico, Renaissance humanism sought to illuminate the relationship between humans and God and to define humans not only as physical beings but divinely inspired beings as well.

Education in the Renaissance

The humanist movement had a profound effect on education. Renaissance humanists believed that human beings could be dramatically changed by education. They wrote books on education and developed secondary schools based on their ideas. Most famous was the school founded in 1423 by Vittorino da Feltre at Mantua, where the ruler of that small Italian state, Gian Francesco I Gonzaga, wished to provide a humanist education for his children. Vittorino based much of his educational system on the ideas of classical authors, particularly Cicero and Quintilian.

At the core of humanist schools were the "liberal studies." A treatise on education called *Concerning Character* by Pietro Paolo Vergerio (PYAY-troh PAH-oh-loh vur-JEER-ee-oh) (1370–1444) especially influenced the Renaissance view of the value of the liberal arts. This work stressed the importance of liberal studies as the key to true freedom, enabling individuals to reach their full potential. According to Vergerio, "We call those studies liberal which are worthy of a free man; those studies by which we attain and practice virtue and wisdom; that education which calls forth, trains, and develops those highest gifts of body and mind which ennoble men."[18] The liberal studies included history, moral philosophy, eloquence (rhetoric), letters (grammar and logic), poetry, mathematics, astronomy, and music. The purpose of a liberal education was thus to produce individuals who followed a path of virtue and wisdom and possessed the rhetorical skills with which to persuade others to do the same. Following the Greek precept of a sound mind in a sound body, Vittorino's school at Mantua

PICO DELLA MIRANDOLA AND THE DIGNITY OF MAN

GIOVANNI PICO DELLA MIRANDOLA was one of the foremost intellects of the Italian Renaissance. Pico boasted that he had studied all schools of philosophy, which he tried to demonstrate by drawing up nine hundred theses for public disputation at the age of twenty-four. As a preface to his theses, he wrote his famous *Oration on the Dignity of Man*, in which he proclaimed the unlimited potentiality of human beings.

Pico della Mirandola, *Oration on the Dignity of Man*

At last the best of artisans [God] ordained that that creature to whom He had been able to give nothing proper to himself should have joint possession of whatever had been peculiar to each of the different kinds of being. He therefore took man as a creature of indeterminate nature, and assigning him a place in the middle of the world, addressed him thus: "Neither a fixed abode nor a form that is yours alone nor any function peculiar to yourself have we given you, Adam, to the end that according to your longing and according to your judgment you may have and possess what abode, what form, and what functions you yourself desire. The nature of all other beings is limited and constrained within the bounds of laws prescribed by Us. You, constrained by no limits, in accordance with your own free will, in whose hand We have placed you, shall ordain for yourself the limits of your nature. We have set you at the world's center that you may from there more easily observe whatever is in the world. We have made you neither of heaven nor of earth, neither mortal nor immortal, so that with freedom of choice and with honor, as though the maker and molder of yourself, you may fashion yourself in whatever shape you shall prefer. You shall have the power to degenerate into the lower forms of life, which are brutish. You shall have the power, out of your soul's judgment, to be reborn into the higher forms, which are divine."

O supreme generosity of God the Father, O highest and most marvelous felicity of man! To him it is granted to have whatever he chooses, to be whatever he wills. Beasts as soon as they are born bring with them from their mother's womb all they will ever possess. Spiritual beings, either from the beginning or soon thereafter, become what they are to be for ever and ever. On man when he came into life the Father conferred the seeds of all kinds and the germs of every way of life. Whatever seeds each man cultivates will grow to maturity and bear in him their own fruit. If they be vegetative, he will be like a plant. If sensitive, he will become brutish. If rational, he will grow into a heavenly being. If intellectual, he will be an angel and the son of God.

Q *What did Pico mean by the "dignity of man"? Why would Pico be regarded as one of the Renaissance magi?*

Source: E. Cassirer, P. Kristeller, and J. Randall Jr., *The Renaissance Philosophy of Man* (Chicago: University of Chicago Press, 1948).

also stressed physical education. Pupils were taught the skills of javelin throwing, archery, and dancing and encouraged to run, wrestle, hunt, and swim.

Humanist education was thought to be a practical preparation for life. Its aim was not to create great scholars but rather to produce complete citizens who could participate in the civic life of their communities. As Vittorino said, "Not everyone is obliged to excel in philosophy, medicine, or the law, nor are all equally favored by nature; but all are destined to live in society and to practice virtue."[19] Humanist schools, combining the classics and Christianity, provided the model for the basic education of the European ruling classes until the twentieth century.

Although a small number of children from the lower classes received free educations, humanist schools such as Vittorino's were primarily geared for the education of an elite, the ruling classes of their communities. Also largely absent from such schools were females. Vittorino's only female pupils were the two daughters of the Gonzaga ruler of Mantua. Though these few female students studied the classics and were encouraged to know some history and to ride, dance, sing, play the lute, and appreciate poetry, they were discouraged from learning mathematics and rhetoric. In the educational treatises of the time, religion and morals were thought to "hold the first place in the education of a Christian lady."

HISTORIANS DEBATE **WAS THERE A RENAISSANCE FOR WOMEN?** Historians have disagreed over the benefits of the Renaissance for women. Some maintain that during the Middle Ages upper-class women in particular had greater freedom to satisfy their emotional needs and that upper-class women in the Renaissance experienced a contraction of both social and personal options as they became even more subject to male authority and patterns. Other historians have argued that although conditions remained bleak for most women, some women, especially those in courtly, religious, and intellectual environments, found ways to develop a new sense of themselves as women. This may be especially true of women who were educated in the humanist fashion and went on to establish their own literary careers.

Isotta Nogarola (ee-ZAHT-uh NOH-guh-roll-uh), born to a noble family in Verona, mastered Latin and wrote numerous letters and treatises that brought her praise from male Italian intellectuals. Cassandra Fedele (FAY-duh-lee) of Venice, who learned both Latin and Greek from humanist tutors hired by her family, became well known in Venice for her public recitations of orations. Laura Cereta (say-REE-tuh) was educated in Latin by her father, a physician from Brescia. Laura defended the ability of women to pursue scholarly pursuits (see the box on p. 348).

A WOMAN'S DEFENSE OF LEARNING

AS A YOUNG WOMAN, LAURA CERETA was proud of her learning but was condemned by a male world that found it unseemly for women to be scholars. One monk said to her father, "She gives herself to things unworthy of her—namely, the classics." Before being silenced, Laura Cereta wrote a series of letters, including one to a male critic who had argued that her work was so good it could not have been written by a woman.

Laura Cereta, *Defense of the Liberal Instruction of Women*

My ears are wearied by your carping. You brashly and publicly not merely wonder but indeed lament that I am said to possess as fine a mind as nature ever bestowed upon the most learned man. You seem to think that so learned a woman has scarcely before been seen in the world. You are wrong on both counts....

I would have been silent.... But I cannot tolerate your having attacked my entire sex. For this reason my thirsty soul seeks revenge, my sleeping pen is aroused to literary struggle, raging anger stirs mental passions long chained by silence. With just cause I am moved to demonstrate how great a reputation for learning and virtue women have won by their inborn excellence, manifested in every age as knowledge....

Only the question of the rarity of outstanding women remains to be addressed. The explanation is clear: women have been able by nature to be exceptional, but have chosen lesser goals. For some women are concerned with parting their hair correctly, adorning themselves with lovely dresses, or decorating their fingers with pearls and other gems. Others delight in mouthing carefully composed phrases, indulging in dancing, or managing spoiled puppies. Still others wish to gaze at lavish banquet tables, to rest in sleep, or, standing at mirrors, to smear their lovely faces. But those in whom a deeper integrity yearns for virtue, restrain from the start their youthful souls, reflect on higher things, harden the body with sobriety and trials, and curb their tongues, open their ears, compose their thoughts in wakeful hours, their minds in contemplation, to letters bonded to righteousness. For knowledge is not given as a gift, but [is gained] with diligence. The free mind, not shirking effort, always soars zealously toward the good, and the desire to know grows ever more wide and deep. It is because of no special holiness, therefore, that we [women] are rewarded by God the Giver with the gift of exceptional talent. Nature has generously lavished its gifts upon all people, opening to all the doors of choice through which reason sends envoys to the will, from which they learn and convey its desires. The will must choose to exercise the gift of reason....

I have been praised too much; showing your contempt for women, you pretend that I alone am admirable because of the good fortune of my intellect.... Do you suppose, O most contemptible man on earth, that I think myself sprung [like Athena] from the head of Jove? I am a school girl, possessed of the sleeping embers of an ordinary mind. Indeed I am too hurt, and my mind, offended, too swayed by passions, sighs, tormenting itself, conscious of the obligation to defend my sex. For absolutely everything—that which is within us and that which is without—is made weak by association with my sex.

Q *How did Cereta explain her intellectual interests and accomplishments? Why were Renaissance women rarely taken seriously when they sought educational opportunities and recognition for their intellectual talents? Were any of those factors unique to the Renaissance era?*

Source: Laura Cereta, "Defense of the Liberal Instruction of Women," in *Her Immaculate Hand: Selected Works by and about the Women Humanists of Quattrocentro Italy*, eds. M. King and A. Rabil (Asheville, N.C., Pegasus Press, 2000).

Humanism and History

Humanism had a strong impact on the writing of history. Influenced by Roman and Greek historians, the humanists approached the writing of history differently from the chroniclers of the Middle Ages. The humanists' belief that classical civilization had been followed by an age of barbarism (the Middle Ages), which had in turn been succeeded by their own age, with its rebirth of the study of the classics, enabled them to think in terms of the passage of time, of the past as past. Their division of the past into ancient world, dark ages, and their own age provided a new sense of chronology or periodization in history.

The humanists were also responsible for secularizing the writing of history. Humanist historians reduced or eliminated the role of miracles in historical interpretation, not because they were anti-Christian but because they took a new approach to sources. They wanted to use documents and exercised their newly developed critical skills in examining them. Greater attention was paid to the political events and forces that affected their city-states or larger territorial units. Thus, Leonardo Bruni wrote the *History of the Florentine People*. The new emphasis on secularization was also evident in the humanists' conception of causation in history. Medieval historical literature often portrayed historical events as being caused by God's active involvement in human affairs. Humanists de-emphasized divine intervention in favor of human motives, stressing political forces or the role of individuals in history.

GUICCIARDINI The high point of Renaissance historiography was achieved at the beginning of the sixteenth century in the works of Francesco Guicciardini (frahn-CHESS-koh gwee-char-DEE-nee) (1483–1540). To many historians, his *History of Italy* and *History of Florence* represent the beginning of "modern analytical historiography." To Guicciardini, the purpose of writing history was to teach lessons, but he was so impressed by the complexity of historical events that he felt those lessons were not always obvious. From his extensive background in government and diplomatic affairs, he developed the skills that enabled him to analyze political situations precisely and critically. Emphasizing political and military history, his works relied heavily on personal examples and documentary sources.

The Impact of Printing

The Renaissance witnessed the invention of printing, one of the most important technological innovations of Western civilization. The art of printing made an immediate impact on European intellectual life and thought. Printing from hand-carved wooden blocks had been done in the West since the twelfth century and in China even before that. What was new to Europe in the fifteenth century was multiple printing with movable metal type. The development of printing from movable type was a gradual process that culminated between 1445 and 1450; Johannes Gutenberg (yoh-HAH-nuss GOO-ten-bayrk) of Mainz played an important role in bringing the process to completion. Gutenberg's Bible, completed in 1455 or 1456, was the first true book in the West produced from movable type.

The new printing spread rapidly throughout Europe in the second half of the fifteenth century. Printing presses were established throughout the Holy Roman Empire in the 1460s and within ten years had spread to both western and eastern Europe. Especially well known as a printing center was Venice, home by 1500 to almost one hundred printers who had produced almost 2 million volumes.

By 1500, there were more than a thousand printers in Europe who had published almost 40,000 titles (between 8 million and 10 million copies). Probably 50 percent of these books were religious—Bibles and biblical commentaries, books of devotion, and sermons. Next in importance were the Latin and Greek classics, medieval grammars, legal handbooks, works on philosophy, and an ever-growing number of popular romances.

Printing became one of the largest industries in Europe, and its effects were soon felt in many areas of European life. The printing of books encouraged the development of scholarly research and the desire to attain knowledge. Moreover, printing facilitated cooperation among scholars and helped produce standardized and definitive texts. Printing also stimulated the development of an ever-expanding lay reading public, a development that had an enormous impact on European society. Indeed, without the printing press, the new religious ideas of the Reformation would never have spread as rapidly as they did in the sixteenth century.

The Artistic Renaissance

Q **FOCUS QUESTION:** What were the chief characteristics of Renaissance art, and how did it differ in Italy and northern Europe?

Leonardo da Vinci (dah VEEN-chee), one of the great Italian Renaissance artists, once explained: "Hence the painter will produce pictures of small merit if he takes for his standard the pictures of others, but if he will study from natural objects he will bear good fruit.... Those who take for their standard any one but nature... weary themselves in vain.[20] Renaissance artists considered the imitation of nature their primary goal. Their search for naturalism became an end in itself: to persuade onlookers of the reality of the object or event they were portraying. At the same time, the new artistic standards reflected a new attitude of mind as well, one in which human beings became the focus of attention, the "center and measure of all things," as one artist proclaimed.

Art in the Early Renaissance

Leonardo and other Italians maintained that it was Giotto in the fourteenth century (see Chapter 11) who began the imitation of nature. But what Giotto had begun was not taken up again until the work of Masaccio (muh-ZAH-choh) (1401–1428) in Florence. Masaccio's cycle of frescoes in the Brancacci Chapel has long been regarded as the first masterpiece of Early Renaissance art. With his use of monumental figures, a more realistic relationship between figures and landscape, and visual representation of the laws of perspective, a new realistic style of painting was born. Onlookers become aware of a world of reality that appears to be a continuation of their own world. Masaccio's massive, three-dimensional human figures provided a model for later generations of Florentine artists.

During the fifteenth century, other Florentine painters absorbed and modified this new Renaissance style. Especially important was the development of an experimental trend that took two directions. One emphasized the mathematical side of painting, the working out of the laws of perspective and the organization of outdoor space and light by geometry and perspective. In the work of Paolo Uccello (PAH-oh-loh oo-CHELL-oh) (1397–1475), figures became mere stage props to show off his mastery of the laws of perspective. The other aspect of the experimental trend involved the investigation of movement and anatomical structure. *The Martyrdom of Saint Sebastian* by Antonio Pollaiuolo (pohl-ly-WOH-loh) (ca. 1432–1498) revels in classical motifs and attempts to portray the human body under stress. Indeed, the realistic portrayal of the human nude became one of the foremost preoccupations of Italian Renaissance art. The fifteenth century, then, was a period of experimentation and technical mastery.

During the last decades of the fifteenth century, a new sense of invention emerged in Florence, especially in the circle of artists and scholars who formed part of the court of the city's leading citizen, Lorenzo the Magnificent. One of this group's prominent members was Sandro Botticelli (SAHN-droh bot-i-CHELL-ee) (1445–1510), whose interest in Greek and Roman mythology was well reflected in one of his most famous works, *Primavera* (Spring). The painting is set in the garden of Venus, a garden of eternal spring. Though Botticelli's figures are well defined, they also possess an otherworldly quality that is far removed from the realism that characterized the painting of the Early Renaissance.

Scala/Art Resource, NY

Masaccio, *Tribute Money*. With the frescoes of Masaccio, regarded by many as the first great works of Early Renaissance art, a new realistic style of painting was born. *Tribute Money* was one of a series of frescoes that Masaccio painted in the Brancacci Chapel of the Church of Santa Maria del Carmine in Florence. In *Tribute Money*, Masaccio depicted the biblical story of Jesus's confrontation by a tax collector at the entrance to the town of Capernaum (seen at the center). Jesus sent Peter to collect a coin from the mouth of a fish from Lake Galilee (seen at the left); Peter then paid the tax collector (seen at the right). In illustrating this story from the Bible, Masaccio used a rational system of perspective to create a realistic relationship between the figures and their background; the figures themselves are realistic. As one Renaissance observer said, "The works made before Masaccio's day can be said to be painted, while his are living, real, and natural."

The revolutionary achievements of Florentine painters in the fifteenth century were matched by equally stunning advances in sculpture and architecture. Donato di Donatello (doh-NAH-toh dee doh-nuh-TELL-oh) (1386–1466) spent time in Rome studying and copying the statues of antiquity. His subsequent work in Florence reveals how well he had mastered the essence of what he saw. Among his numerous works was a statue of David, which is the first known life-size, freestanding bronze nude in European art since antiquity. With the severed head of the giant Goliath beneath David's feet, Donatello's statue may have celebrated Florentine heroism in the triumph of Florence over the Milanese in 1428. Like Donatello's other statues, *David* also radiated a simplicity and strength that reflected the dignity of humanity.

Scala/Art Resource, NY

Botticelli, *Primavera*. This work reflects Botticelli's strong interest in classical antiquity. At the center of the painting is Venus, the goddess of love. At the right stands Flora, a Roman goddess of flowers and fertility, while the Three Graces dance playfully at the left. Cupid, the son of Venus, aims his arrow at the Three Graces. At the far left of the picture is Mercury, the messenger of the gods. Later in life, Botticelli experienced a profound religious crisis, leading him to reject his earlier preoccupation with pagan gods and goddesses. He burned many of his early paintings and thereafter produced only religious works.

Filippo Brunelleschi (fee-LEE-poh BROO-nuh-LESS-kee) (1377–1446), a friend of Donatello's, accompanied the latter to Rome. Brunelleschi drew much inspiration from the architectural monuments of Roman antiquity, and when he returned to Florence, he poured his new insights into the creation of a new architecture. His first project involved the challenge of building a dome for the unfinished cathedral of Florence (the Duomo). The cathedral had been started in 1296, but it was Brunelleschi who devised new building techniques and machinery to create a dome, built between 1420 and 1436, that spanned a 140-foot opening.

Donatello, *David*. Donatello's *David* first stood in the courtyard of the Medici Palace. On its base was an inscription praising Florentine heroism and virtue, leading art historians to believe that the statue was meant to commemorate the victory of Florence over Milan in 1428. David's pose and appearance are reminiscent of the nude statues of antiquity.

Scala/Art Resource, NY

Scala/Art Resource, NY

Filippo Brunelleschi, Dome of the Duomo. Brunelleschi was first commissioned to design the dome for the unfinished cathedral of Florence in 1417, but work did not begin until 1420. Although Brunelleschi would have preferred the Roman hemispheric dome, for practical reasons he was forced to elevate the center of the dome and then lessen the weight of the structure by building a thin double shell around a structure of twenty-four ribs. The most important ribs were placed on the outside of the dome (four of them are visible in this photograph).

An even better example of Brunelleschi's new Renaissance architectural style is evident in the Church of San Lorenzo. When the Medici commissioned him to design the church, Brunelleschi, inspired by Roman models, created a church interior very different from that of the great medieval cathedrals. San Lorenzo's classical columns, rounded arches, and coffered ceiling created an environment that did not overwhelm the worshiper materially and psychologically, as Gothic cathedrals did, but comforted as a space created to fit human, not divine, measurements. Like painters and sculptors, Renaissance architects sought to reflect a human-centered world.

The new assertion of human individuality, evident in Early Renaissance art, was also reflected in the new emphasis on portraiture. Patrons appeared in the corners of sacred pictures, and monumental tombs and portrait statues honored many of Florence's prominent citizens. By the mid-fifteenth century, artists were giving an accurate rendering of their subjects' facial features while revealing the inner qualities of their

Scala/Art Resource, NY

Brunelleschi, Interior of San Lorenzo. Cosimo de' Medici contributed massive amounts of money to the rebuilding of the Church of San Lorenzo. As seen in this view of the nave and choir of the church, Brunelleschi's architectural designs were based on the basilica plan borrowed by early Christians from pagan Rome. San Lorenzo's simplicity, evident in its rows of slender Corinthian columns, created a human-centered space.

Scala/Ministero per i Beni e le Attività culturali/Art Resource, NY

Leonardo da Vinci, *The Last Supper*. Leonardo da Vinci was the impetus behind the High Renaissance concern for the idealization of nature, moving from a realistic portrayal of the human figure to an idealized form. Evident in Leonardo's *Last Supper* is his effort to depict a person's character and inner nature by the use of gesture and movement. Unfortunately, Leonardo used an experimental technique in this fresco, which soon led to its physical deterioration.

personalities. The portraits of the duke and duchess of Urbino by Piero della Francesca (ca. 1410–1492) provide accurate representations as well as a sense of both the power and the wealth of the rulers of Urbino (see p. 340).

The Artistic High Renaissance

By the end of the fifteenth century, Italian painters, sculptors, and architects had created a new artistic environment. Many artists had mastered the new techniques for a scientific observation of the world around them and were now ready to move into individualistic forms of creative expression. This final stage of Renaissance art, which flourished between 1480 and 1520, is called the High Renaissance. The shift to the High Renaissance was marked by the increasing importance of Rome as a new cultural center of the Italian Renaissance.

The High Renaissance was dominated by the work of three artistic giants: Leonardo da Vinci (1452–1519), Raphael (1483–1520), and Michelangelo (1475–1564). Leonardo represents a transitional figure in the shift to High Renaissance principles. He carried on the fifteenth-century experimental tradition by studying everything and even dissecting human bodies to see more clearly how nature worked. But Leonardo stressed the need to advance beyond such realism and initiated the High Renaissance's preoccupation with the idealization of nature, or the attempt to generalize from realistic portrayal to an ideal form. Leonardo's *Last Supper*, painted in Milan, is a brilliant summary of fifteenth-century trends in its organization of space and use of perspective to depict subjects three-dimensionally in a two-dimensional medium. But it is also more. The figure of Philip is idealized, and the work embodies profound psychological dimensions. The words of Jesus that "one of you shall betray me" are experienced directly as each of the apostles reveals his personality and his relationship to Jesus. Through gestures and movement, Leonardo hoped to reveal a person's inner life.

Raphael (RAFF-ee-ul) blossomed as a painter at an early age; at twenty-five, he was already regarded as one of Italy's best painters. Raphael was acclaimed for his numerous madonnas, in which he attempted to achieve an ideal of beauty far surpassing human standards. He is well known for his frescoes in the Vatican Palace; his *School of Athens* reveals a world of balance, harmony, and order—the underlying principles of the art of the classical world of Greece and Rome.

Michelangelo (my-kuh-LAN-juh-loh), an accomplished painter, sculptor, and architect, was another giant of the High Renaissance. Fiercely driven by his desire to create, he worked with great passion and energy on a remarkable number of projects. Michelangelo was influenced by Neoplatonism, especially evident in his figures on the ceiling of the Sistine Chapel in Rome. In 1508, Pope Julius II had called Michelangelo to Rome and commissioned him to decorate the chapel ceiling. This colossal project was not completed until 1512. Michelangelo attempted to tell the story of the Fall of Man by depicting nine scenes from the biblical book of Genesis. In his *Creation of Adam* (reproduced at the beginning of this chapter), the well-proportioned figure of Adam awaits the divine spark. Adam, like the other muscular figures on the ceiling, reveals an ideal type of human being with perfect proportions. In good Neoplatonic fashion, the beauty of these figures is meant to be a reflection of divine beauty; the more beautiful the body, the more God-like the figure.

Raphael, *School of Athens*. Raphael arrived in Rome in 1508 and began to paint a series of frescoes commissioned by Pope Julius II for the papal apartments at the Vatican. In *School of Athens*, painted in 1510 or 1511, Raphael created an imaginary gathering of ancient philosophers. In the center stand Plato and Aristotle. At the left is Pythagoras, showing his system of proportions on a slate. At the right is Ptolemy, holding a celestial globe.

Another manifestation of Michelangelo's search for ideal beauty was his *David*, a colossal marble statue commissioned by the Florentine government in 1501 and completed in 1504. Michelangelo maintained that the form of a statue already resided in the uncarved piece of stone: "I only take away the surplus, the statue is already there."[21] Out of a piece of marble that had remained unused for fifty years, Michelangelo created a 14-foot-high figure, the largest sculpture in Italy since the time of Rome. An awe-inspiring hero, Michelangelo's *David* proudly proclaims the beauty of the human body and the glory of human beings.

The High Renaissance was also evident in architecture, especially in the work of Donato Bramante (doh-NAH-toh brah-MAHN-tay) (1444–1514). He came from Urbino but took up residence in Rome, where he designed a small temple on the supposed site of Saint Peter's martyrdom. The Tempietto, or little temple, with its Doric columns surrounding a sanctuary enclosed by a dome, summarized the architectural ideals of the High Renaissance. Columns, dome, and sanctuary form a monumental and harmonious whole. Inspired by antiquity, Bramante had recaptured the grandeur of ancient Rome.

The Artist and Social Status

Early Renaissance artists began their careers as apprentices to masters in craft guilds. Apprentices with unusual talent might eventually become masters and run their own workshops. As in the Middle Ages, artists were still largely viewed as artisans. Since guilds depended on commissions for their projects, patrons played an important role in the art of the Early Renaissance. The wealthy upper classes determined both the content and the purpose of the paintings and pieces of sculpture they commissioned.

By the end of the fifteenth century, a transformation in the position of the artist had occurred. Especially talented individuals, such as Leonardo, Raphael, and Michelangelo, were no longer regarded as artisans but as artistic geniuses with creative energies akin to the divine (see the box on p. 355). Artists were heroes, individuals who were praised more for their creativity than for their competence as craftspeople. Michelangelo, for example, was frequently addressed as "Il Divino"—the Divine One. As society excused their eccentricities and valued their creative genius, the artists of the High Renaissance became the first to embody the modern concept of the artist.

Scala/Art Resource, NY

Michelangelo, *David*. This statue of David, cut from an 18-foot-high piece of marble, exalts the beauty of the human body and is a fitting symbol of the Italian Renaissance's affirmation of human power. Completed in 1504, *David* was moved by Florentine authorities to a special location in front of the Palazzo Vecchio, the seat of the Florentine government.

As respect for artists grew, so did their ability to profit economically from their work and to rise on the social scale. Now welcomed as equals into the circles of the upper classes, they mingled with the political and intellectual elite of their society and became more aware of new intellectual theories, which they then embodied in their art. The Platonic Academy and Renaissance Neoplatonism had an especially important impact on Florentine painters.

The Northern Artistic Renaissance

In trying to provide an exact portrayal of their world, the artists of the north (especially the Low Countries) and Italy took different approaches. In Italy, the human form became the primary vehicle of expression as Italian artists sought to master the technical skills that allowed them to portray humans in realistic settings. The large wall spaces of Italian churches had given rise to the art of fresco painting, but in the north, the prevalence of Gothic cathedrals with their stained-glass windows resulted in more emphasis on illuminated manuscripts and wooden panel painting for altarpieces. The space available in these works was limited, and great care was required to depict each object, leading northern painters to become masters at rendering details.

The most influential northern school of art in the fifteenth century was centered in Flanders. Jan van Eyck (YAHN vahn YK *or* van AYK) (ca. 1390–1441) was among the first to use oil paint, a medium that enabled the artist to use a varied range of colors and create fine details. In the famous *Giovanni Arnolfini and His Bride*, van Eyck's attention to detail is staggering: precise portraits, a glittering chandelier, and a mirror reflecting the objects in the room. Although each detail was rendered as observed, it is evident that van Eyck's comprehension of perspective was still uncertain. His work is truly indicative of northern Renaissance painters, who, in their effort to imitate nature, did so not by mastery of the laws of perspective and proportion but by empirical observation of visual reality and the accurate portrayal of details. Moreover, northern painters placed great emphasis on the emotional intensity of religious feeling and created great works of devotional art, especially in their altarpieces. Michelangelo

National Gallery, London/Art Resource, NY

Van Eyck, *Giovanni Arnolfini and His Bride*. Northern painters took great care in depicting each object and became masters at rendering details. This emphasis on a realistic portrayal is clearly evident in this oil painting, supposedly a portrait of Giovanni Arnolfini, an Italian merchant who had settled in Bruges, and his wife, Giovanna Cenami.

THE GENIUS OF MICHELANGELO

DURING THE RENAISSANCE, ARTISTS CAME to be viewed as creative geniuses with almost divine qualities. One individual who helped create this image was himself a painter. Giorgio Vasari (JOR-joh vuh-ZAHR-ee) was an avid admirer of Italy's great artists and wrote a series of brief biographies of them. This excerpt is taken from his account of Michelangelo.

Giorgio Vasari, *Lives of the Artists*

Michelangelo was much inclined to the labors of art, seeing that everything, however difficult, succeeded with him, he having had from nature a genius very apt and ardent in the noble arts of design. Moreover, in order to be entirely perfect, innumerable times he made anatomical studies, dissecting men's bodies in order to see the principles of their construction and the arrangement of the bones, muscles, veins and nerves; the various movements and all the postures of the human body; and not of men only, but also of animals, and particularly of horses... Of all these he desired to learn the principles and laws in so far as touched his art, and this knowledge he so demonstrated in the works that fell to him to handle that those who attend to no other study than this do now know more. He so executed his works, whether with the brush or with the chisel, that they are almost inimitable, and he gave to his labors such grace and loveliness that he surpassed and vanquished the ancients. He was able to wrest things out of the greatest difficulties with such facility that they do not appear wrought with effort, although whoever draws his works after him finds it very hard to imitate them.

The genius of Michelangelo was recognized in his lifetime, and not, as happens to many, after death, for several of the popes always wished to have him near them, and also Suleiman, emperor of the Turks, Francis of Valois, king of France, the emperor Charles V, the signory of Venice, and finally Duke Cosimo de' Medici. All offered him honorable salaries, for no other reason but to avail themselves of his great genius. This does not happen except to men of great worth, such as he was. It is well known that all the three arts of painting, sculpture, and architecture were so perfect in him, that it is not found that among persons ancient or modern, in all the many years that the sun had been whirling round, God has granted this to any other but Michelangelo. He had imagination of such a kind, and so perfect, and the things conceived by him in idea were such, that often, through not being able to express with the hands conceptions so terrible and grand, he abandoned his works—nay, destroyed many of them.

Q *How do you think Vasari's comments on Michelangelo fostered the image of the Renaissance artist as a "creative genius with almost divine qualities"?*

Source: H. Webster, *Readings in Medieval and Modern History* (Boston: D.C. Heath & Co., 1917), pp. 191–192.

summarized the difference between northern and Italian Renaissance painting in these words:

> In Flanders, they paint, before all things, to render exactly and deceptively the outward appearance of things. The painters choose, by preference, subjects provoking transports of piety, like the figures of saints or of prophets. But most of the time they paint what are called landscapes with plenty of figures. Though the eye is agreeably impressed, these pictures have neither choice of values nor grandeur. In short, this art is without power and without distinction; it aims at rendering minutely many things at the same time, of which a single one would have sufficed to call forth a man's whole application.[22]

By the end of the fifteenth century, however, artists from the north began to study in Italy and were visually influenced by what artists were doing there.

One northern artist of this later period who was greatly affected by the Italians was Albrecht Dürer (AHL-brekht DOO-rur) (1471–1528) from Nuremberg. Dürer made two trips to Italy and absorbed most of what the Italians could teach, as is evident in his mastery of the laws of perspective and Renaissance theories of proportion. He wrote detailed treatises on both subjects. At the same time, as in his famous *Adoration of the Magi*, Dürer did not reject the use of minute details characteristic of northern artists. He did try, however, to integrate those details more harmoniously into his works and, like the Italian artists of the High Renaissance, to achieve a standard of ideal beauty by a careful examination of the human form. Dürer was also the first northern Renaissance artist to provide an account of his life through his letters, a diary, and his self-portraits.

Music in the Renaissance

For much of the fifteenth century, an extraordinary cultural environment was fostered in the domains of the dukes of Burgundy in northern Europe. The court of the dukes attracted some of the best artists and musicians of the time. Among them was Guillaume Dufay (gee-YOHM doo-FAY) (ca. 1400–1474), perhaps the most important composer of his era. Born in northern France, Dufay lived for a few years in Italy and was thus well suited to combine the late medieval style of France with the early Renaissance style of Italy. One of Dufay's greatest contributions was a change in the composition of the Mass. He was the first to use secular tunes to replace Gregorian chants as the fixed melody that served as the basis for the Mass. Dufay also composed a number of secular songs, an important reminder that during the Renaissance, music ceased to be used chiefly in the service of God and moved into the secular world of courts and cities. In Italy and France, the chief form of secular music was the madrigal.

Alte Pinakothek, Munich, Germany/Bridgeman Images

Dürer, *Self-Portrait.* By the end of the fifteenth century, northern artists had begun to study in Italy and to adopt many of the techniques used by Italian painters. Albrecht Dürer masterfully incorporated the laws of perspective and the ideals of proportion into his works. At the same time, he did not abandon the preoccupation with detail typical of northern artists, as seen in this self-portrait done in 1500. Reflecting the Italian Renaissance view of the artist as a genius inspired by God, Dürer presents himself here as a Christlike figure.

The Renaissance madrigal was a poem set to music, and it originated in the fourteenth-century Italian courts. The texts were usually twelve-line poems written in the vernacular, and their theme was emotional or erotic love. By the mid-sixteenth century, most madrigals were written for five or six voices and employed a technique called text painting, in which the music tried to portray the literal meaning of the text. Thus, the melody would rise for the word *heaven* or use a wavelike motion to represent the word *water*. By the mid-sixteenth century, the madrigal had also spread to England, where the most popular form was characterized by the *fa-la-la* refrain like that found in the English carol "Deck the Halls."

The European State in the Renaissance

FOCUS QUESTION: Why do historians sometimes refer to the monarchies of the late fifteenth century as "new monarchies" or "Renaissance states"?

In the first half of the fifteenth century, European states continued the disintegrative patterns of the previous century. In the second half of the century, however, recovery set in, and attempts were made to reestablish the centralized power of monarchical governments. To characterize the results, some historians have used the label "Renaissance states"; others have spoken of the "**new monarchies**," especially those of France, England, and Spain at the end of the fifteenth century (see Map 12.2). Although monarchs in western Europe succeeded to varying degrees at extending their political authority, rulers in central and eastern Europe were often weak and unable to impose their authority.

The Growth of the French Monarchy

The Hundred Years' War had left France prostrate. Depopulation, desolate farmlands, ruined commerce, and independent and unruly nobles had made it difficult for the kings to assert their authority. But the war had also developed a strong degree of French national feeling toward a common enemy that the kings could use to reestablish monarchical power. The need to prosecute the war provided an excuse to strengthen the authority of the king, already evident in the policies of Charles VII (1422–1461) after he was crowned king at Reims. With the consent of the Estates-General, Charles established a royal army composed of cavalry and archers. The Estates-General also granted him the right to levy the *taille*, an annual direct tax usually on land or property, without any need for further approval from the Estates-General. Losing control of the purse meant less power for this parliamentary body.

The process of developing a French territorial state was greatly advanced by King Louis XI (1461–1483), known as the Spider because of his wily and devious ways. By retaining the taille as a permanent tax imposed by royal authority, Louis secured a sound, regular source of income. Louis was not, however, completely successful in repressing the French nobility, whose independence posed a threat to his own state building. A major problem was his supposed vassal, Charles the Bold, duke of Burgundy (1467–1477). Charles attempted to create a middle kingdom between France and Germany, stretching from the Low Countries to Switzerland. Louis opposed his efforts, and when Charles was killed in 1477 fighting the Swiss, Louis added part of Charles's possessions, the duchy of Burgundy, to his own lands. Three years later, the provinces of Anjou, Maine, Bar, and Provence were brought under royal control. Many historians believe that Louis created a base for the later development of a strong French monarchy.

England: Civil War and a New Monarchy

The Hundred Years' War had also strongly affected the other protagonist in that conflict. The cost of the war in its final years and the losses in manpower strained the English economy. Moreover, even greater domestic turmoil came to England when a period of civil wars broke out in the 1450s. These wars pitted the ducal house of Lancaster against the ducal house of York. (The wars are popularly known as the "Wars of the Roses" because Shakespeare a hundred years later created the fiction that a white rose symbolized the Yorkists and a red rose, the Lancasters.) Many aristocratic families of England were drawn

MAP 12.2 **Europe in the Second Half of the Fifteenth Century.** By the second half of the fifteenth century, states in western Europe, particularly France, Spain, and England, had begun the process of modern state building. With varying success, they reined in the power of the church and nobles, increased the ability to levy taxes, and established effective government bureaucracies.

Q *What aspects of Europe's political boundaries help explain why France and the Holy Roman Empire were often at war with each other?*

into the conflict. Finally, in 1485, Henry Tudor, duke of Richmond, defeated the last Yorkist king, Richard III (1483–1485), at Bosworth Field and established the new Tudor dynasty.

As the first Tudor king, Henry VII (1485–1509) worked to reduce internal dissension and establish a strong monarchical government. Henry ended the private wars of the nobility by abolishing "livery and maintenance," the practice by which wealthy aristocrats maintained private armies of followers dedicated to the service of their lord. Since England, unlike France and Spain, did not possess a standing army, the king relied on special commissions to trusted nobles to raise troops for a specific campaign, after which the troops were disbanded. Henry also controlled the irresponsible activity of the nobles by establishing the Court of Star Chamber, which did not use juries and allowed torture to be used to extract confessions.

Henry VII was particularly successful in extracting income from the traditional financial resources of the English monarch, such as the crown lands, judicial fees and fines, and customs duties. By using diplomacy to avoid wars, which are always expensive, the king avoided having to call Parliament on any regular basis to grant him funds. By not overburdening the landed gentry and middle class with taxes, Henry won their favor, and they provided much support for his monarchy. Henry's policies enabled him to leave England with a stable and prosperous government and an enhanced status for the monarchy itself.

The Unification of Spain

During the Middle Ages, several independent Christian kingdoms had emerged in the course of the long reconquest of the Iberian peninsula from the Muslims. Aragon and Castile were the strongest Spanish kingdoms; in the west was the independent monarchy of Portugal; in the north, the small kingdom of Navarre, oriented toward France; and in the south, the Muslim kingdom of Granada (see Map 12.3). Few people at the beginning of the fifteenth century could have predicted the unification of the Iberian kingdoms.

MAP 12.3 The Iberian Peninsula. The marriage of Isabella of Castile to Ferdinand of Aragon laid the foundation for the unification of Spain and its rise as a major European power. The two monarchs instituted military and bureaucratic reforms and forced Jews and Muslims to flee the country.

Q *What aspects of Portugal's geography help explain why it became a major seafaring nation, with little overland trade with Europe?*

A major step in that direction was taken with the marriage of Isabella of Castile (1474–1504) and Ferdinand of Aragon (1479–1516) in 1469. This was a dynastic union of two rulers, not a political union. Both kingdoms maintained their own parliaments (Cortes), courts, laws, coinage, speech, customs, and political organs. Nevertheless, the two rulers worked to strengthen royal control of government, especially in Castile. The royal council, which was supposed to supervise local administration and oversee the implementation of government policies, was stripped of aristocrats and filled primarily with middle-class lawyers. Trained in the principles of Roman law, these officials operated on the belief that the monarchy embodied the power of the state.

Seeking to replace the undisciplined feudal levies they had inherited with a more professional royal army, Ferdinand and Isabella reorganized the military forces of Spain. The development of a strong infantry force as the heart of the new Spanish army made it the best in Europe by the sixteenth century.

Because of its vast power and wealth, Ferdinand and Isabella recognized the importance of controlling the Catholic Church. They secured from the pope the right to select the most important church officials in Spain, virtually guaranteeing the creation of a Spanish Catholic Church in which the clergy became an instrument for the extension of royal power. The monarchs also used their authority over the church to institute reform. Isabella's chief minister, the able and astute Cardinal Ximenes (khee-MAY-ness), restored discipline and eliminated immorality among the monks and secular clergy.

The religious zeal exhibited in Cardinal Ximenes's reform program was also evident in the policy of strict religious uniformity pursued by Ferdinand and Isabella. Of course, it served a political purpose as well: to create unity and further bolster royal power. Spain possessed two large religious minorities, the Jews and Muslims, both of which had generally been tolerated in medieval Spain. Although anti-Semitism had become a fact of life in medieval Europe, Spain had largely remained tolerant. In some areas of Spain, Jews exercised much influence in economic and intellectual affairs. During the fourteenth century, however, increased persecution led the majority of Spanish Jews to convert to Christianity. Although many of these converted Jews came to play important roles in Spanish society, complaints that they were secretly reverting to Judaism prompted Ferdinand and Isabella to ask the pope to introduce the Inquisition into Spain in 1478. Under royal control, the Inquisition worked with cruel efficiency to guarantee the orthodoxy of the converts but had no authority over practicing Jews. Consequently, in 1492, flush with the success of their conquest of Muslim Granada, Ferdinand and Isabella took the drastic step of expelling all professed Jews from Spain. It is estimated that 150,000 out of possibly 200,000 Jews fled.

Ferdinand and Isabella also pursued a policy of battling the Muslims by attacking the kingdom of Granada. The war against this remaining Muslim kingdom lasted eleven years until the final bastion of the city of Granada fell in 1492. Muslims were now "encouraged" to convert to Christianity, and in 1502 Isabella issued a decree expelling all professed Muslims from her kingdom. To a very large degree, the "Most Catholic" monarchs had achieved their goal of absolute religious orthodoxy as a basic ingredient of the Spanish state. To be Spanish was to be Catholic, a policy of uniformity enforced by the Inquisition. It was no accident that Spain became a staunch pillar of the Catholic Church during the era of the Reformation in the sixteenth century (see Chapter 13).

The Holy Roman Empire: The Success of the Habsburgs

Unlike France, England, and Spain, the Holy Roman Empire failed to develop a strong monarchical authority. After 1438, the position of Holy Roman Emperor remained in the hands of the Habsburg dynasty. Having gradually acquired a number of possessions along the Danube, known collectively as Austria, the house of Habsburg had become one of the wealthiest landholders in the empire and by the mid-fifteenth century began to play an important role in European affairs.

Much of the Habsburg success in the fifteenth century was due not to military success but to a well-executed policy of dynastic marriages. As the old Habsburg motto said, "Leave the waging of wars to others! But you, happy Austria, marry; for the realms which Mars [god of war] awards to others, Venus [goddess of love] transfers to you." By marrying his son Maximilian to Mary, the daughter of Duke Charles the Bold of Burgundy, Emperor Frederick III (1440–1493) gained Franche-Comté in east-central France, Luxembourg, and a large part of the Low Countries. The addition of these territories made the Habsburg dynasty an international power and brought it the undying opposition of the French monarchy because the rulers of France feared they would be surrounded by the Habsburgs.

Much was expected of the flamboyant Maximilian I (1493–1519) when he became emperor. Through the Reichstag, the imperial diet or parliament, Maximilian attempted to centralize the administration by creating new institutions common to the entire empire. Opposition from the German princes doomed these efforts, however. Maximilian's only real success lay in his marriage alliances. Philip of Burgundy, the son of Maximilian's marriage to Mary, was married to Joanna, the daughter of Ferdinand and Isabella. Philip and Joanna produced a son, Charles, who, through a series of unexpected deaths, became heir to all three lines, the Habsburg, Burgundian, and Spanish, making him the leading monarch of his age (see Chapter 13).

The Struggle for Strong Monarchy in Eastern Europe

In eastern Europe, rulers struggled to achieve the centralization of their territorial states but faced serious obstacles. Although the population was mostly Slavic, there were islands of other ethnic groups that caused untold difficulties. Religious differences also troubled the area, as Roman Catholics, Greek Orthodox Christians, and pagans confronted each other.

Much of Polish history revolved around a bitter struggle between the crown and the landed nobility until the end of the fifteenth century, when the preoccupation of Poland's rulers with problems in Bohemia and Hungary, as well as war with the Russians and Turks, enabled the aristocrats to reestablish their power. Through their control of the Sejm (SAYM) or national diet, the magnates reduced the peasantry to serfdom by 1511 and established the right to elect their kings. The Polish kings proved unable to establish a strong royal authority.

Bohemia, Poland's neighbor, was part of the Holy Roman Empire, but distrust of the Germans and close ethnic ties to the Poles and Slovaks encouraged the Czechs of Bohemia to associate with their northeastern Slavic neighbors. The Hussite wars (see "The Problems of Heresy and Reform" later in this chapter) led to further dissension and civil war. Because of a weak monarchy, the Bohemian nobles increased their authority and wealth at the expense of both crown and church.

The history of Hungary had been closely tied to that of central and western Europe by its conversion to Roman Catholicism by German missionaries. The church became a large and prosperous institution. Wealthy bishops, along with the great territorial lords, became powerful, independent political figures. For a brief while, Hungary developed into an important European state, the dominant power in eastern Europe. King Matthias Corvinus (muh-THY-uss kor-VY-nuss) (1458–1490) broke the power of the wealthy lords and created a well-organized bureaucracy. Like a typical Renaissance prince, he patronized the new humanist culture, brought Italian scholars and artists to his capital at Buda, and made his court one of the most brilliant outside Italy. After his death, however, Hungary returned to weak rule, and the work of Corvinus was largely undone.

Since the thirteenth century, Russia had been under the domination of the Mongols. Gradually, the princes of Moscow rose to prominence by using their close relationship to the Mongol khans to increase their wealth and expand their possessions. In the reign of the great prince Ivan III (1462–1505), a new Russian state—the principality of Moscow—was born. Ivan III annexed other Russian principalities and took advantage of dissension among the Mongols to throw off their yoke by 1480.

The Ottoman Turks and the End of the Byzantine Empire

The steadily advancing Ottoman Turks increasingly threatened Eastern Europe (see Map 12.4). The Byzantine Empire had, of course, served as a buffer between the Muslim Middle East and

CHRONOLOGY Europe in the Renaissance	
France	
Charles VII	1422–1461
Louis XI the Spider	1461–1483
England	
"War of the Roses"	1450s–1485
Henry VII	1485–1509
Spain	
Isabella of Castile	1474–1504
Ferdinand of Aragon	1479–1516
Marriage of Ferdinand and Isabella	1469
Introduction of Inquisition	1478
Expulsion of the Jews	1492
Expulsion of the Muslims	1502
Holy Roman Empire	
Frederick III	1440–1493
Maximilian I	1493–1519
Eastern Europe	
Battle of Kosovo	1389
Fall of Constantinople and Byzantine Empire	1453
Hungary: Matthias Corvinus	1458–1490
Russia: Ivan III	1462–1505

MAP 12.4 The Ottoman Empire and Southeastern Europe. Long a buffer between Christian Europe and the Muslim Middle East, the Byzantine Empire quickly waned in power and territory after crusaders sacked Constantinople in 1204. The Ottoman Turks slowly gained Byzantine territory and ended the thousand-year empire with the fall of Constantinople in 1453.

Q Why would the Byzantine Empire have found it difficult to make alliances by 1403?

the Latin West for centuries, but it had been severely weakened by the sack of Constantinople in 1204 and its occupation by the West. Although the Palaeologus dynasty (1260–1453) had tried to reestablish Byzantine power in the Balkans after the overthrow of the Latin empire, the threat from the Turks finally doomed the long-lasting empire.

Beginning in northeastern Asia Minor in the thirteenth century, the Ottoman Turks spread rapidly, seizing the lands of the Seljuk Turks and the Byzantine Empire. In 1345, they bypassed Constantinople and moved into the Balkans. Under Sultan Murad (moo-RAHD), Ottoman forces moved through Bulgaria and into the lands of the Serbs, who provided a strong center of opposition under King Lazar (lah-ZAR). But in 1389, at the Battle of Kosovo (KAWSS-suh-voh), Ottoman forces defeated the Serbs; both King Lazar and Sultan Murad perished in the battle. Kosovo became a battlefield long revered and remembered by the Serbs. Not until 1480 were Bosnia, Albania, and the rest of Serbia added to the Ottoman Empire in the Balkans.

In the meantime, in 1453, the Ottomans completed the demise of the Byzantine Empire. With 80,000 troops ranged against only 7,000 defenders, Sultan Mehmet II (meh-MET) laid siege to Constantinople. In their attack on the city, the Turks made use of massive cannons with 26-foot barrels that could launch stone balls weighing up to 1,200 pounds each. Finally, the walls were breached; the Byzantine emperor died in the final battle. Mehmet II, standing before the palace of the emperor, paused to reflect on the passing nature of human glory.

After their conquest of Constantinople, the Ottoman Turks tried to complete their conquest of the Balkans, where they had been established since the fourteenth century. Although they were successful in taking the Romanian territory of Wallachia (wah-LAY-kee-uh) in 1476, the resistance of the Hungarians initially kept the Turks from advancing up the Danube valley. Until the end of the fifteenth century, internal problems and the need to consolidate their eastern frontiers kept the Turks from any further attacks on Europe. But at the beginning of the sixteenth century, the Ottomans would renew their offensive against the West, challenging Hungary, Austria, Bohemia, and Poland and threatening to turn the Mediterranean into a Turkish lake.

The Church in the Renaissance

> **FOCUS QUESTION:** What were the policies of the Renaissance popes, and what impact did those policies have on the Catholic Church?

As a result of the efforts of the Council of Constance, the Great Schism had finally been brought to an end in 1417 (see Chapter 11). The ending of the schism proved to be the council's easiest task; it was much less successful in dealing with the problems of heresy and reform.

The Problems of Heresy and Reform

Heresy was not a new problem, and in the thirteenth century, the church had developed inquisitorial machinery to deal with it. But two widespread movements in the fourteenth and early fifteenth centuries—Lollardy and Hussitism—posed new threats to the church.

WYCLIF AND LOLLARDY English Lollardy was a product of the Oxford theologian John Wyclif (WIK-lif) (ca. 1328–1384), whose disgust with clerical corruption led him to make a far-ranging attack on papal authority and medieval Christian beliefs and practices. Wyclif alleged that there was no basis in Scripture for papal claims of temporal authority and advocated that the popes be stripped of their authority and their property. Believing that the Bible should be a Christian's sole authority, Wyclif urged that it be made available in the vernacular languages so that every Christian could read it. Rejecting all practices not mentioned in Scripture, Wyclif condemned pilgrimages, the veneration of saints, and a whole series of rituals and rites that had developed in the medieval church. Wyclif attracted a number of followers who came to be known as Lollards.

HUS AND THE HUSSITES A marriage between the royal families of England and Bohemia enabled Lollard ideas to spread to Bohemia, where they reinforced the ideas of a group of Czech reformers led by the chancellor of the university at Prague, John Hus (1374–1415). In his call for reform, Hus urged the elimination of the worldliness and corruption of the clergy and attacked the excessive power of the papacy within the Catholic Church. Hus's objections fell on receptive ears, for the Catholic Church, as one of the largest landowners in Bohemia, was already widely criticized. Moreover, many clergymen were German, and the native Czechs' strong resentment of the Germans who dominated Bohemia also contributed to Hus's movement.

The Council of Constance attempted to deal with the growing problem of heresy by summoning John Hus to the council. Granted safe conduct by Emperor Sigismund, Hus went in the hope of a free hearing of his ideas. Instead he was arrested, condemned as a heretic (by a narrow vote), and burned at the stake in 1415. This action turned the unrest in Bohemia into revolutionary upheaval, and the resulting Hussite wars racked the Holy Roman Empire until a truce was arranged in 1436.

REFORM OF THE CHURCH The efforts of the Council of Constance to reform the church were even less successful than its attempt to eradicate heresy. The council passed two reform decrees. *Sacrosancta* (sak-roh-SANK-tuh) stated that a general council of the church received its authority from God; hence, every Christian, including the pope, was subject to its authority. The decree *Frequens* (FREE-kwens) provided for the regular holding of general councils to ensure that church reform would continue. Taken together, *Sacrosancta* and *Frequens* provided for a legislative system within the church superior to the popes.

Decrees alone, however, proved insufficient to reform the church. Councils could issue decrees, but popes had to execute them, and popes would not cooperate with councils that diminished their authority. Beginning as early as Martin V in 1417, successive popes worked steadfastly for thirty years to defeat the conciliar movement. The final blow came in 1460, when Pope Pius II issued the papal bull *Execrabilis* (ek-suh-KRAB-uh-liss), condemning appeals to a council over the head of a pope as heretical.

By the mid-fifteenth century, the popes had reasserted their supremacy over the Catholic Church. No longer, however, did they have any possibility of asserting supremacy over temporal governments as the medieval papacy had. Although the papal monarchy had been maintained, it had lost much moral prestige. In the fifteenth century, the Renaissance papacy contributed to an even further decline in the moral leadership of the popes.

The Renaissance Papacy

The Renaissance papacy encompasses the line of popes from the end of the Great Schism (1417) to the beginnings of the Reformation in the early sixteenth century. The primary concern of the papacy is governing the Catholic Church as its spiritual leader. But as heads of the church, popes had temporal preoccupations as well, and the story of the Renaissance papacy is really an account of how the latter came to overshadow the popes' spiritual functions.

The manner in which Renaissance popes pursued their interests in the Papal States and Italian politics, especially their use of intrigue and even bloodshed, seemed shocking. Of all the Renaissance popes, Julius II (1503–1513) was most involved in war and politics. The fiery "warrior-pope" personally led armies against his enemies, much to the disgust of pious Christians, who viewed the pope as a spiritual leader. As one intellectual wrote, "How, O bishop standing in the room of the Apostles, dare you teach the people the things that pertain to war?"

To further their territorial aims in the Papal States, the popes needed loyal servants. Because they were not hereditary monarchs, popes could not build dynasties over several generations and came to rely on the practice of **nepotism** to promote their families' interests. Pope Sixtus IV (1471–1484), for example, made five of his nephews cardinals and gave them an abundance of church offices to build up their finances (the word *nepotism* is in fact derived from the Latin *nepos*, meaning "nephew"). Alexander VI (1492–1503), a member of the Borgia family who was known for his debauchery and sensuality, raised

Scala/Ministero per i Beni e le Attività culturali/Art Resource, NY

A Renaissance Pope: Leo X. The Renaissance popes allowed secular concerns to overshadow their spiritual duties. Shown here is the Medici pope Leo X. Raphael portrays the pope as a collector of books, looking up after examining an illuminated manuscript with a magnifying glass. At left is the pope's cousin Guilio, a cardinal. Standing behind the pope is Luigi de' Rossi, another relative who had also been made a cardinal.

one son, one nephew, and the brother of one mistress to the cardinalate. A Venetian envoy stated that Alexander, "joyous by nature, thought of nothing but the aggrandizement of his children." Alexander scandalized the church by encouraging his son Cesare to carve out a state for himself from the territories of the Papal States in central Italy.

CHRONOLOGY The Church in the Renaissance	
Council of Constance	1414–1418
Burning of John Hus	1415
End of the Great Schism	1417
Pius II issues the papal bull *Execrabilis*	1460
The Renaissance papacy	
Sixtus IV	1471–1484
Alexander VI	1492–1503
Julius II	1503–1513
Leo X	1513–1521

The Renaissance popes were great patrons of Renaissance culture, and their efforts made Rome a cultural leader at the beginning of the sixteenth century. For the warrior-pope Julius II, the patronage of Renaissance culture was mostly a matter of policy as he endeavored to add to the splendor of his pontificate by tearing down the Basilica of Saint Peter, which had been built by the emperor Constantine, and beginning construction of the greatest building in Christendom, the present Saint Peter's Basilica.

Julius's successor, Leo X (1513–1521), was also a patron of Renaissance culture, not as a matter of policy but as a deeply involved participant. Such might be expected of the son of Lorenzo de' Medici. Made an archbishop at the age of eight and a cardinal at thirteen, he acquired a refined taste in art, manners, and social life among the Florentine Renaissance elite. He became pope at the age of thirty-seven, reportedly remarking to the Venetian ambassador, "Let us enjoy the papacy, since God has given it to us." Raphael was commissioned to do paintings, and the construction of Saint Peter's was accelerated as Rome became the literary and artistic center of the Renaissance.

CHAPTER SUMMARY

Beginning in Italy, the Renaissance was an era that rediscovered and was influenced by the culture of ancient Greece and Rome. It was also a time of recovery from the difficulties of the fourteenth century as well as a period of transition that witnessed a continuation of the economic, political, and social trends that had begun in the High Middle Ages.

The Renaissance was also a movement in which intellectuals and artists proclaimed a new vision of humankind and raised fundamental questions about the value and importance of the individual. The humanists or intellectuals of the age called their period (from the mid-fourteenth to the mid-sixteenth century) an age of rebirth, believing that they had restored arts and letters to new glory. Humanism was an intellectual movement based on the study of the classical literary works of Greece and Rome. The goal of a humanist education was to produce individuals of virtue and wisdom. Civic humanism posited that the ideal citizen was not only an intellectual but also an active participant in the life of the state.

The Renaissance is perhaps best known for its artistic brilliance. Renaissance artists in Italy sought not only to persuade onlookers of the reality of the object they were portraying, but also to focus attention on human beings as "the center

and measure of all things." This new Renaissance style was developed, above all, in Florence, but at the end of the fifteenth century, Renaissance art moved into a new phase in which Rome became the new cultural center. In the works of Leonardo da Vinci, Raphael, and Michelangelo, the High Renaissance ideal of beauty was convincingly portrayed.

The Renaissance in Europe was also an era of "new monarchies," best seen in England, France, and Spain. Monarchs in these countries limited the private armies of the aristocracy, raised taxes, created professional armies, and in the process were able to reestablish the centralized power of monarchical governments. At the same time, the Renaissance popes became increasingly mired in political and temporal concerns that overshadowed their spiritual responsibilities.

Of course, the intellectuals and artists of the Renaissance wrote and painted for the upper classes, and the brilliant intellectual, cultural, and artistic accomplishments of the Renaissance were products of and for the elite. The ideas of the Renaissance did not have a broad base among the masses of the people. The Renaissance did, however, raise new questions about medieval traditions. In advocating a return to the early sources of Christianity and criticizing current religious practices, the humanists raised fundamental issues about the Catholic Church, which was still an important institution. In the sixteenth century, as we shall see in the next chapter, the intellectual renaissance of the fifteenth century gave way to a religious renaissance that touched the lives of people, including the masses, in new and profound ways.

CHAPTER TIMELINE

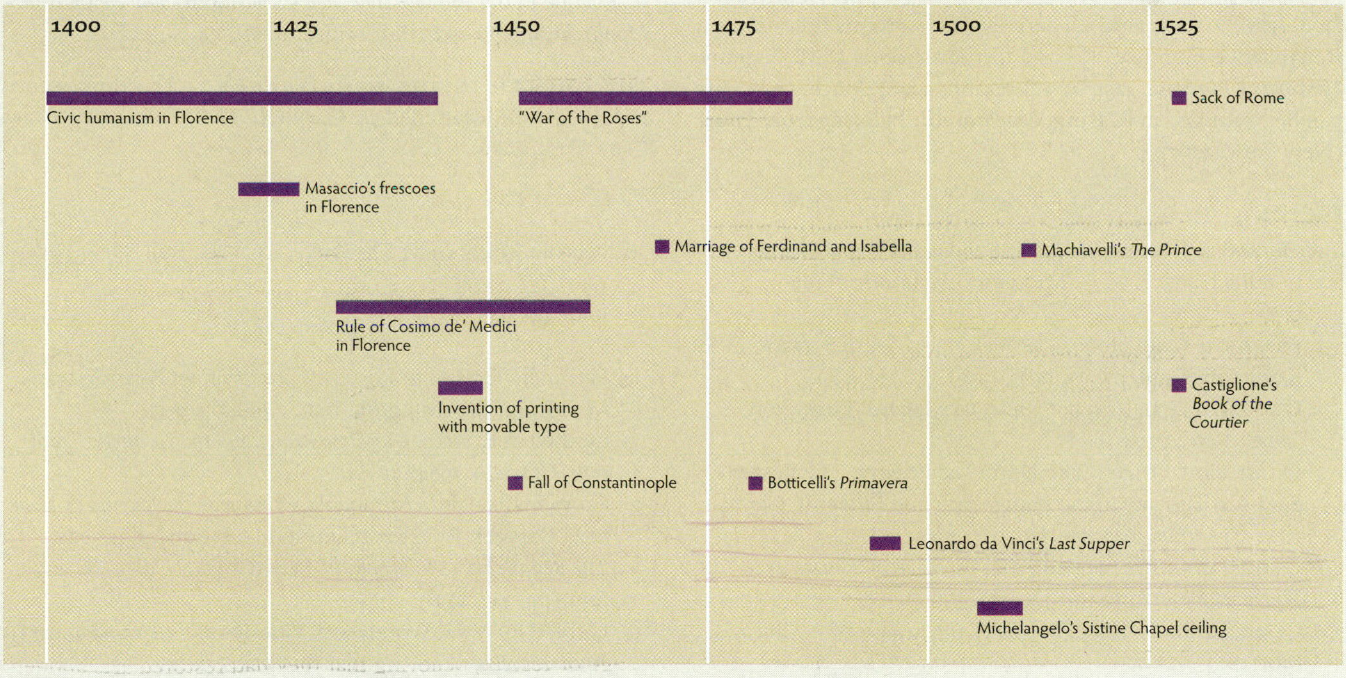

CHAPTER REVIEW

Upon Reflection

Q What was the pattern of political development in Renaissance Italy? What new political practices (statecraft) did the Italians contribute to Europe, and how were these new political practices reflected in the work of Machiavelli?

Q What was the relationship between Italian Renaissance humanism and Italian Renaissance art?

Q What impact did the policies of the Renaissance popes have on the Catholic Church?

Key Terms

Renaissance (p. 332)
estates (p. 334)
individualism (p. 343)
secularism (p. 343)
humanism (p. 343)
civic humanism (p. 343)
Neoplatonism (p. 346)
Hermeticism (p. 346)
pantheism (p. 346)
new monarchies (p. 356)
nepotism (p. 361)

Suggestions for Further Reading

GENERAL WORKS ON THE RENAISSANCE General works on the Renaissance in Europe include **M. L. King, *The Renaissance in Europe*** (New York, 2005), and **J. Hale, *The Civilization of Europe in the Renaissance*** (New York, 1994). Also valuable are **T. K. Rabb, *The Last Days of the Renaissance*** (New York, 2006), and **Alexander Lee, *The Ugly Renaissance: Sex, Greed, Violence and Depravity in an Age of Beauty*** (New York, 2013).

FAMILY AND MARRIAGE On family and marriage, see **C. Klapisch-Zuber, *Women, Family, and Ritual in Renaissance Italy*** (Chicago, 1985). On women, see **M. L. Brown** and **K. B. McBride, *Women's Roles During the Renaissance*** (New York, 2005).

ITALIAN CITY-STATES For studies of the Italian city-states, see **J. M. Najemy, ed., *Italy in the Age of the Renaissance, 1300–1550*** (Oxford, 2004). There is an enormous literature on Renaissance Florence. A good introduction is **J. M. Najemy, *History of Florence, 1200–1575*** (London, 2006). Machiavelli's life can be examined in **R. King, *Machiavelli: Philosopher of Power*** (New York, 2007).

RENAISSANCE HUMANISM A brief introduction to Renaissance humanism can be found in **C. G. Nauert Jr., *Humanism and the Culture of Renaissance Europe***, 2nd ed. (Cambridge, 2006). See also **R. Mackenny, *Renaissances: The Cultures of Italy, c. 1300–c. 1600*** (New York, 2004).

RENAISSANCE ART Good surveys of Renaissance art include **J. T. Paoletti** and **G. M. Radke, *Art, Power, and Patronage in Renaissance Italy***, 3rd ed. (Upper Saddle River, N.J., 2003); **C. Bucci** and **S. Buricchi, *Renaissance Art*** (New York, 2007); **R. Turner, *Renaissance Florence: The Invention of a New Art*** (New York, 1997); and **P. F. Brown, *Art and Life in Renaissance Venice*** (Upper Saddle River, N.J., 2005).

POLITICAL DEVELOPMENTS On the political development of Europe in the Renaissance, see **C. Mulgan, *The Renaissance Monarchies, 1469–1558*** (Cambridge, 1998).

THE CHURCH IN THE RENAISSANCE The Renaissance papacy can be examined in **G. Noel, *The Renaissance Popes*** (New York, 2006).

Notes

1. Quoted in J. Burckhardt, *The Civilization of the Renaissance in Italy*, trans. S. G. C. Middlemore (London, 1960), p. 81.
2. Baldassare Castiglione, *The Book of the Courtier*, trans. C. S. Singleton (Garden City, N.Y., 1959), pp. 288–289.
3. Quoted in D. L. Jensen, *Renaissance Europe* (Lexington, Mass., 1981), p. 94.
4. Quoted in I. Origo, "The Domestic Enemy: The Eastern Slaves in Tuscany in the Fourteenth and Fifteenth Centuries," *Speculum* 30 (1955): 333.
5. Quoted in G. Brucker, ed., *Two Memoirs of Renaissance Florence* (New York, 1967), p. 132.
6. Quoted in M. L. King, *Women of the Renaissance* (Chicago, 1991), p. 3.
7. Quoted in G. Brucker, ed., *The Society of Renaissance Florence* (New York, 1971), p. 190.
8. Quoted in A. Lee, *The Ugly Renaissance: Sex, Greed, Violence and Depravity in an Age of Beauty* (New York, 2013), p. 25.
9. Quoted in G. Mattingly, *Renaissance Diplomacy* (Baltimore, 1964), p. 42.
10. Ibid., p. 95.
11. Niccolò Machiavelli, *The Prince*, trans. G. Bull (New York, 1991), pp. 90–91.
12. Ibid., pp. 96, 101.
13. Ibid., p. 60.
14. Petrarch, "Epistle to Posterity," *Letters from Petrarch*, trans. M. Bishop (Bloomington, Ind., 1966), pp. 6–7.
15. Quoted in F. Yates, *Giordano Bruno and the Hermetic Tradition* (Chicago, 1964), p. 211.
16. Giovanni Pico della Mirandola, *Oration on the Dignity of Man*, in E. Cassirer, P. O. Kristeller, and J. H. Randall Jr., eds., *The Renaissance Philosophy of Man* (Chicago, 1948), p. 225.
17. Ibid., pp. 247, 249.
18. Quoted in W. H. Woodward, *Vittorino da Feltre and Other Humanist Educators* (Cambridge, 1897), p. 102.
19. Quoted in I. Origo, *The Light of the Past* (New York, 1959), p. 136.
20. Quoted in Elizabeth G. Holt, ed., *A Documentary History of Art* (Garden City, N.Y., 1957), vol. 1, p. 286.
21. Quoted in R. M. Letts, *The Cambridge Introduction to Art: The Renaissance* (Cambridge, 1981), p. 86.
22. Quoted in J. Huizinga, *The Waning of the Middle Ages* (Garden City, N.Y., 1956), p. 265.

CHAPTER 13

REFORMATION AND RELIGIOUS WARFARE IN THE SIXTEENTH CENTURY

bpk, Berlin/Art Resource, NY

A nineteenth-century engraving showing Luther before the Diet of Worms

CHAPTER OUTLINE AND FOCUS QUESTIONS

Prelude to Reformation

Q What were the chief ideas of the Christian humanists, and how did they differ from the ideas of the Protestant reformers?

Martin Luther and the Reformation in Germany

Q What were Martin Luther's main disagreements with the Roman Catholic Church, and what political, economic, and social conditions help explain why the movement he began spread so quickly across Europe?

The Spread of the Protestant Reformation

Q What were the main tenets of Lutheranism, Zwinglianism, Anabaptism, and Calvinism, and how did they differ from each other and from Catholicism? What impact did political, economic, and social conditions have on the development of these four reform movements?

The Social Impact of the Protestant Reformation

Q What impact did the Protestant Reformation have on society in the sixteenth century?

The Catholic Reformation

Q What measures did the Roman Catholic Church take to reform itself and to combat Protestantism in the sixteenth century?

Politics and the Wars of Religion in the Sixteenth Century

Q What role did politics, economic and social conditions, and religion play in the European wars of the sixteenth century?

Critical Thinking

Q *Where and how did the reform movements take hold, and how did the emergence of these reform movements affect the political and social realms where they were adopted?*

Connections to Today

Q *How are the religious controversies of the sixteenth century related to religious and social conditions in the Western world today?*

ON APRIL 18, 1521, a lowly monk stood before the emperor and princes of Germany in the city of Worms. He had been called before this august gathering to answer charges of heresy, charges that could threaten his very life. The monk was confronted with a pile of his books and asked if he wished to defend them all or reject a part. Courageously, Martin Luther defended them all and asked to be shown where any part was in error on the basis of "Scripture and plain reason." The emperor was outraged by Luther's response and made his own position clear the next day: "Not only I, but you of this noble German nation, would be forever disgraced if by our negligence not only heresy but the very suspicion of heresy were to survive. After having heard yesterday the obstinate defense of Luther, I regret that I have so long delayed in proceeding against him and his false teaching. I will have no more to do with him."[1] Luther's appearance at Worms set the stage for a serious challenge to the authority of the Catholic Church. This was by no means the first crisis in the church's fifteen-hundred-year history, but its consequences were more far-reaching than anyone at Worms in 1521 could have imagined.

Throughout the Middle Ages, the Christian church had continued to assert its primacy of position. It had overcome defiance of its temporal authority by emperors and kings, and challenges to its doctrines had been crushed by the Inquisition and combated by new religious orders that carried its message of salvation to all the towns and villages of medieval Europe. The growth of the papacy had paralleled the growth of the church, but by the end of the Middle Ages, challenges to papal authority from the rising power of monarchical states had resulted in a loss of papal temporal authority. An even greater threat to papal authority and church unity arose in the sixteenth century when the Reformation shattered the unity of Christendom.

The movement begun by Martin Luther when he made his dramatic stand quickly spread across Europe, a clear indication of dissatisfaction with Catholic practices. Within a short time, new forms of religious practices, doctrines, and organizations, including Zwinglianism, Calvinism, Anabaptism, and Anglicanism, were attracting adherents all over Europe. Although seemingly helpless to stop the new Protestant churches, the Catholic Church also underwent a reformation and managed to revive its fortunes by the mid-sixteenth century. All too soon, the doctrinal divisions between Protestants and Catholics led to a series of religious wars that dominated the history of western Europe in the second half of the sixteenth century.

Prelude to Reformation

FOCUS QUESTION: What were the chief ideas of the Christian humanists, and how did they differ from the ideas of the Protestant reformers?

Martin Luther's reform movement was by no means the first. During the second half of the fifteenth century, the new classical learning that was part of Italian Renaissance humanism spread to northern Europe and spawned a movement called **Christian (northern Renaissance) humanism** whose major goal was the reform of Christianity.

Christian or Northern Renaissance Humanism

Like their Italian counterparts, northern humanists cultivated knowledge of the classics, the bond that united all humanists into a kind of international fellowship. In returning to the writings of antiquity, northern humanists (also called Christian humanists because of their profound preoccupation with religion) focused on the sources of early Christianity, the Holy Scriptures and the writings of such church fathers as Augustine, Ambrose, and Jerome. In these early Christian writings, they discovered a simple religion that they came to feel had been distorted by the complicated theological arguments of the Middle Ages.

The most important characteristic of northern humanism was its reform program. Convinced of the ability of human beings to reason and improve themselves, the northern humanists felt that through education in the sources of classical, and especially Christian, antiquity, they could instill a true inner piety or an inward religious feeling that would bring about a reform of the church and society. For this reason, Christian humanists supported schools, brought out new editions of the classics, and prepared new editions of the Bible and writings of the church fathers. In the preface to his edition of the Greek New Testament, the famous humanist Erasmus wrote:

> I disagree very much with those who are unwilling that Holy Scripture, translated into the vulgar tongue, be read by the uneducated, as if Christ taught such intricate doctrines that they could scarcely be understood by very few theologians, or as if the strength of the Christian religion consisted in men's ignorance of it. . . . I would that even the lowliest women read the Gospels and the Pauline Epistles. And I would that they were translated into all languages so that they could be read and understood not only by Scots and Irish but also by Turks and Saracens. . . . Would that, as a result, the farmer sing some portion of them at the plow, the weaver hum some parts of them to the movement of his shuttle, the traveler lighten the weariness of the journey with stories of this kind![2]

This belief in the power of education would remain an important characteristic of European civilization. Like later intellectuals, Christian humanists believed that to change society, they must first change the human beings who compose it. Although some critics have called the Christian humanists naive, they were in fact merely optimistic. The turmoil of the Reformation, however, shattered much of this intellectual optimism, as the lives and careers of two of the most prominent Christian humanists, Desiderius Erasmus and Thomas More, illustrate.

ERASMUS The most influential of all the Christian humanists was Desiderius Erasmus (dez-ih-DEER-ee-uss ih-RAZZ-mus) (1466–1536), who formulated and popularized the reform program of Christian humanism. Born in Holland, Erasmus was educated at one of the schools of the Brothers of the Common Life (see Chapter 11). He wandered to France, England, Italy, Germany, and Switzerland, conversing everywhere in the classical Latin that might be called his mother tongue. The *Handbook of the Christian Knight*, printed in 1503, reflected his preoccupation with religion. He called his conception of religion "the philosophy of Christ," by which he meant that Christianity should be a guiding philosophy for the direction of daily life rather than the system of dogmatic beliefs and practices that the medieval church seemed to stress. In other words, he emphasized inner piety and de-emphasized the external forms of religion (such as the sacraments, pilgrimages, fasts, veneration of saints, and relics). To return to the simplicity

Scala/Art Resource, NY

Erasmus. Desiderius Erasmus was the most influential of the northern Renaissance humanists. He sought to restore Christianity to the early simplicity found in the teachings of Jesus. This portrait of Erasmus was painted in 1523 by Hans Holbein the Younger, who had formed a friendship with the great humanist while they were both in Basel.

of the early church, people needed to understand the original meaning of the Scriptures and the writings of the early church fathers. Because Erasmus thought that the standard Latin edition of the Bible, known as the Vulgate, contained errors, he edited the Greek text of the New Testament from the earliest available manuscripts and published it, along with a new Latin translation, in 1516. Erasmus also wrote *Annotations*, a detailed commentary on the Vulgate Bible itself. In his day, Erasmus's work on the New Testament was considered his most outstanding achievement, and Martin Luther himself would use Erasmus's work as the basis for his German translation of the New Testament.

To Erasmus, the reform of the church meant spreading an understanding of the philosophy of Jesus, providing enlightened education in the sources of early Christianity, and making common-sense criticisms of the abuses in the church. This last is especially evident in *The Praise of Folly*, written in 1509, in which Erasmus engaged in humorous yet effective criticism of the most corrupt practices of his own society. He was especially harsh on the abuses within the ranks of the clergy (see the box on p. 368).

In another satirical work, *Julius Excluded from Heaven*, Erasmus pilloried the Renaissance papacy in the person of Julius II, the "warrior pope" (see Chapter 12). When Julius dies, he appears before the gates of heaven, expecting a quick entry. When St. Peter denies him entrance because of Julius' misdeeds, Julius threatens to raise an army and storm heaven itself.

Erasmus's program did not achieve the reform of the church that he so desired. His moderation and his emphasis on education were quickly overwhelmed by the passions of the Reformation. Undoubtedly, though, his work helped prepare the way for the Reformation; as contemporaries proclaimed, "Erasmus laid the egg that Luther hatched." Yet Erasmus eventually disapproved of Luther and the Protestant reformers. He had no intention of destroying the unity of the medieval Christian church; rather, his whole program was based on reform within the church.

THOMAS MORE The son of a London lawyer, Thomas More (1478–1535) received the benefits of a good education. Although trained in the law, he took an avid interest in the new classical learning and became proficient in both Latin and Greek. Like the Italian humanists, who believed in putting their learning at the service of the state, More embarked on a public career that ultimately took him to the highest reaches of power as lord chancellor of England.

His career in government service, however, did not keep More from the intellectual and spiritual interests that were so dear to him. He was well acquainted with other English humanists and became an intimate friend of Erasmus. He made translations from Greek authors and wrote both prose and poetry in Latin. A devout man, he spent many hours in prayer and private devotions. Contemporaries praised his household as a shining model of Christian family life.

More's most famous work, and one of the most controversial of his age, was *Utopia*, written in 1516. This literary masterpiece is an account of the idealistic life and institutions of the community of Utopia (Greek for "nowhere"), an imaginary island in the vicinity of the recently discovered New World. It reflects More's own concerns with the economic, social, and political problems of his day. He presented a new social system in which cooperation and reason replaced power and fame as the proper motivating agents for human society. Utopian society, therefore, was based on communal ownership rather than private property. All residents of Utopia worked nine hours a day, regardless of occupation, and were rewarded according to their needs. Possessing abundant leisure time and relieved of competition and greed, Utopians were free to lead wholesome and enriching lives.

In serving King Henry VIII, More came face to face with the abuses and corruption he had criticized in *Utopia*. But he did not allow idealism to outweigh his own ultimate realism, and in *Utopia* itself he justified his service to the king:

> If you can't completely eradicate wrong ideas, or deal with inveterate vices as effectively as you could wish, that's no reason for turning your back on public life altogether. . . . On the other hand, it's no use attempting to put across entirely new ideas, which will obviously carry no weight with people who are prejudiced against them. You must go to work indirectly. You must handle everything as tactfully as you can, and what you can't put right you must try to make as little wrong as possible. For things will never be perfect, until human beings are perfect—which I don't expect them to be for quite a number of years.[3]

ERASMUS: IN PRAISE OF FOLLY

THE PRAISE OF FOLLY IS ONE OF THE MOST famous pieces of literature produced in the sixteenth century. Erasmus, who wrote it in a short time during a visit to the home of Thomas More, considered it a "little diversion" from his "serious work." Yet both contemporaries and later generations have appreciated "this laughing parody of every form and rank of human life." In this selection, Erasmus belittles one of his favorite objects of scorn, the monks. They were, however, merely one of the many groups he disparaged.

Erasmus, *The Praise of Folly*

Those who are the closest to these [the theologians] in happiness are generally called "the religious" or "monks," both of which are deceiving names, since for the most part they stay as far away from religion as possible and frequent every sort of place. I [Folly] cannot, however, see how any life could be more gloomy than the life of these monks if I did not assist them in many ways. Though most people detest these men so much that accidentally meeting one is considered to be bad luck, the monks themselves believe that they are magnificent creatures. One of their chief beliefs is that to be illiterate is to be of a high state of sanctity, and so they make sure that they are not able to read. Another is that when braying out their gospels in church they are making themselves very pleasing and satisfying to God, when in fact they are uttering these psalms as a matter of repetition rather than from their hearts. . . .

Moreover, it is amusing to find that they insist that everything be done in fastidious detail, as if employing the orderliness of mathematics, a small mistake in which would be a great crime. Just so many knots must be on each shoe and the shoelace may be of only one specified color; just so much lace is allowed on each habit; the girdle must be of just the right material and width; the hood of a certain shape and capacity; their hair of just so many fingers' length; and finally they can sleep only the specified number of hours per day. Can they not understand that, because of a variety of bodies and temperaments, all this equality of restrictions is in fact very unequal? Nevertheless, because of all this detail that they employ they think that they are superior to all other people. And what is more, amid all their pretense of Apostolic charity, the members of one order will denounce the members of another order clamorously because of the way in which the habit has been belted or the slightly darker color of it. . . .

Many of them work so hard at protocol and at traditional fastidiousness that they think one heaven hardly a suitable reward for their labors; never recalling, however, that the time will come when Christ will demand a reckoning of that which he had prescribed, namely charity, and that he will hold their deeds of little account. One monk will then exhibit his belly filled with every kind of fish; another will profess a knowledge of over a hundred hymns. Still another will reveal a countless number of fasts that he has made, and will account for his large belly by explaining that his fasts have always been broken by a single large meal. Another will show a list of church ceremonies over which he has officiated so large that it would fill seven ships.

Q *What are Erasmus's main criticisms of monks? What do you think he hoped to achieve by this satirical attack on monastic practices? How do you think the circulation of many printed copies of such attacks would have affected popular attitudes toward the Catholic Church?*

Source: Erasmus, "The Praise of Folly," in *The Essential Erasmus*, trans. J. P. Dolan (New York: Dutton Signet, 1964).

More's religious devotion and belief in the universal Catholic Church ultimately proved even more important than his service to the king, however. While in office, More's intolerance of heresy led him to advocate persecution of those who would fundamentally change the Catholic Church. Moreover, always the man of conscience, More willingly gave up his life opposing England's break with the Roman Catholic Church over the divorce of King Henry VIII.

Church and Religion on the Eve of the Reformation

Corruption in the Catholic Church was another factor that spurred people to want reform. No doubt the failure of the Renaissance popes to provide spiritual leadership had affected the spiritual life of all Christendom. The papal court's preoccupation with finances had an especially strong impact on the clergy. So did the economic changes of the fourteenth and fifteenth centuries. Increasingly, nobles or wealthy members of the bourgeoisie held the highest positions among the clergy. Moreover, to increase their revenues, high church officials (bishops, archbishops, and cardinals) took over more than one church office. This so-called **pluralism** led in turn to absenteeism: church officeholders ignored their duties and hired underlings who sometimes lacked the proper qualifications. Complaints about the ignorance and ineptness of parish priests became widespread in the fifteenth century.

THE SEARCH FOR SALVATION While many of the leaders of the church were failing to meet their responsibilities, ordinary people were clamoring for meaningful religious expression and certainty of salvation. As a result, for some the salvation process became almost mechanical. As more and more people sought certainty of salvation through veneration of relics, collections of such objects grew. Frederick the Wise, elector of Saxony and Martin Luther's prince, had amassed more than 19,000 relics to which were attached indulgences that could reduce one's time in purgatory by nearly 2 million years. (An indulgence, you will recall, is a remission, after death, of all or part of the punishment for sin.) Other people sought certainty of salvation in the popular mystical movement known as the Modern Devotion, which downplayed religious dogma and stressed the need to follow the teachings of Jesus. Thomas à Kempis, author of *The Imitation of Christ*, wrote that "truly, at the day of judgment we shall not be examined by what we have read, but what we have done; not how well we have spoken, but how religiously we have lived."

What is striking about the revival of religious piety in the fifteenth century—whether expressed through such external forces as the veneration of relics and the buying of indulgences or the mystical path—was its adherence to the orthodox beliefs and practices of the Catholic Church. The agitation for certainty of salvation and spiritual peace occurred within the framework of the "holy mother Church." But disillusionment grew as the devout experienced the clergy's inability to live up to their expectations. The deepening of religious life, especially in the second half of the fifteenth century, found little echo among the worldly-wise clergy, and this environment helps explain the tremendous and immediate impact of Luther's ideas.

CALLS FOR REFORM At the same time, several sources of reform were already at work within the Catholic Church at the end of the fifteenth and the beginning of the sixteenth century. Especially noticeable were the calls for reform from the religious orders of the Franciscans, Dominicans, and Augustinians. Members of these groups put particular emphasis on preaching to laypeople. One of the popular preachers was Johannes Geiler of Kaisersberg (KY-zerz-bayrk), who denounced the corruption of the clergy.

The Oratory of Divine Love, first organized in Italy in 1497, was not a religious order but an informal group of clergy and laymen who worked to foster reform by emphasizing personal spiritual development and outward acts of charity. The "philosophy of Christ," advocated by the Christian humanist Erasmus, was especially appealing to many of them. The Oratory's members included a number of cardinals who favored church reform. A Spanish archbishop, Cardinal Ximenes, was especially active in using Christian humanism to reform the church. To foster spirituality among the people, he had a number of religious writings, including Thomas à Kempis's *The Imitation of Christ*, translated into Spanish.

Martin Luther and the Reformation in Germany

> **FOCUS QUESTION:** What were Martin Luther's main disagreements with the Roman Catholic Church, and what political, economic, and social conditions help explain why the movement he began spread so quickly across Europe?

The Protestant Reformation began with a typical medieval question: What must I do to be saved? Martin Luther, a deeply religious man, found an answer that did not fit within the traditional teachings of the late medieval church. Ultimately, he split with that church, destroying the religious unity of western Christendom. That other people were concerned with the same question is evident in the rapid spread of the Reformation. But religion was so entangled in the social, economic, and political forces of the period that the Protestant reformers' hope of transforming the church quickly proved illusory.

The Early Luther

Martin Luther was born in Germany on November 10, 1483. His father wanted him to become a lawyer, so Luther enrolled at the University of Erfurt, where he received his bachelor's degree in 1502. Three years later, after becoming a master in the liberal arts, the young man began to study law. But Luther was not content, not in small part due to his long-standing religious inclinations. That summer, while returning to Erfurt after a brief visit home, he was caught in a ferocious thunderstorm and vowed that if he survived unscathed, he would become a monk. He then entered the monastic order of the Augustinian Hermits in Erfurt, much to his father's disgust. In the monastery, Luther focused on his major concern, the assurance of salvation. The traditional beliefs and practices of the church seemed unable to relieve his obsession with this question, especially evident in his struggle with the sacrament of penance or **confession**. The sacraments were a Catholic's chief means of receiving God's grace; confession offered the opportunity to have one's sins forgiven. Luther spent hours confessing his sins, but he was always doubtful. Had he remembered all of his sins? Even more, how could a hopeless sinner be acceptable to a totally just and all-powerful God? Luther threw himself into his monastic routine with a vengeance:

> I was indeed a good monk and kept my order so strictly that I could say that if ever a monk could get to heaven through monastic discipline, I was that monk. . . . And yet my conscience would not give me certainty, but I always doubted and said, "You didn't do that right. You weren't contrite enough. You left that out of your confession." The more I tried to remedy an uncertain, weak and troubled conscience with human traditions, the more I daily found it more uncertain, weaker and more troubled.[4]

Despite his strenuous efforts, Luther achieved no certainty.

To help overcome his difficulties, his superiors recommended that the monk study theology. He received his doctorate in 1512 and then became a professor in the theological faculty at the University of Wittenberg (VIT-ten-bayrk), lecturing on the Bible. Sometime between 1513 and 1516, through his study of the Bible, he arrived at an answer to his problem.

Catholic doctrine had emphasized that both faith and good works were required for a Christian to achieve personal salvation. In Luther's eyes, human beings, weak and powerless in the sight of an almighty God, could never do enough good works to merit salvation. Through his study of the Bible, especially his work on Paul's Epistle to the Romans, Luther rediscovered another way of viewing this problem. To Luther, humans are saved not through their good works but through faith in the promises of God, made possible by the sacrifice of Jesus on

Scala/Art Resource, NY

Martin Luther and Katherina von Bora. This double portrait of Martin Luther and his wife was done by Lucas Cranach the Elder in 1529. By this time, Luther's reforms had begun to make an impact in many parts of Germany. Luther married Katherina von Bora in 1525, thus creating a new model of family life for Protestant ministers.

the cross. The doctrine of salvation or justification by grace through faith alone became the primary doctrine of the Protestant Reformation (**justification** is the act by which a person is made deserving of salvation). Because Luther had arrived at this doctrine from his study of the Bible, the Bible became for Luther, as for all other Protestants, the chief guide to religious truth. Justification by faith and the Bible as the sole authority in religious affairs were the twin pillars of the Protestant Reformation.

THE INDULGENCE CONTROVERSY Luther did not see himself as either a revolutionary innovator or a heretic, but his involvement in the indulgence controversy propelled him into an open confrontation with church officials and forced him to see the theological implications of justification by faith alone. In 1517, Pope Leo X had issued a special jubilee indulgence to finance the ongoing construction of Saint Peter's Basilica in Rome. Johann Tetzel, a rambunctious Dominican, hawked the indulgences in Germany with the slogan "As soon as the coin in the coffer rings, the soul from purgatory springs."

Greatly distressed by the sale of indulgences, Luther was certain that people who relied on these pieces of paper to assure themselves of salvation were guaranteeing their eternal damnation instead. Angered, he issued his Ninety-Five Theses, although scholars are unsure whether he nailed them to a church door in Wittenberg, as is traditionally alleged, or mailed them to his ecclesiastical superior. In either case, his theses were a stunning indictment of the abuses in the sale of indulgences (see the box on p. 371). It is doubtful that Luther intended any break with the church over the issue of indulgences. If the pope had clarified the use of indulgences, as Luther wished, he would probably have been satisfied, and the controversy would have ended. But Pope Leo X did not take the issue seriously and is even reported to have said that Luther was simply "some drunken German who will amend his ways when he sobers up." Thousands of copies of a German translation of the Ninety-Five Theses were quickly printed and were received sympathetically in a Germany that had a long tradition of dissatisfaction with papal policies and power.

Of course, Luther was not the first theologian to criticize the powers of the papacy. As we saw in Chapter 12, John Wyclif at the end of the fourteenth century and John Hus at the beginning of the fifteenth century had attacked the excessive power of the papacy. Luther was certainly well aware of John Hus's fate at the Council of Constance, where he was burned at the stake on charges of heresy.

THE QUICKENING REBELLION The controversy reached an important turning point with the Leipzig Debate in July 1519. In Leipzig, Luther's opponent, the capable Catholic theologian Johann Eck, forced Luther to move beyond indulgences and deny the authority of popes and councils. During the debate, Eck also identified Luther's ideas with those of John Hus, the condemned heretic. Luther was now compelled to see the consequences of his new theology. At the beginning of 1520, he proclaimed: "Farewell, unhappy, hopeless, blasphemous Rome! The Wrath of God has come upon you, as you deserve. We have cared for Babylon, and she is not healed: let us then, leave her, that she may be the habitation of dragons, spectres, and witches."[5] At the same time, Luther was convinced that he was doing God's work and had to proceed regardless of the consequences.

In three pamphlets published in 1520, Luther moved toward a more definite break with the Catholic Church. The *Address to the Nobility of the German Nation* was a political tract written

LUTHER AND THE NINETY-FIVE THESES

TO MOST HISTORIANS, THE PUBLICATION of Luther's Ninety-Five Theses marks the beginning of the Reformation. To Luther, they were simply a response to what he considered Johann Tetzel's blatant abuses in selling indulgences. Although written in Latin, Luther's statements were soon translated into German and disseminated widely across Germany. They made an immense impression on Germans already dissatisfied with the ecclesiastical and financial policies of the papacy.

Martin Luther, *Selections from the Ninety-Five Theses*

5. The Pope has neither the will nor the power to remit any penalties, except those which he has imposed by his own authority, or by that of the canons [canon law].
20. Therefore the Pope, when he speaks of the plenary remission of all penalties, does not mean simply of all, but only of those imposed by himself.
21. Thus those preachers of indulgences are in error who say that, by the indulgences of the Pope, a man is loosed and saved from all punishment.
27. They preach man [It is mere human talk], who say that the soul flies out of purgatory as soon as the money thrown into the chest rattles.
28. It is certain, that, when the money rattles in the chest, avarice and gain may be increased, but the suffrage of the Church depends on the will of God alone.
50. Christians should be taught, that, if the Pope were acquainted with the exactions of the preachers of pardons, he would prefer that the Basilica of St. Peter should be burnt to ashes, than that it should be built up with the skin, flesh, and bones of his sheep.
81. This license in the preaching of pardons makes it no easy thing, even for learned men, to protect the reverence due to the Pope against the calumnies, or, at all events, the keen questionings, of the laity;
82. As, for instance: Why does not the Pope empty purgatory for the sake of most holy charity and of the supreme necessity of souls,—this being the most just of all reasons,—if he redeems an infinite number of souls for the sake of that most fatal thing, money, to be spent on building a basilica—this being a slight reason?
86. Again: Why does not the Pope, whose riches are at this day more ample than those of the wealthiest of the wealthy, build the one Basilica of St. Peter with his own money, rather than with that of poor believers?
90. To repress these scruples and arguments of the laity by force alone, and not to solve them by giving reasons, is to expose the Church and the Pope to the ridicule of their enemies, and to make Christian men unhappy.
94. Christians should be exhorted to strive to follow Christ their head through pains, deaths, and hells;
95. And thus trust to enter heaven through many tribulations, rather than in the security of peace.

Q *What were the major ideas of Luther's Ninety-Five Theses? Why did they have such a strong appeal in Germany?*

Source: P. Schaff, *History of the Christian Church*, vol. VI (New York: Charles Scribner's Sons, 1916), pp. 161–166.

in German in which Luther called on the German princes to overthrow the papacy in Germany and establish a reformed German church. The *Babylonian Captivity of the Church*, written in Latin for theologians, attacked the sacramental system as the means by which the pope and church had held the real meaning of the Gospel captive for a thousand years. Luther called for the reform of monasticism and for the clergy to marry. Though virginity is good, he argued, marriage is better, and freedom of choice is best. *On the Freedom of a Christian Man* was a short treatise on the doctrine of salvation. It is faith alone, not good works, that justifies, frees, and brings salvation through Jesus. Being saved and freed by his faith in Jesus, however, does not free the Christian from doing good works. Rather, he performs good works out of gratitude to God. "Good works do not make a good man, but a good man does good works."[6]

Unable to accept Luther's forcefully worded dissent from traditional Catholic teachings, the church excommunicated him in January 1521. He was also summoned to appear before the Reichstag (RYKHSS-tahk), the imperial diet of the Holy Roman Empire, in Worms (WURMZ *or* VORMPS), convened by the recently elected Emperor Charles V (1519–1556). Expected to recant the heretical doctrines he had espoused, Luther refused and made the famous reply that became the battle cry of the Reformation:

> Since then Your Majesty and your lordships desire a simple reply, I will answer without horns and without teeth. Unless I am convicted by Scripture and plain reason—I do not accept the authority of popes and councils, for they have contradicted each other—my conscience is captive to the Word of God. I cannot and I will not recant anything, for to go against conscience is neither right nor safe. Here I stand, I cannot do otherwise. God help me. Amen.[7]

Emperor Charles was outraged at Luther's audacity and gave his opinion that "a single friar who goes counter to all Christianity for a thousand years must be wrong." By the Edict of Worms, Martin Luther was made an outlaw within the empire. His works were to be burned, and Luther himself was to be captured and delivered to the emperor. Instead, Luther's prince, the Elector of Saxony, sent him into hiding at the Wartburg (VART-bayrk) Castle, where he remained for nearly a year (see "Film & History" on p. 372).

FILM & HISTORY

Photos 12/Alamy Stock Photo

Watch *Luther* (2003), which depicts the early life and career of Martin Luther, largely from a Lutheran point of view. The movie focuses on some of the major events in Luther's early life, such as his years in a monastery, his study for a doctorate in theology at the University of Wittenberg, the writing of his Ninety-Five Theses, and his dramatic stand at the Diet of Worms. The movie is based more on legends about Luther than on a strict adherence to the historical facts.

Q *What historical errors can you find in this portrayal of Luther's career? Does the film reveal what made Luther a rebel? Why or why not?*

The Rise of Lutheranism

At the beginning of 1522, Luther returned to Wittenberg in Electoral Saxony and began to organize a reformed church. While at the Wartburg Castle, Luther's foremost achievement was his translation of the New Testament into German. Within twelve years, his German New Testament had sold almost 200,000 copies. Lutheranism had wide appeal and spread rapidly, but not primarily through the written word since only 4 to 5 percent of people in Germany were literate. And most of these were in urban areas.

Instead, the primary means of disseminating Luther's ideas was the sermon. The preaching of evangelical sermons, based on a return to the original message of the Bible, found favor throughout Germany. In city after city, the arrival of preachers presenting Luther's teachings was soon followed by a public debate in which the new preachers proved victorious. State authorities then instituted a reform of the church.

Also useful to the spread of the Reformation were pamphlets illustrated with vivid woodcuts portraying the pope as a hideous Antichrist and titled with catchy phrases such as "I Wonder Why There Is No Money in the Land" (which, of course, was an attack on papal greed). Luther also insisted on the use of music as a means to teach the Gospel, and his own composition, "A Mighty Fortress Is Our God," became the battle hymn of the Reformation:

With our power nothing is done.
We are soon lost.
But for us fights the mighty one
Whom God himself has chosen.
You ask, who is this?
He is called Jesus Christ
The Lord God of hosts.
And there is no other God.
He must hold the field forever.[8]

THE SPREAD OF LUTHER'S IDEAS Lutheranism spread to both princely and ecclesiastical states in northern and central Germany as well as to two-thirds of the free imperial cities,

bpk, Berlin/Kupferstichkabinett, SMB/Jörg P. Anders//Art Resource, NY

Woodcut: Luther Versus the Pope. In the 1520s, after Luther's return to Wittenberg, his teachings began to spread rapidly, ending ultimately in a reform movement supported by state authorities. Pamphlets containing picturesque woodcuts were important in the spread of Luther's ideas. In the woodcut shown here, the crucified Jesus attends Luther's service on the left, while on the right the pope is at a table selling indulgences.

especially those of southern Germany, where prosperous burghers, for both religious and secular reasons, became committed to Luther's cause. Nuremberg, where an active city council led by the dynamic city secretary Lazarus Spengler (SCHPEN-ler) brought about a conversion as early as 1525, was the first imperial city to convert to Lutheranism. Luther had visited the city in 1518 and made a number of friends and supporters there, including some prominent men. Albrecht Dürer, the artist (see Chapter 12) said, "In my opinion, it is exactly here that Luther has helped to clarify the situation by making it a point to trust God more than oneself, worldly works, and the laws of human beings."[9] At its outset, the Reformation in Germany was largely an urban phenomenon. Three-fourths of the early converts to the reform movement were from the clergy, many of them from the upper classes, which made it easier for them to work with the ruling elites in the cities.

A series of crises in the mid-1520s made it apparent, however, that spreading the word of God was not as easy as Luther had originally envisioned—the usual plight of most reformers. Luther experienced dissent within his own ranks in Wittenberg from people such as Andreas Carlstadt (KARL-shtaht), who wished to initiate a more radical reform by abolishing all relics, images, and the Mass. Luther had no sooner dealt with them than he began to face opposition from the Christian humanists. Many had initially supported Luther, believing that he shared their goal of reforming the abuses within the church. But when it became apparent that Luther's movement threatened the unity of Christendom, the older generation of Christian humanists, including Erasmus, broke with the reformer. A younger generation of Christian humanists, however, played a significant role in Lutheranism. When Philip Melanchthon (muh-LANK-tun) (1497–1560) arrived in Wittenberg in 1518 at the age of twenty-one to teach Greek and Hebrew, he was immediately attracted to Luther's ideas and became a staunch supporter.

THE PEASANTS' WAR Luther's greatest challenge in the mid-1520s, however, came from the Peasants' War. Peasant dissatisfaction in Germany stemmed from several sources. Many peasants had not been touched by the gradual economic improvement of the early sixteenth century. In some areas, especially southwestern Germany, influential local lords continued to abuse their peasants, and new demands for taxes and other services caused them to wish for a return to "the good old days." Social discontent soon became entangled with religious revolt as peasants looked to Martin Luther, believing that he would support them. It was not Luther, however, but one of his ex-followers, the radical Thomas Müntzer (MOON-tsur), himself a pastor, who inflamed the peasants against their rulers with his fiery language: "Strike while the iron is hot!" Revolt first erupted in southwestern Germany in June 1524 and spread northward and eastward.

Luther reacted quickly and vehemently against the peasants. In his pamphlet *Against the Robbing and Murdering Hordes of Peasants*, he called on the German princes to "smite, slay and stab" the stupid and stubborn peasantry (see the box on p. 374). Luther, who knew how much his reformation of the church depended on the full support of the German princes and magistrates, supported the rulers, although he also blamed them for helping to set off the rebellion by their earlier harsh treatment of the peasants. To Luther, the state and its rulers were ordained by God and given the authority to maintain the peace and order necessary for the spread of the Gospel. It was the duty of princes to put down all revolts. By May 1525, the German princes had ruthlessly suppressed the peasant hordes. By this time, Luther found himself ever more dependent on state authorities for the growth and maintenance of his reformed church.

CHRONOLOGY	Luther's Reform Movement
Ninety-Five Theses	1517
Leipzig Debate	1519
Diet and Edict of Worms	1521
Peasants' War	1524–1525

Organizing the Church

Justification by faith alone was the starting point for most of Protestantism's major doctrines. Since Luther downplayed the role of good works in salvation, the sacraments also had to be redefined. No longer regarded as merit-earning works, they were now viewed as divinely established signs signifying the promise of salvation. Based on his interpretation of scriptural authority, Luther kept only two of the Catholic Church's seven sacraments—baptism and the Lord's Supper. Baptism signified rebirth through grace. Regarding the Lord's Supper, Luther denied the Catholic doctrine of **transubstantiation**, which taught that the substance of the bread and wine consumed in the rite is miraculously transformed into the body and blood of Jesus. Yet he continued to insist on the real presence of Jesus's body and blood in the bread and wine given as a testament to God's forgiveness of sin.

Luther's emphasis on the importance of Scripture led him to reject the Catholic belief that the authority of Scripture must be supplemented by the traditions and decrees of the church. The word of God as revealed in the Bible was sufficient authority in religious affairs. A hierarchical priesthood was thus unnecessary since all Christians who followed the word of God were their own priests, constituting a "priesthood of all believers." Even though Luther thus considered the true church to be an invisible entity, the difficulties of actually establishing a reformed church led him to believe that a tangible, organized church was needed. Since the Catholic ecclesiastical hierarchy had been scrapped, Luther came to rely increasingly on the princes or state authorities to organize and guide the new Lutheran reformed churches. He had little choice. Secular authorities in Germany, as elsewhere, were soon playing an important role in church affairs. By 1530, in the German states that had converted to Lutheranism, both princes and city councils appointed officials who visited churches in their territories and regulated matters of worship. The Lutheran churches in Germany (and later in Scandinavia) quickly became territorial

LUTHER AND THE "ROBBING AND MURDERING HORDES OF PEASANTS"

THE PEASANTS' WAR OF 1524–1525 encompassed a series of uprisings by German peasants who were suffering from economic changes they did not comprehend. Led by radical religious leaders, the revolts quickly became entangled with the religious revolt set in motion by Luther's defiance of the church. But it was soon clear that Luther himself did not believe in any way in social revolution. This excerpt is taken from Luther's pamphlet written in May 1525 at the height of the peasants' power but not published until after their defeat.

Martin Luther, *Against the Robbing and Murdering Hordes of Peasants*

The peasants have taken on themselves the burden of three terrible sins against God and man, by which they have abundantly merited death in body and soul. In the first place they have sworn to be true and faithful, submissive and obedient, to their rulers, as Christ commands, when he says, "Render unto Caesar the things that are Caesar's," and in Romans XIII, "Let everyone be subject unto the higher powers." Because they are breaking this obedience, and are setting themselves against the higher powers, willfully and with violence, they have forfeited body and soul, as faithless, perjured, lying, disobedient knaves and scoundrels are wont to do. . . .

In the second place, they are starting a rebellion, and violently robbing and plundering monasteries and castles which are not theirs, by which they have a second time deserved death in body and soul, if only as highwaymen and murderers. . . . For rebellion is not simple murder, but is like a great fire, which attacks and lays waste a whole land. . . . Therefore, let everyone who can, smite, slay and stab, secretly or openly, remembering that nothing can be more poisonous, hurtful or devilish than a rebel. . . .

In the third place, they cloak this terrible and horrible sin with the Gospel, call themselves "Christian brothers," receive oaths and homage, and compel people to hold with them to these abominations. Thus, they become the greatest of all blasphemers of God and slanderers of his holy Name, serving the devil, under the outward appearance of the Gospel, thus earning death in body and soul ten times over. . . . It does not help the peasants, when they pretend that, according to Genesis I and II, all things were created free and common, and that all of us alike have been baptized. . . . For baptism does not make men free in body and property, but in soul; and the Gospel does not make goods common. . . . Since the peasants, then, have brought both God and man down upon them and are already so many times guilty of death in body and soul . . . I must instruct the worldly governors how they are to act in the matter with a clear conscience.

First, I will not oppose a ruler who, even though he does not tolerate the Gospel, will smite and punish these peasants without offering to submit the case to judgment. For he is within his rights, since the peasants are not contending any longer for the Gospel, but have become faithless, perjured, disobedient, rebellious murderers, robbers and blasphemers, whom even heathen rulers have the right and power to punish; nay, it is their duty to punish them, for it is just for this purpose that they bear the sword, and are "the ministers of God upon him that doeth evil."

Q *What does this passage tell you about the political interests and sympathies of key religious reformers like Luther? Were the reformers really interested in bringing about massive social changes to accompany their religious innovations?*

Source: E. G. Rupp and B. Drewery, *Martin Luther: Documents of Modern History* (London: Palgrave Macmillan, 1970).

or state churches in which the state supervised and disciplined church members.

As part of the development of these state-dominated churches, Luther also instituted new religious services to replace the Mass. These featured a worship service consisting of a vernacular liturgy that focused on Bible reading, preaching the word of God, and song. Following his own denunciation of clerical celibacy, Luther married a former nun, Katherina von Bora (kat-uh-REE-nuh fun BOH-rah), in 1525. His union provided a model of married and family life for the new Protestant minister.

Germany and the Reformation: Religion and Politics

From its very beginning, the fate of Luther's movement was closely tied to political affairs. In 1519, Charles I, king of Spain and grandson of Emperor Maximilian (see Chart 13.1), was elected Holy Roman Emperor as Charles V. Charles ruled over an immense empire, consisting of Spain and its overseas possessions, the traditional Austrian Habsburg lands, Bohemia, Hungary, the Low Countries, and the kingdom of Naples in southern Italy (see Map 13.1). The extent of his possessions was reflected in the languages he used. He said once that he spoke Spanish to God, Italian to women, French to men, and German to his horse. Politically, Charles wanted to maintain his dynasty's control over his enormous empire; religiously, he hoped to preserve the unity of the Catholic faith throughout his empire. Despite Charles's strengths, his empire was overextended, and he spent a lifetime in futile pursuit of his goals. Four major problems—the French, the papacy, the Turks, and Germany's internal situation—cost him both his dream and his health. At the same time, the emperor's problems gave Luther's

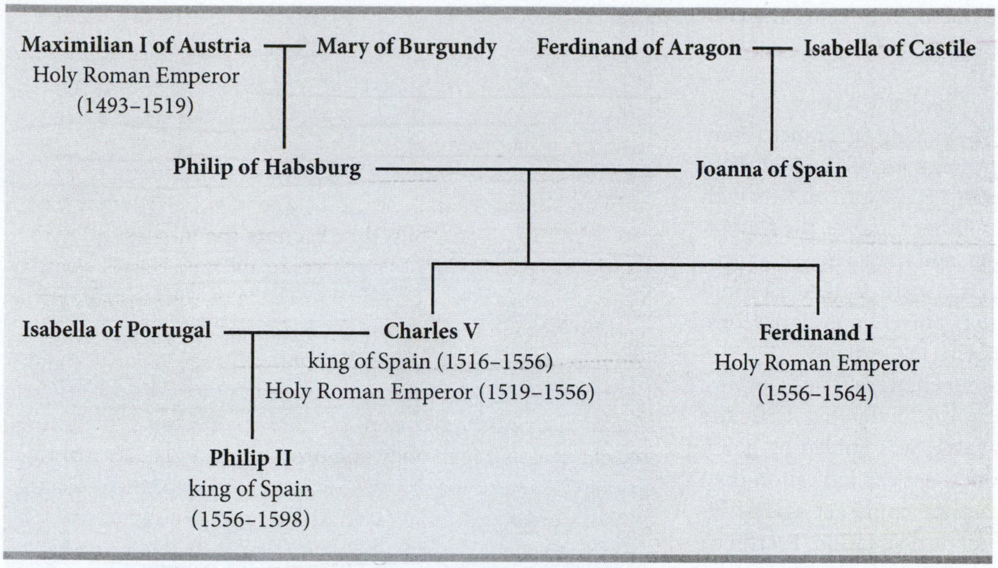

Chart 13.1 The Habsburgs as Holy Roman Emperors and Kings of Spain

MAP 13.1 The Empire of Charles V. Charles V spent much of his reign fighting wars in Italy, against France and the Ottoman Empire, and within the borders of the Holy Roman Empire. He failed in his main goal to secure Europe for Catholicism: the Peace of Augsburg in 1555 recognized the equality of Catholicism and Lutheranism and let each German prince choose his realm's religion.

Q *Why would France feel threatened by the empire of Charles V?*

movement time to grow and organize before facing the concerted onslaught of the Catholic forces.

THE FRENCH AND THE PAPACY Charles V's chief political concern was his rivalry with the Valois king of France, Francis I (1515–1547). Encircled by the possessions of the Habsburg empire, Francis became embroiled in a series of conflicts with Charles over disputed territories in southern France, the Netherlands, the Rhineland, northern Spain, and Italy. These conflicts, known as the Habsburg-Valois Wars, were fought intermittently for twenty-four years (1521–1544), preventing Charles from concentrating on the Lutheran problem in Germany.

Meanwhile, Charles faced two other enemies. The Habsburg emperor expected papal cooperation in dealing with the Lutheran heresy. Papal policy, however, was guided by political considerations, not religious ones, a clear indication that, like the Catholic king of France, a pope could act against his religious interests because of the political situation. Fearful of Charles's power in Italy, Pope Clement VII (1523–1534) joined the side of Francis I in the second Habsburg-Valois War (1527–1529), with catastrophic results. In April 1527, the Spanish-imperial army of Charles V went berserk while attacking Rome and gave the capital of Catholicism a fearful and bloody sacking. Sobered by the experience, Clement came to terms with the emperor, and by 1530, Charles V stood supreme over much of Italy.

THE OTTOMAN EMPIRE In the meantime, Charles V also faced problems in the eastern part of his empire. In the fifteenth century, the Ottoman Turks had overrun Constantinople and established control over much of the Balkans in southeastern Europe (see Chapter 12). Now, in the first decades of the sixteenth century, the Ottomans posed a new threat to Europe. Ottoman armies had taken control of much of the North African coast and captured the Christian island of Rhodes. Under their new leader, Suleiman (SOO-lay-mahn) the Magnificent (1520–1566), Ottoman forces had defeated and killed King Louis of Hungary, Charles's brother-in-law, at the Battle of Mohács (MOH-hach) in 1526. Subsequently, the Ottomans overran most of Hungary, moved into Austria, and advanced as far as Vienna, where they were finally repulsed in 1529. The emperor and much of Christian Europe breathed a sigh of relief but still remained fearful of another Ottoman attack.

POLITICS IN GERMANY By the end of 1529, Charles was ready to deal with Germany. The second Habsburg-Valois War had ended, the Turks had been defeated temporarily, and the pope had been subdued. The internal political situation in the Holy Roman Empire was not in his favor, however. Germany was a land of several hundred territorial states: princely states, ecclesiastical principalities, and free imperial cities. Though all owed loyalty to the emperor, Germany's medieval development had enabled these states to become quite independent of imperial authority. They had no desire to have a strong emperor.

Charles's attempt to settle the Lutheran problem at the Diet of Augsburg in 1530 proved completely inadequate,

Charles V. Charles V sought to maintain religious unity throughout his vast empire by keeping all his subjects within the bounds of the Catholic Church. Due to his conflict with Francis I of France and his difficulties with the Turks, the papacy, and the German princes, Charles was never able to check the spread of Lutheranism. This portrait of Charles V is by the Venetian painter Titian.

and the emperor wound up demanding that the Lutherans return to the Catholic Church by April 15, 1531. In February 1531, fearful of Charles's intentions, eight princes and eleven imperial cities—all Lutheran—formed a defensive alliance known as the Schmalkaldic League. These Protestant German states vowed to assist each other "whenever any one of us is attacked on account of the Word of God and the doctrine of the Gospel." Religion was dividing the empire into two armed camps.

The renewed threat of the Turks against Vienna forced Charles once again to seek compromise instead of war with the Protestant authorities. From 1532 to 1535, Charles was forced to fight off an Ottoman, Arab, and Barbary attack on the Mediterranean coasts of Italy and Spain. Two additional

CHRONOLOGY	Politics and the German Reformation
First Habsburg-Valois War	1521–1525
Second Habsburg-Valois War	1527–1529
Defeat of the Turks at Vienna	1529
Diet of Augsburg	1530
Third Habsburg-Valois War	1535–1538
Fourth Habsburg-Valois War	1542–1544
Schmalkaldic Wars	1546–1555
Peace of Augsburg	1555

Habsburg-Valois Wars (1535–1538 and 1542–1544) soon followed and kept Charles preoccupied with military campaigns in southern France and the Low Countries. Finally, Charles made peace with Francis in 1544 and the Turks in 1545. Fifteen years after the Diet of Augsburg, Charles was finally free to resolve his problem in Germany.

By the time of Luther's death in February 1546, all hopes of a peaceful compromise had faded. Charles brought a sizable imperial army of German, Dutch, Italian, and Spanish troops to do battle with the Protestants. In the first phase of the Schmalkaldic Wars (1546–1547), the emperor's forces decisively defeated the Lutherans at the Battle of Mühlberg (MOOL-bayrk). Charles V was at the zenith of his power, and the Protestant cause seemed doomed.

Appearances proved misleading, however. The Schmalkaldic League was soon reestablished, and the German Protestant princes allied themselves with the new French king, Henry II (1547–1559)—a Catholic—to revive the war in 1552. This time Charles was less fortunate and had to negotiate a truce. Exhausted by his efforts to maintain religious orthodoxy and the unity of his empire, Charles abandoned German affairs to his brother Ferdinand, abdicated all of his titles in 1556, and retired to his country estate in Spain to spend the remaining two years of his life in solitude.

An end to religious warfare in Germany came in 1555 with the Peace of Augsburg, which marked an important turning point in the history of the Reformation. The agreement formally acknowledged the division of Christianity, with Lutheranism granted equal legal standing with Catholicism. Moreover, the peace settlement accepted the right of each German ruler to determine the religion of his subjects (but not the right of the subjects to choose their religion). Charles's hope for a united empire had been completely dashed, and the ideal of medieval Christian unity was irretrievably lost. The rapid proliferation of new Protestant groups served to underscore that new reality.

The Swiss Cantons

The Spread of the Protestant Reformation

FOCUS QUESTIONS: What were the main tenets of Lutheranism, Zwinglianism, Anabaptism, and Calvinism, and how did they differ from each other and from Catholicism? What impact did political, economic, and social conditions have on the development of these four reform movements?

For both Catholics and Protestant reformers, Luther's heresy raised the question of what constituted the correct interpretation of the Bible. The inability to agree on this issue led not only to theological confrontations but also to bloody warfare as each Christian group was unwilling to admit that it could be wrong.

Lutheranism in Scandinavia

In 1397, the Union of Kalmar had brought about the unification of Denmark, Norway, and Sweden under the rule of one monarch, the king of Denmark. This union, however, failed to achieve any real social or political unification of the three states, particularly since the independent-minded landed nobles worked to frustrate any increase in monarchical centralization. By the beginning of the sixteenth century, the union was on the brink of disintegration. In 1520, Christian II (1513–1523) of Denmark, ruler of the three Scandinavian kingdoms, was overthrown by Swedish barons led by Gustavus Vasa. Three years later, Vasa became king of an independent Sweden (1523–1560) and took the lead in establishing a Lutheran Reformation in his country and by the 1530s had created a Swedish Lutheran National Church.

Meanwhile, the Danish nobility had also deposed Christian II as the king of Denmark. He was succeeded by his uncle, who became Frederick I (1523–1533). Frederick encouraged Lutheran preachers to spread their evangelical doctrines and to introduce a Lutheran liturgy into the Danish church service. In the 1530s, under Frederick's successor, Christian III (1534–1559), a Lutheran state church was installed with the king as the supreme authority in all ecclesiastical affairs. Christian was also instrumental in spreading Lutheranism to Norway. By the 1540s, Scandinavia had become a Lutheran stronghold. Like the German princes, the Scandinavian monarchs had been the dominant force in establishing state-run churches.

The Zwinglian Reformation

In the sixteenth century, the Swiss Confederation was a loose association of thirteen self-governing states called cantons. Theoretically part of the Holy Roman Empire, they had become virtually independent in 1499. The six forest cantons were democratic republics; the seven urban cantons, which included Zürich, Bern, and Basel, were for the most part governed by city councils controlled by narrow oligarchies of wealthy citizens.

Ulrich Zwingli (OOL-rikh TSFING-lee) (1484–1531) was a product of the Swiss forest cantons. The precocious son of a relatively prosperous peasant, the young Zwingli eventually obtained both bachelor of arts and master of arts degrees. During his university education at Vienna and Basel, Zwingli was strongly influenced by Christian humanism. Ordained a priest in 1506, he accepted a parish post in rural Switzerland until his appointment as a cathedral priest in the Great Minster of Zürich in 1518. Through his preaching there, Zwingli began the Reformation in Switzerland.

Zwingli's preaching of the Gospel caused such unrest that in 1523 the city council held a public disputation or debate in the town hall. The disputation became a standard method of spreading the Reformation to many cities. It gave an advantage to reformers, since they had the power of new ideas and Catholics were not used to defending their teachings. The victory went to Zwingli's party, and the council declared that "Mayor, Council and Great Council of Zürich, in order to do away with disturbance and discord, have upon due deliberation and consultation decided and resolved that Master Zwingli should continue as heretofore to proclaim the Gospel and the pure sacred Scripture."[10]

REFORMS IN ZÜRICH Over the next two years, a city council strongly influenced by Zwingli promulgated evangelical reforms in Zürich. Zwingli looked to the state to supervise the church. He declared that a church without the magistrate is "mutilated and incomplete." The city council abolished relics and images, removed all paintings and decorations from the churches, and replaced them with whitewashed walls. As Zwingli remarked, "The images are not to be endured; for all that God has forbidden, there can be no compromise."[11] A new liturgy consisting of Scripture reading, prayer, and sermons replaced the Mass, and music was eliminated from the service as a distraction from the pure word of God. Monasticism, pilgrimages, the veneration of saints, clerical celibacy, and the pope's authority were all abolished as remnants of papal Christianity. Zwingli's movement soon spread to other cities in Switzerland, including Bern in 1528 and Basel in 1529.

A FUTILE SEARCH FOR UNITY By 1528, Zwingli's reform movement faced a serious political problem as the forest cantons remained staunchly Catholic. Zürich feared that they would ally with the Habsburgs. To counteract this danger, Zwingli attempted to build a league of evangelical cities by seeking an agreement with Luther and the German reformers. An alliance between them seemed possible, since the Reformation had spread to the southern German cities, especially Strasbourg, where Martin Bucer (1491–1551) had instituted a moderate reform movement containing characteristics of both Luther's and Zwingli's movements. Both the German and the Swiss reformers realized the need for unity to defend against imperial and conservative opposition.

Gianni Dagli Orti/The Art Archive at Art Resource, NY

Zwingli. Ulrich Zwingli began the Reformation in Switzerland through his preaching in Zürich. Zwingli's theology was accepted in Zürich and soon spread to other Swiss cities. This portrait of Zwingli was done by an unknown artist in the early sixteenth century.

Protestant political leaders, especially Landgrave Philip of Hesse, fearful that Charles V would take advantage of the division between the reformers, attempted to promote an alliance of the Swiss and German reformed churches by persuading the leaders of both groups to attend a colloquy (conference) at Marburg to resolve their differences. Able to agree on virtually everything else, the gathering splintered over the interpretation of the Lord's Supper (see the box on p. 379). Zwingli believed that the scriptural words "This is my body" and "This is my blood" should be taken symbolically, not literally. To Zwingli, the Lord's Supper was only a meal of remembrance, and he refused to accept Luther's insistence on the real presence of the body and blood of Jesus "in, with, and under the bread and wine." The Marburg Colloquy of 1529 produced no agreement and no evangelical alliance. It was a foretaste of the issues that would divide one reform group from another and lead to the creation of different Protestant groups.

In October 1531, war erupted between the Swiss Protestant and Catholic cantons. Zürich's army was routed, and Zwingli was found wounded on the battlefield. His enemies killed him, cut up his body, burned the pieces, and scattered the ashes. This Swiss civil war of 1531 provided an early indication of what religious passions would lead to in the sixteenth century. Unable to find peaceful ways to agree on the meaning of the Gospel, the disciples of Christianity resorted to violence and decision by force. When he heard of Zwingli's death, Martin Luther, who

OPPOSING VIEWPOINTS

A Reformation Debate: Conflict at Marburg

DEBATES PLAYED A CRUCIAL ROLE in the Reformation period. They were a primary instrument in introducing the Reformation into innumerable cities as well as a means of resolving differences among like-minded Protestant groups. This selection contains an excerpt from the vivacious and often brutal debate between Luther and Zwingli over the sacrament of the Lord's Supper at Marburg in 1529. The two protagonists failed to reach agreement.

The Marburg Colloquy, 1529

THE HESSIAN CHANCELLOR FEIGE: My gracious prince and lord [Landgrave Philip of Hesse] has summoned you for the express and urgent purpose of settling the dispute over the sacrament of the Lord's Supper. . . . Let everyone on both sides present his arguments in a spirit of moderation, . . . Now then, Doctor Luther, you may proceed.

LUTHER: Noble prince, gracious lord! Undoubtedly the colloquy is well intentioned. . . . Although I have no intention of changing my mind, which is firmly made up, I will nevertheless present the grounds of my belief and show where the others are in error. . . . Your basic contentions are these: In the last analysis you wish to prove that a body cannot be in two places at once, and you produce arguments about the unlimited body which are based on natural reason. I do not question how Christ can be God and man and how the two natures can be joined. For God is more powerful than all our ideas, and we must submit to his word.

Prove that Christ's body is not there where the Scripture says, "This is my body!" Rational proofs I will not listen to. It is God who commands, "Take, eat, this is my body." I request, therefore, valid scriptural proof to the contrary.

ZWINGLI: I insist that the words of the Lord's Supper must be figurative. This is ever apparent, and even required by the article of faith: "taken up into heaven, seated at the right hand of the Father." Otherwise, it would be absurd to look for him in the Lord's Supper at the same time that Christ is telling us that he is in heaven. One and the same body cannot possibly be in different places. . . .

LUTHER: I call upon you as before: your basic contentions are shaky. Give way, and give glory to God!

ZWINGLI: And we call upon you to give glory to God and to quit begging the question. The issue at stake is this: Where is the proof of your position? . . . You're trying to outwit me. I stand by this passage in the sixth chapter of John, verse 63, and shall not be shaken from it. You'll have to sing another tune.

LUTHER: You're being obnoxious.

ZWINGLI: (*excitedly*) Don't you believe that Christ was attempting in John 6 to help those who did not understand?

LUTHER: You're trying to dominate things! You insist on passing judgment . . . It is your point that must be proved, not mine. But let us stop this sort of thing. It serves no purpose.

ZWINGLI: It certainly does! It is for you to prove that the passage in John 6 speaks of a physical repast.

LUTHER: You express yourself poorly and make about as much progress as a cane standing in a corner. You're going nowhere.

ZWINGLI: No, no, no! This is the passage that will break your neck!

LUTHER: Don't be so sure of yourself. Necks don't break this way. You're in Hesse, not Switzerland.

Q *How did the positions of Zwingli and Luther on the sacrament of the Lord's Supper differ? What was the purpose of this debate? Based on this example, why do you think Reformation debates led to further hostility rather than compromise and unity between religious and sectarian opponents? What implications did this have for the future of the Protestant Reformation?*

Source: "The Marburg Colloquy," in *Great Debates of the Reformation*, ed. D. Ziegler (New York: Modern Library, 1969).

had not forgotten the confrontation at Marburg, is supposed to have remarked that Zwingli "got what he deserved."

The Radical Reformation: The Anabaptists

Although many reformers were ready to allow the state to play an important, if not dominant, role in church affairs, some people rejected this kind of magisterial reformation and favored a far more radical reform movement. Collectively called the Anabaptists, these radicals were actually members of a large variety of groups who shared some common characteristics. Anabaptism was especially attractive to the peasants, weavers, miners, and artisans who had been adversely affected by the economic changes of the age.

THE IDEAS OF THE ANABAPTISTS Anabaptists everywhere held certain ideas in common. All felt that the true Christian church was a voluntary association of believers who had undergone spiritual rebirth and had then been baptized into the church. Anabaptists advocated adult rather than infant baptism. No one, they believed, should be forced to accept the truth of the Bible. They also tried to return literally to the practices and spirit of early Christianity. Adhering to the accounts of early Christian communities in the New Testament, they followed a strict sort of democracy in which all believers were considered equal. Each church chose its own minister, who might be any member of the community, since all Christians were considered priests (though women were often excluded). Those chosen as ministers had the duty to lead services, which were very simple and contained nothing not found in the early church. Like early Christians, Anabaptists, who called themselves "Christians" or "Saints," accepted that they would have to suffer for their faith. Anabaptists rejected theological speculation in favor of simple Christian living according to what they believed was the pure word of God. The Lord's Supper was interpreted as a remembrance, a meal of fellowship celebrated in the evening in private houses according to Jesus's example.

Unlike the Catholics and other Protestants, most Anabaptists believed in the complete separation of church and state. Not only was government to be excluded from the realm of religion, but it was not even supposed to exercise political jurisdiction over real Christians. Human law had no power over those whom God had saved. Anabaptists refused to hold political office or bear arms because many took the commandment "Thou shall not kill" literally, although some Anabaptist groups did become quite violent. Their political beliefs as much as their religious beliefs caused the Anabaptists to be regarded as dangerous radicals who threatened the very fabric of sixteenth-century society. Indeed, the chief thing Protestants and Catholics could agree on was the need to stamp out the Anabaptists.

VARIETIES OF ANABAPTISTS One early group of Anabaptists known as the Swiss Brethren arose in Zürich. Their ideas, especially adult baptism, frightened Zwingli, and they were expelled from the city in 1523. Because the first members of the Swiss Brethren who were baptized as adults had already been baptized as children (in the Catholic Church), their opponents labeled them Anabaptists or Rebaptists. Under Roman law, such people were subject to the death penalty.

As the teachings of the Swiss Brethren spread through southern Germany, the Austrian Habsburg lands, and Switzerland, Anabaptists suffered ruthless persecution, especially after the Peasants' War of 1524–1525, when the upper classes resorted to repression. Virtually eradicated in Germany, Anabaptist survivors emerged in Moravia and Poland, and in the Netherlands, Anabaptism took on a strange form.

In the 1530s, the city of Münster, in Westphalia in northwestern Germany near the Dutch border, was the site of an Anabaptist uprising that determined the fate of Dutch Anabaptism. Seat of a powerful Catholic prince-bishop, Münster had experienced severe economic disasters, including crop failure and plague. Although converted to Lutheranism in 1532, Münster experienced a more radical mass religious hysteria that led to legal recognition for the Anabaptists. Soon Münster became a haven for Anabaptists from the surrounding neighborhood, especially the more wild-eyed variety known as Melchiorites, who adhered to a vivid **millenarianism**. They believed that the end of the world was at hand and that they would usher in the kingdom of God with Münster as the New Jerusalem. By the end of February 1534, these millenarian Anabaptists had taken control of the city, driven out everyone they considered godless or unbelievers, burned all books except the Bible, and proclaimed communal ownership of all property. Eventually, the leadership of this New Jerusalem fell into the hands of one man, John of Leiden, who proclaimed himself king of the New Jerusalem. As king, he would lead the elect from Münster out to cover the entire world and purify it of evil by the sword in preparation for Jesus's Second Coming and the creation of a New Age. In this new kingdom, John of Leiden believed, all goods would be held in common and the saints would live without suffering.

But it was not to be. As the Catholic prince-bishop of Münster gathered a large force and laid siege to the city, the new king repeatedly had to postpone the ushering forth from Münster. Finally, after many inhabitants had starved, a joint army of Catholics and Lutherans recaptured the city in June 1535 and executed the radical Anabaptist leaders in gruesome fashion. The New Jerusalem had ceased to exist.

Purged of its fantasies and its more extreme elements, Dutch Anabaptism reverted to its pacifist tendencies, especially evident in the work of Menno Simons (1496–1561), the man most responsible for rejuvenating Dutch Anabaptism. A popular leader, Menno dedicated his life to the spread of a peaceful, evangelical Anabaptism that stressed separation from the world in order to truly emulate the life of Jesus. Simons imposed strict discipline on his followers and banned those who refused to conform to the rules. The Mennonites, as his followers were called, spread from the Netherlands into northwestern Germany and eventually into Poland and Lithuania as well as the New World. Both the Mennonites and the Amish, who are also descended from the Anabaptists, maintain communities in the United States and Canada today.

The Reformation in England

The English Reformation was initiated by King Henry VIII (1509–1547), who wanted to divorce his first wife, Catherine of Aragon, because she had failed to produce a male heir. Furthermore, Henry had fallen in love with Anne Boleyn (BUH-lin *or* buh-LIN), a lady-in-waiting to Queen Catherine. Anne's unwillingness to be only the king's mistress and the king's desire to have a legitimate male heir made their marriage imperative, but the king's first marriage stood in the way.

Henry relied on Cardinal Wolsey, the highest-ranking English church official and lord chancellor to the king, to obtain from Pope Clement VII an annulment of the king's marriage. Normally, the pope might have been willing to oblige, but the sack of Rome in 1527 had made the pope dependent on the Holy Roman Emperor Charles V, who happened to be the nephew of Queen Catherine. Discretion dictated delay in granting the English king's request. Impatient with the process, Henry dismissed Wolsey in 1529.

Two new advisers now became the king's agents in fulfilling his wishes. These were Thomas Cranmer (1489–1556), who became archbishop of Canterbury in 1532, and Thomas Cromwell (1485–1540), the king's principal secretary after the fall of Wolsey. They advised the king to obtain an annulment of his marriage in England's own ecclesiastical courts. The most important step toward this goal was an act of Parliament cutting off all appeals from English church courts to Rome, a piece of legislation that essentially abolished papal authority in England. Henry no longer needed the pope to obtain his annulment. He was now in a hurry because Anne Boleyn had become pregnant and he had secretly married her in January 1533 to legitimize the expected heir. In May, as archbishop of Canterbury and head of the highest ecclesiastical court in England, Thomas Cranmer ruled that the king's marriage to Catherine was "null and absolutely void" and then validated Henry's marriage to Anne. At the beginning of June, Anne was crowned queen. Three months later, a child was born. Much to the king's disappointment, the baby was a girl, whom they named Elizabeth.

In 1534, Parliament completed the break of the Church of England with Rome by passing the Act of Supremacy, which declared that the king was "taken, accepted, and reputed the only supreme head on earth of the Church of England." This meant that the English monarch now controlled the church in all matters of doctrine, clerical appointments, and discipline. In addition, Parliament passed the Treason Act, making it punishable by death to deny that the king was the supreme head of the church.

One who challenged the new order was Thomas More, the humanist and former lord chancellor, who saw clearly to the heart of the issue: loyalty to the pope in Rome was now treason in England. More refused to support the new laws and was duly tried for treason. At his trial, he asked, rhetorically, what the effect of the actions of the king and Parliament would be: "Therefore am I not bound . . . to conform my conscience to the Council of one realm [England] against the general Council of Christendom?"[12] Because his conscience could not accept the victory of the national state over the church, nor would he, as a Christian, bow his head to a secular ruler in matters of faith, More was beheaded in London on July 6, 1535.

Recent research that emphasizes the strength of Catholicism in England suggests that Thomas More was not alone in his view of the new order. In fact, one historian has argued that Catholicism was vibrant in England in both the fifteenth and sixteenth centuries; in his view, the English Reformation was alien to many English people.

THE NEW ORDER Thomas Cromwell worked out the details of the Tudor government's new role in church affairs based on the centralized power exercised by the king and Parliament. Cromwell also came to his extravagant king's financial rescue with a daring plan for the dissolution of the monasteries. About four hundred religious houses were closed in 1536, and the king confiscated their lands and possessions. Many were sold to nobles, gentry, and some merchants. The king added enormously to his treasury and also to his ranks of supporters, who now had a stake in the new Tudor order.

Although Henry VIII had broken with the papacy, little change occurred in matters of doctrine, theology, and ceremony. Some of his supporters, such as Archbishop Thomas Cranmer, wished to have a religious reformation as well as an administrative one, but Henry was unyielding. Nevertheless, some clergymen ignored Henry on the matter of priestly celibacy and secretly married.

The final decade of Henry's reign was preoccupied with foreign affairs, factional intrigue, and a continued effort to find the perfect wife. Henry soon tired of Anne Boleyn and had her beheaded in 1536 on a charge of adultery. His third wife, Jane Seymour, produced the long-awaited male heir but died twelve

National Museum Wales/Bridgeman Images

Henry VIII and His Successors. This allegorical painting of the Tudor succession, entitled *The Family of Henry VIII*, was done by an English artist about forty years after the death of Henry VIII. King Henry sits on his throne under the Tudor Coat of arms. At the far left is the figure of a Roman soldier representing the god of war. Next is Philip II of Spain, the husband of Mary Tudor, who stands at his right. To the right of Henry stand Edward, Elizabeth, and two female figures who represent peace and plenty.

days later. His fourth marriage, to Anne of Cleves, a German princess, was arranged for political reasons. Henry relied on a painted portrait of Anne when he made the arrangements, but he was disappointed at her physical appearance when he saw her in person and soon divorced her. His fifth wife, Catherine Howard, was more attractive but less moral. When she committed adultery, Henry had her beheaded. His last wife was Catherine Parr, who married the king in 1543 and outlived him. Henry was succeeded by the underage and sickly Edward VI (1547–1553), the son of his third wife.

Since the new king was only nine years old at the time of his accession to the throne, real control of England passed to a council of regency. During Edward's reign, Archbishop Cranmer and others inclined toward Protestant doctrines were able to move the Church of England in a more Protestant direction. New acts of Parliament instituted the right of the clergy to marry, eliminated images, and authorized a revised Protestant liturgy that was elaborated in a new prayer book and liturgical guide known as the Book of Common Prayer. These rapid changes in doctrine and liturgy aroused much opposition and prepared the way for the reaction that occurred when Mary, Henry's first daughter by Catherine of Aragon, came to the throne.

REACTION UNDER MARY Mary (1553–1558) was a Catholic who fully intended to restore England to the Roman Catholic fold. But her restoration of Catholicism, achieved by joint action of the monarch and Parliament, aroused opposition. There was widespread antipathy to Mary's unfortunate marriage to Philip II, son of Charles V and the future king of Spain. Philip was strongly disliked in England, and Mary's foreign policy of alliance with Spain aroused further hostility, especially when her forces lost Calais, the last English possession in France after the Hundred Years' War. The burning of more than three hundred Protestant heretics aroused further ire against "bloody Mary." As a result of her policies, Mary managed to achieve the opposite of what she had intended: England was more Protestant by the end of her reign than it had been at the beginning. When she came to power, Protestantism had become identified with church destruction and religious anarchy. Now people identified it with English resistance to Spanish interference. Mary's death in 1558 ended the restoration of Catholicism in England.

John Calvin and Calvinism

Of the second generation of Protestant reformers, one stands out as the systematic theologian and organizer of the Protestant movement—John Calvin (1509–1564). Calvin received a remarkably diverse education in humanistic studies and law in his native France. He was also influenced by Luther's writings, which were being circulated and read by French intellectuals as early as 1523. In 1533, Calvin experienced a religious crisis that determined the rest of his life's work. He described it in these words:

> God, by a sudden conversion, subdued and brought my mind to a teachable frame, which was more hardened in such matters than might have been expected from one at my early period of life. Having thus received some taste and knowledge of true godliness, I was immediately inflamed with so intense a desire to make progress therein, although I did not leave off other studies, I yet pursued them with less ardor.[13]

Calvin's conversion was solemn and straightforward. He was so convinced of the inner guidance of God that he became the most determined of all the Protestant reformers.

After his conversion and newfound conviction, Calvin was no longer safe in Paris, since King Francis I periodically persecuted Protestants. Eventually, Calvin made his way to Basel, where in 1536 he published the first edition of the *Institutes of the Christian Religion*, a masterful synthesis of Protestant thought that immediately secured his reputation as one of the new leaders of Protestantism.

CALVIN'S IDEAS On most important doctrines, Calvin stood very close to Luther. He adhered to the doctrine of justification by faith alone to explain how humans achieved salvation. Calvin also placed much emphasis on the absolute sovereignty of God or the "power, grace, and glory of God." Thus, "God asserts his possession of omnipotence, and claims our

The Reformed Church of France, Paris, France/Bridgeman Images

John Calvin. After a conversion experience, John Calvin abandoned his life as a humanist and became a reformer. In 1536, Calvin began working to reform the city of Geneva, where he remained until his death in 1564. This is a seventeenth-century portrait of Calvin done by a member of the Swiss school.

acknowledgment of this attribute; not such as is imagined by sophists, vain, idle, and almost asleep, but vigilant, efficacious, operative and engaged in continual action."[14]

One of the ideas derived from his emphasis on the absolute sovereignty of God—**predestination**—gave a unique cast to Calvin's teachings, although Luther also believed in this principle. This "eternal decree," as Calvin called it, meant that God had predestined some people to be saved (the elect) and others to be damned (the reprobate). According to Calvin, "He has once for all determined, both whom he would admit to salvation, and whom he would condemn to destruction.[15] Calvin identified three tests that might indicate possible salvation: an open profession of faith, a "decent and godly life," and participation in the sacraments of baptism and communion. In no instance did Calvin ever suggest that worldly success or material wealth was a sign of election. Significantly for the future of Calvinism, although Calvin himself stressed that there could be no absolute certainty of salvation, some of his followers did not always make this distinction. The practical psychological effect of predestination was to give some later Calvinists an unshakable conviction that they were doing God's work on earth. It is no accident that Calvinism became the activist international form of Protestantism.

To Calvin, the church was a divine institution responsible for preaching the word of God and administering the sacraments. Calvin kept the same two sacraments as other Protestant reformers, baptism and the Lord's Supper. Baptism was a sign of the remission of sins. Calvin believed in the real presence of Jesus in the sacrament of the Lord's Supper, but only in a spiritual sense. Jesus's body is at the right hand of God and thus cannot be in the sacrament, but to the believer, Jesus is spiritually present in the Lord's Supper.

CHRONOLOGY	New Reform Movements
The Zwinglian Reformation	
Zwingli made cathedral priest at Zürich	1518
Reform adopted in Zürich	1523
Marburg Colloquy	1529
The Anabaptists	
Anabaptists expelled from Zürich	1523
New Jerusalem in Münster	1534–1535
The Reformation in England	
Henry VIII	1509–1547
Act of Supremacy	1534
Edward VI	1547–1553
Mary	1553–1558
Calvin and Calvinism	
Institutes of the Christian Religion	1536
Calvin begins ministry in Geneva	1536
Ecclesiastical Ordinances	1541

CALVIN'S GENEVA Before 1536, John Calvin had essentially been a scholar. But in that year, he took up a ministry in Geneva that lasted, except for a brief exile (1538–1541), until his death in 1564. Calvin achieved a major success in 1541 when the city council accepted his new church constitution, known as the Ecclesiastical Ordinances.

This document created a church government that used both clergy and laymen in the service of the church. The Consistory, a special body for enforcing moral discipline, was set up as a court to oversee the moral life and doctrinal purity of Genevans (see the box on p. 384). As its power increased, the Consistory went from "fraternal corrections" to the use of public penance and excommunication. More serious cases could be turned over to the city council for punishments greater than excommunication. During Calvin's last years, stricter laws against blasphemy were enacted and enforced with banishment and public whippings.

Calvin's success in Geneva enabled the city to become a vibrant center of Protestantism. John Knox, the Calvinist reformer of Scotland, called it "the most perfect school of Christ on earth." Following Calvin's lead, missionaries trained in Geneva were sent to all parts of Europe. Calvinism became established in France, the Netherlands, Scotland, and central and eastern Europe. By the mid-sixteenth century, Calvinism had replaced Lutheranism as the international form of Protestantism, and Calvin's Geneva stood as the fortress of the Reformation.

The Social Impact of the Protestant Reformation

FOCUS QUESTION: What impact did the Protestant Reformation have on society in the sixteenth century?

Because Christianity was such an integral part of European life, it was inevitable that the Reformation would have an impact on the family, education, and popular religious practices.

The Family

For centuries, Catholicism had praised the family and sanctified its existence by making marriage a sacrament. But the Catholic Church's high regard for abstinence from sex as the surest way to holiness made the celibate state of the clergy preferable to marriage. Nevertheless, because not all men could remain chaste, marriage offered the best means to control sexual intercourse and give it a purpose, the procreation of children. To some extent, this attitude persisted among the Protestant reformers; Luther, for example, argued that sex in marriage allowed one to "make use of this sex in order to avoid sin," and Calvin advised that every man should "abstain from marriage only so long as he is fit to observe celibacy." If "his power to tame lust fails him," then he must marry.

But the Reformation did bring some change to the conception of the family. Both Catholic and Protestant clergy preached sermons advocating a more positive approach to family relationships. The Protestants were especially important in

CALVIN'S RULES FOR THE CHURCH IN GENEVA

JOHN CALVIN HAD EMPHASIZED IN HIS reform movement that the church should have the ability to enforce proper behavior. Consequently, the Ecclesiastical Ordinances of 1541, the constitution of the church in Geneva, provided for an order of elders whose function was to cooperate with the pastors in maintaining discipline, "to watch over the conduct of every individual," as Calvin expressed it. These selections from Calvin's plan demonstrate the organization of the elders and some of the rules that were expected to be followed in Geneva.

Plan for the Elders and Consistory and Rules for the Church in Geneva

The office of the elders is to watch over the conduct of every individual, to admonish lovingly those whom they see doing wrong or leading an irregular life. When there is need, they should lay the matter before the body deputed to inflict paternal disciple [that is, the Consistory] of which they are members. As the Church is organized, it is best that the elders be chosen, two from the small council, four from the council of sixty, and six from the council of two hundred [the councils constituted the government of the city of Geneva]; they should be men of good life and honest, without reproach and beyond suspicion, above all, God-fearing without reproach and endowed with spiritual prudence. And they should be so chosen they be distributed in each quarter of the city, so that they can have an eye on everything. . . .

The elders, who have been described, shall assemble once a week with the ministers, namely Thursday morning, to see if there be any disorders in the Church and discuss together such remedies as shall be necessary. . . . If any one shall in contempt refuse to appear before them, it shall be their duty to inform the council, so that it may supply a remedy. . . .

Those who are found to have rosaries or idols to adore, let them be sent before the consistory, and in addition to the reproof they receive there, let them be sent before the council. Let the same be done with those who go on a pilgrimage. Those who observe feasts or [Catholic] fasts should only be admonished. Those who go to mass shall, besides being admonished, be sent before the council, and it shall consider the propriety of punishing the offenders by imprisonment or special fines, as it judges best.

He who blasphemes, swearing by the body or blood of our Lord, or in like manner, shall kiss the earth for the first offense, pay five sous for the second and ten for the third. He who contradicts the word of God shall be sent before the consistory for reproof, or before the council for punishment, as the case may require. If any one sings indecent songs, or dances or otherwise, he shall be kept in prison three days and then sent to the council.

Q *Why did Calvin and Geneva put so much emphasis on the role of the Consistory? What specific Catholic practices did Calvin and Geneva wish to stop?*

Source: J. H. Robinson, *Readings in European History*, vol. 2 (Boston: Ginn & Company, 1906), pp. 133–134.

developing this new view of the family. Because Protestantism had eliminated any idea of special holiness for celibacy, abolishing both monasticism and a celibate clergy, the family could be placed at the center of human life, and a new stress on "mutual love between man and wife" could be extolled. But were doctrine and reality the same? For more radical religious groups, at times they were (see the box on p. 385). One Anabaptist wrote to his wife before his execution, "My faithful helper, my loyal friend. I praise God that he gave you to me, you who have sustained me in all my trial."[16] But more often reality reflected the traditional roles of husband as the ruler and wife as the obedient servant whose chief duty was to please her husband. Luther stated it clearly:

> The rule remains with the husband, and the wife is compelled to obey him by God's command. He rules the home and the state, wages war, defends his possessions, tills the soil, builds, plants, etc. The woman on the other hand is like a nail driven into the wall . . . so the wife should stay at home and look after the affairs of the household, as one who has been deprived of the ability of administering those affairs that are outside and that concern the state. She does not go beyond her most personal duties.[17]

Obedience to her husband was not a wife's only role; her other important duty was to bear children. To Calvin and Luther, this function of women was part of the divine plan. God punishes women for the sins of Eve by the burdens of procreation and feeding and nurturing their children, but, said Luther, "it is a gladsome punishment if you consider the hope of eternal life and the honor of motherhood which had been left to her."[18] Although the Protestant reformers sanctified this role of woman as mother and wife, viewing it as a holy vocation, Protestantism also left few alternatives for women. Because monasticism had been destroyed, life as a nun was no longer available; for most Protestant women, family life was their only destiny. At the same time, by emphasizing the father as "ruler" and hence the center of household religion, Protestantism even removed the woman from her traditional role as controller of religion in the home.

Protestant reformers called on men and women to read the Bible and participate in religious services together. In this way, the reformers did provide a stimulus for the education of girls so that they could read the Bible and other religious literature. The city council of Zwickau, for example, established a girls' school in 1525. But these schools were designed to encourage

A PROTESTANT WOMAN

IN THE INITIAL ZEAL OF THE PROTESTANT REFORMATION, women were frequently allowed to play unusual roles. Katherine Zell of Germany (ca. 1497–1562) first preached beside her husband in 1527. After the deaths of her two children, she devoted the rest of her life to helping her husband and their reform faith. This selection is taken from one of her letters to the city of Strasbourg to defend herself against Ludwig Rabus, a Lutheran minister who had criticized her activities.

A Letter to the Whole Citizenship of the City of Strasbourg from Katherine Zell

So that you, dear Strasbourg, may know why I have first introduced this long speech about how I was loved in my youth and marriage (a speech that should be unnecessary!) so read now also what disrespect and judgment I have received in my old age. Therefore I have put here the letter that Mr. Ludwig sent to me. See how he ascribes to me insult, dishonor and godlessness together with all errors and heresies before God and human beings. He hands me over to the devil, with whom (God be praised) I have nothing to do forever, but I belong to my Lord Jesus Christ, who with His own blood redeemed me from the devil. So besides showing Rabus's letter I also seek to give a full accounting of my faith to anyone who wants it. In this account you may see whether my good husband's faith and mine are alike or unlike or whether my confidence and faith in the Lord Jesus have changed or not. However, I will clearly show Rabus that he and others have not kept to the pure knowledge of Jesus Christ as the old architects of our church taught us, . . .

Well then, this is now enough. However, if Mr. Ludwig is not satisfied with his injudicious condemnation of me, a poor solitary women, then I want to take God as my helper and further recount my dear husband's and my faith, teaching and life, and let anyone who wants to do so judge who has fallen away or climbed out of the right way! Now, dear Strasbourg, read this letter that Mr. Ludwig Rabus sent to me and judge without any favor and ill humor toward him or me. If I am owed this and have behaved as he describes, then I will gladly bear my punishment. But I believe that no Jew would give me such a testimony and bring such a judgment on me. I am also assured in my heart that I stand before my Lord Christ and His heavenly Father in a fitting way through the power of His Spirit; I stand before Him through the great and high merit of Christ in whom I believe, who also will bring to light this wicked letter or witness by Mr. Ludwig (which lies about me) on the great day of His glorious appearance, when all the books of the conscience with stand open. Yes, here I stand also before many people who know me, who know my life story and have seen me from youth: as a young woman in my father's house, in my marriage, and now in my grieving widowhood—let them also judge this matter between Mr. Ludwig and me.

Q *What was Katherine Zell's argument against Ludwig Rabus? Of what Protestant sect do you think she was a member?*

Source: Elsie McKee, *Church Mother: The Writings of a Protestant Reformer in Sixteenth-Century Germany* (Chicago: University of Chicago Press, 2006), pp. 230–231.

proper moral values rather than intellectual development and really did little to improve the position of women in society. Likewise, when women attempted to take more active roles in religious life, reformers—Lutheran and Calvinist alike—shrank back in horror. To them, the equality of the Gospel did not mean overthrowing the inequality of social classes or the sexes. Calvin also made clear what he thought of women rulers: "the government of women . . . is utterly at variance with the legitimate order of nature. . . . For a female rule badly organized is like a tyranny, and is to be tolerated until God sees fit to overthrow it."[19] Overall, the Protestant Reformation did not noticeably transform women's subordinate place in society.

Education in the Reformation

The Reformation had an important effect on the development of education in Europe. Renaissance humanism had significantly altered the content of education, and Protestant educators were very successful in implementing and using humanist methods in Protestant secondary schools and universities. Unlike the humanist schools, however, which had been mostly for an elite, the sons and a few daughters of the nobility and wealthier bourgeoisie, Protestant schools were aimed at a much wider audience. Protestantism created an increased need for at least a semiliterate body of believers who could read the Bible for themselves.

While adopting the classical emphasis of humanist schools, Protestant reformers broadened the base of the people being educated. Convinced of the need to provide the church with good Christians and good pastors as well as the state with good administrators and citizens, Martin Luther advocated that all children should have the opportunity of an education provided by the state. To that end, he urged the cities and villages of Saxony to establish schools paid for by the public. Luther's ideas were shared by his Wittenberg co-worker Philip Melanchthon, whose educational efforts earned him the title of *Praecepter Germaniae* (PREE-sep-tur gayr-MAHN-ee-ee), the Teacher of Germany. In his scheme for education in Saxony, Melanchthon divided students into three classes or divisions based on their age or capabilities.

Following Melanchthon's example, the Protestants in Germany were responsible for introducing the gymnasium, or secondary school, where the humanist emphasis on the liberal arts based on instruction in Greek and Latin was combined with religious instruction. Most famous was the school in Strasbourg

Öffentliche Kunstsammlung, Basel/Giraudon/Bridgeman Images

A Sixteenth-Century Classroom. Protestants in Germany developed secondary schools that combined instruction in the liberal arts with religious education. This scene from a painting by Ambrosius Holbein shows a schoolmaster instructing a pupil in the alphabet while his wife helps a little girl.

founded by Johannes Sturm in 1538, which served as a model for other Protestant schools. John Calvin's Genevan Academy, founded in 1559, was organized in two distinct parts. The "private school" or gymnasium was divided into seven classes for young people who were taught Latin and Greek grammar and literature as well as logic. In the "public school," students were taught philosophy, Hebrew, Greek, and theology. The Genevan Academy, which eventually became a university, came to concentrate on preparing ministers to spread the Calvinist view of the Gospel.

Religious Practices and Popular Culture

The Protestant reformers' attacks on the Catholic Church led to radical changes in religious practices. The Protestant Reformation abolished or severely curtailed such customary practices as indulgences, the veneration of relics and saints, pilgrimages, monasticism, and clerical celibacy. The elimination of saints put an end to the numerous celebrations of religious holy days and changed a community's sense of time. Thus, in Protestant communities, religious ceremonies and imagery, such as processions and statues, tended to be replaced with individual private prayer, family worship, and collective prayer and worship at the same time each week on Sunday.

In addition to abolishing saints' days and religious carnivals, some Protestant reformers even tried to eliminate customary forms of entertainment. The Puritans (as English Calvinists were called), for example, attempted to ban drinking in taverns, dramatic performances, and dancing. Dutch Calvinists denounced the tradition of giving small presents to children on the feast of Saint Nicholas, in early December. Many of these Protestant attacks on popular culture were unsuccessful, however. The importance of taverns in English social life made it impossible to eradicate them, and celebrating at Christmastime persisted in the Dutch Netherlands.

The Catholic Reformation

FOCUS QUESTION: What measures did the Roman Catholic Church take to reform itself and to combat Protestantism in the sixteenth century?

By the mid-sixteenth century, Lutheranism had become established in parts of Germany and Scandinavia, and Calvinism in parts of Switzerland, France, the Netherlands, and eastern Europe (see Map 13.2). In England, the split from Rome had resulted in the creation of a national church. The situation in Europe did not look particularly favorable for the Roman Catholic Church. Yet constructive, positive forces were already at work within the Catholic Church.

HISTORIANS DEBATE Catholic Reformation or Counter-Reformation?

There is no doubt that the Catholic Church underwent a revitalization in the sixteenth century. But was this reformation a **Catholic Reformation** or a Counter-Reformation? Some historians prefer to call it a "Counter-Reformation" to focus on the aspects that were a direct reaction against the Protestant movement. Historians who prefer to use "Catholic Reformation" point out that elements of reform were already present in the Catholic Church at the end of the fifteenth century and the beginning of the sixteenth, and that by the mid-sixteenth century, they came to be directed by a revived and reformed papacy, giving the church new strength.

No doubt, both positions on the nature of the reformation of the Catholic Church contain elements of truth. The Catholic Reformation revived the best features of medieval Catholicism and then adjusted them to meet new conditions, as is most apparent in the revival of mysticism and monasticism. The emergence of a new mysticism, closely tied to the traditions of Catholic piety, was especially evident in the life of the Spanish mystic Saint Teresa of Avila (1515–1582). A nun of the Carmelite

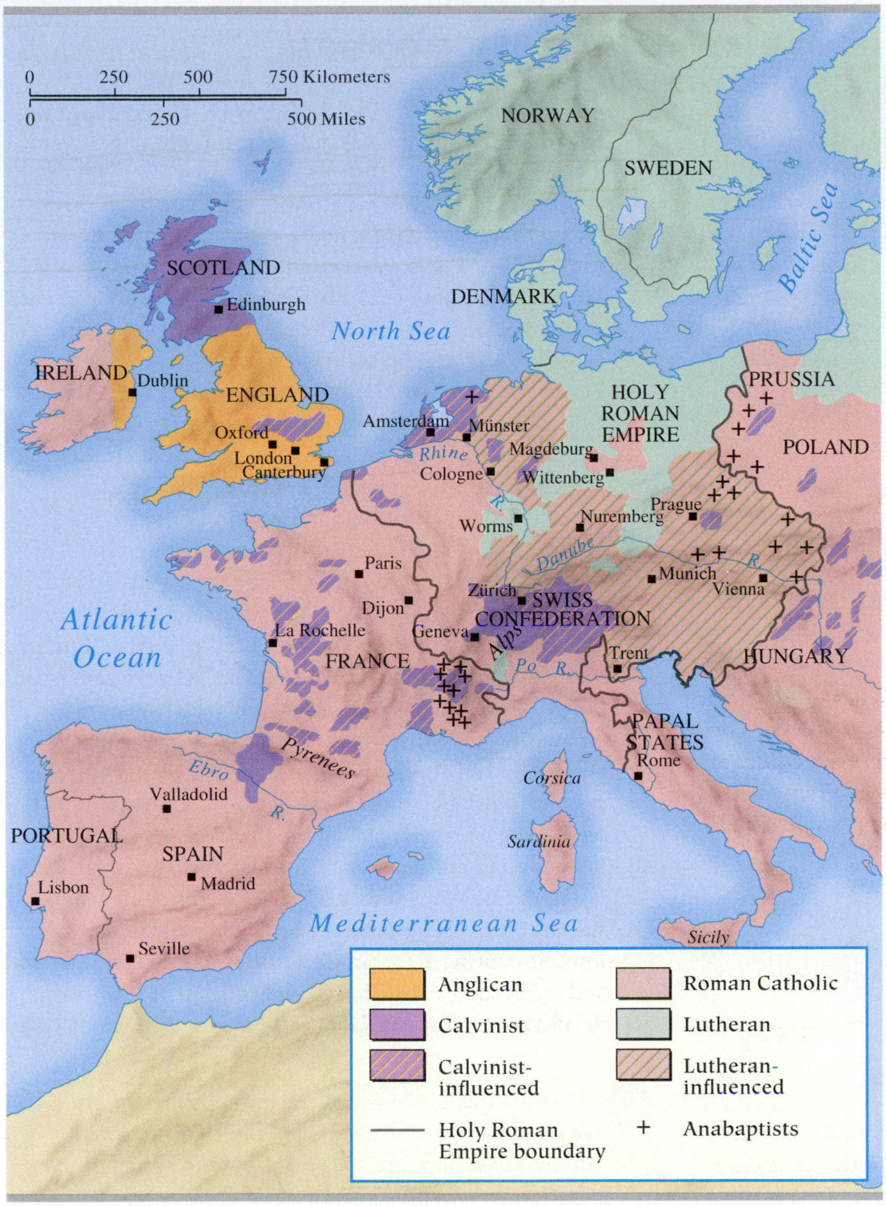

MAP 13.2 Catholics and Protestants in Europe by 1560. The Reformation continued to evolve beyond the basic split of the Lutherans from the Catholics. Several Protestant sects broke away from the teachings of Martin Luther, each with a separate creed and different ways of worship. In England, Henry VIII broke with the Catholic Church for political and dynastic reasons.

Q *Which areas of Europe were solidly Catholic, which were solidly Lutheran, and which were neither?*

order, Teresa experienced mystical visions that she claimed resulted in the ecstatic union of her soul with God. But Teresa also believed that mystical experience should lead to an active life of service on behalf of her Catholic faith. Consequently, she founded a new order of barefoot Carmelite nuns and worked to foster their mystical experiences.

The regeneration of religious orders also proved valuable to the reform of Catholicism. Old orders, such as the Benedictines and Dominicans, were reformed and renewed. The Capuchins emerged when a group of Franciscans decided to return to the simplicity and poverty of Saint Francis of Assisi, the medieval founder of the Franciscan order. In addition to caring for the sick and the poor, the Capuchins focused on preaching the Gospel directly to the people and emerged as an effective force against Protestantism. New religious orders and brotherhoods were also created. The Theatines, founded in 1524, placed their emphasis on reforming the secular clergy and encouraging those clerics to fulfill their duties among the laity. The Theatines also founded orphanages and hospitals to care for the victims of war and plague. The Ursulines, a new order of nuns founded in Italy in 1535, focused their attention on establishing schools for the education of girls.

The Society of Jesus

Of all the new religious orders, the most important was the Society of Jesus, known as the Jesuits, who became the chief instrument of the Catholic Reformation. The Society of Jesus was founded by a Spanish nobleman, Ignatius of Loyola (ig-NAY-shuss of loi-OH-luh) (1491–1556), whose injuries in battle cut short his military career. Loyola experienced a spiritual torment similar to Luther's but, unlike Luther, resolved his problems not by a new doctrine but by a decision to submit his will to the will of the church. Unable to be a real soldier, he vowed to be a soldier of God. Over a period of twelve years, Loyola prepared for his

LOYOLA AND OBEDIENCE TO "OUR HOLY MOTHER, THE HIERARCHICAL CHURCH"

IN HIS *SPIRITUAL EXERCISES*, Ignatius of Loyola developed a systematic program for "the conquest of self and the regulation of one's life" for service to the hierarchical Catholic Church. Ignatius's supreme goal was the commitment of the Christian to active service under Jesus's banner in the Church of Christ (the Catholic Church). In the final section of *The Spiritual Exercises*, Loyola explained the nature of that commitment in a series of "Rules for Thinking with the Church."

Ignatius of Loyola, "Rules for Thinking with the Church"

The following rules should be observed to foster the true attitude of mind we ought to have in the Church militant.

1. We must put aside all judgment of our own, and keep the mind ever ready and prompt to obey in all things the true Spouse of Jesus Christ, our holy Mother, the hierarchical Church.
2. We should praise sacramental confession, the yearly reception of the Most Blessed Sacrament [the Lord's Supper], and praise more highly monthly reception, and still more weekly Communion. . . .
3. We ought to praise the frequent hearing of Mass, the singing of hymns, psalmody, and long prayers whether in the church or outside. . . .
4. We must praise highly religious life, virginity, and continency; and matrimony ought not be praised as much as any of these.
5. We should praise vows of religion, obedience, poverty, chastity, and vows to perform other works of supererogation conducive to perfection. . . .
6. We should show our esteem for the relics of the saints by venerating them and praying to the saints. We should praise visits to the Station Churches, pilgrimages, indulgences, jubilees, the lighting of candles in churches.
7. We must praise the regulations of the Church, with regard to fast and abstinence, for example, in Lent, on Ember Days, Vigils, Fridays, and Saturdays.
8. We ought to praise not only the building and adornment of churches, but also images and veneration of them according to the subject they represent.
9. Finally, we must praise all the commandments of the Church, and be on the alert to find reasons to defend them, and by no means in order to criticize them.
10. We should be more ready to approve and praise the orders, recommendations, and way of acting of our superiors than to find fault with them. Though some of the orders, etc., may not have been praiseworthy, yet to speak against them, either when preaching in public or in speaking before the people, would rather be the cause of murmuring and scandal than of profit. As a consequence, the people would become angry with their superiors, whether secular or spiritual. But while it does harm in the absence of our superiors to speak evil of them before the people, it may be profitable to discuss their bad conduct with those who can apply a remedy. . . .
13. If we wish to proceed securely in all things, we must hold fast to the following principle: What seems to me white, I will believe black if the hierarchical Church so defines. For I must be convinced that in Christ our Lord, the bridegroom, and in His spouse the Church, only one Spirit holds sway, which governs and rules for the salvation of souls.

Q *What are the fundamental assumptions that inform Loyola's rules for "thinking with the church"? What do these assumptions tell you about the nature of the Catholic reform movement?*

Source: Ignatius of Loyola, "Rules for Thinking with the Church," in *The Spiritual Exercises of St. Ignatius of Loyola*, trans. L. J. Puhl (Baltimore: Loyola University Press, 1951).

lifework by prayer, pilgrimages, going to school, and working out a spiritual program in his brief but powerful book, *The Spiritual Exercises*. This was a training manual for spiritual development emphasizing exercises by which the human will could be strengthened and made to follow the will of God as manifested through his instrument, the Catholic Church (see the box above).

Loyola gathered together a small group of individuals who were eventually recognized as a religious order, the Society of Jesus, by a papal bull in 1540. The new order was grounded on the principles of absolute obedience to the papacy, a strict hierarchical order for the society, the use of education to achieve its goals, and a dedication to engage in "conflict for God." The Jesuits' organization came to resemble the structure of a military command. A two-year novitiate weeded out all but the most dedicated adherents. Executive leadership was put in the hands of a general, who nominated all important positions in the order and was to be revered as the absolute head of the order. Loyola served as the first general of the order until his death in 1556. A special vow of absolute obedience to the pope made the Jesuits an important instrument for papal policy.

ACTIVITIES OF THE JESUITS The Jesuits pursued three major activities. They established highly disciplined schools, borrowing freely from humanist schools for their educational methods. To the Jesuits, the thorough education of young people was crucial to combating the advance of Protestantism.

Scala/Art Resource, NY

Ignatius of Loyola. The Jesuits became the most important new religious order of the Catholic Reformation. Shown here in a sixteenth-century painting by an unknown artist is Ignatius of Loyola, founder of the Society of Jesus. Loyola is seen kneeling before Pope Paul III, who officially recognized the Jesuits in 1540.

In the course of the sixteenth century, the Jesuits took over the premier academic posts in Catholic universities, and by 1600, they were the most famous educators in Europe.

Another prominent Jesuit activity was the propagation of the Catholic faith among non-Christians. Francis Xavier (ZAY-vee-ur) (1506–1552), one of the original members of the Society of Jesus, carried the message of Catholic Christianity to the East. After converting tens of thousands in India, he traveled to Malacca and the Moluccas before reaching Japan in 1549. He spoke highly of the Japanese: "They are a people of excellent morals—good in general and not malicious."[20] Thousands of Japanese, especially in the southernmost islands, became Christians. In 1552, Xavier set out for China but died of a fever before he reached the mainland.

Although conversion efforts in Japan proved short-lived, Jesuit activity in China, especially that of the Italian Matteo Ricci (ma-TAY-oh REE-chee) (1552–1610), was more long-lasting. Recognizing the Chinese pride in their own culture, the Jesuits attempted to draw parallels between Christian and Confucian concepts and to show the similarities between Christian morality and Confucian ethics. For their part, the missionaries were impressed with many aspects of Chinese civilization, and reports of their experiences heightened European curiosity about this great society on the other side of the world.

The Jesuits were also determined to carry the Catholic banner and fight Protestantism. Jesuit missionaries succeeded in restoring Catholicism to parts of Germany and eastern Europe. Poland was largely won back for the Catholic Church through Jesuit efforts.

A Revived Papacy

The involvement of the Renaissance papacy in dubious finances and Italian political and military affairs had given rise to numerous sources of corruption. The meager steps taken to control corruption left the papacy still in need of serious reform, and it took the jolt of the Protestant Reformation to bring it about.

The pontificate of Pope Paul III (1534–1549) proved to be a turning point in the reform of the papacy. Raised in the lap of Renaissance luxury, Paul III continued Renaissance papal practices by appointing his nephews as cardinals, involving himself in politics, and patronizing arts and letters on a lavish scale. Nevertheless, he perceived the need for change and expressed it decisively. He made advocates of reform, such as Gasparo Contarini (GAHS-puh-roh kahn-tuh-REE-nee) and Gian Pietro Caraffa (JAHN PYAY-troh kuh-RAH-fuh), cardinals. In 1535, Paul took the audacious step of appointing a reform commission to study the condition of the church. The commission's report in 1537 blamed the church's problems on the corrupt policies of popes and cardinals. Paul III also formally recognized the Jesuits and summoned the Council of Trent (see the next section).

A decisive turning point in the direction of the Catholic Reformation and the nature of papal reform came in the 1540s. In 1541, a colloquy had been held at Regensburg in a final attempt to settle the religious division peacefully. Here Catholic moderates, such as Cardinal Contarini, who favored concessions to Protestants in the hope of restoring Christian unity, reached a compromise with Protestant moderates on a number of doctrinal issues. When Contarini returned to Rome with these proposals, Cardinal Caraffa and other hardliners, who regarded all compromise with Protestant innovations as heresy, accused him of selling out to the heretics. It soon became apparent that the conservative reformers were in the ascendancy when Caraffa was able to persuade Paul III to establish the Roman Inquisition or Holy Office in 1542 to ferret out doctrinal errors. There was to be no compromise with Protestantism.

When Cardinal Caraffa was chosen pope as Paul IV (1555–1559), he so increased the power of the Inquisition that even liberal cardinals were silenced. This "first true pope of the Catholic Counter-Reformation," as he has been called, also created the Index of Forbidden Books, a list of books that Catholics were not allowed to read. It included all the works of Protestant theologians as well as authors considered "unwholesome," a category general enough to include the works of Erasmus. Rome, the capital of Catholic Christianity, was rapidly becoming Fortress Rome; any hope of restoring Christian unity by compromise was fast fading. The activities of the Council of Trent made compromise virtually impossible.

The Council of Trent

In 1542, Pope Paul III took the decisive step of calling for a general council of Christendom to resolve the religious differences created by the Protestant revolt. It was not until March 1545, however, that a group of cardinals, archbishops, bishops, abbots, and theologians met in the city of Trent on the border between Germany and Italy and initiated the Council of Trent. But a variety of problems, including an outbreak of plague,

CHRONOLOGY The Catholic Reformation	
Pope Paul III	1534–1549
Papal recognition of Society of Jesus (Jesuits)	1540
Establishment of Roman Inquisition (Holy Office)	1542
Council of Trent	1545–1563
Pope Paul IV	1555–1559

war between France and Spain, and the changing of popes, prevented the council from holding regular annual meetings. Nevertheless, the council met intermittently in three major sessions between 1545 and 1563. Moderate Catholic reformers hoped that the council would make compromises in formulating doctrinal definitions that would encourage Protestants to return to the church. Conservatives, however, favored an uncompromising restatement of Catholic doctrines in strict opposition to Protestant positions. After a struggle, the latter group won.

The final doctrinal decrees of the Council of Trent reaffirmed traditional Catholic teachings in opposition to Protestant beliefs. The council affirmed Scripture and tradition as equal authorities in religious matters; only the church could interpret Scripture. Other decrees declared both faith and good works to be necessary for salvation and upheld the seven sacraments, the Catholic doctrine of transubstantiation, and clerical celibacy. The council also affirmed the belief in purgatory and in the efficacy of indulgences, although it prohibited the hawking of indulgences. Of the reform decrees that were passed, the most important established theological seminaries in every diocese for the training of priests.

After the Council of Trent, the Roman Catholic Church possessed a clear body of doctrine and a unified church under the acknowledged supremacy of the popes, who had triumphed over bishops and councils. The Roman Catholic Church had become one Christian denomination among many with an organizational framework and doctrinal pattern that would not be significantly altered for four hundred years. With renewed confidence, the Catholic Church entered a new phase of its history.

Politics and the Wars of Religion in the Sixteenth Century

FOCUS QUESTION: What role did politics, economic and social conditions, and religion play in the European wars of the sixteenth century?

By the middle of the sixteenth century, Calvinism and Catholicism had become activist religions dedicated to spreading the word of God as they interpreted it. Although this struggle for the minds and hearts of Europeans is at the heart of the religious wars of the sixteenth century, economic, social, and political forces also played an important role in these conflicts. Of the sixteenth-century religious wars, none were more momentous or shattering than the French civil wars known as the French Wars of Religion.

The French Wars of Religion (1562–1598)

Religion was the engine that drove the French civil wars of the sixteenth century. Concerned by the growth of Calvinism, the French kings tried to stop its spread by persecuting Calvinists but had little success. **Huguenots** (HYOO-guh-nots), as the French Calvinists were called, came from all levels of society: artisans and shopkeepers hurt by rising prices and a rigid guild system, merchants and lawyers in provincial towns whose local privileges were tenuous, and members of the nobility. Possibly 40 to 50 percent of the French nobility became Huguenots, including the house of Bourbon (boor-BOHN), which stood next to the Valois (val-WAH) in the royal line of succession and ruled the southern French kingdom of Navarre (nuh-VAHR). The conversion of so many nobles made the Huguenots a potentially dangerous political threat to monarchical power. Though the Calvinists constituted only about 10 percent of the population, they were a strong-willed and well-organized minority.

The Catholic majority greatly outnumbered the Calvinist minority. The Valois monarchy was staunchly Catholic, and its control of the Catholic Church gave it little incentive to look on Protestantism favorably. When King Henry II was killed accidentally in a tournament in 1559, he was succeeded by a series of weak and neurotic sons, two of whom were dominated by their mother, Catherine de' Medici (1519–1589). As regent for her sons, the moderate Catholic Catherine looked to religious compromise as a way to defuse the political tensions but found to her consternation that both sides possessed their share of religious fanatics unwilling to make concessions. The extreme Catholic party—known as the ultra-Catholics—favored strict opposition to the Huguenots and was led by the Guise (GEEZ) family. Possessing the loyalty of Paris and large sections of northern and northwestern France through their client-patronage system, the Guises could recruit and pay for large armies and received support abroad from the papacy and Jesuits who favored the family's uncompromising Catholic position.

But religion was not the only factor contributing to the French civil wars. Resentful of the growing power of monarchical centralization, towns and provinces were only too willing to join a revolt against the monarchy. This was also true of the nobility, and because so many of them were Calvinists, they formed an important base of opposition to the crown. The French Wars of Religion, then, presented a major constitutional crisis for France and temporarily halted the development of the French centralized territorial state. The claim of the state's ruling dynasty to a person's loyalties was temporarily superseded by loyalty to one's religious belief. For some people, the unity of France was less important than religious truth. But there also emerged in France a group of public figures who placed politics before religion and believed that no religious truth was worth the ravages of civil war. These **politiques** (puh-lee-TEEKS) ultimately prevailed, but not until both sides were exhausted by bloodshed.

COURSE OF THE STRUGGLE The wars erupted in 1562 when the powerful duke of Guise massacred a peaceful congregation of Huguenots at Vassy. In the decade of the 1560s, the Huguenots held their own. Though too small a group to conquer France, their armies were so good at defensive campaigns that they could not be defeated either, despite the infamous Saint Bartholomew's Day massacre.

This massacre of Huguenots occurred in August 1572 at a time when the Catholic and Calvinist parties had apparently been reconciled through the marriage of the sister of the reigning Valois king, Charles IX (1560–1574), and Henry of Navarre, the Bourbon ruler of Navarre. Henry was the son of Jeanne d'Albret (ZHAHN dahl-BRAY), queen of Navarre, who had been responsible for introducing Calvinist ideas into her kingdom. Henry was also the acknowledged political leader of the Huguenots, and many Huguenots traveled to Paris for the wedding.

But the Guise family persuaded the king and his mother, Catherine de' Medici, that this gathering of Huguenots posed a threat to them. Charles and his advisers decided to eliminate the Huguenot leaders with one swift blow. According to one French military leader, Charles and his advisers believed that civil war would soon break out anyway and that "it was better to win a battle in Paris, where all the leaders were, than to risk it in the field and fall into a dangerous and uncertain war."[21]

The massacre began early in the day on August 24 when the king's guards sought out and killed some prominent Huguenot leaders. These murders soon unleashed a wave of violence that gripped the city of Paris. For three days, frenzied Catholic mobs roamed the streets of Paris, killing Huguenots in an often cruel and bloodthirsty manner. According to one eyewitness account: "Then they took her [Françoise Lussault] and dragged her by the hair a long way through the streets, and spying the gold bracelets on her arms, without having the patience to unfasten them, cut off her wrists."[22] Three days of killing left three thousand Huguenots dead, although not Henry of Navarre, who saved his life by promising to turn Catholic. Thousands more were killed in provincial towns. The massacre boomeranged, however, because it discredited the Valois dynasty without ending the conflict.

The fighting continued. The Huguenots rebuilt their strength, and in 1576, the ultra-Catholics formed a "Holy League," vowing to exterminate heresy and seat a true Catholic champion—Henry, duke of Guise—on the French throne in place of the ruling king, Henry III (1574–1589), who had succeeded his brother Charles IX. The turning point in the conflict came in the War of the Three Henries in 1588–1589. Henry, duke of Guise, in the pay of Philip II of Spain, seized Paris and forced King Henry III to make him chief minister. To rid himself of Guise influence, Henry III assassinated the duke of Guise and then joined with Henry of Navarre (who meanwhile had returned to Calvinism), who was next in line to the throne, to crush the Catholic Holy League and retake the city of Paris. Although successful, Henry III was assassinated in 1589 by a monk who was repelled by the spectacle of a Catholic

Musée Cantonal des Beaux-Arts, Lausanne//De Agostini Picture Library/G. Dagli Orti/Bridgeman Images

The Saint Bartholomew's Day Massacre. Although the outbreak of religious war seemed unlikely in France, the collapse of the strong monarchy with the death of Henry II unleashed forces that led to a series of civil wars. Pictured here is the Saint Bartholomew's Day massacre of 1572. This contemporary painting by the Huguenot artist François Dubois vividly depicts a number of the incidents of that day when approximately three thousand Huguenots were murdered in Paris.

CHRONOLOGY	The French Wars of Religion (1562–1598)
Duke of Guise massacres Huguenot congregation at Vassy	1562
Saint Bartholomew's Day massacre	1572
Henry III	1574–1589
Formation of the Holy League	1576
War of the Three Henries	1588–1589
Assassination of Henry III	1589
Coronation of Henry IV	1594
Edict of Nantes	1598

king cooperating with a Protestant. Henry of Navarre now claimed the throne. Realizing, however, that Catholic France would never accept him, Henry took the logical way out and converted once again to Catholicism. With his coronation in 1594, the French Wars of Religion finally came to an end.

Nevertheless, the religious problem persisted until the Edict of Nantes (NAHNT) was issued in 1598. The edict acknowledged Catholicism as the official religion of France but guaranteed the Huguenots the right to worship in selected places in every district and allowed them to retain a number of fortified towns for their protection. In addition, Huguenots were allowed to enjoy all political privileges, including the holding of public offices. Although the Edict of Nantes recognized the rights of the Protestant minority and ostensibly the principle of religious toleration, it did so only out of political necessity, not out of conviction.

Philip II and Militant Catholicism

The greatest advocate of activist Catholicism in the second half of the sixteenth century was King Philip II of Spain (1556–1598), the son and heir of Charles V. Philip's reign ushered in an age of Spanish greatness, both politically and culturally.

The first major goal of Philip II was to consolidate and secure the lands he had inherited from his father. These included Spain, the Netherlands, and possessions in Italy (see Map 13.3) and the New World. For Philip, this meant strict conformity to Catholicism, enforced by aggressive use of the Spanish Inquisition, and the establishment of strong, monarchical authority. The latter was not an easy task because Philip had inherited a governmental structure in which each of the various states and territories of his empire stood in an individual relationship to the king. Philip did manage, however, to expand royal power in Spain by making the monarchy less dependent on the traditional landed

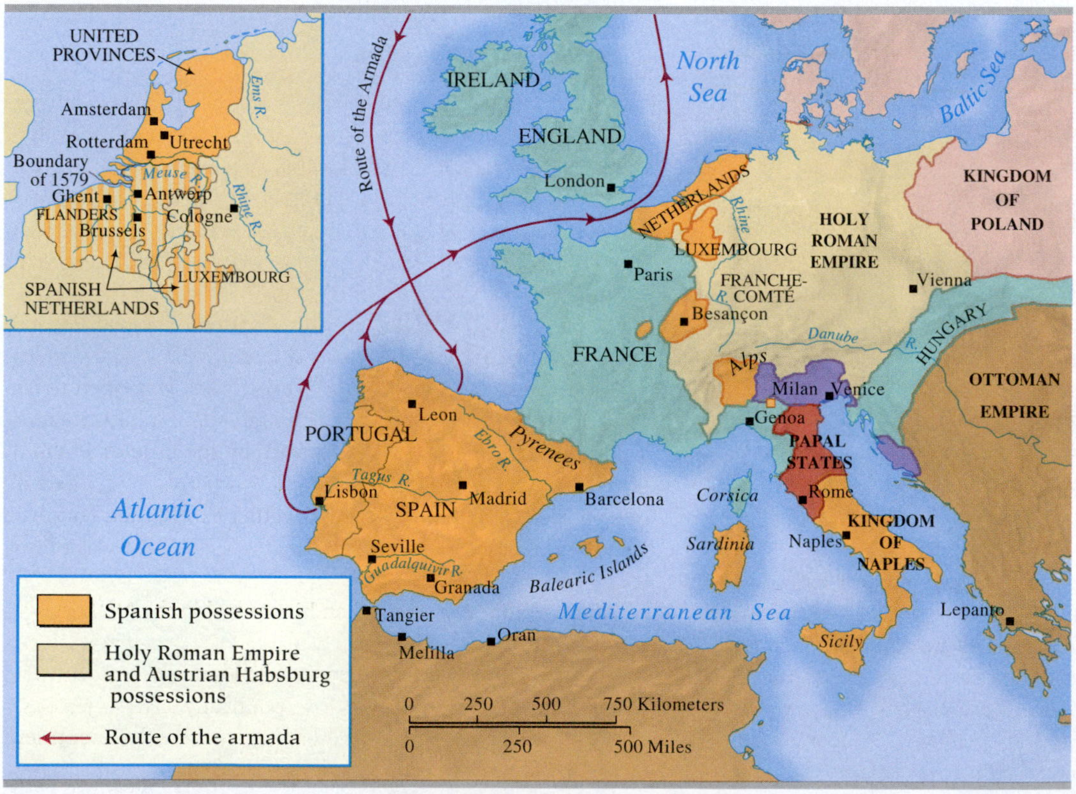

MAP 13.3 The Height of Spanish Power Under Philip II. Like his father, Charles V, Philip II, the "Most Catholic King," was a champion of the Catholic cause against Protestantism. He sought to maintain Habsburg control in the Netherlands by combating a Protestant revolt, a rebellion eventually supported by Queen Elizabeth of England. Spain's attempt to invade England in 1588 ended in disaster.

Q *Why would England feel threatened by Spanish territory in the Netherlands?*

Scala/Art Resource, NY

Philip of Spain. This portrait by Titian depicts Philip II of Spain. The king's attempts to make Spain a great power led to large debts and crushing taxes, and his military actions in defense of Catholicism ended in failure and misfortune in both France and the Netherlands.

aristocracy. Philip tried to be the center of the whole government and supervised the work of all departments, even down to the smallest details. Unwilling to delegate authority, he failed to distinguish between important and trivial matters and fell weeks behind on state correspondence, where he was inclined to make marginal notes and even correct spelling. One Spanish official said, "If God used the Escorial [the royal palace where Philip worked] to deliver my death sentence, I would be immortal."

One of Philip's aims was to make Spain a dominant power in Europe. To a great extent, Spain's preeminence depended on a prosperous economy fueled by its importation of gold and silver from its New World possessions, its agriculture, its commerce, and its industry, especially in textiles, silk, and leather goods. The importation of silver also had detrimental effects, however, as it helped set off a spiraling inflation that disrupted the Spanish economy, eventually hurting both textile production and agriculture. Moreover, the expenses of war, especially after 1580, proved devastating to the Spanish economy. American gold and silver never constituted more than 20 percent of the royal revenue, leading the government to impose a crushing burden of direct and indirect taxes. Even then the government was forced to borrow. Philip repudiated his debts seven times; still, two-thirds of state income went to pay interest on the debt by the end of his reign. The attempt to make Spain a great power led to its decline after Philip's reign.

Crucial to an understanding of Philip II is the importance of Catholicism to the Spanish people and their ruler. Driven by a heritage of crusading fervor, the Spanish had little difficulty seeing themselves as a nation of people divinely chosen to save Catholic Christianity from the Protestant heretics. Philip II, the "Most Catholic King," became the champion of Catholicism throughout Europe, a role that led to spectacular victories and equally spectacular defeats for the Spanish king. Spain's leadership of a holy league against Turkish encroachments in the Mediterranean, especially the Muslim attack on the island of Cyprus, resulted in a stunning victory over the Turkish fleet at the Battle of Lepanto (LEH-pahn-toh *or* LIH-pan-toh) in 1571. Philip's greatest misfortunes came from his attempt to crush the revolt in the Netherlands and his tortured relations with Queen Elizabeth of England.

Revolt of the Netherlands

As one of the richest parts of Philip's empire, the Spanish Netherlands was of great importance to the Most Catholic King. The Netherlands consisted of seventeen provinces (the modern Netherlands, Belgium, and Luxembourg). The seven northern provinces were largely Germanic in culture and Dutch speaking, while the French- and Flemish-speaking southern provinces were closely tied to France. Situated at the commercial crossroads of northwestern Europe, the Netherlands had become prosperous through commerce and a flourishing textile industry. Because of its location, the Netherlands was open to the religious influences of the age. Though some inhabitants had adopted Lutheranism or Anabaptism, by the time of Philip II, Calvinism was also making inroads. These provinces had no real political bond holding them together except their common ruler, and that ruler was Philip II, a foreigner who was out of touch with the local situation.

Philip II hoped to strengthen his control in the Netherlands, regardless of the traditional privileges of the separate provinces. This was strongly opposed by the nobles, towns, and provincial states, which stood to lose politically if their jealously guarded privileges and freedoms were weakened. Resentment against Philip increased when the residents of the Netherlands realized that the taxes they paid were being used for Spanish interests. Finally, religion became a major catalyst for rebellion when Philip attempted to crush Calvinism. Violence erupted in 1566 when Calvinists—especially nobles—began to destroy statues and stained-glass windows in Catholic churches. Philip responded by sending the duke of Alva with 10,000 veteran Spanish and Italian troops to crush the rebellion.

The repressive policies of the duke proved counterproductive. The levying of a permanent sales tax alienated many merchants and commoners, who now joined the nobles and Calvinists in the struggle against Spanish rule. A special tribunal, known as the Council of Troubles (nicknamed the Council of Blood by the Dutch), inaugurated a reign of terror in which even powerful aristocrats were executed. As a result, the revolt now became organized, especially in the northern provinces, where William of Nassau, the prince of Orange, also known as William the Silent, and Dutch pirates known as the "Sea Beggars" mounted growing resistance. In 1573, Philip removed the duke of Alva and shifted to a more conciliatory policy to bring an end to the costly revolt.

William of Orange wished to unify all seventeen provinces, a goal seemingly realized in 1576 with the Pacification of Ghent. This agreement stipulated that all the provinces would stand together under William's leadership, respect religious differences, and demand that the Spanish troops be withdrawn. But religious differences proved too strong for any lasting union. When the duke of Parma, the next Spanish leader, arrived in the Netherlands, he astutely played on the religious differences of the provinces and split their united front. The southern provinces formed a Catholic union—the Union of Arras—in 1579 and accepted Spanish control. To counter this, William of Orange organized the seven northern, Dutch-speaking states into a Protestant union—the Union of Utrecht—determined to oppose Spanish rule. The Netherlands was now divided along religious, geographic, and political lines into two hostile camps. The struggle dragged on until 1609, when a twelve-year truce ended the war, virtually recognizing the independence of the northern provinces. These "United Provinces" soon emerged as the Dutch Republic, although the Spanish did not formally recognize them as independent until 1648. The ten southern provinces remained a Spanish possession (see Map 13.3).

CHRONOLOGY	Philip II and Militant Catholicism
Philip II	1556–1598
Outbreak of revolt in the Netherlands	1566
Battle of Lepanto	1571
Spanish armada	1588
Twelve-year truce (Spain and Netherlands)	1609
Independence of the United Provinces	1648

The England of Elizabeth

After the death of Queen Mary in 1558, her half-sister Elizabeth (1558–1603) ascended the throne of England. During Elizabeth's reign, England rose to prominence as the relatively small island kingdom became the leader of the Protestant nations of Europe, laid the foundations for a world empire, and experienced a cultural renaissance.

The daughter of King Henry VIII and Anne Boleyn, Elizabeth had had a difficult early life. During Mary's reign, she had even been imprisoned for a while and had learned early to hide

Stapleton Collection/Corbis

Procession of Queen Elizabeth I. Intelligent and learned, Elizabeth Tudor was familiar with Latin and Greek and spoke several European languages. Served by able administrators, Elizabeth ruled for nearly forty-five years and generally avoided open military action against any major power. This picture, painted near the end of her reign, shows the queen in a ceremonial procession with her courtiers.

QUEEN ELIZABETH I: "I HAVE THE HEART OF A KING"

QUEEN ELIZABETH I RULED ENGLAND from 1558 to 1603 with a consummate skill that contemporaries considered unusual in a woman. Though shrewd and paternalistic, Elizabeth, like other sixteenth-century monarchs, depended for her power on the favor of her people. When England faced the threat of an invasion by the Spanish armada of Philip II in 1588, Elizabeth sought to rally her troops with a speech at Tilbury, a town on the Thames River. This selection is taken from her speech.

Queen Elizabeth I, Speech to the Troops at Tilbury

My loving people, we have been persuaded by some, that are careful of our safety, to take heed how we commit ourselves to armed multitudes, for fear of treachery; but I assure you, I do not desire to live to distrust my faithful and loving people. Let tyrants fear; I have always so behaved myself that, under God, I have placed my chiefest strength and safeguard in the loyal hearts and good will of my subjects. And therefore I am come amongst you at this time, not as for my recreation or sport, but being resolved, in the midst and heat of the battle, to live or die amongst you all; to lay down, for my God, and for my kingdom, and for my people, my honor and my blood, even in the dust. I know I have but the body of a weak and feeble woman; but I have the heart of a king, and of a king of England, too; and think foul scorn that Parma or Spain, or any prince of Europe, should dare to invade the borders of my realm: to which, rather than any dishonor should grow by me, I myself will take up arms; I myself will be your general, judge, and rewarder of every one of your virtues in the field. I know already, by your forwardness, that you have deserved rewards and crowns; and we do assure you, on the word of a prince, they shall be duly paid you. In the mean my lieutenant general shall be in my stead, than whom never prince commanded a more noble and worthy subject; not doubting by your obedience to my general, by your concord in the camp and by your valor in the field, we shall shortly have a famous victory over the enemies of my God, of my kingdom, and of my people.

Q *What qualities evident in Elizabeth's speech would have endeared her to her listeners? How was her popularity connected to the events of the late sixteenth century?*

Source: Elizabeth I's Speech to the Troops at Tilbury in 1588.

her true feelings from both private and public sight. Intelligent, cautious, and self-confident, she moved quickly to solve the difficult religious problem she had inherited from Mary, who had become extremely unpopular when she tried to return England to the Catholic fold.

RELIGIOUS POLICY Elizabeth's religious policy was based on moderation and compromise. As a ruler, she wished to prevent England from being torn apart over matters of religion. Parliament cooperated with the queen in initiating the Elizabethan religious settlement in 1559. The Catholic legislation of Mary's reign was repealed, and the new Act of Supremacy designated Elizabeth as "the only supreme governor of this realm, as well in all spiritual or ecclesiastical things or causes, as temporal." She used this title rather than "supreme head of the church," which had been used by both Henry VIII and Edward VI, because she did not want to upset the Catholics, who considered the pope the supreme head, or radical Protestants, who thought that Christ alone was head of the church. The Act of Uniformity restored the church service of the Book of Common Prayer from the reign of Edward VI with some revisions to make it more acceptable to Catholics. The Thirty-Nine Articles, a new confession of faith, defined theological issues midway between Lutheranism and Calvinism. Elizabeth's religious settlement was basically Protestant, but it was a moderate Protestantism that avoided overly subtle distinctions and extremes.

The new religious settlement worked, at least to the extent that it smothered religious differences in England in the second half of the sixteenth century. Two groups, however, the Catholics and the Puritans, continued to oppose it. One of Elizabeth's greatest challenges came from her Catholic cousin, Mary, queen of Scots, who was next in line to the English throne. Mary was ousted from Scotland by rebellious Calvinist nobles in 1568 and fled for her life to England. There Elizabeth placed her under house arrest and for fourteen years tolerated her involvement in a number of ill-planned Catholic plots designed to kill Elizabeth and replace her on the throne with the Catholic Mary. Finally, in 1587, after Mary became embroiled in a far more serious plot, Elizabeth had her cousin beheaded to end the threats to her regime.

Potentially more dangerous to Anglicanism in the long run were the **Puritans**. The word *Puritan* first appeared in 1564 when it was used to refer to Protestants within the Anglican Church who, inspired by Calvinist theology, wanted to remove any trace of Catholicism from the Church of England. Elizabeth managed to keep the Puritans in check during her reign.

Elizabeth proved as adept in government and foreign policy as in religious affairs (see the box above). She was well served administratively by the principal secretary of state. The talents of Sir William Cecil and Sir Francis Walsingham, who together held the office for thirty-two years, ensured much of Elizabeth's success in foreign and domestic affairs. Elizabeth also handled Parliament with much skill; it met only thirteen times during her entire reign.

FOREIGN POLICY Caution, moderation, and expediency also dictated Elizabeth's foreign policy. Fearful of other countries' motives, Elizabeth realized that war could be disastrous for her island kingdom and her own rule. Unofficially, however, she encouraged English seamen to raid Spanish ships and colonies. Francis Drake was especially adept at plundering Spanish fleets loaded with gold and silver from Spain's New World empire.

FILM & HISTORY

Watch *Elizabeth* (1998), which opens with Queen Mary pursuing her dream of restoring Catholicism to England as she contemplates signing a death warrant for her Protestant half-sister Elizabeth. But she refuses to do so before dying in 1558. Elizabeth becomes queen and is portrayed in her early years of rule as an uncertain monarch who "rules from the heart instead of the mind," as one adviser tells her. The strength of the movie, which contains numerous historical inaccuracies, is the performance of Cate Blanchett, who captures some of the characteristics of Queen Elizabeth I.

Q *What historical inaccuracies do you find in the movie? What is convincing about the portrait of Queen Elizabeth?*

While encouraging English piracy and providing clandestine aid to French Huguenots and Dutch Calvinists to weaken France and Spain, Elizabeth pretended complete aloofness and avoided alliances that would force her into war with any major power (see "Film & History" above). Gradually, however, Elizabeth was drawn into more active involvement in the Netherlands. This move accelerated the already mounting friction between Spain and England. After years of resisting the idea of invading England as impractical, Philip II of Spain was finally persuaded to do so by advisers who assured him that the people of England would rise against their queen when the Spaniards arrived. Moreover, Philip was easily convinced that the revolt in the Netherlands would never be crushed as long as England provided support for it. In any case, a successful invasion of England would mean the overthrow of heresy and the return of England to Catholicism, surely an act in accordance with the will of God. Accordingly, Philip ordered preparations for a fleet of warships that would rendezvous with the army of the duke of Parma in Flanders and escort his troops across the English Channel for the invasion.

THE SPANISH ARMADA The armada proved to be a disaster. The Spanish fleet that finally set sail had neither the ships nor the troops that Philip had planned to send. A conversation between a papal emissary and an officer of the Spanish fleet before the armada departed reveals the fundamental flaw:

> "And if you meet the English armada in the Channel, do you expect to win the battle?" "Of course," replied the Spaniard.
>
> "How can you be sure?" [asked the emissary].
>
> "It's very simple. It is well known that we fight in God's cause. So, when we meet the English, God will surely arrange matters so that we can grapple and board them, either by sending some strange freak of weather or, more likely, just by depriving the English of their wits. If we can come to close quarters, Spanish valor and Spanish steel (and the great masses of soldiers we shall have on board) will make our victory certain. But unless God helps us by a miracle the English, who have faster and handier ships than ours, and many more long-range guns, and who know their advantage just as well as we do, will never close with us at all, but stand aloof and knock us to pieces with their culverins [cannons], without our being able to do them any serious hurt. So," concluded the captain, and one fancies a grim smile, "we are sailing against England in the confident hope of a miracle."[23]

The hoped-for miracle never materialized. The Spanish fleet, battered by a number of encounters with the English, sailed back to Spain by a northward route around Scotland and Ireland, where it was further battered by storms. Although the English and Spanish would continue their war for another sixteen years, the defeat of the Spanish armada guaranteed for the time being that England would remain a Protestant country. Although Spain made up for its losses within a year and a half, the defeat was a psychological blow to the Spaniards.

CHAPTER SUMMARY

When the Augustinian monk Martin Luther burst onto the scene with a series of theses on indulgences, few people suspected that his observations would eventually split all of Europe along religious lines. But the yearning for reform of the church and meaningful religious experiences caused a seemingly simple dispute to escalate into a powerful movement.

Martin Luther established the twin pillars of the Protestant Reformation: the doctrine of justification by faith alone and the Bible as the sole authority in religious affairs. Although Luther felt that his revival of Christianity based on his interpretation of the Bible should be acceptable to all, others soon appeared who also read the Bible but interpreted it in different ways. Protestantism fragmented into different sects—Zwinglianism, Calvinism, Anglicanism, Anabaptism—which, though united in their dislike of Catholicism, were themselves divided over the interpretation of the sacraments and religious practices. As reform ideas spread, religion and politics became ever more intertwined.

Although the peace of Augsburg in 1555 legally acknowledged Lutheranism in the Holy Roman Empire, it had lost much of its momentum and outside of Scandinavia had scant ability to attract new supporters. Its energy was largely replaced by the new Protestant form of Calvinism, which had a clarity of doctrine and a fervor that made it attractive to a whole new generation

of Europeans. But while Calvinism's activism enabled it to spread across Europe, Catholicism was also experiencing its own revival. New religious orders based on reform, a revived and reformed papacy, and the Council of Trent, which reaffirmed traditional Catholic doctrine, gave the Catholic Church a renewed vitality.

By the middle of the sixteenth century, it was apparent that the religious passions of the Reformation era had brought an end to the religious unity of medieval Europe. The religious division (Catholics versus Protestant) was instrumental in beginning a series of religious wars that were complicated by economic, social, and political forces that also played a role. The French Wars of Religion, the revolt of the Netherlands against Philip II of Spain, and the conflict between Philip II and Elizabeth of England, which led to the failed attempt of the Spanish armada to invade England, were the major struggles in the sixteenth-century religious wars.

That people who were disciples of the Apostle of Peace would kill each other over their beliefs aroused skepticism about Christianity itself. As one German writer put it, "Lutheran, popish, and Calvinistic, we've got all these beliefs here, but there is some doubt about where Christianity has got."[24] It is surely no accident that the search for a stable, secular order of politics and for order in the universe through natural laws soon came to play important roles. Before we look at this search for order in the seventeenth century, however, we need first to look at the adventures that plunged Europe into its new role in the world.

CHAPTER TIMELINE

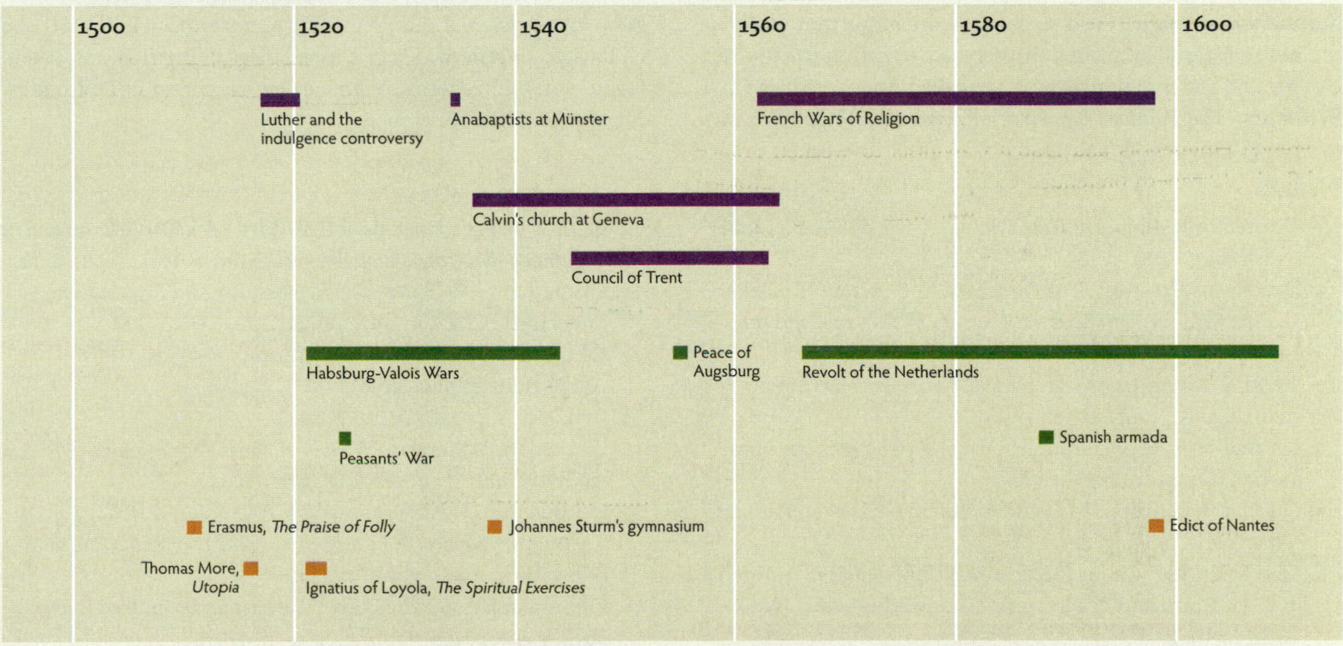

CHAPTER REVIEW

Upon Reflection

Q If attempts at reform of the Catholic Church were unsuccessful in the fifteenth century, why did they succeed during the sixteenth-century Reformation?

Q What role did politics play in the establishment of Lutheranism and Anglicanism?

Q Elizabeth of England and Philip II of Spain were two of Europe's most famous monarchs in the second half of the sixteenth century. Compare and contrast their methods of ruling and their foreign policy. Which was a more successful ruler? Why?

Key Terms

Christian (northern Renaissance) humanism (p. 366)
pluralism (p. 368)
confession (p. 369)
justification (p. 370)
transubstantiation (p. 373)
millenarianism (p. 380)
predestination (p. 383)
Catholic Reformation (p. 386)
Huguenots (p. 390)
politiques (p. 390)
Puritans (p. 395)

Suggestions for Further Reading

THE REFORMATION For a general history of the era of the Reformation, see **M. Greengrass, *Christendom Destroyed: Europe 1517–1648*** (New York, 2014). Basic surveys of the Reformation period include **J. D. Tracy, *Europe's Reformations, 1450–1650*,** 2nd ed. (Oxford, 2006), and **D. MacCulloch, *The Reformation*** (New York, 2003).

NORTHERN RENAISSANCE HUMANISM The development of humanism outside Italy is examined in **C. G. Nauert Jr., *Humanism and the Culture of Renaissance Europe*,** 2nd ed. (Cambridge, 2006).

LUTHER AND LUTHERANISM On Martin Luther's life, see **H. A. Oberman, *Luther: Between God and the Devil*** (New Haven, Conn., 2006), and the brief biography by **M. Marty, *Martin Luther*** (New York, 2004). On the role of Charles V, see **W. Maltby, *The Reign of Charles V*** (New York, 2002).

SPREAD OF THE PROTESTANT REFORMATION **W. P. Stephens's *Zwingli*** (Oxford, 1994) is an important study of the man's ideas. The most comprehensive account of the various groups and individuals who are called Anabaptists is **G. H. Williams, *The Radical Reformation*,** 2nd ed. (Kirksville, Mo., 1992). On the English Reformation, see **N. L. Jones, *English Reformation: Religion and Cultural Adaptation*** (London, 2002). On Calvinism, see **W. G. Naphy, *Calvin and the Consolidation of the Genevan Reformation*** (Philadelphia, 2003).

SOCIAL IMPACT OF THE REFORMATION On the impact of the Reformation on the family, see **J. F. Harrington, *Reordering Marriage and Society in Reformation Germany*** (New York, 1995). On women, see **K. Stjerna, *Women and the Reformation*** (New York, 2008).

CATHOLIC REFORMATION A good introduction to the Catholic Reformation can be found in **M. A. Mullett, *The Catholic Reformation*** (London, 1999). Also valuable is **R. P. Hsia, *The World of Catholic Renewal, 1540–1770*,** 2nd ed. (Cambridge, 2006).

WARS OF RELIGION For a good introduction to the French Wars of Religion, see **R. J. Knecht, *The French Wars of Religion, 1559–1598*,** 3rd ed. (New York, 2010). On Philip II, see **G. Parker, *Imprudent King: A New Life of Philip II*** (New Haven, Conn. 2014). Elizabeth's reign can be examined in **D. Loades, *Elizabeth I*** (New York, 2006).

Notes

1. Quoted in R. Bainton, *Here I Stand: A Life of Martin Luther* (Nashville, 1978), p. 183.
2. Desiderius Erasmus, *The Paraclesis*, in *Christian Humanism and the Reformation: Selected Writings of Erasmus*, 3rd ed., J. Olin, ed. (New York, 1987), p. 101.
3. Thomas More, *Utopia*, trans. Paul Turner (Harmondsworth, U.K., 1965), p. 76.
4. Quoted in A. E. McGrath, *Reformation Thought: An Introduction* (Oxford, 1988), p. 72.
5. Quoted in G. Rupp, *Luther's Progress to the Diet of Worms* (New York, 1964), p. 82.
6. Martin Luther, *On the Freedom of a Christian Man*, quoted in E. G. Rupp and B. Drewery, eds., *Martin Luther* (New York, 1970), p. 50.
7. Quoted in R. Bainton, *Here I Stand: A Life of Martin Luther*, pp. 181–182.
8. Author's translation of Martin Luther's lyrics, second verse of *Ein feste Burg ist unser Gott*.
9. Quoted in A. Dürer, *The Writings of Albrecht Dürer*, ed. and trans. (New York, 1958), p. 157.
10. Quoted in D. L. Jensen, *Reformation Europe* (Lexington, Mass., 1981), p. 83.
11. Quoted in L. P. Wandel, *Voracious Idols and Violent Hands: Iconoclasm in Reformation Zürich, Strasbourg, and Basel* (New York, 1995), p. 81.
12. Quoted in A. G. Dickens and D. Carr, eds., *The Reformation in England to the Accession of Elizabeth I* (New York, 1968), p. 72.
13. Quoted in L. W. Spitz, *The Renaissance and Reformation Movements* (Chicago, 1971), p. 414.
14. John Calvin, *Institutes of the Christian Religion*, trans. J. Allen (Philadelphia, 1936), vol. 1, p. 220.
15. Ibid., vol. 1, p. 228; vol. 2, p. 181.
16. Quoted in R. Bainton, *Women of the Reformation in Germany and Italy* (Minneapolis, 1971), p. 154.
17. Quoted in B. S. Anderson and J. P. Zinsser, *A History of Their Own: Women in Europe from Prehistory to the Present* (New York, 1988), vol. 1, p. 259.
18. Quoted in J. A. Phillips, *Eve: The History of an Idea* (New York, 1984), p. 105.
19. Quoted in J. Zophy, *A Short History of Renaissance and Reformation Europe*, 3rd ed. (Upper Saddle River, N.J., 2003), p. 227.
20. Quoted in J. O'Malley, *The First Jesuits* (Cambridge, Mass., 1993), p. 76.
21. Quoted in R. J. Knecht, *The French Wars of Religion, 1559–1598*, 2nd ed. (New York, 1996), p. 47.
22. Quoted in M. P. Holt, *The French Wars of Religion, 1562–1629* (Cambridge, 1995), p. 86.
23. Quoted in G. Mattingly, *The Armada* (Boston, 1959), pp. 216–217.
24. Quoted in T. Schieder, *Handbuch der Europäischen Geschichte* (Stuttgart, 1979), vol. 3, p. 579.

CHAPTER 14

EUROPE AND THE WORLD: NEW ENCOUNTERS, 1500–1800

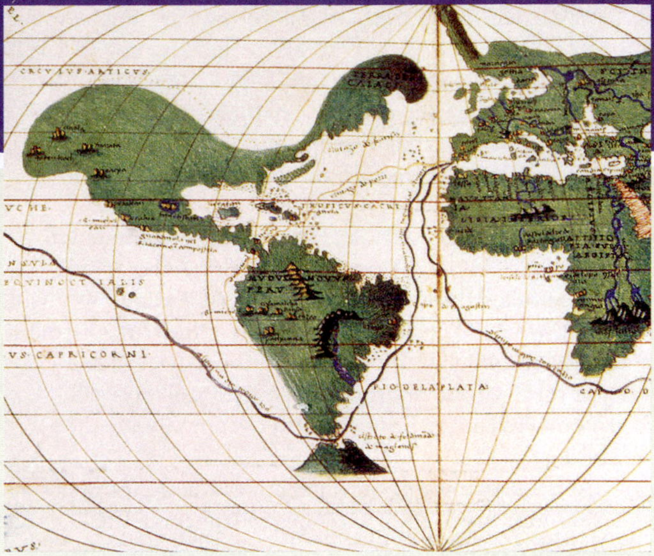

A 1536 Mercator projection map showing the route of Ferdinand Magellan's first circumnavigation of the world

The Everett Collection, Inc.

CHAPTER OUTLINE AND FOCUS QUESTIONS

On the Brink of a New World

Q Why did Europeans begin to embark on voyages of discovery and expansion at the end of the fifteenth century?

New Horizons: The Portuguese and Spanish Empires

Q How did Portugal and Spain acquire their overseas empires, and how did their empires differ?

New Rivals on the World Stage

Q How did the arrival of the Dutch, British, and French on the world scene in the seventeenth and eighteenth centuries affect Africa, Southeast Asia, India, China, and Japan? What were the main features of the African slave trade, and what effects did it have on Africa?

The Impact of European Expansion

Q How did European expansion affect both the conquered and the conquerors?

Toward a World Economy

Q What was mercantilism, and what was its relationship to colonial empires?

Critical Thinking

Q *What was the relationship between European overseas expansion and political, economic, and social developments in Europe?*

Connections to Today

Q *Considering both the benefits and the consequences, what are the similarities and differences between the overseas trade that developed in the seventeenth and eighteenth centuries and the global trade of the twenty-first century?*

WHILE MANY EUROPEANS were occupied with the problems of dynastic expansion and religious reform, others were taking voyages that propelled Europeans far beyond the medieval walls in which they had been enclosed for almost a thousand years. One of these adventurers was the Portuguese explorer Ferdinand Magellan. Convinced that he could find a sea passage to Asia through America, Magellan persuaded the king of Spain to finance an exploratory voyage. On August 10, 1519, Magellan set sail on the Atlantic with five ships and a Spanish crew of 277 men. After a stormy and difficult crossing of the Atlantic, Magellan's fleet moved down the coast of South America, searching for the elusive strait that would take him through. His Spanish ship captains thought he was crazy: "The fool is obsessed with his search for a strait," one remarked. "On the flame of his ambition he will crucify us all." At last, in October 1520, he found it, passing through a narrow waterway (later named the Strait of Magellan) and emerging into an unknown ocean that he called the Pacific Sea. Magellan reckoned that it would then be a short distance to the Spice Islands of the East, but he was badly mistaken. Week after week, he and his crew sailed on across the Pacific as their food supplies dwindled. According to one account, "When their last biscuit had gone, they scraped the maggots out of the casks, mashed them and served them as gruel. They made cakes out of sawdust soaked with the urine of rats—the rats themselves, as delicacies, had long since been hunted to extinction." At last they reached the islands that would later be called the Philippines (after King Philip II of Spain), where Magellan met his death at the hands of the natives. Although only one of his original fleet of five ships survived and returned to Spain, Magellan is still remembered as the first person to circumnavigate the world.

At the beginning of the sixteenth century, European adventurers like Magellan had begun launching small fleets into the vast reaches of the Atlantic Ocean. They were hardly aware that they were beginning a new era, not only for Europe, but for the peoples of Asia, Africa, and the Americas as well. Nevertheless, the voyages of these Europeans marked the beginning of a process that led to radical changes in the political, economic, and cultural life of the entire world.

Between 1500 and 1800, European power engulfed the world. In the Americas, Europeans established colonies that spread their laws, religions, and cultures. In the island regions of Southeast Asia, Europeans firmly established their rule. In other parts of Asia and in Africa, their activities ranged from trading goods to trafficking in humans, permanently altering the lives of the local peoples. In all regions touched by European expansion, the indigenous peoples faced exposure to new diseases, alteration of their religions and customs, and the imposition of new laws.

On the Brink of a New World

FOCUS QUESTION: Why did Europeans begin to embark on voyages of discovery and expansion at the end of the fifteenth century?

Nowhere has the dynamic and even ruthless energy of Western civilization been more apparent than in its expansion into the rest of the world. By the late sixteenth century, the Atlantic seaboard had become the center of a commercial activity that raised Portugal and Spain and later the Dutch Republic, England, and France to prominence. The age of expansion was a crucial factor in the European transition from the agrarian economy of the Middle Ages to a commercial and industrial capitalistic system. Expansion also brought Europeans into new and lasting contacts with non-European peoples that inaugurated a new age of world history in the sixteenth century.

The Motives for Expansion

For almost a millennium, Catholic Europe had been confined to one geographic area. Its one major attempt to expand beyond those frontiers, the Crusades, had largely failed. Of course, Europe had never completely lost touch with the outside world: the goods of Asia and Africa made their way into medieval castles, the works of Muslim philosophers were read in medieval universities, and in the ninth and tenth centuries, the Vikings had even made their way to the eastern fringes of North America. But in all cases, contacts with non-European civilizations remained limited until the end of the fifteenth century, when Europeans embarked on a remarkable series of overseas journeys. What caused Europeans to undertake such dangerous voyages to the ends of the earth?

FANTASTIC LANDS Europeans had long felt the lure of lands outside Europe as a result of a large body of fantasy literature about "other worlds" that blossomed in the Middle Ages. In the fourteenth century, the author of *The Travels of John Mandeville* spoke of realms (which he had never seen) filled with precious stones and gold. Other lands were more frightening and considerably less appealing. In one country, "the folk be great giants of twenty-eight foot long, or thirty foot long. . . . And they eat more gladly man's flesh than any other flesh." Farther north was a land inhabited by "full cruel and evil women. And they have precious stones in their eyes. And they be of that kind that if they behold any man with wrath they slay him at once with the beholding."[1] Other writers, however, enticed Europeans with descriptions of mysterious Christian kingdoms: the magical kingdom of Prester John in Africa and a Christian community in southern India that was supposedly founded by Thomas, an apostle of Jesus.

ECONOMIC MOTIVES Although Muslim control of Central Asia cut Europe off from the countries farther east, the Mongol conquests in the thirteenth century had reopened the doors. The most famous medieval travelers to the East were the Polos of Venice. Niccolò and Maffeo, merchants from Venice, accompanied by Niccolò's son Marco, undertook the lengthy journey to the court of the great Mongol ruler Khubilai Khan (1259–1294) in 1271. An account of Marco's experiences, the *Travels*, was the most informative of all the descriptions of Asia by medieval European travelers (see the box on p. 401). Others followed the Polos, but in the fourteenth century, the conquests of the Ottoman Turks and then the breakup of the Mongol Empire reduced Western traffic to the East. With the closing of the overland routes, a number of people in Europe became interested in the possibility of reaching Asia by sea to gain access to the spices and other precious items of the region. Christopher Columbus had a copy of Marco Polo's *Travels* in his possession when he began to envision his epoch-making voyage across the Atlantic Ocean.

An economic motive thus loomed large in European expansion in the Renaissance. Merchants, adventurers, and government officials had high hopes of finding new areas of trade, especially more direct access to the spices of the East. These continued to come to Europe via Arab intermediaries but were

MARCO POLO'S *TRAVELS*

ONE OF THE MOST POPULAR TEXTS in late medieval Europe was *The Travels of Marco Polo*, in which the Venetian merchant Marco Polo recounted the story of his journeys throughout East and South Asia. His description of the city of Kinsay—modern Hangzhou (HAHNG-joh) in eastern China—heavily influenced Europeans' conception of Asia.

Marco Polo, "Description of the Great City of Kinsay"

When you have left the city of Changan and have traveled for three days through a splendid country, passing a number of towns and villages, you arrive at the most noble city of Kinsay, a name which is as much as to say in our tongue "The City of Heaven," as I told you before. . . .

First and foremost, then, the document stated the city of Kinsay to be so great that it hath a hundred miles of compass. And there are in it twelve thousand bridges of stone, for the most part so lofty that a great fleet could pass beneath them. . . .

The document aforesaid also stated that the number and wealth of the merchants, and the amount of goods that passed through their hands, was so enormous that no man could form a just estimate thereof. . . .

All the streets are paved with stone or brick, as indeed are all the highways throughout Manzi, so that you ride and travel in every direction without inconvenience. . . .

There is another thing I must tell you. It is the custom for every burgess of this city, and in fact for every description of person in it, to write over his door his own name, the name of his wife, and those of his children, his slaves, and all the inmates of his house, and also the number of animals that he keeps. And if any one dies in the house then the name of that person is erased, and if any child is born its name is added. So in this way the sovereign is able to know exactly the population of the city. . . .

In this part [of the city] are ten principal markets, though besides these there are a vast number of others in the different parts of the town. . . . In each of the squares is held a market three days in the week, frequented by 40,000 or 50,000 persons, who bring thither for sale every possible necessary of life, so that there is always an ample supply of every kind of meat and game, as of roebuck, red-deer, fallow-deer, hares, rabbits, partridges, pheasants, francolins, quails, fowls, capons, and of ducks and geese an infinite quantity; for so many are bred on the Lake that for a Venice groat of silver you can have a couple of ducks. . . .

Those markets make a daily display of every kind of vegetables and fruits; and among the latter there are in particular certain pears of enormous size, weighing as much as ten pounds apiece. . . .

To give you an example of the vast consumption in this city let us take the article of *pepper*; and that will enable you in some measure to estimate what must be the quantity of victual, such as meat, wine, groceries, which have to be provided for the general consumption. Now Messer Marco heard it stated by one of the Great Khan's officers of customs that the quantity of pepper introduced daily for consumption into the city of Kinsay amounted to 43 loads, each load being equal to 223 lbs.

The houses of the citizens are well built and elaborately finished; and the delight they take in decoration, in painting and in architecture, leads them to spend in this way sums of money that would astonish you.

Q *What does this description of the city of Kinsay tell us about Europe in the late thirteenth century? Why would Asia appeal to European merchants who read Marco Polo's account?*

Source: H. Yule, ed., trans., *The Book of Ser Marco Polo*, vol. 1 (London: John Murray, 1903), pp. 185–193, 200–208.

outrageously expensive. In addition to the potential profits to be made from the spice trade, many European explorers and conquerors did not hesitate to express their desire for material gain in the form of gold and other precious metals. One Spanish conquistador (kahn-KEESS-tuh-dor) explained that the purpose of their mission to the New World was to "serve God and His Majesty, to give light to those who were in darkness, and to grow rich, as all men desire to do."[2]

RELIGIOUS ZEAL The conquistador's statement expressed another major reason for the overseas voyages—religious zeal. A crusading mentality was particularly strong in Portugal and Spain, where the Muslims had largely been driven out in the Middle Ages. Contemporaries of Prince Henry the Navigator of Portugal (see "The Development of a Portuguese Maritime Empire" later in this chapter) said that he was motivated by "his great desire to make increase in the faith of our Lord Jesus Christ and to bring him all the souls that should be saved." Although most scholars believe that the religious motive was secondary to economic considerations, it would be foolish to overlook the genuine desire of explorers and conquistadors, let alone missionaries, to convert the heathen to Christianity. Hernàn Cortés (hayr-NAHN kor-TAYSS *or* kor-TEZ), the conqueror of Mexico, asked his Spanish rulers if it was not their duty to ensure that the native Mexicans "are introduced into and instructed in the holy Catholic faith" and predicted that if "the devotion, trust and hope which they now have in their idols turned so as to repose with the divine power of the true God . . . they would work many miracles."[3] Spiritual and secular affairs were closely intertwined in the sixteenth century. No doubt, the desire for grandeur and glory as well as plain intellectual curiosity and a spirit of adventure also played some role in European expansion.

The Means for Expansion

If "God, glory, and gold" were the primary motives, what made the voyages possible? First of all, the expansion of Europe was connected to the growth of centralized monarchies during the Renaissance. Although historians still debate the degree of that centralization, the reality is that Renaissance expansion was a state enterprise. By the second half of the fifteenth century, European monarchies had increased both their authority and their resources and were in a position to turn their energies beyond their borders. For France, that meant the invasion of Italy, but for Portugal, a state not strong enough to pursue power in Europe, it meant going abroad. The Spanish monarchy was strong enough by the sixteenth century to pursue power both in Europe and beyond.

MAPS At the same time, Europeans had achieved a level of wealth and technology that enabled them to make a regular series of voyages beyond Europe. Although the highly schematic and symbolic medieval maps were of little help to sailors, the ***portolani*** (pohr-tuh-LAH-nee), or charts made by medieval navigators and mathematicians in the thirteenth and fourteenth centuries, were more useful. With details on coastal contours, distances between ports, and compass readings, these charts proved of great value for voyages in European waters. But because the portolani were drawn on a flat scale and took no account of the curvature of the earth, they were of little use for longer overseas voyages. Only when seafarers began to venture beyond the coast of Europe did they begin to accumulate information about the actual shape of the earth. By the end of the fifteenth century, cartography had developed to the point that Europeans possessed fairly accurate maps of the known world.

One of the most important world maps available to Europeans at the end of the fifteenth century was that of Ptolemy (TAHL-uh-mee), an astronomer of the second century C.E. Ptolemy's work, the *Geography*, had been known to Arab geographers as early as the eighth century, but it was not until the fifteenth century that a Latin translation was made of the work. Printed editions of Ptolemy's *Geography*, which contained his world map, became available from 1477 on. Ptolemy's map (see the accompanying illustration) showed the world as spherical with three major landmasses—Europe, Asia, and Africa—and only two oceans. In addition to showing the oceans as considerably smaller than the landmasses, Ptolemy had also drastically underestimated the circumference of the earth, which led Columbus and other adventurers to believe that it would be feasible to sail west from Europe to reach Asia.

SHIPS AND SAILING Europeans had also developed remarkably seaworthy ships as well as new navigational techniques. European shipbuilders had mastered the use of the axial rudder (an import from China) and had learned to combine the use of lateen sails with a square rig. With these innovations, they could construct ships mobile enough to sail against the wind and engage in naval warfare and also large enough to mount heavy cannons and carry a substantial amount of goods over long distances. Previously, sailors had used a quadrant and their knowledge of

Huntington Library/Superstock

Ptolemy's World Map. Contained in the Latin translation of Ptolemy's *Geography* was this world map, which did not become available to Europeans until the late 1400s. Scholars quickly accepted it as the most accurate map of its time. The twelve "wind faces," meant to show wind currents around the earth, were a fifteenth-century addition to the ancient map.

the position of the Pole Star to ascertain their latitude. Below the equator, however, this technique was useless. Only with the assistance of new navigational aids such as the compass and the astrolabe were they able to explore the high seas with confidence.

A final spur to exploration was the growing knowledge of the wind patterns in the Atlantic Ocean. The first European fleets sailing southward along the coast of West Africa had found their efforts to return hindered by the strong winds that blew steadily from the north along the coast. By the late fifteenth century, however, sailors had learned to tack out into the ocean, where they were able to catch westerly winds in the vicinity of the Azores that brought them back to the coast of western Europe. Christopher Columbus used this technique in his voyages to the Americas, and others relied on their new knowledge of the winds to round the continent of Africa in search of the Spice Islands.

New Horizons: The Portuguese and Spanish Empires

FOCUS QUESTION: How did Portugal and Spain acquire their overseas empires, and how did their empires differ?

Portugal took the lead in the European age of expansion when it began to explore the coast of Africa under the sponsorship of Prince Henry the Navigator (1394–1460). His motives were a blend of seeking a Christian kingdom as an ally against the Muslims, acquiring trade opportunities for Portugal, and spreading Christianity.

The Development of a Portuguese Maritime Empire

In 1419, Prince Henry founded a school for navigators on the southwestern coast of Portugal. Shortly thereafter, Portuguese fleets began probing southward along the western coast of Africa in search of gold, which had been carried northward from south of the Atlas Mountains in central Morocco for centuries. In 1441, Portuguese ships reached the Senegal River, just north of Cape Verde, and brought home a cargo of black Africans, most of whom were then sold as slaves to wealthy buyers elsewhere in Europe. Within a few years, an estimated one thousand slaves were shipped annually from the area back to Lisbon.

Through regular expeditions, the Portuguese gradually crept down the African coast, and in 1471, they discovered a new source of gold along the southern coast of the hump of West Africa (an area that would henceforth be known to Europeans as the Gold Coast). A few years later, they established contact with the state of Bakongo, near the mouth of the Zaire (Congo) River in Central Africa. To facilitate trade in gold, ivory, and slaves (some slaves were brought back to Lisbon, while others were bartered to local merchants for gold), the Portuguese leased land from local rulers and built stone forts along the coast.

THE PORTUGUESE IN INDIA Hearing reports of a route to India around the southern tip of Africa, Portuguese sea captains continued their probing. In 1488, Bartholomeu Dias (bar-toh-loh-MAY-oo DEE-ush) (ca. 1450–1500) took advantage of westerly winds in the South Atlantic to round the Cape of Good Hope, but he feared a mutiny from his crew and returned (see Map 14.1). Ten years later, a fleet under the command of Vasco da Gama (VAHSH-koh dah GAHM-uh) (ca. 1460–1524) rounded the cape and stopped at several ports controlled by Muslim merchants along the coast of East Africa. Da Gama's fleet then crossed the Arabian Sea and reached the port of Calicut, on the southwestern coast of India, on May 18, 1498. On arriving in Calicut, da Gama announced to his surprised hosts that he had come in search of "Christians and spices." He found no Christians, but he did find the spices he sought. Although he lost two ships en route, da Gama's remaining vessels returned to Europe with their holds filled with ginger and cinnamon, a cargo that earned the investors a profit of several thousand percent.

Portuguese fleets returned annually to the area, seeking to destroy Arab shipping and establish a monopoly in the spice trade. In 1509, a Portuguese armada defeated a combined fleet of Turkish and Indian ships off the coast of India and began to impose a blockade on the entrance to the Red Sea to cut off the flow of spices to Muslim rulers in Egypt and the Ottoman Empire. The following year, seeing the need for a land base in

Portuguese in India. The Portuguese continued their exploration of India after gaining control of Goa in 1509 by moving northwards into the territory of Gujarat. This painting by a Mughal artist portrays the killing of Bahadur Shah, leader of the Gujarat sultanate, by a Portuguese convoy in 1537 after Bahadur Shah had formed an alliance with the Portuguese in an attempt to regain control of his sultanate after it was conquered by the Mughals.

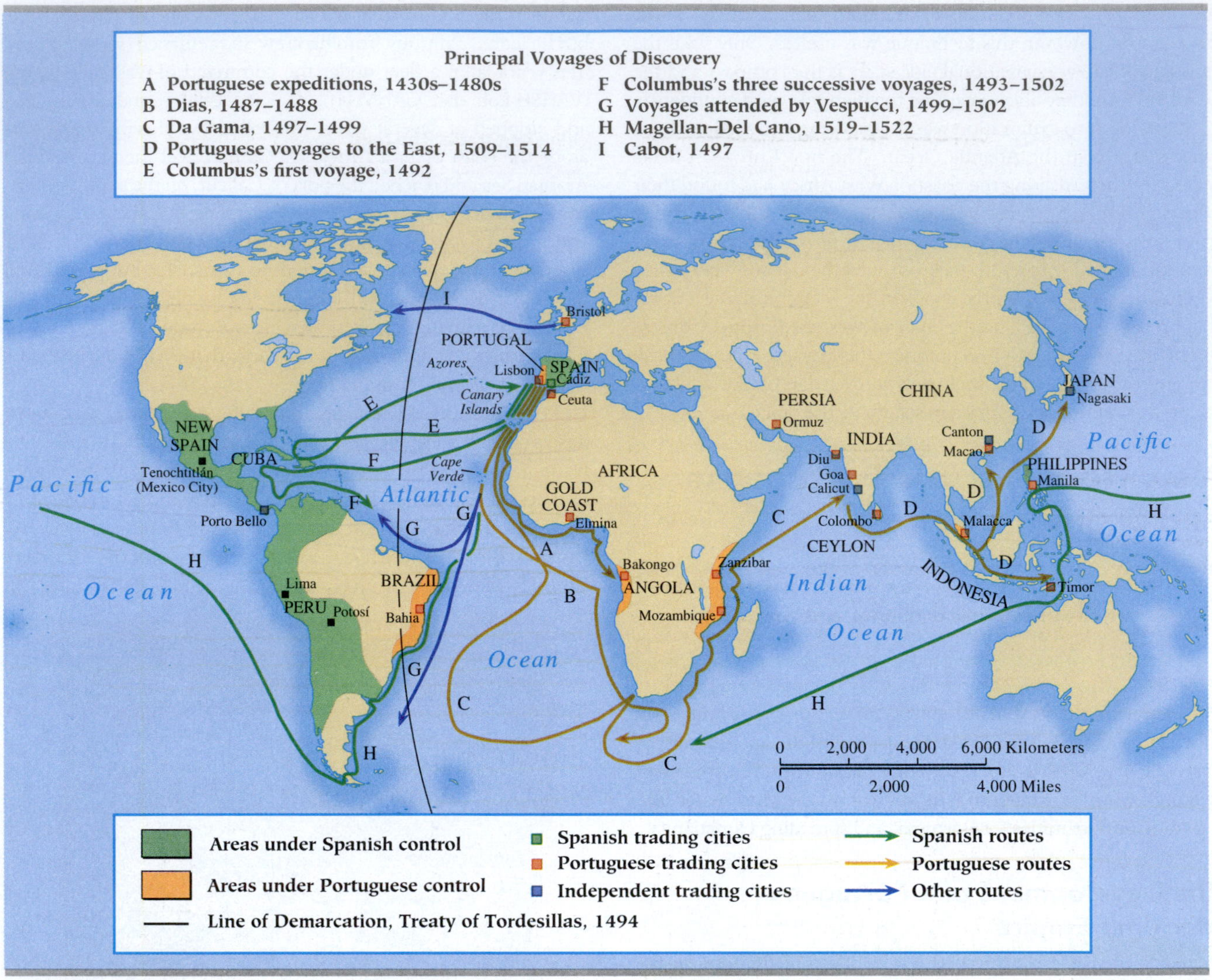

MAP 14.1 Discoveries and Possessions in the Fifteenth and Sixteenth Centuries. Desire for wealth was the main motivation of the early explorers, though spreading Christianity was also an important factor. Portugal under Prince Henry the Navigator initiated the first voyages in the early fifteenth century; Spain's explorations began at the century's end.

Q *Which regions of the globe were primarily explored by Portugal, and which were the main focus of Spain's voyages?*

the area, Admiral Afonso de Albuquerque (ah-FAHN-soh day AL-buh-kur-kee) (ca. 1462–1515) set up port facilities at Goa (GOH-uh), on the western coast of India south of present-day Mumbai (Bombay). Goa henceforth became the headquarters for Portuguese operations throughout the entire region.

IN SEARCH OF SPICES In the early sixteenth century, the Portuguese expanded their search for spices (see "Images of Everyday Life" on p. 405). In 1511, Albuquerque sailed into the harbor of Malacca (muh-LAK-uh) on the Malay peninsula. Its Muslim rulers had transformed Malacca into a thriving port and a major stopping point in the spice trade. After a short but bloody battle, the Portuguese seized the city and massacred the local Arab population. This slaughter initiated a fierce and brutal struggle between the Portuguese and the Arabs. According to one account, "To enhance the terror of his name he [Albuquerque] always separated Arabs from the other inhabitants of a captured city, and cut off the right hand of the men, and the noses and ears of the women."[4] By seizing Malacca, the Portuguese had not only weakened Arab control of the spice trade but obtained a major port en route to the Moluccas (muh-LUHK-uhz), then known as the Spice Islands.

From Malacca, the Portuguese launched expeditions farther east, to China and the Spice Islands. There they signed a treaty with a local ruler for the purchase and export of cloves to the European market. The new trading empire was now complete. Within a few years, the Portuguese had managed to seize control of the spice trade from Muslim traders and had garnered substantial profits for the Portuguese monarchy. Nevertheless, the Portuguese Empire remained limited, consisting only of trading posts on the coasts of

IMAGES OF EVERYDAY LIFE

Spices and World Trade

PEPPER, CINNAMON, NUTMEG, AND other spices from the East had long been a part of European life. The illustration at the top right from a fifteenth-century French manuscript shows pepper being harvested in Malabar, in southwestern India. Europeans' interest in finding a direct route to the Spice Islands intensified after the fall of Constantinople to the Ottoman Turks in 1453 caused the price of pepper to increase thirtyfold. The Venetians had played a dominant role in the spice trade via Constantinople, as is evident in the Venetian fresco shown at the bottom right. It depicts a spice seller's shop with a wide variety of spices for sale. Vasco da Gama's success in locating a route to the East by sailing around Africa shifted much of the control over the spice trade into Portuguese hands. Following the establishment in 1518 of a fort in Ceylon, the center of cinnamon production, the Portuguese were able to dominate Europe's cinnamon trade. The third illustration shows a portrait of da Gama from ca. 1600. The artist depicted the explorer holding a large stick of cinnamon in his right hand, an indication of the significance of the spice to his legacy and its role in his expeditions. Without the desire for spices, men such as da Gama and Christopher Columbus might not have ventured around Africa or across the Atlantic Ocean, thereby opening and forever altering European trade.

Bibliothèque Nationale, Paris/Archives Charmet/The Bridgeman Art Library

Gianni Dagli Orti/The Art Archive at Art Resource, NY

Scala/Art Resource, NY

India and China. The Portuguese lacked the power, the population, and the desire to colonize the Asian regions.

Why were the Portuguese so successful? Basically, their success was a matter of guns and seamanship. The first Portuguese fleet to arrive in Indian waters was relatively modest in size, consisting of three ships and twenty guns, a force sufficient for self-defense and intimidation but not for serious military operations. Later Portuguese fleets, which began to arrive with regularity early in the sixteenth century, were more heavily armed and were able not only to intimidate but also to inflict severe defeats if necessary on local naval and land forces. The Portuguese by no means possessed a monopoly on the use of firearms and explosives, but their effective use of naval technology, their heavy guns that could be mounted in the hulls of their sturdy vessels, and their tactics gave them military superiority over lightly armed rivals that they were able to exploit until the arrival of other European forces several decades later.

Voyages to the New World

While the Portuguese were seeking access to the spice trade of the Indies by sailing eastward through the Indian Ocean, the Spanish were attempting to reach the same destination by sailing westward across the Atlantic. Although the Spanish came to overseas discovery and exploration after the initial efforts of Henry the Navigator, their greater resources enabled them to establish a far grander overseas empire than that of the Portuguese—and one that was quite different.

THE VOYAGES OF COLUMBUS An important figure in the history of Spanish exploration was an Italian known as Christopher Columbus (1451–1506). Knowledgeable Europeans were aware that the world was round but had little understanding of its circumference or the extent of the continent of Asia. Convinced that the circumference of the earth was less than contemporaries believed and that Asia was larger than people thought, Columbus felt that Asia could be reached by sailing west instead of around Africa. After being rejected by the Portuguese, he persuaded Queen Isabella of Spain to finance his exploratory expedition.

With a crew of ninety men and three ships, the *Santa María*, the *Niña*, and the *Pinta*, Columbus set sail on August 3, 1492.

Museo Navale, Genova-Pegli/SuperStock

Christopher Columbus. Columbus was an Italian explorer who worked for the queen of Spain. He has become a symbol for two entirely different perspectives. To some, he was a great and heroic explorer who discovered the New World; to others, especially in Latin America, he was responsible for beginning a process of invasion that led to the destruction of an entire way of life. Because Columbus was never painted during his lifetime, the numerous portraits of him are more fanciful than accurate. The portrait shown here was probably done by the Italian painter Ridolfo Ghirlandaio.

CHRONOLOGY	The Portuguese and Spanish Empires in the Sixteenth Century
Bartholomeu Dias sails around the tip of Africa	1488
The voyages of Columbus	1492–1502
Treaty of Tordesillas	1494
Vasco da Gama lands at Calicut in India	1498
Portuguese seize Malacca	1511
Landing of Portuguese ships in southern China	1514
Magellan's voyage around the world	1519–1522
Spanish conquest of Mexico	1519–1522
Pizarro's conquest of the Inca	1530–1535

On October 12, he reached the Bahamas and then went on to explore the coastline of Cuba and the northern shores of Hispaniola (present-day Haiti and the Dominican Republic). Columbus believed that he had reached Asia, and in his reports to Queen Isabella and King Ferdinand upon his return to Spain, he assured them not only that he would eventually find gold but also that they had a golden opportunity to convert the natives—whom Columbus persisted in calling "Indians"—to Christianity (see the box on p. 407). In three subsequent voyages (1493, 1498, 1502), Columbus sought in vain to find a route to the Asian mainland. In his four voyages, Columbus landed on all the major islands of the Caribbean and the mainland of Central America, still convinced that he had reached the Indies in Asia.

NEW VOYAGES Although Columbus clung to his belief until his death, other explorers soon realized that he had discovered a new frontier altogether. State-sponsored explorers joined the race to the New World. A Venetian seaman, John Cabot, explored the New England coastline of the Americas under a license from King Henry VII of England. The continent of South America was discovered accidentally by the Portuguese sea captain Pedro Cabral (kuh-BRAL) in 1500. Amerigo Vespucci (ahm-ay-REE-goh vess-POO-chee), a Florentine, accompanied several voyages and wrote a series of letters describing the geography of the New World. The publication of these letters led to the use of the name "America" (after Amerigo) for the new lands.

The first two decades of the sixteenth century witnessed numerous overseas voyages that explored the eastern coasts of both North and South America. Vasco Nuñez de Balboa (VAHS-koh NOON-yez day bal-BOH-uh) (1475–1519), a Spanish explorer, led an expedition across the Isthmus of Panama and reached the Pacific Ocean in 1513. Perhaps the most dramatic of all these expeditions was the journey of Ferdinand Magellan (1480–1521) in 1519. After passing through the strait named after him at the southern tip of South America, he sailed across the Pacific Ocean and reached the Philippines, where he was killed by the natives. Although only one of his fleet of five ships completed the return voyage to Spain, Magellan's name is still associated with the first known circumnavigation of the earth.

COLUMBUS LANDS IN THE NEW WORLD

ON RETURNING FROM AMERICA, which he believed was the coast of Asia, Christopher Columbus wrote about his experience. In this passage from a letter describing his first voyage, he tells of his arrival on the island of Hispaniola (Haiti). Historians believe that Columbus wrote this letter for public consumption.

Letter to Raphael Sanchez, Treasurer to the King and Queen of Spain

Thirty-three days after my departure from Cadiz I reached the Indian sea, where I discovered many islands, thickly peopled, of which I took possession without resistance in the name of our most illustrious Monarch, by public proclamation and with unfurled banners. To the first of these islands, I gave the name of the blessed Savior (San Salvador), relying upon whose protection I had reached this as well as the other islands; to each of these I also gave a name. . . .

The inhabitants of both sexes in this island, and in all the others which I have seen, or of which I have received information, go always naked as they were born, with the exception of some of the women, who use the covering of a leaf, or small bough, or an apron of cotton which they prepare for that purpose. None of them are possessed of any iron, neither have they weapons, being unacquainted with, and indeed incompetent to use them, not from any deformity of body (for they are well-formed), but because they are timid and full of fear. . . . As soon however as they see that they are safe, and have laid aside all fear, they are very simple and honest, and exceedingly liberal with all they have; none of them refusing any thing he may possess when he is asked for it. . . . They also give objects of great value for trifles, and content themselves with very little or nothing in return.

I however forbade that these trifles and articles of no value (such as pieces of dishes, plates, and glass, keys, and leather straps) should be given to them, although if they could obtain them, they imagined themselves to be possessed of the most beautiful trinkets in the world. . . . Thus, they bartered, like idiots, cotton and gold for fragments of bows, glasses, bottles, and jars. . . .

In all these islands there is no difference of physiognomy, of manners, or of language, but they all clearly understand each other, a circumstance very propitious for the realization of what I conceive to be the principal wish of our most serene King, namely, the conversion of these people to the holy faith of Christ, to which indeed, as far as I can judge, they are very favorable and well-disposed. . . .

Finally, to compress into a few words the entire summary of my voyage and speedy return, and of the advantages derivable there from, I promise, that with a little assistance afforded me by our most invincible sovereigns, I will procure them as much gold as they need, and as great a quantity of spices and cotton. . . . Let Christ rejoice on earth, as he rejoices in heaven in the prospect of the salvation of the souls of so many nations hitherto lost. Let us also rejoice as well on account of the exaltation of our faith as on account of the increase of our temporal prosperity, of which not only Spain but all Christendom will be partakers.

Q *What evidence in Columbus's comments suggests that his remarks were made mainly for public consumption and not just for the Spanish court? What elements in society might have responded to his statements, and why?*

Source: R. H. Major, ed., trans., *Letters by Christopher Columbus* (London: Hakluyt Society, 1843), pp. 35–43.

The Europeans referred to the newly discovered territories as the New World, even though they held flourishing civilizations populated by millions of people. But the Americas were indeed new to the Europeans, who quickly saw opportunities for conquest and exploitation. The Spanish, in particular, were interested because the 1494 Treaty of Tordesillas (tor-day-SEE-yass) had divided up the newly discovered world into separate Portuguese and Spanish spheres of influence, and it turned out that most of South America (except for the eastern hump) fell within the Spanish sphere (see Map 14.1 on p. 404). Hereafter the route east around the Cape of Good Hope was to be reserved for the Portuguese while the route across the Atlantic was assigned to Spain.

The Spanish Empire in the New World

The Spanish conquerors known as **conquistadors** were hardy individuals motivated by a typical sixteenth-century blend of glory, greed, and religious crusading zeal. Although authorized by the Castilian crown, these groups were financed and outfitted privately, not by the government. Their superior weapons, organizational skills, and determination brought the conquistadors incredible success. They also benefited from rivalries among the native peoples and the decimation of the native peoples by European diseases (see "Disease in the New World" later in this chapter).

EARLY CIVILIZATIONS IN MESOAMERICA Before the Spaniards arrived in the New World, Mesoamerica (modern Mexico and Central America) had already hosted a number of flourishing civilizations. Beginning around 300 C.E., on the Yucatán peninsula a people known as the Maya (MY-uh) had built one of the most sophisticated civilizations in the Americas. The Maya built splendid temples and pyramids, were accomplished artists, and developed a sophisticated calendar, as accurate as any in existence in the world at that time. The Maya were an agrarian people who cleared the dense rain forests, developed farming,

The Maya

and built a patchwork of city-states. Mayan civilization came to include much of Central America and southern Mexico. For unknown reasons, Mayan civilization began to decline around 800 and had collapsed less than a hundred years later.

Sometime during the early twelfth century C.E., a people known as the Aztecs began a long migration that brought them to the Valley of Mexico. They established their capital at Tenochtitlán (tay-nawch-teet-LAHN) between 1325 and 1345 on an island in the middle of Lake Texcoco (now the location of Mexico City). For the next hundred years, the Aztecs built their city, constructing temples, other public buildings, houses, and causeways of stone across Lake Texcoco to the north, south, and west, linking the many islands to the mainland. At the beginning of the fifteenth century, they built an aqueduct to bring fresh water from a spring 4 miles away. Tenochtitlán benefited from commercial routes that brought goods from as far away as the Gulf of Mexico and the Inca Empire in northern South America. By 1500, flourishing trade and agricultural growth supported cities of over 80,000 inhabitants, with some estimates as high as 200,000 inhabitants, larger than most European cities of the time.

The Aztecs

The Aztecs were outstanding warriors, and while they were building their capital city, they also set out to bring the entire area around the city under their control. By the early fifteenth century, they had become the leading city-state in the lake region. For the remainder of the fifteenth century, the Aztecs consolidated their rule over much of what is modern Mexico, from the Atlantic to the Pacific Ocean and as far south as the Guatemalan border. The new kingdom was not a centralized state but a collection of semi-independent territories governed by local lords. The Aztec ruler confirmed these rulers in their authority in return for the payment of tribute. This loose political organization would later contribute to the downfall of the Aztec Empire.

SPANISH CONQUEST OF THE AZTEC EMPIRE In 1519, a Spanish expedition under the command of Hernán Cortés (1485–1547) landed at Veracruz, on the Gulf of Mexico. He marched to the city of Tenochtitlán (see the box on p. 409) at the head of a small contingent of troops (550 soldiers and 16 horses); as he went, he made alliances with city-states that had tired of the oppressive rule of the Aztecs. Especially important was Tlaxcala (tuh-lah-SKAH-lah), a state that the Aztecs had not been able to conquer. In November, Cortés arrived at Tenochtitlán, where he received a friendly welcome from the Aztec monarch Moctezuma (mahk-tuh-ZOO-muh) (often called Montezuma). At first, Moctezuma believed that his visitor was a representative of Quetzalcoatl (KWET-sul-koh-AHT-ul), the god who had departed from his homeland centuries before and had promised that he would return. Riddled with fears, Moctezuma offered gifts of gold to the foreigners and gave them a palace to use while they were in the city.

But the Spaniards quickly wore out their welcome. They took Moctezuma hostage and proceeded to pillage the city. In the fall of 1520, one year after Cortés had arrived, the local population revolted and drove the invaders from the city. Many of the Spaniards were killed, but the Aztecs soon experienced new disasters. As one Aztec related, "At about the time that the Spaniards had fled from Mexico, there came a great sickness, a pestilence, the smallpox." With no natural immunity to the diseases of the Europeans, many Aztecs fell sick and died (see "Disease in the New World" later in this chapter). Meanwhile, Cortés received fresh soldiers from his new allies; the state of Tlaxcala alone provided 50,000 warriors. After four months, the city capitulated.

The Spaniards then embarked on a new wave of destruction. The pyramids, temples, and palaces were leveled, and the stones were used to build Spanish government buildings and churches. The rivers and canals were filled in. The mighty Aztec Empire on mainland Mexico was no more. Between 1531 and 1550, the Spanish gained control of northern Mexico.

THE INCA In the late fourteenth century, the Inca were a small community in the area of Cuzco (KOOS-koh), a city located at an altitude of 10,000 feet in the mountains of southern Peru. In the

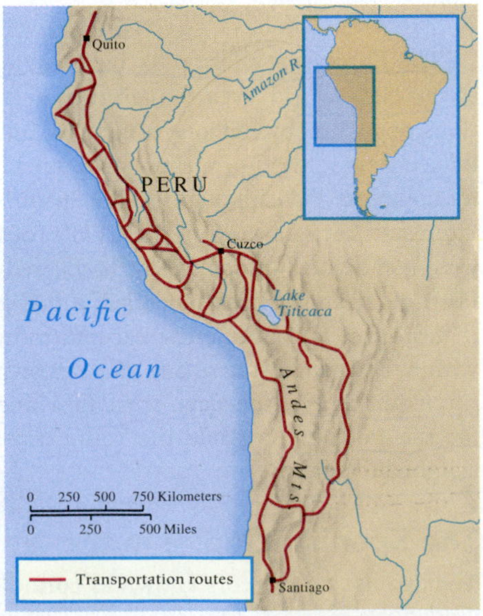

The Inca

THE SPANISH CONQUISTADOR: CORTÉS AND THE CONQUEST OF MEXICO

HERNÁN CORTÉS WAS A MINOR SPANISH nobleman who came to the New World in 1504 to seek his fortune. Contrary to his superior's orders, Cortés waged an independent campaign of conquest and overthrew the Aztec Empire in Mexico (1519–1522). Cortés wrote a series of five reports to Emperor Charles V to justify his action. The second report includes a description of Tenochtitlán, the capital of the Aztec Empire. The Spanish conquistador and his men were obviously impressed by this city, awesome in its architecture yet built by people who lacked European technology, such as wheeled vehicles and tools of hard metal.

Cortés's Description of Tenochtitlán

The great city Tenochtitlán is built in the midst of this salt lake, and it is two leagues from the heart of the city to any point on the mainland. Four causeways lead to it, all made by hand and some twelve feet wide. The city itself is as large as Seville or Cordoba. The principal streets are very broad and straight, the majority of them being of beaten earth, but a few and at least half of the smaller thoroughfares are waterways along which they pass in their canoes. Moreover, even the principal streets have openings at regular distances so that the water can freely pass from one to another, and these openings which are very broad are spanned by great bridges of huge beams, very stoutly put together, so firm indeed that over many of them ten horsemen can ride at once. . . .

The city has many open squares in which markets are continuously held and the general business of buying and selling proceeds. One square in particular is twice as big as that of Salamanca and completely surrounded by arcades where there are daily more than 60,000 folk buying and selling. Every kind of merchandise such as may be met with in every land is for sale there, whether of food and victuals, or ornaments of gold and silver, or lead, brass, copper, tin, precious stones, bones, shells, snails and feathers; limestone for building is likewise sold there, stone both rough and polished, bricks burnt and unburnt, wood of all kinds and in all stages of preparation. . . . There are houses as it were of apothecaries where they sell medicines made from these herbs, both for drinking and for use as ointments and salves. There are barbers' shops where you may have your hair washed and cut. There are other shops where you may obtain food and drink. . . .

Finally, to avoid being wordy in telling all the wonders of this city, I will simply say that the manner of living among the people is very similar to that in Spain, and considering that this is a barbarous nation shut off from a knowledge of the true God or communication with enlightened nations, one may well marvel at the orderliness and good government which is everywhere maintained.

The actual service of Montezuma and those things which call for admiration by their greatness and state would take so long to describe that I assure your Majesty I do not know where to begin with any hope of ending. For as I have already said, what could there be more astonishing than that a barbarous monarch such as he should have reproductions made in gold, silver, precious stones, and feathers of all things to be found in his land, and so perfectly reproduced that there is no goldsmith or silversmith in the world who could better them, nor can one understand what instrument could have been used for fashioning the jewels. . . .

Q *What did Cortés focus on in his description of this Aztec city? Why do you think he felt justified in overthrowing the Aztec Empire?*

Source: J. H. Parry, *The European Reconnaissance: Selected Documents* (New York: Harper & Row, 1968).

1440s, however, under the leadership of their powerful ruler Pachakuti (pah-chah-KOO-tee), the Inca launched a campaign of conquest that eventually brought the entire region under their control. Pachakuti created a highly centralized state. Cuzco, the capital, was transformed from a city of mud and thatch into an imposing city of stone. Under Pachakuti and his immediate successors, Topa Inca and Huayna Inca (the word *Inca* means "ruler"), the boundaries of the Inca Empire were extended as far as Ecuador, central Chile, and the edge of the Amazon basin. The empire included perhaps 12 million people.

Pachakuti divided his realm into four quarters, each ruled by a governor. The quarters were in turn divided into provinces, each also ruled by a governor. The governors were usually chosen from relatives of the royal family. Each province was supposed to contain about 10,000 residents. At the top of the entire system was the emperor, who was believed to be descended from the sun god.

The Inca were great builders. One major project was a system of 24,800 miles of roads that extended from the border of modern-day Colombia to a point south of modern-day Santiago, Chile. Two major roadways extended in a north-south direction, one through the Andes Mountains and the other along the coast, with connecting routes between them. Rest houses, located a day's walk apart, and storage depots were placed along the roads. The Inca also built various types of bridges, including some of the finest examples of suspension bridges in premodern times, over the ravines and waterways.

SPANISH CONQUEST OF THE INCA EMPIRE The Inca Empire was still flourishing when the first Spanish expeditions arrived in the area. In December 1530, Francisco Pizarro (frahn-CHESS-koh puh-ZAHR-oh) (ca. 1475–1541) landed on the Pacific coast of South America with a band of about 180 men, but like Cortés, he had steel weapons, gunpowder, and horses, none of which were familiar to his hosts. Pizarro was also lucky because the Inca Empire had already succumbed to an epidemic of smallpox. Like the Aztecs, the Inca had no immunities to European diseases, and all too soon, smallpox was devastating entire villages. In another stroke of good fortune for Pizarro, even the Inca emperor was a victim. Upon the emperor's death, two sons claimed the throne, setting off a civil war. Pizarro took advantage of the situation by seizing Atahualpa (ah-tuh-WAHL-puh), whose forces had just defeated his brother's. Armed only with stones, arrows, and light spears, Incan soldiers were no match for the charging horses of the Spanish, let alone their guns and cannons. After executing Atahualpa, Pizarro and his soldiers, aided by their Incan allies, marched on Cuzco and captured the Incan capital. By 1535, Pizarro had established a capital at Lima for a new colony of the Spanish Empire.

ADMINISTRATION OF THE SPANISH EMPIRE Spanish policy toward the Indians of the New World was a combination of confusion, misguided paternalism, and cruel exploitation. Whereas the conquistadors made decisions based on expediency and their own interests, Queen Isabella declared the native peoples to be subjects of Castile and instituted the Spanish ***encomienda*** (en-koh-MYEN-dah), an economic and social system that permitted the conquering Spaniards to collect tribute from the Indians and use them as laborers. In return, the holders of an encomienda were supposed to protect the Indians, pay them wages, and supervise their spiritual needs. In practice, this meant that the settlers were free to implement the paternalistic system of the government as they pleased. Three thousand miles from Spain, Spanish settlers largely ignored their government and brutally used the Indians to pursue their own economic interests. Indians were put to work on plantations and in the lucrative gold and silver mines. In Peru, the Spanish made use of the mita, a system that allowed authorities to draft native labor to work in the silver mines.

Forced labor, starvation, and especially disease took a fearful toll of Indian lives. Voices were raised to protest the harsh treatment of the Indians, especially by Dominican friars. In a 1510 sermon, Antón Montecino startled churchgoers in Santo Domingo by saying:

> And you are heading for damnation . . . for you are destroying an innocent people. For they are God's people, these innocents, whom you destroyed. By what right do you make them die? Mining gold for you in your mines or working for you in your fields, by what right do you unleash enslaving wars upon them? They lived in peace in this land before you came, in peace in their own homes. They did nothing to harm you to cause you to slaughter them wholesale.[5]

In 1542, largely in response to the publications of Bartolomé de Las Casas (bahr-toh-loh-MAY day lahs KAH-sahs), a Dominican friar who championed the Indians (see the box on p. 411), the government abolished the encomienda system and provided more protection for the natives.

In the New World, Spanish nobles recreated the urban cities of Spain by constructing ordered towns built around a central plaza. The Spanish built their first town, Santo Domingo, in 1501 on the island of Hispaniola; by 1580, they had constructed 240 towns, with Mexico City and Lima being the largest. By 1600, over 250 thousand Spanish émigrés had arrived from Spain to fill their streets.

The Spanish developed an administrative system based on viceroys to administer their new territories. Spanish possessions were initially divided into two major administrative units: New Spain (Mexico, Central America, and the Caribbean islands), with its center in Mexico City, and Peru (western South America), governed by a **viceroy** in Lima. According to legislation of 1542, "the kingdoms of New Spain and Peru are to be ruled and governed by viceroys, who shall represent our royal person, hold the superior government, do and administer justice equally to all our subjects and vassals, and concern themselves with everything that will promote the calm, peace, ennoblement and pacification of those provinces."[6] Each viceroy served as the king's chief civil and military officer and was aided by advisory groups called ***audiencias*** (ow-dee-en-SEE-uss), which also functioned as supreme judicial bodies.

By papal agreement, the Catholic monarchs of Spain were given extensive rights over ecclesiastical affairs in the New World. They could appoint all bishops and clergy, build churches, collect fees, and supervise the various religious orders that sought to convert the heathen. Catholic missionaries converted and baptized hundreds of thousands of Indians in the early years of the conquest.

The mass conversion of the Indians brought the organizational and institutional structures of Catholicism to the New World. Dioceses, parishes, cathedrals, schools, and hospitals—all the trappings of civilized European society—soon appeared in the Spanish Empire. So, too, did the Spanish Inquisition, established first in Peru in 1570 and in Mexico the following year.

Disease in the New World

When Columbus reached the Caribbean island of Hispaniola in 1492, he brought more than gunpowder, horses, attack dogs, and soldiers to the shores of the New World. With no natural resistance to European diseases, the Indians of America were ravaged by smallpox, influenza, measles, and pneumonic plague, and later by typhus, yellow fever, and cholera.

Smallpox, a highly contagious disease, was spread through droplets in the air or direct contact with contaminated objects, such as clothing. In 1518, a smallpox epidemic erupted and quickly spread along trade routes from the Caribbean to Mesoamerica, killing a third of the Indian population. The disease ultimately reached Tenochtitlán and helped make

LAS CASAS AND THE SPANISH TREATMENT OF THE AMERICAN NATIVES

BARTOLOMÉ DE LAS CASAS (1474–1566) participated in the conquest of Cuba and received land and Indians in return for his efforts. But in 1514 he underwent a radical transformation and came to believe that the Indians had been cruelly mistreated by his fellow Spaniards. He became a Dominican friar and spent the remaining years of his life (he lived to the age of ninety-two) fighting for the Indians. This selection is taken from his most influential work, which is known to English readers as *The Tears of the Indians*. This work was largely responsible for the "black legend" of the Spanish as inherently "cruel and murderous fanatics." Most scholars feel that Las Casas may have exaggerated his account in order to shock his contemporaries into action.

Bartolomé de Las Casas, *The Tears of the Indians*

There is nothing more detestable or more cruel, than the tyranny which the Spaniards use toward the Indians for the getting of pearl. Surely the infernal torments cannot much exceed the anguish that they endure, by reason of that way of cruelty; for they put them under water some four or five ells [15 to 18 feet] deep, where they are forced without any liberty of respiration, to gather up the shells wherein the pearls are; sometimes they come up again with nets full of shells to take breath, but if they stay any while to rest themselves, immediately comes a hangman row'd in a little boat, who as soon as he has well beaten them, drags them again to their labor. Their food is nothing but filth, and the very same that contains the pearl, with a small portion of that bread which that country affords; in the first where of there is little nourishment; and as for the latter, it is made with great difficulty, besides that they have not enough of that neither for sustenance; they lie upon the ground in fetters, lest they should run away; and many times they are drown'd in this labor, and are never seen again till they swim upon the top of the waves: oftentimes they also are devoured by certain sea monsters, that are frequent in those seas. Consider whether this hard usage of the poor creatures be consistent with the precepts which God commands concerning charity to our neighbor, by those that cast them so undeservedly into the dangers of a cruel death, causing them to perish without any remorse or pity, or allowing them the benefit of the sacraments, or the knowledge of religion; it being impossible for them to live any time under the water; and this death is so much the more painful, by reason that by the constricting of the breast, while the lungs strive to do their office, the vital parts are so afflicted that they die vomiting the blood out of their mouths. Their hair also, which is by nature black, is hereby changed and made of the same color with that of the sea wolves; their bodies are also so besprinkled with the froth of the sea, that they appear rather like monsters than men.

Q *In what ways did this account help create the image of the Spaniards as "cruel and murderous fanatics"? What motives may have prompted Las Casas to make this critique, and how might his opinions have affected the broader standing of Spain in the global politics of the age?*

Source: Bartolomé de Las Casas, *The Tears of the Indians* (Williamstown, Mass.: The John Lilburne Company Publishers, 1970).

possible its conquest by Hernán Cortés. When the Spaniards reentered the city in 1521, they found an appalling scene, as reported by Bernal Díaz (ber-NAHL DEE-ass), who accompanied Cortés:

> We could not walk without treading on the bodies and heads of dead Indians. I have read about the destruction of Jerusalem, but I do not think the mortality was greater there than here in Mexico, where most of the warriors who had crowded in from all the provinces and subject towns had died. As I have said, the dry land and the stockades were piled with corpses. Indeed, the stench was so bad that no one could endure it. . . . Even Cortés was ill from the odors which assailed his nostrils.[7]

Smallpox ravaged the Aztecs. The Inca suffered a similar fate from smallpox and measles as well.

Throughout the sixteenth century, outbreaks of Old World diseases continued to spark epidemics that killed off large proportions of the local populations. By 1630, smallpox had reached New England. The ferocity of the epidemics left few survivors to tend the crops, leading to widespread starvation and higher mortality rates. Although scholarly estimates vary drastically, a reasonable guess is that 30 to 40 percent of the local populations died. On Hispaniola alone, out of an initial population of 100,000 Indians when Columbus arrived in 1492, only 300 survived by 1570. The population of central Mexico, estimated at roughly 11 million in 1519, had declined to 6.5 million by 1540 and 2.5 million by the end of the sixteenth century.

The high mortality rates among the native populations resulted in a shortage of workers for the Europeans, which led them to turn to Africa for the labor needed for the silver

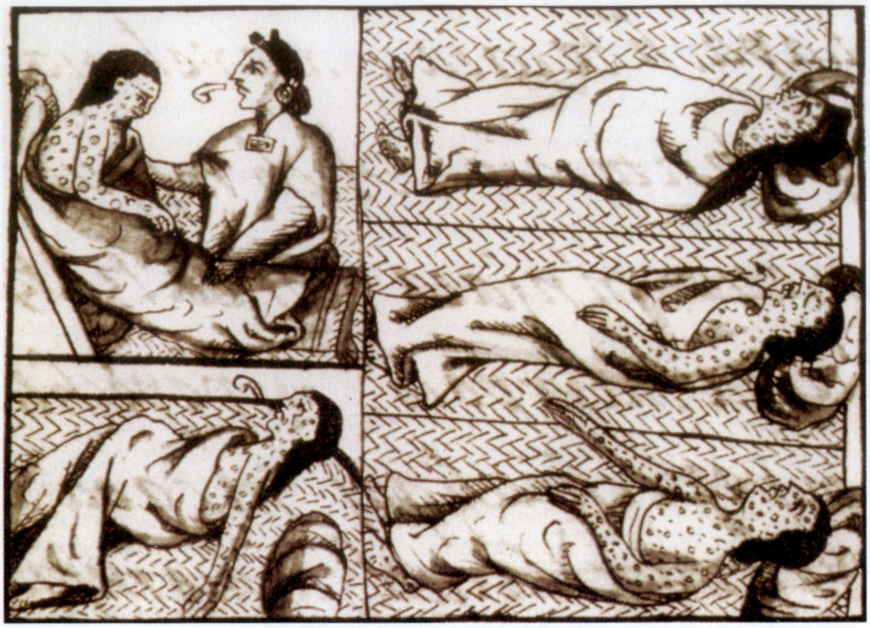

Biblioteca Laurenziana, Florence//NYPL/Science Source/Getty Images

Aztec Victims of Smallpox. The indigenous populations of the New World had no immunities to the diseases of the Old World, such as smallpox. By 1520, smallpox had spread throughout the Caribbean and Mesoamerica. This sixteenth-century drawing by a Franciscan friar portrays Native Americans afflicted with smallpox. The pustules that often covered the body are clearly depicted. The figure at the lower right twists in agony, reflecting the immense pain experienced by those who contracted the disease.

mines and sugar plantations (see "Africa: The Slave Trade" later in this chapter). Despite the Europeans' technological advantages, the biological weapons that they brought with them from the Old World proved to have an even greater impact on the Americas.

New Rivals on the World Stage

FOCUS QUESTIONS: How did the arrival of the Dutch, British, and French on the world scene in the seventeenth and eighteenth centuries affect Africa, Southeast Asia, India, China, and Japan? What were the main features of the African slave trade, and what effects did it have on Africa?

Portugal and Spain had been the first Atlantic nations to take advantage of the age of exploration, starting in the late fifteenth century, and both had become great colonial powers. In the seventeenth century, however, their European neighbors to the north—first the Dutch and then the French and English—moved to replace the Portuguese and Spanish and create their own colonial empires. The new rivals and their rivalry soon had an impact on much of the rest of the world—in Africa, Asia, and the Americas.

Africa: The Slave Trade

Although the primary objective of the Portuguese in sailing around Africa was to find a sea route to the Spice Islands, they soon discovered that profits could be made in Africa itself. So did other Europeans.

The Portuguese built forts on both the western and eastern coasts of Africa and tried, above all, to dominate the trade in gold. During the mid-seventeenth century, however, the Dutch seized a number of Portuguese forts along the West African coast and at the same time took control of much of the Portuguese trade across the Indian Ocean.

The Dutch East India Company, a trading company established in 1602 under government sponsorship, also set up a settlement in southern Africa, at the Cape of Good Hope, to serve as a base to supply food and other provisions to Dutch ships en route to the Spice Islands. Eventually, however, it developed into a permanent colony. Dutch farmers, known as Boers, began to settle in areas outside the city of Cape Town. The area's moderate climate and freedom from tropical diseases made it attractive for Europeans to settle there.

The European exploration of the African coastline did not affect most Africans living in the interior of the continent, but for peoples living on or near the coast, the impact was great indeed. As the trade in slaves increased during the sixteenth through the eighteenth centuries, thousands and then millions of Africans were removed from their homes and forcibly shipped to plantations in the New World.

ORIGINS OF THE SLAVE TRADE Traffic in slaves was not new. As in other areas of the world, slavery had been practiced in Africa since ancient times. In the fifteenth century, it continued at a fairly steady level. The primary market for African slaves was the Middle East, where most were used as domestic servants. Slavery also existed in many European countries, where some slaves from Africa or war captives from the regions north of the Black Sea were used as household help or agricultural workers.

At first, the Portuguese simply replaced European slaves with African ones. During the second half of the fifteenth century, about a thousand slaves were taken to Portugal each year. Most ended up serving as domestic servants for affluent families in Europe. But the discovery of the Americas in the 1490s and the planting of sugarcane in South America and the islands of the Caribbean changed the situation drastically.

Cane sugar had first been introduced to Europeans from the Middle East during the Crusades. At the end of the fifteenth century, the Portuguese set up sugar plantations worked by African laborers on an island off the central coast of Africa. During the sixteenth century, sugarcane plantations were set up along the eastern coast of Brazil and on several islands in the Caribbean, reaching 195 in number by 1600. Because the growing of cane sugar demands both skill and large quantities of labor, the new plantations required more workers than could be provided by the small American Indian population in the New World, decimated by diseases imported from the Old World. Since the climate and soil of much of West Africa were not conducive to the cultivation of sugar, African slaves began to be shipped to Brazil and the Caribbean to work on the plantations. The first were sent from Portugal, but in 1518, a Spanish ship carried the first boatload of African slaves directly from Africa to the New World.

GROWTH OF THE SLAVE TRADE During the next two centuries, the trade in slaves grew dramatically and became part of the **triangular trade** connecting Europe, Africa, and the American continents that characterized the new Atlantic economy (see Map 14.2). European merchant ships (primarily those of England, France, Spain, Portugal, and the Dutch Republic) carried European manufactured goods, such as guns, gin, and cloth, to Africa, where they were traded for a cargo of slaves. The slaves were then shipped to the Americas and sold. European merchants then bought tobacco, molasses, sugar, rum, coffee, and raw cotton and shipped them back to Europe to be sold in European markets.

An estimated 275,000 enslaved Africans were exported to other countries during the sixteenth century, with 2,000 going annually to the Americas alone. The total climbed to over a million in the seventeenth century and jumped to 6 million in the eighteenth century, when the trade spread from West and Central Africa to East Africa. Even during the nineteenth century, when Great Britain and other European countries tried to end the slave trade, nearly 2 million were exported. Altogether as many as 10 million African slaves were transported to the Americas between the sixteenth and nineteenth centuries. About half were transported in British ships, with the rest divided among French, Dutch, Portuguese, Danish, and later, American ships.

One reason for the astonishing numbers of slaves, of course, was the high death rate. The journey of slaves from Africa to the Americas became known as the **Middle Passage**, the middle leg of the triangular trade route. African slaves were closely

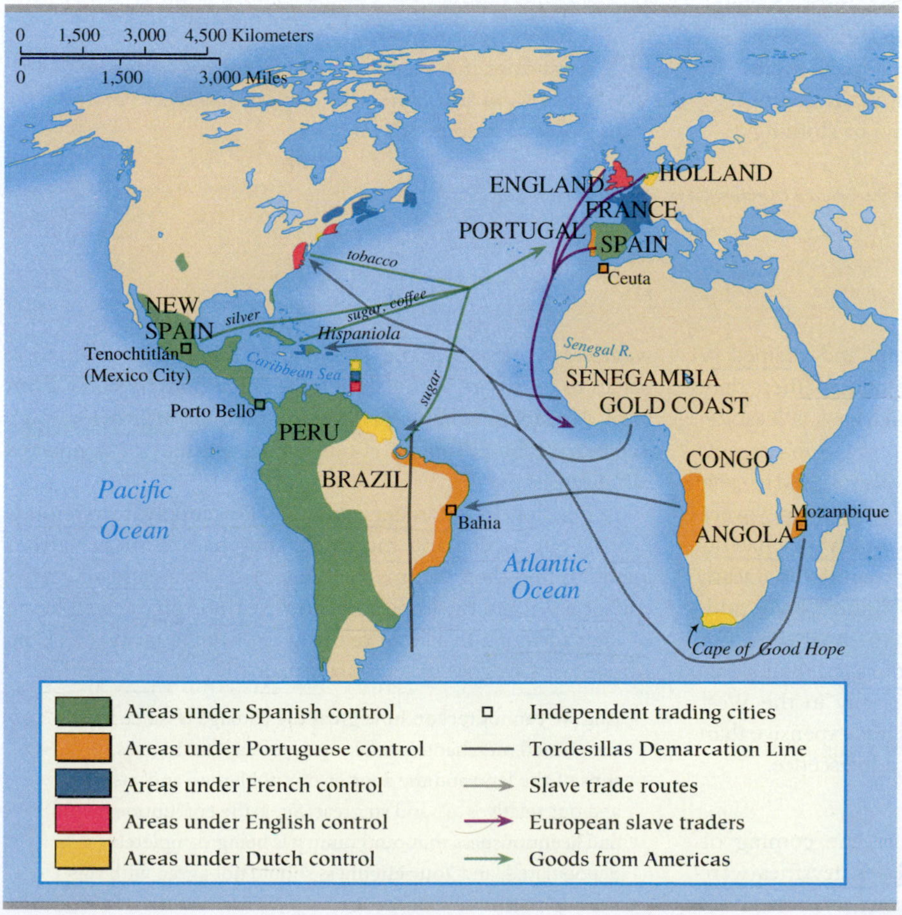

MAP 14.2 Triangular Trade Route in the Atlantic Economy. As the trade in slaves grew, it became part of the triangular trade route that characterized the Atlantic economy, involving the exchange of goods and slaves between the western coast of Europe, the slave depots on the African coast, and the ports of North and South America.

What were the important source regions for slaves, and where were most of the slaves taken?

THE ATLANTIC SLAVE TRADE

ONE OF THE MOST ODIOUS PRACTICES of early modern Western society was the Atlantic slave trade, which reached its height in the eighteenth century. Blacks were transported in densely packed cargo ships from the western coast of Africa to the Americas to work as slaves in the plantation economy. Not until late in the eighteenth century did a rising chorus of voices raise serious objections to this trade in human beings. This excerpt presents a criticism of the slave trade from an anonymous French writer.

Diary of a Citizen

As soon as the ships have lowered their anchors off the coast of Guinea, the price at which the captains have decided to buy the captives is announced to the Negroes who buy prisoners from various princes and sell them to Europeans. Presents are sent to the sovereign who rules over that particular part of the coast, and permission to trade is given. Immediately the slaves are brought by inhuman brokers like so many victims dragged to a sacrifice. White men who covet that portion of the human race receive them in a little house they have erected on the shore, where they have entrenched themselves with two pieces of cannon and twenty guards. As soon as the bargain is concluded, the Negro is put in chains and led aboard the vessel, where he meets his fellow sufferers. . . .

The vessel sets sail for the Antilles, and the Negroes are chained in a hold of the ship. . . . Twice a day some disgusting food is distributed to them. Their consuming sorrow and the sad state to which they are reduced would make them commit suicide if they were not deprived of all the means for an attempt upon their lives. Without any kind of clothing it would be difficult to conceal from the watchful eyes of the sailors in charge any instrument apt to alleviate their despair. The fear of a revolt, such as sometimes happens on the voyage from Guinea, is the basis of a common concern and produces as many guards as there are men in the crew. The slightest noise or a secret conversation among two Negroes is punished with utmost severity. All in all, the voyage is made in a continuous state of alarm on the part of the white men, who fear a revolt, and in a cruel state of uncertainty on the part of the Negroes, who do not know the fate awaiting them.

When the vessel arrives at a port in the Antilles, they are taken to a warehouse where they are displayed, like any merchandise, to the eyes of buyers. The plantation owner pays according to the age, strength, and health of the Negro he is buying. He has him taken to his plantation, and there he is delivered to an overseer who then and there becomes his tormentor. In order to domesticate him, the Negro is granted a few days of rest in his new place, but soon he is given a hoe and a sickle and made to join a work gang. Then he ceases to wonder about his fate; he understands that only labor is demanded of him. But he does not know yet how excessive this labor will be. As a matter of fact, his work begins at dawn and does not end before nightfall; it is interrupted for only two hours at dinnertime. The food a full-grown Negro is given each week consists of two pounds of salt beef or cod and two pots of tapioca meal. . . .

Q *What does this account reveal about the nature of the slave trade and white attitudes toward blacks in the eighteenth century?*

Source: R. Foster and E. Foster, eds., *European Society in the Eighteenth Century* (New York: Walker & Co., 1969).

packed into cargo ships, 300 to 450 per ship, and chained in holds without sanitary facilities or room to stand up; there they remained during the voyage to America, which took at least 100 days (see the box above). Mortality rates averaged 10 percent; longer journeys due to storms or adverse winds resulted in even higher death rates. The Africans who survived the journey were subject to high death rates from diseases to which they had little or no immunity and dysentery from poor sanitation. Death rates were lower for slaves born and raised in the New World: the new generation developed immunity to many of the more fatal diseases. Owners, however, rarely encouraged their slaves to have children. Many slave owners, especially in the West Indies, believed that buying a new slave was less expensive than raising a child from birth to working age at adolescence.

CONDUCT OF THE SLAVE TRADE Before the coming of Europeans in the fifteenth century, most slaves in Africa were prisoners of war. Many served as domestic servants or as wageless workers for the local ruler. When Europeans first began to take part in the slave trade, they bought slaves from local African merchants at slave markets in return for gold, guns, or other European goods such as textiles or copper or iron utensils.

At first, local slave traders obtained their supply from regions nearby, but as demand increased, they had to move farther inland to find their victims. In a few cases, local rulers became concerned about the impact of the slave trade on the well-being of their societies. In a letter to the king of Portugal in 1526, King Affonso of Congo (Bakongo) complained:

> And we cannot reckon how great the damage is, since the mentioned merchants are taking every day our natives, sons of the land and the sons of our noblemen and vassals and our relatives . . . and so great, Sir, is the corruption and licentiousness that our country is being completely depopulated, and Your Highness should not agree with this nor accept it as in your service.[8]

The Sale of Slaves. In the eighteenth century, the slave trade was a highly profitable commercial enterprise. This painting shows a Western slave merchant negotiating with a local African leader over slaves at Gorée, Senegal, in West Africa in the late eighteenth century.

But Europeans as well as other Africans generally ignored protests from Africans. As a general rule, local rulers viewed the slave trade as a source of income, and many sent raiders into defenseless villages in search of unsuspecting victims.

Historians once thought that Europeans controlled the terms of the slave trade and were able to obtain victims at bargain prices. It is now clear, however, that African middlemen—merchants, local elites, or rulers—were active in the process and were often able to dictate the price and number of slaves to European purchasers. Payment to the slave merchant was often made in goods, such as textiles, furniture, and guns.

EFFECTS OF THE SLAVE TRADE The effects of the slave trade varied from area to area. Of course, it had tragic effects on the lives of the slaves and their families. There was also an economic price as the importation of cheap manufactured goods from Europe undermined local cottage industries and forced countless families into poverty. The slave trade also led to the depopulation of some areas and deprived many African communities of their youngest and strongest men and women.

The political effects of the slave trade were also devastating. The need to maintain a constant supply of slaves led to increased warfare and violence as African chiefs and their followers, armed with guns acquired from the trade in slaves, increased their raids and wars on neighboring peoples. A few Europeans lamented what they were doing to traditional African societies. One Dutch slave trader remarked, "From us they have learned strife, quarrelling, drunkenness, trickery, theft, unbridled desire for what is not one's own, misdeeds unknown to them before, and the accursed lust for gold."[9] Nevertheless, the slave trade continued, with devastating effects for some African states.

Despite a rising chorus of humanitarian sentiments from European intellectuals, the use of black slaves remained largely acceptable to Western society. Europeans continued to view blacks as inferior beings fit primarily for slave labor. Not until the Society of Friends, known as the Quakers, began to criticize slavery in the 1770s and exclude from their church any member adhering to slave trafficking did European sentiment for the abolition of slavery begin to build. Even then, it was not until the radical stage of the French Revolution in the 1790s that the French abolished slavery. The British followed suit in 1807. Despite the elimination of the African source, slavery continued in the newly formed United States until the Civil War of the 1860s.

The West in Southeast Asia

Portugal's efforts to dominate the trade of Southeast Asia were never totally successful. The Portuguese lacked both the numbers and the wealth to overcome local resistance and colonize the Asian regions. Portugal's empire was simply too large and Portugal too small to maintain it. One Portuguese chronicler lamented, "My country, oh my country. Too heavy is the task that has been laid on your shoulders. Day after day I watch the ships leaving your shores filled always with your best and bravest men. And too many do not return. . . . Who then is left to till the fields, to harvest the grapes, to keep the enemy on our frontiers at bay?"[10] By the end of the sixteenth century, new European rivals had entered the fray.

One of them was Spain. The Spanish had established themselves in the region when Magellan landed in the Philippines. Although he was killed there, the Spanish were able to gain control over the Philippines, which eventually became a major Spanish base in the trade across the Pacific. Spanish ships carried silk and other luxury goods to Mexico in return for silver from the mines of Mexico.

The primary threat to the Portuguese Empire in Southeast Asia, however, came with the arrival of the Dutch and the English, who were better financed than the Portuguese. The shift in power began in the early seventeenth century when the Dutch seized a Portuguese fort in the Moluccas and then gradually pushed the Portuguese out of the spice trade. During the next fifty years, the Dutch occupied most of the Portuguese coastal forts along the trade routes throughout the Indian Ocean, including the island of Ceylon (today's Sri Lanka), and seized Malacca in 1641. The aggressive Dutch drove the English traders out of the spice market as well, eventually restricting the English to a single port on the southern coast of Sumatra.

The Dutch also began to consolidate their political and military control over the entire area. On the island of Java, where they had established a fort at Batavia (buh-TAY-vee-uh) (modern Jakarta) in 1619, the Dutch found that it was necessary to bring the inland regions under their control to protect their position. On Java and the neighboring island of Sumatra, the Dutch East

India Company established pepper plantations, which soon became the source of massive profits for Dutch merchants in Amsterdam. By the end of the eighteenth century, the Dutch had succeeded in bringing almost the entire Indonesian archipelago under their control.

The arrival of the Europeans had less impact on mainland Southeast Asia, where strong monarchies in Burma—now Myanmar (MYAN-mahr)—Thailand, and Vietnam resisted foreign encroachment. In the sixteenth century, the Portuguese established limited trade relations with several mainland states, including Thailand, Burma, Vietnam, and the remnants of the old Angkor kingdom in Cambodia. By the early seventeenth century, other nations had followed and had begun to compete actively for trade and missionary privileges. To obtain economic advantages, the Europeans soon became involved in local factional disputes. In general, however, these states were able to unite and drive the Europeans out.

Southeast Asia, ca. 1700

In Vietnam, the arrival of Western merchants and missionaries coincided with a period of internal conflict among ruling groups in the country. Expansion had led to a civil war that temporarily divided the country into two separate states, one in the south and one in the north. After their arrival in the mid-seventeenth century, the European powers began to take sides in local politics, with the Portuguese and the Dutch supporting rival factions. The Europeans also set up trading posts for their merchants, but by the end of the seventeenth century, when it became clear that economic opportunities were limited, most of them were abandoned. French missionaries attempted to remain, but their efforts were blocked by the authorities, who viewed converts to Catholicism as a threat to the prestige of the Vietnamese emperor (see "Global Perspectives" on p. 417).

Private Collection/The Bridgeman Art Library

Europe in Asia. As Europeans began to move into parts of Asia, they reproduced many of the physical surroundings of their homeland in the port cities they built there. This is evident in comparing these two scenes. Below is a seventeenth-century view of Batavia, which the Dutch built as their headquarters on the northern coast of Java in 1619. The scene at the left is from a sixteenth-century engraving of Amsterdam. This Dutch city had become the financial and commercial capital of Europe. It was also the chief port for the ships of the Dutch East India Company, which brought the spices of the East to Europe.

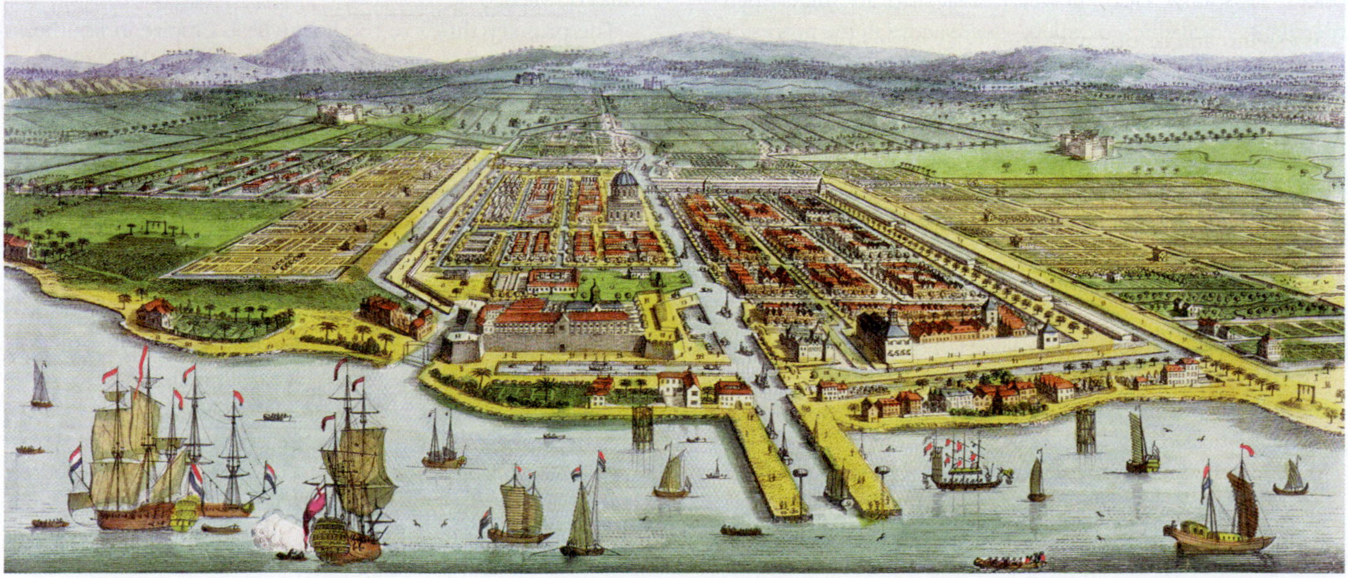

The Art Archive at Art Resource, NY

GLOBAL PERSPECTIVES

West Meets East: An Exchange of Royal Letters

ECONOMIC GAIN WAS NOT THE ONLY motivation of Western rulers who wished to establish a European presence in the East. In 1681, King Louis XIV of France wrote a letter to the king of Tonkin (the Trinh family head, then acting as viceroy to the Vietnamese emperor) asking permission for Christian missionaries to proselytize in Vietnam. The king of Tonkin politely declined the request.

A Letter to the King of Tonkin from Louis XIV

Most high, most excellent, most mighty and most magnanimous Prince, our very dear and good friend, may it please God to increase your greatness with a happy end!

We hear from our subjects who were in your Realm what protection you accorded them. We appreciate this all the more since we have for you all the esteem that one can have for a prince as illustrious through his military valor as he is commendable for the justice which he exercises in his Realm. We have even been informed that you have not been satisfied to extend this general protection to our subjects but, in particular, that you gave effective proofs of it to Messrs. Deydier and de Bourges. We would have wished that they might have been able to recognize all the favors they received from you by having presents worthy of you offered you; but since the war which we have had for several years, in which all of Europe had banded together against us, prevented our vessels from going to the Indies, at the present time, when we are at peace after having gained many victories and expanded our Realm through the conquest of several important places, we have immediately given orders to the Royal Company to establish itself in your kingdom as soon as possible, and have commanded Messrs. Deydier and de Bourges to remain with you in order to maintain a good relationship between our subjects and yours, also to warn us on occasions that might present themselves when we might be able to give you proofs of our esteem and of our wish to concur with your satisfaction as well as with your best interests.

By way of initial proof, we have given orders to have brought to you some presents which we believe might be agreeable to you. But the one thing in the world which we desire most, both for you and for your Realm, would be to obtain for your subjects who have already embraced the law of the only true God of heaven and earth, the freedom to profess it, since this law is the highest, the noblest, the most sacred and especially the most suitable to have kings reign absolutely over the people.

We are even quite convinced that, if you knew the truths and the maxims which it teaches, you would give first of all to your subjects the glorious example of embracing it. We wish you this incomparable blessing together with a long and happy reign, and we pray God that it may please Him to augment your greatness with the happiest of endings.

Written at Saint-Germain-en-Laye, the 10th day of January, 1681,

Your very dear and good friend,
Louis

Answer from the King of Tonkin to Louis XIV

The King of Tonkin sends to the King of France a letter to express to him his best sentiments, saying that he was happy to learn that fidelity is a durable good of man and that justice is the most important of things. Consequently practicing of fidelity and justice cannot but yield good results. Indeed, though France and our Kingdom differ as to mountains, rivers, and boundaries, if fidelity and justice reign among our villages, our conduct will express all of our good feelings and contain precious gifts. Your communication, which comes from a country which is a thousand leagues away, and which proceeds from the heart as a testimony of your sincerity, merits repeated consideration and infinite praise. Politeness toward strangers is nothing unusual in our country. There is not a stranger who is not well received by us. How then could we refuse a man from France, which is the most celebrated among the kingdoms of the world and which for love of us wishes to frequent us and bring us merchandise? These feelings of fidelity and justice are truly worthy to be applauded. As regards your wish that we should cooperate in propagating your religion, we do not dare to permit it, for there is an ancient custom, introduced by edicts, which formally forbids it. Now, edicts are promulgated only to be carried out faithfully; without fidelity nothing is stable. How could we disdain a well-established custom to satisfy a private friendship? . . .

We beg you to understand well that this is our communication concerning our mutual acquaintance. This then is my letter. We send you herewith a modest gift, which we offer you with a glad heart.

This letter was written at the beginning of winter and on a beautiful day.

Q *What are the underlying beliefs and approaches of these two rulers? How are they alike? How are they different? What is King Tonkin's justification for refusing Louis XIV's request? What is the significance of the way the two rulers date their letters?*

Source: H. J. Benda and J. A. Larkin, eds. *The World of Southeast Asia: Selected Historical Readings* (New York: Harper & Row, 1967).

Why were the mainland states better able to resist the European challenge than the states in the Malay world? One factor, no doubt, was the cohesive nature of these states. The mainland states in Burma, Thailand, and Vietnam had begun to define themselves as distinct political entities. The Malay states had less cohesion. Moreover, the Malay states were victims of their own resources. The spice trade was enormously profitable. European merchants and rulers were determined to gain control of the sources of the spices, and that determination led them to take direct control of the Indonesian archipelago.

The French and British in India

When a Portuguese fleet arrived at the port of Calicut in the spring of 1498, the Indian subcontinent was divided into a number of Hindu and Muslim kingdoms. But it was on the verge of a new era of unity that would be brought about by a foreign dynasty called the Mughals (MOO-guls).

THE MUGHAL EMPIRE The founders of the Mughal Empire were not natives of India but came from the mountainous region north of the Ganges River valley. The founder of the dynasty, Babur (BAH-burr) (1483–1530), had an illustrious background. His father was descended from the great Asian conqueror Tamerlane; his mother, from the Mongol conqueror Genghis Khan. It was Akbar (AK-bar) (1556–1605), Babur's grandson, however, who brought Mughal rule to most of India, creating the greatest Indian empire since the Mauryan dynasty nearly two thousand years earlier. By the mid-seventeenth century, however, wars of succession and declining revenue led to the collapse of the Mughal Empire as Mughal nobles asserted their control over various territories. By the mid-eighteenth century the Mughals controlled little more territory than Delhi and its surrounding area. The vacuum of power created by the demise of the Mughals opened the door for European trading companies seeking to capitalize on the lucrative trade between India and Europe.

The Mughal Empire

THE IMPACT OF THE WESTERN POWERS As we have seen, the first Europeans to arrive in India were the Portuguese. At first, Portugal dominated regional trade in the Indian Ocean, but at the end of the sixteenth century, the English and the Dutch arrived on the scene. Soon both powers were competing with Portugal, and with each other, for trading privileges in the region.

During the first half of the seventeenth century, the English presence in India steadily increased. By 1650, English trading posts had been established at Surat (a thriving port along the northwestern coast of India), Fort William (now the great city of Calcutta) near the Bay of Bengal, and Madras (now Chennai) on the southeastern coast. From Madras, English ships carried Indian-made cotton goods to the East Indies, where they were bartered for spices, which were shipped back to England.

English success in India attracted rivals, including the Dutch and the French. The Dutch abandoned their interests to concentrate on the spice trade in the middle of the seventeenth century, but the French were more persistent and established their own forts on the east coast. For a brief period, the French competed successfully with the British, even capturing the British fort at Madras.

But the British were saved by the military genius of Sir Robert Clive (CLYV), an aggressive British empire-builder who eventually became the chief representative of the East India Company in India. (The East India Company had been founded as a joint-stock company in 1600—see "The Growth of Commercial Capitalism" later in this chapter.) The British were aided as well by the refusal of the French government to provide financial support for French efforts in far-off India. Eventually, the French were restricted to the fort at Pondicherry and a handful of small territories on the southeastern coast.

In the meantime, Clive began to consolidate British control in Bengal, where the local ruler had attacked Fort William and imprisoned the local British population in the "Black Hole of Calcutta" (an underground prison for holding the prisoners, many of whom died in captivity). In 1757, a small British force numbering about three thousand defeated a Mughal-led army more than ten times its size in the Battle of Plassey (PLASS-ee). As part of the spoils of victory, the British East India Company received from the now-decrepit Mughal court the authority to impose and collect taxes from over 20 million people in the area surrounding Calcutta. During the Seven Years' War (1756–1763), the British forced the French to withdraw completely from India (see Chapter 18).

To officials of the East India Company, the expansion of their authority into the interior of the subcontinent probably seemed like a simple economic decision. It made sense to seek regular revenues that would pay for increasingly expensive military operations in India. In a letter to the company's directors in London, Clive described the potential of the East India Company's future in India:

> I can assert with some degree of confidence that this rich and flourishing kingdom may be totally subdued by so small a force as two thousand Europeans . . . [The Indians are] indolent, luxurious, ignorant and cowardly beyond all conception . . . [They] attempt everything by treachery rather than force . . . What is it, then, can enable us to secure our present acquisitions or improve upon them but such a force as leaves nothing to the power of treachery and ingratitude?[11]

To historians, it marks a major step in the gradual transfer of all of the Indian subcontinent to the British East India Company and later, in 1858, to the British crown as a colony (see Chapter 24).

China

In 1514, a Portuguese fleet dropped anchor off the coast of China. It was the first direct contact between the Chinese Empire and Europe since the journeys of Marco Polo two hundred years earlier. At the time, the Chinese thought little of the event. China appeared to be at the height of its power as the most magnificent civilization on earth. Its empire stretched from the steppes of Central Asia to the China Sea, from the Gobi Desert to the tropical rain forests of Southeast Asia. From the lofty perspective of the imperial throne in Beijing, the Europeans could only be seen as an unusual form of barbarian. To the Chinese ruler, the rulers of all other countries were simply "younger brothers" of the Chinese emperor, who was regarded as the Son of Heaven.

THE MING AND QING DYNASTIES By the time the Portuguese fleet arrived off the coast of China, the Ming dynasty, which ruled from 1369 to 1644, had already begun a new era of greatness in Chinese history. Under a series of strong rulers, China extended its rule into Mongolia and Central Asia. The Ming even briefly reconquered Vietnam. Along the northern frontier, they strengthened the Great Wall and made peace with the nomadic tribesmen who had troubled China for centuries.

The Qing Empire

But the days of the Ming dynasty were numbered. In the 1630s, a major epidemic devastated the population in many areas. The suffering caused by the epidemic helped spark a peasant revolt led by Li Zicheng (lee zee-CHENG). In 1644, Li and his forces occupied the capital of Beijing. The last Ming emperor committed suicide by hanging himself from a tree in the palace gardens.

The overthrow of the Ming dynasty created an opportunity for the Manchus, a farming and hunting people who lived northeast of China in the area known today as Manchuria. The Manchus conquered Beijing, and Li Zicheng's army fell. The victorious Manchus then declared the creation of a new dynasty with the reign title of the Qing ("Pure").

The Qing (CHING) were blessed with a series of strong early rulers who pacified the country, corrected the most serious social and economic ills, and restored peace and prosperity. Two Qing monarchs, Kangxi (KAHNG-shee) and Qian-long (CHAN-loong), ruled China for well over a century, from the middle of the seventeenth century to the end of the eighteenth. They were responsible for much of the greatness of Manchu China.

WESTERN INROADS Although China was at the height of its power and glory in the mid-eighteenth century, the first signs of internal decay in the Manchu dynasty were beginning to appear. Qing military campaigns along the frontier were expensive and placed heavy demands on the treasury. At the same time, increasing pressure on the land because of population growth led to economic hardship for many peasants and even rebellion.

Unfortunately for China, the decline of the Qing dynasty occurred just as Europe was increasing pressure for more trade. The first conflict had come from the north, where Russian traders sought skins and furs. Formal diplomatic relations between China and Russia were established in 1689 and provided for regular trade between the two countries.

Dealing with the foreigners who arrived by sea was more difficult. By the end of the seventeenth century, the English had replaced the Portuguese as the dominant force in European trade. Operating through the East India Company, which served as both a trading unit and the administrator of English territories in Asia, the English established their first trading post at Canton in 1699.

Over the next several decades, trade with China, notably the export of tea and silk to England, increased rapidly. To limit contacts between Europeans and Chinese, the Qing government confined all European traders to a small island just outside the city walls of Canton and permitted them to reside there only from October through March.

For a while, the British accepted this system, which brought considerable profit to the East India Company. But by the end of the eighteenth century, some British traders had begun to demand access to other cities along the Chinese coast and insist that the country be opened to British manufactured goods. In 1793, a British mission under Lord Macartney visited Beijing to press for liberalization of trade restrictions.

AN IMPERIAL EDICT TO THE KING OF ENGLAND

IN 1793, THE BRITISH EMISSARY Lord Macartney visited the Qing Empire to request the opening of trading relations between his country and China. Emperor Qianlong's reply, addressed to King George III of England, illustrates how the imperial court in Beijing viewed the world. King George cannot have been pleased.

An Imperial Edict to the King of England

You, O King, are so inclined toward our civilization that you have sent a special envoy across the seas to bring to our Court your memorial of congratulations on the occasion of my birthday and to present your native products as an expression of your thoughtfulness. On perusing your memorial, so simply worded and sincerely conceived, I am impressed by your genuine respectfulness and friendliness and greatly pleased.

As to the request made in your memorial, O King, to send one of your nationals to stay at the Celestial Court to take care of your country's trade with China, this is not in harmony with the state system of our dynasty and will definitely not be permitted. Traditionally people of the European nations who wished to tender some service under the Celestial Court have been permitted to come to the capital. But after their arrival they are obliged to wear Chinese court costumes, are placed in a certain residence and are never allowed to return to their own countries. This is the established rule of the Celestial Dynasty with which presumably you, O King, are familiar. Now you, O King, wish to send one of your nationals to live in the capital, but he is not like the Europeans, who come to Beijing as Chinese employees, live there and never return home again, nor can he be allowed to go and come and maintain any correspondence. This is indeed a useless undertaking. . . .

The Celestial Court has pacified and possessed the territory within the four seas. Its sole aim is to do its utmost to achieve good government and to manage political affairs, attaching no value to strange jewels and precious objects. The various articles presented by you, O King, this time are accepted by my special order to the office in charge of such functions in consideration of the offerings having come from a long distance with sincere good wishes. As a matter of fact, the virtue and prestige of the Celestial Dynasty having spread far and wide, the kings of the myriad nations come by land and sea with all sorts of precious things. Consequently there is nothing we lack, as your principal envoy and others have themselves observed. We have never set much store on strange objects, nor do we need any more of your country's manufactures.

Q *What reasons does Qianlong give for denying Britain's request to open diplomatic and trading relations with China? Do his comments indicate any ignorance about the West at the end of the eighteenth century? If he had known more, would his response have been different? Why or why not?*

Source: S. Teng and J. K. Fairbank, *China's Response to the West: A Documentary Survey* (Cambridge, Mass.: Harvard University Press, 1982).

But Emperor Qianlong expressed no interest in British products (see the box above). An exasperated Macartney compared the Chinese Empire to "an old, crazy, first-rate man-of-war" that had once awed its neighbors "merely by her bulk and appearance" but was now destined under incompetent leadership to be "dashed to pieces on the shore." The Chinese would later pay for their rejection of the British request (see Chapter 24).

Japan

At the end of the fifteenth century, Japan was at a point of near anarchy, but in the course of the sixteenth century, a number of powerful individuals achieved the unification of Japan. One of them, Tokugawa Ieyasu (toh-koo-GAH-wah ee-yeh-YAH-soo) (1543–1616), took the title of shogun ("general") in 1603, an act that initiated the most powerful and longest lasting of all the Japanese shogunates. The Tokugawa rulers completed the restoration of central authority and remained in power until 1868.

OPENING TO THE WEST Portuguese traders had landed on the islands of Japan in 1543, and in a few years, Portuguese ships began stopping at Japanese ports on a regular basis to take part in the regional trade between Japan, China, and Southeast Asia. The first Jesuit missionary, Francis Xavier, arrived in 1549 and had some success in converting the local population to Christianity.

Initially, the visitors were welcomed. Tobacco, clocks, eyeglasses, and other European goods fascinated the curious Japanese, and local nobles were interested in purchasing all types of European weapons and armaments. Japanese rulers found the new firearms especially helpful in defeating their enemies and unifying the islands. The effect on Japanese military architecture was especially striking, as local lords began to erect castles in stone on the European model.

The success of the Catholic missionaries, however, provoked a strong reaction against the presence of Westerners. When the missionaries interfered in local politics, Tokugawa Ieyasu, newly come to power, expelled all missionaries. Japanese Christians were now persecuted. When a group of Christian peasants on the island of Kyushu revolted in 1637, they were bloodily suppressed.

The European merchants were the next to go. The government closed the two major foreign trading posts on the island of Hirado and at Nagasaki (nah-gah-SAH-kee). Only a small Dutch community in Nagasaki was allowed to remain in Japan.

RMN-Grand Palais/Art Resource, NY

The Portuguese Arriving at Nagasaki. Portuguese traders landed accidentally in Japan in 1543. In a few years, they arrived regularly, taking part in a regional trade network involving Japan, China, and Southeast Asia. In these panels, done in black lacquer and gold leaf, we see a late-sixteenth-century Japanese interpretation of the first Portuguese landing at Nagasaki.

The Dutch, unlike the Spanish and Portuguese, had not allowed missionary activities to interfere with their trade interests. But the conditions for staying were strict. Dutch ships were allowed to dock at Nagasaki harbor just once a year and could remain for only two or three months.

The Americas

In the sixteenth century, Spain and Portugal had established large colonial empires in the Americas. Portugal continued to profit from its empire in Brazil. The Spanish also maintained an enormous South American empire, but Spain's importance as a commercial power declined rapidly in the seventeenth century because of a drop in the output of the silver mines and the poverty of the Spanish monarchy. By the beginning of the seventeenth century, both Portugal and Spain found themselves with new challenges to their American empires from the Dutch, English, and French, who increasingly sought to create their own colonial empires in the New World.

The West Indies

WEST INDIES Both the French and English colonial empires in the New World included large parts of the West Indies. The English held Barbados, Jamaica, and Bermuda, and the French possessed Saint-Domingue, Martinique, and Guadeloupe. On these tropical islands, both the English and the French developed plantation economies, worked by African slaves, which produced tobacco, cotton, coffee, and sugar, all products increasingly in demand in Europe.

The "sugar factories," as the sugar plantations in the Caribbean were called, played an especially prominent role. By the early eighteenth century, sugar was Britain's main export from its American colonies. By the last two decades of the century, the British colony of Jamaica, one of Britain's most important, was producing 50,000 tons of sugar annually with the slave labor of 200,000 blacks. The French colony of Saint-Domingue (later Haiti) had 500,000 slaves working on three thousand plantations. This colony produced 100,000 tons of sugar a year, but at the expense of a high death rate from the brutal treatment of the slaves. It is not surprising that Saint-Domingue was the site of the first successful slave uprising in 1793 (see Chapter 19).

BRITISH NORTH AMERICA Although Spain claimed all of North America as part of its American overseas empire, other nations largely ignored its claim. The British argued that "prescription without possession availeth nothing." The Dutch were among the first to establish settlements on the North American continent. Their activities began after 1609 when Henry Hudson, an English explorer hired by the Dutch, discovered the river that bears his name. Within a few years, the Dutch had established the mainland colony of New Netherland, which stretched from the mouth of the Hudson River as far north as

Album/Art Resource, NY

A Sugar Mill in the West Indies. Cane sugar was one of the most valuable products produced in the West Indies. By 1700, sugar was replacing honey as a sweetener for increasing numbers of Europeans. This seventeenth-century French illustration shows the operation of a sugar mill in the French West Indies.

Albany, New York. Present-day names such as Staten Island and Harlem remind us that it was the Dutch who initially settled the Hudson River valley. In the second half of the seventeenth century, competition from the English and French and years of warfare with those rivals led to the decline of the Dutch commercial empire. In 1664, the English seized the colony of New Netherland and renamed it New York; soon afterward, the Dutch West India Company went bankrupt.

In the meantime, the English had begun to establish their own colonies in North America. The first permanent English settlement in America was Jamestown, founded in 1607 in modern Virginia. It barely survived, making it evident that the colonizing of American lands was not necessarily conducive to quick profits. But the desire to practice one's own religion, combined with economic interests, could lead to successful colonization, as the Massachusetts Bay Company demonstrated. The Massachusetts colony had 4,000 settlers in its early years but by 1660 had swelled to 40,000. By the end of the seventeenth century, the English had established control over most of the eastern seaboard of the present United States.

British North America came to consist of thirteen colonies. They were thickly populated, containing about 1.5 million people by 1750, and were also prosperous. Supposedly run by the British Board of Trade, the Royal Council, and Parliament, these thirteen colonies had legislatures that tended to act independently. Merchants in such port cities as Boston, Philadelphia, New York, and Charleston resented and resisted regulation from the British government.

The British colonies in both North America and the West Indies were assigned roles in keeping with mercantilist theory (see "Mercantilism" later in this chapter). They provided raw materials, such as cotton, sugar and tobacco, for the mother country while buying the latter's manufactured goods. Navigation acts regulated what could be taken from and sold to the colonies. Theoretically, the system was supposed to provide a balance of trade favorable to the mother country.

FRENCH NORTH AMERICA The French also established a colonial empire in North America. Already in 1534, the French explorer Jacques Cartier (ZHAK kar-TYAY) had discovered the Saint Lawrence River and laid claim to Canada as a French possession. It was not until 1608, however, when Samuel de Champlain (shahm-PLAN *or* SHAM-playn) established a settlement at Quebec that the French began to take a more serious interest in Canada as a colony. In 1663, Canada was made the property of the French crown and administered by a French governor like a French province.

CHRONOLOGY	New Rivals on the World Stage
Portuguese traders land in Japan	1543
British East India Company formed	1600
Dutch East India Company formed	1602
English settlement at Jamestown	1607
Champlain establishes settlement at Quebec	1608
Dutch fort established at Batavia	1619
Dutch seize Malacca from the Portuguese	1641
English seize New Netherland	1664
English establish trading post at Canton	1699
Battle of Plassey	1757
French cede Canada to British	1763
British mission to China	1793

French North America was run autocratically as a vast trading area, where valuable furs, leather, fish, and timber were acquired. The inability of the French state to get its people to emigrate to its Canadian possessions, however, left the territory thinly populated. By the mid-eighteenth century, there were only about 15,000 French Canadians, most of whom were hunters, trappers, missionaries, or explorers. The French failed to provide adequate men or money, allowing their European wars to take precedence over the conquest of the North American continent. Already in 1713, by the Treaty of Utrecht, the French began to cede some of their American possessions to their British rival. As a result of the Seven Years' War, they would surrender the rest of their Canadian lands in 1763 (see Chapter 18).

British and French rivalry was also evident in the Spanish and Portuguese colonial empires in Latin America. The decline of Spain and Portugal had led these two states to depend even more on resources from their colonies, and they imposed strict mercantilist rules to keep others out. Spain, for example, tried to limit all trade with its colonies to Spanish ships. But the British and French were too powerful to be excluded. The British cajoled the Portuguese into allowing them into the lucrative Brazilian trade. The French, however, were the first to break into the Spanish Latin American market when the French Bourbons became kings of Spain at the beginning of the eighteenth century. Britain's first entry into Spanish American markets came in 1713, when the British were granted the privilege, known as the *asiento* (ah-SYEN-toh), of transporting 4,500 slaves a year to Spanish Latin America.

The Impact of European Expansion

FOCUS QUESTION: How did European expansion affect both the conquered and the conquerors?

Between 1500 and 1800, the Atlantic nations of Europe moved into all parts of the world. The first had been Spain and Portugal, the two great colonial powers of the sixteenth century, followed by the Dutch, who built their colonial empire in the seventeenth century as Portugal and Spain declined. The Dutch were soon challenged by the British and French, who outstripped the others in the eighteenth century while becoming involved in a bitter rivalry. By the end of the eighteenth century, it appeared that Great Britain would become the great European imperial power. European expansion had a great impact on both the conquered and the conquerors.

The Conquered

Different regions experienced different effects from the European expansion. The native American civilizations, which had their own unique qualities and a degree of sophistication not much appreciated by Europeans, were virtually destroyed. In addition to devastating losses of population from European diseases, ancient social and political structures were ripped up and replaced by European institutions, religion, language, and culture. In Africa, the real demographic impact of the slave trade is uncertain due to a lack of records; however, estimates of the population in West Africa suggest that the slave trade negated any population growth, rather than causing a decline. Politically and socially, the slave trade encouraged the growth of territories in West Africa, such as Dahomey and Benin, where the leaders waged internal wars to secure more slaves to trade for guns and gunpowder. Without the slave trade, these territories became susceptible to European control in the nineteenth century. The Portuguese trading posts in the East had little direct impact on native Asian civilizations, although Dutch control of the Indonesian archipelago was more pervasive. China and Japan were still little affected by Westerners, although India was subject to ever-growing British encroachment.

In Central and South America, a new civilization arose that we have come to call Latin America. It was a multiracial society. Spanish and Portuguese settlers who arrived in the Western Hemisphere were few in number relative to the native Indians; many of the newcomers were males who not only used female natives for their sexual pleasure but married them as well. Already by 1501, Spanish rulers had authorized intermarriage between Europeans and native American Indians, whose offspring became known as mestizos (mess-TEE-zohz). Another group of people brought to Latin America were the Africans. Over a period of three centuries, possibly as many as 8 million slaves were brought to Spanish and Portuguese America to work the plantations. Africans also contributed to Latin America's multiracial character. Mulattoes (muh-LAH-toh)—the offspring of Africans and whites—joined mestizos and descendants of whites, Africans, and native Indians to produce a unique society in Latin America. Unlike Europe, and unlike British North America, which remained a largely white offshoot of Europe, Latin America developed a multiracial society with less rigid attitudes about race.

The European presence also affected the ecology of the conquered areas. Europeans brought horses, sheep, goats, pigs and cattle to the Americas, which revolutionized the life of the Indians. The Americas were well suited for the European animals. Since they had few predators and plenty of land to roam, the new animals rapidly increased in number. Explorer Hernando De Soto arrived in Florida in 1539 with thirteen pigs; they increased to 700 by 1542. Cattle farming supplanted the Indian agricultural practice of growing maize (Indian corn), eventually leading to the development of large estates for raising cattle. South America would later become a great exporter of beef. Europeans also brought new crops, such as wheat and cane sugar, to be cultivated on large plantations by native or imported slave labor. In their trips to other parts of the world, Europeans also carried New World plants with them. Thus, Europeans introduced sweet potatoes and maize to Africa in the sixteenth century.

CATHOLIC MISSIONARIES Although there were some Protestant missionaries in the world outside Europe, Catholic missionaries were far more active in spreading Christianity. From the beginning of their conquest of the New World, Spanish and Portuguese rulers were determined to Christianize the native peoples. This policy gave the Catholic Church an

THE MISSION

IN 1609, TWO JESUIT PRIESTS EMBARKED on a missionary calling with the Guaraní Indians in eastern Paraguay. Eventually, the Jesuits established more than thirty missions in the region. Well organized and zealous, the Jesuits transformed their missions into profitable businesses. This description of a Jesuit mission in Paraguay was written by Félix de Azara, a Spanish soldier and scientist.

Félix de Azara, Description and History of Paraguay and Rio de la Plata

Having spoken of the towns founded by the Jesuit fathers, and of the manner in which they were founded, I shall discuss the government which they established in them. . . . In each town resided two priests, a curate and a subcurate, who had certain assigned functions. The subcurate was charged with all the spiritual tasks, and the curate with every kind of temporal responsibility. . . .

The curate allowed no one to work for personal gain; he compelled everyone, without distinction of age or sex, to work for the community, and he himself saw to it that all were equally fed and dressed. For this purpose the curates placed in storehouses all the fruits of agriculture and the products of industry, selling in the Spanish towns their surplus of cotton, cloth, tobacco, vegetables, skins, and wood, transporting them in their own boats down the nearest rivers, and returning with implements and whatever else was required.

From the foregoing one may infer that the curate disposed of the surplus funds of the Indian towns, and that no Indian could aspire to own private property. This deprived them of any incentive to use reason or talent, since the most industrious, able, and worthy person had the same food, clothing, and pleasures as the most wicked, dull, and indolent. It also follows that although this form of government was well designed to enrich the communities it also caused the Indian to work at a languid pace, since the wealth of his community was of no concern to him.

It must be said that although the Jesuit fathers were supreme in all respects, they employed their authority with a mildness and a restraint that command admiration. They supplied everyone with abundant food and clothing. They compelled the men to work only half a day, and did not drive them to produce more. Even their labor was given a festive air, for they went in procession to the fields, to the sound of music . . . and the music did not cease until they had returned in the same way they had set out. They gave them many holidays, dances, and tournaments, dressing the actors. . . . in the most costly European garments, but they permitted the women to act only as spectators.

They likewise forbade the women to sew; this occupation was restricted to the musicians, sacristans, and acolytes. But they made them spin cotton; and the cloth that the Indians wove, after satisfying their own needs, they sold together with the surplus cotton in the Spanish towns, as they did with the tobacco, vegetables, wood, and skins. The curate and . . . subcurate had their own plain dwellings, and they never left them except to take the air in the great enclosed yard of their college. They never walked through the streets of the town or entered the house of any Indian or let themselves be seen by any woman—or indeed, by any man, except for those indispensable few through whom they issued their orders.

Q *How were the missions organized to enable the missionaries to control most aspects of the Indians' lives? Why was this deemed necessary?*

Source: B. Keen, ed., *Latin American Civilization*, vol. I (Boston: Houghton Mifflin, 1974), pp. 223–224.

important role to play in the New World, one that added considerably to church power. Catholic missionaries—especially the Dominicans, Franciscans, and Jesuits—fanned out to different parts of the Spanish Empire.

To facilitate their efforts, missionaries brought Indians together into villages, where they could be converted, taught trades, and encouraged to grow crops. These missions enabled the missionaries to control the lives of the Indians and helped ensure that they would remain docile members of the empire (see the box above and "Film & History"). Missions generally benefited the missionaries more than the Indians. In frontier districts such as California and Texas, missions also served as military barriers to foreign encroachment.

The Catholic Church constructed hospitals, orphanages, and schools. Monastic schools instructed Indian students in the rudiments of reading, writing, and arithmetic. The Catholic Church also provided outlets for women other than marriage.

FILM & HISTORY

Warner Brothers/Courtesy The Everett Collection, Inc

Watch ***The Mission***, a cinematic reconstruction of San Carlos, a Jesuit mission in Spanish territory on the border of Paraguay, led by the compelling Father Gabriel. The film follows the activities of Father Gabriel, who has been able to win over the Guaraní Indians and establish a community based on communal livelihood and property. *The Mission* depicts the tragic end of the Jesuit missionaries after Spain agrees to turn over the Guaraní territory in Paraguay to Portugal.

Q *How accurately does the film portray Indian life under Jesuit control? How does the film portray Europeans and their interaction with the native civilizations?*

Nunneries were places of prayer and quiet contemplation, but women in religious orders, many of them of aristocratic background, often lived well and worked outside their establishments by running schools and hospitals. Indeed, one of these nuns, Sor Juana Inés de la Cruz (SAWR HWAH-nuh ee-NAYSS day lah KROOZ) (1651–1695), was one of seventeenth-century Latin America's best-known literary figures. She wrote poetry and prose and promoted the education of women.

Christian missionaries also made the long voyage to China on European merchant ships. The Jesuits were among the most active and the most effective. Many of the early Jesuit missionaries to China were highly educated men who were familiar with European philosophical and scientific developments. They brought along clocks and various other instruments that impressed Chinese officials and made them more open to Western ideas.

The Jesuits used this openness to promote Christianity. To make it easier for the Chinese to accept Christianity, the Jesuits pointed to similarities between Christian morality and Confucian ethics. The Italian priest Matteo Ricci described the Jesuit approach:

> In order that the appearance of a new religion might not arouse suspicion among the Chinese people, the Jesuit Fathers did not speak openly about religious matters when they began to appear in public. . . . They did, however, try to teach this pagan people in a more direct way, namely, by virtue of their example and by the sanctity of their lives. In this way they attempted to win the good will of the people and little by little to dispose their minds to receive what they could not be persuaded to accept by word of mouth. . . . From the time of their entrance they wore the ordinary Chinese outer garment, which was somewhat similar to their own religious habits; a long robe reaching down to the heels and with very ample sleeves, which are much in favor with the Chinese.[12]

The efforts of the Christian missionaries reached their height in the early eighteenth century. Several hundred Chinese officials became Catholics, as did an estimated 300,000 ordinary Chinese. But ultimately squabbling among the religious orders themselves undermined the Christian effort. To make it easier for the Chinese to convert, the Jesuits had allowed the new Catholics to continue the practice of ancestor worship. Jealous Dominicans and Franciscans complained to the pope, who condemned the practice. Soon Chinese authorities began to suppress Christian activities throughout China.

The Jesuits also had some success in Japan, where they converted a number of local nobles. By the end of the sixteenth century, thousands of Japanese on the southernmost islands of Kyushu and Shikoku had become Christians. But the Jesuit practice of destroying local idols and shrines and turning some temples into Christian schools or churches caused a severe reaction. When a new group of Spanish Franciscans continued the same policies, the government ordered the execution of nine missionaries and a number of their Japanese converts. When missionaries continued to interfere in local politics, Tokugawa Ieyasu expelled all missionaries. Japanese Christians were now persecuted.

The Conquerors

For some Europeans, expansion abroad brought the possibility of obtaining land, riches, and social advancement. One Spaniard commented in 1572 that many "poor young men" had left Spain for Mexico, where they hoped to acquire landed estates and call themselves "gentlemen." Although some wives accompanied their husbands abroad, many ordinary European women found new opportunities for marriage in the New World because of the lack of white women. Indeed, as one commentator bluntly put it, even "a whore, if handsome, [can] make a wife for some rich planter."[13] In the violence-prone world of early Spanish America, a number of women also found themselves rich after their husbands were killed unexpectedly. In one area of Central America, women owned about 25 percent of the landed estates by 1700.

European expansion also had other economic effects on the conquerors. Wherever they went in the New World, Europeans looked for sources of gold and silver. One Aztec commented that the Spanish conquerors "longed and lusted for gold. Their bodies swelled with greed, and their hunger was ravenous; they hungered like pigs for that gold."[14] Rich silver deposits were found and exploited in Mexico and southern Peru (modern Bolivia). When the mines at Potosí in Peru opened in 1545, the value of precious metals imported into Europe quadrupled. Between 1503 and 1650, an estimated 16 million kilograms (more than 35 million pounds) of silver and 185,000 kilograms (407,000 pounds) of gold entered the port of Seville and set off a price revolution that affected the Spanish economy.

But gold and silver were only two of the products that became part of the exchange between the New World and the Old. Historians refer to the reciprocal importation and exportation of plants and animals between Europe and the Americas as the **Columbian Exchange** (see Map 14.3). While Europeans were bringing horses, cattle, and wheat to the New World, they were taking new agricultural products such as potatoes, chocolate, corn, tomatoes, and tobacco back to Europe. Potatoes became especially popular as a dietary staple in some areas of Europe. High in carbohydrates and rich in vitamins A and C, potatoes could be easily stored for winter use and enabled more people to survive on smaller plots of land. This improvement in nutrition was soon reflected in a rapid increase in population. Other products, such as cochineal, a red dye discovered in Mexico, gave European artists and artisans a "perfect red" for their paintings and cloth.

The European lifestyle was greatly affected by new products from abroad. In addition to new foods, new drinks also appeared in Europe. Chocolate, which had been brought to Spain from Aztec Mexico, became a common drink by 1700. The first coffee and tea houses opened in London in the 1650s and spread rapidly to other parts of Europe. In the eighteenth century, a craze for Chinese furniture and porcelain spread among the upper classes. Chinese ideas would also have an impact on intellectual attitudes (see Chapter 17).

European expansion, which was in part a product of European rivalries, also deepened that competition and increased the tensions among European states. Bitter conflicts arose over the cargoes coming from the New World and Asia. The

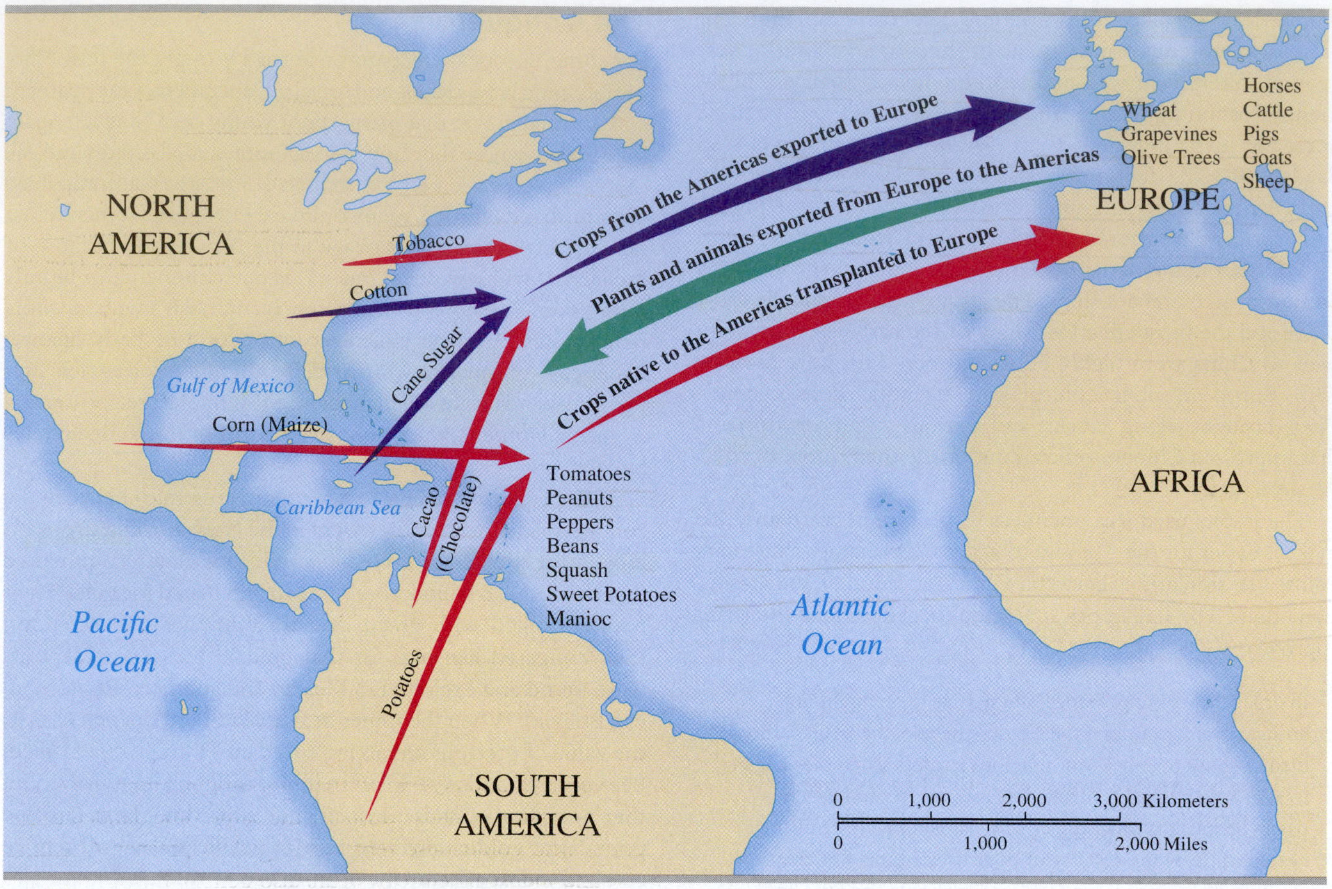

MAP 14.3 The Columbian Exchange. In addition to their diseases, which killed vast numbers of indigenous inhabitants of the Americas, Europeans transplanted many of their crops and domestic animals to the New World. Europeans also imported plants from the New World that improved food production and nutrition in Europe.

Q *Where were the main source regions for native plants imported into Europe?*

Anglo-Dutch trade wars and the British-French rivalry over India and North America became part of a new pattern of worldwide warfare in the eighteenth century (see Chapter 18). Bitter rivalries also led to state-sponsored piracy as governments authorized private captains to attack enemy shipping and keep part of the proceeds for themselves.

In the course of their expansion, Europeans also came to have a new view of the world. When the travels began in the fifteenth century, Europeans were dependent on maps that were often fanciful and inaccurate. Their explorations helped them create new maps that gave a more realistic portrayal of the world, as well as new techniques called map projections that allowed them to represent the round surface of a sphere on a flat piece of paper. The most famous of these is the Mercator projection, the work of a Flemish cartographer, Gerardus Mercator (juh-RAHR-dus mur-KAY-tur) (1512–1594). A Mercator projection is what mapmakers call a conformal projection. It tries to show the true shape of landmasses, but only in a limited area. On the Mercator projection, the shapes of lands near the equator are quite accurate, but the farther away from the equator they lie, the more exaggerated their size becomes. For example, the island of Greenland on a Mercator projection appears to be larger than the continent of South America. In fact, Greenland is about one-ninth the size of South America. Nevertheless, the Mercator projection was valuable to ship captains. Every straight line on a Mercator projection is a line of true direction, whether north, south, east, or west. For four centuries, ship captains were very grateful to Mercator.

The psychological impact of colonization on the colonizers is difficult to evaluate but hard to deny. Europeans were initially startled by the discovery of new peoples in the Americas. Some deemed them inhuman and thus fit to be exploited for labor. Others, however, found them to be refreshingly natural and as yet untouched by European corruption. But even the latter group still believed that the Indians should be converted—if not forcefully, at least peacefully—to Christianity. Overall, the relatively easy European success in dominating native peoples (be they Africans or Indians) reinforced Christian Europe's belief in the inherent superiority of European civilization and religion. The Scientific Revolution of the seventeenth century (see Chapter 16), the Enlightenment of the eighteenth (see Chapter 17), and the imperialism

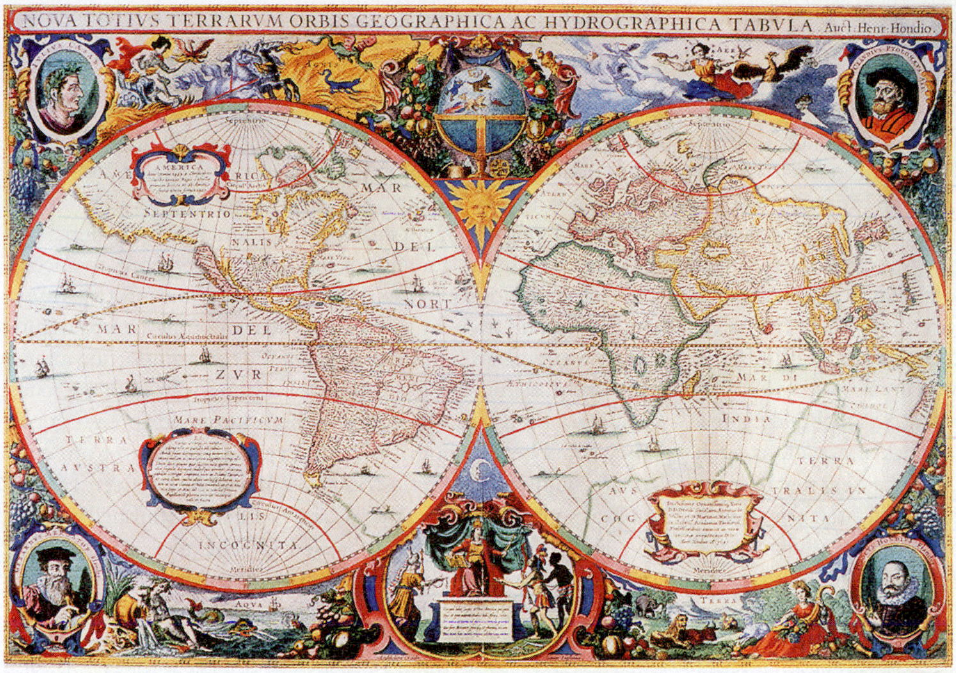

The Huntington Library, San Marino, CA/SuperStock

A Seventeenth-Century World Map. This beautiful world map was prepared in 1630 by Henricus Hondius. The four portraits are of Caesar, the Roman statesman; Ptolemy, the second-century astronomer; Mercator, the Flemish cartographer whose map projection Hondius followed; and Hondius himself. By comparing this map with the map created by Ptolemy on p. 402, one can see how much Europeans had learned about the shape of the world by the seventeenth century.

of the nineteenth (see Chapter 24) would all bolster this Eurocentric perspective, which has pervaded Western civilization's relations with the rest of the world.

Toward a World Economy

FOCUS QUESTION: What was mercantilism, and what was its relationship to colonial empires?

During the High Middle Ages, Europeans had engaged in a commercial revolution that created new opportunities for townspeople in a basically agrarian economy. Although this commercial thrust was slowed by the devastating crises of the fourteenth century, Europe's discovery of the world outside in the fifteenth century led to an even greater burst of commercial activity and the inception of a world market.

Economic Conditions in the Sixteenth Century

Inflation became a major economic problem in the sixteenth and early seventeenth centuries. This so-called **price revolution** was a Europe-wide phenomenon, although it affected different areas at different times. Though the inflation rate was probably a relatively low 2 to 3 percent a year, it was noticeable in a Europe accustomed to stable prices. Foodstuffs were most subject to price increases, especially evident in the price of wheat. An upward surge in wheat prices was first noticed in the Mediterranean area—in Spain, southern France, and Italy—and reached its peak there in the 1590s.

Although precise data are lacking, economic historians believe that as a result of the price revolution, wages failed to keep up with price increases. Wage earners, especially agricultural laborers and salaried workers in urban areas, saw their standard of living drop. At the same time, landed aristocrats, who could raise rents, managed to prosper. Commercial and industrial entrepreneurs also benefited from the price revolution because of rising prices, expanding markets, and relatively cheaper labor costs. Some historians regard this profit inflation as a valuable stimulus to investment and the growth of capitalism, helping to explain the economic expansion and prosperity of the sixteenth century. Governments were likewise affected by inflation. They borrowed heavily from bankers and imposed new tax burdens on their subjects, often stirring additional discontent.

The causes of the price revolution are a subject of much historical debate. Already in the 1560s, European intellectuals associated the rise in prices with the great influx of precious metals from the New World. Although this view was accepted for a long time, many economic historians now believe that the increase in population in the sixteenth century played an important role in creating inflationary pressures. A growing population increased the demand for land and food and drove up prices for both.

The Growth of Commercial Capitalism

The flourishing European trade of the sixteenth century revolved around three major areas: the Mediterranean in the south, the Low Countries and the Baltic region in the north, and central Europe, whose inland trade depended on the Rhine and Danube Rivers. As overseas trade expanded, however, the Atlantic seaboard began to play a more important role, linking the Mediterranean, Baltic, and central European trading areas together and making the whole of Europe into a more integrated market that was all the more vulnerable to price shifts. With their cheaper and faster ships, the Dutch came to monopolize both European and world trade, although they were increasingly challenged by the English and French in the seventeenth century.

The commercial expansion of the sixteenth and seventeenth centuries was made easier by new forms of commercial organization, especially the **joint-stock company**. Individuals bought shares in a company and received dividends on their investment while a board of directors ran the company and made the important business decisions. The return on investments could be spectacular. During its first ten years, investors received 30 percent on their money from the Dutch East India Company, which opened the Spice Islands and Southeast Asia to Dutch activity. The joint-stock company made it easier to raise large amounts of capital for world trading ventures.

Enormous profits were also being made in shipbuilding and in mining and metallurgy, where technological innovations, such as the use of pumps and new methods of extracting metals from ores, proved highly successful. The mining industry was closely tied to sixteenth-century family banking firms. In exchange for arranging large loans to Charles V, Jacob Fugger (YAH-gawp FOO-gurr) was given a monopoly over silver, copper, and mercury mines in the Habsburg possessions of central Europe that produced profits in excess of 50 percent per year. Though these close relationships between governments and entrepreneurs could lead to stunning successes, they could also be precarious. The House of Fugger went bankrupt at the end of the sixteenth century when the Habsburgs defaulted on their loans.

By the seventeenth century, the traditional family banking firms were no longer able to supply the numerous services needed for the expanding commercial capitalism. New institutions arose to take their place. The city of Amsterdam created the Bank of Amsterdam in 1609 as both a deposit and a transfer institution and the Amsterdam Bourse, or Exchange, where the trading of stocks replaced the exchange of goods. By the first half of the seventeenth century, the Amsterdam Exchange had emerged as the hub of the European business world, just as Amsterdam itself had replaced Antwerp as the greatest commercial and banking center of Europe.

Despite the growth of commercial capitalism, most of the European economy still depended on an agricultural system that had experienced few changes since the thirteenth century. At least 80 percent of Europeans still worked on the land. Almost all of the peasants of western Europe were free of serfdom, although many still owed a variety of feudal dues to the nobility. Despite the expanding markets and rising prices, European peasants saw little or no improvement in their lot as they faced increased rents and fees and higher taxes imposed by the state. In eastern Europe, the peasants' position even worsened as they were increasingly tied to the land in a new serfdom enforced by powerful landowners (see Chapter 15).

Mercantilism

In the seventeenth century, a set of economic tendencies that historians call **mercantilism** came to dominate economic practices. Fundamental to mercantilism was the belief that the total volume of trade was unchangeable. Therefore, states protected their economies by following certain practices: hoarding precious metals, implementing protectionist trade policies, promoting colonial development, increasing shipbuilding, supporting trading companies, and encouraging the manufacturing of products to be used in trade.

According to the mercantilists, the prosperity of a nation depended on a plentiful supply of bullion (gold and silver). For this reason, it was desirable to achieve a favorable balance of trade in which goods exported were of greater value than those imported, promoting an influx of gold and silver payments that would increase the quantity of bullion. Furthermore, to encourage exports, governments should stimulate and protect export industries and trade by granting trade monopolies, encouraging investment in new industries through subsidies, importing foreign artisans, and improving transportation systems by building roads, bridges, and canals. By imposing high tariffs on foreign goods, they could be kept out of the country and prevented from competing with domestic industries. Colonies were also deemed valuable as sources of raw materials and markets for finished goods.

The mercantilists also focused on the role of the state, believing that state intervention in some aspects of the economy was desirable for the sake of the national good. Government regulations to ensure the superiority of export goods, the construction of roads and canals, and the granting of subsidies to create trade companies were all predicated on government involvement in economic affairs.

Overseas Trade and Colonies: Movement Toward Globalization

Mercantilist theory on the role of colonies was matched in practice by Europe's overseas expansion. With the development of colonies and trading posts in the Americas and the East, Europeans embarked on an adventure in international commerce in the seventeenth century. Although some historians speak of a nascent world economy, we should remember that local, regional, and intra-European trade still predominated. At the end of the seventeenth century, for example, English imports totaled 360,000 tons, but only 5,000 tons came from the East Indies. About one-tenth of English and Dutch exports were shipped across the Atlantic; slightly more went to the East. What made the transoceanic trade rewarding, however, was not the volume but the value of its goods. Dutch, English, and French merchants were bringing back products that were still consumed largely by the wealthy but were beginning to make their way into the lives of artisans and merchants. Pepper and spices from the Indies, West Indian and Brazilian sugar, and Asian coffee and tea were becoming more readily available to European consumers.

Trade within Europe remained strong throughout the eighteenth century as wheat, timber, and naval stores from the Baltic, wines from France, wool and fruit from Spain, and silk from Italy were exchanged along with a host of other products. But this trade increased only slightly while overseas trade boomed. From 1716 to 1789, total French exports quadrupled; intra-European trade, which constituted 75 percent of these exports in 1716, accounted for only 50 percent of the total in 1789. This increase in overseas trade has led some historians to proclaim the emergence of a truly global economy in the eighteenth century. Trade patterns now interlocked Europe, Africa, the East, and the Americas.

CHAPTER SUMMARY

At the end of the fifteenth century, Europeans sailed out into the world in all directions. Beginning in the mid-fifteenth century with a handful of Portuguese ships that ventured southward along the West African coast, bringing back slaves and gold, the process of European expansion accelerated with the epochal voyages of Christopher Columbus to the Americas and Vasco da Gama to the Indian Ocean in the 1490s. The Portuguese Empire was based on trade; Portugal's population was too small for it to establish large colonies. But Spain had greater resources: Spanish conquistadors overthrew both the Aztec and Inca Empires, and Spain created two major administrative units in New Spain and Peru that subjected the native population to Spanish control. Catholic missionaries, under the control of the Spanish crown, brought Christianity, including cathedrals and schools.

Soon a number of other European peoples, including the Dutch, British, and French, had joined in the process of expansion, and by the end of the eighteenth century, they had created a global trade network dominated by Western ships and Western power. Although originally less prized than gold and spices, slaves became a major object of trade, and by the nineteenth century 10 million African slaves had been shipped to the Americas. Slavery was common in Africa, and the African terminus of the trade was in the hands of the Africans, but the insatiable demand for slaves led to increased warfare on that unfortunate continent. It was not until the late 1700s that slavery came under harsh criticism in Europe.

In less than three hundred years, the European age of exploration had changed the shape of the world. In some areas, such as the Americas and the Spice Islands in Asia, it led to the destruction of indigenous civilizations and the establishment of European colonies. In others, such as Africa, India, and mainland Southeast Asia, it left native regimes intact but had a strong impact on local societies and regional trade patterns. Japan and China were least affected.

At the time, many European observers viewed the process in a favorable light. They believed that it not only expanded wealth through world trade and exchanged crops and discoveries between the Old World and the New but also introduced "heathen peoples" to the message of Jesus. No doubt, the conquest of the Americas and expansion into the rest of the world brought out the worst and some of the best of European civilization. The greedy plundering of resources and the brutal repression and enslavement were hardly balanced by attempts to create new institutions, convert the natives to Christianity, and foster the rights of the indigenous peoples. In any event, Europeans had begun to change the face of the world and increasingly saw their culture, with its religion, languages, and technology, as a coherent force to be exported to all corners of the world.

CHAPTER TIMELINE

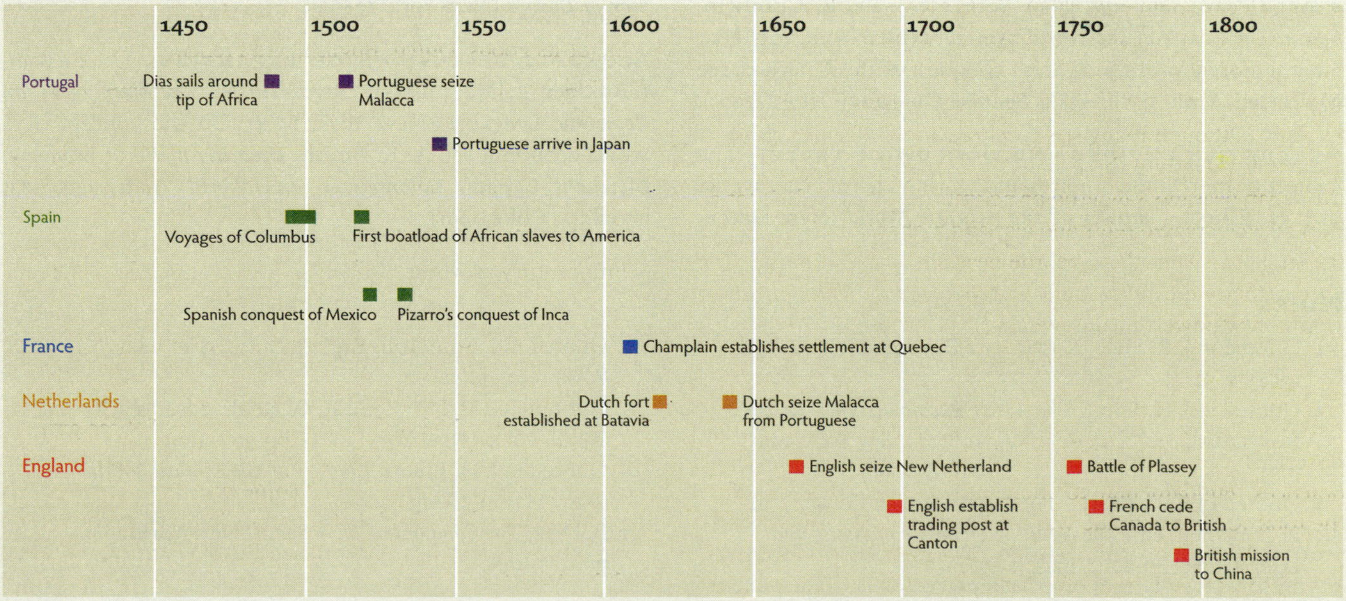

CHAPTER REVIEW

Upon Reflection

Q How did the experiences of the Spanish and Portuguese during the age of exploration differ from those of their French, Dutch, and English counterparts?

Q What role did religion play as a motivation in the age of exploration? Was it as important a motive as economics? Why or why not?

Q Why and how did Japan succeed in keeping Europeans largely away from its territory in the seventeenth century?

Key Terms

portolani (p. 402)
conquistadors (p. 407)
encomienda (p. 410)
viceroy (p. 410)
audiencias (p. 410)
triangular trade (p. 413)
Middle Passage (p. 413)
Columbian Exchange (p. 425)
price revolution (p. 427)
joint-stock company (p. 428)
mercantilism (p. 428)

Suggestions for Further Reading

GENERAL WORKS For general accounts of European discovery and expansion, see **D. Arnold, *Age of Discovery***, 2nd ed. (London, 2002); **R. Fritze, *New Worlds: The Great Voyages of Discovery, 1400–1600*** (Westport, Conn., 2002); **G. J. Ames, *The Globe Encompassed: The Age of European Discovery, 1500–1700*** (Upper Saddle River, N.J., 2007); **P. Morgan** and **N. Canny, eds., *The Oxford Handbook of the Atlantic World, 1450–1850*** (New York, 2011); and **A. Suranyi, *The Atlantic Connection: A History of the Atlantic World, 1450–1900*** (New York, 2015).

PORTUGUESE AND SPANISH EXPANSION On Portuguese expansion, see **R. Crowley, *Conquerors: How Portugal Forged the First Global Empire*** (New York, 2015). On Columbus, see **W. D. Phillips** and **C. R. Phillips, *The Worlds of Christopher Columbus*** (Cambridge, 1992). On the Spanish Empire in the New World, see **H. Kamen, *Empire: How Spain Became a World Power, 1492–1763*** (New York, 2003), and **R. Goodwin, *Spain: The Centre of the World, 1519–1682*** (New York, 2015). For a revisionist view of the Spanish conquest of the Americas, see **M. Restall, *Seven Myths of the Spanish Conquest*** (Oxford, 2003).

MERCANTILE EMPIRES AND WORLDWIDE TRADE The subject of mercantile empires and worldwide trade is covered in **J. H. Elliott, *Empires of the Atlantic World*** (New Haven, Conn., 2006), and **M. J. Seymour, *Transformation of the North Atlantic World, 1492–1763*** (Westport, Conn., 2004). On the African slave trade, see **J. K. Thornton, *Africa and Africans in the Making of the Atlantic World, 1400–1800*** (Cambridge, 1998). On slavery in the New World see **D. B. Davis, *Inhuman Bondage: The Rise and Fall of Slavery in the New World*** (New York, 2008).

IMPACT OF EXPANSION The impact of expansion on European consciousness is explored in **A. Pagden, *European Encounters with the New World: From Renaissance to Romanticism*** (New Haven, Conn., 1993). On the impact of disease, see **N. D. Cook, *Born to Die: Disease and the New World*** (New York, 1998). The human and ecological effects of the interaction of New World and Old World cultures are examined thoughtfully in **A. W. Crosby, *Ecological Imperialism: The Biological Expansion of Europe*** (New York, 1986).

ECONOMIC DIMENSIONS OF EXPANSION On mercantilism, see **L. Magnusson, *Mercantilism: The Shaping of an Economic Language*** (New York, 1994). On the concept of a world economy, see **A. K. Smith, *Creating a World Economy: Merchant Capital, Colonialism, and World Trade, 1400–1825*** (Boulder, Colo., 1991).

Notes

1. Quoted in J. R. Hale, *Renaissance Exploration* (New York, 1968), p. 32.
2. Quoted in J. H. Parry, *The Age of Reconnaissance: Discovery, Exploration, and Settlement, 1450 to 1650* (New York, 1963), p. 33.
3. Quoted in R. B. Reed, "The Expansion of Europe," in R. D. Molen, ed., *The Meaning of the Renaissance and Reformation* (Boston, 1974), p. 308.
4. Quoted in I. Cameron, *Explorers and Exploration* (New York, 1991), p. 42.
5. Quoted in J. H. Parry and R. G. Keith, eds., *New Iberian World*, vol. 2 (New York, 1984), pp. 309–310.
6. Quoted in J. H. Elliott, *Empires of the Atlantic World* (New Haven, Conn., 2006), p. 125.
7. B. Diaz, *The Conquest of New Spain* (New York, 1963) pp. 405–406.

8. Quoted in A. Andrea and J. H. Overfield, *The Human Record: Sources of Global History*, 3rd ed. (Boston, 1998), p. 460.
9. Quoted in B. Davidson, *Africa in History: Themes and Outlines* (New York, 1991), p. 198.
10. Quoted in Cameron, *Explorers and Exploration*, p. 42.
11. Quoted in N. Ferguson, *Empire: The Rise and Demise of the British World Order and the Lessons for Global Power* (New York, 2002), p. 43.
12. Quoted in L. J. Gallagher, ed., trans., *China in the Sixteenth Century: The Journals of Matthew Ricci* (New York, 1953), p. 154.
13. Quoted in G. V. Scammell, *The First Imperial Age: European Overseas Expansion, c. 1400–1715* (London, 1989), p. 62.
14. M. Leon-Portilla, ed., *The Broken Spears: The Aztec Account of the Conquest of Mexico* (Boston, 1969), p. 51.

CHAPTER

15

STATE BUILDING AND THE SEARCH FOR ORDER IN THE SEVENTEENTH CENTURY

Nicolas-René Jollain the Elder's portrait of Louis XIV captures the king's sense of royal grandeur

CHAPTER OUTLINE AND FOCUS QUESTIONS

Social Crises, War, and Rebellions

Q What economic, social, and political crises did Europe experience in the first half of the seventeenth century?

The Practice of Absolutism: Western Europe

Q What was absolutism in theory, and how did its actual practice in France reflect or differ from the theory?

Absolutism in Central, Eastern, and Northern Europe

Q What developments enabled Brandenburg-Prussia, Austria, and Russia to emerge as major powers in the seventeenth century?

Limited Monarchy and Republics

Q What were the main issues in the struggle between king and Parliament in seventeenth-century England, and how were they resolved?

The Flourishing of European Culture

Q How did the artistic and literary achievements of this era reflect the political and economic developments of the period?

Critical Thinking

Q *What theories of government were proposed by Jacques Bossuet, Thomas Hobbes, and John Locke, and how did their respective theories reflect concerns and problems of the seventeenth century?*

Connections to Today

Q *How does the exercise of state power in the seventeenth century compare with the exercise of state power in the twenty-first century? What, if anything, has changed?*

BY THE END of the sixteenth century, Europe was beginning to experience a decline in religious passions and a growing secularization that affected both the political and the intellectual worlds (on the intellectual effects, see Chapter 16). Some historians like to speak of the seventeenth century as a turning point in the evolution of a modern state system in Europe. The ideal of a united Christian Europe gave way to the practical realities of a system of secular states in which matters of state took precedence over the salvation of subjects' souls. By the seventeenth century, the credibility of Christianity had been so weakened through religious wars that more and more Europeans came to think of politics in secular terms.

One response to the religious wars and other crises of the time was a yearning for order. As the internal social and political rebellions and revolts died down, it became apparent that the privileged classes of society—the aristocrats—remained in control, although the various states exhibited important differences in political forms. The most general trend saw an extension of monarchical power as a stabilizing force. This development, which historians have called absolute monarchy or absolutism, was most evident in France during the flamboyant reign of Louis XIV, regarded by some as the perfect embodiment of an absolute monarch. In his memoirs, the duc de Saint-Simon (dook duh san-see-MOHN), who had firsthand experience of French court life, said that Louis was "to the manner born, for he stood out like a king bee because of his height, grace, and beauty (even in the tone of his voice), and because of his princely bearing which was better than good looks." The king's natural grace gave him a special charm as well. He spoke well and learned quickly. He was naturally kind and "he loved glory; he desired peace and good government. He was born prudent, temperate, master of his emotions and his tongue . . . he was born good and just." His life was orderly, and his self-control was impeccable. But even absolute monarchs had imperfections, and Saint-Simon had the courage to point them out: "the king's intelligence was below the average. . . . Praise, or better, adulation pleased him so much that the most fulsome was welcome and the most servile even more delectable." Indeed, "he acquired a pride so colossal that, truly, had not God implanted in his heart the fear of the devil . . . he would have allowed himself to be worshipped."[1]

But absolutism was not the only response to the search for order in the seventeenth century. Other states, such as England, reacted differently to domestic crisis, and another very different system emerged in which monarchs were limited by the power of their representative assemblies. Absolute and limited monarchy were the two poles of seventeenth-century state building.

Social Crises, War, and Rebellions

FOCUS QUESTION: What economic, social, and political crises did Europe experience in the first half of the seventeenth century?

The inflation-fueled prosperity of the sixteenth century showed signs of slackening by the beginning of the seventeenth. Economic contraction was evident in some parts of Europe in the 1620s. In the 1630s and 1640s, as imports of silver from the Americas declined, economic recession intensified, especially in the Mediterranean area. Once the industrial and financial center of Europe in the Renaissance, Italy was now becoming an economic backwater. Spain's economy was also seriously failing by the 1640s.

Population trends of the sixteenth and seventeenth centuries also reveal Europe's worsening conditions. The sixteenth century was a period of expanding population, possibly related to a warmer climate and increased food supplies. It has been estimated that the population of Europe increased from 60 million in 1500 to 85 million by 1600, the first major recovery of the European population since the devastation of the Black Death in the mid-fourteenth century. Records also indicate a leveling off of the population by 1620, however, and even a decline by 1650, especially in central and southern Europe. Only the Dutch, English, and French grew in number in the first half of the seventeenth century. Europe's longtime adversaries—war, famine, and plague—continued to affect population levels. After the middle of the sixteenth century, another "little ice age," when average temperatures fell, affected harvests and caused famines. These problems created social tensions that came to a boil in the witchcraft craze.

The Witchcraft Craze

Hysteria over witchcraft affected the lives of many Europeans in the sixteenth and seventeenth centuries. Witchcraft trials were held in England, Scotland, Switzerland, Germany, some parts of France and the Low Countries, and even in New England in America.

Witchcraft was not a new phenomenon. Its practice had been part of traditional village culture for centuries, but it came to be viewed as both sinister and dangerous when the medieval church began to connect witches to the activities of the devil, thereby transforming witchcraft into a heresy that had to be wiped out. After the establishment of the Inquisition in the thirteenth century, some people were accused of a variety of witchcraft practices and, following the biblical injunction "Thou shalt not suffer a witch to live," were turned over to secular authorities for burning at the stake or, in England, hanging.

THE SPREAD OF WITCHCRAFT What distinguished witchcraft in the sixteenth and seventeenth centuries from these previous developments was the increased number of trials and executions of presumed witches. Perhaps more than 100,000 people throughout Europe were prosecuted on charges of witchcraft. Although larger cities were affected first, the trials spread to smaller towns and rural areas as the hysteria persisted well into the seventeenth century (see the box on p. 434).

The accused witches usually confessed to a number of practices, most often after intense torture. Many said that they had sworn allegiance to the devil and attended sabbats or nocturnal gatherings where they feasted, danced, and even copulated with the devil in sexual orgies. More common, however, were admissions of using evil incantations and special ointments and powders to wreak havoc on neighbors by killing their livestock, injuring their children, or raising storms to destroy their crops.

A number of contributing factors have been suggested to explain why the witchcraft frenzy became so widespread in the sixteenth and seventeenth centuries. Religious uncertainties clearly played some part. Many witchcraft trials occurred in areas where Protestantism had recently been victorious or in regions, such as southwestern Germany, where Protestant-Catholic controversies still raged. As religious passions became inflamed, accusations of being in league with the devil became common on both sides. After all, both Martin Luther and John Calvin had described their personal battles with Satan.

Recently, however, historians have emphasized the importance of social conditions, especially the problems of a society

A WITCHCRAFT TRIAL IN FRANCE

PERSECUTIONS FOR WITCHCRAFT REACHED their high point in the sixteenth and seventeenth centuries when tens of thousands of people were brought to trial. In this excerpt from the minutes of a trial in France in 1652, we can see why the accused witch stood little chance of exonerating herself.

The Trial of Suzanne Gaudry

28 May, 1652. . . . Interrogation of Suzanne Gaudry, prisoner at the court of Rieux. . . . [During interrogations on May 28 and May 29, the prisoner confessed to a number of activities involving the devil.]

Deliberation of the Court—June 3, 1652

The undersigned advocates of the Court have seen these interrogations and answers. They say that the aforementioned Suzanne Gaudry confesses that she is a witch, that she had given herself to the devil, that she had renounced God, Lent, and baptism, that she has been marked on the shoulder, that she has cohabited with the devil and that she has been to the dances. . . .

Third Interrogation—June 27

This prisoner being led into the chamber, she was examined to know if things were not as she had said and confessed at the beginning of her imprisonment.

—Answers no, and that what she has said was done so by force.

Pressed to say the truth, that otherwise she would be subjected to torture . . .

—Answers that she is not a witch. . . .

She was placed in the hands of the officer in charge of torture. . . .

The Torture

This prisoner, before being strapped down, was admonished to maintain herself in her first confessions. . . .

—Says that she denies everything she has said. . . . Feeling herself being strapped down, says that she is not a witch . . . and being a little stretched [on the rack] screams ceaselessly that she is not a witch. . . .

Asked if she did not confess that she had been a witch for twenty-six years.

—Says that she said it, that she retracts it, crying that she is not a witch. . . .

The mark having been probed . . . it was adjudged by the aforesaid doctor and officer truly to be the mark of the devil.

Being more tightly stretched upon the torture-rack, urged to maintain her confessions.

—Said that it was true that she is a witch. Asked how long she has been in subjugation to the devil.

—Answers that it was twenty years ago that the devil appeared to her, being in her lodgings in the form of a man dressed in a little cow-hide and black breeches. . . .

Verdict

July 9, 1652. In the light of the interrogations, answers and investigations made into the charge against Suzanne Gaudry . . . seeing by her own confessions that she is said to have made a pact with the devil, received the mark from him . . . and that following this, she had renounced God, Lent, and baptism and had let herself be known carnally by him. . . . Also, seeing that she is said to have been a part of nocturnal carols and dances.

For expiation of which the advice of the undersigned is that the office of Rieux can legitimately condemn the aforesaid Suzanne Gaudry to death, tying her to a gallows, and strangling her to death, then burning her body and burying it here in the environs of the woods.

Q *Why were women, particularly older women, especially vulnerable to accusations of witchcraft? What "proofs" are offered here that Suzanne Gaudry had consorted with the devil? What does this account tell us about the spread of witchcraft accusations in the seventeenth century?*

Source: A. C. Kors and E. Peters, eds., *Witchcraft in Europe, 1100–1700: A Documentary History* (Philadelphia: University of Pennsylvania Press, 1972).

in turmoil, in explaining the witchcraft hysteria. At a time when the old communal values that stressed working together for the good of the community were disintegrating before the onslaught of a new economic ethic that emphasized looking out for oneself, property owners became more fearful of the growing numbers of poor in their midst and transformed them psychologically into agents of the devil. Old women were particularly susceptible to suspicion. Many of them, no longer the recipients of the local charity available in traditional society, may even have tried to survive by selling herbs, potions, or secret remedies for healing. When problems arose—and there were many in this crisis-laden period—these people were handy scapegoats. Of special concern was the fear that witches harmed mothers and their households or caused male impotence and thus disrupted the social order.

That women were most often the victims of the witch-hunt has led some scholars to argue that the witch hunt was really a woman hunt or "genderized mass murder," arguing that men hunted witches because they caused disorder and were sexual beings in a patriarchal society. Other scholars have rejected this approach and argue first, that men were also accused of witchcraft, and second, that women accused other women of witchcraft. These scholars believe that people in the sixteenth and seventeenth century believed in witchcraft as a constant threat in their society.

Despite scholarly differences about the nature of the witch hunts, there is no doubt that women were the primary victims. Current estimates are that there were 100,000 to 110,000 witch trials between 1450 and 1750 with about 50 percent of the trials leading to executions. Of those executed, 75 to 80 percent were women, many of them older women. A study of the Würzburg, Germany, witch trials reveals that of the 255 executed, 190 were women, 140 were women over forty, and 112 were over fifty.

That women should be the chief victims of witchcraft trials was hardly accidental. Nicholas Rémy, a witchcraft judge in France in the 1590s, found it "not unreasonable that this scum of humanity [witches] should be drawn chiefly from the feminine sex." To another judge, it came as no surprise that witches would confess to sexual experiences with Satan: "The Devil uses them so, because he knows that women love carnal pleasures, and he means to bind them to his allegiance by such agreeable provocations."[2] Of course, witch hunters were not the only ones who held women in such low esteem. Most theologians, lawyers, and philosophers in early modern Europe believed in the natural inferiority of women and thus would have found it plausible that women would be more susceptible to witchcraft.

DECLINE By the mid-seventeenth century, the witchcraft hysteria began to subside. The destruction caused by the religious wars had forced people to accept at least a grudging toleration, tempering religious passions. Moreover, as governments began to stabilize after the period of crisis, fewer magistrates were willing to accept the unsettling and divisive conditions generated by the trials of witches. Finally, by the turn of the eighteenth century, more and more educated people were questioning traditional attitudes toward religion and finding it contrary to reason to believe in the old view of a world haunted by evil spirits.

The Thirty Years' War

Although many Europeans responded to the upheavals of the second half of the sixteenth century with a desire for peace and order, the first fifty years of the seventeenth century continued to be plagued by crises. A devastating war that affected much of Europe and rebellions seemingly everywhere protracted the atmosphere of disorder and violence.

BACKGROUND TO THE WAR Religion, especially the struggle between Catholicism and Calvinism, played an important role in the outbreak of the Thirty Years' War (1618–1648), often called the "last of the religious wars." As the war progressed, however, it became increasingly clear that secular, dynastic-nationalist considerations were far more important. Although much of the fighting during the Thirty Years' War took place in the Germanic lands of the Holy Roman Empire, it became a Europe-wide struggle (see Map 15.1). In fact, some historians view it as part of a larger conflict for European leadership between the Bourbon dynasty of France and the Habsburg dynasties of Spain and the Holy Roman Empire and date it from 1609 to 1659.

The Peace of Augsburg in 1555 had brought an end to religious warfare between German Catholics and Lutherans. Religion, however, continued to play a divisive role in German life as Lutherans and Catholics persisted in vying for control of various principalities. In addition, although the treaty had not recognized the rights of Calvinists, a number of German states had adopted Calvinism as their state church. At the beginning of the seventeenth century, the Calvinist ruler of the Palatinate (puh-LAT-uh-nuht *or* puh-LAT-uh-nayt), the Elector Palatine (PAL-uh-tyn) Frederick IV, assumed the leadership in forming a league of German Protestant states called the Protestant Union. To counteract it, Duke Maximilian of the south German state of Bavaria organized the Catholic League of German states. By 1609, then, Germany was dividing into two armed camps in anticipation of religious war.

A constitutional issue exacerbated the religious division. The desire of the Habsburg emperors to consolidate their authority in the Holy Roman Empire was resisted by the princes, who fought for their "German liberties," their constitutional rights and prerogatives as individual rulers. To pursue their policies, the Habsburg emperors looked to Spain (ruled by another branch of the family) for assistance while the princes turned to the enemies of Spain, especially France, for help against the emperors. The divisions in the Holy Roman Empire and Europe made it almost inevitable that if war did erupt, it would be widespread and difficult to stop.

THE BOHEMIAN PHASE Historians have traditionally divided the Thirty Years' War into four major phases. The Bohemian phase (1618–1625) began in one of the Habsburgs' own territories. In 1617, the Bohemian Estates (primarily the nobles) accepted the Habsburg Archduke Ferdinand as their king but soon found themselves unhappy with their choice. Though many of the nobles were Calvinists, Ferdinand was a devout Catholic who began a process of re-Catholicizing Bohemia and strengthening royal power. The Protestant nobles rebelled against Ferdinand in May 1618 and proclaimed their resistance by throwing two of the Habsburg governors and a secretary out of a window in the royal castle in Prague, the seat of Bohemian government. The Catholic side claimed that their seemingly miraculous escape from death in the 70-foot fall from the castle was due to the intercession of the Virgin Mary, while Protestants pointed out that they fell into a manure pile. The Bohemian rebels now seized control of Bohemia, deposed Ferdinand, and elected as his replacement the Protestant ruler of the Palatinate, Elector Frederick V, who was also the head of the Protestant Union.

Ferdinand, who in the meantime had been elected Holy Roman Emperor, refused to accept his deposition. Realizing that the election of Frederick V, if allowed to stand, could upset the balance of religious and political power in central Europe and give the Protestant forces greater control of the Holy Roman Empire, Ferdinand sought the aid of the imposing forces of Duke Maximilian of Bavaria and the Catholic League. With

MAP 15.1 The Thirty Years' War. The conflict began in the German states as Europe's major powers backed either the northern Protestant Union or the southern Catholic League. As the war progressed, religion receded in importance, replaced by a dynastic struggle between the French Bourbons and the Spanish and Austrian Habsburgs.

Compare this map with Map 13.2. Which countries engaged in the war were predominantly Protestant, which were predominantly Catholic, and which were mixed?

their help, the imperial forces defeated Frederick and the Bohemian nobles at the Battle of White Mountain outside Prague on November 8, 1620. Spanish troops took advantage of Frederick's predicament by invading the Palatinate and conquering it by the end of 1622. The unfortunate Frederick fled into exile in the United Provinces. Reestablished as king of Bohemia, Emperor Ferdinand declared Bohemia a hereditary Habsburg possession, confiscated the land of the Protestant nobles, and established Catholicism as the sole religion. The Spanish renewed their attack on the Dutch, and the forces of Catholicism seemed on the road to victory. But the war was far from over.

THE DANISH PHASE The second phase of the war, the Danish phase (1625–1629), began when King Christian IV of Denmark (1588–1648), a Lutheran, intervened on behalf of the Protestant cause by leading an army into northern Germany. Christian had made an anti-Habsburg and anti-Catholic alliance with the United Provinces and England. He also wanted, however, to gain possession of some Catholic territories in northern Germany to benefit his family.

In the meantime, Ferdinand had gained a new commander for the imperial forces in Albrecht von Wallenstein (AWL-brekht fun VAHL-en-shtyn). A brilliant and enigmatic commander, Wallenstein was a Bohemian nobleman who had taken advantage of Ferdinand's victory to become the country's wealthiest landowner. Wallenstein's forces defeated a Protestant army at Dessau and then continued to operate in northern Germany. The forces of Christian IV, despite substantial aid from their allies, were defeated in 1626 by an army of the Catholic League under Count Tilly and then suffered an even more devastating loss to Wallenstein's forces the following year. Wallenstein now occupied parts of northern Germany, including the Baltic ports of Hamburg, Lübeck, and Bremen. Christian IV's defeat meant the end of Danish supremacy in the Baltic.

DHM/The Bridgman Art Library

The Thirty Years' War: Soldiers Plundering a Farm. This 1620 painting shows a group of soldiers running amok and plundering a farm. This scene was typical of many that occurred during the Thirty Years' War, especially in Germany, where the war caused enormous destruction.

After the success of the imperial armies, Emperor Ferdinand II was at the height of his power and took this opportunity to issue the Edict of Restitution in March 1629. His proclamation prohibited Calvinist worship and restored all property taken by Protestant princes or cities during the past seventy-five years to the Catholic Church. But this sudden growth in the power of the Habsburg emperor frightened many German princes, who feared for their independent status and reacted by forcing the emperor to dismiss Wallenstein.

THE SWEDISH PHASE The Swedish phase (1630–1635) marked the entry of Gustavus Adolphus (goo-STAY-vus uh-DAHL-fuss), king of Sweden (1611–1632), into the war. Gustavus Adolphus was responsible for reviving Sweden and transforming it into a great Baltic power. A military genius, he brought a disciplined and well-equipped Swedish army to northern Germany. He was also a devout Lutheran who felt compelled to aid his coreligionists in Germany.

Gustavus's army swept the imperial forces out of the north and moved into the heart of Germany. In desperation, the imperial side recalled Wallenstein, who was given command of the imperial army that met Gustavus's troops near Leipzig. At the Battle of Lützen (LOOT-sun) in 1632, the Swedish forces prevailed but paid a high price for the victory when the Swedish king was killed in the battle. Although the Swedish forces remained in Germany, they proved much less effective. Despite the loss of Wallenstein, who was assassinated in 1634 on the orders of Emperor Ferdinand, the imperial army decisively defeated the Swedes at the Battle of Nördlingen at the end of 1634 and drove them out of southern Germany. This imperial victory guaranteed that southern Germany would remain Catholic. The emperor used this opportunity to make peace with the German princes by agreeing to annul the Edict of Restitution of 1629. But peace failed to come to war-weary Germany. The Swedes wished to continue, while the French, under the direction of Cardinal Richelieu (REESH-uh-lyoo), the chief minister of King Louis XIII, entered the war directly, beginning the fourth and final phase of the war, the Franco-Swedish phase (1635–1648).

THE FRANCO-SWEDISH PHASE By this time, religious issues were losing their significance. The Catholic French were now supporting the Protestant Swedes against the Catholic Habsburgs of Germany and Spain. The Battle of Rocroi (roh-KRWAH) in 1643

CHRONOLOGY The Thirty Years' War	
Protestant Union	1608
Catholic League	1609
Election of Habsburg Archduke Ferdinand as king of Bohemia	1617
Bohemian revolt against Ferdinand	1618
Bohemian phase	1618–1625
Battle of White Mountain	1620
Danish phase	1625–1629
Edict of Restitution	1629
Swedish phase	1630–1635
Battle of Lützen	1632
Battle of Nördlingen	1634
Franco-Swedish phase	1635–1648
Battle of Rocroi	1643
Peace of Westphalia	1648
Peace of the Pyrenees	1659

proved decisive as the French beat the Spanish and brought an end to Spanish military greatness. The French then moved on to victories over the imperialist-Bavarian armies in southern Germany. By this time, all parties were ready for peace, and after five years of protracted negotiations, the Peace of Westphalia in 1648 officially ended the war in Germany. The war between France and Spain, however, continued until the Peace of the Pyrenees in 1659. By that time, Spain had become a second-class power, and France had emerged as the dominant nation in Europe.

OUTCOMES OF THE WAR What were the results of what one historian has called a "basically meaningless conflict"? The Peace of Westphalia ensured that all German states, including the Calvinist ones, were free to determine their own religion. Territorially, France gained parts of western Germany, part of Alsace, and the three cities of Metz, Toul, and Verdun, giving the French control of the Franco-German border area. While Sweden and the German states of Brandenburg and Bavaria gained some territory in Germany, the Austrian Habsburgs did not really lose any but did see their authority as rulers of Germany further diminished. The more than three hundred states that made up the Holy Roman Empire were recognized as virtually independent, since each received the power to conduct its own foreign policy. The Habsburg emperor had been reduced to a figurehead in the Holy Roman Empire. The Peace of Westphalia also made it clear that religion and politics were now separate. The pope was completely ignored in all decisions at Westphalia, and political motives became the guiding forces in public affairs as religion moved closer to becoming primarily a matter of personal conviction and individual choice. Some historians also argue that the Peace of Westphalia marks the beginning of a modern international order in which sovereign states began to operate as equals within a secular framework.

The economic and social effects of the Thirty Years' War on Germany are still debated. Some areas of Germany were completely devastated, but others remained relatively untouched and even experienced economic growth. The most recent work pictures a damaged economy and a population decline of 15 to 20 percent in the Holy Roman Empire. Although historians may debate the degree of devastation, many people in Germany would have understood this description by a traveler journeying along the Main River in 1636:

> [We] came to a wretched little village called Neukirchen, which we found quite uninhabited yet with one house on fire. Here, since it was now late, we were obliged to stay all night, for the nearest town was four miles away; but we spent that night walking up and down with guns in our hands, and listening fearfully to the sound of shots in the woods around us. . . . Early next morning, His Excellency went to inspect the church and found it had been plundered and that the pictures and the altar had been desecrated. In the churchyard we saw a dead body, scraped out of the grave, while outside the churchyard we found another dead body.[3]

The Thirty Years' War was undoubtedly the most destructive conflict Europeans had yet experienced (see the box on p. 439).

HISTORIANS DEBATE Was There a Military Revolution?

By the seventeenth century, war played an increasingly important role in European affairs. Military power was considered essential to a ruler's reputation and power; thus, the pressure to build an effective military machine was intense. Some historians believe that the changes that occurred in the science of warfare between 1560 and 1660 warrant the title of military revolution.

Medieval warfare, with its mounted knights and supplementary archers, had been transformed in the Renaissance by the employment of infantry armed with pikes and halberds (long-handled weapons combining an axe with a spike) and arranged in massed rectangles known as squadrons or battalions. The use of firearms required adjustments to the size and shape of the massed infantry and made the cavalry less effective.

It was Gustavus Adolphus, the king of Sweden, who developed the first standing army of conscripts, notable for the flexibility of its tactics. The infantry brigades of Gustavus's army were composed of equal numbers of musketeers and pikemen, standing six men deep. They employed the salvo, in which all rows of the infantry fired at once instead of row by row. These salvos of fire, which cut up the massed ranks of the opposing infantry squadrons, were followed by a pike charge, giving the infantry a primarily offensive deployment. Gustavus also used his cavalry in a more mobile fashion. After shooting a pistol volley, they charged the enemy with their swords. Additional flexibility was obtained by using lighter artillery pieces that were more easily moved during battle. All of these changes required coordination, careful training, and better discipline, forcing rulers to move away from undisciplined mercenary forces. Naturally, the success of Gustavus Adolphus led to imitation.

THE DESTRUCTION OF MAGDEBURG IN THE THIRTY YEARS' WAR

AFTER GUSTAVUS ADOLPHUS entered the war, he was finally joined by German Protestant forces after the fall of the Protestant city of Magdeburg to the imperial forces. In this excerpt, a writer of this period gives a vivid description of what happened to Magdeburg and its inhabitants.

An Account of the Destruction of Magdeburg

Thus it came about that the city and all its inhabitants fell into the hands of the enemy, whose violence and cruelty were due in part to their common hatred of the adherents of the Augsburg Confession [Lutherans], and in part to their being embittered by the chain shot which had been fired at them and by the derision and insults that the Magdeburgers had heaped upon them from the ramparts.

Then was there naught but beating and burning, plundering, torture, and murder. Most especially was every one of the enemy bent on securing much booty. When a marauding party entered a house, if its master had anything to give he might thereby purchase respite and protection for himself and his family till the next man, who also wanted something should come along. It was only when everything had been brought forth and there was nothing left to give that the real trouble commenced. Then, what with blows and threats of shooting, stabbing, and hanging, the poor people were so terrified that if they had had anything left they would have brought it forth if it had been buried in the earth or hidden away in a thousand castles. In this frenzied rage, the great and splendid city that had stood like a fair princess in the land was now, in its hour of direct need and unutterable distress and woe, given over to the flames, and thousands of innocent men, women, and children, in the midst of a horrible din of heartrending shrieks and cries, were tortured and put to death in so cruel and shameful a manner that no words would suffice to describe, nor no tears to bewail it . . .

Thus, in a single day this noble and famous city, the pride of the whole country, went up in fire and smoke; and the remnant of its citizens, with their wives and children, were taken prisoner and driven away by the enemy with a noise of weeping and wailing that could be heard from afar, while the cinders and ashes from the town were carried by the wind to . . . distant places . . .

In addition to all this, quantities of sumptuous and irreplaceable house furnishings and movable property of all kinds, such as books, manuscripts, paintings, memorials of all sorts . . . which money could not buy, were either burned or carried away by the soldiers as booty. The most magnificent garments, hangings, silk stuffs, gold and silver lace, linen of all sorts, and other household goods were bought by the army soldiers for a mere song and peddled about by the cart load all throughout the archbishopric of Magdeburg. . . . Gold chains and rings, jewels, and every kind of gold and silver utensils were to be bought from the common soldiers for a tenth of their real value . . .

Q *What does this document reveal about the effect of war on ordinary Europeans? Compare this description with the descriptions of the treatment of civilians in other wars. Does this author exaggerate, or is this description similar to the others?*

Source: J. H. Robinson, *Readings in European History*, vol. 2 (Boston: Ginn & Company, 1906), pp. 211–212.

Some historians have questioned the use of the phrase "military revolution" to describe the military changes from 1560 to 1660, arguing instead that military developments were gradual. In any case, for the rest of the seventeenth century, warfare continued to change. Standing armies, based partly on conscription, grew ever larger and more expensive. Standing armies necessitated better-disciplined and better-trained soldiers and led to the education of officers in military schools. Armies also introduced the use of linear rather than square formations to provide greater flexibility and mobility in tactics. There was also an increased use of firearms as the musket with attached bayonet increasingly replaced the pike in the ranks of the infantry. A naval arms race in the seventeenth century led to more and bigger warships or capital ships known as "ships of the line." By the end of the seventeenth century, most of these had two or three decks and were capable of carrying between fifty and one hundred heavy cannon.

Larger armies and navies could be maintained only by levying heavier taxes, making war a greater economic burden and an ever more important part of the early modern European state. The creation of large bureaucracies to supervise the military resources of the state led to growth in the power of state governments.

Rebellions

Before, during, and after the Thirty Years' War, a series of rebellions and civil wars stemming from the discontent of both nobles and commoners rocked the domestic stability of many European governments. To increase their power, monarchs attempted to extend their authority at the expense of traditional powerful elements who resisted the rulers' efforts. At the same time, to fight their battles, governments increased taxes and created such hardships that common people also rose in opposition.

Between 1590 and 1640, peasant and lower-class revolts erupted in central and southern France, Austria, and Hungary. In the decades of the 1640s and 1650s, even greater unrest occurred. Portugal and Catalonia rebelled against the Spanish government in 1640. The common people in Naples and Sicily revolted against both the government and the landed nobility in 1647. Russia, too, was rocked by urban uprisings in 1641,

1645, and 1648. Nobles rebelled in France from 1648 to 1652 in an effort to halt the growth of royal power. The northern states of Sweden, Denmark, and the United Provinces were not immune from upheavals involving clergy, nobles, and mercantile groups. The most famous and widest-ranging struggle, however, was the civil war and rebellion in England, commonly known as the English Revolution (discussed later in this chapter).

The Practice of Absolutism: Western Europe

FOCUS QUESTION: What was absolutism in theory, and how did its actual practice in France reflect or differ from the theory?

Absolute monarchy or **absolutism** meant that the sovereign power or ultimate authority in the state rested in the hands of a king who claimed to rule by divine right. But what did sovereignty mean? The late-sixteenth-century political theorist Jean Bodin (ZHAHN boh-DAN) believed that sovereign power consisted of the authority to make laws, tax, administer justice, control the state's administrative system, and determine foreign policy. These powers made a ruler sovereign.

One of the chief theorists of **divine-right monarchy** in the seventeenth century was the French theologian and court preacher Bishop Jacques Bossuet (ZHAHK baw-SWAY) (1627–1704), who expressed his ideas in a book titled *Politics Drawn from the Very Words of Holy Scripture*. Bossuet argued first that government was divinely ordained so that humans could live in an organized society. God established kings and through them reigned over all the peoples of the world. Since kings received their power from God, their authority was absolute. They were responsible to no one (including parliaments) except God. For Bossuet, though, his last point was especially important. Because God would hold a king accountable for his actions, Bossuet believed that kings faced serious responsibilities as well as real limits on their power. There was also a large gulf between the theory of absolutism as expressed by Bossuet and the practice of absolutism. A monarch's absolute power was often limited greatly by practical realities.

Absolute Monarchy in France

France during the reign of Louis XIV (1643–1715) has traditionally been regarded as the best example of the practice of absolute monarchy in the seventeenth century. French culture, language, and manners influenced all levels of European society. French diplomacy and wars shaped the political affairs of western and central Europe. The court of Louis XIV seemed to be imitated everywhere in Europe. Of course, the stability of Louis's reign was magnified by the instability that had preceded it.

FOUNDATIONS OF FRENCH ABSOLUTISM: CARDINAL RICHELIEU In the half century before Louis XIV came to power, royal and ministerial governments struggled to avoid the breakdown of the French state. The line between order and anarchy was often a narrow one. The situation was complicated by the fact that both Louis XIII (1610–1643) and Louis XIV were only boys when they succeeded to the throne in 1610 and 1643, respectively, leaving the government dependent on royal ministers. Two especially competent ministers played crucial roles in maintaining monarchical authority.

Cardinal Richelieu, Louis XIII's chief minister from 1624 to 1642, initiated policies that eventually strengthened the power of the monarchy. By eliminating the political and military rights of the Huguenots while preserving their religious privileges, Richelieu transformed the Huguenots into more reliable subjects. Richelieu acted more cautiously in "humbling the pride of the great men," the important French nobility. He understood the influential role played by the nobles in the French state. The dangerous ones were those who asserted their territorial independence when they were excluded from participating in the central government. Proceeding slowly but determinedly, Richelieu developed an efficient network of spies to uncover noble plots and then crushed the conspiracies and executed the conspirators, thereby eliminating a major threat to royal authority.

Cardinal Richelieu. A key figure in the emergence of a strong monarchy in France was Cardinal Richelieu, pictured here in a portrait by Philippe de Champaigne. Chief minister to Louis XIII, Richelieu strengthened royal authority by eliminating the private armies and fortified cities of the Huguenots and by crushing aristocratic conspiracies.

To reform and strengthen the central administration, initially for financial reasons, Richelieu sent out royal officials called **intendants** (anh-tahnh-DAHNHZ *or* in-TEN-dunts) to the provinces to execute the orders of the central government. As the functions of the intendants grew, they came into conflict with provincial governors. Since the intendants were victorious in most of these disputes, they further strengthened the power of the crown. Richelieu proved less capable in financial matters, however. Not only was the basic system of state finances corrupt, but so many people benefited from the system's inefficiency and injustice that the government faced strong resistance when it tried to institute reforms. The *taille* (TY) (an annual direct tax usually levied on land or property) was increased—in 1643 it was two and a half times what it had been in 1610. Richelieu's foreign policy goal of confronting the growing power of the Habsburgs in the Thirty Years' War, however, led to ever-increasing expenditures, which soon outstripped the additional revenues. French debt continued its upward spiral under Richelieu.

CARDINAL MAZARIN Richelieu died in 1642, followed five months later by King Louis XIII, who was succeeded by his son Louis XIV, then but four years old. This necessitated a regency under Anne of Austria, the mother of Louis XIV. But she allowed Cardinal Mazarin (maz-uh-RANH), Richelieu's trained successor, to dominate the government. An Italian who had come to France as a papal legate and then become naturalized, Mazarin attempted to carry on Richelieu's policies until his death in 1661.

The most important event during Mazarin's rule was a revolt of the nobles known as the Fronde (FROHND). As a foreigner, Mazarin was greatly disliked by all elements of the French population. The nobles, who particularly resented the centralized administrative power being built up at the expense of the provincial nobility, temporarily allied with the members of the Parlement (par-luh-MAHNH) of Paris, who opposed the new taxes levied by the government to pay the costs of the Thirty Years' War (Mazarin continued Richelieu's anti-Habsburg policy), and with the people of Paris, who were also angry at the additional taxes. The Parlement of Paris was the most important court in France, with jurisdiction over half of the kingdom, and its members formed the nobles of the robe, the service nobility of lawyers and administrators. These nobles of the robe led the first Fronde (1648–1649), which broke out in Paris and was ended by compromise. The second Fronde, begun in 1650, was led by the nobles of the sword, who were descended from the medieval nobility. They were interested in overthrowing Mazarin for their own purposes: to secure their positions and increase their own power. The second Fronde was crushed by 1652, a task made easier when the nobles began fighting each other instead of Mazarin. With the end of the Fronde, the vast majority of the French concluded that the best hope for stability in France lay in the crown. When Mazarin died in 1661, the greatest of the seventeenth-century monarchs, Louis XIV, took over supreme power.

The Reign of Louis XIV (1643–1715)

The day after Cardinal Mazarin's death, Louis XIV, age twenty-three, expressed his determination to be a real king and the sole ruler of France:

> Up to this moment I have been pleased to entrust the government of my affairs to the late Cardinal. It is now time that I govern them myself. You [secretaries and ministers of state] will assist me with your counsels when I ask for them. I request and order you to seal no orders except by my command. . . . I order you not to sign anything, not even a passport . . . without my command; to render account to me personally each day and to favor no one.[4]

His mother, who was well aware of Louis's proclivity for fun and games and getting into the beds of the maids in the royal palace, laughed aloud at these words. But Louis was quite serious.

Louis proved willing to pay the price of being a strong ruler. He established a conscientious routine from which he seldom deviated. Eager for glory (in the French sense of achieving what was expected of one in an important position), Louis created a grand and majestic spectacle at the court of Versailles (vayr-SY). Consequently, Louis and his court came to set the standard for monarchies and aristocracies all over Europe. Just a few decades after the king's death, the great French writer Voltaire dubbed the period from 1661 to 1715 the "Age of Louis XIV," and historians have tended to call it that ever since.

Although Louis may have believed in the theory of absolute monarchy and consciously fostered the myth of himself as the Sun King, the source of light for all of his people (see "Global Perspectives" on p. 442), historians are quick to point out that the realities fell far short of the aspirations. Despite the centralizing efforts of Cardinals Richelieu and Mazarin, seventeenth-century France still possessed a bewildering system of overlapping authorities. Provinces had their own regional courts, their own local Estates (parliaments), their own sets of laws. Members of the high nobility, with their huge estates and clients among the lesser nobility, still exercised much authority. Both towns and provinces possessed privileges and powers seemingly from time immemorial that they would not easily relinquish.

ADMINISTRATION OF THE GOVERNMENT One of the keys to Louis's power was that he was able to restructure the central policy-making machinery of government because it was part of his own court and household. The royal court located outside the city of Paris at Versailles was an elaborate structure that served different purposes: it was the personal household of the king, the location of central governmental machinery, and the place where powerful subjects came to find favors and offices for themselves and their clients as well as the main arena where rival aristocratic factions jostled for power. The greatest danger to Louis's personal rule came from the very high nobles and princes of the blood (the royal princes), who considered it their natural function to assert the policy-making role of royal ministers. Louis eliminated this threat by removing them from the royal council, the chief administrative body of the king and overseer of the central machinery of government, and enticing them to his court, where he could keep them preoccupied with court life and out of politics. Instead of using the high nobility and royal princes, Louis relied on other nobles for his ministers. His ministers were expected to be subservient; Louis said that he had no intention of "sharing my authority with them."

RMN-Grand Palais/Art Resource, NY

Hu Weibiao/Panorama/The Image Works

GLOBAL PERSPECTIVES

Sun Kings, West and East

AT THE END OF THE SEVENTEENTH CENTURY, two powerful rulers held sway in kingdoms that dominated the affairs of the regions around them. Both rulers saw themselves as favored by divine authority—Louis XIV of France as a divine-right monarch and Kangxi (GANG-zhee) of China as possessing the mandate of Heaven. Thus, both rulers saw themselves not as divine beings but as divinely ordained beings whose job was to govern organized societies. On the left, Louis, who ruled France from 1643 to 1715, is seen in a portrait by Hyacinthe Rigaud (ee-ah-SANT ree-GOH) that captures the king's sense of royal dignity and grandeur. One person at court said of the king: "Louis XIV's vanity was without limit or restraint." On the right, Kangxi, who ruled China from 1661 to 1722, is seen in a portrait that shows him seated in majesty on his imperial throne. A dedicated ruler, Kangxi once wrote, "One act of negligence may cause sorrow all through the country, and one moment of negligence may result in trouble for hundreds and thousands of generations."

Q *Although these rulers practiced very different religions, why did they justify their powers in such a similar fashion?*

Louis's domination of his ministers and secretaries gave him control of the central policy-making machinery of government and thus authority over the traditional areas of monarchical power: the formulation of foreign policy, the making of war and peace, the assertion of the secular power of the crown against any religious authority, and the ability to levy taxes to fulfill these functions. Louis had considerably less success with the internal administration of the kingdom, however. The traditional groups and institutions of French society—the nobles, officials, town councils, guilds, and representative Estates in some provinces—were simply too powerful for the king to have direct control over the lives of his subjects. Consequently,

The Palace of Versailles. Louis XIV spent untold sums of money on the construction of a new palace at Versailles. As is evident from this exterior view, the palace was enormous—more than a quarter of a mile long. In addition to being the royal residence, it also housed the members of the king's government and served as home for thousands of French nobles. As the largest royal residence in Europe, Versailles impressed foreigners and became a source of envy for other rulers.

control of the provinces and the people was achieved largely by bribing the individuals responsible for executing the king's policies. Nevertheless, local officials could still obstruct the execution of policies they disliked, indicating clearly that a so-called absolute monarch was not always absolute. A recent study of Louis's relationship with the **parlements**, however, asserts that he was able to exercise both political and economic control over these provincial law courts, which were responsible for registering new laws sent to them by the king.

RELIGIOUS POLICY The maintenance of religious harmony had long been considered an area of monarchical power. The desire to keep it brought Louis into conflict with the French Huguenots. Louis XIV did not want to allow Protestants to practice their faith in largely Catholic France. Perhaps he was motivated by religion, but it is more likely that Louis, who believed in the motto "One king, one law, one faith," felt that the existence of this minority undermined his own political authority. In October 1685, Louis issued the Edict of Fontainebleau (fawnh-ten-BLOH). In addition to revoking the Edict of Nantes, the new edict provided for the destruction of Huguenot churches and the closing of Protestant schools. It is estimated that 200,000 Huguenots defied the prohibition against their leaving France and sought asylum in England, the United Provinces, and the German states. Although it was once believed that this exodus weakened the French economy, others maintain that an influx of English and Irish political and religious refugees into France offset the loss. Support for the expulsion of the Protestants came from Catholic lay-people, who rejected Protestant legal rights, banned them from government meetings, and destroyed Protestant churches in an effort to regain Catholic control of heavily populated Protestant regions.

FINANCIAL ISSUES The cost of building Versailles and other palaces, maintaining his court, and pursuing his wars made finances a crucial issue for Louis XIV. He was most fortunate in having the services of Jean-Baptiste Colbert (ZHAHNH-bah-TEEST kohl-BAYR) (1619–1683) as controller general of finances. Colbert sought to increase the wealth and power of France through general adherence to mercantilism, which stressed government regulation of economic activities to benefit the state. To decrease the need for imports and increase exports, Colbert founded new luxury industries, such as the royal tapestry works at Beauvais; invited Venetian glass-makers and Flemish clothmakers to France; drew up instructions regulating the quality of goods produced; oversaw the training of workers; and granted special privileges, including tax exemptions, loans, and subsidies, to individuals who established new industries. To improve communications and the transportation of goods internally, he built roads and canals. To decrease imports directly, Colbert raised tariffs on foreign manufactured goods and created a merchant marine to carry French goods.

Although Colbert's policies are given much credit for fostering the development of manufacturing in France, some historians are dubious about the usefulness of many of his mercantilistic policies and question whether Colbert stuck to rigid mercantilistic convictions. Regulations were often evaded, and the imposition of high tariffs brought foreign retaliation. French trading companies entered the scene too late to be really competitive with the English and the Dutch. And above all, Colbert's economic policies, which were geared to making his king more powerful, were ultimately self-defeating. The more revenue Colbert collected to enable the king to make war, the faster Louis depleted the treasury. At the same time, the burden of taxes fell increasingly on the peasants, who still constituted the overwhelming majority of the French population. Nevertheless, some historians argue that although Louis bankrupted the treasury in order to pay for his wars, the economic practices implemented under Colbert, including investment in the shipping and textile industries and improvements in transportation facilities, allowed for greater economic growth in the eighteenth century.

DAILY LIFE AT THE COURT OF VERSAILLES The court of Louis XIV at Versailles set a standard that was soon followed by other European rulers. In 1660, Louis decided to convert a hunting lodge at Versailles, not far from the capital city of Paris, into a chateau. Not until 1688, after untold sums of money had been spent and tens of thousands of workers had labored incessantly, was construction completed on the enormous palace.

Versailles served many purposes. It was the residence of the king, a reception hall for state affairs, an office building for the members of the king's government, and the home of thousands of royal officials and aristocratic courtiers. Versailles also served a practical political purpose. It became home to the high nobility and princes of the blood. By keeping them involved in the myriad activities that made up daily life at the court of Versailles, Louis excluded them from real power while allowing them to share in the mystique of power as companions of the king. Versailles became a symbol for the French absolutist state and the power of the Sun King, Louis XIV. As a visible manifestation of France's superiority and wealth, this lavish court was intended to overawe subjects and impress foreign powers.

RMN-Grand Palais/Art Resource, NY

Interior of Versailles: The Hall of Mirrors. Pictured here is the exquisite Hall of Mirrors at Versailles. Located on the second floor, the hall overlooks the park below. Three hundred and fifty-seven mirrors were placed on the wall opposite the windows to create an illusion of even greater width. Careful planning went into every detail of the interior decoration. Even the doorknobs were specially designed to reflect the magnificence of Versailles. This photo shows the Hall of Mirrors after the restoration work that was completed in June 2007, a project that took three years, cost 12 million euros (more than $16 million), and included the restoration of the Bohemian crystal chandeliers.

THE KING'S DAY BEGINS

THE DUC DE SAINT-SIMON (1675–1755) WAS ONE of many noble courtiers who lived at Versailles and had firsthand experience of court life there. In his *Memoirs,* he left a controversial and critical account of Louis XIV and his court. In this selection, Saint-Simon describes the scene in Louis's bedroom at the beginning of the day.

Duc de Saint-Simon, *Memoirs*

At eight o'clock the chief valet of the room on duty, who alone had slept in the royal chamber, and who had dressed himself, awoke the King. The chief physician, the chief surgeon, and the nurse (as long as she lived) entered at the same time. The latter kissed the King; the others rubbed and often changed his shirt, because he was in the habit of sweating a great deal. At the quarter, the grand chamberlain was called (or, in his absence, the first gentleman of the chamber), and those who had, what was called the grandes entrées [grand entry]. The chamberlain (or chief gentleman) drew back the curtains which had been closed again, and presented the holy water from the vase, at the head of the bed. These gentlemen stayed but a moment, and that was the time to speak to the King, if any one had anything to ask of him; in which case the rest stood aside. When, contrary to custom, nobody had anything to say, they were there but for a few moments. He who had opened the curtains and presented the holy water, presented also a prayer-book. Then all passed into the cabinet [a small room] of the council. A very short religious service being over, the King called, they reentered. The same officer gave him his dressing-gown; immediately after, other privileged courtiers entered, and then everybody, in time to find the King putting on his shoes and stockings, for he did almost everything himself and with address and grace. Every other day we saw him shave himself; and he had a little short wig in which he always appeared, even in bed, and on medicine days. . . .

As soon as he was dressed, he prayed to God, at the side of his bed, where all the clergy present knelt, the cardinals without cushions, all the laity remaining standing; and the captain of the guards came to the balustrade during the prayer, after which the king passed into his cabinet.

He found there, or was followed by all who had the entrée, a very numerous company, for it included everybody in any office. He gave orders to each for the day; thus within a half a quarter of an hour it was known what he meant to do; and then all this crowd left directly.

Q *What were the message and purpose of the royal waking and dressing ceremony for both the nobles and the king? Do you think this account might be biased? Why?*

Source: B. St. John, trans., *The Memoirs of the Duke of Saint-Simon on the Reign of Louis XIV and the Regency*, vol. 3, 8th ed. (London: George Allen, 1913), pp. 221–222.

Life at Versailles became a court ceremony with Louis XIV at the center of it all. The king had little privacy; only when he visited his wife or mother or mistress or met with ministers was he free of the noble courtiers who swarmed about the palace. Most daily ceremonies were carefully staged, such as those attending Louis's rising from bed, dining, praying, attending Mass, and going to bed. A mob of nobles aspired to assist the king in carrying out these solemn activities. It was considered a great honor for a noble to be chosen to hand the king his shirt while dressing (see the box above). But why did nobles participate in so many ceremonies, some of which were so obviously demeaning? Active involvement in the activities at Versailles was the king's prerequisite for obtaining the offices, titles, and pensions that only he could grant. This policy reduced great nobles and ecclesiastics, the "people of quality," to a plane of equality, allowing Louis to exercise control over them and prevent them from interfering in the real lines of power. To maintain their social prestige, the "people of quality" were expected to adhere to rigid standards of court etiquette appropriate to their rank.

Indeed, court etiquette became a complex matter. Nobles and royal princes were arranged in an elaborate order of seniority and expected to follow certain rules of precedence. Who could sit down and on what kind of chair was a subject of much debate. When Philip of Orléans, the king's brother, and his wife Charlotte sought to visit their daughter, the duchess of Lorraine, they encountered problems with Louis. Charlotte explained why in one of her letters:

> The difficulty is that the Duke of Lorraine claims that he is entitled to sit in an armchair in the presence of Philip and myself because the Emperor gives him an armchair. To this the King [Louis] replied that the Emperor's ceremonial is one thing and the King's another, and that, for example, the Emperor gives the cardinals armchairs, whereas here they may never sit at all in the King's presence.[5]

Louis refused to compromise; the duke of Lorraine was only entitled to a stool. The duke balked, and Philip and Charlotte canceled their visit.

Daily life at Versailles also included numerous forms of entertainment. Walks through the gardens, boating trips, performances of tragedies and comedies, ballets, and concerts all provided sources of pleasure. Three evenings a week, from seven to ten, Louis also held an *appartement* (uh-par-tuh-MAHNH) where he was "at home" to his court. The appartement was characterized by a formal informality. Relaxed rules of etiquette even allowed people to sit down in the presence of their superiors. The evening's entertainment began with a concert, followed by games of billiards or cards, and ended with a sumptuous buffet.

THE WARS OF LOUIS XIV Both the increase in royal power that Louis pursued and his desire for military glory led the king to wage war. Under the secretary of war, François-Michel Le Tellier (frahnh-SWAH-mee-SHEL luh tel-YAY), the marquis of Louvois (loo-VWAH), France developed a professional army numbering 100,000 men in peacetime and 400,000 in time of war. Louis made war an almost incessant activity of his reign. To achieve the prestige and military glory befitting the Sun King as well as to ensure the domination of his Bourbon dynasty over European affairs, Louis waged four wars between 1667 and 1713 (see Map 15.2).

In 1667, Louis began his first war by invading the Spanish Netherlands to his north and Franche-Comté to the east. But the Triple Alliance of the Dutch, English, and Swedes forced Louis to sue for peace in 1668 and accept a few towns in the Spanish Netherlands for his efforts. He never forgave the Dutch for arranging the Triple Alliance, and in 1672, after isolating the Dutch, France invaded the United Provinces with some initial success. But the French victories led Brandenburg, Spain, and the Holy Roman Empire to form a new coalition that forced Louis to end the Dutch War by making peace at Nimwegen (NIM-vay-gun) in 1678. While Dutch territory remained intact, France received Franche-Comté from Spain, which served merely to stimulate Louis's appetite for even more land.

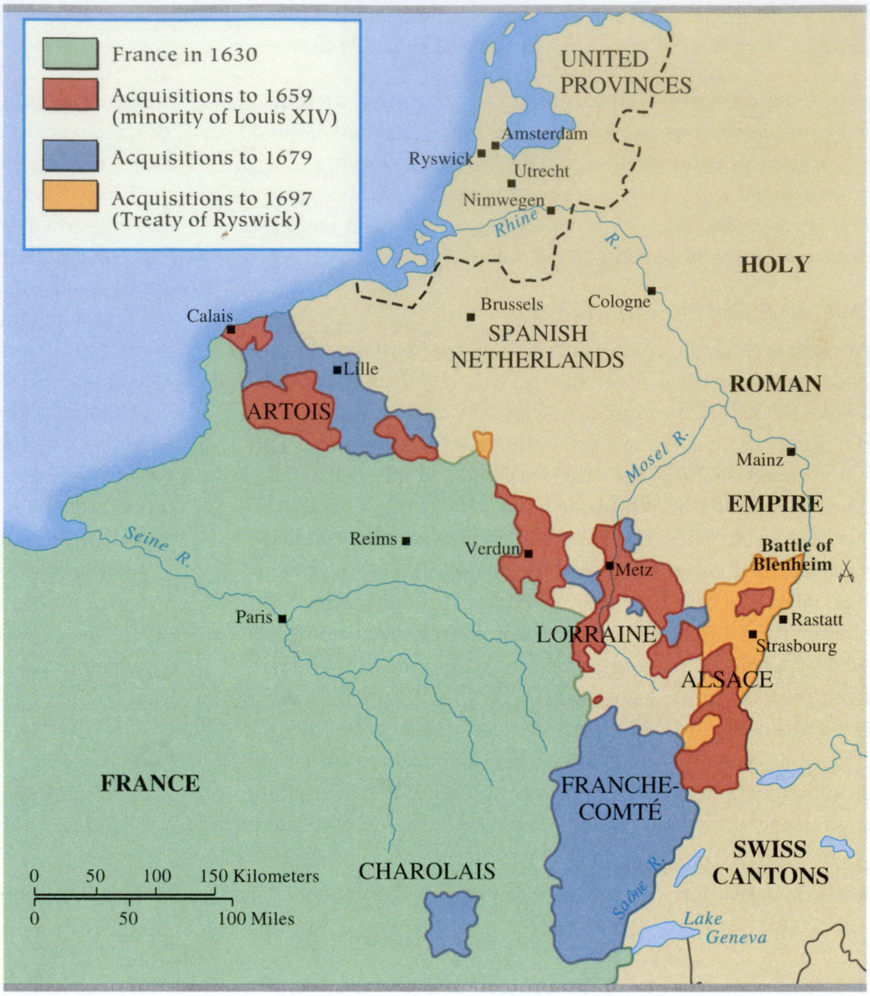

MAP 15.2 **The Wars of Louis XIV.** The Sun King instigated several wars in his efforts to expand the power of France and the Bourbon dynasty. A coalition of European states met each military thrust, however, so Louis's gains were minimal despite the amount of blood spilled and capital spent.

Q *At the expense of what countries did Louis XIV make most of his territorial acquisitions?*

This time, Louis moved eastward against the Holy Roman Empire, which he perceived from his previous war as feeble and unable to resist. The gradual annexation of the provinces of Alsace and Lorraine was followed by the occupation of the city of Strasbourg, a move that led to widespread protest and the formation of a new coalition. The creation of this League of Augsburg, consisting of Spain, the Holy Roman Empire, the United Provinces, Sweden, and England, led to Louis's third war, the War of the League of Augsburg (1689–1697). This bitterly contested eight-year struggle brought economic depression and famine to France. The Treaty of Ryswick (RYZ-wik) ending the war forced Louis to give up most of his conquests in the empire, although he was allowed to keep Strasbourg and part of Alsace. The gains were hardly worth the bloodshed and the misery he had caused the French people.

Louis's fourth war, the War of the Spanish Succession (1702–1713), was over bigger stakes, the succession to the Spanish throne. Charles II, the sickly and childless Habsburg ruler, left the throne of Spain in his will to a grandson of Louis XIV. When the latter became King Philip V of Spain after Charles's death, the suspicion that Spain and France would eventually be united in the same dynastic family caused the formation of a new coalition, determined to prevent a Bourbon hegemony that would mean the certain destruction of the European balance of power. This coalition of England, the United Provinces, Habsburg Austria, and German states opposed France and Spain in a war that dragged on in Europe and the colonial empires in North America for eleven years. In a number of battles, including the memorable defeat of the French forces at Blenheim (BLEN-im) in 1704 by allied troops led by the English commander, John Churchill, duke of Marlborough, the coalition wore down Louis's forces. An end to the war finally came with the Peace of Utrecht in 1713 and of Rastatt in 1714. Although these peace treaties confirmed Philip V as the Spanish ruler, initiating a Spanish Bourbon dynasty that would last into the twentieth century, they also affirmed that the thrones of Spain and France were to remain separated. The Spanish Netherlands, Milan, and Naples were given to Austria, and the emerging state of Brandenburg-Prussia gained additional territories. The real winner at Utrecht, however, was England, which received Gibraltar as well as the French possessions of Newfoundland, Hudson Bay Territory, and Nova Scotia in America. Though France, by its sheer size and position, remained a great power, England had emerged as a formidable naval force.

Only two years after the treaty, the Sun King was dead, leaving France in debt and surrounded by enemies. On his deathbed, the seventy-six-year-old monarch seemed remorseful when he told his successor:

> Soon you will be King of a great kingdom. I urge you not to forget your duty to God; remember that you owe everything to Him. Try to remain at peace with your neighbors. I loved war too much. Do not follow me in that or in overspending. Take advice in everything; try to find the best course and follow it. Lighten your people's burden as soon as possible, and do what I have had the misfortune not to do myself.[6]

Did Louis mean it? Did Louis ever realize how tarnished the glory he had sought had become? Ten years before the end of his reign one of his subjects wrote: "Even the people . . . who have so much loved you, and have placed such trust in you, begin to lose their love, their trust, and even their respect. . . . They believe you have no pity for their sorrows, that you are devoted only to your power and your glory."[7] In any event, the advice to his successor was probably not remembered; his great-grandson was only five years old.

CHRONOLOGY	Absolutism in Western Europe
France	
Louis XIII	1610–1643
Cardinal Richelieu as chief minister	1624–1642
Ministry of Cardinal Mazarin	1642–1661
First Fronde	1648–1649
Second Fronde	1650–1652
Louis XIV	1643–1715
First war (versus Triple Alliance)	1667–1668
Dutch War	1672–1678
Edict of Fontainebleau	1685
War of the League of Augsburg	1689–1697
War of the Spanish Succession	1702–1713
Spain	
Philip III	1598–1621
Philip IV	1621–1665

The Decline of Spain

At the beginning of the seventeenth century, Spain possessed the most populous empire in the world, controlling almost all of South America and a number of settlements in Asia and Africa. To most Europeans, Spain still seemed the greatest power of the age, but the reality was quite different. The treasury was empty; Philip II went bankrupt in 1596 from excessive expenditures on war, and his successor, Philip III, did the same in 1607 by spending a fortune on his court. The armed forces were out-of-date, the government was inefficient, and the commercial class was weak in the midst of a suppressed peasantry, a luxury-loving class of nobles, and an oversupply of priests and monks. Spain continued to play the role of a great power, but appearances were deceiving.

During the reign of Philip III (1598–1621), many of Spain's weaknesses became apparent. Interested only in court luxury or miracle-working relics, Philip III allowed his first minister, the greedy duke of Lerma, to run the country. The aristocratic Lerma's primary interest was accumulating power and wealth for himself and his family. As important offices were filled with his relatives, crucial problems went unsolved.

THE REIGN OF PHILIP IV The reign of Philip IV (1621–1665) seemed to offer hope for a revival of Spain's energies, especially in the capable hands of his chief minister, Gaspar de Guzman (gahs-PAR day goos-MAHN), the count of Olivares (oh-lee-BAH-rayss). This clever, hardworking, and power-hungry statesman dominated the king's every move and worked to revive the interests of the monarchy. A flurry of domestic reform decrees, aimed at curtailing the power of the Catholic Church and the landed aristocracy, was soon followed by a political reform program whose purpose was to further centralize the government of all Spain and its possessions in monarchical hands. All of these efforts met with little real success, however, because both the number (estimated at one-fifth of the population) and the power of the Spanish aristocrats made them too strong to curtail in any significant fashion.

At the same time, most of the efforts of Olivares and Philip were undermined by their desire to pursue Spain's imperial glory and by a series of internal revolts. Spain's involvement in the Thirty Years' War led to a series of frightfully expensive military campaigns that incited internal revolts and years of civil war. Unfortunately for Spain, the campaigns also failed to produce victory. As Olivares wrote to King Philip IV, "God wants us to make peace; for He is depriving us visibly and absolutely of all the means of war."[8] At the Battle of Rocroi in 1643, much of the Spanish army was destroyed.

The defeats in Europe and the internal revolts of the 1640s ended any illusions about Spain's greatness. The actual extent of Spain's economic difficulties is still debated, but there is no question about its foreign losses. The Peace of Westphalia formally recognized Dutch independence in 1648, and the Peace of the Pyrenees with France in 1659 meant the surrender of Artois and the outlying defenses of the Spanish Netherlands as well as certain border regions that went to France.

Absolutism in Central, Eastern, and Northern Europe

FOCUS QUESTION: What developments enabled Brandenburg-Prussia, Austria, and Russia to emerge as major powers in the seventeenth century?

During the seventeenth century, a development of great importance for the modern Western world took place in central and eastern Europe, as three new powers made their appearance: Prussia, Austria, and Russia.

The German States

The Peace of Westphalia, which officially ended the Thirty Years' War in 1648, left each of the states in the Holy Roman Empire virtually autonomous and sovereign. Properly speaking, there was no longer a German state but rather more than three hundred little Germanies. Of these, two emerged as great European powers in the seventeenth and eighteenth centuries.

THE RISE OF BRANDENBURG-PRUSSIA The evolution of Brandenburg into a powerful state was largely the work of the Hohenzollern (hoh-en-TSULL-urn) dynasty, which in 1415 had come to rule the insignificant principality in northeastern Germany. In 1609, the Hohenzollerns inherited some lands in the Rhine valley in western Germany; nine years later, they received the duchy of Prussia (East Prussia). By the seventeenth century, then, the dominions of the house of Hohenzollern, now called Brandenburg-Prussia, consisted of three disconnected masses in western, central, and eastern Germany; only the person of the Hohenzollern ruler connected them (see Map 15.3).

Frederick William the Great Elector (1640–1688), who came to power in the midst of the Thirty Years' War, laid the foundation for the Prussian state. Realizing that Brandenburg-Prussia was a small, open territory with no natural frontiers for defense, Frederick William built a competent and efficient standing army. By 1678, he possessed a force of 40,000 men that absorbed more than 50 percent of the state's revenues. To sustain the army and his own power, Frederick William established the General War Commissariat to levy taxes for the army and oversee its growth and training. The Commissariat soon evolved into an agency for civil government as well. Directly responsible to the elector, the new bureaucratic machine became his chief instrument for governing the state. Many of its officials were members of the Prussian landed aristocracy, the Junkers (YOONG-kers), who also served as officers in the all-important army.

The nobles' support for Frederick William's policies derived from the tacit agreement that he made with them. In order to eliminate the power that the members of the nobility could exercise in their provincial Estates-General, Frederick William made a deal with the nobles. In return for a free hand in running the government (in other words, for depriving the provincial Estates of their power), he gave the nobles almost unlimited power over their peasants, exempted the nobles from taxation, and awarded them the highest ranks in the army and the Commissariat with the understanding that they would not challenge his political control. As for the peasants, the nobles were allowed to appropriate their land and bind them to the soil as serfs. Serfdom was not new to Brandenburg-Prussia, but Frederick William reinforced it through his concessions to the nobles.

To build Brandenburg-Prussia's economy, Frederick William followed the fashionable mercantilist policies, constructing roads and canals and using high tariffs, subsidies, and monopolies for manufacturers to stimulate domestic industry. At the same time, however, he continued to favor the interests of the nobility at the expense of the commercial and industrial middle classes in the towns.

Frederick William laid the groundwork for the Prussian state. His son Frederick III (1688–1713) made one further significant

MAP 15.3 The Growth of Brandenburg-Prussia. Frederick William the Great Elector laid the foundation for a powerful state when he increased the size and efficiency of the army, raised taxes and created an efficient bureaucracy to collect them, and gained the support of the landed aristocracy. Later rulers added more territory.

Why were the acquisitions of Pomerania and West Prussia important for Brandenburg-Prussia's continued rise to power?

contribution: in return for aiding the Holy Roman Emperor, he was officially granted the title of king-in-Prussia. Thus was Elector Frederick III transformed into King Frederick I, ruler of an important new player on the European stage.

THE EMERGENCE OF AUSTRIA The Austrian Habsburgs had long played a significant role in European politics as Holy Roman Emperors, but by the end of the Thirty Years' War, the Habsburg hopes of creating an empire in Germany had been dashed. In the seventeenth century, the house of Austria made an important transition; the German empire was lost, but a new empire was created in eastern and southeastern Europe.

The nucleus of the new Austrian Empire remained the traditional Austrian hereditary possessions: Lower and Upper Austria, Carinthia, Carniola, Styria, and Tyrol (see Map 15.4). To these had been added the kingdom of Bohemia and parts of northwestern Hungary in the sixteenth century.

In the seventeenth century, Leopold I (1658–1705) encouraged the eastward movement of the Austrian Empire, but he was sorely challenged by the revival of Ottoman power. Having moved into Transylvania, the Ottomans eventually pushed westward and laid siege to Vienna in 1683. A European army, led by the Austrians, counterattacked and decisively defeated the Ottomans in 1687. By the Treaty of Karlowitz (KARL-oh-vits) in 1699, Austria took control of Hungary, Transylvania, Croatia, and Slovenia, thus establishing an Austrian Empire in southeastern Europe. At the end of the War of the Spanish Succession, Austria gained the Spanish Netherlands and received formal recognition of its occupation of the Spanish possessions in Italy, namely, Milan, Mantua, Sardinia, and Naples. By the beginning of the eighteenth century, the house of Austria had acquired an empire of considerable size.

The Austrian monarchy, however, never became a highly centralized, absolutist state, primarily because it included so many different national groups. The Austrian Empire remained a collection of territories held together by a personal union. The Habsburg emperor was archduke of Austria, king of Bohemia, and king of Hungary. Each of these territories had its own laws, Estates-General, and political life. The landed aristocrats throughout the empire were connected by a common bond of service to the house of Habsburg, as military officers or government bureaucrats, but no other common sentiment tied the regions together. Nevertheless, by the beginning of the eighteenth century, Austria was a populous empire in central Europe of great potential military strength.

Italy: From Spanish to Austrian Rule

By 1530, Emperor Charles V had managed to defeat the French armies in Italy and become the arbiter of Italy (see Chapter 13). Initially, he was content to establish close ties with many native Italian rulers and allowed them to rule, provided that they recognized his dominant role. But in 1540, he gave the duchy of Milan to his son Philip II and transferred all imperial rights over Italy to the Spanish monarchy.

MAP 15.4 The Growth of the Austrian Empire. The Habsburgs had hoped to establish a German empire, but the results of the Thirty Years' War crushed that dream. So Austria expanded to the east and the south, primarily at the expense of the Ottoman Empire, and also gained the Spanish Netherlands and former Spanish territories in Italy.

Q *In which areas did the Austrian Empire have access to the Mediterranean Sea, and why would that potentially be important?*

From the beginning of Philip II's reign in 1556 until 1713, the Spanish presence was felt everywhere in Italy. Only Florence, the Papal States, and Venice managed to maintain relatively independent policies. At the same time, the influence of the papacy became oppressive in Italy as the machinery of the Catholic Counter-Reformation—the Inquisition, the Index, and the Jesuits—was used to stifle all resistance to the Catholic orthodoxy created by the Council of Trent (see Chapter 13).

At the beginning of the eighteenth century, Italy suffered further from the struggles between France and Spain. But it was Austria, not France, that benefited the most from the War of the Spanish Succession. By gaining Milan, Mantua, Sardinia, and Naples, Austria supplanted Spain as the dominant power in Italy.

Russia: From Fledgling Principality to Major Power

A new Russian state had emerged in the fifteenth century under the leadership of the principality of Moscow and its grand dukes (see Chapter 12). In the sixteenth century, Ivan IV the Terrible (1533–1584), who was the first ruler to take the title of tsar ("Caesar"), expanded the territories of Russia eastward after finding westward expansion blocked by the powerful Swedish and Polish states. Ivan also extended the autocracy of the tsar by crushing the power of the Russian nobility, known as the **boyars** (boh-YARS). Ivan's dynasty came to an end in 1598 and was followed by a resurgence of aristocratic power in a period of anarchy known as the Time of Troubles. It did not end until the Zemsky Sobor (ZEM-skee suh-BOR), or national assembly, chose Michael Romanov (ROH-muh-nahf) (1613–1645) as the new tsar, beginning a dynasty that lasted until 1917.

In the seventeenth century, Muscovite society was highly stratified. At the top was the tsar, who claimed to be a divinely ordained autocratic ruler. Russian society was dominated by an upper class of landed aristocrats who, in the course of the seventeenth century, managed to bind their peasants to the land. An abundance of land and a shortage of peasants made serfdom desirable to the landowners. Townspeople were also controlled. Many merchants were not allowed to move from their cities without government permission or to sell their businesses to anyone outside their class. In the seventeenth century, merchant and peasant revolts as well as a schism in the Russian Orthodox Church created very unsettled conditions. In the midst of these political and religious upheavals, seventeenth-century Moscow was experiencing more frequent contacts with the West, and Western ideas were beginning to penetrate a few Russian circles. Nevertheless, Russia remained largely outside the framework of the West: the Renaissance, the Reformation, and the geographic discoveries of the sixteenth and seventeenth centuries made little impact on Russia. At the end of the seventeenth century, Peter the Great (1689–1725) noticeably accelerated the westernizing process.

THE REIGN OF PETER THE GREAT (1689–1725) Peter the Great was an unusual character. A strong man, towering 6 feet 9 inches tall, Peter was coarse in his tastes and rude in his behavior. He enjoyed a low kind of humor—belching contests, crude jokes, comical funerals—and vicious punishments including floggings, impalings, roastings, and beard burnings (see the box on p. 451). Peter gained a firsthand view of the West when he made a trip there in 1697–1698 and returned to Russia with a firm determination to westernize or Europeanize his realm. He admired European technology and gadgets and desired to transplant these to Russia. Only this kind of modernization could give him the army and navy he needed to make Russia a great power.

As could be expected, one of Peter's first priorities was the reorganization of the army and the creation of a navy. Employing both Russians and Europeans as officers, he conscripted peasants for twenty-five-year stints of service to build a standing army of 210,000 men. Peter has also been given credit for forming the first Russian navy.

Peter also reorganized the central government, partly along Western lines. In 1711, he created the Senate to supervise the administrative machinery of the state while he was away on military campaigns. In time, the Senate became something like a ruling council, but its ineffectiveness caused Peter to borrow the Western institution of "colleges," or boards of administrators entrusted with specific functions, such as foreign affairs, war, and justice. To impose the rule of the central government more effectively throughout the land, Peter divided Russia into eight provinces and later, in 1719, into fifty. Although he hoped to create a "police state," by which he meant a well-ordered community governed in accordance with law, few of his bureaucrats shared his concept of honest service and duty to the state. Peter hoped for a sense of civic duty, but his own forceful personality created an atmosphere of fear that prevented it. He wrote to one administrator, "According to these orders act, act, act. I won't write more, but you will pay with your head if you interpret orders again."[9]

To further his administrative aims, Peter demanded that all members of the landholding class serve in either military or civil offices. Moreover, in 1722, Peter instituted the Table of Ranks to create opportunities for nonnobles to serve the state and join the nobility. He had all civil offices ranked according to fourteen levels and created a parallel list of fourteen grades for all military offices. Every official was then required to begin at level one and work his way up the ranks. When a nonnoble reached the eighth rank, he acquired noble status. Peter's successors did not continue his attempt to create a new nobility based on merit, however.

To obtain the enormous amount of money needed for an army and navy that absorbed as much as four-fifths of the state revenue, Peter adopted Western mercantilistic policies to stimulate economic growth. He tried to increase exports and develop new industries while exploiting domestic resources like the iron mines in the Urals. But his military needs were endless, and he came to rely on the old expedient of simply raising taxes, imposing additional burdens on the hapless peasants, who were becoming ever more oppressed in Peter's Russia.

Peter also sought to establish state control over the Russian Orthodox Church. In 1721, he abolished the position of patriarch and created a body called the Holy Synod to make decisions for the church. At its head stood a **procurator**, a layman

PETER THE GREAT DEALS WITH A REBELLION

DURING HIS FIRST VISIT TO THE WEST IN 1697–1698, Peter received word that the Streltsy, an elite military unit stationed in Moscow, had revolted against his authority. Peter hurried home and crushed the revolt in a very savage fashion. This selection is taken from an Austrian account of how Peter dealt with the rebels.

Peter and the Streltsy

How sharp was the pain, how great the indignation, to which the tsar's Majesty was mightily moved, when he knew of the rebellion of the Streltsy, betraying openly a mind panting for vengeance! He was still tarrying at Vienna, quite full of the desire of setting out for Italy; but, fervid as was his curiosity of rambling abroad, it was, nevertheless, speedily extinguished on the announcement of the troubles that had broken out in the bowels of his realm. Going immediately to Lefort . . . he thus indignantly broke out: "Tell me, Francis, how I can reach Moscow by the shortest way, in a brief space, so that I may wreak vengeance on this great perfidy of my people, with punishments worthy of their abominable crime. Not one of them shall escape with impunity. Around my royal city, which, with their impious efforts, they planned to destroy, I will have gibbets and gallows set upon the walls and ramparts, and each and every one of them will I put to a direful death." Nor did he long delay the plan for his justly excited wrath; he took the quick post, as his ambassador suggested, and in four weeks' time he had got over about 300 miles without accident, and arrived the 4th of September, 1698—a monarch for the well disposed, but an avenger for the wicked.

His first anxiety after his arrival was about the rebellion— in what it consisted, what the insurgents meant, who dared to instigate such a crime. And as nobody could answer accurately upon all points, and some pleaded their own ignorance, others the obstinacy of the Streltsy, he began to have suspicions of everybody's loyalty. . . . No day, holy or profane, were the inquisitors idle; every day was deemed fit and lawful for torturing. There was as many scourges as there were accused, and every inquisitor was a butcher. . . . The whole month of October was spent in lacerating the backs of culprits with the knout and with flames; no day were those that were left alive exempt from scourging or scorching; or else they were broken upon the wheel, or driven to the gibbet, or slain with the ax. . . .

To prove to all people how holy and inviolable are those walls of the city which the Streltsy rashly meditated scaling in a sudden assault, beams were run out from all the embrasures in the walls near the gates, in each of which two rebels were hanged. This day beheld about two hundred and fifty die that death. There are few cities fortified with as many palisades as Moscow has given gibbets to her guardian Streltsy.

Q *How did Peter deal with the revolt of the Streltsy? What does his approach to this problem tell us about the tsar?*

Source: J. H. Robinson, *Readings in European History*, vol. 2 (Boston: Ginn & Co., 1906).

who represented the interests of the tsar and assured Peter of effective domination of the church.

Shortly after his return from the West in 1698, Peter had begun to introduce Western customs, practices, and manners into Russia. He ordered the preparation of the first Russian book of etiquette to teach Western manners. Among other things, it pointed out that it was not polite to spit on the floor or to scratch oneself at dinner. Because Europeans at that time did not wear beards or traditional long-skirted coats, Russian beards had to be shaved and coats shortened, a reform Peter personally enforced at court by shaving off his nobles' beards and cutting their coats at the knees with his own hands. Outside the court, barbers and tailors planted at town gates enforced the edicts by cutting the beards and cloaks of those who entered or left. Many Russians, as a result, according to one observer, regarded the tsar as a tyrant, "and there were many old Russians who, after having their beards shaved off, saved them preciously, in order to have them placed in their coffins, fearing that they would not be allowed to enter heaven without their beards."[10]

One group of Russians benefited greatly from Peter's cultural reforms—women. Having watched women mixing freely with men in Western courts, Peter shattered the seclusion of upper-class Russian women and demanded that they remove the traditional veils that covered their faces. Peter also decreed that social gatherings be held three times a week in the large houses of Saint Petersburg where men and women could mix for conversation, card games, and dancing, which Peter had learned in the West. The tsar also now insisted that women could marry of their own free will.

RUSSIA AS A MILITARY POWER The object of Peter's domestic reforms was to make Russia into a great state and a military power. His primary goal was to "open a window to the West," meaning a port easily accessible to Europe. This could only be achieved on the Baltic, but at that time the Baltic coast was controlled by Sweden, the most important power in northern Europe. Desirous of these lands, Peter, with the support of Poland and Denmark, attacked Sweden in the summer of 1700 believing that the young king of Sweden, Charles XII, could easily be defeated. Charles, however, proved to be a brilliant general. He smashed the Danes, flattened the Poles, and with a well-disciplined force of only 8,000 men, routed the Russian army of 40,000 at the Battle of Narva (1700). The Great Northern War (1701–1721) soon ensued.

Peter the Great. Peter the Great wished to westernize Russia, especially in the realm of technical skills. His goal was the creation of a strong army and navy and the acquisition of new territory in order to make Russia a great power. Jean Marc Nattier, a French artist, painted this portrait of the tsar dressed in military armor in 1717.

But Peter fought back. He reorganized his army along western lines and at the Battle of Poltava (pul-TAH-vuh) in 1709 defeated Charles's army decisively. Although the war dragged on for another twelve years, the Peace of Nystadt (NEE-shtaht) in 1721 gave formal recognition to what Peter had already achieved: the acquisition of Estonia, Livonia, and Karelia (see Map 15.5). Sweden had become a second-rate power, and Russia was now the great European state Peter had wanted. And he was building it a fine capital. Early in the war, in the northern marshlands along the Baltic, Peter had begun to construct a new city, Saint Petersburg, his window on the West and a symbol that Russia was looking westward to Europe. Though its construction cost the lives of thousands of peasants, Peter completed the city during his lifetime. It remained the Russian capital until 1917.

Peter modernized and westernized Russia to the extent that it became a great military power and, by his death in 1725, an important member of the European state system. But his policies were also detrimental to Russia. Westernization was a bit of a sham because Western culture reached only the upper classes, and the real object of the reforms, the creation of a strong military, only added more burdens to the masses of the Russian people. The forceful way in which Peter the Great

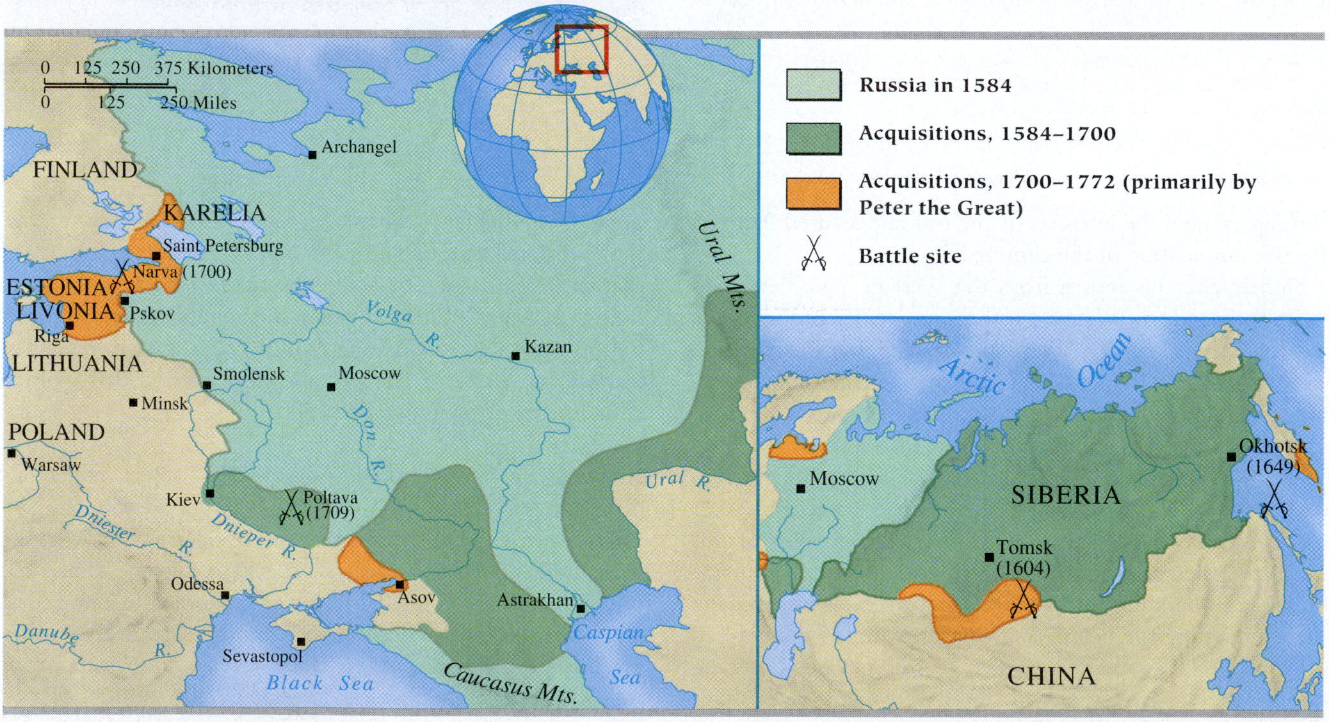

MAP 15.5 Russia: From Principality to Nation-State. Russia had expanded its territory since its emergence in the fifteenth century. Peter the Great modernized the country, instituting administrative and tax reforms and building up the military. He won territory on the Baltic from Sweden, enabling Russia to have a port at Saint Petersburg.

Q *Why would the westward expansion of Russia during Peter's reign affect the international balance of power in Europe?*

imposed westernization led his people to distrust Europe and Western civilization rather than embrace them.

The Great Northern States

As the economic thoroughfare for the products of eastern Europe and the West, the Baltic Sea bestowed special importance on the lands surrounding it. In the sixteenth century, Sweden had broken its ties with Denmark and emerged as an independent state (see Chapter 13). Despite their common Lutheran religion, Denmark's and Sweden's territorial ambitions in northern Europe kept them in almost constant rivalry during the seventeenth century.

DENMARK Under Christian IV (1588–1648), Denmark seemed a likely candidate for expansion, but it met with little success. The system of electing monarchs forced the kings to share their power with the Danish nobility, who exercised strict control over the peasants who worked their lands. Danish ambitions for ruling the Baltic were severely curtailed by the losses they sustained in the Thirty Years' War and later in the so-called Northern War (1655–1660) with Sweden.

Danish military losses led to a constitutional crisis in which a meeting of Denmark's Estates brought to pass a bloodless revolution in 1660. The power of the nobility was curtailed, a hereditary monarchy was reestablished, and a new absolutist constitution was proclaimed in 1665. Under Christian V (1670–1699), a centralized administration was instituted with the nobility as the chief officeholders.

SWEDEN Compared with Denmark, Sweden seemed a relatively poor country, and historians have had difficulty explaining why it played such a large role in European affairs in the seventeenth century. Sweden's economy was weak, and the monarchy was still locked in conflict with the powerful Swedish nobility. During the reign of Gustavus Adolphus (1611–1632), his wise and dedicated chief minister, Axel Oxenstierna (AHK-sul OOK-sen-shur-nah), persuaded the king to adopt a new policy in which the nobility formed a "First Estate" occupying the bureaucratic positions of an expanded central government. This created a stable monarchy and freed the king to raise a formidable army and participate in the Thirty Years' War, only to be killed in battle in 1632.

Sweden entered a period of severe political crisis after the death of Gustavus Adolphus. His daughter Christina (1633–1654) proved to be far more interested in philosophy and religion than ruling. Her tendency to favor the interests of the nobility caused the other estates of the Riksdag (reeks-TAGH), Sweden's parliament—the burghers, clergy, and peasants—to protest. In 1654, tired of ruling and wishing to become a Catholic, which was forbidden in Sweden, Christina abdicated in favor of her cousin, who became King Charles X (1654–1660). His accession to the throne defused a potentially explosive peasant revolt against the nobility.

Charles X reestablished domestic order, but it was his successor, Charles XI (1660–1697), who did the painstaking work of building the Swedish monarchy along the lines of an absolute monarchy. By retaking control of the crown lands and the revenues attached to them from the nobility, Charles managed to weaken the independent power of the nobles. He built up a bureaucracy, subdued both the Riksdag and the church, improved the army and navy, and left to his son, Charles XII (1697–1718), a well-organized Swedish state that dominated northern Europe. In 1693, he and his heirs were acclaimed as "absolute, sovereign kings, responsible for their actions to no man on earth."

Sweden in the Seventeenth Century

Charles XII was primarily interested in military affairs. Though he was energetic and regarded as a brilliant general, his grandiose plans and strategies, which involved Sweden in conflicts with Poland, Denmark, and Russia, proved to be Sweden's undoing. By the time he died in 1718, Charles XII had lost much of Sweden's northern empire to Russia, and Sweden was no longer a first-class northern power.

The Ottoman Empire

After conquering Constantinople in 1453, the Ottoman Turks tried to complete their conquest of the Balkans, where they had been established since the fourteenth century (see Map 15.6).

Although they were successful in taking the Romanian territory of Wallachia in 1476, the resistance of the Hungarians kept them from advancing up the Danube valley. From 1480 to 1520, internal problems and the need to consolidate their eastern frontiers kept the Turks from any further attacks on Europe. The reign of Sultan Suleiman (SOO-lay-mahn) I the Magnificent (1520–1566), however, brought the Turks back to Europe's attention. Advancing up the Danube, the Turks seized Belgrade in 1521 and Hungary by 1526, although their attempts to conquer Vienna in 1529 were repulsed. At the same time, the Turks extended their power into the western Mediterranean, threatening to turn it into a Turkish lake until the Spanish destroyed a large Turkish fleet at Lepanto (in modern-day Greece) in 1571. Despite the defeat, the Turks continued to hold nominal control over the southern shores of the Mediterranean.

Although Europeans frequently spoke of new Christian Crusades against the "infidel" Turks, by the beginning of the seventeenth century European rulers seeking alliances and trade concessions were treating the Ottoman Empire like another European power. The Ottoman Empire possessed a highly effective governmental system, especially when it was led by strong sultans or powerful grand viziers (prime ministers). The splendid capital, Constantinople, had a population far larger than that of any European city. Nevertheless, Ottoman politics periodically degenerated into bloody intrigues as factions fought each other for influence and the throne. In one particularly gruesome practice, a ruling sultan would murder his brothers to avoid challenges to his rule. Despite the periodic bouts of civil chaos, a well-trained bureaucracy of civil servants continued to administer state affairs efficiently.

A well-organized military system also added to the strength of the Ottoman Empire. Especially outstanding were the **Janissaries** (JAN-nih-say-reez), composed of Christian boys who had been taken from their parents, converted to the

MAP 15.6 The Ottoman Empire. In the sixteenth and seventeenth centuries, the Ottoman Empire possessed an effective bureaucracy and military. During this period, it conquered much of the Balkans and made inroads into eastern Europe; by 1699, however, it had lost the farthest reaches of its European territory and would never again pose a serious threat to Europe.

Q *In what region did the Ottomans make the greatest territorial gains in the sixteenth century?*

Muslim faith, and subjected to rigid military discipline to form an elite core of 8,000 troops personally loyal to the sultan.

In the first half of the seventeenth century, the Ottoman Empire was a "sleeping giant." Occupied by domestic bloodletting and severely threatened by a challenge from Persia, the Ottomans were content with the status quo in eastern Europe. But under a new line of grand viziers in the second half of the seventeenth century, the Ottoman Empire again took the offensive. By 1683, the Ottomans had marched through the Hungarian plain and laid siege to Vienna. Repulsed by a mixed army of Austrians, Poles, Bavarians, and Saxons, the Turks retreated and were pushed out of Hungary by a new European coalition. Although they retained the core of their empire, the Ottoman Turks would never again be a threat to Europe.

The Limits of Absolutism

In recent decades, historical studies of local institutions have challenged the traditional picture of absolute monarchs. We now recognize that their power was far from absolute, and it is misleading to think that they actually controlled the lives of their subjects. In 1700, government for most people still meant the local institutions that affected their lives: local courts, local tax collectors, and local organizers of armed forces. Kings and ministers might determine policies and issue guidelines, but they still had to function through local agents and had no guarantee that their wishes would be carried out. A mass of urban and provincial privileges, liberties, and exemptions (including from taxation) and a whole host of corporate bodies and interest groups—provincial and national Estates, clerical officials, officeholders who had bought or inherited their positions, and provincial nobles—limited what monarchs could achieve. The most successful rulers were not those who tried to destroy the old system but rather those like Louis XIV, who knew how to use the old system to their advantage. Above all other considerations stood the landholding nobility. Everywhere in the seventeenth century, the landed aristocracy played an important role in the European monarchical system. As military officers, judges, officeholders, and landowners in control of vast, untaxed estates, their power remained immense. In some places, their strength put severe limits on how effectively even absolute monarchs could rule.

CHRONOLOGY	Absolutism in Central, Eastern, and Northern Europe
Brandenburg Prussia	
Hohenzollerns established in Brandenburg	1415
Hohenzollerns acquire East Prussia	1618
Frederick William the Great Elector	1640–1688
Elector Frederick III (King Frederick I)	1688–1713
Austrian Empire	
Leopold I	1658–1705
Turkish siege of Vienna	1683
Treaty of Karlowitz	1699
Russia	
Ivan IV the Terrible	1533–1584
Time of Troubles	1598–1613
Michael Romanov	1613–1645
Peter the Great	1689–1725
First trip to the West	1697–1698
Great Northern War	1701–1721
Construction of Saint Petersburg begins	1703
Battle of Poltava	1709
Denmark	
Christian IV	1588–1648
Christian V	1670–1699
Sweden	
Gustavus Adolphus	1611–1632
Christina	1633–1654
Charles X	1654–1660
Charles XI	1660–1697
Charles XII	1697–1718

Limited Monarchy and Republics

FOCUS QUESTION: What were the main issues in the struggle between king and Parliament in seventeenth-century England, and how were they resolved?

Almost everywhere in Europe in the seventeenth century, kings and their ministers were in control of central governments that sought to impose order by strengthening their powers. But not all European states followed the pattern of absolute monarchy. In eastern Europe, the Polish aristocracy controlled a virtually powerless king. In western Europe, two great states—the Dutch Republic and England—successfully resisted the power of hereditary monarchs.

The Weakness of the Polish Monarchy

Much of Polish history revolved around the bitter struggle between the crown and the landed nobility. The dynastic union of Jagiello (yahg-YEL-oh), grand prince of Lithuania, with the Polish queen Jadwiga (yahd-VEE-guh) resulted in a large Lithuanian-Polish state in 1386, although it was not until 1569 that a formal merger occurred between the two crowns. The union of Poland and Lithuania under the Jagiello dynasty had created the largest kingdom in Christendom at the beginning of the fifteenth century. As a result, Poland-Lithuania played a major role in eastern Europe in the fifteenth century and also ruled much of Ukraine by the end of the sixteenth century. Poland-Lithuania had a rather unique governmental system in that assemblies of nobles elected the king and carefully limited royal power. The power of the nobles also enabled them to keep the Polish peasantry in a state of serfdom.

In 1572, when the Jagiello dynasty came to an end, a new practice arose of choosing outsiders as kings, with the idea that they would bring in new alliances. When the throne was awarded to the Swede Sigismund III (1587–1631), the new king dreamed of creating a vast Polish empire that would include Russia and possibly Finland and Sweden. Poland not only failed to achieve this goal but by the end of the seventeenth century had become a weak, decentralized state.

It was the elective nature of the Polish monarchy that reduced it to impotence. The Sejm (SAYM), or Polish diet, was a two-chamber assembly in which landowners completely dominated the few townspeople and lawyers who were also members. To be elected to the kingship, prospective monarchs had to agree to share power with the Sejm (in effect with the nobles) in matters of taxation, foreign and military policy, and the appointment of state officials and judges. The power of the Sejm had disastrous results for central monarchical authority, for the real aim of most of its members was to ensure that central authority would not affect their local interests. The acceptance of the liberum veto in 1652, whereby the meetings of the Sejm could be stopped by a single dissenting member, reduced government to virtual chaos.

Poland in the Seventeenth Century

Poland, then, was basically a confederation of semi-independent estates of landed nobles. By the late seventeenth century, it had also become a battleground for foreign powers, who found the nation easy to invade but difficult to rule.

The Golden Age of the Dutch Republic

The seventeenth century has often been called the golden age of the Dutch Republic as the United Provinces held center stage as one of Europe's great powers. Like France and England, the United Provinces was an Atlantic power, underlining the importance of the shift of political and economic power from the Mediterranean basin to the countries on the Atlantic seaboard. As a result of the sixteenth-century revolt of the Netherlands, the seven northern provinces, which began to call themselves the United Provinces of the Netherlands in 1581, became the core of the modern Dutch state. The Peace of Westphalia officially recognized the new state in 1648.

With independence came internal dissension. There were two chief centers of political power in the new state. Each province had an official known as a stadholder (STAD-hohl-dur) who was responsible for leading the army and maintaining order. Beginning with William of Orange and his heirs, the house of Orange occupied the stadholderate in most of the seven provinces and favored the development of a centralized government with themselves as hereditary monarchs. The States General, an assembly of representatives from every province, opposed the Orangist ambitions and advocated a decentralized or republican form of government. For much of the seventeenth century, the republican forces were in control. But in 1672, burdened with war against both France and England, the United Provinces turned to William III (1672–1702) of the house of Orange to establish a monarchical regime. But his death in 1702 without a direct heir enabled the republican forces to gain control once more, although the struggle persisted throughout the eighteenth century.

Underlying Dutch prominence in the seventeenth century was economic prosperity, fueled by the role of the Dutch as carriers of European trade. But warfare proved disastrous to the Dutch Republic. Wars with France and England placed heavy burdens on Dutch finances and manpower. English shipping began to challenge what had been Dutch commercial supremacy, and by 1715, the Dutch were experiencing a serious economic decline.

LIFE IN SEVENTEENTH-CENTURY AMSTERDAM By the beginning of the seventeenth century, Amsterdam had replaced Antwerp as the financial and commercial capital of Europe. In 1570, Amsterdam had 30,000 inhabitants; by 1610, that number had doubled as refugees poured in, especially from the Spanish Netherlands. In 1613, this rapid growth caused the city government to approve an "urban expansion plan" that increased the city's territory from 500 to 1,800 acres through the construction of three large concentric canals. Builders prepared plots for the tall, narrow-fronted houses that were characteristic of the city by hammering wooden columns through the mud to the firm sand underneath. The canals in turn made it possible for merchants and artisans to use the upper stories of their houses as storerooms for their goods. Wares carried by small boats were hoisted to the top windows of these dwellings by block and tackle beams fastened to the gables of the roofs. Amsterdam's physical expansion was soon matched by its population as the city grew to 200,000 by 1660.

The exuberant expansion of Amsterdam in the seventeenth century owed much to the city's role as the commercial and financial center of Europe. But what had made this possible? For one thing, Amsterdam merchants possessed vast fleets of ships, many of which were used for the lucrative North Sea herring catch. Amsterdam-based ships were also important carriers for the products of other countries. The Dutch invention of the *fluyt* (FLYT), a shallow-draft ship of large capacity, enabled them to transport enormous quantities of cereals, timber, and iron.

Amsterdam merchants unloaded their cargoes at Dam Square, and the city soon became a crossroads for the exchange of many of Europe's chief products. Amsterdam was also, of course, the chief port for the Dutch West Indian and East Indian trading companies. Moreover, city industries turned imported raw materials into finished goods, making Amsterdam an important producer of woolen cloth, refined sugar and tobacco products, glass, beer, paper, books, jewelry, and leather goods. Some of the city's great wealth came from war profits: by 1700, Amsterdam was the principal supplier of military goods in Europe; its gun foundries had customers throughout the Continent.

Another factor in Amsterdam's prosperity was its importance as a financial center. Trading profits provided large quantities of capital for investment. The city's financial role was greatly facilitated by the foundation in 1609 of the Exchange Bank of Amsterdam, long the greatest public bank in northern Europe. The city also founded the Amsterdam Stock Exchange for speculating in commodities.

IMAGES OF EVERYDAY LIFE

Dutch Domesticity

DURING THE GOLDEN AGE OF THE DUTCH REPUBLIC, Dutch painters delighted in painting scenes of domestic life, especially the lives of the wealthy burghers who prospered from trade, finance, and manufacturing. The Dutch painter Pieter de Hooch (PEE-ter duh HOHKH) specialized in painting pictures of Dutch interiors, as can be seen in three of his paintings. In *The Mother* (below left), de Hooch portrays a tranquil scene of a mother with her infant and small daughter. The spotless, polished floors reflect the sunlight streaming in through the open door. The rooms are clean and in good order. Household manuals, such as The *Experienced and Knowledgeable Hollands Householder,* provided detailed outlines of the cleaning tasks that should be performed each day of the week. In *The Linen Cupboard* (below right), a Dutch mother, assisted by her daughter, is shown storing her clean sheets in an elegant cupboard in another well-polished Dutch room. The Chinese porcelain on top of the cupboard and the antique statue indicate that this is the residence of a wealthy family. In *Two Women Teach a Child to Walk* (at the right), the artist again shows a well-furnished and spotless interior. A small girl is learning to walk, assisted by a servant holding straps attached to a band around the girl's head to keep her from falling.

Erich Lessing/Art Resource, NY

bpk, Berlin/Art Resource, NY

Rijksmuseum, Amsterdam//Alinari/Art Resource, NY

At the very top of Amsterdam's society stood a select number of very prosperous manufacturers, shipyard owners, and merchants whose wealth enabled them to control the city's government. In the first half of the seventeenth century, the Calvinist background of the wealthy Amsterdam burghers led them to adopt a simple lifestyle. They wore dark clothes and lived in substantial but simply furnished houses known for their steep, narrow stairways. The oft-quoted phrase that "cleanliness is next to godliness" was literally true for these self-confident Dutch burghers. Their houses were spotless and orderly (see "Images of Everyday Life" above); foreigners often commented that Dutch housewives always seemed to be scrubbing. But in the second half of the seventeenth century, the wealthy burghers began to reject their Calvinist heritage, a transformation that is especially evident in their more elaborate and colorful clothes.

England and the Emergence of Constitutional Monarchy

One of the most prominent examples of resistance to absolute monarchy came in seventeenth-century England, where king and Parliament struggled to determine the role each should play in governing the nation. But a deep and profound religious controversy complicated the struggle over this political issue. With the victory of Parliament came the foundation for constitutional monarchy by the end of the seventeenth century.

KING JAMES I AND PARLIAMENT Upon the death of Queen Elizabeth in 1603, the Tudor dynasty became extinct, and the Stuart line of rulers was inaugurated with the accession to the throne of Elizabeth's cousin, King James VI of Scotland (son of Mary, queen of Scots), who became James I (1603–1625) of England. Although used to royal power as king of Scotland, James understood little about the laws, institutions, and customs of the English. He espoused the divine right of kings, the belief that kings receive their power directly from God and are responsible to no one except God. This viewpoint alienated Parliament, which had grown accustomed under the Tudors to act on the premise that monarch and Parliament together ruled England as a "balanced polity." Parliament expressed its displeasure with James's claims by refusing his requests for additional monies needed by the king to meet the increased cost of government. Parliament's power of the purse proved to be its trump card in its relationship with the king.

James's religious policy also alienated some members of Parliament. The Puritans—Protestants in the Anglican Church inspired by Calvinist theology—wanted James to eliminate the episcopal system of church organization used in the Church of England (in which the bishop or *episcopos* played the major administrative role) in favor of a Presbyterian model (used in Scotland and patterned after Calvin's church organization in Geneva, where ministers and elders—also called presbyters—played an important governing role). James refused because he realized that the Anglican Church, with its bishops appointed by the crown, was a major support of monarchical authority. But the Puritans were not easily cowed and added to the rising chorus of opposition to the king. Many of England's **gentry**, mostly well-to-do landowners below the level of the nobility, had become Puritans, and these Puritan gentry not only formed an important and substantial part of the House of Commons, the lower house of Parliament, but also held important positions locally as justices of the peace and sheriffs. It was not wise to alienate them.

CHARLES I AND THE MOVE TOWARD REVOLUTION The conflict that had begun during the reign of James came to a head during the reign of his son, Charles I (1625–1649). In 1628, Parliament passed the Petition of Right, which the king was supposed to accept before being granted any tax revenues. This petition prohibited taxation without Parliament's consent, arbitrary imprisonment, the quartering of soldiers in private houses, and the declaration of martial law in peacetime. Although he initially accepted it, Charles later reneged on the agreement because of its limitations on royal power. In 1629, Charles decided that since he could not work with Parliament, he would not summon it to meet. From 1629 to 1640, Charles pursued a course of personal rule, which forced him to find ways to collect taxes without the cooperation of Parliament. One expedient was a tax called ship money, a levy on seacoast towns to pay for coastal defense, which was now collected annually by the king's officials throughout England and used to finance other government operations besides defense. This use of ship money aroused opposition from middle-class merchants and landed gentry, who objected to the king's attempts to tax without Parliament's consent.

The king's religious policy also proved disastrous. His marriage to Henrietta Maria, the Catholic sister of King Louis XIII of France, aroused suspicions about the king's own religious inclinations. Even more important, however, the efforts of Charles and William Laud, the archbishop of Canterbury, to introduce more ritual into the Anglican Church struck the Puritans as a return to Catholic popery. Grievances mounted. Charles might have survived unscathed if he could have avoided calling Parliament, which alone could provide a focus for the many cries of discontent throughout the land. But when the king and Archbishop Laud attempted to impose the Anglican Book of Common Prayer on the Scottish Presbyterian Church, the Scots rose up in rebellion against the king. Financially strapped and unable to raise troops to defend against the Scots, the king was forced to call Parliament into session. Eleven years of frustration welled up to create a Parliament determined to deal the king his due.

In its first session, from November 1640 to September 1641, the so-called Long Parliament (because it lasted in one form or another from 1640 to 1660) took a series of steps that placed severe limitations on royal authority. These included the abolition of arbitrary courts; the abolition of taxes that the king had collected without Parliament's consent, such as ship money; and the passage of the revolutionary Triennial Act, which specified that Parliament must meet at least once every three years, with or without the king's consent. By the end of 1641, one group in Parliament was prepared to go no further, but a group of more radical parliamentarians pushed for more change, including the elimination of bishops in the Anglican Church. When the king tried to take advantage of the split by arresting some members of the more radical faction in Parliament, a large group in Parliament led by John Pym and his fellow Puritans decided that the king had gone too far. England slipped into civil war.

CIVIL WAR IN ENGLAND Parliament proved victorious in the first phase of the English Civil War (1642–1646). Most important to Parliament's success was the creation of the New Model Army, which was composed primarily of more extreme Puritans known as the Independents, who believed they were doing battle for the Lord. It is striking to read in the military reports of Oliver Cromwell (1599–1658), one of the group's leaders, such statements as "Sir, this is none other but the hand of God; and to Him alone belongs the glory." We might also attribute some of the credit to Cromwell himself, since his crusaders were well disciplined and trained in the latest military tactics. Supported by the New Model Army, Parliament ended the first phase of the civil war with the capture of King Charles I in 1646.

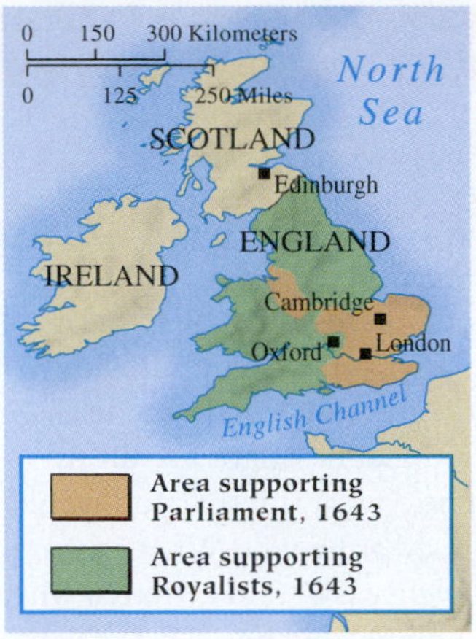

Civil War in England

A split now occurred in the parliamentary forces. A Presbyterian majority wanted to disband the army and restore Charles I with a Presbyterian state church. The army, composed mostly of the more radical Independents, who opposed an established Presbyterian church, marched on London in 1647 and began negotiations with the king. Charles took advantage of this division to flee and seek help from the Scots. Enraged by the king's treachery, Cromwell and the army engaged in a second civil war (1648) that ended with Cromwell's victory and the capture of the king. This time, Cromwell was determined to achieve a victory for the army's point of view. The Presbyterian members of Parliament were purged, leaving a Rump Parliament of fifty-three members of the House of Commons who then tried and condemned the king on a charge of treason and adjudged that "he, the said Charles Stuart, as a tyrant, traitor, murderer, and public enemy to the good people of this nation, shall be put to death by the severing of his head from his body." On January 30, 1649, Charles was beheaded, a most uncommon act in the seventeenth century. The revolution had triumphed, and the monarchy in England had been destroyed, at least for the moment.

City Art Gallery, Leeds, UK//Getty Images

Oliver Cromwell. Oliver Cromwell was a dedicated Puritan who helped form the New Model Army and defeat the forces supporting King Charles I. Unable to work with Parliament, he came to rely on military force to rule England. Cromwell is pictured here in 1649, on the eve of his military campaign in Ireland.

CROMWELL AND NEW GOVERNMENTS After the death of the king, the Rump Parliament abolished the monarchy and the House of Lords and proclaimed England a republic or commonwealth (1649–1653). This was not an easy period for Cromwell. As commander in chief of the army, he had to crush a Catholic uprising in Ireland, which he accomplished with a brutality that earned him the eternal enmity of the Irish people, as well as an uprising in Scotland on behalf of the son of Charles I.

Cromwell also faced opposition at home, especially from more radically minded groups who took advantage of the upheaval in England to push their agendas. The Levellers, for example, advocated such advanced ideas as freedom of speech, religious toleration, and a democratic republic, arguing for the right to vote for all male householders over the age of twenty-one. The Levellers also called for annual Parliaments, women's equality with men, and government programs to care for the poor. As one Leveller said, "The poorest he that is in England has a life to live as the greatest he." To Cromwell, a country gentleman, only people of property had the right to participate in the affairs of state, and he warned in a fit of rage: "I tell you . . . you have no other way to deal with these men but to break them or they will break you; and make void all that work that, with so many years' industry, toil, and pains, you have done . . . I tell you again, you are necessitated to break them."[11] And break them he did; Cromwell smashed the radicals by force. More than a century would pass before their ideas of democracy and equality became fashionable.

At the same time that Cromwell was dealing with the Levellers, he also found it difficult to work with the Rump Parliament and finally dispersed it by force. As the members of Parliament departed (in April 1653), he shouted after them, "It's you that have forced me to do this. . . . I have sought the Lord night and day that He would slay me rather than put upon me the doing of this work."[12] With the certainty of one who is convinced he is right, Cromwell had destroyed both king and Parliament (see "Opposing Viewpoints" on p. 460).

The army provided a new government when it drew up the Instrument of Government, England's first and only written constitution. Executive power was vested in the Lord Protector (a position held by Cromwell) and legislative power in a reconstituted Parliament. But the new system failed to work. Cromwell found it difficult to work with Parliament, especially when its members debated his authority and advocated once again the creation of a Presbyterian state church. In 1655, Cromwell dissolved Parliament and divided the country into eleven regions, each ruled by a major general who served virtually as a military governor. To meet the cost of military government, Cromwell levied a 10 percent land tax on all former Royalists. Unable to establish a constitutional basis for a working

OPPOSING VIEWPOINTS

Oliver Cromwell: Three Perspectives

OLIVER CROMWELL WAS A STRONG LEADER with firm religious convictions. The first selection, taken from a letter written after the defeat of the king's forces at Naseby in 1645, reveals Cromwell's feelings about the reasons for his military victory. The next selection, also by Cromwell, is taken from his comments after his army's massacre of Catholic forces at Drogheda (DRAW ih-duh) in Catholic Ireland. The third selection is by Edmund Ludlow, a general on Cromwell's side who broke with Cromwell after the latter had become Lord Protector. The final selection by Edward Hyde, the first earl of Clarendon, a supporter of King Charles I and later Charles II, presents a royalist view of Cromwell.

Oliver Cromwell on the Victory at Naseby

Sir, this is none other but the hand of God; and to Him alone belongs the glory, wherein none are to share with Him. The general [Fairfax] served you with all faithfulness and honor: and the best commendations I can give him is, that I dare say he attributes all to God, and would rather perish than assume to himself. Which is an honest and a thriving way, and yet as much for bravery may be given to him, in this action, as to a man.

Cromwell on the Massacre at Drogheda

The next day, the other two towers were summoned, in one of which was about six or seven score; but they refused to yield themselves, and we knowing that hunger must compel them, set only good guards to secure them from running away until their stomachs were come down. From one of the said towers, notwithstanding their condition, they killed and wounded some of our men. When they submitted, their officers were knocked on the head, and every tenth man of the soldiers killed, and the rest shipped for the Barbados. The soldiers in the other tower were all spared, as to their lives only, and shipped likewise for the Barbados.

I am persuaded that this is a righteous judgment of God upon these barbarous wretches, who have imbrued their hands in so much innocent blood; and that it will tend to prevent the effusion of blood for the future, which are the satisfactory grounds to such actions, which otherwise cannot but work remorse and regret.

Edmund Ludlow, *Memoirs*

Then I drew near to the council-table, where Cromwell charged me with dispersing treasonable books in Ireland, and with endeavoring to render the officers of the army disaffected, by discoursing to them concerning new models of Government. I acknowledged that I had caused some papers to be dispersed in Ireland, but denied that they justly could be called treasonable. . . .

"You do well," said he, "to reflect on our fears. . . . I now require you to give assurance not to act against the Government." I desired to be excused in that particular, reminding him of the reasons I had formerly given him for my refusal, adding that I was in his power, and that he might use me as he thought fit. "Pray then," said he, "what is it that you would have? May not every man be as good as he will? What can you desire more than you have?" "It were easy," said I, "to tell what we would have." "What is that, I pray?" said he. "That which we fought for," said I, "that the nation might be governed by its own consent." "I am," said he, "as much for a government by consent as any man; but where shall we find that consent? Amongst the Prelatical, Presbyterian, Independent, Anabaptist, or Leveling Parties?" I answered, "Amongst those of all sorts who had acted with fidelity and affection to the public."

Lord Clarendon, *The History of the Rebellion and Civil Wars in England*

He was one of those men . . . whom his very enemies could not condemn without commending him at the same time: for he could never have done half that mischief without great parts of courage, industry, and judgment. He must have had a wonderful understanding in the natures and humors of men, and as great a dexterity in applying them; who, from a private and obscure birth (though of a good family), without interest or estate, alliance or friendship, could raise himself to such a height, and compound and knead such opposite and contradictory tempers, humors, and interests into a consistence, that contributed to his designs, and to their own destruction; whilst himself grew insensibly powerful enough to cut off those by whom he had climbed, in the instant that they projected to demolish their own building. What [a Roman writer] said of Cinna [a Roman politician] may very justly be said of him: he attempted those things which no good man dared have ventured on; and achieved those in which none but a valiant and great man could have succeeded. Without doubt, no man with more wickedness ever attempted any thing, or brought to pass what he desired more wickedly, more in the face and contempt of religion, and moral honesty; yet wickedness as great as his could never have accomplished those trophies, without the assistance of a great spirit, an admirable circumspection and sagacity, and a most magnanimous resolution.

Q *What motivated Cromwell's political and military actions? What was Edmund Ludlow's criticism of Cromwell, and how did Cromwell respond? In what ways did Edward Hyde see both good and bad features in Cromwell? How do you explain the differences in these three perspectives?*

Sources: Oliver Cromwell on the Victory at Naseby and on the Massacre at Drogheda, in T. Carlyle, ed., *The Letters and Speeches of Oliver Cromwell*, vols. 1 and 3 (New York: G.P. Putnam's Sons, 1904); E. Ludlow, *Memoirs*, in C. H. Firth, *The Memoirs of Edmund Ludlow*, vol. 2 (Oxford: Oxford University Press, 1894); Lord Clarendon, *The History of the Rebellion and Civil Wars in England*, vol. 6 (Oxford: Oxford University Press, 1839).

government, Cromwell had resorted to military force to maintain the rule of the Independents, ironically using even more arbitrary policies than those of Charles I.

Oliver Cromwell died in 1658. After floundering for eighteen months, the military establishment decided that arbitrary rule by the army was no longer feasible and reestablished the monarchy in the person of Charles II, the eldest son of Charles I (see Chart 15.1). The restoration of the Stuart monarchy ended England's time of troubles, but it was not long before yet another constitutional crisis arose.

RESTORATION OF THE MONARCHY After eleven years of exile, Charles II (1660–1685) returned to England. As he entered London amid the acclaim of the people, he remarked cynically, "I never knew that I was so popular in England." The restoration of the monarchy and the House of Lords did not mean, however, that the work of the English Revolution was undone. Parliament kept much of the power it had won: its role in government was acknowledged, the necessity for its consent to taxation was accepted, and arbitrary courts were still abolished. Yet Charles continued to push his own ideas, some of which were clearly out of step with many of the English people. A serious religious problem disturbed the tranquility of Charles II's reign. After the restoration of the monarchy, a new Parliament (the Cavalier Parliament) met in 1661 and restored the Anglican Church as the official church of England. In addition, laws were passed to force everyone, particularly Catholics and Puritan Dissenters, to conform to the Anglican Church. Charles, however, was sympathetic to and perhaps even inclined toward Catholicism. Moreover, Charles's brother James, heir to the throne, did not hide the fact that he was a Catholic. Parliament's suspicions were therefore aroused in 1672 when Charles took the audacious step of issuing the Declaration of Indulgence, which suspended the laws that Parliament had passed against Catholics and Puritans. Parliament would have none of it and induced the king to suspend the declaration. Propelled by a strong anti-Catholic sentiment, Parliament then passed the Test Act of 1673, specifying that only Anglicans could hold military and civil offices.

A purported Catholic plot to assassinate King Charles and place his brother James on the throne, though soon exposed as imaginary, inflamed Parliament to attempt to pass a bill that would have barred James from the throne as a professed Catholic. Although these attempts failed, the debate over the bill created two political groupings: the Whigs, who wanted to exclude James and establish a Protestant king with toleration of Dissenters, and the Tories, who supported the king, despite their dislike of James as a Catholic, because they believed that Parliament should not tamper with the lawful succession to the throne. To foil these efforts, Charles dismissed Parliament in 1681, relying on French subsidies to rule alone. When he died in 1685, his Catholic brother came to the throne.

The accession of James II (1685–1688) virtually guaranteed a new constitutional crisis for England. An open and devout Catholic, his attempt to further Catholic interests made religion once more a primary cause of conflict between king and Parliament. Contrary to the Test Act, James named Catholics to high positions in the government, army, navy, and universities.

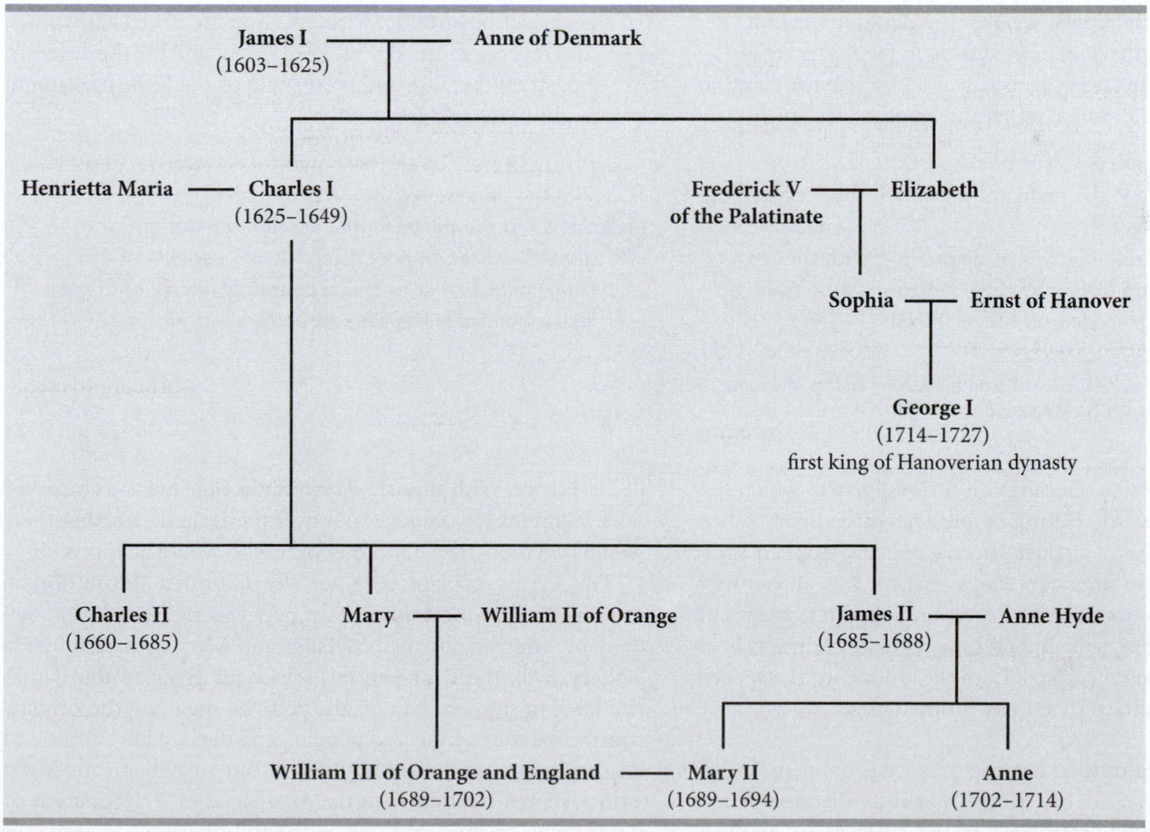

Chart 15.1 A Simplified Look at the Stuart Dynasty

THE BILL OF RIGHTS

IN 1688, THE ENGLISH EXPERIENCED yet another revolution, a bloodless one in which the Stuart king James II was replaced by Mary, James's daughter, and her husband, William of Orange. After William and Mary had assumed power, Parliament passed the Bill of Rights, which specified the rights of Parliament and laid the foundation for a constitutional monarchy.

The Bill of Rights

Whereas the said late King James II having abdicated the government, and the throne being thereby vacant, his Highness the prince of Orange (whom it has pleased Almighty God to make the glorious instrument of delivering this kingdom from popery and arbitrary power) did (by the device of the lords spiritual and temporal, and diverse principal persons of the Commons) cause letters to be written to the lords spiritual and temporal, being Protestants, and other letters to the several counties, cities, universities, boroughs, and Cinque Ports, for the choosing of such persons to represent them, as were of right to be sent to parliament, to meet and sit at Westminster upon the two and twentieth day of January, in this year 1689, in order to such an establishment as that their religion, laws, and liberties might not again be in danger of being subverted; upon which letters elections have been accordingly made.

And thereupon the said lords spiritual and temporal and Commons, pursuant to their respective letters and elections, being now assembled in a full and free representation of this nation, taking into their most serious consideration the best means for attaining the ends aforesaid, do in the first place (as their ancestors in like case have usually done), for the vindication and assertion of their ancient rights and liberties, declare:

1. That the pretended power of suspending laws, or the execution of laws, by regal authority, without consent of parliament is illegal.
2. That the pretended power of dispensing with the laws, or the execution of law by regal authority, as it has been assumed and exercised of late, is illegal.
3. That the commission for erecting the late court of commissioners for ecclesiastical causes, and all other commissions and courts of like nature, are illegal and pernicious.
4. That levying money for or to the use of the crown by pretense of prerogative, without grant of parliament, for longer time or in other manner than the same is or shall be granted, is illegal.
5. That it is the right of the subjects to petition the king, and all commitments and prosecutions for such petitioning are illegal.
6. That the raising or keeping a standing army within the kingdom in time of peace, unless it be with consent of parliament, is against law.
7. That the subjects which are Protestants may have arms for their defense suitable to their conditions, and as allowed by law.
8. That election of members of parliament ought to be free.
9. That the freedom of speech, and debates or proceedings in parliament, ought not to be impeached or questioned in any court or place out of parliament.
10. That excessive bail ought not to be required, nor excessive fines imposed, nor cruel and unusual punishments inflicted.
11. That jurors ought to be duly impaneled and returned, and jurors which pass upon men in trials for high treason ought to be freeholders.
12. That all grants and promises of fines and forfeitures of particular persons before conviction are illegal and void.
13. And that for redress of all grievances, and for the amending, strengthening, and preserving of the laws, parliament ought to be held frequently.

Q *How did the Bill of Rights lay the foundation for a constitutional monarchy? What key aspects of this document testify to the exceptional nature of English state politics in the seventeenth century?*

Source: *The Statutes: Revised Edition*, vol. 2 (London: Eyre and Spottiswoode, 1871), pp. 10–12.

In 1687, he issued a new Declaration of Indulgence, which suspended all laws barring Catholics and Dissenters from office. Parliamentary outcries against James's policies stopped short of rebellion because members knew that he was an old man and that his successors were his Protestant daughters Mary and Anne, born to his first wife. But on June 10, 1688, a son was born to James II's second wife, also a Catholic. Suddenly, the specter of a Catholic hereditary monarchy loomed large.

A GLORIOUS REVOLUTION A group of seven prominent English noblemen invited William of Orange, husband of James's daughter Mary, to invade England. William and Mary raised an army and invaded England while James, his wife, and their infant son fled to France. With almost no bloodshed, England had embarked on a "Glorious Revolution," not over the issue of whether there would be a monarchy but rather over who would be monarch.

The events of late 1688 set the Glorious Revolution in motion. The far more important part was the Revolution Settlement, which confirmed William and Mary as monarchs. In January 1689, the Convention Parliament asserted that James had tried to subvert the constitution "by breaking the original contract between king and people" and declared the throne of England vacant. It then offered the throne to William and Mary, who accepted it along with the provisions of a declaration of rights, later enacted into law as the Bill of Rights in 1689 (see the box above). The Bill of Rights affirmed Parliament's right to make laws and levy taxes and made it impossible for kings to oppose or do without Parliament by stipulating that standing armies could be raised only with the consent of Parliament. Both elections of members and debates in Parliament had to be free, meaning that the king could not interfere. The rights of citizens to petition the sovereign, keep arms, have a jury trial, and not be subject to excessive bail were also confirmed. The Bill of Rights helped fashion a system of government based on the rule of law and a freely elected Parliament, thus laying the foundation for a constitutional monarchy.

The Bill of Rights did not settle the religious questions that had played such a large role in England's troubles in the seventeenth century. The Toleration Act of 1689 granted Puritan Dissenters the right of free public worship (Catholics were still excluded), although they did not yet have full civil and political equality since the Test Act was not repealed. Although the Toleration Act did not mean complete religious freedom and equality, it marked a departure in English history: few people would ever again be persecuted for religious reasons.

Many historians have viewed the Glorious Revolution as the end of the seventeenth-century struggle between king and Parliament. By deposing one king and establishing another, Parliament had demolished the divine-right theory of kingship (William was, after all, king by grace of Parliament, not God) and confirmed its right to participate in the government. Parliament did not have complete control of the government, but it now had an unquestioned role in affairs of state. Over the next century, it would gradually prove to be the real authority in the English system of constitutional monarchy.

RESPONSES TO REVOLUTION The English revolutions of the seventeenth century prompted very different responses from two English political thinkers—Thomas Hobbes and John Locke. Thomas Hobbes (1588–1679), who lived during the English Civil War, was alarmed by the revolutionary upheavals in his contemporary England. Hobbes's name has since been associated with the state's claim to absolute authority over its subjects, a topic that he elaborated in his major treatise on political thought known as the *Leviathan* (luh-VY-uh-thun), published in 1651.

Hobbes claimed that in the state of nature, before society was organized, human life was "solitary, poor, nasty, brutish, and short." Humans were guided not by reason and moral ideals but by animalistic instincts and a ruthless struggle for self-preservation. To save themselves from destroying each other (the "war of every man against every man"), people contracted to form a commonwealth, which Hobbes called "that great Leviathan (or rather, to speak more reverently, that mortal god) to which we owe our peace and defense." This commonwealth placed its collective power into the hands of a sovereign authority, preferably a single ruler, who served as executor, legislator, and judge. This absolute ruler possessed unlimited power. In Hobbes's view, subjects may not rebel; if they do, they must be suppressed.

John Locke (1632–1704) viewed the exercise of political power quite differently from Hobbes and argued against the absolute rule of one man. Locke's experience of English politics during the Glorious Revolution was incorporated into a political work called *Two Treatises of Government*. Like Hobbes, Locke began with the state of nature before human existence became organized socially. But unlike Hobbes, Locke believed that humans lived then in a state of equality and freedom rather than a state of war. In this state of nature, humans had certain inalienable natural rights—to life, liberty, and property. Like Hobbes, Locke did not believe all was well in the state of nature. Since there was no impartial judge in the state of nature, people found it difficult to protect these rights. So they mutually agreed to establish a government to ensure the protection of their rights. This agreement established mutual obligations: government would protect the rights of the people while the people would act reasonably toward government. But if a government broke this agreement—for example, if a monarch failed to live up to his obligation to protect the people's rights or claimed absolute authority and made laws without the consent of the community—the people might form a new government. For Locke, however, the community of people was primarily the landholding aristocracy who were represented in Parliament, not the landless masses. Locke was hardly an advocate of political democracy, but his ideas proved important to both the Americans and the French in the eighteenth century and were used to support demands for constitutional government, the rule of law, and the protection of rights.

CHRONOLOGY	Limited Monarchy and Republics
Poland	
Merger of Poland and Lithuania	1569
Sigismund III	1587–1631
Beginning of liberum veto	1652
United Provinces	
Official recognition of United Provinces	1648
House of Orange	
William III	1672–1702
England	
James I	1603–1625
Charles I	1625–1649
Petition of Right	1628
First Civil War	1642–1646
Second Civil War	1648
Execution of Charles I	1649
Commonwealth	1649–1653
Death of Cromwell	1658
Restoration of monarchy	1660
Charles II	1660–1685
Cavalier Parliament	1661
Declaration of Indulgence	1672
Test Act	1673
James II	1685–1688
Declaration of Indulgence	1687
Glorious Revolution	1688
Bill of Rights	1689

The Flourishing of European Culture

FOCUS QUESTION: How did the artistic and literary achievements of this era reflect the political and economic developments of the period?

In the midst of religious wars and the growth of absolutism, European culture continued to flourish. The era was blessed with a number of prominent artists and writers.

The Changing Faces of Art

After the Renaissance, European art passed through a number of stylistic stages. The artistic Renaissance came to an end when a new movement called Mannerism emerged in Italy in the 1520s and 1530s.

MANNERISM The Reformation's revival of religious values brought much political turmoil. Especially in Italy, the worldly enthusiasm of the Renaissance gave way to anxiety, uncertainty, suffering, and a yearning for spiritual experience. **Mannerism** reflected this environment in its deliberate attempt to break down the High Renaissance principles of balance, harmony, and moderation (the term *Mannerism* derives from critics who considered their contemporary artists to be second-rate imitators, painting "in the manner of" Michelangelo's late style). Italian Mannerist painters deliberately distorted the rules of proportion by portraying elongated figures that conveyed a sense of suffering and a strong emotional atmosphere filled with anxiety and confusion.

Mannerism spread from Italy to other parts of Europe and perhaps reached its apogee in the work of El Greco (1541–1614). Doménikos Theotocópoulos (called "the Greek"—El Greco) was from Crete, but after studying in Venice and Rome, he moved in the 1570s to Spain, where he became a church painter in Toledo. El Greco's elongated and contorted figures, portrayed in unusual shades of yellow and green against an eerie background of turbulent grays, reflect the artist's desire to create a world of intense emotion.

THE BAROQUE PERIOD A new movement—the **Baroque** (buh-ROHK)—eventually replaced Mannerism. The Baroque began in Italy in the last quarter of the sixteenth century and spread to the rest of Europe, where it was most wholeheartedly embraced by the Catholic reform movement, and especially at the Catholic courts of the Habsburgs in Madrid, Prague, Vienna, and Brussels. Although it was resisted in France, England, and the Netherlands, eventually the Baroque style spread to all of Europe and to Latin America.

Baroque artists sought to bring together the classical ideals of Renaissance art with the spiritual feelings of the sixteenth-century religious revival. The Baroque painting style was known for its use of dramatic effects to arouse the emotions. In large part, though, Baroque art and architecture reflected the search for power that was so important to the seventeenth-century ethos. Baroque churches and palaces were magnificent and richly detailed. Kings and princes wanted other kings and princes as well as their subjects to be in awe of their power.

National Gallery of Art, Washington, DC//SuperStock

El Greco, *Laocoön*. Mannerism reached its height in the work of El Greco. Born in Crete, trained in Venice and Rome, and settling finally in Spain, El Greco worked as a church painter in Toledo. Pictured here is his version of the *Laocoön*, a Hellenistic sculpture discovered in Rome in 1506. The elongated, contorted bodies project a world of suffering while the somber background scene of the city of Toledo and the threatening sky add a sense of terror and doom.

Baroque painting was known for its use of dramatic effects to heighten emotional intensity. This style was especially evident in the works of the Flemish master Peter Paul Rubens (1577–1640), a prolific artist and an important figure in the spread of the Baroque from Italy to other parts of Europe. In his artistic masterpieces, bodies in violent motion, heavily fleshed nudes, a dramatic use of light and shadow, and rich, sensuous pigments converge to express intense emotions. The restless forms and constant movement blend together into a dynamic unity.

Perhaps the greatest figure of the Baroque was the Italian architect and sculptor Gian Lorenzo Bernini (ZHAHN loh-RENT-zoh bur-NEE-nee) (1598–1680), who completed Saint Peter's Basilica at the Vatican and designed the vast colonnade enclosing the piazza in front of it. Action, exuberance, profusion, and dramatic effects mark the work of Bernini in the interior of Saint Peter's, where his *Throne of Saint Peter* hovers in midair, held by the hands of the four great doctors of the Catholic Church. Above the chair, rays of golden light drive a mass of clouds and angels toward the spectator. In his most striking sculptural work, the *Ecstasy of Saint Theresa*, Bernini depicts a moment of mystical experience in the life of the sixteenth-century Spanish saint. The elegant draperies and the expression on her face create a sensuously real portrayal of physical ecstasy.

Less well known than the male artists who dominated the art world of seventeenth-century Italy but prominent in her own right was Artemisia Gentileschi (ar-tuh-MEE-zhuh jen-tuh-LESS-kee) (1593–1653). Born in Rome, she studied painting under her father's direction. In 1616, she moved to Florence and began a successful career as a painter. At the age of twenty-three, she became the first woman to be elected to the Florentine Academy of Design. Although she was known internationally in her day as a portrait painter, her fame now rests on a series of pictures of heroines from the Old Testament. Most famous is *Judith Beheading Holofernes*, a dramatic rendering of the biblical scene in which Judith slays the Assyrian general Holofernes to save her besieged town from the Assyrian army.

FRENCH CLASSICISM In the second half of the seventeenth century, France replaced Italy as the cultural leader of Europe. Rejecting the Baroque style as overly showy and impassioned, the French remained committed to the classical values of the High Renaissance. French late classicism, with its emphasis

RMN-Grand Palais/Art Resource, NY

Peter Paul Rubens, *The Landing of Marie de'Mediciat Marseilles.* Peter Paul Rubens played a key role in spreading the Baroque style from Italy to other parts of Europe. In *The Landing of Marie de' Medici at Marseilles*, Rubens made dramatic use of light and color, bodies in motion, and luxurious nudes to heighten the emotional intensity of the scene. This was one of a cycle of twenty-one paintings dedicated to the queen mother of France.

Cornaro Chapel, S. Maria della Vittoria, Rome//Scala/Art Resource, NY

Gian Lorenzo Bernini, *Ecstasy of Saint Theresa.* One of the great artists of the Baroque period was the Italian sculptor and architect Gian Lorenzo Bernini. The *Ecstasy of Saint Theresa*, created for the Cornaro Chapel in the Church of Santa Maria della Vittoria in Rome, was one of Bernini's most famous sculptures. Bernini sought to convey visually Theresa's mystical experience when, according to her description, an angel pierced her heart repeatedly with a golden arrow.

on clarity, simplicity, balance, and harmony of design, was a rather austere version of the High Renaissance style. Its triumph reflected the shift in seventeenth-century French society from chaos to order. Though it rejected the emotionalism and high drama of the Baroque, French classicism continued the Baroque's conception of grandeur in the portrayal of noble subjects, especially those from classical antiquity.

DUTCH REALISM A brilliant flowering of Dutch painting paralleled the supremacy of Dutch commerce in the seventeenth century. Wealthy patricians and burghers of Dutch urban society commissioned works of art for their guild halls, town halls, and private dwellings. The subject matter of many Dutch paintings reflected the interests of this burgher society: portraits of themselves, group portraits of their military companies and guilds, landscapes, seascapes, genre scenes, still lives, and the interiors of their residences. Neither classical nor Baroque, Dutch painters were primarily interested in the realistic portrayal of secular everyday life.

This interest in painting scenes of everyday life is evident in the work of Judith Leyster (LESS-tur) (ca. 1609–1660), who established her own independent painting career, a remarkable occurrence in seventeenth-century Europe. Leyster became the first female member of the painting Guild of Saint Luke in Haarlem, which enabled her to set up her own workshop and take on three male pupils. Musicians playing their instruments, women sewing, children laughing while playing games, and actors performing all form the subject matter of Leyster's paintings of everyday Dutch life.

© National Gallery of Art, Washington, DC/Alamy Stock Photo

Judith Leyster, *Self-Portrait*. Although Judith Leyster was a well-known artist to her Dutch contemporaries, her fame diminished soon after her death. In the late nineteenth century, a Dutch art historian rediscovered her work. In Leyster's *Self-Portrait*, painted in 1635, she is seen pausing in her work painting one of the scenes of daily life that made her such a popular artist in her own day.

Alinari/Art Resource, NY

Artemisia Gentileschi, *Judith Beheading Holofernes*. Artemisia Gentileschi painted a series of pictures portraying scenes from the lives of courageous Old Testament women. In this painting, a determined Judith, armed with her victim's sword, struggles to saw off the head of Holofernes. Gentileschi realistically and dramatically shows the gruesome nature of Judith's act.

The finest product of the golden age of Dutch painting was Rembrandt van Rijn (REM-brant vahn RYN) (1606–1669). During his early career, Rembrandt painted opulent portraits and grandiose scenes that were often quite colorful. He was prolific and successful, but he turned away from materialistic success to follow his own artistic path; in the process, he lost public support and died bankrupt.

Although Rembrandt shared the Dutch predilection for realistic portraits, he became more introspective as he grew older. He refused to follow his contemporaries, whose pictures were largely secular; half of his own paintings depicted scenes from biblical tales. Since the Protestant tradition of hostility to religious pictures had discouraged artistic expression, Rembrandt stands out as the one great Protestant painter of the seventeenth century.

A Wondrous Age of Theater

In England and Spain, writing reached new heights between 1580 and 1640. All of these impressive new works were written in the vernacular. Except for academic fields, such as theology, philosophy, jurisprudence, and the sciences, Latin was no longer

DEA Picture Library/Getty Images

Rembrandt van Rijn, *The Night Watch*. The Dutch enjoyed a golden age of painting during the seventeenth century. The burghers and patricians of Dutch urban society commissioned works of art, and these quite naturally reflected the burghers' interests. In his painting *The Night Watch*, Rembrandt portrays the two leaders and sixteen members of a civic militia preparing for a parade in the city of Amsterdam.

a universal literary language. The greatest age of English literature is often called the Elizabethan era because much of the English cultural flowering of the late sixteenth and early seventeenth centuries occurred during the reign of Queen Elizabeth I. Elizabethan literature exhibits the exuberance and pride associated with England's international exploits at the time. Of all the forms of Elizabethan literature, none expressed the energy and intellectual versatility of the era better than drama. And of all the dramatists, none is more famous than William Shakespeare (1564–1616).

WILLIAM SHAKESPEARE Shakespeare was the son of a prosperous glovemaker from Stratford-upon-Avon. When he appeared in London in 1592, Elizabethans were already addicted to the stage. In Greater London, as many as six theaters were open six afternoons a week. London theaters ranged from the Globe, which was a circular unroofed structure holding three thousand spectators, to the Blackfriars, which was roofed and held only five hundred. In the former, an admission charge of a penny or two enabled even the lower classes to attend; the higher prices in the latter ensured an audience of the well-to-do. Elizabethan audiences varied greatly, putting pressure on playwrights to write works that pleased nobles, lawyers, merchants, and even vagabonds.

William Shakespeare was a "complete man of the theater." Although best known for writing plays, he was also an actor and shareholder in the chief company of the time, the Lord Chamberlain's Company, which played in theaters as diverse as the Globe and the Blackfriars. Shakespeare has long been recognized as a universal genius. A master of the English language, he was instrumental in codifying a language that was still in transition. His technical proficiency, however, was matched by an incredible insight into human psychology. In tragedies as well as comedies, Shakespeare exhibited a remarkable understanding of the human condition (see the box on p. 468).

SPAIN'S GOLDEN CENTURY The theater was also one of the most creative forms of expression during Spain's golden century. As in England, actors' companies ran the first professional

WILLIAM SHAKESPEARE: IN PRAISE OF ENGLAND

WILLIAM SHAKESPEARE IS ONE OF THE MOST famous playwrights of the Western world. He was a universal genius, outclassing all others in his psychological insights, depth of characterization, imaginative skills, and versatility. His historical plays reflected the patriotic enthusiasm of the English in the Elizabethan era, as this excerpt from *Richard II* illustrates.

William Shakespeare, *Richard II*

This royal throne of kings, this sceptered isle,
This earth of majesty, this seat of Mars,
This other Eden, demi-Paradise,
This fortress built by Nature for herself
Against infection and the hand of war,
This happy breed of men, this little world,
This precious stone set in the silver sea,
Which serves it in the office of a wall
Or as a moat defensive to a house
Against the envy of less happier lands—
This blessed plot, this earth, this realm, this England,
This nurse, this teeming womb of royal kings,
Feared by their breed and famous by their birth,
Renowned for their deeds as far from home,
For Christian service and true chivalry,
As is the sepulcher in stubborn Jewry [the Holy Sepulcher in Jerusalem]
Of the world's ransom, blessed Mary's Son—
This land of such dear souls, this dear dear land,
Dear for her reputation through the world,
Is now leased out, I die pronouncing it,
Like a tenement or pelting farm.
England, bound in with the triumphant sea,
Whose rocky shore beats back the envious siege
Of watery Neptune, is now bound in with shame,
With inky blots and rotten parchment bonds.
That England, what was wont to conquer others,
Hath made a shameful conquest of itself.
Ah, would the scandal vanish with my life,
How happy then were my ensuing death!

Q *Why is William Shakespeare aptly described as not merely a playwright, but a "complete man of the theater"? Which countries might Shakespeare have meant by the phrase "the envy of less happier lands"?*

Source: G. B. Harrison, ed. *Shakespeare, The Complete Works* (New York: Harcourt Brace & World, 1952).

theaters, which were established in Seville and Madrid in the 1570s. Soon a public playhouse could be found in every large town, including Mexico City in the New World. Touring companies brought the latest Spanish plays to all parts of the Spanish Empire.

Beginning in the 1580s, Lope de Vega (LOH-pay day VAY-guh) (1562–1635) set the agenda for playwrights. Like Shakespeare, he was from a middle-class background. He was an incredibly prolific writer; almost one-third of his fifteen hundred plays survive, which have been characterized as witty, charming, action packed, and realistic. Lope de Vega made no apologies for the fact that he wrote his plays to please his audiences. In a treatise on drama written in 1609, he stated that the foremost duty of the playwright was to satisfy public demand. Shakespeare undoubtedly believed the same thing, since his livelihood depended on public approval, but Lope de Vega was considerably more cynical about it: he remarked that if anyone thought he had written his plays for fame, "undeceive him and tell him that I wrote them for money."

FRENCH DRAMA As the great age of theater in England and Spain was drawing to a close around 1630, a new dramatic era began to dawn in France that lasted into the 1680s. Unlike Shakespeare in England and Lope de Vega in Spain, French playwrights wrote more for an elite audience and were forced to depend on royal patronage. Louis XIV used theater as he did art and architecture—to attract attention to his monarchy.

French dramatists cultivated a style that emphasized the clever, polished, and correct over the emotional and imaginative. Many of the French works of the period derived both their themes and their plots from classical Greek and Roman sources, especially evident in the works of Jean-Baptiste Racine (ZHAHNH-bah-TEEST ra-SEEN) (1639–1699). In *Phèdre*, which has been called his best play, Racine followed closely the plot of *Hippolytus* by the Greek tragedian Euripides. Like the ancient tragedians, Racine, who perfected the French neoclassical tragic style, focused on conflicts, such as between love and honor or inclination and duty, that characterized and revealed the tragic dimensions of life.

Jean-Baptiste Molière (ZHAHNH-bah-TEEST mohl-YAYR) (1622–1673) enjoyed the favor of the French court and benefited from the patronage of King Louis XIV. Molière wrote, produced, and acted in a series of comedies that often satirized the religious and social world of his time. In *Tartuffe*, he ridiculed religious hypocrisy. His satires, however, sometimes got him into trouble. The Paris clergy did not find *Tartuffe* funny and had it banned for five years. Only the protection of the king saved Molière from more severe harassment.

To many historians, the seventeenth century has assumed extraordinary proportions. The divisive effects of the Reformation had been assimilated and the concept of a united Christendom, held as an ideal since the Middle Ages, had been irrevocably destroyed by the religious wars, making possible the emergence of a system of nation-states in which power politics took on an increasing significance. The growth of political thought focusing on the secular origins of state power reflected the changes that were going on in seventeenth-century society.

Within those states, there slowly emerged some of the machinery that made possible a growing centralization of power. In those states called absolutist, strong monarchs with the assistance of their aristocracies took the lead in providing the leadership for greater centralization. In this so-called age of absolutism, Louis XIV, the Sun King of France, was the model for other rulers. His palace of Versailles, where the nobles were entertained and controlled by ceremony and etiquette, symbolized his authority. Louis revoked his grandfather's Edict of Nantes, and he fought four costly wars, mainly to acquire lands on France's eastern borders. Strong monarchy also prevailed in central and eastern Europe, where three new powers made their appearance: Prussia, Austria, and Russia. Peter the Great attempted to westernize Russia, especially militarily, and built Saint Petersburg, a new capital city, as his window on the west.

But not all European states followed the pattern of absolute monarchy. Especially important were developments in England, where a series of struggles between king and Parliament took place in the seventeenth century. The conflict between the Stuart kings, who were advocates of divine-right monarchy, and Parliament led to civil war and the creation of a republic and then a military dictatorship under Oliver Cromwell. After his death, the Stuart monarchy was restored, but a new conflict led to the overthrow of James II and the establishment of a new order. The landed aristocracy gained power at the expense of the monarchs, thus laying the foundations for a constitutional government in which Parliament provided the focus for the institutions of centralized power. In all the major European states, a growing concern for power and dynamic expansion led to larger armies and greater conflict. War remained an endemic feature of Western civilization.

But the search for order and harmony continued, evident in art and literature. At the same time, religious preoccupations and values were losing ground to secular considerations. The seventeenth century was a period of transition toward the more secular spirit that has characterized modern Western civilization to the present. No stronger foundation for this spirit could be found than in the new view of the universe that was ushered in by the Scientific Revolution of the seventeenth century, and it is to that story that we turn in the next chapter.

CHAPTER TIMELINE

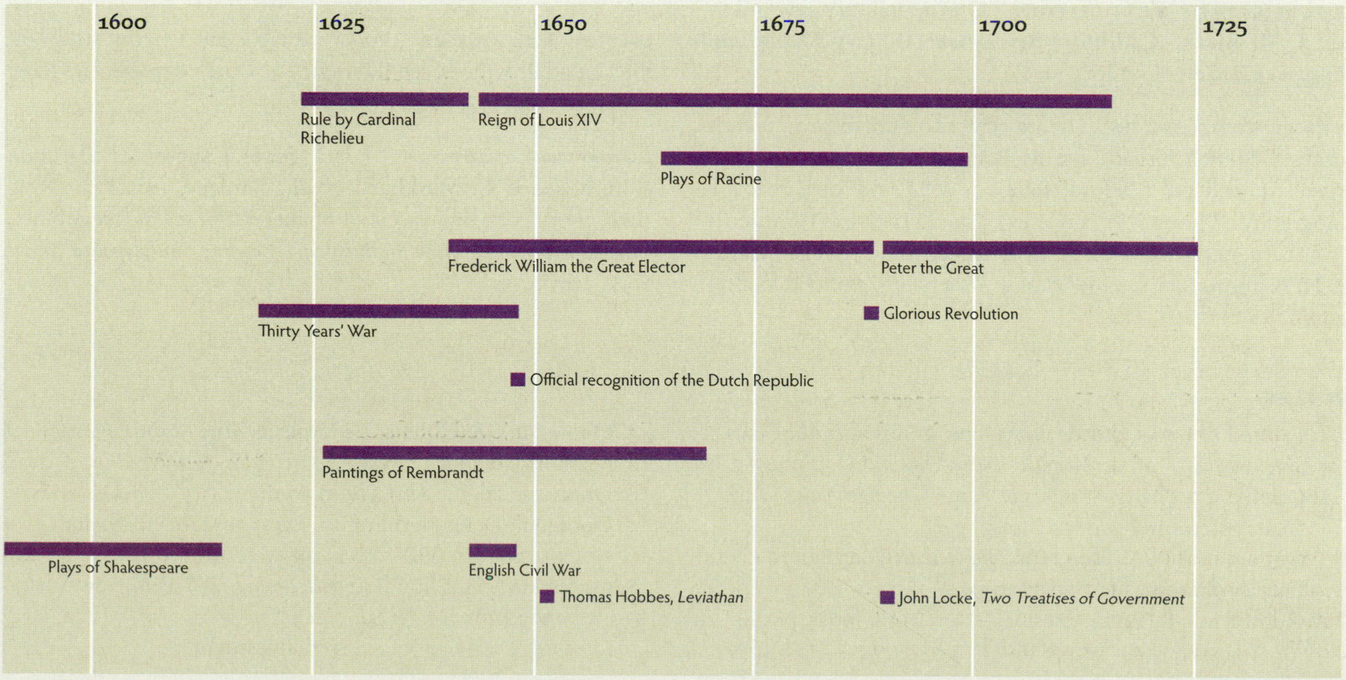

CHAPTER REVIEW

Upon Reflection

Q What does the witchcraft craze tell us about European society in the sixteenth and seventeenth centuries?

Q What did Louis XIV hope to accomplish in his domestic and foreign policies? To what extent did he succeed?

Q What role did the nobility play in Poland and England?

Key Terms

absolutism (p. 440)
divine-right monarchy (p. 440)
intendants (p. 441)
parlements (p. 443)
boyars (p. 450)
procurator (p. 450)
Janissaries (p. 454)
gentry (p. 458)
Mannerism (p. 464)
Baroque (p. 464)

Suggestions for Further Reading

GENERAL WORKS For general works on the seventeenth century, see **T. Munck, *Seventeenth-Century Europe, 1598–1700*,** 2nd ed. (London, 2005); **Q. Deakin, *Expansion, War, and Rebellion, 1598–1661*** (Cambridge, 2000); and **J. Bergin, *Seventeenth-Century Europe, 1598–1715*** (Oxford, 2001).

WITCHCRAFT CRAZE The story of the witchcraft frenzy can be examined in **R. Briggs, *Witches and Neighbors: The Social and Cultural Context of European Witchcraft*,** 2nd ed. (Oxford, 2002), **L. Roper, *Witch Craze: Terror and Fantasy in Baroque Germany*** (New Haven, Conn., 2006).

THIRTY YEARS' WAR The fundamental study of the Thirty Years' War is **P. H. Wilson, *The Thirty Years War: Europe's Tragedy*** (Cambridge, Mass., 2009). For a brief study, see **R. Bonney, *The Thirty Years' War, 1618–1648*** (Oxford, 2002).

THE MILITARY REVOLUTION On the military revolution, see **J. M. Black, *A Military Revolution? Military Change and European Society*** (London, 1996).

FRANCE AND SPAIN For a succinct account of seventeenth-century French history, see **R. Briggs, *Early Modern France, 1560–1715*,** 2nd ed. (Oxford, 1998). A solid and very readable biography of Louis XIV is **A. Levi, *Louis XIV*** (New York, 2004). A good general work on seventeenth-century Spanish history is **H. Kamen, *Spain, 1469–1714: A Society of Conflict*** (London, 2014).

CENTRAL AND EASTERN EUROPE On the German states, see **P. H. Wilson, *The Holy Roman Empire, 1495–1806*,** 2nd ed. (New York, 2011). On the creation of Austria, see **P. S. Fichtner,** *The Habsburg Monarchy, 1490–1848* (New York, 2003). On Austria and Prussia, see **P. H. Wilson, *Absolutism in Central Europe*** (New York, 2000).

RUSSIA On *Peter the Great*, see **P. Bushkovitz,** *Peter the Great* (Oxford, 2001).

ENGLISH REVOLUTIONS Good general works on the period of the English Revolutions include **M. A. Kishlansky, *A Monarchy Transformed*** (London, 1997), and **D. Purkiss, *The English Civil War*** (New York, 2006). On Oliver Cromwell, see **P. Gaunt, M. Weems,** and **B. Wallis, *Oliver Cromwell*** (New York, 2004), and **P. Little, *Oliver Cromwell: New Perspectives*** (New York, 2008).

UNITED PROVINCES For a valuable but lengthy study on the United Provinces, see **J. Israel, *The Dutch Republic: Its Rise, Greatness, and Fall*** (New York, 1998).

EUROPEAN CULTURE For a general survey of Baroque culture, see **F. C. Marchetti et al., *Baroque, 1600–1770*** (New York, 2005). For a biography of Shakespeare, see **S. Greenblatt, *Will in the World: How Shakespeare Became Shakespeare*** (New York, 2005).

Notes

1. Quoted in Louis, duc de Saint-Simon, *Versailles, the Court and Louis XIV*, ed. L. Norton (New York, 1958), pp. 247–248.
2. Quoted in J. Klaits, *Servants of Satan: The Age of the Witch Hunts* (Bloomington, Ind., 1985), p. 68.
3. Quoted in P. H. Wilson, *The Thirty Years War: Europe's Tragedy* (Cambridge, Mass., 2009), p. 783.
4. Quoted in J. B. Wolf, *Louis XIV* (New York, 1968), p. 134.
5. Quoted in J. B. Collins, *The State in Early Modern France* (Cambridge, 1995), p. 130.
6. Quoted in Wolf, *Louis XIV*, p. 618.
7. Quoted in D. H. Pennington, *Europe in the Seventeenth Century*, 2nd ed. (New York, 1989), p. 494.
8. Quoted in J. H. Elliot, *Imperial Spain, 1469–1716* (New York, 1963), p. 306.

9. Quoted in B. H. Sumner, *Peter the Great and the Emergence of Russia* (New York, 1962), p. 122.
10. Quoted in the account of Peter by an eighteenth-century French writer in J. H. Robinson, *Readings in European History*, vol. 2 (Boston, 1906), p. 311.
11. Quoted in S. Schama, *A History of Britain*, vol. 2: *The Wars of the British, 1603–1776* (New York, 2001), pp. 182, 185.
12. T. Carlyle, *Oliver Cromwell's Letters and Speeches: with Elucidations*, vol. II, (London: Chapman & Hall, 1893), p. 250.

CHAPTER

16

TOWARD A NEW HEAVEN AND A NEW EARTH: THE SCIENTIFIC REVOLUTION AND THE EMERGENCE OF MODERN SCIENCE

Erich Lessing/Art Resource, NY

A nineteenth-century painting of Galileo before the Holy Office in the Vatican in 1633

CHAPTER OUTLINE AND FOCUS QUESTIONS

Background to the Scientific Revolution

Q What developments during the Middle Ages and the Renaissance contributed to the Scientific Revolution of the seventeenth century?

Toward a New Heaven: A Revolution in Astronomy

Q What did Copernicus, Kepler, Galileo, and Newton contribute to a new vision of the universe, and how did it differ from the Ptolemaic conception of the universe?

Advances in Medicine and Chemistry

Q What did Paracelsus, Vesalius, and Harvey contribute to a scientific view of medicine?

Women in the Origins of Modern Science

Q What role did women play in the Scientific Revolution?

Toward a New Earth: Descartes, Rationalism, and a New View of Humankind

Q Why is Descartes considered the "founder of modern rationalism"?

The Scientific Method and the Spread of Scientific Knowledge

Q How were the ideas of the Scientific Revolution spread, and what impact did they have on society and religion?

Critical Thinking

Q *In what ways were the intellectual, political, social, and religious developments of the seventeenth century related?*

Connections to Today

Q *What scientific discoveries of the twentieth and twenty-first centuries have had as great an impact on society as those of the Scientific Revolution?*

IN ADDITION TO the political, economic, social, and international crises of the seventeenth century, we need to add an intellectual one. The Scientific Revolution questioned and ultimately challenged conceptions and beliefs about the nature of the external world and reality that had crystallized into a rather strict orthodoxy by the Later Middle Ages. Derived from the works of ancient Greeks and Romans and grounded in Christian thought, the medieval worldview had become formidable. But the breakdown of Christian unity during the Reformation and the subsequent religious wars had created an environment in which Europeans became more comfortable with challenging both the ecclesiastical and the political realms. Should it surprise us that a challenge to intellectual authority soon followed?

The Scientific Revolution taught Europeans to view the universe and their place in it in a new way. The shift from an earth-centered to a sun-centered cosmos had an emotional as well as an intellectual effect on the people who understood it. Thus, the Scientific Revolution, popularized in the eighteenth-century Enlightenment, stands as the major force in the transition to the largely secular, rational, and materialistic perspective that has defined the modern Western mentality since its full acceptance in the nineteenth and twentieth centuries.

The transition to a new worldview, however, was far from easy. In the seventeenth century, the Italian scientist Galileo Galilei (gal-li-LAY-oh GAL-li-lay), an outspoken advocate of the new worldview, found that his ideas were strongly opposed by the authorities of the Catholic Church. Galileo's position was clear: "I hold the sun to be situated motionless in the center of the revolution of the celestial bodies, while the earth rotates on its axis and revolves about the sun." Moreover, "nothing physical that sense-experience sets before our eyes . . . ought to be called in question (much less condemned) upon the testimony of Biblical passages."[1] But the church had a different view, and in 1633, Galileo, now sixty-eight and in ill health, was called before the dreaded Inquisition in Rome. He was kept waiting for two months before he was tried and found guilty of heresy and disobedience. Completely shattered by the experience, he denounced his errors: "I curse and detest the said errors and heresies contrary to the Holy Church." Legend holds that when he left the trial room, Galileo muttered to himself: "And yet it does move!" Galileo had been silenced, but his writings remained, and they spread throughout Europe. The Inquisition had failed to stop the new ideas of the Scientific Revolution.

In one sense, the Scientific Revolution was not a revolution. It was not characterized by the explosive change and rapid overthrow of traditional authority that we normally associate with the word *revolution*. The Scientific Revolution did overturn centuries of authority, but only in a gradual and piecemeal fashion. Nevertheless, its results were truly revolutionary. The Scientific Revolution was a key factor in setting Western civilization along its modern secular and materialistic path.

Background to the Scientific Revolution

FOCUS QUESTION: What developments during the Middle Ages and the Renaissance contributed to the Scientific Revolution of the seventeenth century?

To say that the **Scientific Revolution** brought about a dissolution of the medieval worldview is not to say that the Middle Ages was a period of scientific ignorance. Many educated Europeans took an intense interest in the world around them since it was, after all, "God's handiwork" and therefore an appropriate subject for study. Late medieval scholastic philosophers had advanced mathematical and physical thinking in many ways, but the subjection of these thinkers to a strict theological framework and their unquestioning reliance on a few ancient authorities, especially Aristotle and Galen, limited where they could go. Many "natural philosophers," as medieval scientists were called, preferred refined logical analysis to systematic observations of the natural world. A number of changes and advances in the fifteenth and sixteenth centuries may have played a major role in helping "natural philosophers" abandon their old views and develop new ones.

Ancient Authors and Renaissance Artists

Whereas medieval scholars had made use of Aristotle, Galen, and Ptolemy in Latin translations to develop many of their positions in the fields of physics, medicine, and astronomy, the Renaissance humanists had mastered Greek and made available new works of Galen, Ptolemy, and Archimedes as well as Plato and the pre-Socratics. These writings made it apparent that other thinkers in antiquity had contradicted the unquestioned authorities of the Middle Ages, Aristotle and Galen. The desire to discover which school of thought was correct stimulated new scientific work that sometimes led to a complete rejection of the classical authorities.

Renaissance artists have also been credited with making an impact on scientific study. Their desire to imitate nature led them to a close observation of nature. Their accurate renderings of rocks, plants, animals, and human anatomy established new standards for the study of natural phenomena. At the same time, the "scientific" study of the problems of perspective and correct anatomical proportions led to new insights. "No painter," one Renaissance artist declared, "can paint well without a thorough knowledge of geometry."[2] Renaissance artists were frequently called on to be practicing mathematicians as well. Leonardo da Vinci devised "war machines," and Albrecht Dürer made designs for the fortifications of cities.

Technological Innovations and Mathematics

Technical problems such as accurately calculating the tonnage of ships also stimulated scientific activity because they required careful observation and precise measurements. The discovery of the New World and increased trading furthered the need for improved navigational and mathematical knowledge. The relationship between technology and the Scientific Revolution was not a simple one, however, for many technological experts did not believe in abstract or academic learning. Moreover, the early institutions that supported the academic study of technology, such as Spain's Casa de Contractación, or House of Trade, regarded their technological discoveries as state secrets and kept them hidden from the public. Indeed, many of the technical innovations of the Middle Ages and the Renaissance were accomplished outside the universities by people who emphasized practical rather than theoretical knowledge. In any case, the invention of new instruments and machines, such as the telescope and the microscope, often made new scientific discoveries possible. The printing press had an indirect but crucial role in spreading innovative ideas quickly and easily.

Mathematics, so fundamental to the scientific achievements of the sixteenth and seventeenth centuries, was promoted in the Renaissance by the rediscovery of the works of ancient mathematicians and the influence of Plato, who had emphasized the importance of mathematics in explaining the universe. Applauded as the key to navigation, military science, and geography, mathematics was also regarded as the key to understanding the nature of things. According to Leonardo da Vinci, since God eternally geometrizes, nature is inherently mathematical: "Proportion is not only found in numbers and measurements but also in sounds, weights, times, positions, and in whatsoever power there may be."[3] Moreover, mathematical reasoning was seen as promoting a degree of certainty that was otherwise impossible. In the words of Leonardo da Vinci: "There is no certainty where one can neither apply any of the mathematical sciences nor any of those which are based upon the mathematical sciences."[4] Copernicus, Kepler, Galileo, and Newton were all great mathematicians who believed that the secrets of nature were written in the language of mathematics.

Renaissance Magic

Another factor in the origins of the Scientific Revolution may have been magic. Renaissance magic was the preserve of an intellectual elite from all of Europe. By the end of the sixteenth century, Hermetic magic had become fused with alchemical thought into a single intellectual framework. This tradition believed that the world was a living embodiment of divinity. Humans, who it was believed also had that spark of divinity within, could use magic, especially mathematical magic, to understand and dominate the world of nature or employ the powers of nature for beneficial purposes. Hermetic magicians, who experimented with natural objects, were considered to be practitioners of idolatry because of their practice of distorting nature. However, it was their engagement with experimentation that perhaps contributed to the later practice of "experimental philosophy" or empirical science based upon observation. Was it Hermeticism, then, that inaugurated the shift in consciousness that made the Scientific Revolution possible, since the desire to control and dominate the natural world was a crucial motivating force in the Scientific Revolution? One scholar has argued:

> It is a movement of the will which really originates an intellectual movement. A new center of interest arises, surrounded by emotional excitement; the mind turns where the will has directed it and new attitudes, new discoveries follow. Behind the emergence of modern science there was a new direction of the will toward the world, its marvels, and mysterious workings, a new longing and determination to understand those workings and to operate with them.[5]

"This time," the author continues, "the return to the occult [Hermetic tradition] stimulates the genuine science."[6] Scholars debate the issue, but histories of the Scientific Revolution frequently overlook the fact that the great names we associate with the revolution in cosmology—Copernicus, Kepler, Galileo, and Newton—all had a serious interest in Hermetic ideas and the fields of astrology and alchemy. The mention of these names also reminds us of one final consideration in the origins of the Scientific Revolution: it largely resulted from the work of a handful of great intellectuals.

Toward a New Heaven: A Revolution in Astronomy

FOCUS QUESTION: What did Copernicus, Kepler, Galileo, and Newton contribute to a new vision of the universe, and how did it differ from the Ptolemaic conception of the universe?

The greatest achievements in the Scientific Revolution of the sixteenth and seventeenth centuries came in the fields most dominated by the ideas of the Greeks—astronomy, mechanics, and medicine. The cosmological views of the Later Middle Ages had been built on a synthesis of the ideas of Aristotle, Ptolemy (the greatest astronomer of antiquity, who lived in the second century C.E.), and Christian theology. In the resulting Ptolemaic (tahl-uh-MAY-ik) or **geocentric conception**, the

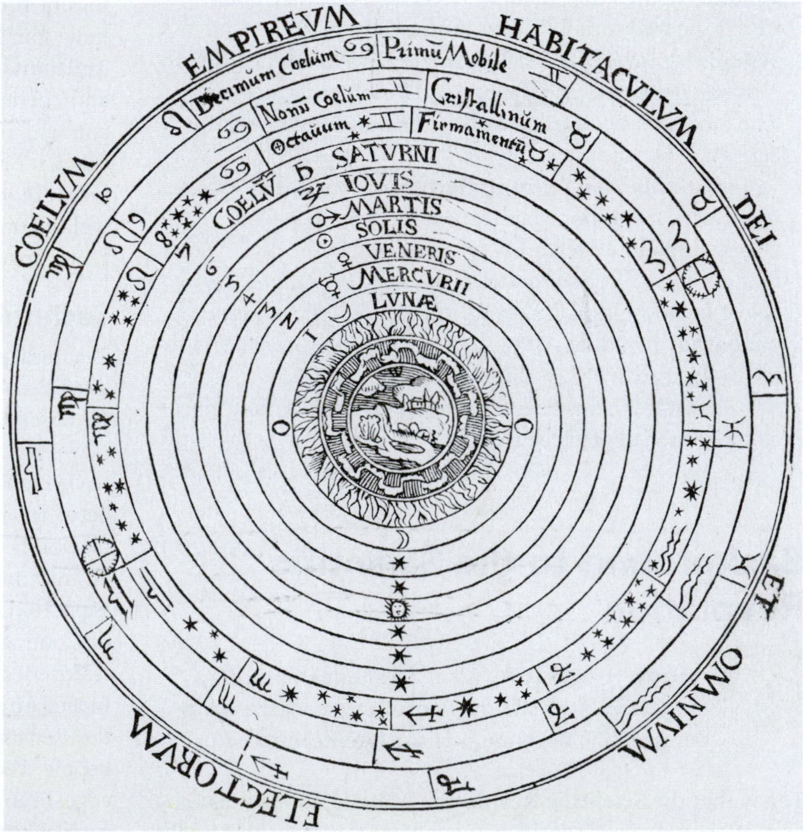

Image Select/Art Resource, NY

Medieval Conception of the Universe. As this sixteenth-century illustration shows, the medieval cosmological view placed the earth at the center of the universe, surrounded by a series of concentric spheres. The earth was imperfect and constantly changing, whereas the heavenly bodies that surrounded it were perfect and incorruptible. Beyond the tenth and final sphere was heaven, where God and all the saved souls were located. (The circles read from the center outward as follows: 1. Moon, 2. Mercury, 3. Venus, 4. Sun, 5. Mars, 6. Jupiter, 7. Saturn, 8. Firmament (of the Stars), 9. Crystalline Sphere, 10. Prime Mover; and around the outside, Empyrean Heaven—Home of God and All the Elect, that is, saved souls.)

universe was seen as a series of concentric spheres with a fixed or motionless earth at its center. Composed of the material substances of earth, air, fire, and water, the earth was imperfect and constantly changing. The spheres that surrounded the earth were made of a crystalline, transparent substance and moved in circular orbits around the earth. Circular movement, according to Aristotle, was the most "perfect" kind of motion and hence appropriate for the "perfect" heavenly bodies thought to consist of a nonmaterial, incorruptible "quintessence." These heavenly bodies, pure orbs of light, were embedded in the moving, concentric spheres, which in 1500 were believed to number ten. Working outward from the earth, eight spheres contained the moon, Mercury, Venus, the sun, Mars, Jupiter, Saturn, and the fixed stars. The ninth sphere imparted to the eighth sphere of the fixed stars its motion, and the tenth sphere was frequently described as the prime mover that moved itself and imparted motion to the other spheres. Beyond the tenth sphere was the Empyrean Heaven—the location of God and all the saved souls. This Christianized Ptolemaic universe, then, was finite. It had a fixed outer boundary in harmony with Christian thought and expectations. God and the saved souls were at one end of the universe, and humans were at the center. They had been given power over the earth, but their real purpose was to achieve salvation.

This conception of the universe, however, did not satisfy professional astronomers, who wished to ascertain the precise paths of the heavenly bodies across the sky. Finding that their observations did not always correspond to the accepted scheme, astronomers tried to "save appearances" by developing an elaborate system of devices. They proposed, for example, that the planetary bodies traveled on epicycles, concentric spheres within spheres, that would enable the paths of the planets to correspond more precisely to observations while adhering to Aristotle's ideas of circular planetary movement.

Copernicus

Nicolaus Copernicus (nee-koh-LAU-uss kuh-PURR-nuh-kuss) (1473–1543) had studied both mathematics and astronomy first at Krakow in his native Poland and later at the Italian universities of Bologna and Padua. Before he left Italy in 1506, he had become aware of ancient views that contradicted the Ptolemaic, earth-centered conception of the universe. Between 1506 and 1530, he completed the manuscript of his famous book, *On the Revolutions of the Heavenly Spheres*, but his own timidity and fear of ridicule from fellow astronomers kept him from publishing it until May 1543, shortly before his death.

Copernicus was not an accomplished observational astronomer and relied on his predecessors for his data. But he was a mathematician who felt that Ptolemy's geocentric system was too complicated and failed to accord with the observed motions of the heavenly bodies (see the box on p. 476). Copernicus hoped that his **heliocentric** or sun-centered **conception** would offer a simpler and more accurate explanation.

Copernicus argued that the universe consisted of eight spheres with the sun motionless at the center and the sphere of the fixed stars at rest in the eighth sphere. The planets revolved around the sun in the order of Mercury, Venus, the earth, Mars, Jupiter, and Saturn. The moon, however, revolved

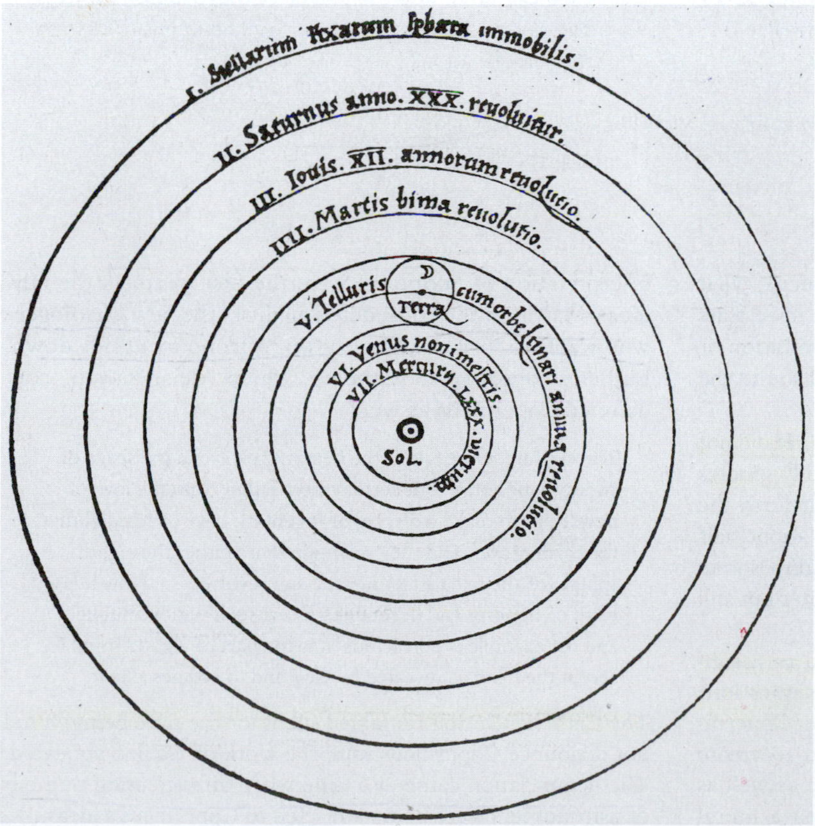

Image Select/Art Resource, NY

The Copernican System. The Copernican system was presented in *On the Revolutions of the Heavenly Spheres*, published shortly before Copernicus's death. As shown in this illustration from the first edition of the book, Copernicus maintained that the sun was the center of the universe and that the planets, including the earth, revolved around it. Moreover, the earth rotated daily on its axis. (The circles read from the inside out as follows: 1. Sun; 2. Mercury, orbit of 80 days; 3. Venus; 4. Earth, with the moon, orbit of one year; 5. Mars, orbit of 2 years; 6. Jupiter, orbit of 12 years; 7. Saturn, orbit of 30 years; 8. Immobile Sphere of the Fixed Stars.)

ON THE REVOLUTIONS OF THE HEAVENLY SPHERES

NICOLAUS COPERNICUS BEGAN A REVOLUTION in astronomy when he argued that the sun and not the earth was at the center of the universe. Expecting controversy and scorn, Copernicus hesitated to publish the work in which he put forth his heliocentric theory. He finally relented, however, and managed to see a copy of it just before he died.

Nicolaus Copernicus, *On the Revolutions of the Heavenly Spheres*

For a long time, then, I reflected on this confusion in the astronomical traditions concerning the derivation of the motions of the universe's spheres. I began to be annoyed that the movements of the world machine, created for our sake by the best and most systematic Artisan of all [God], were not understood with greater certainty by the philosophers, who otherwise examined so precisely the most insignificant trifles of this world. For this reason I undertook the task of rereading the works of all the philosophers which I could obtain to learn whether anyone had ever proposed other motions of the universe's spheres than those expounded by the teachers of astronomy in the schools. And in fact first I found in Cicero that Hicetas supposed the earth to move. Later I also discovered in Plutarch that certain others were of this opinion. I have decided to set his words down here, so that they may be available to everybody:

> *Some think that the earth remains at rest. But Philolaus the Pythagorean believes that, like the sun and moon, it revolves around the fire in an oblique circle. Heraclides of Pontus and Ecphantus the Pythagorean make the earth move, not in a progressive motion, but like a wheel in a rotation from the west to east about its own center.*

Therefore, having obtained the opportunity from these sources, I too began to consider the mobility of the earth. And even though the idea seemed absurd, nevertheless I knew that others before me had been granted the freedom to imagine any circles whatever for the purpose of explaining the heavenly phenomena. Hence I thought that I too would be readily permitted to ascertain whether explanations sounder than those of my predecessors could be found for the revolution of the celestial spheres on the assumption of some motion of the earth.

Having thus assumed the motions which I ascribe to the earth later on in the volume, by long and intense study I finally found that if the motions of the other planets are correlated with the orbiting of the earth, and are computed for the revolution of each planet, not only do their phenomena follow therefrom but also the order and size of all the planets and spheres, and heaven itself is so linked together that in no portion of it can anything be shifted without disrupting the remaining parts and the universe as a whole . . .

Hence I feel no shame in asserting that this whole region engirdled by the moon, and the center of the earth, traverse this grand circle amid the rest of the planets in an annual revolution around the sun. Near the sun is the center of the universe. Moreover, since the sun remains stationary, whatever appears as a motion of the sun is really due rather to the motion of the earth.

Q *What major new ideas did Copernicus discuss in this excerpt? What was the source of these ideas? Why might one say that European astronomers had finally destroyed the Middle Ages?*

Source: Copernicus, in E. Rosen, trans., *The Complete Works* (London: Palgrave Macmillan, 1978).

around the earth. Moreover, according to Copernicus, what appeared to be the movement of the sun and the fixed stars around the earth was really explained by the daily rotation of the earth on its axis and the journey of the earth around the sun each year.

Copernicus, however, was basically conservative. He did not reject Aristotle's principle of the existence of heavenly spheres moving in circular orbits. As a result, when he put forth the calculations to prove his new theory, he retained about half of Ptolemy's epicycles and wound up with a system somewhat simpler than that of the Alexandrian astronomer but still extremely complicated.

Nevertheless, the shift from an earth-centered to a sun-centered system was significant and raised serious questions about Aristotle's astronomy and physics despite Copernicus's own adherence to Aristotle. It also seemed to create uncertainty about the human role in the universe as well as God's location. Protestant reformers, adhering to a literal interpretation of Scripture, were the first to attack the new ideas. Martin Luther thundered against "the new astrologer" who wants to turn the whole art of astronomy upside down. Luther's cohort at Wittenberg, Philip Melanchthon, condemned Copernicus as well:

> The eyes are witness that the heavens revolve in the space of twenty-four hours. But certain men, either from the love of novelty, or to make a display of ingenuity, have concluded that the earth moves, and they maintain that neither the eighth sphere [of the fixed stars] nor the sun revolves. . . . Now it is a want of honesty and decency to assert such notions publicly, and the example is pernicious. It is the part of a good mind to accept the truth as revealed by God and to acquiesce in it.[7]

The Catholic Church remained silent for the time being; it did not denounce Copernicus until the work of Galileo appeared. The denunciation came at a time when an increasing number of astronomers were being attracted to Copernicus's ideas.

Brahe

Copernicus did not have a great impact immediately, but doubts about the Ptolemaic system were growing. Johannes Kepler took the next step in destroying the geocentric conception and supporting the Copernican system. It has been argued, however, that Kepler's work would not have occurred without the material provided by Tycho Brahe (TY-koh BRAH).

A Danish nobleman, Tycho Brahe (1546–1601) was granted possession of an island near Copenhagen by King Frederick II. On it, Brahe built the elaborate Uraniborg Castle, which he outfitted with a library, observatories, and instruments he had designed for more precise astronomical observations. For twenty years, Brahe patiently concentrated on compiling a detailed record of his observations of the positions and movements of the stars and planets, a series of observations described as the most accurate up to that time. This body of data led him to reject the Aristotelian-Ptolemaic system, but at the same time he was unable to accept Copernicus's suggestion that the earth actually moved. Brahe's last years were spent in Prague as imperial mathematician to Emperor Rudolf II, who took a keen interest in astronomy, astrology, and the Hermetic tradition. While he was in Prague, Brahe took on an assistant by the name of Johannes Kepler.

The Art Archive/Art Resource, NY

Tycho Brahe. His work at the Uraniborg observatory provided astronomers with the best data on the position of the celestial bodies. He published his results in *Of More Recent Phenomena of the Ethereal World* in 1588. He is depicted here in a sixteenth-century Dutch oil painting with a silver nose; his own nose was cut off during a duel.

Kepler

Johannes Kepler (yoh-HAHN-us KEP-lur) (1571–1630) had been destined by his parents for a career as a Lutheran minister. While studying theology at the university at Tübingen (TOO-bing-un), however, he fell under the influence of Michael Mästlin (MEST-lin), Germany's best-known astronomer, and spent much time pursuing his real interests—mathematics and astronomy. He abandoned theology and became a teacher of mathematics and astronomy at Graz in Austria.

Kepler's work illustrates well the narrow line that often separated magic and science in the early Scientific Revolution. An avid astrologer, Kepler had a keen interest in Hermetic mathematical magic. In a book written in 1596, he elaborated on his theory that the universe was constructed on the basis of geometric figures, such as the pyramid and the cube. Believing that the harmony of the human soul (a divine attribute) was mirrored in the numerical relationships existing between the planets, he focused much of his attention on discovering the "music of the spheres." Kepler was also a brilliant mathematician and astronomer and, after Brahe's death, succeeded him as imperial mathematician to Rudolf II. There he gained possession of Brahe's detailed astronomical data and, using them, arrived at his three laws of planetary motion. These laws may have confirmed Kepler's interest in the "music of the spheres," but more important, they confirmed Copernicus's heliocentric theory while modifying it in some ways. Above all, they drove another nail into the coffin of the Aristotelian-Ptolemaic system.

Kepler published his first two laws of planetary motion in 1609. Although at Tübingen he had accepted Copernicus's heliocentric ideas, in his first law he rejected Copernicus by showing that the orbits of the planets around the sun were not circular but elliptical, with the sun at one focus of the ellipse rather than at the center. In his second law, he demonstrated that the speed of a planet is greater when it is closer to the sun and decreases as its distance from the sun increases. This proposition destroyed a fundamental Aristotelian tenet that Copernicus had shared—that the motion of the planets was steady and unchanging. Published ten years later, Kepler's third law established that the square of a planet's period of revolution is proportional to the cube of its average distance from the sun. In other words, planets with larger orbits revolve at a slower average velocity than those with smaller orbits.

Kepler's three laws effectively eliminated the idea of uniform circular motion as well as the idea of crystalline spheres revolving in circular orbits. The basic structure of the traditional Ptolemaic system had been disproved, and people had been freed to think in new ways about the actual paths of planets revolving around the sun in elliptical orbits. By the end of Kepler's life, the Ptolemaic system was rapidly losing ground to the new ideas (see the box on p. 478). Important questions remained unanswered, however: What were the planets made of? And how could motion in the universe be explained? It was an Italian scientist who achieved the next important breakthrough to a new cosmology by answering the first question and making important strides toward answering the second.

KEPLER AND THE EMERGING SCIENTIFIC COMMUNITY

THE EXCHANGE OF LETTERS BETWEEN INTELLECTUALS was an important avenue for scientific communication. After receiving a copy of Johannes Kepler's first major work, the Italian Galileo Galilei wrote to Kepler, inaugurating a correspondence between them. This selection contains samples of their letters to each other.

Galileo to Kepler, Padua, August 4, 1597

Your book . . . reached me not days ago but only a few hours ago, and as this Paulus just informed me of his return to Germany, I should think myself indeed ungrateful if I should not express to you my thanks by this letter. I thank you . . . for having deemed me worthy of such a proof of your friendship. . . . So far I have read only the introduction, but have learned from it . . . your intentions and congratulate myself on the good fortune of having found such a man as a companion in the exploration of truth. For it is deplorable that there are so few who seek the truth. . . . But this is not the place to mourn about the misery of our century but to rejoice with you about such beautiful ideas proving the truth. . . . I would certainly dare to approach the public with my ways of thinking if there were more people of your mind. As this is not the case, I shall refrain from doing so. . . . I shall always be at your service. Farewell, and do not neglect to give me further good news of yourself.

Yours in sincere friendship,
Galilaeus Galilaeus
Mathematician at the Academy of Padua

Kepler to Galileo, Graz, October 13, 1597

I received your letter of August 4 on September 1. It was a double pleasure to me. First because I became friends with you, the Italian, and second because of the agreement in which we find ourselves concerning Copernican cosmography. . . .

I would, however, have wished that you who have such a keen insight into everything would choose another way to reach your practical aims. By the strength of your personal example you advise us . . . to go out of the way of general ignorance and warn us against exposing ourselves to the furious attacks of the scholarly crowd. . . . But after the beginning of a tremendous enterprise has been made in our time, and furthered by so many learned mathematicians, and after the statement that the earth moves can no longer be regarded as something new, would it not be better to pull the rolling wagon to its destination with united effort? . . . For it is not only you Italians who do not believe that they move unless they feel it, but we in Germany, too, in no way make ourselves popular with this idea. Yet there are ways in which we protect ourselves against these difficulties. . . . Be of good cheer, Galileo, and appear in public. If I am not mistaken there are only a few among the distinguished mathematicians of Europe who would dissociate themselves from us. So great is the power of truth. If Italy seems less suitable for your publication and if you have to expect difficulties there, perhaps Germany will offer us more freedom. . . . Please let me know, at least privately if you do not want to do so publicly, what you have discovered in favor of Copernicus.

Q *What does the correspondence between Galileo and Kepler reveal about an emerging spirit of scientific inquiry? What other notable achievements must European society have reached even to make this exchange of letters possible? What aspects of European material culture made the work of these scientists easier?*

Source: C. Baumgardt, *Johannes Kepler, Life and Letters* (New York: Philosophical Library, 1951).

Galileo

Galileo Galilei (1564–1642) taught mathematics, first at Pisa and later at Padua, one of the most prestigious universities in Europe. Galileo was the first European to make systematic observations of the heavens by means of a telescope, thereby inaugurating a new age in astronomy. He had heard of a Flemish lens grinder who had created a "spyglass" that magnified objects seen at a distance and soon constructed his own after reading about it. Instead of peering at terrestrial objects, Galileo turned his telescope to the skies and made a remarkable series of discoveries: mountains and craters on the moon, four moons revolving around Jupiter, the phases of Venus, and sunspots. Galileo's observations demolished yet another aspect of the traditional cosmology in that the universe seemed to be composed of material substance similar to that of the earth rather than ethereal or perfect and unchanging substance.

Galileo's revelations, published in *The Starry Messenger* in 1610 (see the box above), stunned his contemporaries and probably did more to make Europeans aware of the new picture of the universe than the mathematical theories of Copernicus and Kepler did. The English ambassador in Venice wrote to the chief minister of King James I in 1610:

> I send herewith unto His Majesty the strangest piece of news . . . that he has ever yet received from any part of the world; which is the annexed book of the Mathematical Professor at Padua [Galileo], who by the help of an optical instrument . . . has discovered four new planets rolling about the sphere of Jupiter. . . . So upon the whole subject he has first overthrown all former astronomy. . . . By the next ship your Lordship shall receive from me one of the above instruments [a telescope], as it is bettered by this man.[8]

THE STARRY MESSENGER

THE ITALIAN GALILEO GALILEI WAS THE FIRST European to use a telescope to make systematic observations of the heavens. His observations, as reported in *The Starry Messenger* in 1610, stunned European intellectuals by revealing that the celestial bodies were not perfect and immutable but composed of material substance similar to that of the earth. In this selection, Galileo describes how he devised a telescope and what he saw with it.

Galileo Galilei, *The Starry Messenger*

About ten months ago a report reached my ears that a Dutchman had constructed a telescope, by the aid of which visible objects, although at a great distance from the eye of the observer, were distinctly seen as if near; and some proofs of its most wonderful performances were reported, which some gave credence to, but others contradicted. A few days after, I received confirmation of the report in a letter written from Paris by a noble Frenchman, Jacques Badovere, which finally determined me to give myself up to inquire into the principle of the telescope, and then to consider the means by which I might compass the invention of a similar instrument, which a little while after I succeeded in doing, through deep study of the theory of Refraction; and I prepared a tube, at first of lead, in the ends of which I fitted two glass lenses, both plane on one side, but on the other side one spherically convex, and the other concave. Then bringing my eye to the concave lens I saw objects satisfactorily large and near, for they appeared one-third of the distance off and nine times larger than when they are seen with the natural eye alone. I shortly afterwards constructed another telescope with more nicety, which magnified objects more than sixty times. At length, by sparing neither labour nor expense, I succeeded in constructing for myself an instrument so superior that objects seen through it appear magnified nearly a thousand times, and more than thirty times nearer than if viewed by the natural powers of sight alone.

It would be altogether a waste of time to enumerate the number and importance of the benefits which this instrument may be expected to confer, when used by land or sea. But without paying attention to its use for terrestrial objects, I betook myself to observations of the heavenly bodies; and first of all, I viewed the Moon as near as if it was scarcely two semi-diameters of the Earth distant. After the Moon, I frequently observed other heavenly bodies, both fixed stars and planets, with incredible delight; and, when I saw their very great number, I began to consider about a method by which I might be able to measure their distances apart. . . .

Now let me review the observations made by me during the two months just past, again inviting the attention of all who are eager for true philosophy to the beginnings which led to the sight of the most important phenomena.

Let me speak first of the surface of the Moon, which is turned towards us. For the sake of being understood more easily, I distinguish two parts in it, which I call respectively the brighter and the darker. The brighter part seems to surround and to pervade the whole hemisphere; but the darker part discolors, like a sort of cloud, discolors the Moon's surface and makes it appear covered with spots. . . . These spots have never been observed by any one before me; and from my observations of them, often repeated, I have been led to the opinion which I have expressed, namely that I feel sure that the surface of the Moon is not perfectly smooth, free from inequalities, and exactly spherical, as a large school of philosophers considers with regard to the Moon and the other heavenly bodies, but that, on the contrary, it is full of inequalities, uneven, full of hollows and protuberances, just like the surface of the Earth itself, which is varied everywhere by lofty mountains and deep valleys.

Q *What was the significance of Galileo's invention? What impressions did he receive of the moon? Why were his visual discoveries so stunning, and how did he go about publicizing them?*

Source: E. S. Carlo, *The Sidereal Messenger of Galileo Galilei: And a Part of the Preface to Kepler's Dioptrics Containing the Original Account of Galileo's Astronomical Discoveries* (London: Rivingtons, 1880), pp. 10–11, 14–15.

During a trip to Rome, scholars received Galileo as a conquering hero. Grand Duke Cosimo II of Florence offered him a new position as his court mathematician, which Galileo readily accepted. But even in the midst of his newfound acclaim, Galileo found himself increasingly suspect by the authorities of the Catholic Church.

GALILEO AND THE INQUISITION In *The Starry Messenger*, Galileo had revealed himself as a firm proponent of Copernicus's heliocentric system. The Roman Inquisition (or Holy Office) of the Catholic Church condemned Copernicanism and ordered Galileo to reject the Copernican thesis. As one cardinal commented, "The intention of the Holy Spirit is to teach us not how the heavens go, but how to go to heaven." The report of the Inquisition ran:

> That the doctrine that the sun was the center of the world and immovable was false and absurd, formally heretical and contrary to Scripture, whereas the doctrine that the earth was not the center of the world but moved, and has further a daily motion, was philosophically false and absurd and theologically at least erroneous.[9]

Galileo was told, however, that he could continue to discuss Copernicanism as long as he maintained that it was not a fact but a mathematical supposition. It is apparent from the Inquisition's response that the church attacked the Copernican system

SuperStock

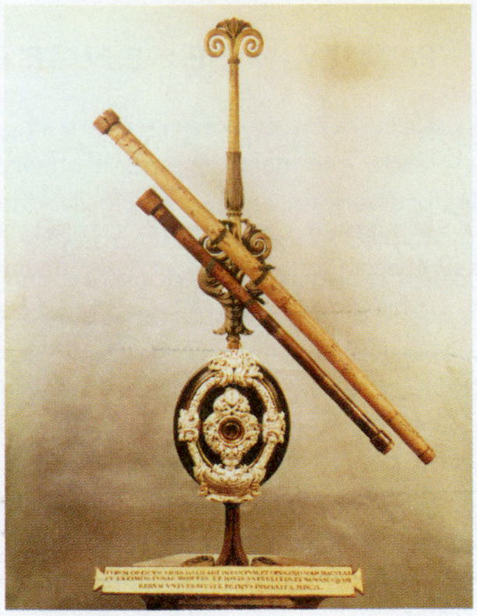

Scala/Art Resource, NY

The Telescope. The invention of the telescope enabled Europeans to inaugurate a new age in astronomy. Shown here is Johannes Hevelius (huh-VAY-lee-uss), an eminent German-Polish astrologer (1611–1697), making an observation with his telescope. Hevelius's observations were highly regarded. He located his telescope on the roof of his own house, and by the 1660s, his celestial observatory was considered one of the best in Europe. The photograph above shows Galileo's original telescope, built in 1609.

because it threatened not only Scripture but also an entire conception of the universe (see "Opposing Viewpoints" on p. 481). The heavens were no longer a spiritual world but a world of matter. Humans were no longer at the center, and God was no longer in a specific place. The new system raised such uncertainties that it seemed prudent simply to condemn it.

Galileo, however, never really accepted his condemnation. In 1632, he published his most famous work, *Dialogue on the Two Chief World Systems: Ptolemaic and Copernican*. Unlike most scholarly treatises, it was written in Italian rather than Latin, making it more widely available to the public, which no doubt alarmed the church authorities. The work took the form of a dialogue among Simplicio, a congenial but somewhat stupid supporter of Aristotle and Ptolemy; Sagredo, an open-minded layman; and Salviati, a proponent of Copernicus's ideas. There is no question who wins the argument, and the *Dialogue* was quickly perceived as a defense of the Copernican system. Galileo was dragged once more before the Inquisition in 1633, found guilty of teaching the condemned Copernican system, and forced to recant his errors. Placed under house arrest on his estate near Florence, he spent the remaining eight years of his life studying mechanics, a field in which he made significant contributions.

GALILEO AND THE PROBLEM OF MOTION One of the problems that fell under the heading of mechanics was the principle of motion. The Aristotelian conception, which dominated the late medieval world, held that an object remained at rest unless a force was applied against it. If a force was constantly exerted, then the object moved at a constant rate, but if it was removed, then the object stopped. This conception encountered some difficulties, especially with a projectile thrown out of a cannon. Late medieval theorists had solved this problem by arguing that the rush of air behind the projectile kept it in motion. The Aristotelian principle of motion also raised problems in the new Copernican system. In the Ptolemaic system, the concentric spheres surrounding the earth were weightless, but in the Copernican system, if a constant force had to be applied to objects to cause movement, then what power or force kept the heavy earth and other planets in motion?

Galileo made two contributions to the problem of motion. First, he demonstrated by experiments that if a uniform force was applied to an object, it would move at an accelerated speed rather than a constant speed. Moreover, Galileo discovered the principle of inertia when he argued that a body in motion continues in motion forever unless deflected by an external force. Thus, a state of uniform motion is just as natural as a state of rest. Before Galileo, natural philosophers had tried to explain motion; now their task was to explain changes in motion.

The condemnation of Galileo by the Inquisition, coming at a time of economic decline, seriously undermined further scientific work in Italy, which had been at the forefront of scientific innovation. Leadership in science now passed to the northern countries, especially England, France, and the Dutch Netherlands. By the 1630s and 1640s, no reasonable

OPPOSING VIEWPOINTS

A New Heaven? Faith Versus Reason

IN 1614, GALILEO WROTE A LETTER TO THE Grand Duchess Christina of Tuscany in which he explained why his theory that the earth rotated around the sun was not necessarily contrary to Scripture. To Galileo, it made little sense for the church to determine the nature of physical reality on the basis of biblical texts that were subject to different interpretations. One year later, Cardinal Robert Bellarmine, a Jesuit and now a member of the church's Inquisition, wrote a letter to one of Galileo's followers that laid out the Catholic Church's approach to the issue of Galileo's theory.

Galileo, Letter to the Grand Duchess Christina, 1614

Some years ago, as Your Serene Highness well knows, I discovered in the heavens many things that had not been seen before our own age. The novelty of these things, as well as some consequences which followed from them in contradiction to the physical notions commonly held among academic philosophers, stirred up against me no small number of professors—as if I had placed these things in the sky with my own hands in order to upset nature and overturn the sciences. . . .

Contrary to the sense of the Bible and the intention of the holy Fathers, if I am not mistaken, they would extend such authorities until even in purely physical matters—where faith is not involved—they would have us altogether abandon reason and the evidence of our senses in favor of some biblical passage, though under the surface meaning of its words this passage may contain a different sense. . . .

The reason produced for condemning the opinion that the earth moves and the sun stands still is that in many places in the Bible one may read that the sun moves and the earth stands still. Since the Bible cannot err, it follows as a necessary consequence that anyone takes an erroneous and heretical position who maintains that the sun is inherently motionless and the earth movable.

With regard to this argument, I think in the first place that it is very pious to say and prudent to affirm that the holy Bible can never speak untruth—whenever its true meaning is understood. But I believe nobody will deny that it is often very abstruse, and may say things which are quite different from what its bare words signify. Hence, in expounding the Bible if one were always to confine oneself to the unadorned grammatical meaning, one might fall into error. Not only contradictions and propositions far from true might thus be made to appear in the Bible, but even grave heresies and follies. Thus, it would be necessary to assign to God feet, hands, and eyes, as well as corporeal and human affections, such as anger, repentance, hatred, and sometimes even the forgetting of things past and ignorance of those to come. These propositions uttered by the Holy Ghost were set down in that manner by the sacred scribes in order to accommodate them to the capacities of the common people, who are rude and unlearned. For the sake of those who deserve to be separated from the herd, it is necessary that wise expositors should produce the true senses of such passages, together with the special reasons for which they were set down in these words. . . .

This being granted, I think that in discussions of physical problems we ought to begin not from the authority of scriptural passages, but from sense-experiences and necessary demonstrations; for the holy Bible and the phenomena of nature proceed alike from the divine Word. . . . For that reason it appears that nothing physical which sense-experience sets before our eyes, or which necessary demonstrations prove to us, ought to be called in question (much less condemned) upon the testimony of biblical passages which may have some different meaning beneath their words.

Robert Bellarmine, Letter to Paolo Foscarini, 1615

First. I say that it seems to me that Your Reverence and Galileo did prudently to content yourself with speaking hypothetically, and not absolutely, as I have always believed that Copernicus spoke. For to say that, assuming the earth moves and the sun stands still, all the appearances are saved better than with eccentrics and epicycles, is to speak well; there is no danger in this, and it is sufficient for mathematicians. But to want to affirm that the sun really is fixed in the center of the heavens and only revolves around itself (i.e., turns upon its axis) without traveling from east to west, and that the earth is situated in the third sphere and revolves with great speed around the sun, is a very dangerous thing, not only by irritating all the philosophers and scholastic theologians, but also by injuring our holy faith and rendering the Holy Scriptures false. For Your Reverence has demonstrated many ways of explaining Holy Scripture, but you have not applied them in particular, and without a doubt you would have found it most difficult if you had attempted to explain all the passages which you yourself have cited.

Second. I say that, as you know, the Council [of Trent] prohibits expounding the Scriptures contrary to the common agreement of the holy Fathers. And if Your Reverence would read not only the Fathers but also the commentaries of modern writers on Genesis, Psalms, Ecclesiastes and Josue, you would find that all agree in explaining literally (*ad litteram*) that the sun is in the heavens and moves swiftly around the earth, and that the earth is far from the heavens and stands immobile in the center of the universe. Now consider whether in all prudence the Church could encourage giving to Scripture a sense contrary to the holy Fathers and all the Latin and Greek commentators. Nor may it be answered that this is not a matter of faith, for if it is not a matter of faith from the point of view of the subject matter, it is on the part of the ones who have spoken. . . .

(continued)

(*Continued*)

Third. I say that if there were a true demonstration that the sun was in the center of the universe and the earth in the third sphere, and that the sun did not travel around the earth but the earth circled the sun, then it would be necessary to proceed with great caution in explaining the passages of Scripture which seemed contrary, and we would rather have to say that we did not understand them than to say that something was false which has been demonstrated. But I do not believe that there is any such demonstration; none has been shown to me. It is not the same thing to show that the appearances are saved by assuming that the sun really is in the center and the earth in the heavens. I believe that the first demonstration might exist, but I have grave doubts about the second, and in a case of doubt, one may not depart from the Scriptures as explained by the holy Fathers.

Q *What does Galileo think is the difference between knowledge about the natural world and knowledge about the spiritual world? What does Galileo suggest that his opponents should do before dismissing his ideas? In what ways does Cardinal Bellarmine attempt to refute Galileo's ideas? Why did Galileo's ideas represent a threat to the Catholic Church?*

Source: Galileo, Letter to the Grand Duchess Christina, 1614, in S. Drake, trans., *Discoveries and Opinions of Galileo* (New York: Doubleday, 1957); Robert Bellarmine, Letter to Paolo Foscarini, 1615, in J. J. Langford, *Galileo, Science, and the Church* (New York: Desclee, 1966).

astronomer could overlook that Galileo's discoveries, combined with Kepler's mathematical laws, had made nonsense of the Aristotelian-Ptolemaic world system and clearly established the reasonableness of the Copernican model. Nevertheless, the problem of explaining motion in the universe and tying together the ideas of Copernicus, Galileo, and Kepler had not yet been solved. This would be the work of an Englishman who has long been considered the greatest genius of the Scientific Revolution.

Newton

Born in the English village of Woolsthorpe in 1642, Isaac Newton was an unremarkable young man until he attended Cambridge University. His first great burst of creative energy came in 1666, when fear of the plague closed Cambridge and forced him to return to Woolsthorpe for eighteen months. There Newton discovered his creative talents: "In those days I was in the prime of my life for invention and minded mathematics and philosophy more than at any time since."[10] During this period, he invented the calculus, a mathematical means of calculating rates of change; began his investigations into the composition of light; and inaugurated his work on the law of universal gravitation. Two years after his return to Cambridge, in 1669, he accepted a chair in mathematics at the university. During a second intense period of creativity from 1684 to 1686, he wrote his famous *Principia* (prin-SIP-ee-uh) (see the box on p. 483). After a nervous breakdown in 1693, he sought and received an administrative post as warden of the royal mint and was advanced to master of the mint by 1699, a post he held until his death in 1727. Made president of the Royal Society (see "The Scientific Societies" later in this chapter) in 1703 and knighted in 1705 for his great achievements, Sir Isaac Newton is to this day the only English scientist to be buried in Westminster Abbey.

NEWTON AND THE OCCULT Although Newton occupies a very special place in the history of modern science, we need to remember that he, too, remained extremely interested in aspects of the occult world. He left behind hundreds of manuscript pages of his studies of alchemy, and in fact, his alchemical experiments were a major feature of his life until he moved to London in 1696 to become warden of the royal mint. The British economist John Maynard Keynes said of Newton after examining his manuscripts in 1936:

> Newton was not the first of the age of reason. He was the last of the magicians. . . . He looked on the whole universe and all that is in it as a riddle, as a secret which could be read by applying pure thought to certain evidence, certain mystic clues which God had laid about the world to allow a sort of philosopher's treasure hunt to the esoteric brotherhood. He believed that these clues were to be found partly in the evidence of the heavens and in the constitution of elements . . . but also partly in certain papers and traditions handed down by the brethren in an unknown chain back to the original cryptic revelation in Babylonia.[11]

Although Newton may have considered himself a representative of the Hermetic tradition, he chose, it has been recently argued, for both political and psychological reasons to repress that part of his being, and it is as the "symbol of Western science" that he came to be viewed.

UNIVERSAL LAW OF GRAVITATION Newton's major work, the "hinge point of modern scientific thought," was his *Mathematical Principles of Natural Philosophy*, known simply as the *Principia*, the first word of its Latin title. In this work, the last highly influential book in Europe to be written in Latin, Newton spelled out the mathematical proofs demonstrating his universal law of gravitation. Newton's work was the culmination of the theories of Copernicus, Kepler, and Galileo. Though each had undermined some part of the Aristotelian-Ptolemaic cosmology, until Newton no one had pieced together a coherent synthesis for a new cosmology.

In the first book of the *Principia*, Newton defined the basic concepts of mechanics by elaborating the three laws of motion:

NEWTON'S RULES OF REASONING

IN 1687, ISAAC NEWTON PUBLISHED HIS MASTERPIECE, the *Mathematical Principles of Natural Philosophy*, or *Principia*. In this work, Newton demonstrated the mathematical proofs for his universal law of gravitation and completed the new cosmology begun by Copernicus, Kepler, and Galileo. He also described the rules of reasoning by which he arrived at his universal law.

Isaac Newton, *Rules of Reasoning in Philosophy*

Rule 1

We are to admit no more causes of natural things than such as are both true and sufficient to explain their appearances.

To this purpose the philosophers say that Nature does nothing in vain, and more is in vain when less will serve; for Nature is pleased with simplicity, and affects not the pomp of superfluous causes.

Rule 2

Therefore to the same natural effects we must, as far as possible, assign the same causes.

As to respiration in a man and in a beast; the descent of stones in Europe and in America; the light of our culinary fire and of the sun; the reflection of light in the earth and in the planets.

Rule 3

The qualities of bodies, which admit neither intensification nor remission of degrees, and which are found to belong to all bodies within the reach of our experiments, are to be esteemed the universal qualities of all bodies whatsoever.

For since qualities of bodies are only known to us by experiments, we are to hold for universal all such as universally agree with experiments; and such as are not liable to diminution can never be quite taken away.

Rule 4

In experimental philosophy we are to look upon propositions inferred by general induction from phenomena as accurately or very nearly true, notwithstanding any contrary hypotheses that may be imagined, till such time as other phenomena occur, by which they may either be made more accurate, or liable to exceptions.

This rule we must follow, that the argument of induction may not be evaded by hypotheses.

Q *What are Newton's rules of reasoning? How important were they to the development of the Scientific Revolution? How would following these rules change a person's view of the world, of European religious traditions, and of ancient "science"?*

Source: Newton, *The Mathematical Principles of Natural Philosophy* (London, 1803), pp. 160–162.

National Portrait Gallery, London/The Bridgeman Art Library

Isaac Newton. With a single law, that of universal gravitation, Isaac Newton was able to explain all motion in the universe. His great synthesis of the work of his predecessors created a new picture of the cosmos, one in which the universe was viewed as a great machine operating according to natural laws. Enoch Seeman painted this portrait of Newton one year before his death.

every object continues in a state of rest or uniform motion in a straight line unless deflected by a force, the rate of change of motion of an object is proportional to the force acting on it, and to every action there is always an equal and opposite reaction. In book 3, Newton applied his theories of mechanics to the problems of astronomy by demonstrating that these three laws of motion govern the planetary bodies as well as terrestrial objects. Integral to his whole argument was the universal law of gravitation, which explained why the planetary bodies did not go off in straight lines but continued in elliptical orbits about the sun. In mathematical terms, Newton explained that every object in the universe was attracted to every other object with a force (gravity) that is directly proportional to the product of their masses and inversely proportional to the square of the distances between them.

The implications of Newton's universal law of gravitation were enormous, even though another century would

CHRONOLOGY	Important Works of the Scientific Revolution
Copernicus, *On the Revolutions of the Heavenly Spheres*	1543
Vesalius, *On the Fabric of the Human Body*	1543
Galileo, *The Starry Messenger*	1610
Harvey, *On the Motion of the Heart and Blood*	1628
Galileo, *Dialogue on the Two Chief World Systems*	1632
Cavendish, *Grounds of Natural Philosophy*	1668
Newton, *Principia*	1687

pass before they were widely recognized. Newton had demonstrated that one universal law, mathematically proved, could explain all motion in the universe, from the movements of the planets in the celestial world to an apple falling from a tree in the terrestrial world. The secrets of the natural world could be known by human investigations. At the same time, the Newtonian synthesis created a new cosmology in which the world was seen largely in mechanistic terms. The universe was one huge, regulated, and uniform machine that operated according to natural laws in absolute time, space, and motion. Although Newton believed that God was "everywhere present" and acted as the force that moved all bodies on the basis of the laws he had discovered, later generations dropped his spiritual assumptions. Newton's **world-machine**, conceived as operating absolutely in time, space, and motion, dominated the Western worldview until the twentieth century, when the Einsteinian revolution, based on the concept of relativity, superseded the Newtonian mechanistic concept.

Newton's ideas were soon accepted in England, possibly out of national pride and conviction and, as has been argued recently, for political reasons (see "Science and Society" later in this chapter). Natural philosophers on the continent resisted Newton's ideas, and it took much of the eighteenth century before they were generally accepted everywhere in Europe. They were also reinforced by developments in other fields, especially medicine.

Advances in Medicine and Chemistry

FOCUS QUESTION: What did Paracelsus, Vesalius, and Harvey contribute to a scientific view of medicine?

Although the Scientific Revolution of the sixteenth and seventeenth centuries is associated primarily with the dramatic changes in astronomy and mechanics that precipitated a new perception of the universe, a third field that had been dominated by Greek thought in the Later Middle Ages, that of medicine, also experienced a transformation. Late medieval medicine was dominated not by the teachings of Aristotle but by those of the Greek physician Galen (GAY-len), who had lived in the second century C.E.

Galen's influence on the medieval medical world was pervasive in anatomy, physiology, and disease. Galen had relied on animal, rather than human, dissection to arrive at a picture of human anatomy that was quite inaccurate in many instances. Even when Europeans began to practice human dissection in the Later Middle Ages, instruction in anatomy still relied on Galen. While a professor read a text of Galen, an assistant dissected a cadaver for illustrative purposes. Physiology, or the functioning of the body, was also dominated by Galenic hypotheses, including the belief that there were two separate blood systems. One controlled muscular activities and contained bright red blood moving upward and downward through the arteries; the other governed the digestive functions and contained dark red blood that ebbed and flowed in the veins.

Treatment of disease was highly influenced by Galen's doctrine of four bodily humors: blood, considered warm and moist; yellow bile, warm and dry; phlegm, cold and moist; and black bile, cold and dry. Since disease was supposedly the result of an imbalance of humors that could be discerned from the quantity and color of urine, the examination of a patient's urine became the chief diagnostic tool. Although purging and bleeding to remedy the imbalance were often harmful to patients, treatment with traditional herbal medicines sometimes proved beneficial.

Paracelsus

Three figures are associated with the changes in medicine in the sixteenth and seventeenth centuries: Paracelsus (par-uh-SELL-suss), Andreas Vesalius (ahn-DRAY-uss vuh-SAY-lee-uss), and William Harvey. Philippus Aureolus von Hohenheim (1493–1541), who renamed himself Paracelsus ("greater than Celsus," an ancient physician), traveled widely and may have been awarded a medical degree from the University of Ferrara in Italy. He achieved a moment of glory when he was appointed city physician and professor of medicine at Basel in 1527. But this, like so many other appointments, proved short-lived due to his vanity and quick temper. He could never disguise his contempt for universities and physicians who did not agree with his new ideas:

> I am *monarcha medicorum*, monarch of physicians, and I can prove to you what you cannot prove. . . . It was not the constellations that made me a physician: God made me. . . . I need not don a coat of mail or a buckler against you, for you are not learned or experienced enough to refute even one word of mine. . . . Let me tell you this: every little hair on my neck knows more than you and all your scribes, and my shoebuckles are more learned than your Galen and Avicenna, and my beard has more experience than all your high colleges.[12]

Paracelsus was not easy to get along with, and he was forced to wander from one town to another until his death in 1541.

Paracelsus rejected the work of both Aristotle and Galen and attacked the universities as centers of their moribund philosophy. He and his followers hoped to replace the traditional system with a new chemical philosophy that was based on a new understanding of nature derived from fresh observation and experiment. This chemical philosophy was in turn closely connected to a view of the universe based on the macrocosm-microcosm analogy. According to this view, a human being was a small replica (microcosm) of the larger world (macrocosm). All parts of the universe were represented within each person. As Paracelsus said, "For the sun and the moon and all planets, as well as the stars and the whole chaos, are in man. . . . For what is outside is also inside; and what is not outside man is not inside. The outer and the inner are one thing."[13] In accordance with the macrocosmic-microcosmic principle, Paracelsus believed that the chemical reactions of the universe as a whole were reproduced in human beings on a smaller scale. Disease, then, was not caused by an imbalance of the four humors, as Galen had argued, but was due to chemical imbalances that were localized in specific organs and could be treated by chemical remedies.

Although others had used chemical remedies, Paracelsus and his followers differed from them in giving careful attention to the proper dosage of their chemically prepared metals and minerals. Paracelsus had turned against the Galenic principle that "contraries cure" in favor of the ancient Germanic folk principle that "like cures like." The poison that caused a disease would be its cure if used in proper form and quantity. Despite the apparent effectiveness of this use of toxic substances as treatment (Paracelsus did have a strong reputation for actually curing his patients), his opponents viewed it as the practice of a "homicide physician." Later generations came to regard Paracelsus more favorably, and historians who have stressed Paracelsus's concept of disease and recognition of "new drugs" for medicine have viewed him as a father of modern medicine. Others have argued that his macrocosmic-microcosmic philosophy and use of "like cures like" drugs make him the forerunner of both homeopathy and the holistic medicine of the postmodern era.

Vesalius

The new anatomy of the sixteenth century was the work of Andreas Vesalius (1514–1564). His study of medicine at Paris involved him in the works of Galen. Especially important to him was a recently discovered text of Galen, *On Anatomical Procedures*, that led Vesalius to emphasize practical research as the principal avenue for understanding human anatomy. After receiving a doctorate in medicine at the University of Padua in 1536, he accepted a position there as professor of surgery. In 1543, he published his masterpiece, *On the Fabric of the Human Body*.

This book was based on his personal dissection of a body to illustrate what he was discussing. Vesalius's anatomical treatise presented a careful examination of the individual organs and general structure of the human body. The book would not have been feasible without both the artistic advances of the Renaissance and technical developments in the art of printing. Together, they made possible the creation of illustrations superior to any done before.

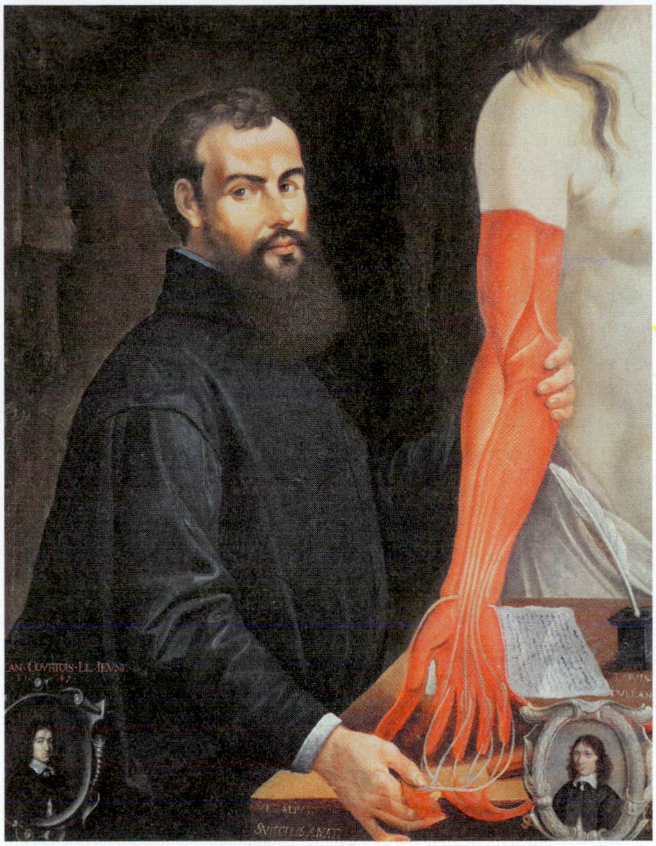

Andreas Vesalius. In this seventeenth-century French portrait of Andreas Vesalius, Vesalius is portrayed with one of his cadavers. His work established new understanding of the human body while the developments in artistic representation during the Renaissance allowed for more accurate representations of his findings, as seen here.

Vesalius's hands-on approach to teaching anatomy enabled him to rectify some of Galen's most glaring errors. He did not hesitate, for example, to correct Galen's assertion that the great blood vessels originated from the liver since his own observations made it apparent that they came from the heart. Nevertheless, Vesalius still clung to a number of Galen's erroneous assertions, including the Greek physician's ideas on the ebb and flow of two kinds of blood in the veins and arteries. It was not until William Harvey's work on the circulation of the blood nearly a century later that this Galenic misperception was corrected.

William Harvey

William Harvey (1578–1657) attended Cambridge University and later Padua, where he received a doctorate in medicine in 1602. His reputation rests on his book *On the Motion of the Heart and Blood*, published in 1628. Although questions had been raised in the sixteenth century about Galen's physiological principles, no major break from his system had occurred. Harvey's work, which was based on meticulous observations and experiments, led him to demolish the ancient Greek's erroneous contentions. Harvey demonstrated that the heart and not the liver was the beginning point of the circulation of blood in the body, that the same blood flows in both veins and arteries, and most important, that the blood makes a complete circuit as it passes through the body. His efforts did not come without an ethical cost, however. Harvey chose as his experimental subjects people who had been convicted of murder or treason and operated on them while they were alive in order to assess certain organ function, such as the process of digestion. Although Harvey's work dealt a severe blow to Galen's theories, his ideas did not begin to achieve general recognition until the 1660s, when capillaries, which explained how the blood passed from the arteries to the veins, were discovered. Harvey's theory of the circulation of the blood laid the foundation for modern physiology.

Chemistry

Although Paracelsus had proposed a new chemical philosophy in the sixteenth century, it was not until the seventeenth and eighteenth centuries that a science of chemistry arose. Robert Boyle (1627–1691) was one of the first scientists to conduct controlled experiments. His pioneering work on the properties of gases led to Boyle's law, which states that the volume of a gas varies with the pressure exerted on it. Boyle also rejected the medieval belief that all matter consisted of the same components in favor of the view that matter is composed of atoms, which he called "little particles of all shapes and sizes" and which would later be known as the chemical elements.

In the eighteenth century, Antoine Lavoisier (AHN-twahn lah-vwah-ZYAY) (1743–1794) invented a system of naming the chemical elements, much of which is still used today. In helping to show that water is a compound of oxygen and hydrogen, he demonstrated the fundamental rules of chemical combination. Many regard him as the founder of modern chemistry. Lavoisier's wife, Marie-Anne, was her husband's scientific collaborator. She learned English in order to translate the work of British chemists for her husband and made engravings to illustrate his scientific experiments. Marie-Anne Lavoisier is a reminder that women too played a role in the Scientific Revolution.

Women in the Origins of Modern Science

FOCUS QUESTION: What role did women play in the Scientific Revolution?

During the Middle Ages, except for members of religious orders, women who sought a life of learning were severely hampered by the traditional attitude that a woman's proper role was as a daughter, wife, and mother. But in the late fourteenth and early fifteenth centuries, new opportunities for elite women emerged as enthusiasm for the new secular learning called humanism led Europe's privileged and learned men to encourage women to read and study classical and Christian texts. The ideal of a humanist education for some of the daughters of Europe's elite persisted into the seventeenth century, but only for some privileged women.

Margaret Cavendish

Much as they were drawn to humanism, women were also attracted to the Scientific Revolution. Unlike females educated formally in humanist schools, women interested in science had to obtain a largely informal education. European nobles had the leisure and resources that gave them easy access to the world of learning. This door was also open to noblewomen who could participate in the informal scientific networks of their fathers and brothers. One of the most prominent female scientists of the seventeenth century, Margaret Cavendish (KAV-un-dish) (1623–1673), came from an aristocratic background. Cavendish was not a popularizer of science for women but a participant in the crucial scientific debates of her time. Despite her achievements, however, she was excluded from membership in the Royal Society (see "The Scientific Societies" later in this chapter), although she was once allowed to attend a meeting. She wrote a number of works on scientific matters, including *Observations upon Experimental Philosophy* and *Grounds of Natural Philosophy*, published in 1668. In these works, she did not hesitate to attack what she considered the defects of the rationalist and empiricist approaches to scientific knowledge and was especially critical of the growing belief that through science,

AS400 DB/Bettman/Corbis

Margaret Cavendish. Shown in this portrait is Margaret Cavendish, the duchess of Newcastle. She was a prolific writer, responsible for plays, biographies, poetry, and prose romances, as well as works in philosophy and science. Unlike most female authors of the time, who wrote anonymously, she used her own name on her works.

MARGARET CAVENDISH: THE EDUCATION OF WOMEN

MARGARET CAVENDISH'S HUSBAND, WHO WAS THIRTY YEARS HER SENIOR, encouraged her to pursue her literary interests. In addition to scientific works, she wrote plays, an autobiography, and a biography of her husband titled *The Life of the Thrice Noble, High and Puissant Prince William Cavendish, Duke, Marquess and Earl of Newcastle.* The autobiography and biography led one male literary critic to call her "a mad, conceited and ridiculous woman." In an essay titled "The Philosophical and Physical Opinions," she discussed the constraints placed upon women, including education.

Margaret Cavendish, "The Philosophical and Physical Opinions"

But to answer those objections that are made against me, as first how should I come by so much experience as I have expressed in my several books to have? I answer: I have had by relation the long and much experience of my lord, who hath lived to see and be in many changes of fortune and to converse with many men of sundry nations, ages, qualities, tempers, capacities, abilities, wits, humours, fashions and customs.

And as many others, especially wives, go from church to church, from ball to ball . . . gossiping from house to house, so when my lord admits me to his company I listen with attention to his edifying discourse and I govern myself by his doctrine: I dance a measure with the muses, feast with sciences, or sit and discourse with the arts.

The second is that, since I am no scholar, I cannot know the names and terms of art and the divers and several opinions of several authors. I answer: that I must have been a natural fool if I had not known and learnt them, for they are customarily taught all children from the nurse's breast, being ordinarily discoursed of in every family that is of quality, and the family from whence I sprung are neither natural idiots or ignorant fools, but the contrary, for they were rational, learned, understanding and witty. . . .

But as I have said my head was so full of my own natural fantasies, as it had not room for strangers to board therein, and certainly natural reason is a better tutor than education. For though education doth help natural reason to a more sudden maturity, yet natural reason was the first educator: for natural reason did first compose commonwealths, invented arts and science, and if natural reason hath composed, invented and discovered, I know no reason but natural reason may find out what natural reason hath composed, invented and discovered with the help of education. . . .

Q *What arguments does Cavendish make to defend her right and ability to be an author?*

Source: K. Aughterson, *Renaissance Woman: A Sourcebook* (London: Routledge, 1995); pp. 286–288.

humans would be masters of nature: "We have no power at all over natural causes and effects . . . for man is but a small part. . . . His powers are but particular actions of Nature, and he cannot have a supreme and absolute power."[14]

As an aristocrat (she was the duchess of Newcastle), Cavendish was a good example of the women in France and England who worked in science (see the box above). In Germany, women interested in science came from a different background. There the tradition of female participation in craft production enabled some women to become involved in observational science, especially entomology and astronomy. Between 1650 and 1710, one of every seven German astronomers was a woman.

Maria Merian

A good example of female involvement in the Scientific Revolution stemming from the craft tradition was Maria Sibylla Merian (MAY-ree-un) (1647–1717), who had established a reputation as an important entomologist by the beginning of the eighteenth century. Merian's training came from working in her father's workshop, where she learned the art of illustration, a training of great importance since her exact observation of insects and plants was demonstrated through the superb illustrations she made. In 1699, she undertook an expedition into the wilds of the Dutch colony of Surinam in South America to collect and draw samples of plants and insect life. This led to her major scientific work, the *Metamorphosis of the Insects of Surinam*, in which she used sixty illustrations to show the reproductive and developmental cycles of Surinam's insect life.

Maria Winkelmann

The craft organization of astronomy also gave women opportunities to become involved in science. Those who did worked in family observatories; hence, daughters and wives received training as apprentices to fathers or husbands. The most famous of the female astronomers in Germany was Maria Winkelmann (VINK-ul-mahn) (1670–1720). She was educated by her father and uncle and received advanced training in astronomy from a nearby self-taught astronomer. When she married Gottfried Kirch, Germany's foremost astronomer, she became his assistant at the astronomical observatory operated in Berlin by the Academy of Science. She made some original contributions, including a hitherto undiscovered comet, as her husband related:

> Early in the morning (about 2:00 A.M.) the sky was clear and starry. Some nights before, I had observed a variable star, and

> my wife (as I slept) wanted to find and see it for herself. In so doing, she found a comet in the sky. At which time she woke me, and I found that it was indeed a comet. . . . I was surprised that I had not seen it the night before.[15]

Moreover, Winkelmann corresponded with the famous scientist Gottfried Leibniz (who invented the calculus independently of Newton), who praised her effusively as "a most learned woman who could pass as a rarity." When her husband died in 1710, she applied for a position as assistant astronomer for which she was highly qualified. As a woman—with no university degree—she was denied the post by the Berlin Academy, which feared that it would establish a precedent by hiring a woman ("mouths would gape"). Winkelmann continued to do much of the work at the Berlin Academy once her son Christoph was appointed astronomer.

Winkelmann's difficulties with the Berlin Academy reflect the obstacles women faced in being accepted in scientific work, which was considered a male preserve. Although no formal statutes excluded women from membership in the new scientific societies, no woman was invited to join either the Royal Society of England or the French Academy of Sciences until the twentieth century. All of these women scientists were exceptional, since a life devoted to any kind of scholarship was still viewed as being at odds with the domestic duties women were expected to perform.

Debates on the Nature of Women

The nature and value of women had been the subject of an ongoing, centuries-long debate known as the **querelles des femmes** (keh-REL day FAHM)—arguments about women. Male opinions in the debate were largely a carryover from medieval times and were not favorable. Women were portrayed as inherently base, prone to vice, easily swayed, and "sexually insatiable." Hence, men needed to control them. Learned women were viewed as having overcome female liabilities to become like men. One man in praise of a woman scholar remarked that her writings were so good that you "would hardly believe they were done by a woman at all."

In the early modern era, women joined this debate by arguing against these male images of women. They argued that women also had rational minds and could grow from education. Further, since most women were pious, chaste, and temperate, there was no need for male authority over them. These female defenders of women emphasized education as the key to women's ability to move into the world. How, then, did the changes brought by the Scientific Revolution affect this debate over the nature of women? In an era of intellectual revolution in which traditional authorities were being overthrown, we might expect significant change in men's views of women. But by and large, instead of becoming an instrument for liberation, science was used to find new support for the old, stereotypical views about a woman's place in the scheme of things.

An important project in the new anatomy of the sixteenth and seventeenth centuries was the attempt to illustrate the human body and skeleton. For Vesalius, the portrayal of physical differences between males and females was limited to external bodily form (the outlines of the body) and the sexual organs. Vesalius saw no difference in skeletons and portrayed them as the same for men and women. It was not until the eighteenth century, in fact, that a new anatomy finally prevailed. Drawings of female skeletons between 1730 and 1790 varied, but females tended to have a larger pelvic area, and, in some instances, female skulls were portrayed as smaller than those of males. Eighteenth-century studies on the anatomy and physiology of sexual differences provided "scientific evidence" to reaffirm the traditional inferiority of women. The larger pelvic area "proved" that women were meant to be childbearers, and the larger skull "demonstrated" the superiority of the male mind. Male-dominated science had been used to "prove" male social dominance.

At the same time, during the seventeenth and eighteenth centuries, women even lost the traditional spheres of influence they had possessed, especially in the science-related art of midwifery. Women serving as midwives had traditionally been responsible for birthing. Similar to barber-surgeons or apothecaries (see Chapter 17), midwives had acquired their skills through apprenticeship. But the impact of the Scientific Revolution caused traditional crafts to be upgraded and then even professionalized as males took over. When medical men entered this arena, they also began to use devices and techniques derived from the study of anatomy. These were increasingly used to justify the male takeover of the traditional role of midwives. By the end of the eighteenth century, midwives were simply accessories to the art they had once controlled, except among the poor. Since little money was to be made in serving the lower classes, midwives were allowed to continue to practice their traditional art among them.

Overall, the Scientific Revolution reaffirmed traditional ideas about women. Male scientists used the new science to spread the view that women were inferior by nature, subordinate to men, and suited by nature to play a domestic role as nurturing mothers. The widespread distribution of books ensured the continuation of these ideas. Jean de La Bruyère (ZHAHNH duh lah broo-YARE), the seventeenth-century French moralist, was typical when he remarked that an educated woman was like a gun that was a collector's item, "which one shows to the curious, but which has no use at all, any more than a carousel horse."[16]

Toward a New Earth: Descartes, Rationalism, and a New View of Humankind

> **FOCUS QUESTION:** Why is Descartes considered the founder of modern rationalism?

The fundamentally new conception of the universe contained in the cosmological revolution of the sixteenth and seventeenth centuries inevitably had an impact on the Western

RMN-Grand Palais/Art Resource, NY

Descartes. René Descartes was one of the primary figures in the Scientific Revolution. Claiming to use reason as his sole guide to truth, Descartes posited a sharp distinction between mind and matter. He is shown here in a portrait done around 1649 by Frans Hals, one of the painters of the Dutch golden age who was famous for his portraits, especially that of Descartes.

view of humankind. Nowhere is this more evident than in the work of René Descartes (ruh-NAY day-KART) (1596–1650), an extremely important figure in Western history. Descartes began by reflecting the doubt and uncertainty that seemed pervasive in the confusion of the seventeenth century and ended with a philosophy that dominated Western thought until the twentieth century.

Descartes was born into a family of the French lower nobility. After a Jesuit education, he studied law at Poitiers but traveled to Paris to study by himself. In 1618, at the beginning of the Thirty Years' War, Descartes volunteered for service in the army of Maurice of Nassau, but he seems to have been interested less in military action than in traveling and finding leisure time to think. On the night of November 10, 1619, Descartes underwent what one historian has called an experience comparable to the "ecstatic illumination of the mystic." Having perceived in one night the outlines of a new rational-mathematical system, with a sense of divine approval he made a new commitment to mind, mathematics, and a mechanical universe. For the rest of his life, Descartes worked out the details of his vision.

The starting point for Descartes's new system was doubt, as he explained at the beginning of his most famous work, the *Discourse on Method*, written in 1637:

> From my childhood, I have been familiar with letters; and as I was given to believe that by their help a clear and certain knowledge of all that is useful in life might be acquired, I was ardently desirous of instruction. But as soon as I had finished the entire course of study, at the close of which it is customary to be admitted into the order of the learned, I completely changed my opinion. For I found myself involved in so many doubts and errors, that I was convinced I had advanced no farther in all my attempts at learning, than the discovery of my own ignorance.[17]

Descartes decided to set aside all that he had learned and begin again. One fact seemed beyond doubt—his own existence:

> But immediately upon this I observed that [while] I thus wished to think that all was false, it was absolutely necessary that I who thus thought, should be [something]; and as I observed that this truth, *I think*, [*therefore*] *I am*, was so certain and of such evidence, that no ground of doubt, however extravagant, could be alleged by the Sceptics capable of shaking it, I concluded that I might without scruple accept it as the first principle of the Philosophy of which I was in search.[18]

With this emphasis on the mind, Descartes asserted that he would accept only those things that his reason said were true.

From his first postulate, Descartes deduced an additional principle, the separation of mind and matter. Descartes argued that since "the mind cannot be doubted but the body and material world can, the two must be radically different." From this came an absolute duality between mind and body that has been called **Cartesian dualism**. Using mind or human reason, the path to certain knowledge, and its best instrument, mathematics, humans can understand the material world because it is pure mechanism, a machine that is governed by its own physical laws because it was created by God, the great geometrician.

Descartes's conclusions about the nature of the universe and human beings had important implications. His separation of mind and matter allowed scientists to view matter as dead or inert, as something that was totally separate from themselves and could be investigated independently by reason. The split between mind and body led Westerners to equate their identity with mind and reason rather than with the whole organism. Descartes has rightly been called the father of modern **rationalism** (see the box on p. 490). His books were placed on the papal Index of Forbidden Books and condemned by many Protestant theologians. The radical Cartesian split between mind and matter, and between mind and body, had devastating implications not only for traditional religious views of the universe but also for how Westerners viewed themselves.

THE FATHER OF MODERN RATIONALISM

RENÉ DESCARTES HAS LONG BEEN VIEWED as the founder of modern rationalism and modern philosophy because he believed that human beings could understand the world—itself a mechanical system—by the same rational principles inherent in mathematical thinking. In his *Discourse on Method*, he elaborated on his approach to discovering truth.

René Descartes, *Discourse on Method*

In place of the numerous precepts which have gone to constitute logic, I came to believe that the four following rules would be found sufficient, always provided I took the firm and unswerving resolve never in a single instance to fail in observing them.

The first was to accept nothing as true which I did not evidently know to be such, that is to say, scrupulously to avoid precipitance and prejudice, and in the judgments I passed to include nothing additional to what had presented itself to my mind so clearly and so distinctly that I could have no occasion for doubting it.

The second, to divide each of the difficulties I examined into as many parts as may be required for its adequate solution.

The third, to arrange my thoughts in order, beginning with things the simplest and easiest to know, so that I may then ascend little by little, as it were step by step, to the knowledge of the more complex, and in doing so, to assign an order of thought even to those objects which are not of themselves in any such order of precedence.

And the last, in all cases to make enumerations so complete, and reviews so general, that I should be assured of omitting nothing.

Those long chains of reasonings, each step simple and easy, which geometers are wont to employ in arriving even at the most difficult of their demonstrations, have led me to surmise that all the things we human beings are competent to know are interconnected in the same manner, and that none are so remote as to be beyond our reach or so hidden that we cannot discover them—that is, provided we abstain from accepting as true what is not thus related, i.e., keep always to the order required for their deduction one from another. And I had no great difficulty in determining what the objects are with which I should begin, for that I already knew, namely, that it was with the simplest and easiest. Bearing in mind, too, that of all those who in time past have sought for truth in the sciences, the mathematicians alone have been able to find any demonstrations, that is to say, any reasons which are certain and evident, I had no doubt that it must have been by a procedure of this kind that they had obtained them.

Q *Describe Descartes's principles of inquiry and compare them with Newton's rules of reasoning. What are the main similarities between these systems of thinking?*

Source: N. K. Smith, trans., *Descartes' Philosophical Writings* (London: Palgrave.Macmillan, 1958).

The Scientific Method and the Spread of Scientific Knowledge

Q **FOCUS QUESTION:** How were the ideas of the Scientific Revolution spread, and what impact did they have on society and religion?

During the seventeenth century, scientific learning and investigation began to increase dramatically. Major universities in Europe established new chairs of science, especially in medicine. Royal and princely patronage of individual scientists became an international phenomenon.

The Scientific Method

Of great importance to the work of science was establishing the proper means to examine and understand the physical realm. This development of a **scientific method** was crucial to the evolution of science in the modern world.

FRANCIS BACON Curiously enough, it was an Englishman with few scientific credentials who attempted to put forth a new method of acquiring knowledge that made an impact on English scientists in the seventeenth century and other European scientists in the eighteenth century. Francis Bacon (1561–1626), a lawyer and lord chancellor, rejected Copernicus and Kepler and misunderstood Galileo. And yet in his unfinished work, *The Great Instauration*, he called for his contemporaries "to commence a total reconstruction of sciences, arts, and all human knowledge, raised upon the proper foundations." Bacon did not doubt humans' ability to know the natural world, but he believed that they had proceeded incorrectly: "The entire fabric of human reason which we employ in the inquisition of nature is badly put together and built up, and like some magnificent structure without foundation."

Bacon's new foundation—a correct scientific method—was to be built on inductive principles. Rather than beginning with assumed first principles from which logical conclusions could be deduced, he urged scientists to proceed from the particular to the general. From carefully organized experiments and thorough, systematic observations, correct generalizations could be developed.

Bacon was clear about what he believed his method could accomplish. His concern was for practical results rather than for pure science. He stated that "the true and lawful goal of the sciences is none other than this: that human life be endowed with new discoveries and power." He wanted science to contribute to the "mechanical arts" by creating devices that would benefit industry, agriculture, and trade. Bacon was prophetic when he said that he was "laboring to lay the foundation, not of any sect or doctrine, but of human utility and power." And how would this "human power" be used? To "conquer nature in action."[19] The control and domination of nature became a central proposition of modern science and the technology that accompanied it. Only in the twentieth century did some scientists begin to ask whether this assumption might not be at the heart of the earth's ecological crisis.

DESCARTES Descartes proposed a different approach to scientific methodology by emphasizing deduction and mathematical logic. As Descartes explained in the *Discourse on Method*, each step in an argument should be as sharp and well founded as a mathematical proof:

> Those long chains of reasonings, each step simple and easy, which geometers are wont to employ in arriving even at the most difficult of their demonstrations, have led me to surmise that all the things we human beings are competent to know are interconnected in the same manner, and that none are so remote as to be beyond our reach or so hidden that we cannot discover them—that is, provided we abstain from accepting as true what is not thus related, i.e., keep always to the order required for their deduction one from another.[20]

Descartes believed, then, that one could start with self-evident truths, comparable to geometric axioms, and deduce more complex conclusions. His emphasis on deduction and mathematical order complemented Bacon's stress on experiment and induction. It was Sir Isaac Newton who synthesized them into a single scientific methodology by uniting Bacon's **empiricism** with Descartes's rationalism. This scientific method began with systematic observations and experiments, which were used to arrive at general concepts. New deductions derived from these general concepts could then be tested and verified by precise experiments.

The scientific method, of course, was valuable in answering the question of *how* something works, and its success in doing this gave others much confidence in the method. It did not attempt to deal with the question of *why* something happens or the purpose and meaning behind the world of nature. This allowed religion to retain its central importance in the seventeenth century (see "Science and Religion" later in this chapter).

The Spread of Scientific Knowledge

Also important to the work of science was the emergence of new learned societies and journals that enabled the new scientists to communicate their ideas to each other and to disseminate them to a wider, literate public.

THE SCIENTIFIC SOCIETIES The first of these scientific societies appeared in Italy, but those of England and France were ultimately of greater significance. The English Royal Society evolved out of informal gatherings of scientists at London and Oxford in the 1640s, although it did not receive a formal charter from King Charles II until 1662. The French Royal Academy of Sciences also arose out of informal scientific meetings in Paris during the 1650s. In 1666, Louis XIV formally recognized the group. The French Academy received abundant state support and remained under government control; the state appointed its members and paid their salaries. In contrast, the Royal Society of England received little government encouragement, and its fellows simply co-opted new members.

RMN-Grand Palais/Art Resource, NY

Louis XIV and Colbert Visit the Academy of Sciences. In the seventeenth century, individual scientists received royal and princely patronage, and a number of learned societies were established. In France, Louis XIV, urged on by his controller general, Jean-Baptiste Colbert, gave formal recognition to the French Academy in 1666. In this painting by Henri Testelin, Louis XIV is shown seated, surrounded by Colbert and members of the French Royal Academy of Sciences.

IMAGES OF EVERYDAY LIFE

The Science of Collecting

THE ART OF COLLECTING WAS AN IMPORTANT part of scientific culture. Early scientists maintained their relevance to the scientific community by their collections of drawings and specimens. Wealthy patrons were able to amass thousands of species of plants and insects as well as gems and scientific instruments for academic study. The prestige of one's collection could lead to scientific posts. Sir Hans Sloane (1660–1753), portrayed with his drawings of plants (see photo, right), was an English physician who had spent fifteen months in Jamaica as a personal physician to the West Indies fleet in 1687. He collected around 800 species to bring back to England. His large collection fostered his position as president of the Royal College of Physicians and the Royal Society and also served as the foundation for the British Museum. Various collections were kept in drawers, seen in this photo of specimens of beetles in the Jans Sloane collection (see below, left). These private collections consisted of objects collected around the globe, as did the public collections found in botanical gardens. In France, the Royal Botanical Garden, founded in 1640, served as the leading center of botany in Europe; its gardens were divided into quarters representing Europe, Asia, Africa, and the Americas, as seen in a French drawing (see below, right).

National Portrait Gallery, London, UK/Bridgeman Images

National History Museum, London, UK/Bridgeman Images

Scala/White Images/Art Resource, NY

Early on, both the English and the French scientific societies formally emphasized the practical value of scientific research. The Royal Society created a committee to investigate technological improvements for industry; the French Academy collected tools and machines (see "Images of Everyday Life" above). This concern with the practical benefits of science proved short-lived, however, as both societies came to focus their primary interest on theoretical work in mechanics and astronomy. The construction of observatories at Paris in 1667 and at Greenwich, England, in 1675 greatly facilitated research in astronomy by both groups. Although both the English and the French societies made useful contributions to scientific knowledge in the second half of the seventeenth century, their true significance was that they demonstrated the benefits of science proceeding as a cooperative venture.

Scientific journals furthered this concept of cooperation. The French *Journal des Savants* (zhoor-NAHL day sah-VAHNH), published weekly beginning in 1665, printed results of experiments as well as general scientific knowledge. Its format appealed to both scientists and the educated public interested in the new science. In contrast, the *Philosophical Transactions* of the Royal Society, also initiated in 1665, published papers of its members and learned correspondence and was aimed at practicing scientists. It became a prototype for the scholarly journals of later learned and academic societies and a crucial instrument for circulating news of scientific and academic activities.

SCIENCE AND SOCIETY The importance of science in the history of modern Western civilization is usually taken for granted. No doubt the Industrial Revolution of the nineteenth century provided tangible proof of the effectiveness of science and ensured its victory over Western minds. But how did science become such an integral part of Western culture in the seventeenth and eighteenth centuries? Recent research has stressed that one cannot simply assert that people perceived that science was a rationally superior system. Several factors, however, might explain the relatively rapid acceptance of the new science.

It has been argued that the literate mercantile and propertied elites of Europe were attracted to the new science because it offered new ways to exploit resources for profit. Some of the early scientists made it easier for these groups to accept the new ideas by showing how they could be applied directly to specific industrial and technological needs. Galileo, for example, consciously sought an alliance between science and the material interests of the educated elite when he assured his listeners that the science of mechanics would be quite useful "when it becomes necessary to build bridges or other structures over water." At the same time, Galileo stressed that science was fit for the "minds of the wise" and not for "the shallow minds of the common people." This made science part of the high culture of Europe's wealthy elites at a time when that culture was being increasingly separated from the popular culture of the lower classes (see Chapter 17).

It has also been argued that political interests used the new scientific conception of the natural world to bolster social stability. One scholar has argued that "no single event in the history of early modern Europe more profoundly shaped the integration of the new science into Western culture than did the English Revolution (1640–1660)."[21] Fed by their millenarian expectations that the end of the world would come and usher in a thousand-year reign of the saints, Puritan reformers felt it was important to reform and renew their society. They seized on the new science as a socially useful instrument to accomplish this goal. The Puritan Revolution's role in the acceptance of science, however, stemmed even more from the reaction to the radicalism spawned by the revolutionary ferment. The upheavals of the Puritan Revolution gave rise to groups, such as the Levellers, Diggers, and Ranters, who advocated not only radical political ideas but also a new radical science based on Paracelsus and the natural magic associated with the Hermetic tradition. The propertied and educated elites responded vigorously to these challenges to the established order by supporting the new mechanistic science and appealing to the material benefits of science. Hence, the founders of the Royal Society were men who wanted to pursue an experimental science that would remain detached from radical reforms of church and state. Although willing to make changes, they now viewed those changes in terms of an increase in food production and commerce.

At the same time, princes and kings who were providing patronage for scientists were doing so not only for prestige but also for practical reasons, especially the military applications of the mathematical sciences. The use of gunpowder, for example, gave new importance to ballistics and metallurgy. Rulers, especially absolute ones, were also concerned about matters of belief in their realms and recognized the need to control and manage the scientific body of knowledge, as we have seen in the French Academy. In appointing its members and paying their salaries, Louis XIV was also ensuring that the members and their work would be under his control.

Science and Religion

In Galileo's struggle with the inquisitorial Holy Office of the Catholic Church, we see the beginning of the conflict between science and religion that has marked the history of modern Western civilization. Since time immemorial, theology had seemed to be the queen of the sciences. It was natural that the churches would continue to believe that religion was the final measure of all things. The emerging scientists, however, tried to draw lines between the knowledge of religion and the knowledge of "natural philosophy" or nature. Galileo had clearly felt that it was unnecessary to pit science against religion when he wrote:

> In discussions of physical problems we ought to begin not from the authority of scriptural passages, but from sense-experiences and necessary demonstrations; for the holy Bible and the phenomena of nature proceed alike from the divine word, the former as the dictate of the Holy Ghost and the latter as the observant executrix of God's commands. It is necessary for the Bible, in order to be accommodated to the understanding of every man, to speak many things which appear to differ from the absolute truth so far as the bare meaning of the words is concerned. But Nature, on the other hand, is inexorable and immutable; she never transgresses the laws imposed upon her, or cares a whit whether her abstruse reasons and methods of operation are understandable to men.[22]

To Galileo, it made little sense for the church to determine the nature of physical reality on the basis of biblical texts that were subject to radically divergent interpretations. The church, however, decided otherwise in Galileo's case and lent its great authority to one scientific theory, the Aristotelian-Ptolemaic cosmology, no doubt because it fit so well with its own philosophical views of reality. But the church's decision had tremendous consequences, just as the rejection of Darwin's ideas did in the nineteenth century. For educated individuals, it established a dichotomy between scientific investigations and religious beliefs. As the scientific beliefs triumphed, it became almost inevitable that religious beliefs would suffer, leading to a growing secularization in European intellectual life—precisely what the church had hoped to combat by opposing Copernicanism. Many seventeenth-century intellectuals were both religious and scientific and believed that the implications of this split would be tragic. Some believed that the split was largely unnecessary, while others felt the need to combine God, humans, and a mechanistic universe into a new philosophical synthesis. Two individuals—Spinoza and Pascal—illustrate the wide diversity in the response of European intellectuals to the implications of the cosmological revolution of the seventeenth century.

SPINOZA Benedict de Spinoza (spi-NOH-zuh) (1632–1677) was a philosopher who grew up in the relatively tolerant atmosphere of Amsterdam. He was excommunicated from the Amsterdam synagogue at the age of twenty-four for rejecting the tenets of Judaism. Ostracized by the local Jewish community and major Christian churches alike, Spinoza lived a quiet, independent life, earning a living by grinding optical lenses and refusing to accept an academic position in philosophy at the University of Heidelberg for fear of compromising his freedom of thought. Spinoza read a great deal of the new scientific literature and was influenced by Descartes.

Spinoza was unwilling to accept the implications of Descartes's ideas, especially the separation of mind and matter and the apparent separation of an infinite God from the finite world of matter. God was not simply the creator of the universe; he was the universe. All that is is in God, and nothing can be apart from God. This philosophy of pantheism (or monism) was set out in Spinoza's book *Ethics Demonstrated in the Geometrical Manner*, which was not published until after his death.

To Spinoza, human beings are not "situated in nature as a kingdom within a kingdom" but are as much a part of God or nature or the universal order as other natural objects. The failure to understand God had led to many misconceptions—for one, that nature exists only for one's use:

> As they find in themselves and outside themselves many means which assist them not a little in their search for what is useful, for instance, eyes for seeing, teeth for chewing, herbs and animals for yielding food, the sun for giving light, the sea for breeding fish, they come to look on the whole of nature as a means for obtaining such conveniences.[23]

Furthermore, unable to find any other cause for the existence of these things, they attributed them to a creator-God who must be worshiped to gain their ends: "Hence also it follows, that everyone thought out for himself, according to his abilities, a different way of worshiping God, so that God might love him more than his fellows, and direct the whole course of nature for the satisfaction of his blind cupidity and insatiable avarice." Then, when nature appeared unfriendly in the form of storms, earthquakes, and diseases, "they declared that such things happen, because the gods are angry at some wrong done them by men, or at some fault committed in their worship," rather than realizing "that good and evil fortunes fall to the lot of pious and impious alike."[24] Likewise, human beings made moral condemnations of others because they failed to understand that human emotions, "passions of hatred, anger, envy and so, considered in themselves, follow from the same necessity and efficacy of nature" and "nothing comes to pass in nature in contravention to her universal laws." To explain human emotions, like everything else, we need to analyze them as we would the movements of planets: "I shall, therefore, treat of the nature and strength of my emotions according to the same method as I employed heretofore in my investigations concerning God and the mind. I shall consider human actions and desires in exactly the same manner as though I were concerned with lines, planes, and solids."[25] Everything has a rational explanation, and humans are capable of finding it. In using reason, people can find true happiness. Their real freedom comes when they understand the order and necessity of nature and achieve detachment from passing interests.

PASCAL Blaise Pascal (BLEZ pass-KAHL) (1623–1662) was a French scientist who sought to keep science and religion united.

Blaise Pascal (1623–62) (oil on canvas), Champaigne, Philippe de (1602–74)/Private Collection/Bridgeman Images

Blaise Pascal. Blaise Pascal was a brilliant scientist and mathematician who hoped to keep science and Christianity united. In his *Pensées*, he made a passionate argument on behalf of the Christian religion. He is pictured here in a portrait by Philippe de Champaigne, a well-known French portrait painter of the Baroque period.

CHRONOLOGY	Consequences of the Revolution: Important Works
Bacon, *The Great Instauration*	1620
Descartes, *Discourse on Method*	1637
Pascal, *Pensées*	1669
Spinoza, *Ethics Demonstrated in the Geometrical Manner*	1677

An accomplished scientist and a brilliant mathematician, he excelled at both the practical, by inventing a calculating machine, and the abstract, by devising a theory of chance or probability and doing work on conic sections. After a profound mystical vision on the night of November 23, 1654, which assured him that God cared for the human soul, he devoted the rest of his life to religious matters. He planned to write an "apology for the Christian religion" but died before he could do so. He did leave a set of notes for the larger work, however, which in published form became known as the *Pensées* (pahn-SAY) (*Thoughts*).

In the *Pensées* (see the box below), Pascal tried to convert rationalists to Christianity by appealing to both their reason and their emotions. Humans were, he argued, frail creatures, often deceived by their senses, misled by reason, and battered by their emotions. And yet they were beings whose very nature involved thinking: "Man is but a reed, the weakest in nature; but he is a thinking reed."[26]

Pascal was determined to show that the Christian religion was not contrary to reason: "If we violate the principles of reason, our religion will be absurd, and it will be laughed at." Christianity, he felt, was the only religion that recognized people's true state of being as both vulnerable and great. To a Christian, a human being was both fallen and at the same time God's special creation. But it was not necessary to emphasize one at the expense of the other—to view humans as only rational or only hopeless. Pascal even had an answer for skeptics in his famous wager. God is a reasonable bet; it is worthwhile to assume that God exists. If he does, then we win all; if he does not, we lose nothing.

Despite his own background as a scientist and mathematician, Pascal refused to rely on the scientist's world of order and rationality to attract people to God: "If we submit

PASCAL: "WHAT IS A MAN IN THE INFINITE?"

PERHAPS NO INTELLECTUAL IN THE SEVENTEENTH CENTURY gave greater expression to the uncertainties generated by the cosmological revolution than Blaise Pascal, himself a scientist. Pascal's work, the *Pensées*, consisted of notes for a large unfinished work justifying the Christian religion. In this selection, Pascal presents his musings on the human place in an infinite world.

Blaise Pascal, *Pensées*

Let man then contemplate the whole of nature in her full and grand majesty, and turn his vision from the low objects which surround him. Let him gaze on that brilliant light, set like an eternal lamp to illumine the universe; let the earth appear to him a point in comparison with the vast circle described by the sun; and let him wonder at the fact that this vast circle is itself but a very fine point in comparison with that described by the stars in their revolution round the firmament. But if our view be arrested there, let our imagination pass beyond; it will sooner exhaust the power of conception than nature that of supplying material for conception. The whole visible world is only an imperceptible atom in the ample bosom of nature. No idea approaches it. We may enlarge our conceptions beyond all imaginable space; we only produce atoms in comparison with the reality of things. It is an infinite sphere, the centre of which is everywhere, the circumference nowhere. In short it is the greatest sensible mark of the almighty power of God, that imagination loses itself in that thought.

Returning to himself, let man consider what he is in comparison with all existence; let him regard himself as lost in this remote corner of nature; and from the little cell in which he finds himself lodged, I mean the universe, let him estimate at their true value the earth, kingdoms, cities, and himself. What is a man in the Infinite? . . .

For in fact what is man in nature? A Nothing in comparison with the Infinite, an All in comparison with the Nothing, a mean between nothing and everything. Since he is infinitely removed from comprehending the extremes, the end of things and their beginning are hopelessly hidden from him in an impenetrable secret, he is equally incapable of seeing the nothing from which he was made, and the Infinite in which he is swallowed up. What will he do then, but perceive the appearance of the middle of things, in an eternal despair of knowing either their beginning or their end. All things proceed from the Nothing, and are borne towards the Infinite. Who will follow these marvellous processes? The Author of these wonders understands them. None other can do so.

Q *Why did Pascal question whether human beings could achieve scientific certainty? What is the significance of Pascal's thoughts for modern science?*

Source: The Project Gutenberg EBook of Pascal's *Pensées*. Accessed from http://www.gutenberg.org/files/18269/18269-h/18269-h.htm.

everything to reason, there will be no mystery and no supernatural element in our religion." In the new cosmology of the seventeenth century, "finite man," Pascal believed, was lost in the new infinite world, a realization that frightened him: "The eternal silence of those infinite spaces strikes me with terror." The world of nature, then, could never reveal God: "Because they have failed to contemplate these infinites, men have rashly plunged into the examination of nature, as though they bore some proportion to her. . . . Their assumption is as infinite as their object." A Christian could only rely on a God who through Jesus cared for human beings. In the final analysis, after providing reasonable arguments for Christianity, Pascal came to rest on faith. Reason, he believed, could take people only so far: "The heart has its reasons of which the reason knows nothing." As a Christian, faith was the final step: "The heart feels God, not the reason. This is what constitutes faith: God experienced by the heart, not by the reason."[27]

In retrospect, it is obvious that Pascal failed to achieve his goal of uniting Christianity and science. The gap between science and traditional religion grew ever wider as Europe continued along its path of secularization. Of course, traditional religions were not eliminated, nor is there any evidence that churches had yet lost their followers. That would happen later. Nevertheless, more and more of the intellectual, social, and political elites began to act on the basis of secular rather than religious assumptions.

CHAPTER SUMMARY

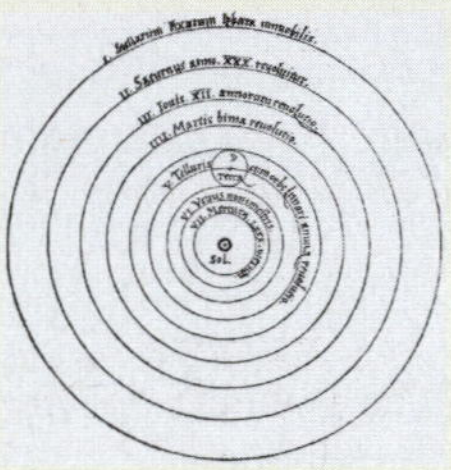

The Scientific Revolution represents a major turning point in modern Western civilization. In the Scientific Revolution, the Western world overthrew the medieval, Aristotelian-Ptolemaic worldview and geocentric universe and arrived at a new conception of the universe: the sun at the center, the planets as material bodies revolving around the sun in elliptical orbits, and an infinite rather than finite world. This new conception of the heavens was the work of a number of brilliant individuals: Nicolaus Copernicus, who theorized a heliocentric, or sun-centered, universe; Johannes Kepler, who discovered that planetary orbits were elliptical; Galileo Galilei, who, by using a telescope and observing the moon and sunspots, discovered that the universe seemed to be composed of material substance; and Isaac Newton, who tied together all of these ideas with his universal law of gravitation. The contributions of each individual built on the work of the others, thus establishing one of the basic principles of the new science—cooperation in the pursuit of new knowledge.

With the changes in the conception of "heaven" came changes in the conception of "earth." The work of Bacon and Descartes left Europeans with the separation of mind and matter and the belief that by using only reason they could in fact understand and dominate the world of nature. The development of a scientific methodology furthered the work of the scientists, and the creation of scientific societies and learned journals spread its results. The Scientific Revolution was more than merely intellectual theories. It also appealed to nonscientific elites because of its practical implications for economic progress and for maintaining the social order, including the waging of war.

Although traditional churches stubbornly resisted the new ideas and a few intellectuals pointed to some inherent flaws, nothing was able to halt the supplanting of the traditional ways of thinking by new ways of thinking that created a more fundamental break with the past than that represented by the breakup of Christian unity in the Reformation.

The Scientific Revolution forced Europeans to change their conception of themselves. At first, some were appalled and even frightened by its implications. Formerly, humans on earth had viewed themselves as being at the center of the universe. Now the earth was only a tiny planet revolving around a sun that was itself only a speck in a boundless universe. Most people remained optimistic despite the apparent blow to human dignity. After all, had Newton not demonstrated that the universe was a great machine governed by natural laws? Newton had found one—the universal law of gravitation. Could others not find other laws? Were there not natural laws governing every aspect of human endeavor that could be found by the new scientific method? Thus, as we shall see in the next chapter, the Scientific Revolution leads us logically to the Enlightenment in the eighteenth century.

CHAPTER TIMELINE

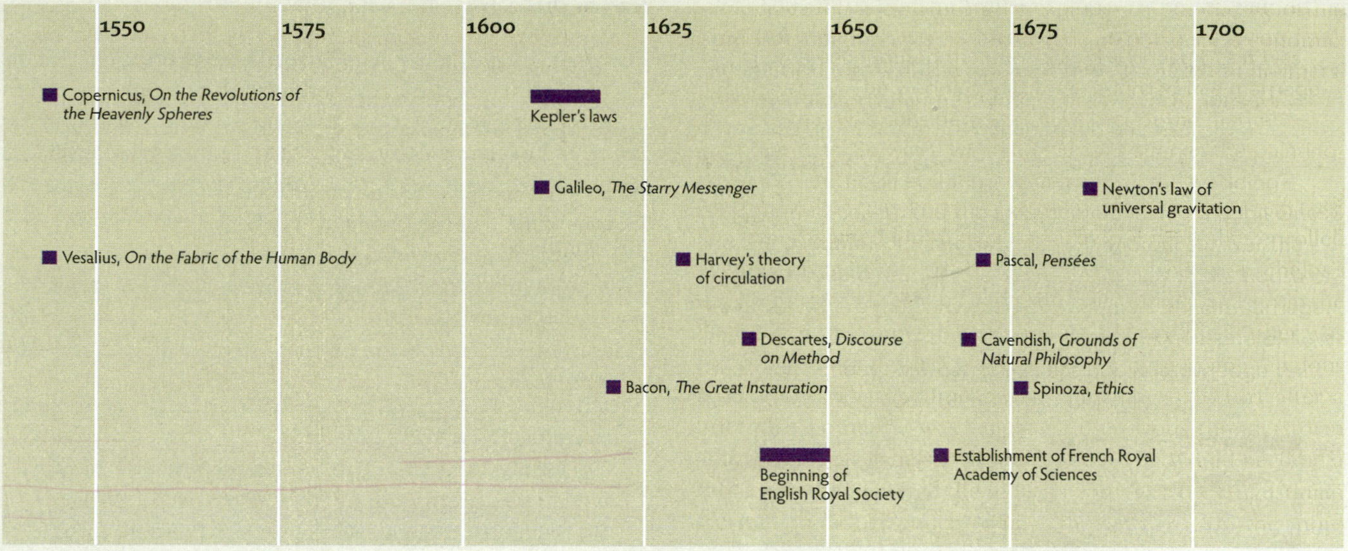

CHAPTER REVIEW

Upon Reflection

Q How do you explain the emergence of the Scientific Revolution?

Q What do we mean by the "Newtonian world-machine," and what is its significance?

Q Compare the methods used by Bacon and Descartes. Would Pascal agree with their methods and interests? Why or why not?

Key Terms

Scientific Revolution (p. 473)
geocentric conception (p. 474)
heliocentric conception (p. 475)
world-machine (p. 484)
querelles des femmes (p. 488)
Cartesian dualism (p. 489)
rationalism (p. 489)
scientific method (p. 490)
empiricism (p. 491)

Suggestions for Further Reading

GENERAL WORKS General surveys of the entire Scientific Revolution include **J. Henry, *The Scientific Revolution and the Origins of Modern Science***, 2nd ed. (London, 2002), and **D. Wootton, *The Invention of Science: A New History of the Scientific Revolution*** (New York, 2015). See also **P. Dear, *Revolutionizing the Sciences: European Knowledge and Its Ambitions, 1500–1700*** (Princeton, N.J., 2001). On the Scientific Revolution in global perspective, see **T. Hoff, *Intellectual Curiosity and the Scientific Revolution: A Global Perspective*** (Cambridge, U.K., 2011), and **W. E. Burns, *The Scientific Revolution in Global Perspective*** (New York, 2015). On the relationship of magic to the beginnings of the Scientific Revolution, see the pioneering work by **F. Yates, *The Rosicrucian Enlightenment*** (London, 1975). On the relationship between Renaissance artists and the Scientific Revolution, see **P. H. Smith, *Body of the Artisan: Art and Experience in the Scientific Revolution*** (Chicago, 2006).

A REVOLUTION IN ASTRONOMY On the important figures of the revolution in astronomy, see **H. Margolis, *It Started with Copernicus: How Turning the World Inside Out Led to the Scientific Revolution*** (New York, 2002); **D. Wootton, *Galileo: Watcher of the Stars***, (New Haven, Conn., 2013); **M. Casper, *Johannes Kepler***, trans. **C. D. Hellman** (London, 1959), the standard biography; **R. S. Westfall, *The Life of Isaac Newton*** (New York, 1993); and **P. Fara, *Newton: The Making of Genius*** (New York, 2004).

ADVANCES IN MEDICINE For a general survey of medicine and the Scientific Revolution, see **M. Lindemann, *Medicine and Society in Early Modern Europe*** (Cambridge, 2010). The worldview of Paracelsus can be examined in **P. Ball, *The Devil's Doctor: Paracelsus and the World of Renaissance Magic and Science*** (New York, 2006). The standard biography of Vesalius is **C. D. O'Malley, *Andreas Vesalius of Brussels, 1514–1564***

(Berkeley, Calif., 1964). The work of Harvey is discussed in **G. Whitteridge, *William Harvey and the Circulation of the Blood*** (London, 1971).

IMPACT OF SCIENCE The importance of Francis Bacon in the early development of science is underscored in **P. Zagorin, *Francis Bacon*** (Princeton, N.J., 1998). A good introduction to the work of Descartes can be found in **G. Radis-Lewis, *Descartes: A Biography*** (Ithaca, N.Y., 1998).

WOMEN AND SCIENCE On the subject of women and early modern science, see the comprehensive and highly informative work by **L. Schiebinger, *The Mind Has No Sex? Women in the Origins of Modern Science*** (Cambridge, Mass., 1989) and **K. Park, *Secrets of Women: Gender, Generation, and the Origins of Human Dissection*** (New York, 2010).

SCIENCE AND SOCIETY The social and political context for the triumph of science in the seventeenth and eighteenth centuries is examined in **M. C. Jacobs, *The Cultural Meaning of the Scientific Revolution*** (New York, 1988). On the relationship of science and industry, see **S. Gaukroger, *The Emergence of a Scientific Culture: Science and the Shaping of Modernity, 1210–1685*** (Oxford, 2006).

Notes

1. Galileo, *Discoveries and Opinions*, tr. and ed. S. Drake (Garden City, N.Y., 1957), pp. 177, 180.
2. Quoted in A. G. R. Smith, *Science and Society in the Sixteenth and Seventeenth Centuries* (London, 1972), p. 59.
3. E. MacCurdy, *The Notebooks of Leonardo da Vinci* (London, 1948), vol. 1, p. 634.
4. Ibid., p. 636.
5. F. Yates, *Giordano Bruno and the Hermetic Tradition* (New York, 1964), p. 448.
6. Ibid., p. 450.
7. Quoted in Smith, *Science and Society*, p. 97.
8. L. P. Smith, *Life and Letters of Sir Henry Wotton* (Oxford, 1907), vol. 1, pp. 486–487.
9. Quoted in J. H. Randall, *The Making of the Modern Mind* (Boston, 1926), p. 234.
10. Quoted in Smith, *Science and Society*, p. 124.
11. Quoted in B. J. Dobbs, *The Foundations of Newton's Alchemy* (Cambridge, 1975), pp. 13–14.
12. Jolande Jacobi, ed., *Paracelsus: Selected Writings* (New York, 1965), pp. 5–6.
13. Ibid., p. 21.
14. Quoted in L. Schiebinger, *The Mind Has No Sex? Women in the Origins of Modern Science* (Cambridge, Mass., 1989), pp. 52–53.
15. Ibid., p. 85.
16. Quoted in P. Stock, *Better than Rubies: A History of Women's Education* (New York, 1978), p. 16.
17. *The Method, Meditations, and Selections from the Principles of Descartes*, Sixth Edition, John Veitch, trans. (William Blackwood and Sons: Edinburgh and London, 1879), pp. 5–6.
18. Ibid., p. 33.
19. Francis Bacon, *The Great Instauration*, trans. Jerry Weinberger (Arlington Heights, Ill., 1989), pp. 2, 8, 16, 21.
20. Descartes, *Discourse on Method*, in *Philosophical Writings*, p. 75.
21. M. C. Jacob, *The Cultural Meaning of the Scientific Revolution* (New York, 1988), p. 73.
22. Stillman Drake, ed., trans., *Discoveries and Opinions of Galileo* (New York, 1957), p. 182.
23. Benedict de Spinoza, *Ethics*, trans. R. H. M. Elwes (New York, 1955), pp. 75–76.
24. Ibid., p. 76.
25. Spinoza, *Letters*, quoted in Randall, *The Making of the Modern Mind*, p. 247.
26. Blaise Pascal, *Pensées*, trans. J. M. Cohen (Harmondsworth, U.K., 1961), p. 100.
27. Ibid., pp. 31, 52–53, 164, 165.

CHAPTER

17

THE EIGHTEENTH CENTURY: AN AGE OF ENLIGHTENMENT

© RMN-Grand Palais/Art Resource, NY

Portrait of Madame Geoffrin

CHAPTER OUTLINE AND FOCUS QUESTIONS

The Enlightenment

Q What intellectual developments led to the emergence of the Enlightenment? Who were the leading figures of the Enlightenment, and what were their main contributions? In what type of social environment did the philosophes thrive, and what role did women play in that environment?

Culture and Society in the Enlightenment

Q What innovations in art, music, and literature occurred in the eighteenth century? How did popular culture differ from high culture in the eighteenth century?

Religion and the Churches

Q How did popular religion differ from institutional religion in the eighteenth century?

Critical Thinking

Q *What was the relationship between the Scientific Revolution and the Enlightenment?*

Connections to Today

Q *What intellectual movements today parallel the philosophes of the Enlightenment in challenging accepted ideas about government, religion, women, and the economy?*

THE EARTH-SHATTERING WORK of the "natural philosophers" in the Scientific Revolution had affected only a relatively small number of Europe's educated elite. In the eighteenth century, this changed dramatically as a group of intellectuals known as the philosophes popularized the ideas of the Scientific Revolution and used them to undertake a dramatic reexamination of all aspects of life. In Paris, the cultural capital of Europe, women took the lead in bringing together groups of men and women to discuss the new ideas of the philosophes. At her fashionable home on the rue Saint-Honoré, Marie-Thérèse de Geoffrin (ma-REE-tay-RAYZ duh zhoh-FRANH), the wife of a wealthy merchant, held sway over gatherings that became the talk of France and even Europe. Distinguished foreigners, including a future king of Sweden and a future king of Poland, competed to receive invitations. When Madame Geoffrin made a visit to Vienna, she was so well received that she exclaimed, "I am better known here than a couple of yards from my own house." Madame Geoffrin was an amiable but firm hostess who allowed wide-ranging discussions as long as they remained in good taste. When she found that artists and philosophers did not mix particularly well (the artists were high-strung and the philosophers talked too much), she set up separate meetings. Artists were invited only on Mondays, philosophers, on Wednesdays. These gatherings were among the many avenues for the spread of the ideas of the philosophes. And those ideas had such a widespread impact on their society that historians ever since have called the eighteenth century the Age of Enlightenment.

For most of the philosophes, "enlightenment" included the rejection of traditional Christianity. The religious wars and intolerance of the sixteenth and seventeenth centuries had so alienated intellectuals that they were open and even eager to embrace the new ideas of the Scientific Revolution. Whereas the great scientists of the seventeenth century believed that their work exalted God, the intellectuals of the eighteenth century read those scientific conclusions a different way and increasingly turned their backs on Christian orthodoxy. Consequently, European intellectual life in the eighteenth century was marked by the emergence of the secularization that has characterized the modern Western mentality ever since. Ironically, at the same time that reason and materialism were beginning to replace faith and worship, a great outburst of religious sensibility manifested itself in music and art. Clearly, the growing secularization of the eighteenth century had not yet captured the hearts and minds of all European intellectuals and artists.

The Enlightenment

FOCUS QUESTIONS: What intellectual developments led to the emergence of the Enlightenment? Who were the leading figures of the Enlightenment, and what were their main contributions? In what type of social environment did the philosophes thrive, and what role did women play in that environment?

In 1784, the German philosopher Immanuel Kant (i-MAHN-yoo-el KAHNT) (1724–1804) defined the **Enlightenment** as "man's leaving his self-caused immaturity." Whereas earlier periods had been handicapped by the inability to "use one's intelligence without the guidance of another," Kant proclaimed as the motto of the Enlightenment: "Dare to know! Have the courage to use your own intelligence!" The eighteenth-century Enlightenment was a movement of intellectuals who dared to know. They were greatly impressed with the accomplishments of the Scientific Revolution, and when they used the word *reason*—one of their favorite words—they were advocating the application of the scientific method to the understanding of all life. All institutions and all systems of thought were subject to the rational, scientific way of thinking if only people would free themselves from the shackles of old, worthless traditions, especially religious ones. If Isaac Newton could discover the natural laws regulating the world of nature, they too, by using reason, could find the laws that governed human society. This belief in turn led them to hope that they could make progress toward a better society than the one they had inherited. *Reason, natural law, hope, progress*—these were the buzz words in the heady atmosphere of the eighteenth century.

The Paths to Enlightenment

The intellectuals of the eighteenth century were especially influenced by the revolutionary thinkers of the seventeenth century. What were the major intellectual changes that culminated in the intellectual movement of the Enlightenment?

THE POPULARIZATION OF SCIENCE Although the intellectuals of the eighteenth century were much influenced by the scientific ideas of the seventeenth, they did not always acquire this knowledge directly from the original sources. Newton's *Principia* was not an easy book to read or comprehend. Scientific ideas were spread to ever-widening circles of educated Europeans not so much by scientists themselves as by popularizers. Especially important as the direct link between the Scientific Revolution of the seventeenth century and the philosophes of the eighteenth was Bernard de Fontenelle (bayr-NAHR duh fawnt-NELL) (1657–1757), secretary of the French Royal Academy of Science from 1691 to 1741.

Although Fontenelle performed no scientific experiments and made no scientific discoveries, he possessed a deep knowledge of all the scientific work of earlier centuries and his own time. Moreover, he was able to communicate that body of scientific knowledge in a clear and even witty fashion that appealed to his upper-class audiences in a meaningful way. One of his most successful books, *Plurality of Worlds*, was actually presented in the form of an intimate conversation between a lady aristocrat and her lover who are engaged in conversation under the stars. What are they discussing? "Tell me," she exclaims, "about these stars of yours." Her lover proceeds to tell her of the tremendous advances in cosmology after the foolish errors of their forebears:

> There came on the scene a certain German, one Copernicus, who made short work of all those various circles, all those solid skies, which the ancients had pictured to themselves. The former he abolished; the latter, he broke in pieces. Fired with the noble zeal of a true astronomer, he took the earth and spun it very far away from the center of the universe, where it had been installed, and in that center he put the sun, which had a far better title to the honor.[1]

In the course of two evenings under the stars, the lady learned the basic fundamentals of the new mechanistic universe. So too did scores of the educated elite of Europe.

Thanks to Fontenelle, science was no longer the monopoly of experts but part of literature. He was especially fond of downplaying the religious backgrounds of the seventeenth-century scientists. Himself a skeptic, Fontenelle contributed to the growing **skepticism** toward religion at the end of the seventeenth century by portraying the churches as enemies of scientific progress.

A NEW SKEPTICISM The great scientists of the seventeenth century, including Kepler, Galileo, and Newton, had pursued their work in a spirit of exalting God, not undermining Christianity. But as scientific knowledge spread, more and more educated men and women began to question religious truths and values. Skepticism about religion and a growing secularization of thought were especially evident in the work of Pierre Bayle (PYAYR BELL) (1647–1706), who remained a Protestant while becoming a leading critic of traditional religious attitudes.

The Popularization of Science in the Age of Enlightenment. During the Enlightenment, the ideas of the Scientific Revolution were spread and popularized in a variety of ways. Scientific societies funded by royal and princely patrons were especially valuable in providing outlets for the spread of new scientific ideas. This illustration shows the German prince Frederick Christian visiting his Academy of Sciences in 1739. Note the many instruments of the new science around the rooms—human skeletons, globes, microscopes, telescopes, and orreries (mechanical models of the solar system).

Archivio di Stato, Bologna//Alinari/Art Resource, NY

Bayle attacked superstition, religious intolerance, and dogmatism. In his view, compelling people to believe a particular set of religious ideas (as Louis XIV was doing at the time in Bayle's France) was wrong. It simply created hypocrites and in itself was contrary to what religion should be about. Individual conscience should determine one's actions. Bayle argued for complete religious toleration, maintaining that the existence of many religions would benefit rather than harm the state.

THE IMPACT OF TRAVEL LITERATURE Skepticism about both Christianity and European culture itself was nourished by travel reports. As we saw in Chapter 14, Europeans had embarked on voyages of discovery to other parts of the world in the late fifteenth and sixteenth centuries. In the course of the seventeenth century, traders, missionaries, medical practitioners, and explorers began to publish an increasing number of travel books that gave accounts of many different cultures. Then, too, the new geographic adventures of the eighteenth century, especially the discovery of the Pacific island of Tahiti and of New Zealand and Australia by James Cook, aroused much enthusiasm. Cook's *Travels*, an account of his journey, became a best-seller. Educated Europeans responded to these accounts of lands abroad in different ways. For some intellectuals, exotic peoples, such as the natives of Tahiti, presented an image of a "natural man" who was far happier than many Europeans. One intellectual wrote:

> The life of savages is so simple, and our societies are such complicated machines! The Tahitian is close to the origin of the world, while the European is closer to its old age. . . . [The Tahitians] understand nothing about our manners or our laws, and they are bound to see in them nothing but shackles disguised in a hundred different ways. Those shackles could only provoke the indignation and scorn of creatures in whom the most profound feeling is a love of liberty.[2]

The idea of the "noble savage" would play an important role in the political work of some philosophes.

The travel literature of the seventeenth and eighteenth centuries also led to the realization that there were highly developed civilizations with different customs in other parts of the world. China was especially singled out. One German university professor praised Confucian morality as superior to the intolerance of Christianity. Some European intellectuals began to evaluate their own civilization relative to others. Practices that had seemed to be grounded in reason now appeared to be merely matters of custom. Certainties about European practices gave way to **cultural relativism**.

Cultural relativism was accompanied by religious skepticism. As these travel accounts made clear, the Christian perception of God was merely one of many. Some people were devastated by this revelation: "Some complete their demoralization by extensive travel, and lose whatever shreds of religion remained to them. Every day they see a new religion, new customs, new rites."[3]

As Europeans were exposed to growing numbers of people around the world who were different from themselves, some intellectuals also began to classify people into racial groups. One group espoused polygenesis, or the belief in separate human species; others argued for monogenesis, or the belief in one human species characterized by racial variations. Both groups were especially unsympathetic to Africans and placed them in the lowest rank of humankind. In his *Encyclopedia*, the intellectual Denis Diderot (see "Diderot and the *Encyclopedia*" later in this chapter) maintained that all Africans were black and characterized the Negro as a "new species of mankind."

THE LEGACY OF LOCKE AND NEWTON The intellectual inspiration for the Enlightenment came primarily from two Englishmen, Isaac Newton and John Locke, acknowledged by the philosophes as great minds. Newton was frequently singled out for praise as the "greatest and rarest genius that ever rose for the ornament and instruction of the species." One English poet declared: "Nature and Nature's Laws lay hid in Night; God said, 'Let Newton be,' and all was Light." Enchanted by the grand design of the Newtonian world-machine, the intellectuals of the Enlightenment were convinced that by following Newton's rules of reasoning, they could discover the natural laws that governed politics, economics, justice, religion, and the arts.

John Locke's theory of knowledge especially influenced the philosophes. Locke studied medicine at Oxford University before joining the household of Lord Ashley as a general counselor before fleeing for the Netherlands in 1683 where he wrote his *Essay Concerning Human Understanding* in 1690. Locke denied Descartes's belief in innate ideas, instead he argued that every person was born with a *tabula rasa* (TAB-yuh-luh RAH-suh), a blank mind:

> Let us then suppose the mind to be, as we say, white paper, void of all characters, without any ideas. How comes it to be furnished? Whence comes it by that vast store which the busy and boundless fancy of man has painted on it with an almost endless variety? Whence has it all the materials of reason and knowledge? To this I answer, in one word, from experience. . . . Our observation, employed either about external sensible objects or about the internal operations of our minds perceived and reflected on by ourselves, is that which supplies our understanding with all the materials of thinking.[4]

Our knowledge, then, is derived from our environment, not from heredity; from reason, not from faith. Locke's philosophy implied that people were molded by their environment, by the experiences that they received through their senses from their surrounding world. By changing the environment and subjecting people to proper influences, they could be changed and a new society created. And how should the environment be changed? Newton had already paved the way by showing how reason enabled enlightened people to discover the natural laws to which all institutions should conform. No wonder the philosophes were enamored of Newton and Locke. Taken together, their ideas seemed to offer the hope of a "brave new world" built on reason.

The Philosophes and Their Ideas

The intellectuals of the Enlightenment were known by the French term *philosophe* (fee-loh-ZAWF), although not all of them were French and few were actually philosophers. The **philosophes** were literary people, professors, journalists, statesmen, economists, political scientists, and above all, social reformers. They came from both the nobility and the middle class, and a few even stemmed from lower origins. Although it was a truly international and **cosmopolitan** movement, the Enlightenment also enhanced the dominant role being played by French culture. Paris was its recognized capital, and most of the leaders of the Enlightenment were French (see Map 17.1). The French philosophes in turn affected intellectuals elsewhere and created a movement that engulfed the entire Western world, including the British and Spanish colonies in America.

Although the philosophes faced different political circumstances depending on the country in which they lived, they shared common bonds as part of a truly international movement. They were called philosophers, but what did philosophy mean to them? The role of philosophy was to change the world, not just discuss it. As one writer said, the philosophe is one who "applies himself to the study of society with the purpose of making his kind better and happier." To the philosophes, rationalism did not mean the creation of a grandiose system of thought to explain all things. Reason was scientific method, an appeal to facts and experience. A spirit of rational criticism was to be applied to everything, including religion and politics.

The philosophes' call for freedom of expression is a reminder that their work was done in an atmosphere of censorship. The philosophes were not free to write whatever they chose. State censors decided what could be published, and protests from any number of government bodies could result in the seizure of books and the imprisonment of their authors, publishers, and sellers. The philosophes found ways to get around state censorship. Some published under pseudonyms or anonymously or abroad, especially in Holland. The use of double meanings, such as talking about the Persians when they meant the French, became standard procedure for many. Books were also published and circulated secretly or in manuscript form to avoid the censors.

Although the philosophes constituted a kind of "family circle" bound together by common intellectual bonds, they often disagreed. Spanning almost a century, the Enlightenment evolved over time, with each succeeding generation becoming more radical as it built on the contributions of the previous one. A few people, however, dominated the landscape completely, and we might best begin our survey of the ideas of the philosophes by looking at three French giants—Montesquieu, Voltaire, and Diderot.

MONTESQUIEU AND POLITICAL THOUGHT Charles de Secondat, the baron de Montesquieu (MOHN-tess-kyoo) (1689–1755), came from the French nobility. He received a classical education and then studied law. In his first work, the *Persian Letters*, published in 1721, he used the format of two Persians supposedly traveling in western Europe and sending their impressions back home to enable him to criticize French institutions, especially the Catholic Church and the French monarchy. Much of the program of the French Enlightenment is contained in this work: the attack on traditional religion, the advocacy of religious toleration, the denunciation of slavery, and the use of reason to liberate human beings from their prejudices.

Montesquieu's most famous work, *The Spirit of the Laws*, was published in 1748. This treatise was a comparative study of governments in which Montesquieu attempted to apply the scientific method to the social and political arena to ascertain the "natural laws" governing the social relationships of human beings. Montesquieu distinguished three basic kinds of governments: republics, suitable for small states and based on citizen involvement; monarchy, appropriate for middle-sized states and grounded in the ruling class's adherence to law; and despotism, apt for large empires and dependent on fear to inspire obedience. Montesquieu used England as an example of the

MAP 17.1 **The Enlightenment in Europe.** "Have the courage to use your own intelligence!" Kant's words epitomize the role of the individual in using reason to understand all aspects of life—the natural world and the sphere of human nature, behavior, and institutions.

Q *Which countries or regions were at the center of the Enlightenment, and what could account for peripheral regions being less involved?*

second category, and it was his praise and analysis of England's constitution that led to his most far-reaching and lasting contribution to political thought—the importance of checks and balances created by means of a **separation of powers** (see the box on p. 504). He believed that England's system, with its separate executive, legislative, and judicial powers that served to limit and control each other, provided the greatest freedom and security for a state. In large part, Montesquieu misread the English situation and insisted on a separation of powers because he wanted the nobility of France (of which he was a member) to play an active role in running the French government. The translation of his work into English two years after publication ensured that it would be read by American philosophes, such as Benjamin Franklin, James Madison, John Adams, Alexander Hamilton, and Thomas Jefferson, who incorporated its principles into the U.S. Constitution (see Chapter 19).

VOLTAIRE AND THE ENLIGHTENMENT The greatest figure of the Enlightenment was François-Marie Arouet (frahn-SWAH-ma-REE ahr-WEH), known simply as Voltaire (vohl-TAYR) (1694–1778). Son of a prosperous middle-class family from Paris, Voltaire received a classical education in Jesuit schools. Although he studied law, he wished to be a writer and achieved his first success as a playwright. By his mid-twenties, Voltaire had been hailed as the successor to Racine (see Chapter 15) for his tragedy *Œdipe* and his epic *Henriade* on his favorite king,

THE SEPARATION OF POWERS

THE ENLIGHTENMENT AFFECTED THE NEW WORLD of America as much as it did the old world of Europe. American philosophes were well aware of the ideas of European Enlightenment thinkers. This selection from Montesquieu's *Spirit of the Laws* enunciates the "separation of powers" doctrine.

Montesquieu, "Of the Constitution of England"

In every government there are three sorts of power: the legislative; the executive in respect to things dependent on the law of nations; and the executive in regard to matters that depend on the civil law.

By virtue of the first, the prince or magistrate enacts temporary or perpetual laws, and amends or abrogates those that have been already enacted. By the second, he makes peace or war, sends or receives embassies, establishes the public security, and provides against invasions. By the third, he punishes criminals, or determines the disputes that arise between individuals. The latter we shall call the judiciary power, and the other simply the executive power of the state.

The political liberty of the subject is a tranquility of mind arising from the opinion each person has of his safety. In order to have this liberty, it is requisite the government be so constituted as one man need not be afraid of another.

When the legislative and executive powers are united in the same person, or in the same body of magistrates, there can be no liberty; because apprehensions may arise, lest the same monarch or senate should enact tyrannical laws, to execute them in a tyrannical manner.

Again, there is no liberty, if the judiciary power be not separated from the legislative and executive. Were it joined with the legislative, the life and liberty of the subject would be exposed to arbitrary control; for the judge would be then the legislator. Were it joined to the executive power, the judge might behave with violence and oppression.

There would be an end of everything, were the same man or the same body, whether of the nobles or of the people, to exercise those three powers, that of enacting laws, that of executing the public resolutions, and of trying the causes of individuals.

Q *As seen in this excerpt, what is Montesquieu's doctrine of the separation of powers? What are the underlying moral and political justifications for this system of government? How was this doctrine incorporated into the U.S. Constitution?*

Source: N. L. Torrey, *Les Philosophes* (New York: G. P. Putnam's Sons, 1961).

Henry IV. His wit made him a darling of the Parisian intellectuals but also involved him in a quarrel with a dissolute nobleman that forced him to flee France and live in England for almost two years.

Well received in English literary and social circles, the young playwright was much impressed by England. His *Philosophic Letters on the English*, written in 1733, expressed a deep admiration of English life, especially its freedom of the press, its political freedom, and its religious toleration. In judging the English religious situation, he made the famous remark that if there were two religions, they would cut each other's throats; but since there are thirty religions, "they live together peacefully and happily." Although he clearly exaggerated the freedoms England possessed, in a roundabout way Voltaire had managed to criticize many of the ills oppressing France, especially royal absolutism and the lack of religious toleration and freedom of thought. The criticism of absolute monarchy by Voltaire and other philosophes reflected the broader dissatisfaction of middle-class individuals with their society. In the course of

RMN-Grand Palais/Art Resource, NY

Voltaire. François-Marie Arouet, better known as Voltaire, achieved his first success as a playwright. A philosophe, Voltaire was well known for his criticism of traditional religion and his support of religious toleration. Maurice-Quentin de La Tour painted this portrait of Voltaire holding one of his books in 1736.

THE ATTACK ON RELIGIOUS INTOLERANCE

VOLTAIRE'S LUCID PROSE, BITING SATIRE, AND clever wit caused his works to be widely read and all the more influential. These two selections present different sides of Voltaire's attack on religious intolerance. The first is from a straightforward treatise, *The Ignorant Philosopher*, and the second is from his only real literary masterpiece, the novel *Candide*, in which he used humor to make the same fundamental point about religious intolerance.

Voltaire, *The Ignorant Philosopher*

The contagion of fanaticism then still subsists. . . . The author of the *Treatise upon Toleration* has not mentioned the shocking executions wherein so many unhappy victims perished in the valleys of Piedmont. He has passed over in silence the massacre of six hundred inhabitants of Valtelina, men, women, and children, who were murdered by the Catholics in the month of September, 1620. I will not say it was with the consent and assistance of the archbishop of Milan, Charles Borome, who was made a saint. Some passionate writers have averred this fact, which I am very far from believing; but I say, there is scarce any city or borough in Europe, where blood has not been spilt for religious quarrels; I say, that the human species has been perceptibly diminished, because women and girls were massacred as well as men; I say, that Europe would have had a third larger population, if there had been no theological disputes. In fine, I say, that so far from forgetting these abominable times, we should frequently take a view of them, to inspire an eternal horror for them; and that it is for our age to make reparation by toleration, for this long collection of crimes, which has taken place through the want of toleration, during sixteen barbarous centuries. Let it not then be said, that there are no traces left of that shocking fanaticism, of the want of toleration; they are still everywhere to be met with, even in those countries that are esteemed the most humane. The Lutheran and Calvinist preachers, were they masters, would, perhaps, be as little inclined to pity, as obdurate, as insolent as they upbraid their antagonists with being.

Voltaire, *Candide*

At last he [Candide] approached a man who had just been addressing a big audience for a whole hour on the subject of charity. The orator peered at him and said:

"What is your business here? Do you support the Good Old Cause?"

"There is not effect without a cause," replied Candide modestly. "All things are necessarily connected and arranged for the best. It was my fate to be driven from Lady Cunégonde's presence and made to run the gantlet, and now I have to beg my bread until I can earn it. Things should not have happened otherwise."

"Do you believe that the Pope is Antichrist, my friend?" said the minister.

"I have never heard anyone say so," replied Candide; "but whether he is or he isn't, I want some food."

"You don't deserve to eat," said the other. "Be off with you, you villain, you wretch! Don't come near me again or you'll suffer for it."

The minister's wife looked out of the window at that moment, and seeing a man who was not sure that the Pope was Antichrist, emptied over his head a chamber pot, which shows to what lengths ladies are driven by religious zeal.

Q *Compare the two approaches that Voltaire uses to address the problem of religious intolerance. Do you think one is more effective? Why?*

Sources: Voltaire, *The Ignorant Philosopher* and *Candide*, in J. Butt, trans., *Candide or Optimism* (London: Penguin Classics, 1947).

the eighteenth century, this would help lead to revolutionary upheavals in France and other countries (see Chapter 19).

Voltaire returned to France to discover his *Philosophic Letters* banned by the state, sending Voltaire into exile to Cirey, near France's eastern border, where he lived in semi-seclusion on the estate of his mistress, the marquise du Châtelet (mahr-KEEZ duh shat-LAY) (1706–1749). Herself an early philosophe, the marquise was one of the first intellectuals to adopt the ideas of Isaac Newton, and in 1759 her own translation of Newton's famous *Principia* was published. While Voltaire lived with her at her château at Cirey, the two collaborated on a book about the natural philosophy of Newton.

Voltaire eventually settled on a magnificent estate at Ferney. Located in France near the Swiss border, Ferney gave Voltaire the freedom to write what he wished. By this time, through his writings, inheritance, and clever investments, Voltaire had become wealthy and now had the leisure to write an almost endless stream of pamphlets, novels, plays, letters, and histories.

Although he touched on all of the themes of importance to the philosophes, Voltaire was especially well known for his criticism of traditional religion and his strong attachment to the ideal of religious toleration (see the box above). He lent his prestige and skills as a polemicist to fighting cases of intolerance in France. The most famous incident was the Calas affair. Jean Calas (ZHAHNH ka-LAH) was a Protestant from Toulouse who was accused of murdering his own son to stop him from becoming a Catholic. Tortured to confess his guilt, Calas died shortly thereafter. An angry and indignant Voltaire published devastating broadsides that aroused public opinion and forced a retrial in which Calas was exonerated when it was proved that his son had actually committed suicide. The family was paid an indemnity, and Voltaire's appeals for toleration appeared all the more reasonable. In 1763, he penned

DIDEROT QUESTIONS CHRISTIAN SEXUAL STANDARDS

DENIS DIDEROT WAS ONE OF THE BOLDEST thinkers of the Enlightenment. In his *Supplement to the Voyage of Bougainville,* he constructed a dialogue between Orou, a Tahitian who symbolizes the wisdom of a philosophe, and a chaplain who defends Christian sexual mores. The dialogue gave Diderot the opportunity to criticize the practice of sexual chastity and monogamy.

Denis Diderot, *Supplement to the Voyage of Bougainville*

[Orou, speaking to the Chaplain:] "You are young and healthy and you have just had a good supper. He who sleeps alone sleeps badly; at night a man needs a woman at his side. Here is my wife and here are my daughters. Choose whichever one pleases you most, but if you would like to do me a favor, you will give your preference to my youngest girl, who has not yet had any children. . . ."

The chaplain replied that his religion, his holy orders, his moral standards and his sense of decency all prevented him from accepting Orou's invitation.

Orou answered: "I don't know what this thing is that you call religion, but I can only have a low opinion of it because it forbids you to partake of an innocent pleasure to which Nature, the sovereign mistress of us all, invites everybody. It seems to prevent you from bringing one of your fellow creatures into the world, from doing a favor asked of by a father, a mother and their children, from repaying the kindness of a host, and from enriching a nation by giving it an additional citizen. . . . Look at the distress you have caused to appear on the faces of these four women—they are afraid you have noticed some defect in them that arouses your distaste. . . ."

The Chaplain: "You don't understand—it's not that. They are all four of them equally beautiful. But there is my religion! My holy orders! . . . [God] spoke to our ancestors and gave them laws . . . he ordained that certain actions are good and others he forbade them to do as being evil."

Orou: "I see. And one of these evil actions which he has forbidden is that of a man who goes to bed with a woman or girl. But in that case, why did he make two sexes?"

The Chaplain: "In order that they might come together—but only when certain conditions are satisfied and only after certain initial ceremonies one man belongs to one woman and only to her; one woman belongs to one man and only to him."

Orou: "For their whole lives?"

The Chaplain: "For their whole lives. . . ."

Orou: "I find these strange precepts contrary to nature, and contrary to reason. . . . Furthermore, your laws seem to me to be contrary to the general order of things. For in truth is there anything so senseless as a precept that forbids us to heed the changing impulses that are inherent in our being, or commands that require a degree of constancy which is not possible, that violate the liberty of both male and female by chaining them perpetually to one another? . . . I don't know what your great workman [God] is, but I am very happy that he never spoke to our forefathers, and I hope that he never speaks to our children, for if he does, he may tell them the same foolishness, and they may be foolish enough to believe it."

Q *What attack does Diderot make on Christian sexual standards? What does this passage say about enlightened conceptions of nature and the place of physical pleasure in healthy human life?*

Source: J. Barzun and R. Bowen, trans., *Diderot: Rameau's Nephew and Other Works* (Indianapolis: Hackett Publishing Company, 1956).

his *Treatise on Toleration*, in which he argued that religious toleration had created no problems for England and Holland and reminded governments that "all men are brothers under God." As he grew older, Voltaire became ever more strident in his denunciations. "Crush the infamous thing," he thundered repeatedly—the infamous thing being religious fanaticism, intolerance, and superstition.

Throughout his life, Voltaire championed not only religious tolerance but also **deism**, a religious outlook shared by most other philosophes. Deism was built on the Newtonian world-machine, which suggested the existence of a mechanic (God) who had created the universe. Voltaire said, "In the opinion that there is a God, there are difficulties, but in the contrary opinion there are absurdities." To Voltaire and most other philosophes, God had no direct involvement in the world he had created and allowed it to run according to its own natural laws. God did not extend grace or answer prayers or perform miracles, as Christians liked to believe. Jesus might be a "good fellow," as Voltaire called him, but he was not divine, as Christianity claimed.

DIDEROT AND THE *ENCYCLOPEDIA* Denis Diderot (duh-NEE DEE-droh) (1713–1784), the son of a skilled craftsman from eastern France, became a freelance writer so that he could study many subjects and read in many languages. One of his favorite topics was Christianity, which he condemned as fanatical and unreasonable. As he grew older, his literary attacks on Christianity grew more vicious. Of all religions, he maintained, Christianity was the worst, "the most absurd and the most atrocious in its dogma" (see the box above). Near the end of his life, he argued for an essentially materialistic conception of life: "This world is only a mass of molecules."

Diderot's most famous contribution to the Enlightenment was the twenty-eight-volume *Encyclopedia, or Classified Dictionary of the Sciences, Arts, and Trades*, that he edited and called the "great work of his life." Its purpose, according to Diderot, was to "change the general way of thinking." It did precisely that in becoming a major weapon of the philosophes' crusade against the old French society. The contributors included many philosophes who expressed their major concerns. They attacked religious superstition and advocated toleration as well as a program for social, legal, and political improvements that would lead to a society that was more cosmopolitan, more tolerant, more humane, and more reasonable. In later editions, the price of the *Encyclopedia* was drastically reduced, dramatically increasing its sales and making it available to doctors, clergy, teachers, lawyers, and even military officers. The ideas of the Enlightenment were spread even further as a result.

THE NEW "SCIENCE OF MAN" The Enlightenment belief that Newton's scientific methods could be used to discover the natural laws underlying all areas of human life led to the emergence in the eighteenth century of what the philosophes called the "science of man," or what we would call the social sciences. In a number of areas, philosophes arrived at natural laws that they believed governed human actions. If these "natural laws" seem less than universal to us, it reminds us how much the philosophes were people of their times reacting to the conditions they faced. Nevertheless, their efforts did at least lay the foundations for the modern social sciences.

That a science of man was possible was a strong belief of the Scottish philosopher David Hume (1711–1776). An important figure in the history of philosophy, Hume has also been called "a pioneering social scientist." In his *Treatise on Human Nature*, which he subtitled "An Attempt to Introduce the Experimental Method of Reasoning into Moral Subjects," Hume argued that observation and reflection, grounded in "systematized common sense," made conceivable a "science of man." Careful examination of the experiences that constituted human life would lead to the knowledge of human nature that would make this science possible.

The Physiocrats and Adam Smith have been viewed as founders of the modern discipline of economics. The leader of the Physiocrats was François Quesnay (frahn-SWAH keh-NAY) (1694–1774), a highly successful French court physician. Quesnay and the Physiocrats claimed they would discover the natural economic laws that governed human society. Their first principle was that land constituted the only source of wealth and that wealth itself could be increased only by agriculture because all other economic activities were unproductive and sterile. Even the state's revenues should come from a single tax on land rather than the hodgepodge of inequitable taxes and privileges currently in place. In stressing the economic primacy of agricultural production, the Physiocrats were rejecting the mercantilist emphasis on the significance of money—that is, gold and silver—as the primary determinants of wealth (see Chapter 14).

Their second major "natural law" of economics also represented a repudiation of mercantilism, specifically, its emphasis on a controlled economy for the benefit of the state. Instead, the Physiocrats stressed that the existence of the natural economic forces of supply and demand made it imperative that individuals should be left free to pursue their own economic self-interest. In doing so, all of society would ultimately benefit. Consequently, they argued that the state should in no way interrupt the free play of natural economic forces by government regulation of the economy but rather should just leave it alone, a doctrine that subsequently became known by its French name, ***laissez-faire*** (less-ay-FAYR) (noninterference; literally, "let people do as they choose").

The best statement of laissez-faire was made in 1776 by a Scottish philosopher, Adam Smith (1723–1790), in his *Inquiry into the Nature and Causes of the Wealth of Nations*, known simply as *The Wealth of Nations*. In the process of enunciating three basic principles of economics, Smith presented a strong attack on mercantilism. First, he condemned the mercantilist use of tariffs to protect home industries. If one country can supply another country with a product cheaper than the latter can make it, it is better to purchase the product than to produce it. To Smith, free trade was a fundamental economic principle. Smith's second principle was his labor theory of value. Like the Physiocrats, he claimed that gold and silver were not the source of a nation's true wealth, but unlike the Physiocrats, he did not believe that land was either. Rather labor—the labor of individual farmers, artisans, and merchants—constituted the true wealth of a nation. Finally, like the Physiocrats, Smith believed that the state should not interfere in economic matters; indeed, he assigned to government only three basic functions: to protect society from invasion (army), defend individuals from injustice and oppression (police), and keep up certain public works, such as roads and canals, that private individuals could not afford. Thus, in Smith's view, the state should stay out of the lives of individuals. In emphasizing the economic liberty of the individual, the Physiocrats and Adam Smith laid the foundation for what became known in the nineteenth century as **economic liberalism**.

THE LATER ENLIGHTENMENT By the late 1760s, a new generation of philosophes who had grown up with the worldview of the Enlightenment began to move beyond their predecessors' beliefs. Baron Paul d'Holbach (dawl-BAHK) (1723–1789), a wealthy German aristocrat who settled in Paris, preached a doctrine of strict atheism and materialism. In his *System of Nature*, written in 1770, he argued that everything in the universe consisted of matter in motion. Human beings were simply machines; God was a product of the human mind and was unnecessary for leading a moral life. People needed only reason to live in this world: "Let us persuade men to be just, beneficent, moderate, sociable; not because the gods demand it, but because they must please men. Let us advise them to abstain from vice and crimes; not because they will be punished in the other world, but because they will suffer for it in this."[5] Holbach shocked almost all of his fellow philosophes with his uncompromising atheism. Most intellectuals remained more comfortable with deism and feared the effect of atheism on society.

Marie-Jean de Condorcet (ma-REE-ZHAHNH duh kohn-dor-SAY) (1743–1794), another French philosophe, made an exaggerated claim for progress. Condorcet was a victim of the turmoil of the French Revolution and wrote his chief work, *The Progress of the Human Mind*, while in hiding during the Reign of Terror (see Chapter 19). His survey of human history convinced him that humans had progressed through nine stages of history. Now, with the spread of science and reason, humans were about to enter the tenth stage, one of perfection, in which they will see that "there is no limit to the perfecting of the powers of man; that human perfectibility is in reality indefinite, that the progress of this perfectibility . . . has no other limit than the duration of the globe upon which nature has placed us." Shortly after composing this work, the prophet of humankind's perfection died in a French revolutionary prison.

ROUSSEAU AND THE SOCIAL CONTRACT No one was more critical of the work of his predecessors than Jean-Jacques Rousseau (ZHAHNH-ZHAHK roo-SOH) (1712–1778). Born in Geneva, he was orphaned at a young age and spent his youth wandering about France and Italy holding various jobs. Largely self-educated, he returned to school for a while to study music and the classics (he could afford to do so after becoming the paid lover of an older woman). Eventually, he made his way to Paris, where he was introduced into the circles of the philosophes. He never really liked the social life of the cities, however, and frequently withdrew into long periods of solitude.

Musée d'Art et d'Histoire, Geneva//Erich Lessing/Art Resource, NY

Jean-Jacques Rousseau. By the late 1760s, a new generation of philosophes arose who began to move beyond and even to question the beliefs of their predecessors. Of the philosophes of the late Enlightenment, Rousseau was perhaps the most critical of his predecessors. Shown here is a portrait of Rousseau by Maurice-Quentin de La Tour.

Rousseau's political beliefs were presented in two major works. In his *Discourse on the Origins of the Inequality of Mankind*, Rousseau began with humans in their primitive condition (or state of nature—see Chapter 15), where they were happy. There were no laws, no judges; all people were equal. But what had gone wrong?

> The first man who, having enclosed a piece of ground, thought of saying, This is mine, and found people simple enough to believe him, was the true founder of civil society. How many crimes, wars, murders; how much misery and horror the human race would have been spared if someone had pulled up the stakes and filled in the ditch, and cried to his fellow men: "Beware of listening to this impostor. You are lost if you forget that the fruits of the earth belong to everyone and that the earth itself belongs to no one!"[6]

To preserve their private property, people adopted laws and governors. In so doing, they rushed headlong not to liberty but into chains. "What then is to be done? Must societies be totally abolished? . . . Must we return again to the forest to live among bears?" No, civilized humans could "no longer subsist on plants or acorns or live without laws and magistrates." Government was an evil, but a necessary one.

In his celebrated treatise *The Social Contract*, published in 1762, Rousseau tried to harmonize individual liberty with governmental authority (see the box on p. 509). The social contract was basically an agreement on the part of an entire society to be governed by its general will. If any individual wished to follow his own self-interest, he should be compelled to abide by the general will. "This means nothing less than that he will be forced to be free," said Rousseau, because the general will represented a community's highest aspirations, whatever was best for the entire community. Thus, liberty was achieved through being forced to follow what was best for all people because, he believed, what was best for all was best for each individual. True freedom is adherence to laws that one has imposed on oneself. To Rousseau, because everybody was responsible for framing the general will, the creation of laws could never be delegated to a parliamentary institution:

> Thus, the people's deputies are not and could not be its representatives; they are merely its agents; and they cannot decide anything finally. Any law which the people has not ratified in person is void; it is not law at all. The English people believes itself to be free; it is gravely mistaken; it is free only during the election of Members of Parliament; as soon as the Members are elected, the people is enslaved; it is nothing.[7]

This is an extreme and idealistic statement, but it is the ultimate statement of participatory democracy.

Another influential treatise by Rousseau also appeared in 1762. Titled *Émile*, it is one of the Enlightenment's most important works on education. Written in the form of a novel, the work is really a general treatise "on the education of the natural man." Rousseau's fundamental concern was that education should foster rather than restrict children's natural instincts. Life's experiences had shown Rousseau the importance of the promptings of the heart, and what he sought was a balance

A SOCIAL CONTRACT

ALTHOUGH JEAN-JACQUES ROUSSEAU WAS ONE of the French philosophes, he has also been called "the father of Romanticism." His political ideas have proved extremely controversial. Though some people have hailed him as the prophet of democracy, others have labeled him an apologist for totalitarianism. This selection is taken from one of his most famous books, *The Social Contract*.

Jean-Jacques Rousseau, *The Social Contract*

Book 1, Chapter 6: "The Social Pact"

"How to find a form of association which will defend the person and goods of each member with the collective force of all, and under which each individual, while uniting himself with the others, obeys no one but himself, and remains as free as before." This is the fundamental problem to which the social contract holds the solution. . . .

Book 1, Chapter 7: "The Sovereign"

Despite their common interest, subjects will not be bound by their commitment unless means are found to guarantee their fidelity.

For every individual as a man may have a private will contrary to, or different from, the general will that he has as a citizen. His private interest may speak with a very different voice from that of the public interest; his absolute and naturally independent existence may make him regard what he owes to the common cause as a gratuitous contribution, the loss of which would be less painful for others than the payment is onerous for him; and fancying that the artificial person which constitutes the state is a mere rational entity, he might seek to enjoy the rights of a citizen without doing the duties of a subject. The growth of this kind of injustice would bring about the ruin of the body politic.

Hence, in order that the social pact shall not be an empty formula, it is tacitly implied in that commitment—which alone can give force to all others—that whoever refused to obey the general will shall be constrained to do so by the whole body, which means nothing other than that he shall be forced to be free; for this is the condition which, by giving each citizen to the nation, secures him against all personal dependence, it is the condition which shapes both the design and the working of the political machine, and which alone bestows justice on civil contracts—without it, such contracts would be absurd, tyrannical and liable to the grossest abuse.

Q *What was Rousseau's concept of the social contract? What implications did it have for political thought, especially in regard to the development of democratic ideals?*

Source: Jean-Jacques Rousseau, *The Social Contract*, trans. M. Cranston (London: Penguin Classics, 1968).

between heart and mind, between sentiment and reason. This emphasis on heart and sentiment made him a precursor of the intellectual movement called **Romanticism** that dominated Europe at the beginning of the nineteenth century.

But Rousseau did not necessarily practice what he preached. His own five children born to his illiterate serving girl were sent to foundling homes, where many children died young. Rousseau also viewed women as "naturally" different from men: "To fulfill [a woman's] functions, an appropriate physical constitution is necessary to her. . . . She needs a soft sedentary life to suckle her babies. How much care and tenderness does she need to hold her family together." In *Émile*, Sophie, who was Émile's intended wife, was educated for her role as wife and mother by learning obedience and the nurturing skills that would enable her to provide loving care for her husband and children. Not everyone in the eighteenth century agreed with Rousseau, however, making ideas of gender an important issue in the Enlightenment.

THE "WOMAN'S QUESTION" IN THE ENLIGHTENMENT For centuries, men had dominated the debate about the nature and value of women. In general, many male intellectuals had argued that the base nature of women made them inferior to men and made male domination of women necessary (see Chapter 16). In the seventeenth and eighteenth centuries, many male thinkers reinforced this view by arguing that it was based on "natural" biological differences between men and women. Like Rousseau, they argued that the female constitution destined women to be mothers. Male writers, in particular, were critical of the attempts of some women in the Enlightenment to write on intellectual issues, arguing that women were by nature intellectually inferior to men. Nevertheless, some Enlightenment thinkers offered more positive views of women. Diderot, for example, maintained that men and women were not all that different, and Voltaire asserted that "women are capable of all that men are" in intellectual affairs.

It was women thinkers, however, who added new perspectives to the "woman's question" by making specific suggestions for improving the condition of women. Mary Astell (AST-ul) (1666–1731), daughter of a wealthy English coal merchant, argued in 1697 in *A Serious Proposal to the Ladies* that women needed to become better educated. Men, she believed, would resent her proposal, "but they must excuse me, if I be as partial to my own sex as they are to theirs, and think women as capable of learning as men are, and that it becomes them as well."[8] In a later work titled *Some Reflections upon Marriage*, Astell argued for the equality of the sexes in marriage: "If absolute sovereignty be not necessary in a state, how comes it to be so in a family?

CHRONOLOGY	Works of the Philosophes
Montesquieu, *Persian Letters*	1721
Voltaire, *Philosophic Letters on the English*	1733
Hume, *Treatise on Human Nature*	1739–1740
Montesquieu, *The Spirit of the Laws*	1748
Voltaire, *The Age of Louis XIV*	1751
Diderot, *Encyclopedia*	1751–1765
Rousseau, *The Social Contract; Émile*	1762
Voltaire, *Treatise on Toleration*	1763
Beccaria, *On Crimes and Punishments*	1764
Holbach, *System of Nature*	1770
Smith, *The Wealth of Nations*	1776
Gibbon, *The Decline and Fall of the Roman Empire*	1776–1788
Wollstonecraft, *Vindication of the Rights of Woman*	1792
Condorcet, *The Progress of the Human Mind*	1794

For if arbitrary power is evil in itself, and an improper method of governing rational and free agents, it ought not be practiced anywhere. . . . If all men are born free, how is it that all women are born slaves?"[9]

The strongest statement for the rights of women in the eighteenth century was advanced by the English writer Mary Wollstonecraft (WULL-Stun-kraft) (1759–1797), viewed by many as the founder of modern European **feminism**. In *Vindication of the Rights of Woman*, written in 1792, Wollstonecraft pointed out two contradictions in the views of women held by such Enlightenment thinkers as Rousseau. To argue that women must obey men, she said, was contrary to the beliefs of the same individuals that a system based on the arbitrary power of monarchs over their subjects or slave owners over their slaves was wrong. The subjection of women to men was equally wrong. In addition, she argued, the Enlightenment was based on the ideal that reason is innate in all human beings. If women have reason, then they are entitled to the same rights that men have. Women, Wollstonecraft declared, should have equal rights with men in education and in economic and political life as well (see "Opposing Viewpoints" on p. 511).

The Social Environment of the Philosophes

The social background of the philosophes varied considerably, from the aristocratic Montesquieu to the lower-middle-class Diderot and Rousseau. The Enlightenment was not the preserve of any one class, although obviously its greatest appeal was to the aristocracy and upper middle classes of the major cities. The common people, especially the peasants, were little affected by the Enlightenment.

Of great importance to the Enlightenment was the spread of its ideas to the literate elite of European society. Although the publication and sale of books and treatises were crucial to this process, the salon was also a factor. **Salons** came into being in the seventeenth century but rose to new heights in the eighteenth. These were the elegant drawing rooms in the urban houses of the wealthy where invited philosophes and guests gathered to engage in witty, sparkling conversations that often centered on the ideas of the philosophes. In France's rigid hierarchical society, the salons were important in bringing together writers and artists with aristocrats, government officials, and wealthy bourgeoisie.

As hostesses of the salons, women found themselves in a position to affect the decisions of kings, sway political opinion, and influence literary and artistic taste. Salons provided havens for people and views unwelcome in the royal court. When French authorities suppressed the *Encyclopedia*, Marie-Thérèse de Geoffrin (1699–1777), a wealthy bourgeois widow whose father had been a valet, welcomed the encyclopedists to her salon and offered financial assistance to complete the work in secret. Madame Geoffrin was not without rivals, however. The marquise du Deffand (mahr-KEEZ duh duh-FAHNH) (1697–1780) had abandoned her husband in the provinces and established herself in Paris, where her ornate drawing room attracted many of the Enlightenment's great figures, including Montesquieu, Hume, and Voltaire.

Although women ran the salons, the reputation of a salon depended on the stature of the males a hostess was able to attract (see "Images of Everyday Life" on p. 512). Despite this male domination, both French and foreign observers complained that females exerted undue influence in French political affairs. Though exaggerated, this perception led to the decline of salons during the French Revolution.

The salons served an important role in promoting conversation and sociability between upper-class men and women as well as spreading the ideas of the Enlightenment. But other means of spreading Enlightenment ideas were also available. Coffeehouses, cafés, reading clubs, and public lending libraries established by the state were gathering places for the exchange of ideas. Learned societies were formed in cities throughout Europe and America. At such gatherings as the Select Society of Edinburgh, Scotland, and the American Philosophical Society in Philadelphia, lawyers, doctors, and local officials gathered to discuss enlightened ideas. Secret societies also developed. The most famous was the Freemasons, established in London in 1717, France and Italy in 1726, and Prussia in 1744. It was no secret that the Freemasons were sympathetic to the ideas of the philosophes.

Culture and Society in the Enlightenment

> **FOCUS QUESTIONS:** What innovations in art, music, and literature occurred in the eighteenth century? How did popular culture differ from high culture in the eighteenth century?

The intellectual adventure fostered by the philosophes was accompanied by both traditional practices and important changes in eighteenth-century culture and society.

OPPOSING VIEWPOINTS

Women in the Age of the Enlightenment: Rousseau and Wollstonecraft

THE "WOMAN'S QUESTION"—THE DEBATE ABOUT the nature and value of women—continued to be discussed in the eighteenth century. In *Émile*, Jean-Jacques Rousseau reflected the view of many male thinkers when he argued that there were natural biological differences between men and women that made women mothers rather than intellectuals. Some women thinkers, however, presented new perspectives. Mary Wollstonecraft, for example, responded to an unhappy childhood in a large family by seeking to lead an independent life. Few occupations were available for middle-class women in her day, but she survived by working as a teacher, chaperone, and governess to aristocratic children. All the while, she wrote and developed her ideas on the rights of women. The selection that follows is taken from her *Vindication of the Rights of Woman*, the work that won her a reputation as the foremost British feminist thinker of the eighteenth century.

Rousseau, *Émile* (1762)

It follows that woman is made specially to please men. If man ought to please her in turn, it is due to a less direct necessity. His merit is in his power; he pleases by the sole fact of his strength. . . .

The strictness of the relative duties of the two sexes is not and cannot be the same. When woman complains on this score about unjust man-made inequality, she is wrong. This inequality is not a human institution—or, at least, it is the work not of prejudice but of reason. It is up to the sex that nature has charged with the bearing of children to be responsible for them to the other sex. Doubtless it is not permitted to anyone to violate his faith, and every unfaithful husband who deprives his wife of the only reward of the austere duties of sex is an unjust and barbarous man. But the unfaithful woman does more; she dissolves the family and breaks all the bonds of nature. . . .

The good constitution of children initially depends on that of their mothers. The first education of men depends on the care of women. . . . Thus, the whole education of women ought to relate to men. To please men, to be useful to them, to make herself loved and honored by them, to raise them when young, to care for them when grown, to counsel them, to console them, to make their lives agreeable and sweet—these are the duties of women at all times, and they ought to be taught from childhood. . . .

The quest for abstract and speculative truths, principles, and axioms in the sciences, for everything that tends to generalize ideas, is not within the competence of women. All their studies ought to be related to practice. . . . Nor do women have sufficient precision and attention to succeed at the exact sciences. And as for the physical sciences, they are for the sex which is more active, gets around more, and sees more objects, the sex which has more strength and uses it more to judge the relations of sensible beings and the laws of nature. Woman, who is weak and who sees nothing outside the house, estimates and judges the forces she can put to work to make up for her weakness.

Mary Wollstonecraft, *Vindication of the Rights of Woman* (1792)

It is a melancholy truth—yet such is the blessed effect of civilization—the most respectable women are the most oppressed; and, unless they have understandings far superior to the common run of understandings, taking in both sexes, they must, from being treated like contemptible beings, become contemptible. How many women thus waste life away the prey of discontent, who might have practiced as physicians, regulated a farm, managed a shop, and stood erect, supported by their own industry, instead of hanging their heads surcharged with the dew of sensibility, that consumes the beauty to which it at first gave luster. . . .

Proud of their weakness, however, [women] must always be protected, guarded from care, and all the rough toils that dignify the mind. If this be the fiat of fate, if they will make themselves insignificant and contemptible, sweetly to waste "life away," let them not expect to be valued when their beauty fades, for it is the fate of the fairest flowers to be admired and pulled to pieces by the careless hand that plucked them. In how many ways do I wish, from the purest benevolence, to impress this truth on my sex; yet I fear that they will not listen to a truth that dear-bought experience has brought home to many an agitated bosom, nor willingly resign the privileges of rank and sex for the privileges of humanity, to which those have no claim who do not discharge its duties. . . .

Would men but generously snap our chains, and be content with the rational fellowship instead of slavish obedience, they would find us more observant daughters, more affectionate sisters, more faithful wives, and more reasonable mothers—in a word, better citizens. We should then love them with true affection, because we should learn to respect ourselves; and the peace of mind of a worthy man would not be interrupted by the idle vanity of his wife.

Q *What did Rousseau believe was the role of women, and how did he think they should be educated? What arguments did Mary Wollstonecraft make on behalf of the rights of women? What picture did she paint of the women of her day? Why did Wollstonecraft suggest that both women and men were at fault for the "slavish" situation of women?*

Sources: Jean-Jacques Rousseau, *Émile; Or on Education*, in A. Bloom, trans. (New York: Basic Books, 1979); Mary Wollstonecraft, *Vindication of the Rights of Woman* (1792).

IMAGES OF EVERYDAY LIFE

Women and the Enlightenment Salon

RMN-Grand Palais/Art Resource, NY

AS HOSTESSES OF SALONS, WOMEN PLAYED a pivotal role in the spread of Enlightenment ideas by providing a place where philosophes could meet and discuss the topics of the day. Salons also offered women access to intellectual stimulus that was generally otherwise denied to them. Throughout Europe, women were barred from any other higher educational opportunities. A hostess of a salon not only provided food and a drawing room where the guests could mingle, but also set the agenda for the evening and dictated the guest list. Two of the most prominent Parisian hostesses were Madame Geoffrin and Madame Necker (neh-KAIR). In the painting on the left, Madame Geoffrin is seen (third on the right) in her salon surrounded by philosophes in her home on the rue Saint-Honore. Her salon was highly popular, with nobles, writers, artists, and financiers in regular attendance. Suzanne Necker, seen in the portrait at the lower right, was the wife of financier Jacques Necker and spent her days preparing for the evening discussions by reading and writing in her journal. Although the Parisian salons were the most famous, by the late eighteenth century, hostesses in Vienna and Berlin were also holding prominent salons. The painting at the lower left depicts Henriette Herz, whose father was the first Jewish physician to practice in Berlin. Herz was one of many notable wealthy women from Jewish families who sponsored salons in Berlin and Vienna.

bpk, Berlin/Nationalgalerie, SMB/Jörg P. Anders/Art Resource, NY

Antoine Watteau, *Return from Cythera*. Antoine Watteau was one of the most gifted painters in eighteenth-century France. His portrayal of aristocratic life reveals a world of elegance, wealth, and pleasure. In this painting, which is considered his masterpiece, Watteau depicts a group of aristocratic lovers about to depart from the island of Cythera, where they have paid homage to Venus, the goddess of love. Luxuriously dressed, they move from the woodlands to a golden barge that is waiting to take them from the island.

Innovations in Art, Music, and Literature

Although the Baroque and neoclassical styles that had dominated the seventeenth century continued into the eighteenth century, by the 1730s a new style known as **Rococo** (ruh-KOH-koh) had begun to influence decoration and architecture all over Europe. Following the death of Louis XIV in 1715, the great nobles of France returned to their townhouses in Paris to host soirées of intellectuals and aristocrats. Within these new spaces, a more delicate art form emerged. Unlike the Baroque, which stressed majesty, power, and movement, Rococo emphasized grace and gentle action. Rococo, derived from the French word *rocaille*, or pebble, rejected strict geometrical patterns and had a fondness for curves; it liked to follow the wandering lines of natural objects, such as seashells and flowers. It made much use of interlaced designs colored in gold with delicate contours and graceful curves. Highly secular, its lightness and charm spoke of the pursuit of pleasure, happiness, and love.

Some of Rococo's appeal is evident already in the work of Antoine Watteau (AHN-twahn wah-TOH) (1684–1721). Watteau created a specific type of Rococo; his paintings portrayed a lyrical view of aristocratic life—refined, sensual, civilized, with gentlemen and ladies in elegant dress—reflecting a world of upper-class pleasure and joy. Underneath that exterior, however, was an element of sadness as the artist revealed the fragility and transitory nature of pleasure, love, and life. Watteau relied upon the use of color rather than representational form to highlight his subjects. Watteau died at the age of thirty-six from tuberculosis. Later artists, such as Jean-Honoré Fragonard (1732–1806), continued Watteau's use of color and subject matter of aristocratic life.

Another aspect of Rococo was that its decorative work could easily be used with Baroque architecture. The palace of Versailles had made an enormous impact on Europe. "Keeping up with the Bourbons" became important as the Austrian emperor, the Swedish king, German princes and prince-bishops, Italian princes, and even a Russian tsar built grandiose palaces. While emulating Versailles's size, they were modeled less after the French classical style of Versailles than after the seventeenth-century Italian Baroque, as modified by a series of brilliant German and Austrian sculptor-architects. This Baroque-Rococo architectural style of the eighteenth century was used in both palaces and churches, and often the same architects designed both. This is evident in the work of one of the greatest architects of the eighteenth century, Balthasar Neumann (BAHL-tuh-zahr NOI-mahn) (1687–1753).

Neumann's two masterpieces are the pilgrimage church of the Vierzehnheiligen (feer-tsayn-HY-li-gen) (Fourteen Saints) in southern Germany and the Bishop's Palace, known as the Residenz, the residential palace of the Schönborn (SHURN-bawn) prince-bishop of Würzburg (VOORTS-boork). Secular and spiritual become easily interchangeable in both buildings as the visitor is greeted by lavish and fanciful ornament; light, bright colors; and elaborate, rich detail. The church is designed without any straight lines, only ovals and circles, contrasting the traditional rectilinear nave, creating a fluidity of motion reflected in the curvilinear gilding on the ceiling.

Jean-Honoré Fragonard, *The Swing*. Fragonard captured the frivolity and decadence of France's aristocracy. In this painting, Fragonard portrays a young lady being pushed on a swing as her suitor sits below her. The lush environs and curvilinear landscape epitomize Rococo's love of nature, while the delicate light and color of the lady's dress highlight the playful moment of her kicking off her shoe.

Vierzehnheiligen, Interior View. Pictured here is the interior of the Vierzehnheiligen, the pilgrimage church designed by Balthasar Neumann. Elaborate detail, blazing light, rich colors, and opulent decoration blend together to create a work of stunning beauty. The pilgrim in search of holiness is struck by an incredible richness of detail. Persuaded by joy rather than fear, the believer is lifted toward heaven on a cloud of rapture.

Despite the popularity of the Rococo style, **neoclassicism** continued to maintain a strong appeal and in the late eighteenth century emerged in France as an established movement. Neoclassical artists wanted to recapture the dignity and simplicity of the classical style of ancient Greece and Rome. Some were especially influenced by the recent excavations of the ancient Roman cities of Herculaneum and Pompeii. Classical elements are evident in the work of Jacques-Louis David (ZHAHK-LWEE dah-VEED) (1748–1825). In the *Oath of the Horatii*, he re-created a scene from Roman history in which the three Horatius brothers swore an oath before their father, proclaiming their willingness to sacrifice their lives for their country. David's neoclassical style, with its moral seriousness and its emphasis on honor and patriotism, made him extremely popular during the French Revolution.

THE DEVELOPMENT OF MUSIC The seventeenth and eighteenth centuries were the formative years of classical music and saw the rise of the opera and oratorio, the sonata, the concerto, and the symphony. The Italians were the first to develop these genres but were soon followed by the Germans, Austrians, and English. As in previous centuries, most musicians depended on a patron—a prince, a well-endowed ecclesiastic, or an aristocrat. The many individual princes, archbishops, and bishops, each with his own court, provided the patronage that made Italy and Germany the musical leaders of Europe.

Many of the techniques of the Baroque musical style, which dominated Europe between 1600 and 1750, were perfected by two composers—Bach and Handel—who stand out as musical geniuses. Johann Sebastian Bach (yoh-HAHN suh-BASS-chun BAHK) (1685–1750) came from a family of musicians. Bach held the post of organist and music director at a number of small German courts before becoming director of church music at the Church of Saint Thomas in Leipzig in 1723. There Bach composed his Mass in B Minor, his *Saint Matthew's Passion*, and the cantatas and motets that have established his reputation as one of the greatest composers of all time. For Bach, music was above all a means to worship God; in his own words, his task in life was to make "well-ordered music in the honor of God."

The other great musical giant of the early eighteenth century, George Frederick Handel (HAN-dul) (1685–1759), was, like Bach, born in Saxony in Germany and in the same year. In contrast to Bach's quiet provincial life, however, Handel experienced a stormy international career and was profoundly secular in temperament. After studying in Italy, where he began his career by writing operas in the Italian manner, in 1712 he moved to England, where he spent most of his adult life attempting to run an opera company. Although patronized by the English royal court, Handel wrote music for large public audiences and was not averse to writing huge, unusual-sounding pieces. The band for his *Fireworks Music*, for example, was supposed to be accompanied by 101 cannons. Although he wrote more than forty operas and much other secular music, the worldly Handel

© RMN-Grand Palais/Art Resource, NY

Jacques-Louis David, *Oath of the Horatii*. The Frenchman Jacques-Louis David was one of the most famous neoclassical artists of the late eighteenth century. To immerse himself in the world of classical antiquity, he painted the *Oath of the Horatii* in Rome. Thanks to its emphasis on patriotic duty, the work became an instant hit in both Paris and Rome.

is, ironically, probably best known for his religious music. His *Messiah* has been called "one of those rare works that appeal immediately to everyone, and yet is indisputably a masterpiece of the highest order."[10]

Although Bach and Handel composed many instrumental suites and concerti, orchestral music did not come to the fore until the second half of the eighteenth century, when new instruments such as the piano appeared. A new musical period, the classical era (1750–1830), also emerged, represented by two great innovators—Haydn and Mozart. Their renown caused the musical center of Europe to shift from Italy and Germany to the Austrian Empire.

Franz Joseph Haydn (FRAHNTS YO-zef HY-dun) (1732–1809) spent most of his adult life as musical director for the wealthy Hungarian princes, the Esterhazy brothers. Haydn was incredibly prolific, composing 104 symphonies in addition to string quartets, concerti, songs, oratorios, and Masses. His visits to England in 1790 and 1794 introduced him to another world, where musicians wrote for public concerts rather than princely patrons. This "liberty," as he called it, induced him to write his two great oratorios, *The Creation* and *The Seasons*, both of which were dedicated to the common people.

The concerto, symphony, and opera all reached their zenith in the works of Wolfgang Amadeus Mozart (VULF-gahng ah-muh-DAY-uss MOH-tsart) (1756–1791), a child prodigy who gave his first harpsichord concert at six and wrote his first opera at twelve. He, too, sought a patron, but his discontent with the overly demanding archbishop of Salzburg forced him to move to Vienna, where his failure to find a permanent patron made his life miserable. Nevertheless, he wrote music prolifically and passionately until he died a debt-ridden pauper at thirty-five (see "Film & History" below). Mozart carried the tradition of

FILM & HISTORY

Warner Bros./The Everett Collection

Watch ***Amadeus***, which was based on the relationship of two eighteenth-century composers, Antonio Salieri and Wolfgang Amadeus Mozart. *Amadeus* is a brilliant film about the musical genius of Mozart. While the movie is accurate in presenting Mozart as a child prodigy and a great composer who died at the young age of thirty-five, the story of the rivalry between Salieri and Mozart is mostly fictional. Nevertheless, *Amadeus* provides viewers with a stunning portrayal of one of the world's greatest composers.

Q *How were musicians paid during the eighteenth century? How did this influence their work?*

Italian comic opera to new heights with *The Marriage of Figaro*, based on a Parisian play of the 1780s in which a valet outwits and outsings his noble employers, and *Don Giovanni*, a "black comedy" about the havoc Don Giovanni wrought on earth before he descended into hell. *The Marriage of Figaro, The Magic Flute*, and *Don Giovanni* are three of the world's greatest operas. Mozart composed with an ease of melody and a blend of grace, precision, and emotion that arguably no one has ever excelled. Haydn remarked to Mozart's father that "your son is the greatest composer known to me either in person or by reputation."

THE DEVELOPMENT OF THE NOVEL The eighteenth century was also decisive in the development of the novel. The novel was not a completely new literary genre but grew out of the medieval romances and the picaresque stories of the sixteenth century. The English are credited with establishing the modern novel as the chief vehicle for fiction writing. With no established rules, the novel was open to much experimentation. It also proved especially attractive to women readers and women writers.

Samuel Richardson (1689–1761) was a printer by trade and did not turn to writing until his fifties. His first novel, *Pamela: or, Virtue Rewarded*, focused on a servant girl's resistance to numerous seduction attempts by her master. Finally, by reading the girl's letters describing her feelings about his efforts, the master realizes that she has a good mind as well as an attractive body and marries her. Virtue is rewarded. *Pamela* won Richardson a large audience as he appealed to the growing cult of sensibility in the eighteenth century—the taste for the sentimental and emotional. Samuel Johnson, another great English writer of the century and an even greater wit, remarked, "If you were to read Richardson for the story . . . you would hang yourself. But you must read him for the sentiment."

Reacting against the moral seriousness of Richardson, Henry Fielding (1707–1754) wrote novels about people without scruples who survived by their wits. His best work was *The History of Tom Jones, a Foundling*, a lengthy novel about the numerous adventures of a young scoundrel. Fielding presented scenes of English life from the hovels of London to the country houses of the aristocracy. In a number of hilarious episodes, he described characters akin to real types in English society. Although he emphasized action rather than inner feeling, Fielding did his own moralizing by attacking the hypocrisy of his age.

THE WRITING OF HISTORY The philosophes were responsible for creating a revolution in the writing of history. Their secular orientation caused them to eliminate the role of God in history and freed them to concentrate on events themselves and search for causal relationships in the natural world. Earlier, the humanist historians of the Renaissance had also placed their histories in purely secular settings, but not with the same intensity and complete removal of God.

The philosophe-historians also broadened the scope of history from the humanists' preoccupation with politics. Politics still predominated in the work of Enlightenment historians, but they also paid attention to economic, social, intellectual, and cultural developments. As Voltaire explained in his masterpiece, *The Age of Louis XIV*: "It is not merely the life of Louis XIV that we propose to write; we have a wider aim in view. We shall endeavor to depict for posterity, not the actions of a single man, but the spirit of men in the most enlightened age the world has ever seen."[11] In seeking to describe the "totality of past human experience," Voltaire initiated the modern ideal of social history.

The weaknesses of these philosophe-historians stemmed from their preoccupations as philosophes. Following the ideals of the classics that dominated their minds, the philosophes sought to instruct as well as entertain. Their goal was to help civilize their age, and history could play a role by revealing its lessons according to their vision. Their emphasis on science and reason and their dislike of Christianity made them less than sympathetic to the period we call the Middle Ages. This is particularly noticeable in the other great masterpiece of eighteenth-century historiography, the six-volume *Decline and Fall of the Roman Empire* by Edward Gibbon (1737–1794). Although Gibbon thought that the decline of Rome had many causes, he portrayed the growth of Christianity as a major reason for Rome's eventual collapse. Like some of the philosophes, Gibbon believed in the idea of progress and, in reflecting on the decline and fall of Rome, expressed his optimism about the future of European civilization and the ability of Europeans to avoid the fate of the Romans.

The High Culture of the Eighteenth Century

Historians and cultural anthropologists have grown accustomed to distinguishing between a civilization's high culture and its popular culture. Whereas **high culture** usually refers to the literary and artistic world of the educated and wealthy ruling classes, **popular culture** refers to the written and unwritten lore of the masses, most of which is passed down orally. By the eighteenth century, European high culture consisted of a learned world of theologians, scientists, philosophers, intellectuals, poets, and dramatists, for whom Latin remained a truly international language. Their work was supported by a wealthy and literate lay group, the most important of whom were the landed aristocracy and the wealthier upper classes in the cities.

Especially noticeable in the eighteenth century was an expansion of both the reading public and publishing. One study revealed that French publishers were issuing about sixteen hundred titles yearly in the 1780s, up from three hundred titles in 1750. Though many of these titles were still aimed at small groups of the educated elite, many were also directed to the new reading public of the middle classes, which included women and even urban artisans. The growth of publishing houses made it possible for authors to make money from their works and be less dependent on wealthy patrons.

An important aspect of the growth of publishing and reading in the eighteenth century was the development of magazines for the general public. Great Britain, an important center for the new magazines, saw 25 periodicals published in 1700, 103 in 1760, and 158 in 1780. Although short-lived, the best known was Joseph Addison and Richard Steele's *Spectator*, begun in 1711.

British Museum, London//UIG via Getty Images

A London Coffeehouse. Coffeehouses first appeared in Venice and Constantinople but quickly spread throughout Europe by the beginning of the eighteenth century. In addition to drinking coffee, patrons of coffeehouses could read magazines and newspapers, exchange ideas, play chess, smoke, and engage in business transactions. In this scene from a London coffeehouse of 1705, well-attired gentlemen make bids on commodities.

Its goal was "to bring Philosophy out of the closets and libraries, schools and colleges, to dwell in clubs and assemblies, at tea-tables and coffeehouses." In keeping with one of the chief intellectual goals of the philosophes, the *Spectator* wished to instruct and entertain at the same time. With its praise of family, marriage, and courtesy, the *Spectator* also had a strong appeal to women. Some of the new magazines were aimed specifically at women, such as *The Female Spectator* in England, which was also edited by a woman, Eliza Haywood, and featured articles by female writers.

Along with magazines came daily newspapers. The first was printed in London in 1702, but by 1780, thirty-seven other English towns had their own newspapers. Filled with news and special features, they were relatively cheap and were provided free in coffeehouses. In 1737, a German visitor to London described the atmosphere of public readership in a coffeehouse:

> The fine Gentleman . . . rises late, puts on a Frock . . . and leaving his Sword at Home . . . goes . . . to some Coffee-house, or Chocolate-house, frequented by the Person he would see; for 'tis a Sort of Rule with the English, to go once a Day at least, to Houses of this Sort, where they talk of Business and News, read the Papers, and often look at one another without opening their lips; and 'tis very well they are so mute; for if they were as talkative as the People of many other Nations, the Coffee-houses would be intolerable, and there would be no hearing what one Man said, where there are so many.[12]

Books, too, received wider circulation through the development of public libraries in the cities as well as private circulating libraries, which offered books for rent.

EDUCATION AND UNIVERSITIES By the eighteenth century, Europe was home to a large number of privately endowed secondary schools, such as the grammar and public schools in England, the gymnasiums in German-speaking lands, and the *collèges* in France and Spain. These schools tended to be elitist, designed to meet the needs of the children of the upper classes of society. Basically, European secondary schools perpetuated the class hierarchy of Europe rather than creating avenues for social mobility. In fact, most of the philosophes reinforced the belief that education should function to keep people in their own social class. Baron d'Holbach said, "Education should teach . . . the rich to use their riches well, the poor to live by honest industry."

The curriculum of these secondary schools still largely concentrated on the Greek and Latin classics with little attention paid to mathematics, the sciences, and modern languages. Complaints from philosophe-reformers, as well as from merchants and other middle-class people who wanted their sons to have a more practical education, led to the development of new schools designed to provide a broader education. In Germany, the first *Realschule* (ray-AHL-shoo-luh) was opened in Berlin in 1747 and offered modern languages, geography,

THE PUNISHMENT OF CRIME

TORTURE AND CAPITAL PUNISHMENT REMAINED common features of European judicial systems well into the eighteenth century. Public spectacles were especially gruesome, as this excerpt from the *Nocturnal Spectator* of Restif de la Bretonne, a French novelist, demonstrates.

Restif de la Bretonne, "The Broken Man"

I went home by way of rue Saint-Antoine and the Place de Grève. Three murderers had been broken on the wheel there, the day before. I had not expected to see any such spectacle, one that I had never dared to witness. But as I crossed the square I caught sight of a poor wretch, pale, half dead, wracked by the pains of the interrogation inflicted on him twenty hours earlier; he was stumbling down from the Hotel de Ville supported by the executioner and the confessor. These two men, so completely different, inspired an inexpressible emotion in me! I watched the latter embrace a miserable man consumed by fever, filthy as the dungeons he came from, swarming with vermin! And I said to myself, "O Religion, here is your greatest glory!" . . .

I saw a horrible sight, even though the torture had been mitigated. . . . The wretch had revealed his accomplices. He was garroted before he was put to the wheel. A winch set under the scaffold tightened a noose around the victim's neck and he was strangled; for a long while the confessor and the hangman felt his heart to see whether the artery still pulsed, and the hideous blows were dealt only after it beat no longer. . . . I left, with my hair standing on end in horror.

Q *What does this selection reveal about the punishment of crime in the eighteenth century? What impact did such descriptions have on the philosophes' attitudes toward the administration of justice as it was carried out by their respective monarchical states?*

Source: L. Asher and E. Fertig, trans., *Les Nuits de Paris; or, The Nocturnal Spectator: A Selection* (New York: Knopf, 1964).

and bookkeeping to prepare boys for careers in business. New schools of this kind were also created for upper-class girls, although they focused primarily on religion and domestic skills.

The most common complaint about universities, especially from the philosophes, was the old-fashioned curriculum that emphasized the classics and Aristotelian philosophy and provided no training in the sciences or modern languages. Before the end of the century, this criticism led to reforms that introduced new ideas in the areas of physics, astronomy, and even mathematics into the universities. It is significant, however, that very few of the important scientific discoveries of the eighteenth century occurred in the universities.

Crime and Punishment

By the eighteenth century, most European states had developed a hierarchy of courts to deal with crimes. Except in England, judicial torture remained an important means of obtaining evidence before a trial. Courts used the rack, thumbscrews, and other instruments to obtain confessions in criminal cases. Punishments for crimes were often cruel and even spectacular. Public executions were a basic part of traditional punishment and were regarded as necessary to deter potential offenders in an age when police forces were too weak to ensure the capture of criminals. Although nobles were executed by simple beheading, lower-class criminals condemned to death were tortured, broken on the wheel, or drawn and quartered (see the box above). The death penalty was still commonly used for property crimes as well as for violent offenses. By 1800, more than two hundred crimes were subject to the death penalty in England. In addition to executions, European states resorted to forced labor in mines, forts, and navies. England also sent criminals as indentured servants to colonies in the New World and, after the American Revolution, to Australia.

Appalled by the unjust laws and brutal punishments of their times, some philosophes sought to create a new approach to justice. The most notable effort was made by an Italian philosophe, Cesare Beccaria (CHAY-zuh-ray buh-KAH-ree-uh) (1738–1794). In his essay *On Crimes and Punishments*, written in 1764, Beccaria argued that punishments should serve only as deterrents, not as exercises in brutality: "Such punishments . . . ought to be chosen as will make the strongest and most lasting impressions on the minds of others, with the least torment to the body of the criminal."[13] Beccaria was also opposed to the use of capital punishment. It was spectacular, but it failed to stop others from committing crimes. Imprisonment—the deprivation of freedom—made a far more lasting impression. Moreover, capital punishment was harmful to society because it set an example of barbarism: "Is it not absurd that the laws, which detest and punish homicide, should, in order to prevent murder, publicly commit murder themselves?"

By the end of the eighteenth century, a growing sentiment against executions and torture led to a decline in both corporal and capital punishment. A new type of prison, in which criminals were placed in cells and subjected to discipline and regular work to rehabilitate them, began to replace the public spectacle of barbarous punishments.

The World of Medicine

In the eighteenth century, a hierarchy of practitioners practiced medicine. At the top stood the physicians, who were university graduates and enjoyed a high social status. Despite the scientific advances of the seventeenth and eighteenth centuries, however, university medical education was still largely conducted in Latin and was based primarily on Galen's work. New methods emphasizing clinical experience did begin to be introduced at the University of Leiden, which replaced Padua as the foremost medical school of Europe in the first half of the seventeenth century, only to be surpassed in the second half of that century by Vienna. A graduate with a doctorate in medicine from a university needed to receive a license before he could be a practicing member of the physicians' elite corporate body. In England, the Royal College of Physicians licensed only one hundred physicians in the early eighteenth century. Only officially licensed physicians could hold regular medical consultations with patients and receive payments, already regarded in the eighteenth century as outrageously high.

Below the physicians were the surgeons, who were still known as barber-surgeons well into the eighteenth century from their original dual occupation. Their primary functions were to bleed patients and perform surgery; the latter was often done crudely, without painkillers and in filthy conditions, because there was no understanding of anesthesia or infection. Bleeding was widely believed to be beneficial in reducing fevers and combating a variety of illnesses.

The surgeons underwent significant changes in the course of the eighteenth century. In the 1740s, they began to separate themselves from the barbers and organize their own guilds. At the same time, they started to undergo additional training by dissecting corpses and studying anatomy more systematically. As they became more effective, the distinction between physicians and surgeons began to break down, and surgeons were examining patients in a fashion similar to physicians by the end of the century. Moreover, surgeons also began to be licensed. In England, the Royal College of Surgeons required clinical experience before granting the license.

Other medical practitioners, such as apothecaries, midwives, and faith healers, primarily served the common people in the eighteenth century. Although their main function was to provide herbs and potions as recommended by physicians, apothecaries or pharmacists also acted independently in diagnosing illnesses and selling remedies. In the course of the eighteenth century, male doctors increasingly supplanted midwives in delivering babies. At the same time, the tradition of faith healing, so prominent in medieval medicine, continued to be practiced, especially in the rural areas of Europe.

Hospitals in the eighteenth century seemed more a problem than an aid in dealing with disease and illness. That conditions were bad is evident in this description by the philosophe Denis Diderot, who characterized the Hôtel-Dieu in Paris, France's "biggest, roomiest, and richest" hospital, in these words:

> Imagine a long series of communicating wards filled with sufferers of every kind of disease who are sometimes packed three, four, five or even six into a bed, the living alongside the dead and dying, the air polluted by this mass of unhealthy bodies, passing pestilential germs of their afflictions from one to the other, and the spectacle of suffering and agony on every hand. That is the Hôtel-Dieu. The result is that many of these poor wretches come out with diseases they did not have when they went in, and often pass them on to the people they go back to live with.[14]

Despite appeals, efforts at hospital reform in the eighteenth century remained ineffectual.

Popular Culture

Popular culture refers to the written and unwritten literature and the social activities and pursuits that are fundamental to the lives of most people. The distinguishing characteristic of popular culture is its collective and public nature. Group activity was especially evident in the festival, a broad name used to cover a variety of celebrations: community festivals in Catholic Europe that celebrated the feast day of the local patron saint; annual festivals, such as Christmas and Easter, that went back to medieval Christianity; and Carnival, the most spectacular form of festival, which was celebrated in Spain, Italy, France, Germany, and Austria. All of these festivals were special occasions when people ate, drank, and celebrated to excess (see "Global Perspectives" on p. 520). In traditional societies, festival was a time for relaxation and enjoyment because much of the rest of the year was a time of unrelieved work. As the poet Thomas Gray said of Carnival in Turin in 1739: "This Carnival lasts only from Christmas to Lent; one half of the remaining part of the year is passed in remembering the last, the other in expecting the future Carnival."[15]

CARNIVAL Carnival was celebrated in the weeks leading up to the beginning of Lent, the forty-day period of fasting and purification preceding Easter. Carnival was, understandably, a time of great indulgence, just the reverse of Lent, when people were expected to abstain from meat, sex, and most recreations. Hearty consumption of food, especially meat and other delicacies, and heavy drinking were the norm during Carnival; so was intense sexual activity. Songs with double meanings that would be considered offensive at other times could be sung publicly at this time of year. A float of Florentine "keymakers," for example, sang this ditty to the ladies: "Our tools are fine, new and useful; We always carry them with us; They are good for anything; If you want to touch them, you can."[16] Finally, Carnival was a time of aggression, a time to release pent-up feelings. Most often this took the form of verbal aggression, since people were allowed to openly insult other people and even criticize their social superiors and authorities. Certain acts of physical violence were also permitted. People pelted each other with apples, eggs, flour, and pigs' bladders filled with water.

TAVERNS AND ALCOHOL The same sense of community evident in festival was also present in the chief gathering places of the common people, the local taverns or cabarets. Taverns functioned as regular gathering places for neighborhood men to talk, play games, conduct small business matters, and drink. In some countries, the favorite drinks of poor people, such as gin in England and vodka in Russia, proved devastating as poor people regularly drank themselves into oblivion. Gin was cheap; the classic sign in English taverns, "Drunk for a penny, dead drunk for two pence," was literally true. In England, the consumption of gin rose from 2 million to 5 million gallons between 1714 and 1733 and declined only when complaints finally led to laws restricting sales in the 1750s. Of course, the rich drank too. Samuel Johnson once remarked that all the decent people in Lichfield got drunk every night and "were not the worse thought of." But unlike the poor, the rich drank port and brandy, usually in large quantities.

This difference in drinking habits between rich and poor reminds us of the ever-widening separation between the elite and the poor in the eighteenth century. In 1500, popular culture was for everyone; a second culture for the elite, it was the only culture for the rest of society. But between 1500 and 1800, the nobility, clergy, and bourgeoisie had abandoned popular culture to the lower classes. This was, of course, a gradual process, and in abandoning the popular festivals, the upper classes were also abandoning the popular worldview as well. The new scientific outlook had brought a new mental world for the upper classes, and they now viewed such things as witchcraft, faith healing, fortune telling, and prophecy as the beliefs of those who were, as one writer said, "of the weakest judgment and reason, as women, children, and ignorant and superstitious persons."

LITERACY AND PRIMARY EDUCATION Popular culture had always included a vast array of traditional songs and stories that were passed down from generation to generation. But popular culture was not entirely based on an oral tradition; a popular literature existed as well. So-called chapbooks, printed on cheap paper, were short brochures sold by itinerant peddlers to the lower classes. They contained both spiritual and secular material: lives of saints and inspirational stories competed with crude satires and adventure stories.

It is apparent from the chapbooks that popular culture did not have to remain primarily oral. Its ability to change was dependent on the growth of literacy. Studies in France indicate that literacy rates for men increased from 29 percent in the late seventeenth century to 47 percent in the late eighteenth century; for women, the increase was from 14 to 27 percent during the same period. Of course, certain groups were more likely to be literate than others. Upper-class elites and the upper middle classes in the cities were mostly all literate. Nevertheless, the figures also indicate dramatic increases for lower-middle-class artisans in urban areas. Recent research in the city of Marseilles, for example, indicates that literacy of male artisans and workers increased from 28 percent in 1710 to 85 percent in 1789, though the rate for women remained at 15 percent. Peasants, who constituted as much as 75 percent of the French population, remained largely illiterate.

The spread of literacy was closely connected to primary education. In Catholic Europe, primary education was largely a matter of local community effort, leading to little real growth. Only in the Habsburg Austrian Empire was a system of state-supported primary schools—*Volkschulen* (FULK-shoo-lun)—established, although only one in four school-age children actually attended.

The emphasis of the Protestant reformers on reading the Bible had led Protestant states to take a greater interest in primary education. Some places, especially the Swiss cantons, Scotland, and the German states of Saxony and Prussia, witnessed the emergence of universal primary schools that

Scala/Art Resource, NY

Newark Museum/Art Resource, NY

GLOBAL PERSPECTIVES

Popular Culture in the West and East

BY THE SEVENTEENTH CENTURY, a popular culture distinct from the elite culture of the nobility was beginning to emerge in the urban worlds of both the West and the East. At the top is a scene from the celebration of Carnival on the Piazza Sante Croce in Florence, Italy. Carnival was a period of festivities before Lent, celebrated primarily in Roman Catholic countries. It became an occasion for indulgence in food, drink, games, and practical jokes as a prelude to the austerity of the forty-day Lenten season from Ash Wednesday to Easter. All of these activities are evident here. On the right below is a festival scene from the pleasure district of Kyoto known as the Gion. Spectators on a balcony are enjoying a colorful parade of floats and costumed performers. The festival originated as a celebration of the passing of a deadly epidemic in medieval Japan.

Q *Do festivals such as these still exist in our day? What purpose do they serve?*

provided a modicum of education for the masses. But effective systems of primary education were hindered by the attitudes of the ruling classes, who feared the consequences of teaching the lower classes anything beyond the virtues of hard work and deference to their superiors. Hannah More, an English writer who set up a network of Sunday schools, made clear the philosophy of her charity school for poor children: "My plan of instruction is extremely simple and limited. They learn on weekdays such coarse work as may fit them for servants. I allow of no writing for the poor. My object is to train up the lower classes in habits of industry and piety."

Religion and the Churches

FOCUS QUESTION: How did popular religion differ from institutional religion in the eighteenth century?

The music of Bach and the pilgrimage and monastic churches of southern Germany and Austria make us aware of a curious fact. Though much of the great art and music of the time was religious, the thought of the time was antireligious as life became increasingly secularized and men of reason attacked the established churches. And yet most Europeans were still Christians. Even many of those most critical of the churches accepted that society could not function without religious faith.

The Institutional Church

In the eighteenth century, the established Catholic and Protestant churches were basically conservative institutions that upheld society's hierarchical structure, privileged classes, and traditions. Although churches experienced change because of new state policies, they did not sustain any dramatic internal changes. In both Catholic and Protestant countries, the parish church run by a priest or pastor remained the center of religious practice. In addition to providing religious services, the parish church kept records of births, deaths, and marriages; provided charity for the poor; supervised whatever primary education there was; and cared for orphans.

CHURCH-STATE RELATIONS Early on, the Protestant Reformation had solved the problem of the relationship between church and state by establishing the principle of state control over the churches. In the eighteenth century, Protestant state churches flourished throughout Europe: Lutheranism in Scandinavia and the north German states; Anglicanism in England; and Calvinism (or Reformed churches) in Scotland, the United Provinces, and some of the Swiss cantons and German states (see Map 17.2). There were also Protestant minorities in other European countries.

In 1700, the Catholic Church still exercised much power in Catholic European states: Spain, Portugal, France, Italy, the Habsburg Empire, Poland, and most of southern Germany. The church also continued to possess enormous wealth. In Spain, three thousand monastic institutions housing 100,000 men and women controlled enormous landed estates.

The Catholic Church remained hierarchically structured. In most Catholic countries, the highest clerics, such as bishops, archbishops, abbots, and abbesses, were members of the upper class, especially the landed nobility, and received enormous revenues from their landed estates and tithes from the faithful. A wide gulf existed between the upper and lower clergy. While the French bishop of Strasbourg, for example, received 100,000 livres a year, parish priests were paid only 500.

In the eighteenth century, the governments of many Catholic states began to seek greater authority over the churches in their countries. This "nationalization" of the Catholic Church meant controlling the papacy and in turn the chief papal agent, the Society of Jesus. The Jesuits had proved extremely successful, perhaps too successful for their own good. They had created special enclaves, virtually states within states, in the French, Spanish, and Portuguese colonies in the New World. As advisers to Catholic rulers, the Jesuits exercised considerable political influence. But the high profile they achieved through their successes attracted a wide range of enemies, and a series of actions soon undermined Jesuit power. The Portuguese monarch destroyed the powerful Jesuit state in Paraguay and then in 1759 expelled the Jesuits from Portugal and confiscated their property. In 1764, they were expelled from France and three years later from Spain and the Spanish colonies. In 1773, when Spain and France demanded that the entire society be dissolved, Pope Clement XIV reluctantly complied. The dissolution of the Jesuit order, an important pillar of Catholic strength, was yet another victory for Catholic governments determined to win control over their churches.

The end of the Jesuits was paralleled by a decline in papal power. Already by the mid-eighteenth century, the papacy played only a minor role in diplomacy and international affairs. The nationalization of the churches by the states meant the loss of the papacy's power to appoint high clerical officials.

TOLERATION AND RELIGIOUS MINORITIES One of the chief battle cries of the philosophes was a call for religious toleration. Out of political necessity, a certain level of tolerance of different creeds had occurred in the seventeenth century, but many rulers still found it difficult to accept. Louis XIV had turned back the clock in France at the end of the seventeenth century, insisting on religious uniformity and suppressing the rights of the Huguenots (see Chapter 15). Many rulers continued to believe that there was only one path to salvation; it was the true duty of a ruler not to allow subjects to be condemned to hell by being heretics. Hence, persecution of heretics continued; the last burning of a heretic took place in 1781.

Nevertheless, some progress was made toward religious toleration. No ruler was more interested in the philosophes' call for religious toleration than Joseph II of Austria. His Toleration Patent of 1781, while recognizing Catholicism's public practice, granted Lutherans, Calvinists, and Greek Orthodox the right to worship privately. In all other ways, all subjects were now equal: "Non-Catholics are in future admitted under dispensation to buy houses and real property, to practice as master craftsmen, to take up academic appointments and posts in public service, and are not to be required to take the oath in any form contrary to their religious tenets."[17]

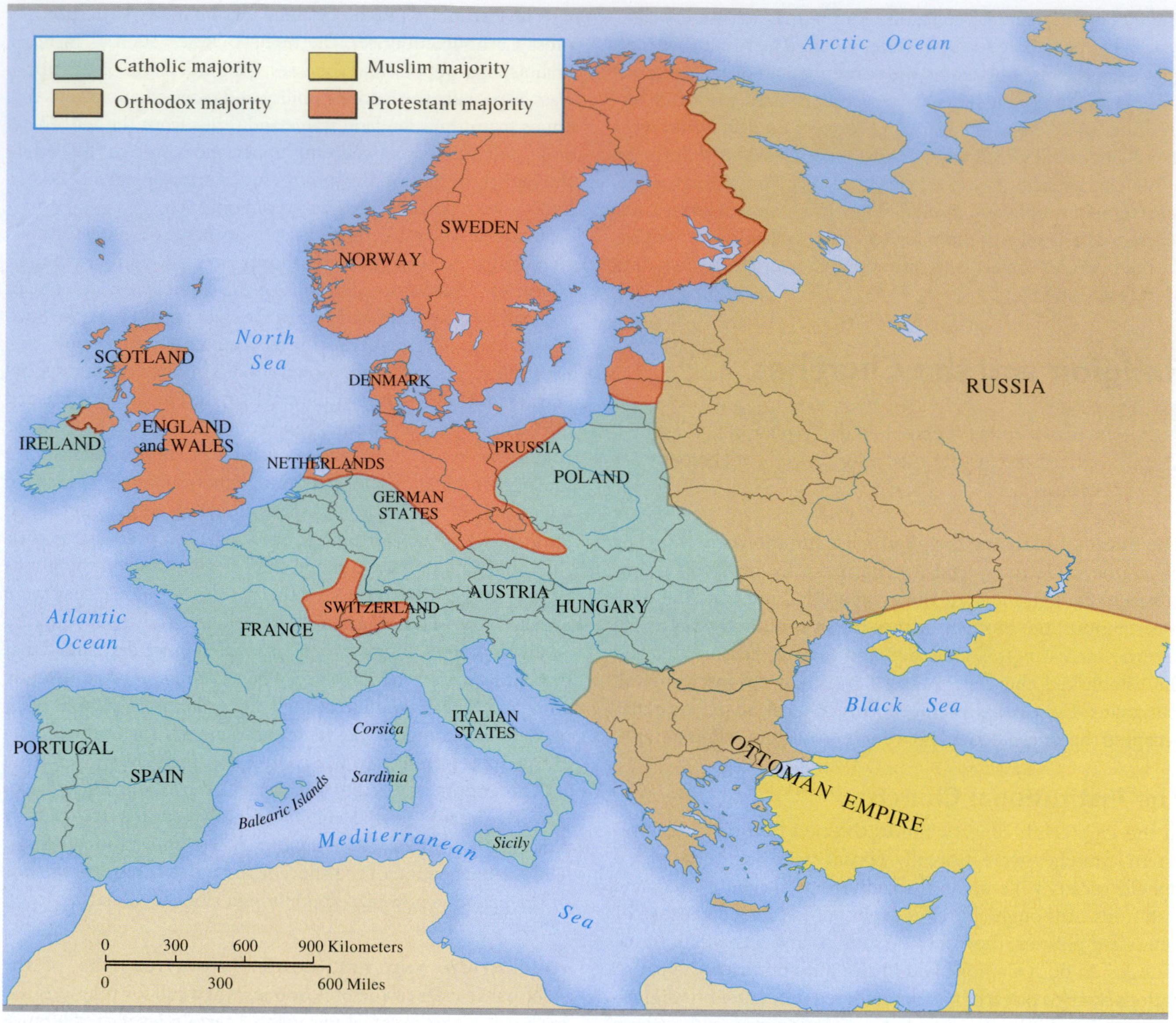

MAP 17.2 Religious Populations of Eighteenth-Century Europe. Christianity was still a dominant force in eighteenth-century Europe—even many of the philosophes remained Christians while attacking the authority and power of the established Catholic and Protestant churches. By the end of the century, however, most monarchs had increased royal power at the expense of religious institutions.

Q *To what extent were religious majorities geographically concentrated in certain areas, and what accounted for this?*

In the Dutch Republic, however, toleration of various religious orders underwent significant changes during the eighteenth century, building upon centuries of varying degrees of religious tolerance towards dissenting groups. Toleration, however, did not equal freedom of religious expression, but rather freedom of conscience as prescribed in article 13 of the Union of Utrecht of 1579. To what degree this freedom was tolerated depended upon the political state, and by 1651, this privilege was granted to the Dutch Reformed Church, or Calvinist Church. All other religions could worship inconspicuously, and non-Reformed citizens were treated as second-class citizens. By the mid-eighteenth century, however, the writings of Enlightenment thinkers fueled heated public debates in the Dutch Republic. By 1796, a Declaration of Human Rights declared the separation of church and state, thus establishing the equality of all Protestant and Roman Catholic citizens in the United Provinces, while Jews were granted civil rights.

TOLERATION AND THE JEWS The Jews remained the despised religious minority of Europe. The largest number of Jews (known as the Ashkenazic Jews) lived in eastern Europe. Except in relatively tolerant Poland, Jews were restricted in their movements, forbidden to own land or hold many jobs, forced to pay burdensome special taxes, and also subject to periodic outbursts of popular wrath. The resulting **pogroms**, in which Jewish communities were looted and massacred, made Jewish existence precarious and dependent on the favor of their territorial rulers.

Another major group was the Sephardic Jews, who had been expelled from Spain in the fifteenth century. Although many had migrated to Turkish lands, some had settled in cities, such as Amsterdam, Venice, London, and Frankfurt, where they were relatively free to participate in the banking and commercial activities that Jews had practiced since the Middle Ages. The highly successful ones came to provide valuable services to rulers, especially in central Europe, where they were known as the court Jews. But even these Jews were insecure because their religion set them apart from the Christian majority and served as a catalyst to social resentment.

Some Enlightenment thinkers in the eighteenth century favored a new acceptance of Jews. They argued that Jews and Muslims were human and deserved the full rights of citizenship despite their religion. Many philosophes denounced persecution of the Jews but made no attempt to hide their hostility and ridiculed Jewish customs. Diderot, for example, said that the Jews had "all the defects peculiar to an ignorant and superstitious nation." Many Europeans favored the assimilation of the Jews into the mainstream of society, but only by the conversion of Jews to Christianity as the basic solution to the "Jewish problem." This, of course, was not acceptable to most Jews.

The Austrian emperor Joseph II attempted to adopt a new policy toward the Jews, although it too was limited. It freed Jews from nuisance taxes and allowed them more freedom of movement and job opportunities, but they were still restricted from owning land and worshiping in public. At the same time, Joseph II encouraged Jews to learn German and work toward greater assimilation into Austrian society.

Popular Religion in the Eighteenth Century

Despite the rise of skepticism and the intellectuals' belief in deism and natural religion, religious devotion remained strong in the eighteenth century.

CATHOLIC PIETY It is difficult to assess precisely the religiosity of Europe's Catholics. The Catholic parish church remained an important center of life for the entire community. How many people went to church regularly cannot be known exactly, but it has been established that 90 to 95 percent of Catholic populations did go to Mass on Easter Sunday, one of the church's most special celebrations. Catholic religiosity proved highly selective, however. Despite the Reformation, much popular devotion was still directed to an externalized form of worship focusing on prayers to saints, pilgrimages, and devotion to relics and images. This bothered many clergymen, who felt that their parishioners were "more superstitious than devout," as one Catholic priest put it. Many common people continued to fear witches and relied on the intervention of the saints and the Virgin Mary to save them from personal disasters caused by the devil.

PROTESTANT REVIVALISM: PIETISM After the initial century of religious fervor that created Protestantism in the sixteenth century, Protestant churches in the seventeenth century had settled down into well-established patterns controlled by state authorities and served by a well-educated clergy. Protestant churches became bureaucratized and bereft of religious enthusiasm. In Germany and England, where rationalism and deism had become influential and moved some theologians to a more "rational" Christianity, the desire of ordinary Protestant churchgoers for greater depths of religious experience led to new and dynamic religious movements.

Pietism (PY-uh-tiz-um) in Germany was a response to this desire for a deeper personal devotion to God. Begun in the seventeenth century by a group of German clerics who wanted their religion to be more personal, Pietism was spread by the teachings of Count Nikolaus von Zinzendorf (NEE-koh-LOWSS fun TSIN-sin-dorf) (1700–1760). To Zinzendorf and his Moravian Brethren, as his sect was called, true religious experience consisted of the mystical dimensions—the personal experience of God—in one's life. He was utterly opposed to what he perceived as the rationalistic approach of orthodox Lutheran clergy, who were being educated in new "rational" ideas. As Zinzendorf commented, "He who wishes to comprehend God with his mind becomes an atheist."

After the civil wars of the seventeenth century, England too had arrived at a respectable, uniform, and complacent state church. A pillar of the establishment, the Anglican Church seemed to offer little spiritual excitement, especially to the

TopFoto/The Image Works

John Wesley. In leading a deep spiritual revival in Britain, John Wesley founded a religious movement that came to be known as Methodism. He loved to preach to the masses, and this 1766 portrait by Nathaniel Hone shows him as he might have appeared before a crowd of people.

THE CONVERSION EXPERIENCE IN WESLEY'S METHODISM

AFTER HIS OWN CONVERSION EXPERIENCE, John Wesley traveled extensively to bring the "glad tidings" of Jesus to other people. It has been estimated that he preached more than 40,000 sermons, some of them to audiences numbering 20,000 listeners. Wesley gave his message wherever people gathered—in the streets, hospitals, private houses, and even pubs. In this selection from his journal, Wesley describes how emotional and even violent conversion experiences could be.

The Journal of the Reverend John Wesley

Sunday, May 20 [1759], being with Mr. B——ll at Everton, I was much fatigued, and did not rise: but Mr. B. did, and observed several fainting and crying out, while Mr. Berridge was preaching: afterwards at Church, I heard many cry out, especially children, whose agonies were amazing: one of the eldest, a girl of ten or twelve years old, was full in my view, in violent contortions of body, and weeping aloud, I think incessantly, during the whole service. . . . The Church was equally crowded in the afternoon, the windows being filled within and without, and even the outside of the pulpit to the very top; so that Mr. B. seemed almost stifled by their breath; yet feeble and sickly as he is, he was continually strengthened, and his voice, for the most part, distinguishable; in the midst of all the outcries. I believe there were present three times more men than women, a great part of whom came from far; thirty of them having set out at two in the morning, from a place thirteen miles off. The text was, *Having a form of godliness, but denying the power thereof.* When the power of religion began to be spoken of, the presence of God really filled the place: and while poor sinners felt the sentence of death in their souls, what sounds of distress did I hear! The greatest number of them who cried or fell, were men: but some women, and several children, felt the power of the same almighty Spirit, and seemed just sinking into hell. This occasioned a mixture of several sounds; some shrieking, some roaring aloud. The most general was a loud breathing, like that of people half strangled and gasping for life: and indeed almost all the cries were like those of human creatures, dying in bitter anguish. Great numbers wept without any noise: others fell down as death: some sinking in silence; some with extreme noise and violent agitation. I stood on the pew-seat, as did a young man in the opposite pew, an able-bodied, fresh, healthy countryman: but in a moment, while he seemed to think of nothing less, down he dropped with a violence inconceivable. The adjoining pews seemed to shake with his fall: I heard afterwards the stamping of his feet; ready to break the boards, as he lay in strong convulsions, at the bottom of the pew. Among several that were struck down in the next pew, was a girl, who was as violently seized as he. . . . Among the children who felt the arrows of the Almighty, I saw a sturdy boy, about eight years old, who roared above his fellows, and seemed in his agony to struggle with the strength of a grown man. His face was as red as scarlet: and almost all on whom God laid his hand, turned either very red or almost black. . . .

The violent struggling of many in the above-mentioned churches, has broken several pews and benches. Yet it is common for people to remain unaffected there, and afterwards to drop down on their way home. Some have been found lying as dead on the road: others, in Mr. B.'s garden; not being able to walk from the Church to his house, though it is not two hundred yards.

Q *What was a conversion experience? How does the emotionalism of this passage relate to enlightened thinkers' fascination with the passions and the workings of human reason?*

Source: *The Journal of the Reverend John Wesley AM*, vol. 2. (Darlington, U.K.: J. M. Dent & Sons Ltd., 1920).

masses of people. The dissenting Protestant groups—Puritans, Quakers, Baptists—were relatively subdued, while the growth of deism seemed to challenge Christianity itself. The desire for deep spiritual experience seemed unmet until the advent of John Wesley.

WESLEY AND METHODISM An ordained Anglican minister, John Wesley (1703–1791) suffered a deep spiritual crisis and underwent a mystical experience: "I felt I did trust in Christ alone for salvation; and an assurance was given me, that He had taken away my sins, even mine, and saved me from the law of sin and death." To Wesley, "the gift of God's grace" assured him of salvation and led him to become a missionary to the English people, bringing the "glad tidings" of salvation to all people, despite opposition from the Anglican Church, which criticized this emotional mysticism or religious enthusiasm as superstitious nonsense. To Wesley, all could be saved by experiencing God and opening the doors to his grace.

In taking the Gospel to the people, Wesley preached to the masses in open fields, appealing especially to the lower classes neglected by the socially elitist Anglican Church. He tried, he said, "to lower religion to the level of the lowest people's capacities." Wesley's charismatic preaching often provoked highly charged and even violent conversion experiences (see the box above). Afterward, converts were organized into so-called Methodist societies or chapels in which they could aid each other in doing the good works that Wesley considered a component of salvation. Although Wesley sought to keep Methodism within the Anglican Church, after his death it became a separate and independent sect. Methodism was an important revival of Christianity and proved that the need for spiritual experience had not been expunged by the eighteenth-century search for reason.

CHAPTER SUMMARY

The eighteenth century was a time of change but also of tradition. The popularization of the ideas of the Scientific Revolution, the impact of travel literature, a new skepticism, and the ideas of Locke and Newton led to what historians call the Age of Enlightenment. Its leading figures were the intellectuals known as philosophes who hoped that they could create a new society by using reason to discover the natural laws that governed it. Like the Christian humanists of the fifteenth and sixteenth centuries, they believed that education could create better human beings and a better human society. Such philosophes as Montesquieu, Voltaire, Diderot, Hume, Quesnay, Smith, Beccaria, Condorcet, and Rousseau attacked traditional religion as the enemy, advocated religious toleration and freedom of thought, criticized their oppressive societies, and created a new "science of man" in economics, politics, and education. In doing so, the philosophes laid the foundation for a modern worldview based on rationalism and secularism.

Although many of the philosophes continued to hold traditional views about women, female intellectuals like Mary Astell and Mary Wollstonecraft began to argue for the equality of the sexes and the right of women to be educated. The Enlightenment appealed largely to the urban middle classes and some members of the nobility, and its ideas were discussed in salons, coffeehouses, reading clubs, lending libraries, and societies like the Freemasons.

Innovation in the arts also characterized the eighteenth century. The cultural fertility of the age is evident in Rococo painting and architecture; the achievements of Bach, Handel, Haydn, and Mozart in music; the birth of the novel in literature; and new directions in education and historical writing.

Although the philosophes attacked the established Christian churches, many Europeans continued to practice their traditional faith. Moreover, a new wave of piety swept both Catholic and Protestant churches, especially noticeable in Protestant Europe with the advent of Pietism in Germany and John Wesley and Methodism in England.

Thus, despite the secular thought and secular ideas that began to pervade the mental world of the ruling elites, most people in eighteenth-century Europe still lived by seemingly eternal verities and practices—God, religious worship, and farming. The most brilliant architecture and music of the age were religious. And yet the forces of secularization were too strong to stop. In the midst of intellectual change, economic, political, and social transformations of great purport were taking shape and would lead, as we shall see in the next two chapters, to both political and social upheavals and even revolution before the century's end.

CHAPTER TIMELINE

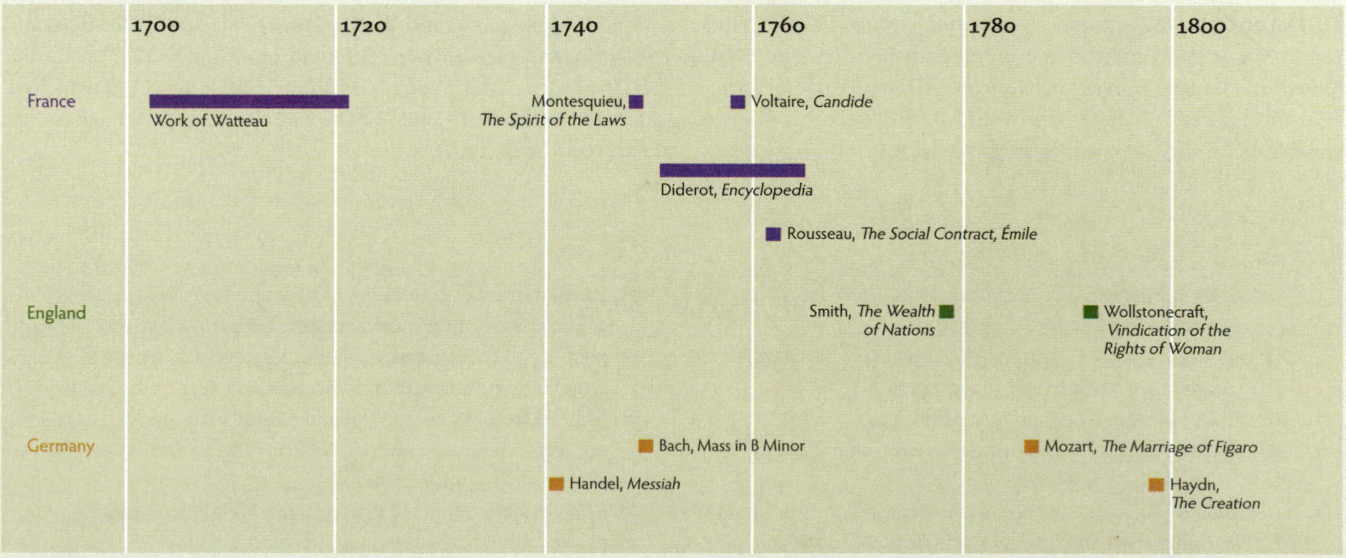

CHAPTER REVIEW

Upon Reflection

Q What contributions did Montesquieu, Voltaire, Diderot, and Rousseau make to the Enlightenment? What did they have in common? How did they differ?

Q What is popular culture, and how was it expressed in the eighteenth century?

Q What kinds of experiences do you associate with popular religion in the eighteenth century? How do you explain the continuing growth of popular religious devotion?

Key Terms

Enlightenment (p. 500)
skepticism (p. 500)
cultural relativism (p. 501)
philosophes (p. 502)
cosmopolitan (p. 502)
separation of powers (p. 503)
deism (p. 506)
laissez-faire (p. 507)
economic liberalism (p. 507)
Romanticism (p. 509)
feminism (p. 510)
salons (p. 510)
Rococo (p. 513)
neoclassicism (p. 514)
high culture (p. 516)
popular culture (p. 516)
pogroms (p. 523)
Pietism (p. 523)

Suggestions for Further Reading

EIGHTEENTH-CENTURY EUROPE Surveys of eighteenth-century Europe include **M. S. Anderson, *Europe in the Eighteenth Century***, 4th ed. (London, 2000); **I. Woloch, *Eighteenth-Century Europe, 1648–1789*** (New York, 1986); and **T. C. W. Blanning, ed., *The Eighteenth Century: Europe, 1689–1815*** (Oxford, 2000).

THE ENLIGHTENMENT Good introductions to the Enlightenment can be found in **D. Outram, *The Enlightenment***, 2nd ed. (Cambridge, 2005), and **A. Pagden, *The Enlightenment and Why It Still Matters*** (New York, 2013). On the social history of the Enlightenment, see **T. Munck, *The Enlightenment: A Comparative Social History, 1721–1794*** (London, 2000). Studies of the major Enlightenment intellectuals include **R. Pearson, *Voltaire Almighty: A Life in Pursuit of Freedom*** (New York, 2005); **J. Fowler, *New Essays on Diderot*** (New York, 2011); and **L. Damrosch, *Jean-Jacques Rousseau: Restless Genius*** (Boston, 2007). On women in the eighteenth century, see **M. E. Wiesner-Hanks, *Women and Gender in Early Modern Europe*** (Cambridge, 2000), and **S. Knott and B. Taylor, eds., *Women, Gender and Enlightenment*** (Basingstoke, 2005).

CULTURE AND SOCIETY On Rococo art, see **E. G. Bahr** and **I. F. Walther, *Rococo*** (New York, 2007). On the coffeehouse, see **E. Markman, *The Coffee House: A Cultural History*** (London, 2004).

POPULAR CULTURE Important studies on popular culture include **P. Burke, *Popular Culture in Early Modern Europe***, 3rd ed. (New York, 2009), and **J. Mullan, ed., *Eighteenth-Century Popular Culture*** (Oxford, 2000).

EIGHTEENTH-CENTURY RELIGIOUS HISTORY A good introduction to the religious history of the eighteenth century can be found in **G. R. Cragg, *The Church and the Age of Reason, 1648–1789*** (London, 1990). On religious toleration, see **O. P. Grell and R. Porter, eds., *Toleration in Enlightenment Europe*** (Cambridge, 2000), and **B. Kaplan, *Divided by Faith: Religious Conflict and the Practice of Toleration in Early Modern Europe*** (Cambridge, Mass., 2007). On John Wesley, see **H. Rack, *Reasonable Enthusiast: John Wesley and the Rise of Methodism***, 3rd ed. (New York, 2002).

Notes

1. Quoted in P. Hazard, *The European Mind, 1680–1715* (New York: Meridian Books, 1963), pp. 304–305.
2. Quoted in D. Outram, *The Enlightenment* (Cambridge: Cambridge University Press, 1995), p. 67.
3. Quoted in Hazard, *The European Mind*, p. 12.
4. John Locke, *An Essay Concerning Human Understanding* (New York, 1964), pp. 89–90.
5. Baron Paul d'Holbach, *Common Sense*, as quoted in F. E. Manuel, ed., *The Enlightenment* (Englewood Cliffs, N.J., 1965), p. 62.
6. Jean-Jacques Rousseau, *A Discourse on Inequality*, trans. M. Cranston (Harmondsworth, U.K., 1984), p. 109.
7. Jean-Jacques Rousseau, *The Social Contract*, trans. M. Cranston (Harmondsworth, U.K., 1968), p. 141.
8. Mary Astell, *A Serious Proposal to the Ladies*, in M. Ferguson, ed., *First Feminists: British Women Writers, 1578–1799* (Bloomington, Ind., 1985), p. 190.
9. Mary Astell, *Some Reflections upon Marriage*, in ibid., p. 193.

10. K. Clark, *Civilization* (New York: Harper & Row, 1969), p. 231.
11. Voltaire, *The Age of Louis XIV*, trans. M. P. Pollack (New York: Dutton, 1961), p. 1.
12. Quoted in B. Kümen, *The European World, 1500–1800* (London: Routledge, 2009), p. 230.
13. Cesare Beccaria, *An Essay on Crimes and Punishments*, trans. E. D. Ingraham (Philadelphia, 1819), pp. 59–60.
14. Quoted in R. Sand, *The Advance to Social Medicine* (London, 1952), pp. 86–87.
15. Quoted in P. Burke, *Popular Culture in Early Modern Europe* (New York, 1978), p. 179.
16. Quoted in ibid., p. 186.
17. Quoted in C. A. Macartney, *The Habsburg and Hohenzollern Dynasties in the Seventeenth and Eighteenth Centuries* (New York, 1970), p. 157.

CHAPTER

18

THE EIGHTEENTH CENTURY: EUROPEAN STATES, INTERNATIONAL WARS, AND SOCIAL CHANGE

A 1793 portrait of Catherine the Great of Russia by Johann Lampi

CHAPTER OUTLINE AND FOCUS QUESTIONS

The European States

Q What were the main developments in France, Great Britain, the Dutch Republic, the Mediterranean states, and the Scandinavian monarchies in the eighteenth century? What do historians mean by the term *enlightened absolutism*, and to what degree did eighteenth-century Prussia, Austria, and Russia exhibit its characteristics?

Wars and Diplomacy

Q How did the concepts of "balance of power" and "reason of state" influence international relations in the eighteenth century? What were the causes and results of the Seven Years' War?

Economic Expansion and Social Change

Q What changes occurred in agriculture, finance, industry, and trade during the eighteenth century?

The Social Order of the Eighteenth Century

Q Who were the main groups making up the European social order in the eighteenth century, and how did the conditions in which they lived differ both between groups and between different parts of Europe?

Critical Thinking

Q *What was the relationship among intellectual, political, economic, and social changes in the eighteenth century?*

Connections to Today

Q *How do the benefits and consequences of the agricultural revolution of the eighteenth century compare with the changes in agricultural production occurring in the twenty-first century?*

HISTORIANS OFTEN DEFINE the eighteenth century as the years from 1715 to 1789. Politically, this makes sense since 1715 marks the end of the age of Louis XIV and 1789 was the year in which the French Revolution erupted. This period has often been portrayed as the final phase of Europe's old order, before the violent upheaval and reordering of society associated with the French Revolution. Europe's old order—still largely agrarian, dominated by kings and landed aristocrats, and grounded in privileges for nobles, clergy, towns, and provinces—seemed to continue a basic pattern that had prevailed in Europe since medieval times. But new ideas and new practices were also beginning to emerge. Just as a new intellectual order based on rationalism and secularism was evolving from the Scientific Revolution and the Enlightenment, demographic, economic, and social patterns were beginning to change in ways that reflected a modern new order.

The ideas of the Enlightenment seemed to proclaim a new political age as well. Catherine the Great, who ruled Russia from 1762 to 1796, wrote to Voltaire, "Since 1746 I have been under the greatest obligations to you. Before that period I read nothing but romances, but by chance your works fell into my hands, and ever since then I have never ceased to read them, and have no desire for books less well written than yours, or less instructive." The empress of Russia also invited Diderot to Russia and, when he arrived, urged him to speak frankly "as man to man." Diderot did, offering her advice for a far-ranging program of political and financial reform. But Catherine's apparent eagerness to make enlightened reforms was tempered by skepticism. She said of Diderot, "If I had believed him everything would have been turned upside down in my kingdom; legislation, administration, finance—all would have been turned topsy-turvy to make room for impractical theories." For Catherine, enlightened reform remained more a dream than a reality, and in the end, the waging of wars to gain more power was more important.

In the eighteenth century, the process of centralization that had characterized the growth of states since the Middle Ages continued as most European states enlarged their bureaucratic machinery and consolidated their governments in order to collect the revenues and build the armies they needed to compete militarily with the other European states. International competition continued to be the favorite pastime of eighteenth-century rulers. Within the European state system, the nations that would dominate Europe until World War I—Britain, France, Austria, Prussia, and Russia—emerged as the five great powers of Europe. Their rivalries led to major wars, which some have called the first world wars because they were fought outside as well as inside Europe. In the midst of this state building and war making, dramatic demographic, economic, and social changes heralded the emergence of a radical transformation in the way Europeans would raise food and produce goods.

The European States

FOCUS QUESTIONS: What were the main developments in France, Great Britain, the Dutch Republic, the Mediterranean states, and the Scandinavian monarchies in the eighteenth century? What do historians mean by the term *enlightened absolutism*, and to what degree did eighteenth-century Prussia, Austria, and Russia exhibit its characteristics?

Monarchs ruled most European states in the eighteenth century. Although the justifications of the previous century for strong monarchy continued to hold sway, divine-right assumptions were gradually superseded by influential utilitarian arguments as Europe became increasingly secularized. The Prussian king Frederick II expressed this new thinking well when explaining the services a monarch must provide for his people:

> These services consisted in the maintenance of the laws; a strict execution of justice; an employment of his whole powers to prevent any corruption of manners; and defending the state against its enemies. It is the duty of this magistrate to pay attention to agriculture; it should be his care that provisions for the nation should be in abundance, and that commerce and industry should be encouraged. He is a perpetual sentinel, who must watch the acts and the conduct of the enemies of the state. . . . If he be the first general, the first minister of the realm, it is not that he should remain the shadow of authority, but that he should fulfill the duties of such titles. He is only the first servant of the state.[1]

The praises of the philosophes reinforced this utilitarian argument.

Enlightened Absolutism?

There is no doubt that Enlightenment thought had some impact on the political development of European states in the eighteenth century. Closely related to the Enlightenment idea of **natural laws** was the belief in **natural rights**, which were thought to be inalterable privileges that ought not to be withheld from any person. These natural rights included equality before the law, freedom of religious worship, freedom of speech and press, and the right to assemble, hold property, and seek happiness. The American Declaration of Independence summarized the Enlightenment concept of natural rights in its opening paragraph: "We hold these truths to be self-evident, that all men are created equal; that they are endowed by their creator with certain unalienable rights; that among these are life, liberty and the pursuit of happiness."

But how were these natural rights to be established and preserved? In the opinion of most philosophes, most people needed the direction provided by an enlightened ruler. What made rulers enlightened? They must allow religious toleration, freedom of speech and press, and the right to hold private property. They must foster the arts, sciences, and education. Above all, their rule must not be arbitrary; they must obey the laws and enforce them fairly for all subjects. Only strong monarchs seemed capable of overcoming vested interests and effecting the reforms society needed. Reforms then should come from above—from the rulers rather than from the people. Distrustful of the masses, the philosophes believed that absolute rulers, swayed by enlightened principles, were the best hope of reforming their societies.

The extent to which rulers actually did so is frequently discussed in the political analyses of Europe in the eighteenth century. Many historians once asserted that a new type of monarchy emerged in the late eighteenth century, which they called enlightened despotism or **enlightened absolutism**. Monarchs such as Frederick II of Prussia, Catherine the Great of Russia, and Joseph II of Austria supposedly followed the advice of the philosophes and ruled by enlightened principles, establishing a path to modern nationhood. Recent scholarship, however, has questioned the usefulness of the concept of enlightened absolutism. We can best determine the extent to which it can be applied by surveying the development of the European states in the eighteenth century and then making a judgment about the enlightened absolutism of the century's later years.

The Atlantic Seaboard States

As a result of the overseas voyages of the sixteenth century, the European economic axis began to shift from the Mediterranean to the Atlantic seaboard. In the seventeenth century, the

English and Dutch expanded as Spain and Portugal declined. By the eighteenth century, Dutch power had waned, and it was left to the English and French to build the commercial empires that created a true global economy.

FRANCE: THE PROBLEMS OF THE FRENCH MONARCHS In the eighteenth century, France experienced an economic revival as the Enlightenment gained strength. The French monarchy, however, was not overly influenced by the philosophes and resisted reforms even as the French aristocracy grew stronger.

Louis XIV had left France with enlarged territories, an enormous debt, an unhappy populace, and a five-year-old great-grandson as his successor. The governing of France fell into the hands first of the regent, the duke of Orléans, whose good intentions were thwarted by his drunken and immoral behavior, and later of Cardinal Fleury (floo-REE), the king's minister. France pulled back from foreign adventures while commerce and trade expanded and the government promoted the growth of industry, especially in coal and textiles. The budget was even balanced for a while. When Fleury died in 1743, Louis XV (1715–1774) decided to rule alone. But Louis was both lazy and weak, and ministers and mistresses soon began to influence the king, control the affairs of state, and undermine the prestige of the monarchy. One mistress—probably the most famous of eighteenth-century Europe—was Madame de Pompadour (ma-DAM duh POM-puh-door). An intelligent and beautiful woman, she charmed Louis XV and gained both wealth and power, often making important government decisions and giving advice on appointments and foreign policy. The loss of an empire in the Seven Years' War, accompanied by burdensome taxes, an ever-mounting public debt, more hungry people, and a court life at Versailles that remained frivolous and carefree, forced even Louis to recognize the growing disgust with his monarchy. Perhaps all might not have been in vain if a competent king had succeeded Louis. But the new king, Louis's twenty-year-old grandson who became Louis XVI (1774–1792), knew little about the operations of the French government and lacked the energy to deal decisively with state affairs (see the box on p. 531). His wife, Marie Antoinette (ma-REE ahn-twahn-NET), was a spoiled Austrian princess who devoted much of her time to court intrigues (see "Film & History" above). As France's financial crises worsened, neither Louis nor his queen seemed able to fathom the depths of despair and discontent that soon led to violent revolution (see Chapter 19).

FILM & HISTORY

Columbia/American Zoetrope/Sony/The Kobal Collection at Art Resource, NY

Watch ***Marie Antoinette*** (2006), a film based on Antonia Fraser's book *Marie Antoinette: A Journey* (2001). The film begins with the marriage of Marie Antoinette, the daughter of Empress Maria Theresa of Austria, to the dauphin Louis, the heir to the French throne. Shot at Versailles, the film chronicles the young life of Marie Antoinette at court and the challenges she faced adapting to courtly life in France. The film incorporates contemporary music and material goods to engage modern viewers, yet the elaborate sets and costumes capture the grandeur and splendor of court life in eighteenth-century France.

Q *What can you discern about courtly life by watching this film? What challenges did Marie Antoinette face at court?*

GREAT BRITAIN: KING AND PARLIAMENT The success of the Glorious Revolution in England had prevented absolutism without clearly inaugurating constitutional monarchy. The

National Portrait Gallery, London/The Bridgeman Art Library

The British House of Commons. A sharing of power between king and Parliament characterized the British political system in the eighteenth century. Parliament was divided into the House of Lords and the House of Commons. This painting shows the House of Commons in session in 1793 during a debate over the possibility of war with France. William Pitt the Younger is addressing the House.

THE FRENCH KING'S BEDTIME

LOUIS XIV HAD USED COURT ETIQUETTE to magnify the dignity of kingship. During the reign of Louis XVI, however, court etiquette degenerated to ludicrous depths. This excerpt from the *Memoirs of the Comtesse de Boigne* describes the king's *coucher* (KOO-shay), the formal ceremony in which the king retired for the night.

Comtesse de Boigne, *Memoirs*

The king [Louis XVI] went to his *coucher*. The so-called *coucher* took place every evening at half past nine. The gentlemen of the court assembled in the bedroom of Louis XVI (but Louis XVI did not sleep there). I believe that all those who had been presented at court were permitted to attend.

The king came in from an adjoining room, followed by his domestic staff. His hair was in curlers, and he was not wearing his decorations. Without paying attention to anybody, he stepped behind the handrail surrounding the bed, and the chaplain on duty was given the prayer book and a tall taperstand with two candles by one of the valets. He then joined the king behind the handrail, handed him the book, and held the taperstand during the king's prayer, which was short. The king then went to the part of the room where the courtiers were, and the chaplain gave the taperstand back to the first valet who, in turn, took it over to a person indicated by the king. This person held it as long as the *coucher* lasted. This distinction was very much sought after. . . .

The king had his coat, vest and finally shirt removed. He was naked to the waist, scratching and rubbing himself as if alone, though he was in the presence of the whole court and often a number of distinguished foreigners.

The first valet handed the nightshirt to the most qualified person. . . . If it was a person with whom the king was on familiar terms, he often played little tricks before donning it, missed it, passed it, and ran away, accompanying this charming nonsense with hearty laughter, making those who were sincerely attached to him suffer. Having donned the nightshirt, he put on his robe and three valets unfastened the belt and the knee buckles of his trousers, which fell down to his feet. Thus attired, hardly able to walk so absurdly encumbered, he began to make the round of the circle.

The duration of this reception was by no means fixed; sometimes it lasted only a few minutes, sometimes almost an hour; it depended on who was there. . . . When the king had enough, he dragged himself backward to an easy chair which had been pushed to the middle of the room and fell heavily into it, raising both legs. Two pages on their knees seized his shoes, took them off, and dropped them on the floor with a thump, which was part of the etiquette. When he heard it, the doorman opened the door and said, "This way, gentlemen." Everybody left, and the ceremony was over. However, the person who held the taperstand was permitted to stay if he had anything special to say to the king. This explains the high price attached to this strange favor.

Q *What does this account reveal about the condition of the French monarchy and the high French aristocracy during the reign of Louis XVI?*

Source: From *Memoirs of the Comtesse de Boigne.* Ed. M. Charles Nicoullaud. New York: Heinemann, 1907.

eighteenth-century British political system was characterized by a sharing of power between king and Parliament, with Parliament gradually gaining the upper hand. (The United Kingdom of Great Britain came into existence in 1707 when the governments of England and Scotland were united; the term *British* came to refer to both English and Scots.) The king chose ministers responsible to himself who set policy and guided Parliament; Parliament had the power to make laws, levy taxes, pass the budget, and indirectly influence the king's ministers. The eighteenth-century British Parliament was dominated by a landed aristocracy that historians usually divide into two groups: the peers, who sat for life in the House of Lords, and the landed gentry, who sat in the House of Commons and served as justices of the peace in the counties. The two groups had much in common: both were landowners with similar economic interests, and they frequently intermarried.

The deputies to the House of Commons were chosen from the boroughs and counties, but not by popular voting. Who was eligible to vote in the boroughs varied wildly, enabling wealthy landed aristocrats to gain support by **patronage** and bribery; the result was a number of "pocket boroughs" controlled by a single person (hence "in his pocket"). The duke of Newcastle, for example, controlled the representatives from seven boroughs. It has been estimated that out of 405 borough deputies, 293 were chosen by fewer than 500 voters. This aristocratic control also extended to the county delegates, two from each of England's forty counties. Although all holders of property worth at least 40 shillings a year could vote, members of the leading landed gentry families were elected over and over again.

In 1714, a new dynasty—the Hanoverians—was established. When the last Stuart ruler, Queen Anne, died without an heir, the crown was offered to the Protestant rulers of the German state of Hanover. Because the first Hanoverian king, George I (1714–1727), did not speak English and neither he nor George II (1727–1760) had much familiarity with the British system, their chief ministers were allowed to handle Parliament. Many historians believe that this exercise of ministerial power was an important step in the development of the modern cabinet system in British government.

CHRONOLOGY	The Atlantic Seaboard States
France	
Louis XV	1715–1774
Louis XVI	1774–1792
Great Britain	
George 1	1714–1727
George II	1727–1760
Robert Walpole	1721–1742
William Pitt the Elder	1757–1761
George III	1760–1820
William Pitt the Younger	1783–1801

Robert Walpole served as prime minister from 1721 to 1742 and pursued a peaceful foreign policy to avoid new land taxes. But new forces were emerging in eighteenth-century England as growing trade and industry led an ever-increasing middle class to favor expansion of trade and world empire. The exponents of empire found a spokesman in William Pitt the Elder, who became prime minister in 1757 and furthered imperial ambitions by acquiring Canada and India in the Seven Years' War.

Despite his successes, Pitt the Elder was dismissed in 1761 by the new king, George III (1760–1820), and replaced by the king's favorite, Lord Bute. Discontent over the electoral system, however, and the loss of the American colonies (see Chapter 19) led to public criticism of the king. In 1780, the House of Commons affirmed that "the influence of the crown has increased, is increasing, and ought to be diminished." King George III managed to avoid drastic change by appointing William Pitt the Younger (1759–1806), son of William Pitt the Elder, as prime minister in 1783. Supported by the merchants, industrial classes, and the king, Pitt managed to stay in power. George III, however, remained an uncertain supporter because of periodic bouts of insanity (he once mistook a tree in Windsor Park for the king of Prussia). Nevertheless, thanks to Pitt's successes, serious reform of the corrupt parliamentary system was avoided for another generation.

THE DECLINE OF THE DUTCH REPUBLIC After its century in the sun, the Dutch Republic or United Netherlands suffered a decline in economic prosperity. Both local and national political affairs were dominated by the oligarchies that governed the Dutch Republic's towns. In the eighteenth century, the struggle continued between these oligarchs (or regents, as they were called, from their governing positions) and the house of Orange, who as stadholders headed the executive branch of government. The regents sought to reduce the power of the Orangists but soon became divided when Dutch burghers who called themselves the Patriots (artisans, merchants, and shopkeepers) began to agitate for democratic reforms that would open up the municipal councils to greater participation than that of the oligarchs. The success of the Patriots, however, led to foreign interference when the Prussian king sent troops to protect his sister, the wife of the Orangist stadholder. The Patriots were crushed, and both Orangists and regents reestablished the old system. The intervention by Prussia serves to remind us of the growing power of the central European states.

Absolutism in Central and Eastern Europe

Of the five major European states, three were located in central and eastern Europe and came to play an increasingly important role in European international politics (see Map 18.1).

PRUSSIA: THE ARMY AND THE BUREAUCRACY Two able Prussian kings in the eighteenth century, Frederick William I and Frederick II, further developed the two major institutions—the army and the bureaucracy—that were the backbone of Prussia. Frederick William I (1713–1740) promoted the evolution of Prussia's highly efficient civil bureaucracy by establishing the General Directory. It served as the chief administrative agent of the central government, supervising military, police, economic, and financial affairs. Frederick William strove to maintain a highly efficient bureaucracy of civil service workers. It had its own code, in which the supreme values were obedience, honor, and service to the king as the highest duty. As Frederick William asserted, "One must serve the king with life and limb, with goods and chattels, with honor and conscience, and surrender everything except salvation. The latter is reserved for God. But everything else must be mine."[2] For his part, Frederick William personally kept a close watch over his officials to ensure that they performed their duties. As the Saxon minister at Berlin related:

> Every day His Majesty gives new proofs of his justice. Walking recently at Potsdam at six in the morning, he saw a post-coach arrive with several passengers who knocked for a long time at the post-house which was still closed. The King, seeing that no one opened the door, joined them in knocking and even knocked in some window-panes. The master of the post then opened the door and scolded the travelers, for no one recognized the King. But His Majesty let himself be known by giving the official some good blows of his cane and drove him from his house and his job after apologizing to the travelers for his laziness. Examples of this sort, of which I could relate several others, make everybody alert and exact.[3]

Close personal supervision of the bureaucracy became a hallmark of the eighteenth-century Prussian rulers.

Under Frederick William I, the rigid class stratification that had emerged in seventeenth-century Brandenburg-Prussia persisted. The nobility or landed aristocracy known as Junkers, who owned large estates with many serfs, still played a dominating role in the Prussian state. The Junkers held a complete monopoly over the officer corps of the Prussian army, which Frederick William passionately continued to expand. By the end of his reign, the army had grown from 45,000 to 83,000 men. Though tenth in geographic area and thirteenth in population among the European states, Prussia had the fourth largest army, after France, Russia, and Austria.

By using nobles as officers, Frederick William ensured a close bond between the nobility and the army and, in turn, the loyalty of the nobility to the absolute monarch. As officers, the Junker nobility became imbued with a sense of service to

MAP 18.1 Europe in 1763. By the middle of the eighteenth century, five major powers dominated Europe—Prussia, Austria, Russia, Britain, and France. Each sought to enhance its power both domestically, through a bureaucracy that collected taxes and ran the military, and internationally, by capturing territory or preventing other powers from doing so.

Q *Given the distribution of Prussian and Habsburg holdings, in what areas of Europe were they most likely to compete for land and power?*

the king or state. All the virtues of the Prussian nobility were, in effect, military virtues: duty, obedience, sacrifice. At the same time, because of its size and reputation as one of the best armies in Europe, the Prussian army was the most important institution in the state. "Prussian militarism" became synonymous with the extreme exaltation of military virtues. Indeed, one Prussian minister around 1800 remarked that "Prussia was not a country with an army, but an army with a country which served as headquarters and food magazine."[4]

The remaining classes in Prussia were considerably less important than the nobility. The peasants were born on their lords' estates and spent most of their lives there or in the army. They had few real rights and even needed their Junker's permission to marry. For the middle class, the only opportunity for any social prestige was in the Prussian civil service, where the ideal of loyal service to the state became a hallmark of the middle-class official. Frederick William allowed and even encouraged men of non-noble birth to serve in important administrative posts. When he died in 1740, only three of his eighteen privy councillors were nobles.

Frederick II, known as the Great (1740–1786), was one of the best-educated and most cultured monarchs of the eighteenth century. He was well versed in Enlightenment thought and even invited Voltaire to live at his court for several years. His father had despised Frederick's intellectual interests and forced him to prepare for a career in ruling (see the box on p. 534). A believer in the king as the "first servant of the state," Frederick the Great became a conscientious ruler who made few innovations in the administration of the state. His diligence in overseeing its operation, however, made the Prussian bureaucracy famous for both its efficiency and its honesty.

For a time, Frederick seemed quite willing to follow the philosophes' recommendations for reform. He established a single code of laws for his territories that eliminated the use of torture except in treason and murder cases. He also granted limited freedom of speech and press as well as religious toleration—no difficult task since he had no strong religious convictions. He did exclude the Jews, levying special taxes on the Jewish subjects and barring them from civil service. Frederick attempted to improve the lives of the peasants by increasing agricultural

FREDERICK THE GREAT AND HIS FATHER

AS A YOUNG MAN, THE FUTURE FREDERICK THE GREAT was quite different from his strict and austere father, Frederick William I. Possessing a high regard for French culture, poetry, and flute playing, Frederick resisted his father's wishes that he immerse himself in governmental and military affairs. Eventually, Frederick capitulated to his father's will and accepted the need to master affairs of state. These letters, written when Frederick was sixteen, illustrate the difficulties in their relationship.

Frederick to His Father, Frederick William I (September 11, 1728)

I have not ventured for a long time to present myself before my dear papa, partly because I was advised against it, but chiefly because I anticipated an even worse reception than usual and feared to vex my dear papa still further by the favor I have now to ask; so I have preferred to put it in writing.

I beg my dear papa that he will be kindly disposed toward me. I do assure him that after long examination of my conscience I do not find the slightest thing with which to reproach myself; but if, against my wish and will, I have vexed my dear papa, I hereby beg most humbly for forgiveness, and hope that my dear papa will give over the fearful hate which has appeared so plainly in his whole behavior and to which I cannot accustom myself. I have always thought hitherto that I had a kind father, but now I see the contrary. However, I will take courage and hope that my dear papa will think this all over and take me again into his favor. Meantime I assure him that I will never, my life long, willingly fail him, and in spite of his disfavor I am still, with most dutiful and childlike respect, my dear papa's

Most obedient and faithful servant and son,
Frederick

Frederick William to His Son Frederick

A bad, obstinate boy, who does not love his father; for when one does one's best, and especially when one loves one's father, one does what he wishes not only when he is standing by but when he is not there to see. Moreover you know very well that I cannot stand an effeminate fellow who has no manly tastes, who cannot ride or shoot (to his shame be it said!), is untidy about his person, and wears his hair curled like a fool instead of cutting it; and that I have condemned all these things a thousand times, and yet there is no sign of improvement. For the rest, haughty, offish as a country lout, conversing with none but a favored few instead of being affable and popular, grimacing like a fool, and never following my wishes out of love for me but only when forced into it, caring for nothing but to have his own way, and thinking nothing else is of any importance. This is my answer.

Frederick William

Q *Based on these documents, why was the relationship between Frederick II and his father such a difficult one? What does this troubled relationship tell you about the effects of ruling on the great monarchs of Europe and their families? What new duties and concerns of rulers (like Frederick William) may have reshaped relations between kings and sons?*

Source: J. H. Robinson, *Readings in European History*, vol. 2 (Boston: Ginn & Co., 1906).

productivity—he imported clover and potatoes from Western Europe and the iron plow, while draining swamps in the lower Oder Valley. Although Frederick was well aware of the philosophes' condemnation of serfdom, he was too dependent on the Prussian nobility to interfere with it or with the hierarchical structure of Prussian society. In fact, Frederick was a social conservative who made Prussian society even more aristocratic than it had been before. Frederick reversed his father's policy of allowing commoners to rise to power in the civil service and reserved the higher positions in the bureaucracy for members of the nobility. Over time the upper ranks of the bureaucracy came close to constituting a hereditary caste.

Like his predecessors, Frederick the Great took a great interest in military affairs and enlarged the Prussian army (to 200,000 men). Unlike his predecessors, he had no objection to using it. Frederick did not hesitate to take advantage of a succession crisis in the Habsburg monarchy to seize the Austrian province of Silesia (sy-LEE-zhuh) for Prussia. This act aroused Austria's bitter hostility and embroiled Frederick in two major wars, the War of the Austrian Succession and the Seven Years' War (see "Wars and Diplomacy" later in this chapter). Although the latter war left his country exhausted, Frederick succeeded in keeping Silesia. After the wars, the first partition of Poland with Austria and Russia in 1772 gave him the Polish territory between Prussia and Brandenburg, bringing greater unity to the scattered lands of Prussia. By the end of his reign, Prussia was recognized as a great European power.

THE AUSTRIAN EMPIRE OF THE HABSBURGS The Austrian Empire had become one of the great European states by the beginning of the eighteenth century. The city of Vienna, center of the Habsburg monarchy, was filled with magnificent palaces and churches built in the Baroque style and became the music capital of Europe. And yet Austria, a sprawling empire composed of many different nationalities, languages, religions, and cultures, found it difficult to provide common laws and a centralized administration for its people.

Empress Maria Theresa (1740–1780), however, stunned by the loss of Austrian Silesia to Prussia in the War of the Austrian Succession, resolved to reform her empire in preparation for the seemingly inevitable next conflict with rival Prussia. Maria

Frederick II. Frederick II was one of the most cultured and best-educated European monarchs. He is seen here in a portrait done five years before his death by the Swiss artist Anton Graff. The painting is regarded as Graff's masterpiece, and contemporaries considered it the best and most accurate portrait of the ruler.

bpk, Berlin/Charlottenburg Castle, Preussische Schlösser und Gärten, Berlin/Jörg P. Anders/Art Resource, NY

Franz Stephan I (1708–65) with his wife Marie-Therese (1717–80) and their children (oil on canvas), Mytens or Meytens, Martin II (1695–1770) (school of) / Château de Versailles, France/Bridgeman Images

Maria Theresa and Her Family. Maria Theresa governed the vast possessions of the Austrian Empire from 1740 to 1780. Of her ten surviving children, Joseph II (shown here in red standing beside his mother) succeeded her; Leopold became grand-duke of Tuscany and the ruler of Austria after Joseph's death; Ferdinand was made duke of Modena; and Marie Antoinette became the wife of King Louis XVI of France.

Theresa curtailed the role of the diets or provincial assemblies in taxation and local administration. Now clergy and nobles were forced to pay property and income taxes to royal officials rather than the diets. The Austrian and Bohemian lands were divided into ten provinces and subdivided into districts, all administered by royal officials rather than representatives of the diets, making part of the Austrian Empire more centralized and more bureaucratic. But these administrative reforms were done for practical reasons—to strengthen the power of the Habsburg state—and were accompanied by the expansion and modernization of the armed forces. Maria Theresa remained staunchly Catholic and conservative and was not open to the philosophes' calls for wider reforms. But her successor was.

Joseph II (1780–1790) was determined to make changes; at the same time, he carried on his mother's chief goal of enhancing Habsburg power within the monarchy and Europe. Joseph's reform program was far-reaching. He abolished serfdom and tried to give the peasants hereditary rights to their holdings. He also instituted a new penal code that abrogated the death penalty and established the principle of equality of all before the law. Joseph introduced drastic religious reforms as well, including complete religious toleration and restrictions on the Catholic Church. His government also supported public education, supplying textbooks and teachers for primary schools. Altogether, Joseph issued 6,000 decrees and 11,000 laws in his effort to transform Austria.

Joseph's reform program proved overwhelming for Austria, however. He alienated the nobility by freeing the serfs and alienated the church by his attacks on the monastic establishment. Even the peasants were unhappy, unable to comprehend the drastic changes inherent in Joseph's policies. His attempt to rationalize the administration of the empire by imposing German as the official bureaucratic language alienated the non-German nationalities. As Joseph complained, there were not enough people for the kind of bureaucracy he needed. His deep sense of failure is revealed in the epitaph he wrote for his gravestone: "Here lies Joseph II, who was unfortunate in everything that he undertook." His successors undid many of his reform efforts.

RUSSIA UNDER CATHERINE THE GREAT The six successors to Peter the Great of Russia all fell under the thumb of the palace guard. The last of these six was Peter III, whose German wife, Catherine, learned Russian and won the favor of the guard. When Peter was murdered by a faction of nobles, Catherine II the Great (1762–1796) emerged as autocrat of all Russia.

Catherine was an intelligent woman who was familiar with the works of the philosophes. She claimed that she wished to reform Russia along the lines of Enlightenment ideas, but she was always shrewd enough to realize that her success depended on the support of the palace guard and the gentry class from which it stemmed. She could not afford to alienate the Russian nobility (see the box "Opposing Viewpoints" on p. 536).

Initially, Catherine seemed eager to pursue reform. She called for the election of an assembly

OPPOSING VIEWPOINTS

Enlightened Absolutism: Enlightened or Absolute?

ALTHOUGH HISTORIANS HAVE USED THE TERM *enlightened absolutism* to describe a new type of monarchy in the eighteenth century, scholars have recently questioned the usefulness of the concept. The three selections below offer an opportunity to evaluate one so-called enlightened monarch, Catherine the Great of Russia. The first selection is from a letter written by the baron de Breteuil, the French ambassador to Russia, giving his impressions of Catherine. In 1767, Catherine convened a legislative commission to prepare a new code of laws for Russia. In her *Instruction*, parts of which form the second selection, she gave the delegates a detailed guide to the principles they should follow. Although the guidelines were culled from the liberal ideas of the philosophes, the commission itself accomplished nothing. The third selection, from a Decree on Serfs (also issued in 1767), reveals Catherine's authoritarian nature.

Letter of the Baron de Breteuil

[Catherine] seems to combine every kind of ambition in her person. Everything that may add luster to her reign will have some attraction for her. Science and the arts will be encouraged to flourish in the empire; projects useful for the domestic economy will be undertaken. She will endeavor to reform the administration of justice and to invigorate the laws; but her policies will be based on Machiavellianism; and I should not be surprised if in this field she rivals the king of Prussia. She will adopt the prejudices of her entourage regarding the superiority of her power and will endeavor to win respect not by the sincerity and probity of her actions but also by an ostentatious display of her strength. Haughty as she is, she will stubbornly pursue her undertakings and will rarely retrace a false step. Cunning and falsity appear to be vices in her character; woe to him who puts too much trust in her.

Catherine II, Proposals for a New Law Code

13. What is the true End of Monarchy? Not to deprive People of their natural Liberty; but to correct their Actions, in order to attain the supreme good. . . .

33. The Laws ought to be so framed, as to secure the Safety of every Citizen as much as possible.

34. The Equality of the Citizens consists in this; that they should all be subject to the same Laws. . . .

123. The Usage of Torture is contrary to all the Dictates of Nature and Reason; even Mankind itself cries out against it, and demands loudly the total Abolition of it. . . .

180. That Law, therefore, is highly beneficial to the Community where it is established, which ordains that every Man be judged by his Peers and Equals. For when the Fate of a Citizen is in Question, all Prejudices arising from the Difference of Rank or Fortune should be stifled; because they ought to have no Influence between the Judges and the Parties accused. . . .

194. No Man ought to be looked upon as guilty, before he has received his judicial Sentence; nor can the Laws deprive him of their Protection, before it is proved that he has forfeited all Right to it. What Right therefore can Power give to any to inflict Punishment upon a Citizen at a Time, when it is yet dubious, whether he is Innocent or guilty?

Catherine II, Decree on Serfs

The Governing Senate . . . has deemed it necessary to make known that the landlords' serfs and peasants . . . owe their landlords proper submission and absolute obedience in all matters, according to the laws that have been enacted from time immemorial by the autocratic forefathers of Her Imperial Majesty and which have not been repealed, and which provide that all persons who dare to incite serfs and peasants to disobey their landlords shall be arrested and taken to the nearest government office, there to be punished forthwith as disturbers of the public tranquillity, according to the laws and without leniency. And should it so happen that even after the publication of the present decree of Her Imperial Majesty any serfs and peasants should cease to give the proper obedience to their landlords . . . and should make bold to submit unlawful petitions complaining of their landlords, and especially to petition Her Imperial Majesty personally, then both those who make the complaints and those who write up the petitions shall be punished by the knout and forthwith deported to Nerchinsk to penal servitude for life and shall be counted as part of the quota of recruits which their landlords must furnish to the army.

Q *What impressions of Catherine do you get from the letter by the French ambassador to Russia? To what extent were the ideas expressed in the proposals for a new law code taken from the writings of the philosophes? What does the decree on serfs reveal about Catherine's view of power? Based on these documents, was Catherine an enlightened monarch? Why or why not?*

Sources: Letter of the Baron de Breteuil and Catherine II, Decree on Serfs, in G. Vernadsky, *A Source Book for Russian History*, vol. 2 (New Haven, Conn.: Yale University Press, 1972); Catherine II, Proposals for a New Law Code, in W. F. Reddaway, *Documents of Catherine the Great* (Cambridge: Cambridge University Press, 1931).

in 1767 to debate the details of a new law code. In her *Instruction*, written as a guide to the deliberations, Catherine questioned the institutions of serfdom, torture, and capital punishment and even advocated the principle of the equality of all people in the eyes of the law. But a year and a half of negotiation produced little real change.

In fact, Catherine's subsequent policies had the effect of strengthening the landholding class at the expense of all others, especially the Russian serfs. To reorganize local government, Catherine divided Russia into fifty provinces, each of which was in turn subdivided into districts ruled by officials chosen by the nobles. In this way, the local nobility became responsible for the day-to-day governing of Russia. Moreover, the gentry were now formed into corporate groups with special legal privileges, including the right to trial by peers and exemption from personal taxation and corporal punishment. The Charter of the Nobility formalized these rights in 1785.

Catherine's policy of favoring the landed nobility led to even worse conditions for the Russian peasantry. The government's attempt to impose restrictions on free peasants in the border districts of the Russian Empire soon led to a full-scale revolt that spread to the Volga valley. It was intensified by the support of the Cossacks, independent tribes of fierce warriors who had at times fought for the Russians against the Turks but now resisted the government's attempt to absorb them into the empire.

An illiterate Cossack, Emelyan Pugachev (yim-yil-YAHN poo-guh-CHAWF), succeeded in welding the disparate elements of discontent into a mass revolt. Beginning in 1773, Pugachev's rebellion spread across southern Russia from the Urals to the Volga River. Initially successful, Pugachev won the support of many peasants when he issued a manifesto in July 1774 freeing all peasants from oppressive taxes and military service. Encouraged by Pugachev to seize their landlords' estates, the peasants responded by killing more than fifteen hundred estate owners and their families. The rebellion soon faltered, however, as government forces rallied and became more effective. Betrayed by his own subordinates, Pugachev was captured, tortured, and executed. The rebellion collapsed completely, and Catherine responded with even greater repression of the peasantry. All rural reform was halted, and serfdom was expanded into newer parts of the empire.

Pugachev's Rebellion

Catherine proved a worthy successor to Peter the Great by expanding Russia's territory westward into Poland and southward to the Black Sea. Russia spread southward by defeating the Ottoman Turks. In the Treaty of Kuchuk-Kainarji (koo-CHOOK-ky-NAR-jee) in 1774, the Russians gained some land and the privilege of protecting Greek Orthodox Christians in the Ottoman Empire. Russian expansion westward occurred at the expense of neighboring Poland. In the three partitions of Poland, Russia gained about 50 percent of Polish territory.

THE DESTRUCTION OF POLAND Poland was an excellent example of why a strong monarchy was needed in early modern Europe. The Polish king was elected by the Polish nobles and forced to accept drastic restrictions on his power, including limited revenues, a small bureaucracy, and a standing army of no more than 20,000 soldiers. For Polish nobles, these limitations eliminated an absolute king; for Poland's powerful neighbors, they were an invitation to meddle in its affairs.

The total destruction of the Polish state in the eighteenth century resulted from the rivalries of its three great neighbors, Austria, Russia, and Prussia. To avoid war, the leaders of these powers decided to compensate themselves by dividing Poland. To maintain the balance of power in central and eastern Europe, the three great powers cynically agreed to the acquisition of roughly equal territories at Poland's expense.

In 1772, Poland lost about 30 percent of its land and 50 percent of its population (see Map 18.2). Austria gained the agriculturally rich district of Galicia, Russia took the largest slice of land in eastern Poland, and Prussia acquired West Prussia, the smallest but most valuable territory because it united two of the chief sections of Prussia.

The remaining Polish state was supposedly independent; in truth, it was dominated by the Russians, who even kept troops on Polish territory. After the Poles attempted to establish a stronger state under a hereditary monarchy in 1791, the Russians gained the support of Austria and Prussia and intervened militarily in May 1792. In the following year, Russia and Prussia undertook a second partition of Polish territory. Finally, after a heroic but hopeless rebellion in 1794–1795 under General Thaddeus Kosciuszko (tah-DAY-oosh kaw-SHOOS-koh), the remaining Polish state was obliterated by Austria, Prussia, and Russia

CHRONOLOGY	Central and Eastern Europe
Prussia	
Frederick William I	1713–1740
Frederick II the Great	1740–1786
Austrian Empire	
Maria Theresa	1740–1780
Joseph II	1780–1790
Russia	
Catherine II the Great	1762–1796
Pugachev's rebellion	1773–1775
Charter of the Nobility	1785
Poland	
First partition	1772
Second partition	1793
Third partition	1795

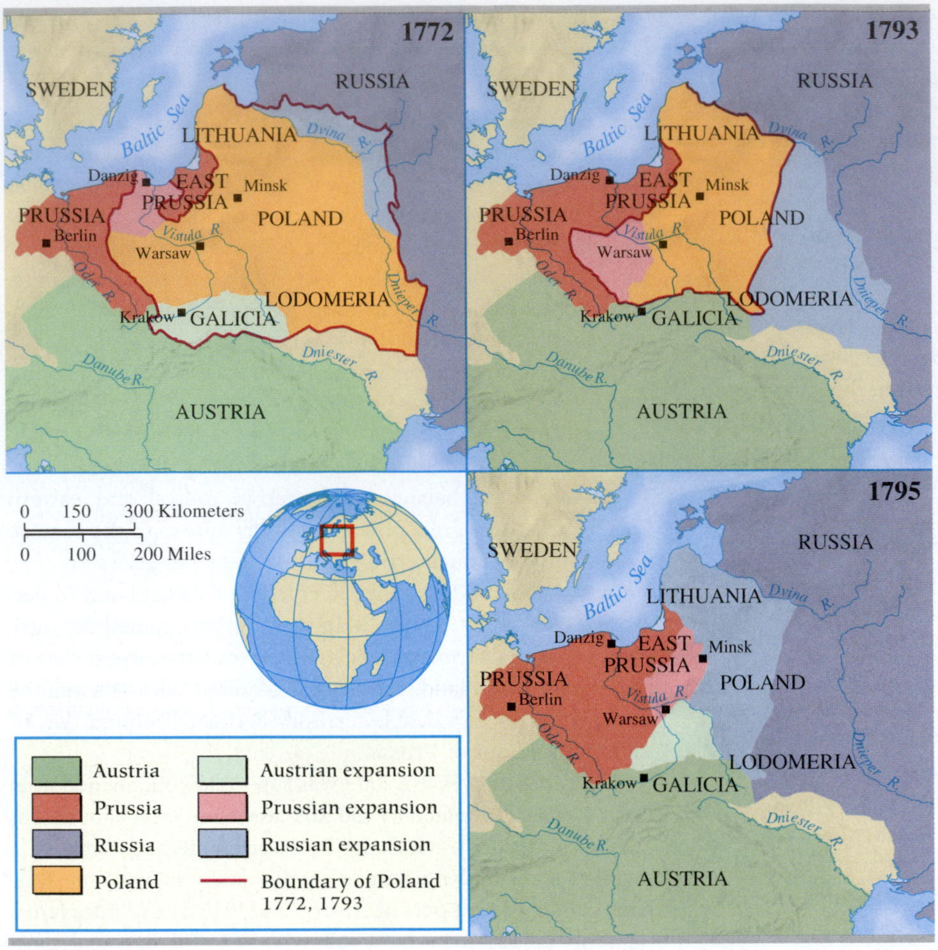

MAP 18.2 The Partitioning of Poland. Crowded by three great powers, Poland lay primarily on a plain with few easily defensible borders. This fact, combined with a weak and ineffectual monarchy, set the stage for Poland's destruction. By 1795, Austria, Prussia (Germany in 1870), and Russia had long borders with each other, a situation that would contribute to the outbreak of World War I in 1914.

Q *Which country gained the most territory at the expense of Poland?*

in the third partition of Poland (1795). Many historians have pointed to Poland's demise as a cogent example of why building a strong, absolutist state was essential to survival in the seventeenth and eighteenth centuries.

The Mediterranean World

At the beginning of the eighteenth century, Spain experienced a change of dynasties from the Habsburgs to the Bourbons. Bourbon rule temporarily rejuvenated Spain and at least provided an opportunity to centralize the institutions of the state. Under Philip V (1700–1746), the laws, administrative institutions, and language of Castile were established in the other Spanish kingdoms, making the king of Castile truly the king of Spain. Moreover, French-style ministries replaced the old conciliar system of government, and officials similar to French *intendants* were introduced into the various Spanish provinces. Since the Treaty of Utrecht in 1713 had taken the Italian territories and the Netherlands away from Spain, the latter now had fewer administrative problems and less drain on its already overtaxed economic resources. In the second half of the eighteenth century, especially during the reign of Charles III (1759–1788), the Catholic Church was also brought under royal control when the king banished the Jesuits and circumscribed the activities of the Inquisition. The king undertook ambitious economic reforms, establishing new roads, canals, textile mills, and banks. He also attempted to reduce the authority of the landed aristocrats by curbing the privileges of the great sheep ranchers. The landed aristocracy continued to exercise substantial power throughout the eighteenth century, however.

PORTUGAL Portugal had experienced decline since the glorious days of empire in the sixteenth century. Nevertheless, during the long ministry of the marquis de Pombal (mar-KEE duh pum-BAHL) (1750–1777), who served as chief minister to a series of Portuguese kings, Portugal experienced a revival. The marquis secured his reputation after the devastating Lisbon earthquake of 1755 that destroyed eighty-five percent of the city's buildings, killing almost fifty thousand people. During his tenure, the nobility and Catholic Church were curtailed and the Portuguese Empire temporarily revived. After Pombal was removed from office, the nobility and church regained much of their power.

THE ITALIAN STATES After the Treaty of Utrecht, Austria had replaced Spain as the dominant force in Italy in the eighteenth century. The duchy of Milan, Sardinia, and the kingdom of Naples were all surrendered to the Habsburg emperors, and Sicily was given to the northern Italian state of Savoy, which was slowly emerging as a state with an appetite for territorial expansion. In 1734, the Bourbons of Spain reestablished control over Naples and Sicily. Though some Italian states, such as

CHRONOLOGY	The Mediterranean World and Scandinavia
Spain	
Philip V, the first Bourbon king	1700–1746
Charles III	1759–1788
Portugal	
Marquis de Pombal	1750–1777
Sweden	
Charles XII	1697–1718
Gustavus III	1771–1792
Denmark	
Christian VII	1766–1808

Venice and Genoa, remained independent, they grew increasingly impotent in international affairs.

The Scandinavian States

In the seventeenth century, Sweden had become the dominant power in northern Europe, but after the Battle of Poltava in 1709, Swedish power declined rapidly. Following the death of the powerful Charles XII in 1718, the Swedish nobility, using the Swedish diet as its instrument, gained control of public life and reduced the monarchy to puppet status. But the division of the nobility into pro-French and pro-Russian factions eventually enabled King Gustavus III (1771–1792) to reassert the power of the monarchy. Gustavus proved to be one of the most enlightened monarchs of his age. By decree, he established freedom of religion, speech, and press and instituted a new code of justice that eliminated the use of torture. Moreover, his economic reforms smacked of laissez-faire: he reduced tariffs, abolished tolls, and encouraged trade and agriculture. In 1792, however, a group of nobles, incensed at these reforms and their loss of power, assassinated the king, but they proved unable to fully restore the rule of the aristocracy.

Denmark also saw an attempt at enlightened reforms by King Christian VII (1766–1808) and his chief minister, John Frederick Struensee (SHTROO-un-zay). Aristocratic opposition stymied their efforts, however, and led to Struensee's death in 1772.

Enlightened Absolutism Revisited

Of the three major rulers traditionally associated most closely with enlightened absolutism—Joseph II, Frederick II, and Catherine the Great—only Joseph II sought truly radical changes based on Enlightenment ideas. Both Frederick and Catherine liked to be cast as disciples of the Enlightenment, expressed interest in enlightened reforms, and even attempted some, but neither ruler's policies seemed seriously affected by Enlightenment thought. Necessities of state and maintenance of the existing system took precedence over reform. Indeed, many historians feel that Joseph, Frederick, and Catherine were all guided primarily by a concern for the power and well-being of their states and that their policies were not all that different from those of their predecessors. In the final analysis, heightened state power was used to amass armies and wage wars to gain more power. Nevertheless, in their desire to build stronger state systems, these rulers did pursue such enlightened practices as legal reform, religious toleration, and the extension of education because these served to create more satisfied subjects and strengthened the state in significant ways.

It would be foolish, however, to overlook the fact that not only military but also political and social realities limited the ability of enlightened rulers to make reforms. Everywhere in Europe, the hereditary aristocracy still held the most power in society. Enlightened reforms were often limited to changes in the administrative and judicial systems that did not seriously undermine the powerful interests of the European nobility. Although aristocrats might join the populace in opposing monarchical extension of centralizing power, as the chief beneficiaries of a system based on traditional rights and privileges for their class, they were certainly not willing to support a political ideology that trumpeted the principle of equal rights for all.

Wars and Diplomacy

FOCUS QUESTIONS: How did the concepts of "balance of power" and "reason of state" influence international relations in the eighteenth century? What were the causes and results of the Seven Years' War?

The philosophes condemned war as a foolish waste of life and resources in stupid quarrels of no value to humankind. Rulers, however, paid little attention to these comments and continued their costly struggles. By the eighteenth century, the European system of self-governing, individual states was grounded largely in the principle of self-interest. Because international relations were based on considerations of power, the eighteenth-century concept of a **balance of power** was predicated on how to counterbalance the power of one state by another to prevent any one state from dominating the others. This balance of power, however, did not imply a desire for peace. Large armies created to defend a state's security were often used for offensive purposes as well. As Frederick the Great of Prussia remarked, "The fundamental rule of governments is the principle of extending their territories." Nevertheless, the regular use of diplomacy served at times to lead to compromise.

The diplomacy of the eighteenth century still focused primarily on dynastic interests, or the desire of ruling families to provide for their dependents and extend their dynastic holdings. But the eighteenth century also saw the emergence of the concept of **reason of state**, on the basis of which a ruler such as Frederick II and a minister such as William Pitt the Elder looked beyond dynastic interests to the long-term future of their states.

International rivalry and the continuing centralization of the European states were closely related. The need for money to support the new standing armies, navies, and weapons of war that had originated in the seventeenth century created its own imperative for more efficient and effective control of power in the hands of bureaucrats who could collect taxes and organize states for the task of winning wars. At the same time, the development of large standing armies ensured that political disputes would periodically be resolved by armed conflict rather than diplomacy. Between 1715 and 1740, Europe seemed to prefer peace. But in 1740, a major conflict erupted over the succession to the Austrian throne.

The War of the Austrian Succession (1740–1748)

Unable to produce a male heir to the Austrian throne, the Habsburg emperor Charles VI (1711–1740) so feared the consequences of the succession of his daughter Maria Theresa that he spent much of his reign negotiating the Pragmatic Sanction, by which various European powers agreed to recognize his daughter as his legal heir.

After Charles's death, however, the Pragmatic Sanction was conveniently pushed aside, especially by Frederick II, who had recently succeeded to the throne of Prussia. The new Prussian ruler took advantage of the new empress to invade Austrian Silesia. The vulnerability of Maria Theresa encouraged France to enter the war against its traditional enemy Austria; in turn, Maria Theresa made an alliance with Great Britain, which feared French hegemony over Continental affairs. All too quickly, the Austrian succession had set off a worldwide conflagration. The war was fought not only in Europe, where Prussia seized Silesia and France occupied the Austrian Netherlands, but in the East, where France took Madras (now Chennai) in India from the British, and in North America, where the British captured the French fortress of Louisbourg at the entrance to the Saint Lawrence River. By 1748, all parties were exhausted and agreed to stop. The peace treaty of Aix-la-Chapelle (ex-lah-shah-PELL) promised the return of all occupied territories except Silesia to their original owners. Prussia's refusal to return Silesia guaranteed another war, at least between the two hostile central European powers of Prussia and Austria.

The Seven Years' War (1756–1763)

Maria Theresa refused to accept the loss of Silesia and prepared for its return by rebuilding her army while working diplomatically through her able foreign minister, Count Wenzel von Kaunitz (VENT-sul fun KOW-nits), to separate Prussia from its chief ally, France. In 1756, Austria achieved what was soon labeled a diplomatic revolution. Bourbon-Habsburg rivalry had been a fact of European diplomacy since the late sixteenth century. But two new rivalries made this old one seem superfluous: Britain and France

MAP 18.3 Battlefields of the Seven Years' War. A major struggle among the five great powers, the Seven Years' War was truly a worldwide conflict. In central Europe, Prussia survived against the combined forces of France, Austria, and Russia, while Britain emerged victorious against France in the struggle for empire, gaining control of French North America and India.

Q *Why were naval strength and ability important in the conflict between Britain and France?*

over colonial empires, and Austria and Prussia over Silesia. France now abandoned Prussia and allied with Austria. Russia, which saw Prussia as a major hindrance to Russian goals in central Europe, joined the new alliance. In turn, Great Britain allied with Prussia. This diplomatic revolution of 1756 now led to another war, with three major areas of conflict: Europe, India, and North America (see Map 18.3). Indeed, the Seven Years' War could be seen, as some historians have argued, as the first world war.

CONFLICT IN EUROPE Europe witnessed the clash of the two major alliances: the British and Prussians against the Austrians, Russians, and French. With his superb army and military prowess, Frederick the Great was able for some time to defeat the Austrian, French, and Russian armies. At the Battle of Rossbach (RAWSS-bahkh) in Saxony in 1757, he won a spectacular victory over combined French-Austrian forces that far outnumbered his own troops. Under attack from three different directions, however, Frederick's forces were gradually worn down and faced utter defeat when they were saved by the death of Tsarina Elizabeth of Russia (1741–1762), which brought her nephew Peter III to power. A great admirer of Frederick the Great, Peter withdrew the Russian troops from the conflict and from the Prussian lands that they had occupied. His withdrawal guaranteed a stalemate and led to a desire for peace. The Peace of Hubertusburg (hoo-BERR-toos-bayrk) ended the European conflict in 1763. All occupied territories were returned, and Austria officially recognized Prussia's permanent control of Silesia.

WAR IN INDIA The Anglo-French struggle in the rest of the world had more decisive results. Known as the Great War for Empire, it was fought in India and North America. The French had returned Madras (muh-DRAS *or* muh-DRAHS) to Britain after the War of the Austrian Succession, but jockeying for power continued as the French and British supported opposing native Indian princes. The British under Robert Clive (1725–1774) ultimately won out, not because they had better forces but because they were more persistent (see the box on p. 542). By the Treaty of Paris in 1763, the French withdrew and left India to the British.

THE FRENCH AND INDIAN WAR By far the greatest conflicts of the Seven Years' War took place in North America, where it was known as the French and Indian War. There were two primary areas of contention. One consisted of the waterways of the Gulf of Saint Lawrence, guarded by the fortress of Louisbourg and by forts near the Great Lakes and Lake Champlain that protected French Quebec and French traders. The other was the unsettled Ohio River valley. As the French moved south from the Great Lakes and north from their garrisons along the Mississippi, they began to establish forts from the Appalachians to the Mississippi River. To British settlers in the thirteen colonies to the east, this French activity threatened to cut off a vast area from British expansion. The French found allies among the Indians, who considered the French traders less threatening than the British settlers.

Despite initial French successes, British fortunes were revived by the efforts of William Pitt the Elder, who was convinced that the destruction of the French colonial empire was a necessary prerequisite for the creation of Britain's own colonial empire. Accordingly, Pitt decided to make a minimal effort in Europe while concentrating resources, especially the British navy, on the colonial war. Although the French troops were greater in number, the ability of the French to use them in the New World was contingent on naval support. The defeat of French fleets in major naval battles in 1759 gave the British an advantage since the French could no longer easily reinforce their garrisons. A series of British victories soon followed. Already in 1758, the British had captured Forts Louisbourg and Duquesne. Then, on the night of September 13, 1759, British forces led by General James Wolfe scaled the heights outside Quebec and defeated the French under General Louis-Joseph Montcalm on the Plains of Abraham. Both generals died in the battle. The British

British Library, London/Erich Lessing/Art Resource, NY

Robert Clive in India. Robert Clive was the leader of the army of the British East India Company. He had been commanded to fight the ruler of Bengal in order to gain trading privileges. After the Battle of Plassey in 1757, Clive and the East India Company took control of Bengal. In this painting by Edward Penny, Clive is shown receiving a grant of money for his injured soldiers from the local nabob or governor of Bengal.

BRITISH VICTORY IN INDIA

THE SUCCESS OF THE BRITISH AGAINST THE French in India was due to Robert Clive. In this excerpt from one of his letters, he describes his famous victory at Plassey, north of Calcutta, on June 23, 1757. This battle demonstrated the inability of native Indian soldiers to compete with Europeans and signified the beginning of British control in Bengal (ben-GAHL). Clive claimed to have a thousand Europeans, two thousand sepoys (SEE-poiz) (local soldiers), and eight cannons available for this battle.

Robert Clive's Account of His Victory at Plassey

At daybreak we discovered the [governor's army] moving toward us, consisting, as we since found, of about fifteen thousand horse and thirty-five thousand foot, with upwards of forty pieces of cannon. They approached apace, and by six began to attack with a number of heavy cannon, supported by the whole army, and continued to play on us very briskly for several hours, during which our situation was of the utmost service to us, being lodged in a large grove with good mud banks. To succeed in an attempt on their cannon was next to impossible, as they were planted in a manner round us and at considerable distances from each other. We therefore remained quiet in our post, in expectation of a successful attack upon their camp at night. About noon the enemy drew off their artillery and retired to their camp. . . .

On finding them make no great effort to dislodge us, we proceeded to take possession of one or two more eminences lying very near an angle of their camp, from whence, and an adjacent eminence in their possession, they kept a smart fire of musketry upon us. They made several attempts to bring out their cannon, but our advanced fieldpieces played so warmly and so well upon them that they were always driven back. Their horse exposing themselves a good deal on this occasion, many of them were killed, and among the rest four or five officers of the first distinction; by which the whole army being visibly dispirited and thrown into some confusion, we were encouraged to storm both the eminence and the angle of their camp, which were carried at the same instant, with little or no loss; though the latter was defended (exclusively of blacks) by forty French and two pieces of cannon; and the former by a large body of blacks, both horse and foot. On this a general rout ensued, and we pursued the enemy six miles, passing upwards of forty pieces of cannon they had abandoned, with an infinite number of carts and carriages filled with baggage of all kinds. . . . It is computed there are killed of the enemy about five hundred. Our loss amounted to only twenty-two killed and fifty wounded, and those chiefly blacks.

Q *In what ways, if any, would Clive's account likely have been different if the Battle of Plassey had occurred in Europe? According to the letter, what role did native Indians seemingly play in the battle? Why does Clive give them such little mention?*

Source: J. H. Robinson, *Readings in European History*, vol. 2 (Boston: Ginn & Co., 1906).

went on to seize Montreal, the Great Lakes area, and the Ohio valley. The French were forced to make peace. By the Treaty of Paris, they ceded Canada and the lands east of the Mississippi to Britain. Their ally Spain transferred Spanish Florida to British control; in return, the French gave their Louisiana territory to the Spanish. By 1763, Great Britain had become the world's greatest colonial power.

CHRONOLOGY The Mid-Century Wars	
War of the Austrian Succession	1740–1748
Peace of Aix-la-Chapelle	1748
Seven Years' War	1756–1763
Diplomatic revolution	1756
Battle of Rossbach	1757
British capture of Forts Duquesne and Louisbourg	1758
Battle of Quebec	1759
Peace of Hubertusburg	1763
Treaty of Paris	1763

European Armies and Warfare

The professional standing army, initiated in the seventeenth century, became a standard feature of eighteenth-century Europe. Especially noticeable was the increase in the size of armies, which paralleled the development of absolutist states. Between 1740 and 1780, the French army grew from 190,000 to 300,000 men; the Prussian, from 83,000 to 200,000; the Austrian, from 108,000 to 282,000; and the Russian, from 130,000 to 290,000.

COMPOSITION OF ARMIES The composition of these armies reflected the hierarchical structure of European society and the great chasm that separated the upper and lower classes. Officers came primarily from the landed aristocracy, which had for centuries regarded military activity as one of its major functions. Middle-class individuals could enter the middle ranks of the officer corps but were largely kept out of the higher ranks.

Rank-and-file soldiers came mostly from the lower classes of society. Some states, such as Prussia and Russia, conscripted able-bodied peasants. But many states realized that this was counterproductive since they could not afford to waste their farmers. For that reason, eighteenth-century armies were partly composed of foreign troops, many from Switzerland or the petty German states. Of the great powers, Britain alone had no regular standing army and relied on mercenaries, evident in its use of German troops in America. Most troops in European armies, especially the French and Austrian, were natives who enlisted voluntarily for six-year terms. Some were not exactly volunteers; often vagabonds and the unemployed were pressed into service. Most, however, came from the lower classes—peasants and also artisans from the cities—who saw the military as an opportunity to escape from hard times or personal problems.

The maritime powers, such as Britain and the Dutch Republic, regarded navies as more important than armies. In the second half of the eighteenth century, the British possessed 174 warships manned by 80,000 sailors. Conditions on these ships were often poor. Diseases such as scurvy and yellow fever were rampant, and crews were frequently press-ganged into duty.

THE NATURE OF WARFARE The dramatic increase in the size of armies and navies did not necessarily result in more destructive warfare in eighteenth-century Europe. For one thing, war was no longer driven by ideology as the religious conflicts of the sixteenth and seventeenth centuries had been. By their very nature, ideological wars are often violent and destructive. Moreover, since the larger armies depended on increased tax revenues, rulers regarded the wanton destruction of civilian taxpayers as foolish. Finally, the costliness of eighteenth-century armies as well as the technology and customary tactics of the age created a system of warfare based on limited objectives.

Since generals were extremely reluctant to risk the destruction of their armies in pitched battles, they came to rely on clever and elaborate maneuvers, rather than direct confrontation. A system of formalities accepted by all sides allowed defeated opponents to withdraw without being captured or destroyed. This mentality also encouraged the construction of vast fortresses to secure major roads and the enormous quantities of supplies needed by eighteenth-century armies. With its own set patterns of tactics, siege warfare often became, as one French critic said disgustedly, "the art of surrendering strongholds honorably after certain conventional formalities." Nevertheless, despite the maneuvering and the sieges, European warfare in the eighteenth century also involved many battles and considerable risk.

Economic Expansion and Social Change

> **FOCUS QUESTION:** What changes occurred in agriculture, finance, industry, and trade during the eighteenth century?

The depressed economic conditions of the seventeenth century began to improve in the early eighteenth century. Rapid population growth, expansion in banking and trade, an agricultural revolution (at least in Britain), the stirrings of industrialization, and an increase in worldwide trade and consumption characterized the economic patterns of the eighteenth century.

Growth of the European Population

Europe's population began to grow around 1750 and experienced a slow but steady rise, with some regional variations. It has been estimated that the total European population rose from around 120 million in 1700 to 140 million by 1750, and then grew to 190 million by 1790; thus, the growth rate in the second half of the century was double that of the first half. Individual states also experienced rapid growth between 1700 and 1790: Russia's population went from 14 million to 28 million (much of it due to territorial expansion); France's, from 20 to 26 or 27 million; Spain's, from 6 to 10 million; Brandenburg-Prussia's, from 1.5 to 5.5 million (over half of this came from territorial acquisition); and Britain's, from 5 or 6 to 9 million. These increases occurred during the same time that several million Europeans were going abroad as colonists.

Perhaps the most important cause of population growth was a decline in the death rate, thanks, no doubt, to more plentiful food and better transportation of food supplies, which led to improved diets and some relief from devastating famines. The introduction of new crops from the Americas, such as corn and potatoes, played an important role in creating a more bountiful and nutritious food supply (see "Was There an Agricultural Revolution?" later in this chapter). Some historians have estimated that at the beginning of the eighteenth century, farmers were producing about 20 to 30 percent more food than they needed to sustain themselves; by 1750, the surplus reached 50 percent.

But a more plentiful food supply was not the only factor contributing to population growth. Also of great significance was the end of the bubonic plague: the last great outbreak in western Europe occurred in 1720 in southern France. In England, a decline in the number of women who remained unmarried during their childbearing years may also have played an important role in population growth. It has been estimated that this number fell from 15 to 7 percent between 1700 and 1800.

Nevertheless, death was still a ubiquitous feature of everyday life. Diseases such as typhus, smallpox, influenza, and dysentery were rampant, especially since hygienic conditions remained poor—little bathing, dirty clothes, and no systematic elimination of human wastes. Despite the improved transportation, famine and hunger could still be devastating.

Family, Marriage, and Birthrate Patterns

The family, rather than the individual, was still at the heart of Europe's social organization. For the most part, people still thought of the family in traditional terms, as a patriarchal institution with the husband dominating his wife and children. The upper classes in particular were still concerned for the family as a "house," an association whose collective interests were more important than those of its individual members. In all social classes, parents, especially the fathers, still generally selected marriage partners for their children, based on the interests of the family (see the box on p. 544). One French noble responded to his son's inquiry about his upcoming marriage: "Mind your own business."

CHILD CARE At the beginning of the eighteenth century, traditional attitudes also prevailed in the care of children. Generally, lower-class women breast-fed their own children because

MARITAL ARRANGEMENTS

IN THE EIGHTEENTH CENTURY, UPPER-CLASS PARENTS continued to choose marriage partners for their children. This practice and the turmoil it could cause are evident in this selection from *The Rivals*, a play written in 1775 by Richard Sheridan. Sheridan was an Irish playwright who quit writing plays in order to pursue a political career. In this scene from *The Rivals*, a father, Sir Anthony Absolute, informs his son, Captain Jack Absolute, of the arrangements he has made for Jack's marriage. Jack, in love with another woman, is dumbfounded by his father's plans.

Richard Sheridan, *The Rivals*

ABSOLUTE: Now, Jack, I am sensible that the income of your commission, and what I have hitherto allowed you, is but a small pittance for a lad of your spirit.

CAPTAIN JACK: Sir, you are very good.

ABSOLUTE: And it is my wish, while yet I live, to have my boy make some figure in the world. I have resolved, therefore, to fix you at once in a noble independence.

CAPTAIN JACK: Sir, your kindness overpowers me—such generosity makes the gratitude of reason more lively than the sensations even of filial affection.

ABSOLUTE: I am so glad you are so sensible of my attention—and you shall be master of a large estate in a few weeks.

CAPTAIN JACK: Let my future life, sir, speak my gratitude; I cannot express the sense I have of your munificence.—Yet, sir, I presume you would not wish me to quit the army?

ABSOLUTE: Oh, that shall be as your wife chooses.

CAPTAIN JACK: My wife, sir!

ABSOLUTE: Ay, ay, settle that between you—settle that between you.

CAPTAIN JACK: A wife, sir, did you say?

ABSOLUTE: Ay, a wife—why, did I not mention her before?

CAPTAIN JACK: Not a word of her, sir.

ABSOLUTE: Odd, so! I musn't forget her though.—Yes, Jack, the independence I was talking of is by marriage—the fortune is saddled with a wife—but I suppose that makes no difference.

CAPTAIN JACK: Sir! Sir! You amaze me!

ABSOLUTE: Why, what the devil's the matter with you, fool? Just now you were all gratitude and duty.

CAPTAIN JACK: I was, sir—you talked of independence and a fortune, but not a word of a wife!

ABSOLUTE: Why—what difference does that make? Odds life, sir! If you had an estate, you must take it with the live stock on it, as it stands!

CAPTAIN JACK: If my happiness is to be the price, I must beg leave to decline the purchase. Pray, sir, who is the lady?

ABSOLUTE: What's that to you, sir? Come, give me your promise to love, and to marry her directly.

CAPTAIN JACK: Sure, sir, this is not very reasonable. . . . You must excuse me, sir, if I tell you, once for all, that in this point I cannot obey you. . . .

ABSOLUTE: Sir, I won't hear a word—not one word! . . .

CAPTAIN JACK: What, sir, promise to link myself to some mass of ugliness!

ABSOLUTE: Zounds! Sirrah! The lady shall be as ugly as I choose: she shall have a hump on each shoulder; she shall be as crooked as the crescent; her one eye shall roll like the bull's in Cox's Museum; she shall have a skin like a mummy, and the beard of a Jew—she shall be all this, sirrah! Yet I will make you ogle her all day, and sit up all night to write sonnets on her beauty.

Source: Richard Sheridan, *The Rivals* (London, 1775).

Q *What does Sheridan suggest about marriage among the upper classes in the eighteenth century? What social, political, and economic considerations were significant in eighteenth-century marriages? Could he be overstating the issue? Why or why not?*

that provided the best nourishment. Moreover, since there were strong taboos in various parts of Europe against sexual intercourse while breastfeeding, mothers might also avoid another immediate pregnancy; if the infant died, they could then have another child. Lower-class women, however, also served as wet nurses for children of the aristocratic and upper middle classes. Mothers from these higher social strata considered breastfeeding undignified and hired wet nurses instead. Even the wives of artisans in the cities, for economic reasons, sent their babies to wet nurses in the countryside if they could, making the practice widespread in the eighteenth century.

In the second half of the eighteenth century, traditional attitudes began to alter, especially in western Europe. The impact of Enlightenment thought, such as Rousseau's *Émile*, and the increasing survival of more infants led to new attitudes toward children. Childhood came to be viewed more and more as a distinct phase in human development. One result was a shift to dressing children in comfortable clothes appropriate to their age rather than in clothes modeled after adult styles. Shops for children's clothes appeared for the first time. The practice of **primogeniture**, in which the eldest son received all or the largest share of the parents' estate and thus was treated as the favorite, also came under attack. All children, it was argued, deserved their parents' attention. Appeals for women to breast-feed their children rather than use wet nurses soon followed. In England, games and toys specifically for children now appeared. The jigsaw puzzle was invented in the 1760s, and books, such as *Little Pretty Pocket-Book* (1744), aimed to please as well as teach children. These changes, however, were largely limited to the upper classes of western European society and did not extend to the peasants. For most Europeans, children were still a source of considerable anxiety. They represented a health risk to the mothers who bore them and more mouths to feed if they survived. In times of economic crisis, children proved such a burden to some families that they resorted to **infanticide** or abandoned their children at foundling homes.

Despite being punishable by death, infanticide remained a solution to the problem of too many children. So many children were being "accidentally" suffocated while in their parents' bed that in Austria in 1784 a law was enacted that forbade parents to place children under five years old in bed with them. More common than infanticide was simply leaving unwanted children at foundling homes or hospitals, which became a favorite charity of the rich in eighteenth-century Europe. The largest of its kind, located in Saint Petersburg, Russia, was founded by members of the nobility. By the end of the century, it was taking in 5,000 new babies a year and caring for 25,000 children at one time.

But severe problems arose as the system became overburdened. One historian has estimated that in the 1770s, one-third of all babies born in Paris were taken to foundling institutions by parents or desperate unmarried mothers, creating serious overcrowding. Foundling institutions often proved fatal for infants. Mortality rates ranged from 50 percent to as high as 90 percent (in a sense making foundling homes a legalized form of infanticide). Children who survived were usually sent to miserable jobs. The suffering of poor children was one of the blackest pages of eighteenth-century European history.

MARRIAGE AND BIRTHRATES In most of Europe, newly married couples established their own households independent of their parents. This nuclear family, which had its beginning in the Middle Ages, had become a common pattern, especially in northwestern Europe. In order to save enough to establish their own households, both men and women (outside the aristocracy) married quite late; the average age for men in northwestern Europe was between twenty-seven and twenty-eight; for women, between twenty-five and twenty-seven.

Late marriages imposed limits on the birthrate; in fact, they might be viewed as a natural form of birth control. But was this limitation offset by the babies born illegitimately? From the low illegitimacy rate of 1 percent in some places in France and 5 percent in some English parishes, it would appear that it was not, at least in the first half of the eighteenth century. After 1750, however, illegitimacy appears to have increased. Studies in Germany, for example, show that rates of illegitimacy increased from 2 percent in 1700 to 5 percent in 1760 and to 10 percent in 1800, followed by an even more dramatic increase in the early nineteenth century.

For married couples, the first child usually appeared within one year of marriage, and additional children came at intervals of two or three years, producing an average of five births per

Yale Center for British Art//Paul Mellon Collection/The Bridgeman Art Library

Children of the Upper Classes. This painting of John Bacon and his family illustrates an important feature of upper-class family life in Great Britain in the first half of the eighteenth century. The children appear as miniature adults, dressed in clothes modeled after the styles of their parents' clothes.

family. It would appear, then, that the birthrate had the potential of causing a significant increase in population. This possibility was restricted, however, because 40 to 60 percent of European women of childbearing age (between fifteen and forty-four) were not married at any given time. Moreover, by the end of the eighteenth century, especially among the upper classes in France and Britain, birth control techniques were being used to limit the number of children. Figures for the French aristocracy indicate that the average number of children declined from six in the period between 1650 and 1700 to three between 1700 and 1750 and to two between 1750 and 1780. These figures are even more significant when one considers that aristocrats married at younger ages than the rest of the population. Coitus interruptus remained the most commonly used form of birth control.

Among the working classes, whether peasants or urban workers, the contributions of women and children to the "family economy" were often crucial. In urban areas, both male and female children either helped in the handicraft manufacturing done in the home or were sent out to work as household servants. In rural areas, children worked on the land or helped in the activities of cottage industry. Married women grew vegetables in small plots, tended livestock, and sold eggs, vegetables, and milk. Wives of propertyless agricultural workers labored in the fields or as textile workers, spinning or knitting. In the cities, wives of artisans helped their husbands at their crafts or worked as seamstresses. The wives of unskilled workers labored as laundresses and cleaners for the rich or as peddlers of food or used clothing to the lower classes. But the family economy was often precarious. Bad harvests in the countryside or a downturn in employment in the cities often reduced people to utter poverty and a life of begging.

HISTORIANS DEBATE Was There an Agricultural Revolution?

Did improvements in agricultural practices and methods in the eighteenth century lead to an **agricultural revolution**? The topic is much debated. Some historians have noted the beginning of agrarian changes already in the seventeenth century, especially in the Low Countries. Others, however, have questioned the use of the term, arguing that significant changes occurred only in England and that even there the upward trend in agricultural production was not maintained after 1750.

Traditional interpretations of the agricultural revolution are characterized by four interrelated factors: more farmland, increased crop yields per acre, healthier and more abundant livestock, and an improved climate. Climatologists believe that the "little ice age" of the seventeenth century declined in the eighteenth, especially evident in moderate summers that provided more ideal growing conditions.

Historians dispute the increase of the amount of land under cultivation and the rate at which more land entered cultivation. The amount of land under cultivation was increased by abandoning the old open-field system, in which part of the land was allowed to lie fallow to renew it and plow it for weeds. The formerly empty fields were now planted with new crops, such as alfalfa, turnips, and clover, which stored nitrogen in their roots and thereby restored the soil's fertility. Turnips could be hoed to remove weeds while the turnips were growing, allowing formerly fallow fields to be in continual use. Historians argue, however, that turnips were not common until the mid-eighteenth century and were not in constant rotation

Eileen Tweedy/The Art Archive at Art Resource, NY

Science and Society/SuperStock

Jethro Tull and the Seed Drill. A major innovation in the new agricultural practices of the eighteenth century was the development of seed drills that enabled farmers to plant seeds in rows and prevent them from being picked up by birds. The seed drill pictured here was invented by Jethro Tull (left), one of the many landed aristocrats who participated in the scientific experimentation of the age.

THE IMPACT OF AGRICULTURAL CHANGES

THE NEW AGRICULTURAL PRACTICES IN ENGLAND, which led to larger farms and increased productivity, also had social repercussions. As common lands were enclosed by large landowners, many small farmers became landless laborers, working for the larger farmers or in the emerging factories. This selection is from a work published in 1795 by David Davies (1742–1819), an English clergyman who analyzed the changes he saw in the countryside.

David Davies, *The Case of Labourers in Husbandry Stated and Considered*

The depriving of all landed property has beggared multitudes. It is plainly agreeable to sound policy, that as many individuals as possible in a state should possess an interest in the soil; because this attaches them strongly to the country and its constitution, and makes them zealous and resolute in defending them. But the gentry of this kingdom seem to have lost sight of this wise and salutary policy. Instead of giving to labouring people a valuable stake in the soil, the opposite measure has so long prevailed, that but few cottages, comparatively, have now any land about them. Formerly many of the lower sort of people [had land on which] they raised for themselves a considerable part of their subsistence. . . . But since these small parcels of ground have been swallowed up in the contiguous farms and enclosures, and the cottages themselves have been pulled down, the families which used to occupy them are crowded together in decayed farmhouses, with hardly ground enough about them for a cabbage garden; and being thus reduced to be mere hirelings, they are of course very liable to come to want. . . .

Thus an amazing number of people have been reduced from a comfortable state of partial independence to the precarious condition of hirelings, who, when out of work, must immediately come to their parish [for welfare]. And the great plenty of working hands always to be had when wanted, having kept down the price of labour below its proper level, the consequence is universally felt in the increased number of dependent poor.

Q *In Davies's eyes, how were the changes in agricultural practices affecting England's small farmers? What did he think would be the consequences of these changes?*

Source: David Davies, *The Case of Labourers in Husbandry Stated and Considered* (London, 1795), pp. 55–56.

until the nineteenth century. Historians also argue that one of the reasons why output increased during this time was due to land reclamation, especially in eastern England. However, the increase of the new crops served another purpose; they provided winter fodder for livestock, enabling landlords to maintain an ever-larger number of animals.

The more numerous livestock increased the amount of meat in the European diet and enhanced food production by making available more animal manure, which was used to fertilize fields and produce larger yields per acre. Landed aristocrats with an interest in the scientific experimentation of the age also adopted innovations that increased yields. In England, Jethro Tull (1674–1741) discovered that using a hoe to keep the soil loose allowed air and moisture to reach plants and enabled them to grow better. He also used a drill to plant seeds in rows instead of scattering them by hand, a method that had lost much seed to the birds. However, some historians argue that the seed drill was not used by farmers on a large scale until the nineteenth century.

The eighteenth century witnessed greater yields of vegetables, including two important American crops, the potato and maize (Indian corn). Although they were not grown in quantity until after 1700, both had been brought to Europe from America in the sixteenth century. The potato became a staple in Germany, the Low Countries, and especially Ireland, where repression by English landlords forced large numbers of poor peasants to survive on small plots of marginal land. The potato took relatively little effort to produce in large quantities. High in carbohydrates and calories, rich in vitamins A and C, it could be easily stored for winter use.

Another argument of the agriculture revolution is whether or not the new crops and agricultural inventions increased food production while lowering the agricultural workforce, consequently altering the size and scale of farms and displacing agricultural workers. The new agricultural techniques were considered best suited to large-scale farms. Large landowners or yeomen farmers enclosed the old open fields, combining many small holdings into larger units. The end of the open-field system led to the demise of the cooperative farming of the village community. As crop yields increased, food prices began to decline, leaving landlords with the prospect of lowered profits. Their response was to enact legislation. Historians are still debating the causes of this legislation and whether or not it forced more innovative farming practices, leading to higher food yields. In England, Parliament was dominated by the landed aristocracy and enacted legislation to allow agricultural lands to be legally enclosed. As a result of these **enclosure acts**, England gradually became a land of large estates, and many small farmers were forced to become wage laborers or tenant farmers working farms of 100 to 500 acres. The enclosure acts allowed landlords to easily evict their tenants while converting the crop fields to meadows to raise sheep and generate income from their wool. The enclosure movement and new agricultural practices largely destroyed the traditional patterns of English village life (see the box above).

Historians continue to debate the timing and degree of an agricultural revolution in England, in part because some historians rely upon economics and pricing of food as a barometer for productivity. The lack of data makes this assessment problematic. However it is difficult to deny the rapid increase in agricultural production by the second half of the eighteenth century. English agriculture, with its noticeable increase in productivity, made possible the feeding of an expanding population while freeing the workforce from agriculture, enabling them to enter a new world of industrialization and urbanization. In other parts of Europe, however, noble privileges and heavy taxes on the peasants prevented the adoption of new agricultural practices. Nobles maintained rights of usage to all lands and often pastured animals on fallow fields; although the animals' manure could fertilize the soil, overgrazing could destroy the fields. In addition, lords often levied taxes on certain crops, such as wheat and rye, which prevented the introduction of fodder crops.

New Methods of Finance

A decline in the supply of gold and silver in the seventeenth century had created a chronic shortage of money that undermined the efforts of governments to meet their needs. The establishment of new public and private banks and the acceptance of paper notes made possible an expansion of credit in the eighteenth century.

Perhaps the best example of this process can be observed in England, where the Bank of England was founded in 1694. Unlike other banks accustomed to receiving deposits and exchanging foreign currencies, the Bank of England also made loans. In return for lending money to the government, the bank was allowed to issue paper "banknotes" backed by its credit. These soon became negotiable and provided a paper substitute for gold and silver coins. In addition, the issuance of government bonds paying regular interest, backed by the Bank of England and the London financial community, created the notion of a public or "national debt" distinct from the monarch's personal debts. This process meant that capital for financing larger armies and other government undertakings could be raised in ever-greater quantities.

These new financial institutions and methods were not risk-free, however. In both Britain and France in the early eighteenth century, speculators provided opportunities for people to invest in colonial trading companies. The French company under John Law was also tied to his attempt to create a national bank and paper currency for France. When people went overboard and drove the price of the stock to incredibly high levels, the bubble burst. Law's company and bank went bankrupt, leading to a loss of confidence in paper money that prevented the formation of a French national bank. Consequently, French public finance developed slowly in the eighteenth century (see Chapter 19).

This was not the case in Britain, however. Despite crises, public confidence in the new financial institutions enabled the British government to borrow large sums of money at relatively low rates of interest, giving it a distinct advantage in the struggle with France. According to a contemporary observer, Britain's public credit was "the permanent miracle of her policy, which has inspired both astonishment and fear in the States of Europe."[5] Despite Britain's growing importance in finance, however, the Dutch Republic remained the leader in Europe's financial life, and Amsterdam continued to be the center of international finance until London replaced it in the nineteenth century. One observer noted in 1769:

> If ten or twelve businessmen of Amsterdam of the first rank meet for a banking operation, they can in a moment send circulating throughout Europe over two hundred million florins in paper money, which is preferred to cash. There is no Sovereign who could do as much. . . . This credit is a power which the ten or twelve businessmen will be able to exert over all the States of Europe, in complete independence of any authority.[6]

As Dutch trade, industry, and power declined, Dutch capitalists were inclined to lend money abroad because they had fewer opportunities at home.

European Industry

The most important product of European industry in the eighteenth century was textiles. Woolen cloth made up 75 percent of Britain's exports in the early part of the century. France, too, was a leader in the production of woolen cloth, and other major states emulated both France and Britain by encouraging the development of their own textile industries.

COTTAGE INDUSTRY Most textiles were still produced by traditional methods. In cities that were textile centers, master artisans used timeworn methods to turn out finished goods in their guild workshops. But by the eighteenth century, textile production was beginning to shift to the countryside in parts of Europe. In the countryside, textiles were produced by the "putting-out" or "domestic" system. A merchant-capitalist

Cottage Industry. One important source of textile production in the eighteenth century was the cottage industry, truly a family enterprise. Shown here is a family at work producing flax. It was customary in the cottage industry for women to spin and wind the yarn.

British Library, London, UK/Bridgeman Images

entrepreneur bought the raw materials, mostly wool and flax, and "put them out" to rural workers, who spun the raw material into yarn and then wove it into cloth on simple looms. Capitalist entrepreneurs sold the finished product, made a profit, and used it to manufacture more. This system became known as the **cottage industry** because spinners and weavers did their work in their own cottages. The cottage industry was truly a family enterprise: women and children could spin while men wove on the looms, enabling rural people to earn incomes to supplement their pitiful wages as agricultural laborers.

NEW METHODS AND NEW MACHINES The cottage system employed traditional methods of manufacturing and spread to many areas of rural Europe in the eighteenth century. But significant changes in industrial production also began to occur in the second half of the century, pushed along by the introduction of cotton, originally imported from India. The importation of raw cotton from slave plantations in the Americas encouraged the production of cotton cloth in Europe, where a profitable market developed because of the growing demand for lightweight cotton clothes that were less expensive than linens and woolens. But the traditional methods of the cottage industry proved incapable of keeping up with the growing demand, leading English cloth entrepreneurs to develop new methods and new machines. The flying shuttle sped up the process of weaving on a loom, thereby increasing the need for large quantities of yarn. In response, Richard Arkwright (1732–1792) invented a "water frame," powered by horse or water, which turned out yarn much faster than cottage spinning wheels. This abundance of yarn, in turn, led to the development of mechanized looms, invented in the 1780s but not widely adopted until the early nineteenth century. By that time, Britain was in the throes of the Industrial Revolution (see Chapter 20), but already at the end of the eighteenth century, rural workers, perceiving that the new machines threatened their traditional livelihood, had begun to call for the machines' destruction (see the box on p. 550).

THE NEW CONSUMERS As agricultural innovations in the eighteenth century reduced the need for agricultural workers, other occupations were expanding. Small merchants, craftspeople, and shopkeepers were growing in number, aided by the developments in industry. This led to the beginnings of a consumer revolution that was primarily centered in England in the eighteenth century. Consumers increasingly purchased a host of newly available goods including china, silverware, cut glass, mahogany furniture, teapots, and ready-made clothing. Porcelain had been imported from China for centuries; however, by the eighteenth century factories on the Continent and in England had bypassed Chinese production. Large showrooms opened in London. The most famous was that of Josiah Wedgwood, whose shop was illuminated by a large skylight and filled with opulent furnishings to show off his wares. By the late eighteenth century, Wedgwood's company exported nearly eighty percent of its wares. The consumer products of the eighteenth century quickly became international commodities.

Mercantile Empires and Worldwide Trade

As we saw in Chapter 14, the growth of commercial capitalism led to integrated markets, joint-stock trading companies, and banking and stock exchange facilities. Mercantilist theory had posited that a nation should acquire as much gold and silver as possible; that it should maintain a favorable balance of trade, or more exports than imports; and that the state should provide subsidies to manufacturers, grant monopolies to traders, build roads and canals, and impose high tariffs to limit imports. Colonies were also seen as valuable sources of raw materials and markets for finished goods. Mercantilist theory on the role of colonies was matched in practice by Europe's overseas expansion. With the development of colonies and trading posts in the Americas, Asia, and Africa, Europeans embarked on an adventure in international commerce. This increase in overseas trade has led some historians to speak of the emergence of a truly global economy in the eighteenth century.

Although trade within Europe still dominated total trade figures, overseas trade boomed in the eighteenth century. As we saw in Chapter 14, of all the goods traded in the eighteenth century, perhaps the most profitable were African slaves. The African slave trade and the plantation economy in the Americas that depended on it were an integral part of the new Atlantic economy, which enabled the nations of western Europe to experience greater prosperity than the states in central and eastern Europe.

During the eighteenth century, trade between European states and their colonies increased dramatically. In 1715, 19 percent of Britain's trade was with its American colonies; by 1785, that figure had risen to 34 percent. The growing trade of Europe with the Americas, Africa, and Asia was also visible in the expansion of merchant fleets. The British, for example, had 3,300 merchant ships carrying 260,000 tons in 1700; by

Bristol. After the discovery of the New World, Bristol became an important British shipping port. By the seventeenth century, it was the second-largest port in the kingdom. Portrayed here in a painting dated 1760 is Bristol's quay, where woods were unloaded and loaded.

THE BEGINNINGS OF MECHANIZED INDUSTRY: THE ATTACK ON NEW MACHINES

ALREADY BY THE END OF THE EIGHTEENTH CENTURY, mechanization was bringing changes to the traditional cottage industry of textile manufacturing. Rural workers who depended on the extra wages earned in their own homes often reacted by attacking the machinery that threatened their livelihoods. This selection is a petition that English woolen workers published in their local newspapers asking that machines no longer be used to prepare wool for spinning.

The Leeds Woolen Workers' Petition (1786)

To the Merchants, Clothiers and all such as wish well to the Staple Manufactory of this Nation.

The Humble ADDRESS and PETITION of Thousands, who labor in the Cloth Manufactory.

The Scribbling-Machines have thrown thousands of your petitioners out of employ, whereby they are brought into great distress, and are not able to procure a maintenance for their families, and deprived them of the opportunity of bringing up their children to labor: We have therefore to request, that prejudice and self-interest may be laid aside, and that you may pay that attention to the following facts, which the nature of the case requires.

The number of Scribbling-Machines extending about seventeen miles southwest of LEEDS, exceed all belief, being no less than *one hundred and seventy!* and as each machine will do as much work in twelve hours, as ten men can in that time do by hand (speaking within bounds) and they working night and day, one machine will do as much work in one day as would otherwise employ twenty men.

As we do not mean to assert any thing but what we can prove to be true, we allow four men to be employed at each machine twelve hours, working night and day, will take eight men in twenty-four hours; so that, upon a moderate computation twelve men are thrown out of employ for every single machine used in scribbling; and as it may be supposed the number of machines in all the other quarters together, nearly equal those in the South-West, full four thousand men are left to shift for a living how they can, and must of course fall to the Parish, if not time relieved. Allowing one boy to be bound apprentice from each family out of work, eight thousand hands are deprived of the opportunity of getting a livelihood.

We therefore hope, that the feelings of humanity will lead those who have it in their power to prevent the use of those machines, to give every discouragement they can to what has a tendency so prejudicial to their fellow-creatures. . . .

We wish to propose a few queries to those who would plead for the further continuance of these machines:

How are those men, thus thrown out of employ to provide for their families; and what are they to put their children apprentice to, that the rising generation may have something to keep them at work, in order that they may not be like vagabonds strolling about in idleness? Some say, Begin and learn some other business.—Suppose we do, who will maintain our families, whilst we undertake the arduous task; and when we have learned it, how do we know we shall be any better for all our pains; for by the time we have served our second apprenticeship, another machine may arise, which may take away that business also. . . .

But what are our children to do; are they to be brought up in idleness? Indeed as things are, it is no wonder to hear of so many executions; for our parts, though we may be thought illiterate men, our conceptions are, that bringing children up to industry, and keeping them employed, is the way to keep them from falling into those crimes, which an idle habit naturally leads to.

Q *What arguments did the Leeds woolen workers use against the new machines? What does the petition reveal about the concept of "progress" at the end of the eighteenth century?*

Source: Leeds Woolen Workers' Petition (Leeds, 1786).

1775, those numbers had increased to 9,400 ships carrying 695,000 tons.

Flourishing trade also had a significant impact on the European economy, especially visible in the growth of towns and cities. The rise of the Atlantic trade led to great prosperity for such port cities as Bordeaux, Nantes, and Marseilles in France; Bristol and Liverpool in Britain; and Lisbon and Oporto in Portugal. Trade also led to the growth of related industries, such as textile manufacturing, sugar refining, and tobacco processing, and to an increase in dock workers, building tradesmen, servants, and numerous service people. Visitors' accounts of their visits to prosperous port cities detail the elegant buildings and affluent lifestyle they encountered.

The Social Order of the Eighteenth Century

Q **FOCUS QUESTION:** Who were the main groups making up the European social order in the eighteenth century, and how did the conditions in which they lived differ both between groups and between different parts of Europe?

The pattern of Europe's social organization, first established in the Middle Ages, continued well into the eighteenth century. Social status was still largely determined not by wealth and economic standing but by the division into the traditional "orders" or "estates" determined by heredity. This divinely sanctioned division of society into traditional orders was supported by Christian teaching, which emphasized the need to fulfill the responsibilities of one's estate. Although Enlightenment intellectuals attacked these traditional distinctions, they did not die easily. In the Prussian law code of 1794, marriage between noble males and middle-class females was forbidden without a government dispensation. Even without government regulation, however, different social groups remained easily distinguished everywhere in Europe by the distinctive, traditional clothes they wore.

Nevertheless, some forces of change were at work in this traditional society. The ideas of the Enlightenment made headway as reformers argued that the concept of an unchanging social order based on privilege was hostile to the progress of society. Not until the revolutionary upheavals at the end of the eighteenth century, however, did the old order finally begin to crumble.

The Peasants

Because society was still mostly rural in the eighteenth century, the peasantry constituted the largest social group, making up as much as 85 percent of Europe's population. There were rather large differences, however, between peasants from area to area. The most important distinction, at least legally, was between the free peasant and the serf. Peasants in Britain, northern Italy, the Low Countries, Spain, most of France, and some areas of western Germany were legally free, though not exempt from burdens. Some free peasants in Andalusia in Spain, southern Italy, Sicily, and Portugal lived in poverty more desperate than that of many serfs in Russia and eastern Germany. In France, 40 percent of free peasants owned little or no land by 1789.

Small peasant proprietors or tenant farmers in western Europe were also not free from compulsory services. Most owed **tithes**, often one-third of their crops. Although tithes were intended for parish priests, in France only 10 percent of the priests received them. Instead the tithes wound up in the hands of towns and aristocratic landowners. Moreover, peasants could still owe a variety of dues and fees. Local aristocrats claimed hunting rights on peasant land and had monopolies over the flour mills, community ovens, and wine and oil presses needed by the peasants. Hunting rights, dues, fees, and tithes were all deeply resented.

Eastern Europe continued to be dominated by large landed estates owned by powerful lords and worked by serfs. Serfdom had come late to the east, having largely been imposed in the sixteenth and seventeenth centuries. Peasants in eastern Germany were bound to the lord's estate, had to perform labor services on the lord's land, and could not marry or move without permission and payment of a tax. By the eighteenth century, landlords also possessed legal jurisdiction, giving them control over the administration of justice. Only in the Habsburg empire had a ruler attempted to improve the lot of the peasants through a series of reforms. With the exception of the clergy and a small merchant class, eighteenth-century Russia, unlike the rest of Europe, was still largely a society of landlords and serfs. Russian peasants were not attached to the land but to the landlord and thus existed in a condition approaching slavery.

THE VILLAGE The local village remained the center of social life for the peasants. The village, especially in western Europe, maintained public order; provided poor relief, a village church, and sometimes a schoolmaster; collected taxes for the central government; maintained roads and bridges; and established common procedures for sowing, plowing, and harvesting crops. But villages were often dominated by the wealthiest peasants and proved highly resistant to innovations, such as new agricultural practices.

THE PEASANT DIET The diet of the peasants in the eighteenth century had not changed much since the Middle Ages. Dark bread, made of roughly ground wheat and rye flour, remained the basic staple. It was quite nourishing and high in vitamins, minerals, and even proteins, since the bran and germ were not removed. Peasants drank water, wine, and beer and ate soups and gruel made of grains and vegetables. The new foods of the eighteenth century, potatoes and American corn, added important elements to the peasant diet. Of course, when harvests were bad, hunger and famine became the peasants' lot in life, making them even more susceptible to the ravages of disease.

The Nobility

The nobles, who constituted only 2 to 3 percent of the European population, played a dominating role in society. Being born a noble automatically guaranteed a place at the top of the social order, with all the attendant special privileges and rights. The legal privileges of the nobility included judgment by their peers, immunity from severe punishment, and exemption from many forms of taxation. Especially in central and eastern Europe, the rights of landlords over their serfs were overwhelming. In Poland until 1768, the nobility even possessed the right of life or death over their serfs.

In many countries, nobles were highly conscious of their unique lifestyle, which set them apart from the rest of society. This did not mean, however, that they were unwilling to bend the conventions of that lifestyle if there were profits to be made. For example, by convention, nobles were expected to live off the yields of their estates. But although nobles almost everywhere talked about trade being beneath their dignity, many were not averse to mercantile endeavors. Many were also all too eager to profit from the exploitation of raw materials found on their estates; as a result, many nobles were involved in industries such as mining, metallurgy, and glassmaking. Their diet also set them off from the rest of society. Aristocrats consumed enormous quantities of meat and fish accompanied by cheeses, nuts, and a variety of sweets.

Nobles also played important roles in military and government affairs. Since medieval times, landed aristocrats had served as military officers. Although monarchs found it impossible to exclude commoners from the ranks of officers, tradition maintained that nobles made the most natural and hence the best officers. Moreover, the eighteenth-century nobility played a significant role in the administrative machinery of state. In some countries, such as Prussia, the entire bureaucracy reflected aristocratic values. Moreover, in most of Europe, landholding nobles controlled much of the local government in their districts.

The nobility or landowning class was not a homogeneous social group, however. Landlords in England leased their land to tenant farmers, while those in eastern Europe used the labor services of serfs. Nobles in Russia and Prussia served the state, but those in Spain and Italy had few official functions. Differences in wealth, education, and political power also led to differences within countries as well. The gap between rich and poor nobles could be enormous. As the century progressed, poor nobles sometimes sank into the ranks of the unprivileged masses of the population. It has been estimated that the number of European nobles declined by one-third between 1750 and 1815.

Although the nobles clung to their privileged status and struggled to keep others out, almost everywhere a person with money found it possible to enter the ranks of the nobility. Rights of nobility were frequently attached to certain lands, so purchasing the lands made one a noble; the acquisition of government offices also often conferred noble status.

THE ARISTOCRATIC WAY OF LIFE: THE COUNTRY HOUSE One aristocrat who survived the French Revolution commented that "no one who did not live before the Revolution" could know the real sweetness of living. Of course, he spoke not for the peasants whose labor maintained the system but for the landed aristocrats. For them, the eighteenth century was a final century of "sweetness" before the Industrial Revolution and bourgeois society diminished their privileged way of life.

In so many ways, the court of Louis XIV had provided a model for other European monarchs, who built palaces and encouraged the development of a court society as a center of culture. As at Versailles, these courts were peopled by members of the aristocracy whose income from rents or officeholding enabled them to participate in this lifestyle. This court society, whether in France, Spain, or Germany, manifested common characteristics: participation in intrigues for the king's or prince's favor, serene walks in formal gardens, and duels to maintain one's honor.

The majority of aristocratic landowners, however, remained on their country estates and did not participate in court society; their large houses continued to give witness to their domination of the surrounding countryside. This was especially true in England, where the court of the Hanoverian kings (Georges I–III, from 1714 to 1820) made little impact on the behavior of upper-class society. English landed aristocrats invested much time, energy, and money in their rural estates, giving the English country house an important role in English social life. One American observer remarked, "Scarcely any persons who hold a leading place in the circles of their society live in London. They have houses in London, in which they stay while Parliament sits, and occasionally visit at other seasons; but their homes are in the country."[7]

Although there was much variety in country houses, many in the eighteenth century were built in the Georgian style (named after the Hanoverian kings). This style was greatly influenced by the classical serenity and sedateness of the sixteenth-century Venetian architect Andrea Palladio (ahn-DRAY-ah puh-LAH-dee-oh), who had specialized in the design of country villas. The Georgian country house combined elegance with domesticity, and its interior was often described as offering visual delight and utility along with the comfort of a home.

The country house also fulfilled a new desire for greater privacy that was reflected in the growing separation between the lower and upper floors. The lower floors were devoted to public activities—dining, entertaining, and leisure (see "Images of Everyday Life" on p. 553). A central entrance hall provided the setting for the ceremonial arrival and departure of guests on formal occasions. From the hall, guests could proceed to a series of downstairs common rooms. The largest was the drawing room (larger houses had two), which contained musical instruments and was used for dances or card games, a favorite pastime. Other common rooms included a formal dining room, informal breakfast room, library, study, gallery, billiard room, and conservatory. The entrance hall also featured a large staircase that led to the upstairs rooms, which consisted of bedrooms for husbands and wives, sons, and daughters. These rooms were used not only for sleeping but also for private activities, such as playing for the children and sewing, writing, and reading for wives. "Going upstairs" literally meant leaving the company of others in the downstairs common rooms to be alone in the privacy of one's bedroom. This eighteenth-century desire for privacy also meant keeping servants at a distance. They were now housed in their own wing of rooms and alerted to their employers' desire for assistance by a new invention—long cords connected to bells in the servants' quarters.

Although the arrangement of the eighteenth-century Georgian house originally reflected male interests, the influence of women was increasingly evident by the second half of the century. Already in the seventeenth century, it had become customary for the sexes to separate after dinner; while the men preoccupied themselves with brandy and cigars in the dining room, women would exit to a "withdrawing room" for their own conversation. In the course of the eighteenth century, the drawing room became a larger, more feminine room with comfortable pieces of furniture grouped casually in front of fireplaces to create a cozy atmosphere.

Aristocratic landowners, especially in Britain, also sought to expand the open space around their country houses to separate themselves from the lower classes in the villages and to remove farmland from their view. Often these open spaces were then enclosed by walls to create parks (as they were called in England) to provide even more privacy. Sometimes entire villages

IMAGES OF EVERYDAY LIFE

The Aristocratic Way of Life

Collection of the Earl of Pembroke, Wilton House, Wilts./Bridgeman Images

Scala/Art Resource, NY

Art Resource, NY

Erich Lessing/Art Resource, NY

THE EIGHTEENTH-CENTURY COUNTRY HOUSE IN Britain fulfilled the desire of aristocrats for both elegance and greater privacy. The painting above at the left, by Richard Wilson, shows a typical English country house of the eighteenth century surrounded by a simple, serene landscape. Thomas Gainsborough's *Conversation in the Park*, above right, captures the relaxed life of two aristocrats in the park of their country estate. The illustration at the lower left shows the formal dining room of a great British country house. In the course of the eighteenth century, upper-class country houses came to be furnished with upholstered furniture and elaborate carpets as aristocrats sought greater comfort. Cabinets with glass windows also became fashionable as a way to display fine china and other objects. Especially desirable were objects from the East, as vast amounts of Chinese and Japanese ceramics were imported into Europe in the eighteenth century. The illustration at the lower right shows Chinese cups without handles, which became extremely fashionable. As seen in the painting, it was even acceptable to pour tea into the saucer in order to cool it.

were destroyed to create a park, causing one English poet to lament the social cost:

> *The man of wealth and pride*
> *Takes up the space that many poor supplied;*
> *Space for his lake, his park's extended bounds,*
> *Space for his horses, equipage and hounds.*[8]

Along with a sense of privacy, parks gave landed aristocrats the ability to reshape their property to meet their leisure needs.

THE ARISTOCRATIC WAY OF LIFE: THE GRAND TOUR One characteristic of the high culture of the Enlightenment was its cosmopolitanism, reinforced by education in the Latin classics and the use of French as an international language. Travel was another manifestation of the Enlightenment's sophistication and interest in new vistas. An important aspect of eighteenth-century travel was the grand tour, in which the sons of aristocrats completed their education by making a tour of Europe's major cities. The English aristocracy in particular regarded the grand tour as crucial to their education. The great-aunt of Thomas Coke wrote to him upon his completion of school: "Sir, I understand you have left Eton and probably intend to go to one of those Schools of Vice, the Universities. If, however, you choose to travel I will give you 500 pounds [about $12,500] per annum."[9] Coke was no fool and went on the grand tour, along with many others. In one peak year alone, 40,000 Englishmen were traveling in Europe.

Travel was not easy in the eighteenth century. Crossing the English Channel could be difficult in rough seas and might take anywhere from three to twelve hours. The trip from France to Italy could be made by sea, where the traveler faced the danger of pirates, or overland by sedan chair over the Alps, where narrow passes made travel an adventure in terror. Inns, especially in Germany, were populated by thieves and the ubiquitous bedbugs. The English in particular were known for spending vast sums of money during their travels; as one observer recounted, "The French usually travel to save money, so that they sometimes leave the places where they sojourn worse off than they found them. The English, on the other hand, come over with plenty of cash, plenty of gear, and servants to wait on them. They throw their money about like lords."[10]

Since the trip was intended to be educational, young Englishmen in particular were usually accompanied by a tutor who ensured that his charges spent time looking at museum collections of natural history and antiquities. But tutors were not able to stop young men from also pursuing wine, women, and song. After crossing the Channel, English visitors went to Paris for a cram course on how to act sophisticated. They then went on to Italy, where their favorite destinations were Florence, Venice, and Rome. In Florence, the studious and ambitious studied art in the Uffizi Gallery. The less ambitious followed a less vigorous routine; according to the poet Thomas Gray, they "get up at twelve o'clock, breakfast till three, dine till five, sleep till six, drink cooling liquors till eight, go to the bridge till ten, sup till two, and so sleep till twelve again." In Venice, where sophisticated prostitutes had flourished since Renaissance times, women were the chief attraction for young English males. As Samuel Johnson remarked, "If a young man is wild, and must run after women and bad company, it is better this should be done abroad." Rome was another "great object of our pilgrimage," where travelers visited the "modern" sights, such as Saint Peter's and, above all, the ancient ruins. To a generation raised on a classical education, souvenirs of ruins and Piranesi's etchings of classical ruins were required purchases. After the accidental rediscovery of the ancient Roman towns of Herculaneum and Pompeii, they became a popular eighteenth-century tourist attraction.

The Inhabitants of Towns and Cities

Townspeople were still a distinct minority of the total population, except in the Dutch Republic, Britain, and parts of Italy. At the end of the eighteenth century, about one-sixth of the French population lived in towns of 2,000 people or more. The biggest city in Europe was London, with 1 million inhabitants, while Paris numbered between 550,000 and 600,000. Altogether, Europe had at least twenty cities in twelve countries with populations over 100,000, including Naples, Lisbon, Moscow, Saint Petersburg, Vienna, Amsterdam, Berlin, Rome, and Madrid. Although urban dwellers were vastly outnumbered by rural inhabitants, towns played an important role in Western culture. The contrasts between a large city, with its education, culture, and material consumption, and the surrounding, often poverty-stricken countryside were striking, evident in this British traveler's account of Russia's Saint Petersburg in 1741:

> The country about Petersburg has full as wild and desert a look as any in the Indies; you need not go above 200 paces out of the town to find yourself in a wild wood of firs, and such a low, marshy, boggy country that you would think God when he created the rest of the world for the use of mankind had created this for an inaccessible retreat for all sorts of wild beasts.[11]

Peasants often resented the prosperity of towns and their exploitation of the countryside to serve urban interests. Palermo in Sicily used one-third of the island's food production while paying only one-tenth of the taxes. Towns lived off the countryside not by buying peasant produce but by acquiring it through tithes, rents, and dues.

Many cities in western and even central Europe had a long tradition of patrician oligarchies that continued to control their communities by dominating town and city councils. Despite their domination, patricians constituted only a small minority of the urban population. Just below the patricians stood an upper crust of the middle classes: non-noble officeholders, financiers and bankers, merchants, wealthy rentiers who lived off their investments, and important professionals, including lawyers. Another large urban group was the petty bourgeoisie or lower middle class, made up of master artisans, shopkeepers, and small traders. Below them were the laborers or working classes. Much urban industry was still carried on in small guild workshops by masters, journeymen, and apprentices. Apprentices who acquired the proper skills became journeymen before entering the ranks of the masters, but increasingly in the eighteenth century, guilds became closed oligarchies as membership was restricted to the relatives of masters. Many skilled artisans were then often forced to become low-paid workers.

Alfredo Dagli Orti/The Art Archive at Art Resource, NY

A Market Square in Naples. Below the wealthy patrician elites who dominated the towns and cities were a number of social groups with a wide range of incomes and occupations. This remarkable diversity is evident in this eighteenth-century painting by Angelo Costa, which shows a fair being held in the chief market square of the Italian city of Naples.

Urban communities also had a large group of unskilled workers who served as servants, maids, and cooks at pitifully low wages.

Despite an end to the ravages of plague, eighteenth-century cities still experienced high death rates, especially among children, because of unsanitary living conditions, polluted water, and a lack of sewerage facilities. One observer compared the stench of Hamburg to an open sewer that could be smelled for miles around. Overcrowding also exacerbated urban problems as cities continued to grow from an influx of rural immigrants. But cities proved no paradise for them as unskilled workers found few employment opportunities. The result was a serious problem of poverty in the eighteenth century.

THE PROBLEM OF POVERTY Poverty was a highly visible problem in the eighteenth century, both in cities and in the countryside (see the box on p. 556). In Venice, licensed beggars made up 3 to 5 percent of the population, and unlicensed beggars may have constituted as much as 13 to 15 percent. Beggars in Bologna were estimated at 25 percent of the population; in Mainz, figures indicate that 30 percent of the people were beggars or prostitutes. Prostitution was often an alternative to begging. In France and Britain by the end of the century, an estimated 10 percent of the people depended on charity or begging for their food.

Earlier in Europe, the poor had been viewed as blessed children of God; assisting them was a Christian duty. A change of attitude that had begun in the latter part of the sixteenth century became even more apparent in the eighteenth century. Charity to poor beggars, it was argued, simply encouraged their idleness and led them to vice and crime. A French official stated, "Beggary is the apprenticeship of crime; it begins by creating a love of idleness which will always be the greatest political and moral evil. In this state the beggar does not long resist the temptation to steal."[12] Although private charitable institutions such as the religious Order of Saint Vincent de Paul and the Sisters of Charity had been founded to help the poor, they were soon overwhelmed by the increased numbers of indigent in the eighteenth century.

Although some "enlightened" officials argued that the state should become involved in the problem, mixed feelings prevented concerted action. Since the sixteenth century, vagrancy and begging had been considered crimes. In the eighteenth century, French authorities attempted to round up vagrants and beggars and incarcerate them for eighteen months to act as a deterrent. This effort accomplished little, however, since the basic problem was socioeconomic. These people had no work. In the 1770s, the French tried to use public works projects, such as road building, to give people jobs, but not enough funds were available to accomplish much. The problem of poverty remained another serious blemish on the quality of eighteenth-century life.

POVERTY IN FRANCE

UNLIKE THE BRITISH, WHO HAD A SYSTEM OF public-supported poor relief, the French responded to poverty with ad hoc policies when conditions became acute. This selection is taken from an *intendant's* report to the controller general at Paris describing his suggestions for a program to relieve the grain shortages expected for the winter months.

M. de la Bourdonnaye, *Intendant* of Bordeaux, to the Controller General, September 30, 1708

Having searched for the means of helping the people of Agen in this cruel situation and having conferred with His Eminence, the Bishop, it seems to us that three things are absolutely necessary if the people are not to starve during the winter.

Most of the inhabitants do not have seed to plant their fields. However, we decided that we would be going too far if we furnished it, because those who have seed would also apply [for more]. Moreover, we are persuaded that all the inhabitants will make strenuous efforts to find some seed, since they have every reason to expect prices to remain high next year. . . .

But this project will come to nothing if the collectors of the *taille* [taxes] continue to be as strict in the exercise of their functions as they have been of late and continue to employ troops [to force collection]. Those inhabitants who have seed grain would sell it to be freed from an oppressive garrison, while those who must buy seed, since they have none left from their harvest and have scraped together a little money for this purchase, would prefer to give up that money [for taxes] when put under police constraint. To avoid this, I feel it is absolutely necessary that you order the receivers-general to reduce their operations during this winter, at least with respect to the poor. . . .

We are planning to import wheat for this region from Languedoc and Quercy, and we are confident that there will be enough. . . . As a protective measure, it would seem wise to establish two small storehouses. Ten thousand ecus [30,000 livres] would be sufficient for each. . . .

A third point demanding our attention is the support of beggars among the poor, as well as of those who have no other resources than their wages. Since there will be very little work, these people will soon be reduced to starvation. We should establish public workshops to provide work as was done in 1693 and 1694. . . . In this manner, we should rid ourselves of those who do not want to work and assure the others a moderate subsistence. For these workshops, we would need about 40,000 livres, or altogether 100,000 livres. The receiver-general of the *taille* of Agen could advance this sum. The 60,000 livres for the storehouses he would get back very soon. I shall await your orders on all of the above.

Marginal Comments by the Controller General

Operations for the collection of the *taille* are to be suspended. The two storehouses are to be established; great care must be taken to put them to good use. The interest on the advances will be paid by the king. His Majesty has agreed to the establishment of the public workshops for the able-bodied poor and is willing to spend up to 40,000 livres on them this winter.

Q *What does this document reveal about the nature of poverty in France in the eighteenth century? How would the growing ranks of the poor in Europe further destabilize society?*

Source: R. Forster and E. Forster, *European Society in the Eighteenth Century* (London: Walker & Co., 1969).

CHAPTER SUMMARY

Everywhere in Europe at the beginning of the eighteenth century, the old order remained strong. Nobles, clerics, towns, and provinces all had privileges, some medieval in origin, others the result of the attempt of monarchies in the sixteenth and seventeenth centuries to gain financial support from their subjects. Everywhere in the eighteenth century, monarchs sought to enlarge their bureaucracies to raise taxes to support the new large standing armies that had originated in the seventeenth century. During the eighteenth century, royal authority was often justified by the service the monarch could give to the state and its people rather than by divine right, creating a form of monarchy that some have labeled "enlightened absolutism." Three rulers, Frederick II of Prussia, Joseph II of Austria, and Catherine the Great of Russia, are traditionally associated with the concept of enlightened absolutism, although only Joseph II truly sought radical change based on Enlightenment ideas. Joseph abolished serfdom, reformed the laws, and granted religious toleration, but his reforms did not outlast his reign. Frederick and Catherine expressed interest in enlightened reforms, but maintenance of the existing political system took precedence over reform. Indeed, many historians believe that Frederick, Catherine, and Joseph were all guided by a policy of using state power to amass armies and wage wars to gain more power.

The existence of these armies made wars more likely. The emergence of five great powers, two of them (France and Britain) in conflict in the East and North America, initiated a new scale of confrontation. The mid-century War of the Austrian Succession and the Seven Years' War were fought not only in Europe but also in North America and India. Frederick the Great was the instigator, desiring Austrian Silesia, but Great Britain was the true victor, driving France from Canada and India. Britain emerged with a worldwide empire and became the world's greatest naval and colonial power. Standing armies became the norm, and everywhere in Europe, increased demands for taxes to support these conflicts led to attacks on the privileged orders and a desire for change not met by the ruling monarchs.

At the same time, the population grew, mainly as a result of a declining death rate and improvements in agriculture; paper money began to compensate for gold and silver; institutions such as the Bank of England mobilized the wealth of the nation through credit; and the beginnings of an industrial revolution emerged in the textile industry. This growth in population, along with dramatic changes in finance, trade, and industry and an increase in poverty, created tensions that undermined the traditional foundations of European society. The inability of the old order to deal meaningfully with these changes led to a revolutionary outburst at the end of the eighteenth century that marked the beginning of the end for that old order.

CHAPTER TIMELINE

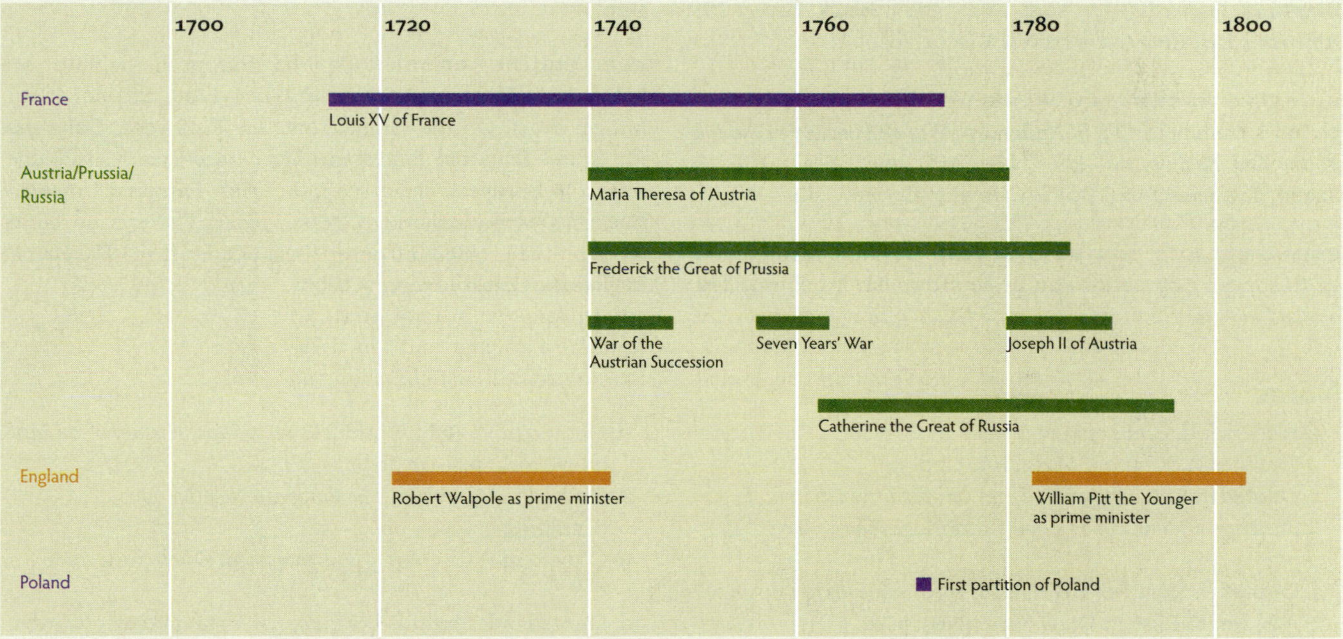

CHAPTER REVIEW

Upon Reflection

Q If you were a philosophe serving Joseph II of Austria or Catherine the Great of Russia, what advice would you give the monarch on the best way to rule his or her country?

Q What were the characteristics of war and diplomacy in the eighteenth century, and how would you compare the nature of war and diplomacy in the eighteenth century with that of the seventeenth century?

Q How and why did the nobility play a dominating role in the European society of the eighteenth century?

Key Terms

natural laws (p. 529)
natural rights (p. 529)
enlightened absolutism (p. 529)
patronage (p. 531)
balance of power (p. 539)
reason of state (p. 539)
primogeniture (p. 544)
infanticide (p. 545)
agricultural revolution (p. 546)
enclosure acts (p. 547)
cottage industry (p. 549)
tithes (p. 551)

Suggestions for Further Reading

GENERAL WORKS For a good introduction to the political history of the eighteenth century, see the relevant chapters in the general works by **Woloch, Anderson,** and **Blanning** listed in Chapter 17. See also **G. Treasure, *The Making of Modern Europe, 1648–1780*** (London, 2003), and **O. Hufton, *Europe: Privilege and Protest, 1730–1789*,** 2nd ed. (London, 2001). On enlightened absolutism, see **D. Beales, *Enlightenment and Reform in Eighteenth-Century Europe*** (New York, 2005). Good biographies of some of Europe's monarchs include **G. MacDonough, *Frederick the Great*** (New York, 2001); **V. Rounding, *Catherine the Great: Love, Sex, and Power*** (New York, 2007); **T. C. W. Blanning, *Joseph II*** (New York, 1994); and **J. Black, *George III: America's Last King*** (New Haven, Conn., 2006).

EIGHTEENTH-CENTURY WARFARE The warfare of this period is examined in **M. S. Anderson, *War and Society in Europe of the Old Regime, 1615–1789*** (New York, 1998). See also **A. J. Szabo, *The Seven Years' War in Europe, 1756–1763*** (Oxford, 2007).

ECONOMIC AND SOCIAL CHANGE A good introduction to European population can be found in **M. W. Flinn, *The European Demographic System, 1500–1820*** (Brighton, 1981). One of the best works on family and marriage patterns is **L. Stone, *The Family, Sex, and Marriage in England, 1500–1800*** (New York, 1977). On England's agricultural revolution debate, see **M. Overton, *Agricultural Revolution in England*** (Cambridge, 1996), and **R. C. Allen, *Enclosure and the Yeoman: The Agricultural Development of the South Midlands, 1450–1850*** (Oxford, 1992). On the consumer revolution, see **M. Berg, *Luxury and Pleasure in Eighteenth-Century Britain*** (Oxford, 2007), and **J. Mokyr, *The Enlightened Economy: An Economic History of Britain 1700–1800*** (New Haven, Conn., 2010).

THE SOCIAL ORDER On the European nobility, see **J. Dewald, *The European Nobility, 1400–1800*,** 2nd ed. (Cambridge, 2004). On the Grand Tour, see **R. Sweet, *Cities and the Grand Tour: The British in Italy, c. 1620–1820*** (Cambridge, 2013). On European cities, see **J. de Vries, *European Urbanization, 1500–1800*** (Cambridge, Mass., 1984). There is no better work on the problem of poverty than **O. Hufton, *The Poor of Eighteenth-Century France*** (Oxford, 1974).

Notes

1. Frederick II, *Forms of Government*, in E. Weber, *The Western Tradition* (Lexington, Mass., 1972), pp. 538, 544.
2. Quoted in R. A. Dorwart, *The Administrative Reforms of Frederick William I of Prussia* (Cambridge, Mass., 1953), p. 36.
3. Quoted in Sidney B. Fay, *The Rise of Brandenburg-Prussia to 1786*, rev. K. Epstein (New York, 1964), p. 92.
4. Quoted in H. Rosenberg, *Bureaucracy, Aristocracy, and Autocracy: The Prussian Experience, 1660–1815* (Cambridge, Mass., 1958), p. 40.
5. Quoted in F. Braudel, *Civilization and Capitalism*, vol. 3 (London, 1984), p. 378.
6. Quoted in ibid., p. 245.
7. Quoted in W. Rybczynski, *Home: A Short History of an Idea* (New York, 1986), p. 105.
8. Quoted in J. Dewald, *The European Nobility, 1400–1800* (Cambridge, 1996), pp. 91–92.
9. Quoted in P. Gay, *Age of Enlightenment* (New York, 1966), p. 87.
10. Quoted in P. Hazard, *The European Mind, 1680–1715* (Cleveland, Ohio, 1963), pp. 6–7.
11. I. Vinogradoff, "Russian Missions to London, 1711–1789: Further Extracts from the Cottrell Papers," *Oxford Slavonic Papers*, New Series (1982), 15: 76.
12. Quoted in J. Kaplow, *The Names of Kings: The Parisian Laboring Poor in the Eighteenth Century* (New York, 1972), p. 134.

CHAPTER

19

A REVOLUTION IN POLITICS: THE ERA OF THE FRENCH REVOLUTION AND NAPOLEON

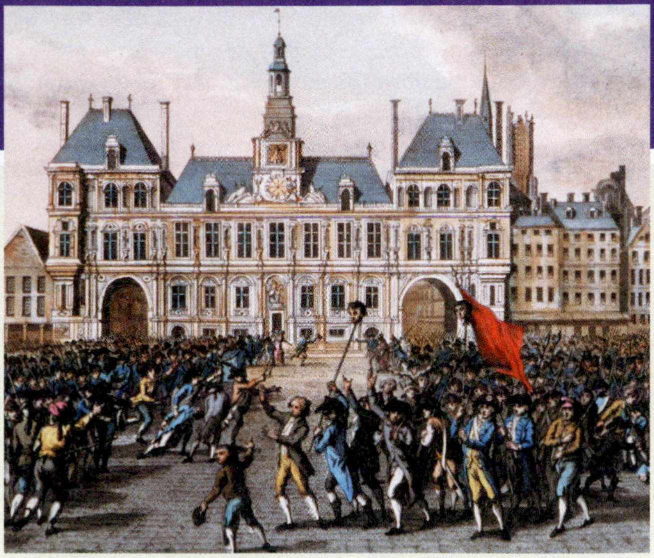

CCI/The Art Archive at Art Resource, NY

The storming of the Bastille

CHAPTER OUTLINE AND FOCUS QUESTIONS

The Beginning of the Revolutionary Era: The American Revolution

Q What were the causes and results of the American Revolution, and what impact did it have on Europe?

Background to the French Revolution

Q What were the long-range and immediate causes of the French Revolution?

The French Revolution

Q What were the main events of the French Revolution between 1789 and 1799? What role did each of the following play in the French Revolution: lawyers, peasants, women, the clergy, the Jacobins, the sans-culottes, the French revolutionary army, and the Committee of Public Safety?

The Age of Napoleon

Q Which aspects of the French Revolution did Napoleon preserve, and which did he destroy?

Critical Thinking

Q *In what ways were the French Revolution, the American Revolution, and the seventeenth-century English revolutions alike? In what ways were they different?*

Connections to Today

Q *What similarities and differences do you see between the French Revolution and contemporary revolutions?*

ON THE MORNING OF JULY 14, 1789, a Parisian mob of eight thousand people in search of weapons streamed toward the Bastille (bass-STEEL), a royal armory filled with arms and ammunition. The Bastille was also a state prison, and although it now held only seven prisoners, in the eyes of these angry Parisians, it was a glaring symbol of the government's despotic policies. The armory was defended by the marquis de Launay (mar-KEE duh loh-NAY) and a small garrison of 114 men. The attack began in earnest in the early afternoon, and after three hours of fighting, de Launay and the garrison surrendered. Angered by the loss of ninety-eight of their members, the victorious mob beat de Launay to death, cut off his head, and carried it aloft in triumph through the streets of Paris. When King Louis XVI was told the news of the fall of the Bastille by the duc de La Rochefoucauld-Liancourt (dook duh lah-RUSH-foo-koh-lee-ahnh-KOOR), he exclaimed, "Why, this is a revolt." "No, Sire," replied the duc, "it is a revolution."

Historians have long assumed that the modern history of Europe began with two major transformations—the French Revolution (discussed in this chapter) and the Industrial Revolution (see Chapter 20). Accordingly, the French Revolution has been portrayed as the major turning point in European political and social history, when the institutions of the "old regime" were destroyed and a new order was created based on individual rights, representative institutions, and a concept of loyalty to the nation rather than the monarch. This perspective does have certain limitations, however.

France was only one of a number of areas in the Western world where the assumptions of the old order were challenged. Although some historians have called the upheavals of the eighteenth and early nineteenth centuries a "democratic revolution," it is probably more appropriate to speak of a liberal movement to extend political rights and power to the bourgeoisie in possession of capital—citizens besides the aristocracy who were literate and had become wealthy through capitalist enterprises in trade, industry, and finance. The years preceding and accompanying the French Revolution included attempts at reform and revolt in the North American colonies, Britain, the Dutch Republic, some Swiss cities, and the Austrian Netherlands. The success of the American and French Revolutions makes them the center of attention for this chapter.

Not all of the decadent privileges that characterized the old European regime were destroyed in 1789, however. The revolutionary upheaval of the era, especially in France, did create new liberal and national political ideals, summarized in the French revolutionary slogan, "Liberty, Equality, Fraternity," that transformed France and were then spread to other European countries through the conquests of Napoleon. After Napoleon's defeat, however, the forces of reaction did their best to restore the old order and resist pressures for reform.

The Beginning of the Revolutionary Era: The American Revolution

Q **FOCUS QUESTION:** What were the causes and results of the American Revolution, and what impact did it have on Europe?

At the end of the Seven Years' War in 1763, Great Britain had become the world's greatest colonial power. In North America, Britain controlled Canada and the lands east of the Mississippi (see Map 19.1). After the war, British policy makers sought to obtain new revenues from the thirteen American colonies to pay for expenses the British army had incurred in defending the colonists. An attempt to levy new taxes by a stamp act in 1765, however, led to riots and the law's quick repeal.

The Americans and the British had different conceptions of empire. The British envisioned a single empire with Parliament as the supreme authority throughout. Only Parliament could make laws for all the people in the empire, including the American colonists. The Americans, in contrast, had their own representative assemblies. They believed that neither the king nor Parliament had any right to interfere in their internal affairs and that no tax could be levied without the consent of an assembly whose members actually represented the people.

Crisis followed crisis in the 1770s until 1776, when the colonists decided to declare their independence from the British Empire. On July 4, 1776, the Second Continental Congress approved a declaration of independence written by Thomas Jefferson (1743–1826) (see the box on p. 562). A stirring political document, the declaration affirmed the Enlightenment's natural rights of "life, liberty, and the pursuit of happiness" and declared the colonies to be "free and independent states absolved from all allegiance to the British crown." The war for American independence had formally begun.

The War for Independence

The war against Great Britain was a great gamble. Britain was a strong European military power with enormous financial resources. The Second Continental Congress had authorized the formation of a Continental Army under George Washington (1732–1799) as commander in chief. Washington, who had had political experience in Virginia and military experience in the French and Indian War, was a good choice for the job. As a southerner, he brought balance to an effort that until that point had been led by New Englanders. Nevertheless, compared with the British forces, the Continental Army consisted of undisciplined amateurs whose terms of service were usually very brief.

Complicating the war effort were the internal divisions within the colonies. Fought for independence, the Revolutionary War was also a civil war, pitting family members and neighbors against one another. The Loyalists, between 15 and 30 percent of the population, questioned whether British policies justified the rebellion. The Loyalists were strongest in New York and Pennsylvania and tended to be wealthy, older, and politically moderate.

Since probably half the colonial population was apathetic at the beginning of the struggle, the patriots, like the Loyalists, constituted a minority of the population. The patriots, however, managed to win over many of the uncommitted, either by persuasion or by force. There were patriots among the rich as well as Loyalists; George Washington owned an estate with 15,000 acres and 150 slaves. But the rich patriots joined an extensive coalition that included farmers and artisans. The wide social spectrum in this coalition had an impact on representative governments in the states after the war. The right to vote was often broadened; Pennsylvania, for example, dropped all property qualifications for voting.

Of great importance to the colonies' cause was the assistance provided by foreign countries that were eager to gain revenge for earlier defeats at the hands of the British. The French supplied arms and money to the rebels from the beginning of the war, and French officers and soldiers also served in Washington's Continental Army. When the British army of General Cornwallis was forced to surrender to a combined American and French army and French fleet under Washington at Yorktown in 1781, the British government decided to call it quits. The Treaty of Paris, signed in 1783, recognized the independence of the American colonies and granted the Americans control of the western territory from the Appalachians to the Mississippi River.

Forming a New Nation

The thirteen American colonies had gained their independence as the United States of America, but a fear of concentrated power and concern for their own interests caused them to have little enthusiasm for establishing a united nation with a strong

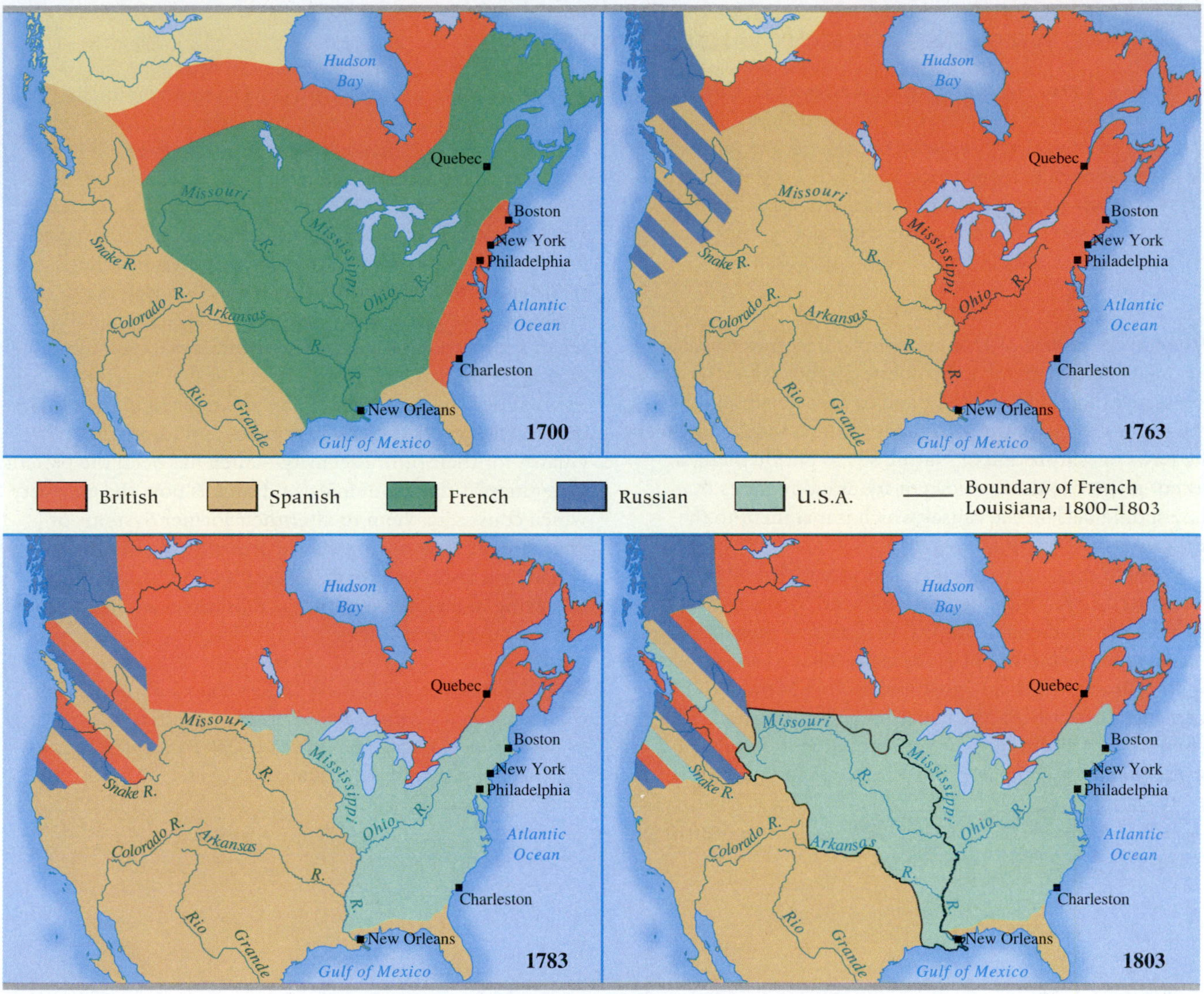

MAP 19.1 North America, 1700–1803. At the end of the Seven Years' War, Britain had gained much territory in eastern North America, but its efforts to obtain new revenues from the American colonies to help pay for the war sparked the American Revolution. The 1803 Louisiana Purchase nearly doubled the size of the United States and spurred westward expansion to the Pacific Ocean.

Q *In what periods was the Mississippi River a national boundary, and why was control of the river important for the United States?*

central government. The Articles of Confederation, ratified in 1781, did little to provide for a strong central government. A movement for a different form of national government soon arose. In the summer of 1787, fifty-five delegates attended a convention in Philadelphia to revise the Articles of Confederation. The convention's delegates—wealthy, politically experienced, well educated—rejected revision and decided to devise a new constitution.

The proposed constitution created a central government distinct from and superior to the governments of the individual states. The national government was given the power to levy taxes, raise a national army, regulate domestic and foreign trade, and create a national currency. The central or federal government was divided into three branches, each with some power to check the functioning of the others. A president would serve as the chief executive with the power to execute laws, veto the legislature's acts, supervise foreign affairs, and direct military forces. Legislative power was vested in the second branch of government, a bicameral legislature composed of the Senate, elected by the state legislatures, and the House of Representatives, elected directly by the people. The Supreme Court and other courts "as deemed necessary" by Congress served as the third branch of government. They would enforce the Constitution as the "supreme law of the land."

The United States Constitution was approved by the states—by a slim margin—in 1788. Important to its success was a promise to add a bill of rights as the new government's first piece of business. Accordingly, in March 1789, the new Congress

THE ARGUMENT FOR INDEPENDENCE

ON JULY 2, 1776, THE SECOND CONTINENTAL CONGRESS adopted a resolution declaring the independence of the American colonies. Two days later, the delegates approved the Declaration of Independence, which gave the reasons for their action. Its principal author was Thomas Jefferson, who basically restated John Locke's theory of revolution (see Chapter 15).

The Declaration of Independence

When in the course of human events it becomes necessary for one people to dissolve the political bands which have connected them with another, and to assume among the Powers of the earth, the separate and equal station to which the Laws of Nature and of Nature's God entitle them, a decent respect to the opinions of mankind requires that they should declare the causes which impel them to the separation.

We hold these truths to be self-evident, that all men are created equal, that they are endowed by their Creator with certain unalienable Rights, that among these are Life, Liberty and the pursuit of Happiness. That to secure these rights, Governments are instituted among Men, deriving their just powers from the consent of the governed, That whenever any Form of Government becomes destructive of these ends, it is the Right of the People to alter or to abolish it and to institute new Government, laying its foundation on such principles and organizing its powers in such form, as to them shall seem most likely to effect their Safety and Happiness. Prudence, indeed, will dictate that Governments long established should not be changed for light and transient causes; and accordingly all experience has shown, that mankind are more disposed to suffer, while evils are sufferable, than to right themselves by abolishing the forms to which they are accustomed. But when a long train of abuses and usurpations, pursuing invariably the same Object evinces a design to reduce them under absolute Despotism, it is their right, it is their duty, to throw off such Government, and to provide new Guards for their future security.—Such has been the patient sufferance of these Colonies; and such is now the necessity which constrains them to alter their former Systems of government. The history of the present King of Great Britain is a history of repeated injuries and usurpations, all having in direct object the establishment of an absolute Tyranny over these States.

Q *What influence did John Locke's theory of revolution have on the American Declaration of Independence? How would a member of the British Parliament have responded to this declaration?*

Source: S. N. Thorpe, *The Federal and State Constitutions* (Washington, DC, 1909), pp. 3–4.

The Declaration of Independence. The Declaration of Independence, approved on July 4, 1776, by the Second Continental Congress, opened the door to the war for American independence. John Trumbull's famous painting, *The Signing of the Declaration*, shows the members of the committee responsible for the Declaration of Independence (from left to right, John Adams, Roger Sherman, Robert Livingston, Thomas Jefferson, and Benjamin Franklin) standing before John Hancock, president of the Second Continental Congress.

proposed twelve amendments to the Constitution; the ten that were ratified by the states have been known ever since as the Bill of Rights. These guaranteed freedom of religion, speech, press, petition, and assembly, as well as the right to bear arms, protection against unreasonable searches and arrests, trial by jury, due process of law, and protection of property rights. Many of these rights were derived from the natural rights philosophy of the eighteenth-century philosophes, which was popular among the American colonists. Is it any wonder that many European intellectuals saw the American Revolution as the embodiment of the Enlightenment's political dreams?

Impact of the American Revolution on Europe

The year 1789 witnessed two far-reaching events, the beginning of a new United States of America and the eruption of the French Revolution. Was there a connection between the two great revolutions of the late eighteenth century?

There is no doubt that the American Revolution had an important impact on Europeans. Books, newspapers, and magazines provided the newly developing reading public with numerous accounts of American events. To many in Europe, it seemed to portend an era of significant changes, including new arrangements in international politics. The Venetian ambassador to Paris astutely observed in 1783 that "if only the union of the [American] provinces is preserved, it is reasonable to expect that, with the favorable effects of time, and of European arts and sciences, it will become the most formidable power in the world."[1] But the American Revolution also meant far more than that. To many Europeans, it proved that the liberal political ideas of the Enlightenment were not the vapid utterances of intellectuals. The rights of man, ideas of liberty and equality, popular sovereignty, the separation of powers, and freedom of religion, thought, and press were not utopian ideals. The Americans had created a new social contract, embodied it in a written constitution, and made the concepts of liberty and representative government a reality. The premises of the Enlightenment seemed confirmed; a new age and a better world could be achieved. As a Swiss philosophe expressed it, "I am tempted to believe that North America is the country where reason and humanity will develop more rapidly than anywhere else."[2]

Europeans obtained much of their information about America from returning soldiers, especially the hundreds of French officers who had served in the American war. One of them, the aristocratic marquis de Lafayette (mar-KEE duh lah-fay-ET), had volunteered for service in America in order to "strike a blow against England," France's old enemy. Closely associated with George Washington, Lafayette returned to France with ideas of individual liberties and notions of republicanism and popular sovereignty. He became a member of the Society of Thirty, a club composed of people from the Paris salons. These "lovers of liberty" would be influential in the early stages of the French Revolution. The Declaration of the Rights of Man and the Citizen (see "Destruction of the Old Regime" later in this chapter) showed unmistakable signs of the influence of the American Declaration of Independence as well as the American state constitutions. Yet for all of its obvious impact, the American Revolution proved in the long run to be far less important to Europe than the French Revolution. The French Revolution was more complex, more violent, and far more radical in its attempt to construct both a new political order and a new social order. The French Revolution provided a model of revolution for Europe and much of the rest of the world; to many analysts, it remains the political movement that truly inaugurated the modern political world.

Background to the French Revolution

FOCUS QUESTION: What were the long-range and immediate causes of the French Revolution?

Although we associate events like the French Revolution with sudden changes, the causes of such events involve long-range problems as well as immediate precipitating forces. **Revolutions**, as has been repeatedly shown, are not necessarily the result of economic collapse and masses of impoverished people hungering for change. In fact, in the fifty years before 1789, France had experienced a period of economic growth due to an expansion of foreign trade and an increase in industrial production, although many people, especially the peasants, failed to share in the prosperity. Thus, the causes of the French Revolution must be found in a multifaceted examination of French society and its problems in the late eighteenth century.

Social Structure of the Old Regime

The long-range or indirect causes of the French Revolution must first be sought in the condition of French society. Before the Revolution, French society was grounded in the inequality of rights or the idea of privilege. During the eighteenth century, the population had increased by forty-four percent from 18 million to 26 million. It was a young country, with 36 percent under the age of twenty, and 40 percent between twenty and forty; and it was divided, as it had been since the Middle Ages, into legal categories known as the three orders or estates.

THE FIRST ESTATE The First Estate consisted of the clergy and numbered about 130,000 people. The church owned approximately 10 percent of the land. Clergy were exempt from the *taille* (TY), France's chief tax, although the church had agreed to pay a "voluntary" contribution every five years to the state. The church was very wealthy; income from church property and other investments produced almost 300 million *livres* annually—half the income of the royal crown. Clergy were also radically divided, since the higher clergy, stemming from aristocratic families, shared the interests of the nobility and lived in palaces and townhouses, while the parish priests were often poor commoners.

THE SECOND ESTATE The Second Estate was the nobility, composed of no more than 350,000 people who nevertheless owned about 25 to 30 percent of the land. Under Louis XV

Bettmann/Corbis

The Three Estates. This French political cartoon from 1789 reveals a critical view of France's privileged orders. Shown in the cartoon is a naked common man held in chains and being ridden by an aristocrat, a clergyman, and a judge. The message is clear: most ordinary French people (the Third Estate) are suffering horribly as a result of the privileges of the First and Second Estates.

and Louis XVI, the nobility had continued to play an important and even crucial role in French society, holding many of the leading positions in the government, the military, the law courts, and the higher church offices. Nobles also controlled much heavy industry in France, either through investment or by ownership of mining and metallurgical enterprises. The French nobility was also divided. The nobility of the robe derived their status from officeholding, a pathway that had often enabled commoners to attain noble rank. These nobles now dominated the royal law courts and important administrative offices. The nobility of the sword claimed to be descendants of the original medieval nobility. As a group, the nobles sought to expand their privileges at the expense of the monarchy—to defend liberty by resisting the arbitrary actions of monarchy, as some nobles asserted—and to maintain their monopoly over positions in the military, church, and government. In 1781, in reaction to the ambitions of aristocrats newly arrived from the bourgeoisie, the Ségur (say-GOO-uh) Law attempted to limit the sale of military officerships to fourth-generation nobles, thus excluding newly enrolled members of the nobility.

Although there were many poor nobles, on the whole the fortunes of the wealthy aristocrats outstripped those of most others in French society. Generally, the nobles tended to marry within their own ranks, making the nobility a fairly closed group. Although their privileges varied from region to region, the very possession of privileges remained a hallmark of the nobility. Common to all were tax exemptions, especially from the *taille*.

THE THIRD ESTATE The Third Estate, the commoners of society, constituted the overwhelming majority of the French population. They were divided by vast differences in occupation, level of education, and wealth. The peasants, who alone constituted 75 to 80 percent of the total population, were by far the largest segment of the Third Estate. They owned about 35 to 40 percent of the land, although their landholdings varied from area to area and more than half had no or little land on which to survive. The landless peasants were day laborers who increasingly migrated to Paris in search of work; they were the first to suffer in hard times. Serfdom no longer existed on any large scale in France, but French peasants still had obligations to their local landlords that they deeply resented. These relics of feudalism included the payment of fees for the use of village facilities, such as the flour mill, community oven, and winepress, as well as tithes to the clergy. The nobility also maintained the right to hunt on peasants' land.

Another part of the Third Estate consisted of skilled artisans, shopkeepers, and other wage earners in the cities. Although the eighteenth century had been a period of rapid urban growth, 90 percent of French towns had fewer than 10,000 inhabitants; only nine cities had more than 50,000. In the eighteenth century, consumer prices, especially the price of bread, rose faster than wages, causing these urban groups to experience a decline in purchasing power. The economic discontent of this segment of the Third Estate—and often simply their struggle for survival—led them to play an important role in the Revolution, especially in the city of Paris. Insubordination, one observer noted, "has been visible among the people for some years now and above all among craftsmen." The towns and cities were also home to large groups of unskilled and often unemployed workers. One magistrate complained that "misery . . . has thrown into the towns people who overburden them with their uselessness, and who find nothing to do, because there is not enough for the people who live there."[3]

About 8 percent, or 2.3 million people, constituted the bourgeoisie or middle class, who owned about 20 to 25 percent of the land. This group included the merchants, industrialists, and bankers who controlled the resources of trade, manufacturing, and finance and benefited from the economic prosperity after 1730. The bourgeoisie also included professional people—lawyers, holders of public offices, doctors, and writers. Many members of the bourgeoisie sought security and status through the purchase of land. They had their own set of grievances because they were often excluded from the social and political privileges monopolized by the nobles. These resentments of the middle class were for a long time assumed to be a major cause of the French Revolution. But although these tensions existed, the situation was not a simple case of a unified bourgeoisie against a unified noble class. As is evident, neither group was monolithic. Nobles were separated by vast differences in wealth and importance. A similar gulf separated wealthy financiers from local lawyers in French provincial towns.

At the upper levels of society, remarkable similarities existed between the wealthier bourgeoisie and the nobility. It was still possible for wealthy middle-class individuals to join the ranks of the nobility by obtaining public offices and entering the nobility of the robe. In fact, between 1774 and 1789, the not insignificant number of 2,500 wealthy bourgeoisie entered the ranks of the nobility. Over the century as a whole, 6,500 new noble families were created. In addition, as we saw in Chapter 18, the aristocrats were also engaging in capitalist activities on their landed estates, such as mining, metallurgy, and glassmaking, and were even investing in foreign trade. Viewed in terms of economic function, many members of the bourgeoisie and nobility formed a single class. Finally, the new and critical ideas of the Enlightenment proved attractive to both aristocrats and bourgeoisie. Members of both groups shared a common world of liberal political thought. The old view that the French Revolution was the result of the conflict between two rigid orders, the bourgeoisie and the nobility, has been enlarged and revised. Both aristocratic and bourgeois elites, long accustomed to a new socioeconomic reality based on wealth and economic achievement, were increasingly frustrated by a monarchical system resting on privileges and on an old and rigid social order based on the concept of estates. The opposition of these elites to the **old order** ultimately led them to take drastic action against the monarchical regime, although they soon split over the question of how far to proceed in eliminating traditional privileges. In a real sense, the Revolution had its origins in political grievances.

Other Problems Facing the French Monarchy

Although the long-range causes of the French Revolution can thus be found in part in the growing frustration at the monarchy's inability to deal with new social realities and problems, other factors were also present. The failure of the French monarchy was exacerbated by specific problems in the 1780s. Although the country had enjoyed fifty years of growth overall, periodic economic crises still occurred. Bad harvests in 1787 and 1788 and the beginnings of a manufacturing depression resulted in food shortages, rising prices for food and other necessities, and unemployment in the cities. The number of poor, estimated by some at almost one-third of the population, reached crisis proportions on the eve of the Revolution. An English traveler noted the misery of the poor in the countryside: "All the country girls and women are without shoes or stockings; and the plowmen at their work have neither sabots nor stockings to their feet. This is a poverty that strikes at the root of national prosperity."[4]

IDEAS OF THE PHILOSOPHES Existing privileges as well as social and political institutions were also coming under increasing criticism. Although the philosophes did not advocate revolution, their ideas circulated widely among the literate bourgeois and noble elites of France. The actual influence of the ideas of the philosophes is difficult to prove, but once the Revolution began, the revolutionary leaders frequently quoted Enlightenment writers, especially Rousseau.

FAILURE TO MAKE REFORMS The French parlements often frustrated efforts at reform. These thirteen law courts, which were responsible for registering royal decrees, could block royal edicts by not registering them. Although Louis XIV had forced them into submission, the parlements had gained new strength in the eighteenth century as they and their noble judges assumed the role of defenders of "liberty" against the arbitrary power of the monarchy. As noble defenders, however, they often pushed their own interests as well, especially by blocking new taxes. This last point reminds us that one of the fundamental problems facing the monarchy was financial.

FINANCIAL CRISIS The immediate cause of the French Revolution was the near collapse of government finances. France experienced a depression from 1778 to 1787 as a result of a loss of overseas markets and overproduction. Prices of grain and wine fell by forty and fifty percent. Peasants faced increasing uncertainty as rent prices remained high due to a rapidly growing population. Poor harvests in 1788 and 1789 sent prices of wheat and rye soaring—leaving many desperate. At a time when France was experiencing economic crises, the government was drastically short of money. Yet French governmental expenditures continued to grow due to costly wars and royal extravagance. The government responded by borrowing. Poor taxation policy contributed to the high debt, with most of the monarchy's funds coming from the peasantry. Unlike Britain, where the Bank of England financed the borrowing of money at low interest rates, France had no central bank, and instead relied on private loans. By 1788, the interest on the debt alone constituted half of government spending. Total debt had reached 4 billion livres (roughly $40 billion). Financial lenders, fearful they would never be repaid, were refusing to lend additional amounts.

The king's finance ministry wrestled with the problem but met with resistance. The parlements refused to assist in fiscal reform, fearing that it would involve higher taxes. In 1786, Charles de Calonne (SHAHRL duh ka-LUNN), the controller general of finance, finding himself unable to borrow any more, proposed a complete revamping of the fiscal and administrative system of the state. To gain support, Calonne convened an "assembly of notables" early in 1787. This gathering of nobles, prelates, and magistrates refused to cooperate, and the government's attempt to go it alone brought further disaster. On the verge of a complete financial collapse, the government was finally forced to call a meeting of the Estates-General, the French parliamentary body that had not met since 1614. By calling the Estates-General, the government was virtually admitting that the consent of the nation was required to raise taxes.

The French Revolution

FOCUS QUESTIONS: What were the main events of the French Revolution between 1789 and 1799? What role did each of the following play in the French Revolution: lawyers, peasants, women, the clergy, the Jacobins, the sans-culottes, the French revolutionary army, and the Committee of Public Safety?

In summoning the Estates-General, the government was merely looking for a way to solve the immediate financial crisis. The monarchy had no wish for a major reform of the government, nor did the delegates who arrived at Versailles come with plans for the revolutionary changes that ultimately emerged. Yet over the next years, through the interplay of the deputies meeting in various legislative assemblies, the common people in the streets of Paris and other cities, and the peasants in the countryside, much of the old regime would be destroyed, and Europe would have a new model for political and social change.

From Estates-General to a National Assembly

The Estates-General consisted of representatives from the three orders of French society. In the elections for the Estates-General, the government had ruled that the Third Estate should get double representation (it did, after all, constitute 97 percent of the population). Consequently, while both the First Estate (the clergy) and the Second (the nobility) had about 300 delegates each, the commoners had almost 600 representatives. Two-thirds of the latter were people with legal training, and three-fourths were from towns with more than two thousand inhabitants, giving the Third Estate a particularly strong legal and urban representation. Of the 282 representatives of the nobility, about 90 were liberal minded, urban oriented, and interested in the enlightened ideas of the century; half of them were under forty years of age. The activists of the Third Estate and the reform-minded individuals among the First and Second Estates had common ties in their youth, urban background, and hostility to privilege. The *cahiers de doléances* (ka-YAY duh doh-lay-AHNSS), or statements of local grievances, which were drafted throughout France during the elections to the Estates-General, advocated a regular constitutional government that would abolish the fiscal privileges of the church and nobility as the major way to regenerate the country.

The Estates-General opened at Versailles on May 5, 1789. It was divided from the start over the question of whether voting should be by order or by head (each delegate having one vote). The Parlement of Paris, consisting of nobles of the robe, had advocated voting by order according to the form used in 1614. Each order would vote separately; each would have veto power over the other two, thus guaranteeing aristocratic control over reforms. But opposition to the Parlement's proposal arose from a group of reformers calling themselves patriots or "lovers of liberty." Although they claimed to represent the nation, they consisted primarily of bourgeoisie and nobles. One group of patriots known as the Society of Thirty drew most of its members from the salons of Paris. The American Revolution had directly influenced some of this largely noble group, but all had been affected by the ideas of the Enlightenment and favored reforms made in the light of reason and utility.

THE NATIONAL ASSEMBLY The failure of the government to assume the leadership at the opening of the Estates-General created an opportunity for the Third Estate to push its demands for voting by head. Since it had double representation, with the assistance of liberal nobles and clerics, it could turn the three estates into a single-chamber legislature that would reform France in its own way. One representative, the Abbé Sieyès (ab-BAY syay-YESS), issued a pamphlet in which he asked, "What is the Third Estate? Everything. What has it been thus far in the political order? Nothing. What does it demand? To become something." Sieyès's sentiment, however, was not representative of the general feeling in 1789. Most delegates still wanted to make changes within a framework of respect for the authority of the king; revival or reform did not mean the overthrow of traditional institutions. When the First Estate declared in favor of voting by order, the Third Estate felt compelled to respond in a significant fashion. On June 17, 1789, the Third Estate voted to constitute itself a "National Assembly" and decided to draw up a constitution. Three days later, on June 20, the deputies of the Third Estate arrived at their meeting place only to find the doors locked; thereupon they moved to a nearby indoor tennis court and swore (in what has come to be known as the Tennis Court Oath) that they would continue to meet until they had produced a French constitution. These actions of June 17 and June 20 constituted the first step in the French Revolution, since the Third Estate had no legal right to act as the National Assembly. This revolution, largely the work of the lawyers of the Third Estate, was soon in jeopardy, however, as the king sided with the First Estate and threatened to dissolve the Estates-General. Louis XVI now prepared to use force. The revolution of the lawyers appeared doomed.

INTERVENTION OF THE COMMON PEOPLE The common people, however, in a series of urban and rural uprisings in July and August 1789, saved the Third Estate from the king's attempt to stop the Revolution. From now on, the common people would be mobilized by both revolutionary and counterrevolutionary politicians and used to support their interests. The common people had their own interests as well and would use the name of the Third Estate to wage a war on the rich, claiming that the aristocrats were plotting to destroy the Estates-General and retain their privileges. This war was not what the deputies of the Third Estate had planned.

The most famous of the urban risings was the fall of the Bastille (see the box on p. 568). The king's attempt to take defensive measures by increasing the number of troops at the arsenals in Paris and along the roads to Versailles served not to intimidate but rather to inflame public opinion. Increased mob activity in Paris led Parisian leaders to form the so-called Permanent Committee to keep order. Needing arms, they organized a popular force to capture the Invalides, a royal armory,

Musée de la Ville de Paris, Musée Carnavalet, Paris/Giraudon/The Bridgeman Art Library

The Tennis Court Oath. Finding themselves locked out of their regular meeting place on June 20, 1789, the deputies of the Third Estate met instead in the nearby tennis courts of the Jeu de Paume and committed themselves to continue to meet until they established a new constitution for France. In this painting, the neoclassical artist Jacques-Louis David presents a dramatic rendering of the Tennis Court Oath.

and on July 14 attacked the Bastille, another royal armory. The Bastille had also been a state prison but now held only seven prisoners (five forgers and two insane persons). There were few weapons there except those in the hands of the small group of defenders. The Bastille was an imposing fortress with eight towers connected by 9-foot-thick walls. It was easily defended, but its commander, the marquis de Launay, was more inclined to negotiate. Although fighting erupted, de Launay refused to open fire with his cannon, and the garrison soon surrendered. In the minds of the Parisians who fought there, the fall of the Bastille was a great victory, and it quickly became a popular symbol of triumph over despotism.

Paris was abandoned to the insurgents, and Louis XVI was soon informed that the royal troops were unreliable. Louis's acceptance of that reality signaled the collapse of royal authority; the king could no longer enforce his will. Louis then confirmed the appointment of the marquis de Lafayette as commander of a newly created citizens' militia known as the National Guard.

At the same time, independently of what was going on in Paris, popular revolutions broke out in numerous cities. In Nantes, permanent committees and national guards were created to maintain order after crowds had seized the chief citadels. This collapse of royal authority in the cities was paralleled by peasant revolutions in the countryside.

PEASANT REBELLIONS AND THE GREAT FEAR A growing resentment of the entire seigneurial system, with its fees and obligations, greatly exacerbated by the economic and fiscal activities of the great estate holders—whether noble or bourgeois—in the difficult decade of the 1780s, created the conditions for a popular uprising. The fall of the Bastille and the king's apparent capitulation to the demands of the Third Estate now encouraged peasants to take matters into their own hands. From July 19 to August 3, peasant rebellions occurred in five major areas of France. Patterns varied. In some places, peasants simply forced their lay and ecclesiastical lords to renounce dues and tithes; elsewhere they burned charters listing their obligations. The peasants were not acting in blind fury; they knew what they were doing. Many also believed that the king supported their actions. As a contemporary chronicler wrote, "For several weeks, news went from village to village. They announced that the Estates-General was going to abolish tithes, quitrents and dues, that the King agreed but that the peasants had to support the public authorities by going themselves to demand the destruction of titles."[5]

The agrarian revolts served as a backdrop to the Great Fear, a vast panic that spread like wildfire through France between July 20 and August 6. Fear of invasion by foreign troops, aided by a supposed aristocratic plot, encouraged the formation of more citizens' militias and permanent committees. The greatest impact of the agrarian revolts and the Great Fear was on the National Assembly meeting in Versailles. We will now examine its attempt to reform France.

Destruction of the Old Regime

One of the first acts of the National Assembly (also called the Constituent Assembly because from 1789 to 1791 it was writing a new constitution) was to destroy the relics of feudalism or aristocratic privileges. To some deputies, this measure was necessary to calm the peasants and restore order in the countryside, although many urban bourgeois were willing to abolish feudalism as a matter of principle. On the night of August 4, 1789, the National Assembly in an astonishing session voted to abolish seigneurial rights as well as the fiscal privileges of nobles, clergy, towns, and provinces.

THE DECLARATION OF THE RIGHTS OF MAN AND THE CITIZEN On August 26, the assembly provided the ideological foundation for its actions and an educational device for the

THE FALL OF THE BASTILLE

ON JULY 14, 1789, PARISIAN CROWDS IN SEARCH OF weapons attacked and captured the royal armory known as the Bastille. It had also been a state prison, and its fall marked the triumph of "liberty" over despotism. This intervention of the Parisian populace saved the Third Estate from Louis XVI's attempted counterrevolution.

A Parisian Newspaper Account of the Fall of the Bastille

First, the people tried to enter this fortress by the rue St.-Antoine, this fortress, which no one has even penetrated against the wishes of this frightful despotism and where the monster still resided. The treacherous governor had put out a flag of peace. So a confident advance was made; a detachment of French Guards, with perhaps five to six thousand armed bourgeois, penetrated the Bastille's outer courtyards, but as soon as some six hundred persons had passed over the first drawbridge, the bridge was raised and artillery fire mowed down several French Guards and some soldiers; the cannon fired on the town, and the people took fright; a large number of individuals were killed or wounded; but then they rallied and took shelter from the fire. . . . Meanwhile, they tried to locate some cannon; they attacked from the water's edge through the gardens of the arsenal, and from there made an orderly siege; they advanced from various directions, beneath a ceaseless round of fire. It was a terrible scene. . . . The fighting grew steadily more intense; the citizens had become hardened to the fire; from all directions they clambered onto the roofs or broke into the rooms; as soon as an enemy appeared among the turrets on the tower, he was fixed in the sights of a hundred guns and mown down in an instant; meanwhile cannon fire was hurriedly directed against the second drawbridge, which it pierced, breaking the chains; in vain did the cannon on the tower reply, for most people were sheltered from it; the fury was at its height; people bravely faced death and every danger; women, in their eagerness, helped us to the utmost; even the children, after the discharge of fire from the fortress, ran here and there picking up the bullets and shot; [and so the Bastille fell and the governor, de Launay, was captured]. . . . Serene and blessed liberty, for the first time, has at last been introduced into this abode of horrors, this frightful refuge of monstrous despotism and its crimes.

Meanwhile, they get ready to march; they leave amidst an enormous crowd; the applause, the outbursts of joy, the insults, the oaths hurled at the treacherous prisoners of war; everything is confused; cries of vengeance and of pleasure issue from every heart; the conquerors, glorious and covered in honor, carry their arms and the spoils of the conquered, the flags of victory, the militia mingling with the soldiers of the fatherland, the victory laurels offered them from every side, all this created a frightening and splendid spectacle. On arriving at the square, the people, anxious to avenge themselves, allowed neither de Launay nor the other officers to reach the place of trial; they seized them from the hands of their conquerors, and trampled them underfoot one after the other. De Launay was struck by a thousand blows, his head was cut off and hoisted on the end of a pike with blood streaming down all sides. . . . This glorious day must amaze our enemies, and finally usher in for us the triumph of justice and liberty. In the evening, there were celebrations.

Q *Why did the fall of the Bastille come to mark the triumph of French "liberty" over despotism? Do you think this Parisian newspaper account might be biased? Why or why not?*

Source: J. Gilchrist and W. J. Murray, eds., *The Press in the French Revolution: A Selection of Documents Taken from the Press of the Revolution for the Years 1789–1794* (London: Ginn & Company, 1971).

nation by adopting the Declaration of the Rights of Man and the Citizen (see "Opposing Viewpoints" on p. 570). This charter of basic liberties reflected the ideas of the major philosophes of the French Enlightenment and also owed much to the American Declaration of Independence and American state constitutions. The declaration began with a ringing affirmation of "the natural and imprescriptible rights of man" to "liberty, property, security, and resistance to oppression." It went on to affirm the destruction of aristocratic privileges by proclaiming an end to exemptions from taxation, freedom and equal rights for all men, and access to public office based on talent. The monarchy was restricted, and all citizens were to have the right to take part in the legislative process. Freedom of speech and press were coupled with the outlawing of arbitrary arrests.

The declaration also raised another important issue. Did the proclamation's ideal of equal rights for "all men" include women? Many deputies insisted that it did, at least in terms of civil liberties, provided that, as one said, "women do not aspire to exercise political rights and functions." Olympe de Gouges (oh-LAMP duh GOOZH), a playwright and pamphleteer, refused to accept this exclusion of women from political rights. Echoing the words of the official declaration, she penned a Declaration of the Rights of Woman and the Female Citizen in which she insisted that women should have the same rights as men (see "Opposing Viewpoints" on p. 570). The National Assembly ignored her demands.

THE WOMEN'S MARCH TO VERSAILLES In the meantime, Louis XVI had remained inactive at Versailles. He did refuse,

Chateau de Versailles, France/Bridgeman Images

The Art Archive/School of Oriental & African Studies/Eileen Tweedy

GLOBAL PERSPECTIVES

Revolution and Revolt in France and China

FRANCE AND CHINA EXPERIENCED REVOLUTIONARY upheaval at the end of the eighteenth century and well into the nineteenth. In both countries, common people often played an important role. At the top is a scene from the storming of the Bastille in Paris in 1789. This early action by the people of Paris ultimately led to the overthrow of the French monarchy. At the bottom is a scene from one of the struggles during the Taiping Rebellion, a major peasant revolt in the mid-nineteenth century in China. An imperial Chinese army is shown recapturing the city of Nanjing from Taiping rebels in 1864.

Q *What role did common people play in revolutionary upheavals in France and China in the eighteenth and nineteenth centuries?*

however, to promulgate the decrees on the abolition of feudalism and the declaration of rights, but an unexpected turn of events soon forced the king to change his mind. On October 5, after marching to the Hôtel de Ville, the city hall, to demand bread, crowds of Parisian women numbering in the thousands set off for Versailles, 12 miles away, to confront the king and the National Assembly. One eyewitness was amazed at the sight of "detachments of women coming up from every direction, armed with broomsticks, lances, pitchforks, swords, pistols and muskets." After meeting with a delegation of these women, who tearfully described how their children were starving for lack of bread, Louis XVI promised them grain supplies for Paris, thinking that this would end the protest. But the women's action had forced the Paris National Guard under Lafayette to follow their lead and march to Versailles. The crowd now insisted that the royal family return to Paris. On October 6, the king complied. As a goodwill gesture, he brought along wagonloads of flour from the palace stores. All were escorted by women armed with pikes (some of which held the severed heads of the king's guards), singing, "We are bringing back the baker, the baker's wife, and the baker's boy" (the king, queen, and their son). The king now accepted the National Assembly's decrees; it was neither the first nor the last occasion when Parisian crowds would affect national politics. The king was virtually a prisoner in Paris, and the National Assembly, now meeting in Paris, would also feel the influence of Parisian insurrectionary politics.

THE CATHOLIC CHURCH The Catholic Church was viewed as an important pillar of the old order, and it soon also felt the impact of reform. Because of the need for money, most of the lands of the church were confiscated, and *assignats* (ah-see-NYAH), a form of paper money, were issued based on the collateral of the newly nationalized church property. The church was also secularized. In July 1790, the new Civil Constitution of the Clergy was put into effect. Both bishops and priests of the Catholic Church were to be elected by the people and paid by the state. All clergy were also required to swear an oath of allegiance to the Civil Constitution. Since the pope forbade it, only 54 percent of the French parish clergy took the oath, and the majority of bishops refused. This was a critical development because the Catholic Church, still an important institution in the life of the French people, now became an enemy of the Revolution. The Civil Constitution has often been viewed as a serious tactical blunder on the part of the National Assembly, for by arousing the opposition of the church, it gave the counterrevolution a popular base from which to operate.

A NEW CONSTITUTION By 1791, the National Assembly had completed a new constitution that established a limited constitutional monarchy. There was still a monarch (now called "king of the French"), but he enjoyed few powers not subject to review by the new Legislative Assembly. The assembly, in which sovereign power was vested, was to sit for two years and consist of 745 representatives chosen by an indirect system of election that preserved power in the hands of the more affluent members of society. A distinction was drawn between active

OPPOSING VIEWPOINTS

The Natural Rights of the French People: Two Views

ONE OF THE IMPORTANT DOCUMENTS OF THE French Revolution, the Declaration of the Rights of Man and the Citizen, was adopted in August 1789 by the National Assembly. The declaration affirmed that "men are born and remain free and equal in rights," that government must protect these natural rights, and that political power is derived from the people. Olympe de Gouges (the pen name used by Marie Gouze) was a butcher's daughter who wrote plays and pamphlets. She argued that the Declaration of the Rights of Man and the Citizen did not apply to women and composed her own Declaration of the Rights of Woman and the Female Citizen in 1791.

Declaration of the Rights of Man and the Citizen

The representatives of the French people, organized as a national assembly, considering that ignorance, neglect, and scorn of the rights of man are the sole causes of public misfortunes and of corruption of governments, have resolved to display in a solemn declaration the natural, inalienable, and sacred rights of man, so that this declaration, constantly in the presence of all members of society, will continually remind them of their rights and their duties. . . . Consequently, the National Assembly recognizes and declares, in the presence and under the auspices of the Supreme Being, the following rights of man and citizen:

1. Men are born and remain free and equal in rights; social distinctions can be established only for the common benefit.
2. The aim of every political association is the conservation of the natural and imprescriptible rights of man; these rights are liberty, property, security, and resistance to oppression.
3. The source of all sovereignty is located in essence in the nation; no body, no individual can exercise authority which does not emanate from it expressly.
4. Liberty consists in being able to do anything that does not harm another person. . . .
6. The law is the expression of the general will; all citizens have the right to concur personally or through their representatives in its formation; it must be the same for all, whether it protects or punishes. All citizens being equal in its eyes are equally admissible to all honors, positions, and public employments, according to their capabilities and without other distinctions than those of their virtues and talents.
7. No man can be accused, arrested, or detained except in cases determined by the law, and according to the forms which it has prescribed. . . .
10. No one may be disturbed because of his opinions, even religious, provided that their public demonstration does not disturb the public order established by law.
11. The free communication of thoughts and opinions is one of the most precious rights of man: every citizen can therefore freely speak, write, and print. . . .
12. The guaranteeing of the rights of man and citizen necessitates a public force; this force is therefore instituted for the advantage of all, and not for the private use of those to whom it is entrusted. . . .
16. Any society in which guarantees of rights are not assured nor the separation of powers determined has no constitution.
17. Property being an inviolable and sacred right, no one may be deprived of it unless public necessity, legally determined, clearly requires such action, and then only on condition of a just and prior indemnity.

Hulton Archive/Getty Images

The Women's March on Versailles. On October 5, 1789, thousands of Parisian women marched to Versailles to confront King Louis XVI and to demand bread for their starving children. This contemporary print shows a group of dedicated marchers returning from Versailles with the King and his guard's heads on pikes.

Declaration of the Rights of Woman and the Female Citizen

Mothers, daughters, sisters, female representatives of the nation ask to be constituted as a national assembly. Considering that ignorance, neglect, or contempt for the rights of woman are the sole causes of public misfortunes and governmental corruption, they have resolved to set forth in a solemn declaration the natural, inalienable, and sacred rights of woman . . .

In consequence, the sex that is superior in beauty as in courage, needed maternal sufferings, recognizes and declares, in the presence and under the auspices of the Supreme Being, the following rights of woman and of the citizeness.

1. Woman is born free and remains equal to man in rights. Social distinctions may be based only on common utility.
2. The purpose of all political association is the preservation of the natural and imprescriptible rights of woman and man. These rights are liberty, property, security, and especially resistance to oppression.
3. The principle of all sovereignty rests essentially in the nation, which is but the reuniting of woman and man; no body and no individual may exercise authority which does not emanate expressly from the nation.
4. Liberty and justice consist in restoring all that belongs to another; hence, the exercise of the natural rights of woman has no other limits than those that the perpetual tyranny of man opposed to them; these limits must be reformed according to the laws of nature and reason. . . .
6. The law should be the expression of the general will; all citizenesses and citizens should take part, in person or by their representatives, in its formation. It must be the same for everyone. All citizenesses and citizens, being equal in its eyes, should be equally admissible to all public dignities, offices, and employments, according to their ability, with no other distinction than that of their virtues and talents.
7. No woman is exempted; she is indicted, arrested, and detained in the cases determined by law. Women like men obey this rigorous law. . . .
10. No one should be disturbed for his fundamental opinions; woman has the right to mount the scaffold; so she should have the right equally to mount the tribune, provided that these manifestations do not trouble public order as established by law.
11. The free communication of thought and opinions is one of the most precious rights of woman, since this liberty assures the recognition of children by their fathers. . . .
12. The safeguard of the rights of woman and citizeness requires public powers. These powers are instituted for the advantage of all, and not for the private benefit of those to whom they are entrusted. . . .
16. Any society in which the guarantee of rights is not assured or the separation of powers not settled has no constitution. The constitution is null and void if the majority of individuals composing the nation has not cooperated in its drafting.
17. Property belongs to both sexes whether united or separate; it is for each of them an inviolable and sacred right, . . .

Q *What "natural rights" does the first document proclaim? To what extent was this document influenced by the writings of the philosophes? What rights for women does the second document enunciate? Given the nature and scope of the arguments in favor of natural rights and women's rights in these two documents, what key effects on European society would you attribute to the French Revolution?*

Sources: P. H. Beik, *The French Revolution* (New York: Walker & Co., 1970); Lynn Hunt, trans., *The French Revolution and Human Rights: A Brief Documentary History* (Boston: Beford/St. Martins, 1996), pp. 124–126.

and passive citizens. Although all had the same civil rights, only active citizens (men over the age of twenty-five paying taxes equivalent in value to three days' unskilled labor) could vote. The active citizens probably numbered 4.3 million in 1790. These citizens did not elect the members of the Legislative Assembly directly but voted for electors (men paying taxes equal in value to ten days' labor). This relatively small group of 50,000 electors chose the deputies. To qualify as a deputy, one had to pay at least a "silver mark" in taxes, an amount equivalent to fifty-four days' labor.

The National Assembly also undertook an administrative restructuring of France. In 1789, it abolished all the old local and provincial divisions and divided France into eighty-three departments, roughly equal in size and population. Departments were in turn divided into districts and communes, all supervised by elected councils and officials who oversaw financial, administrative, judicial, and ecclesiastical institutions within their territories. Although both bourgeois and aristocrats were eligible for offices based on property qualifications, few nobles were elected, leaving local and departmental governments in the hands of the bourgeoisie, especially lawyers of various types.

OPPOSITION FROM WITHIN By 1791, France had moved into a vast reordering of the old regime that had been achieved by a revolutionary consensus that was largely the work of the wealthier members of the bourgeoisie. By mid–1791, however, this consensus faced growing opposition from clerics angered by the Civil Constitution of the Clergy, lower classes hurt by the rise in the cost of living resulting from the inflation of the assignats, peasants who remained opposed to dues that had still not been abandoned, and political clubs offering more radical solutions to the nation's problems. Recent scholarship has placed a greater emphasis on the proliferation of political

RESPONSE TO THE KING'S FLIGHT TO VARENNES

FOLLOWING TWO YEARS OF ARDUOUS DELIBERATIONS, the National Assembly was completing a new constitution before handing over the reigns of power to the king and the Legislative Assembly. The king, however, demonstrated his unwillingness to rule as a constitutional monarch and deserted his people. The response by the people of Paris is described by well-known journalist Louis-Maris Prudhomme in his newspaper.

Response to the King's Flight to Varennes

Louis-Marie Prudhomme, *Révolutions de Paris* (1791)

It was not until ten o'clock in the morning that the municipal government announced, by firing a cannon thrice, the unexpected event of the day. But for three hours the news had already been passing from mouth to mouth and was circulating in all quarters of the city. During these three hours many outrages might have been committed. The king had gone. This news produced a moment of anxiety, and everybody ran in a crowd to the palace of the Tuileries to see if it were true; but every one turned almost immediately to the hall where the National Assembly met, declaring that their king was in there and that Louis XVI might go where he please.

Then the people became curious to visit the apartments vacated by the royal family; they traversed them all, and we questioned the sentinels we found there, "Where, and how, could he have escaped? How could this fat royal person, who complained of the meanness of his lodging, manage to make himself invisible to the sentries, –he whose girth could stop up any passage?" The soldiers of the guard had nothing to say to this. . . .

Far from being "famished for a glimpse of the king," the people proved, by the way in which they took the escape of Louis XVI, that they were sick of the throne and tired of paying for it. If they had known, moreover, that Louis XVI, in his message, which was just then being read in the National Assembly, complained "that he had not been able to find in the palace of the Tuileries the most simple conveniences of life," the people might have been roused to some excess; but they knew their own strength and did not permit themselves any of those little exhibitions of vengeance which are natural to irritated weakness.

They contented themselves with making sport, in their own way, of royalty and of the man who was invested with it. The portrait of the king was taken down from its place of honor and hung on the door. A fruit woman took possession of Antoinette's bed and used it to display her cherries, saying, "It's the nation's turn now to be comfortable." A young girl refused to let them put the queen's bonnet on her head and trampled it with indignation and contempt.

Q *What kinds of responses did the people of Paris have to the king's flight?*

Source: J. H. Robinson, *Readings in European History* (New York: Ginn & Company, 1906), pp. 428–430.

clubs as a primary source of political instability during the revolution. The political clubs grew out of informal gatherings in the coffee houses and public spaces that had accompanied the elections to the Estates General. The most famous were the Jacobins (JAK-uh-binz), who first emerged as a gathering of more radical deputies at the beginning of the Revolution, especially during the events of the night of August 4, 1789. After October 1789, they occupied the former Jacobin convent in Paris. Jacobin clubs also formed in the provinces, where they served primarily as discussion groups. Eventually, they joined together in an extensive correspondence network and by spring 1790 were seeking affiliation with the Parisian club. One year later, there were nine hundred Jacobin clubs in France associated with the Parisian center. Members were usually the elite of their local societies, but they also included artisans and tradespeople.

In addition, by mid-1791, the government was still facing severe financial difficulties due to massive tax evasion. Despite all of their problems, however, the bourgeois politicians in charge remained relatively unified on the basis of their trust in the king. But Louis XVI disastrously undercut them. Quite upset with the whole turn of revolutionary events, he sought to flee France in June 1791 and almost succeeded. Louis XVI, however, stopped for several unplanned rests to have his meals prepared and missed his military escort. Once recognized in Varennes, he could have escaped, but while waiting for a larger military escort, the National Guardsmen and members of the National Assembly arrived instead and brought him back to Paris. The flight to Varennes shattered the illusion of a loyal king (see box above). Though radicals called for the king to be deposed, the members of the National Assembly, fearful of the popular forces in Paris calling for a republic, chose to ignore the king's flight and pretended that he had been kidnapped. In this unsettled situation, with a discredited and seemingly disloyal monarch, the new Legislative Assembly held its first session in October 1791.

Because the National Assembly had passed a "self-denying ordinance" that prohibited the reelection of its members, the composition of the Legislative Assembly turned out to be quite different from that of the National Assembly. The clerics and nobles were largely gone. Most of the representatives were men of property; many were lawyers. Although lacking national reputations, most had gained experience in the new revolutionary politics and prominence in their local areas through the National Guard, the Jacobin clubs, and the many elective offices spawned by the administrative reordering of France. The king made what seemed to be a genuine effort to work with the new Legislative Assembly, but France's relations with the rest of Europe soon led to Louis's downfall.

OPPOSITION FROM ABROAD By this time, most ultra royalists had emigrated, including the Count d'Artois, the king's younger brother, and the Count de Provence (later Louis XVIII). In October 1791, the Legislative Assembly ordered the émigré nobles to return to France or face the loss of their property and be legally classified as traitors. Louis XVI vetoed this law, raising doubts about his willingness to support the new constitution. Meanwhile, some European monarchs had become concerned about the French example and feared that revolution would spread to their countries. On August 27, 1791, Emperor Leopold II of Austria and King Frederick William II of Prussia had issued the Declaration of Pillnitz, which invited other European monarchs to take "the most effectual means . . . to put the king of France in a state to strengthen, in the most perfect liberty, the bases of a monarchical government equally becoming to the rights of sovereigns and to the well-being of the French Nation."[6] European monarchs were too suspicious of each other to undertake such a plan; however, an increasing number of monarchs openly supported the French émigrés, especially in the Rhineland where most émigrés had fled. In January 1791, the Legislative Assembly sent an ultimatum to Austria, demanding that the Holy Roman emperor, Leopold II, expel all French émigrés. The emperor refused, and the Legislative Assembly declared war on Austria on April 20, 1792. Why take such a step in view of its obvious dangers? Many people in France wanted war. Reactionaries hoped that a preoccupation with war would cool off the Revolution; French defeat, which seemed likely in view of the army's disintegration, might even lead to the restoration of the old regime. Leftists hoped that war would consolidate the Revolution at home and spread it to all of Europe.

The French fared badly in the initial fighting. A French army invaded the Austrian Netherlands (Belgium) but was routed, and Paris now feared invasion. In fact, if the Austrians and Prussians had cooperated, they might have seized Paris in May or June. Alarmed by the turn of events, the Legislative Assembly called for 20,000 National Guardsmen from the provinces to come and defend Paris. One group came from Marseilles singing a rousing war song, soon known as the "Marseillaise," that three years later became the French national anthem:

> *Let's go, children of the fatherland*
> *The day of glory has arrived.*
> *Against us, is tyranny*
> *The bloody flag is raised.*
> *The bloody flag is raised.*
> *Do you hear in the countryside*
> *The roar of their fierce soldiers?*
> *They come right into our arms*
> *To slaughter your sons*
> *And your companions.*
> *To arm, citizens!*
> *Form up your battalions!*
> *Let us march, let us march!*
> *That their impure blood will water our fields.*[7]

As fears of invasion grew, a frantic search for scapegoats began; as one observer noted, "Everywhere you hear the cry that the king is betraying us, the generals are betraying us, that nobody is to be trusted; . . . that Paris will be taken in six weeks by the Austrians. . . . We are on a volcano ready to spout flames."[8] Defeats in war coupled with economic shortages in the spring reinvigorated popular groups that had been dormant since the previous summer and led to renewed political demonstrations, especially against the king. Radical Parisian political groups, declaring themselves an insurrectionary commune, organized a mob attack on the royal palace and Legislative Assembly in August 1792, took the king captive, and forced the Legislative Assembly to suspend the monarchy and call for a national convention, chosen on the basis of universal male suffrage, to decide on the future form of government. The French Revolution was about to enter a more radical stage as power passed from the assembly to the new Paris Commune, composed of many who proudly called themselves the **sans-culottes** (sahn-koo-LUT *or* sanz-koo-LAHTSS), ordinary patriots without fine clothes. Although it has become customary to equate the more radical sans-culottes with working people or the poor, many were merchants and better-off artisans who were often the elite of their neighborhoods and trades.

The Radical Revolution

Before the National Convention met, the Paris Commune dominated the political scene. Led by the newly appointed minister of justice, Georges Danton (ZHORZH dahn-TAWNH) (1759–1794), the sans-culottes sought revenge on those who had aided the king and resisted the popular will. The advance of a Prussian army on Paris intensified the fears of treachery. Thousands of presumed traitors were arrested and then massacred as ordinary Parisian tradespeople and artisans solved the problem of overcrowded prisons by mass executions of their inmates. In September 1792, the newly elected National Convention began its sessions. Although it was called to draft a new constitution, it also acted as the sovereign ruling body of France.

Socially, the composition of the National Convention was similar to that of its predecessors. Dominated by lawyers, professionals, and property owners, it also included for the first time a handful of artisans. Two-thirds of the deputies were under age forty-five, and almost all had had political experience as a result of the Revolution. Almost all were also intensely distrustful of the king and his activities. It was therefore no surprise that the convention's first major step on September 21 was to abolish the monarchy and establish a republic. But that was about as far as members of the convention could agree, and the National Convention soon split into factions over the fate of the king. The two most important were the **Girondins** (juh-RAHN-dinz) (so-called because their leaders came from the department of Gironde, located in southwestern France) and the **Mountain** (so-called because its members' seats were on the side of the convention hall where the floor slanted upward). Both were members of the Jacobin club.

DOMESTIC CRISES Representing primarily the provinces, the Girondins came to fear the radical mobs in Paris and were

Execution of the King. At the beginning of 1793, the National Convention decreed the death of the king, and on January 21 of that year, Louis XVI was executed. As seen in this engraving, a new revolutionary device, the guillotine, was used to execute the king.

disposed to keep the king alive as a hedge against future eventualities. The Mountain represented the interests of the city of Paris and owed much of its strength to the radical and popular elements in the city, although the members of the Mountain themselves were middle class. The Mountain won out at the beginning of 1793 when the National Convention found the king guilty of treason by a vote of 387 to 334 and sentenced him to death. On January 21, 1793, the king was executed, and the destruction of the old regime was complete. Now there could be no turning back. But the execution of the king produced further challenges by creating new enemies for the Revolution both at home and abroad while strengthening those who were already its enemies.

Factional disputes between the Girondins and the Mountain were only one aspect of France's domestic crisis in 1792 and 1793. In Paris, the local government was controlled by the Commune, which drew a number of its leaders from the city's artisans and shopkeepers. The Commune favored radical change and put constant pressure on the National Convention, pushing it to ever more radical positions. As one man warned his fellow deputies, "Never forget that you were sent here by the sans-culottes."[9] At the end of May and the beginning of June 1793, the Commune organized a demonstration, invaded the National Convention, and forced the arrest and execution of the leading Girondins, thereby leaving the Mountain in control of the convention.

The National Convention itself still did not rule all of France. The authority of the convention was repudiated in western France, particularly in the department of the Vendée (vahnh-DAY), by peasants who revolted against the new military draft (see "A Nation in Arms" later in this chapter). The Vendean rebellion soon escalated into a full-blown counterrevolutionary appeal: "Long live the king and our good priests. We want our king, our priests and the old regime." Some of France's major provincial cities, including Lyons (LYOHNH) and Marseilles (mar-SAY), also began to break away from the central authority. Arguing as Marseilles did that "it is time for the anarchy of a few men of blood to stop,"[10] these cities favored a decentralized republic to free themselves from the ascendancy of Paris. In no way did they favor breaking up the "indivisible republic."

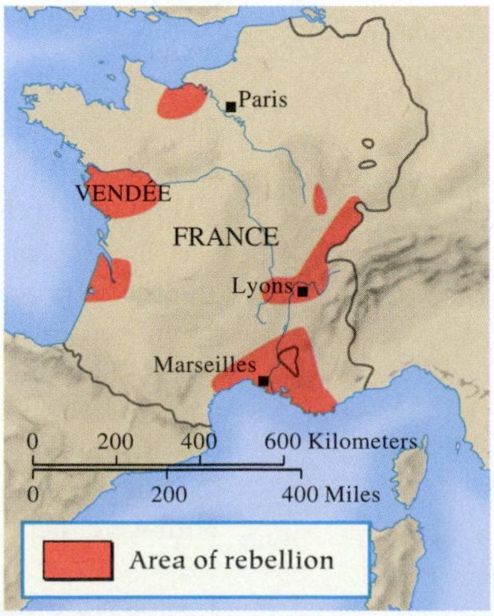

Rebellion in France

FOREIGN CRISIS Domestic turmoil was paralleled by a foreign crisis. Early in 1793, after Louis XVI had been executed, much of Europe—an informal coalition of Austria, Prussia, Spain, Portugal, Britain, and the Dutch Republic—was pitted against France. Carried away by initial successes and their own rhetoric, the French welcomed the struggle. Danton exclaimed to the convention, "They threaten you with kings! You have thrown down your gauntlet to them, and this gauntlet is a king's head, the signal of their coming death."[11] Grossly overextended, the French armies began to experience reverses, and by late spring some members of the anti-French coalition were poised for an invasion of France. If they succeeded, both the Revolution and the revolutionaries would be destroyed and the old regime reestablished. The Revolution had reached a decisive moment.

Gianni Dagli Orti/The Art Archive at Art Resource, NY

Musée de la Ville de Paris, Musée Carnavalet, Paris//Snark/Art Resource

Citizens in the New French Army. To save the Republic from its foreign enemies, the National Convention created a revolutionary army of unprecedented size. The illustration above, from a book of paintings on the French Revolution by the Lesueur brothers, shows three citizens learning to drill, while a young volunteer is being armed and outfitted by his family. The illustration at the left, also by the Lesueur brothers, shows two volunteers joyfully going off to fight.

To meet these crises, the National Convention adopted a program of curbing anarchy and counterrevolution at home while attempting to win the war by a vigorous mobilization of the people. To administer the government, the convention gave broad powers to an executive committee known as the Committee of Public Safety, which was dominated initially by Danton. For the next twelve months, virtually the same twelve members were reelected and gave the country the leadership it needed to weather the domestic and foreign crises of 1793. One of the most important members was Maximilien Robespierre (mak-see-meel-YENH ROHBZ-pyayr) (1758–1794), a small-town lawyer who had moved to Paris as a member of the Estates-General. Politics was his life, and he was dedicated to using power to benefit the people, whom he loved in the abstract though not on a one-to-one basis.

A NATION IN ARMS To meet the crisis and save the Republic from its foreign enemies, the Committee of Public Safety decreed a universal mobilization of the nation on August 23, 1793:

> Young men will fight, young men are called to conquer. Married men will forge arms, transport military baggage and guns and will prepare food supplies. Women, who at long last are to take their rightful place in the revolution and follow their true destiny, will forget their futile tasks: their delicate hands will work at making clothes for soldiers; they will make tents and they will extend their tender care to shelters where the defenders of the Patrie [nation] will receive the help that their wounds require. Children will make lint of old cloth. It is for them that we are fighting: children, those beings destined to gather all the fruits of the revolution, will raise their pure hands toward the skies. And old men, performing their missions again, as of yore, will be guided to the public squares of the cities where they will kindle the courage of young warriors and preach the doctrines of hate for kings and the unity of the Republic.[12]

In less than a year, the French revolutionary government had raised an army of 650,000; by September 1794, it numbered 1,169,000. The Republic's army—a **nation in arms**—was the largest Europe had ever seen. It now pushed the allies back across the Rhine and even conquered the Austrian Netherlands (see Map 19.2). By May 1795, the anti-French coalition of 1793 was breaking up.

Historians have focused on the importance of the French revolutionary army in the creation of modern nationalism. Previously, wars had been fought between governments or ruling dynasties by relatively small armies of professional soldiers.

MAP 19.2 French Expansion During the Revolutionary Wars, 1792–1799. The conservative rulers of Europe, appalled at the republican character of the French Revolution, took up arms to restore the Bourbon monarchy. The French responded with a people's army, the largest ever seen, which pushed the invaders out of France, annexed the Austrian Netherlands and some Italian territory, and created a number of French satellite states.

Q *Why would Austria desire cooperation from the German states if it wanted to wage war on France?*

The new French army, however, was the creation of a "people's" government; its wars were now "people's" wars. The entire nation was to be involved in the war. But when dynastic wars became people's wars, warfare increased in ferocity and lack of restraint. Although innocent civilians had suffered in the earlier struggles, now the carnage became appalling at times. The wars of the French revolutionary era opened the door to the total war of the modern world.

THE COMMITTEE OF PUBLIC SAFETY AND THE REIGN OF TERROR To meet the domestic crisis, the National Convention and the Committee of Public Safety instituted the "Reign of Terror." Revolutionary courts were organized to protect the Republic from its internal enemies, "who either by their conduct, their contacts, their words or their writings, showed themselves to be supporters of tyranny or enemies of liberty" or "who have not constantly manifested their attachment to the revolution."[13] Victims of the Terror ranged from royalists, such as Queen Marie Antoinette, to former revolutionary Girondins, including Olympe de Gouges, the chief advocate for political rights for women, and even included thousands of peasants. Many victims were persons who had opposed the radical activities of the sans-culottes. Robespierre forced through the Convention a law that denied suspects sent before the Revolutionary Tribunal all rights to defend themselves. This law increased the pace of executions. In the course of nine months, 16,000 people were officially killed under the blade of the guillotine, a revolutionary device for the quick and efficient separation of heads from bodies. But the true number of the Terror's victims was probably totaled closer to 250,000 (see the box on p. 577). The bulk of the Terror's executions took place during the Vendée revolt and in cities such as Lyons and Marseilles, places that had been in open rebellion against the authority of the National Convention.

Military force in the form of revolutionary armies was used to bring recalcitrant cities and districts back under the control of the National Convention. Marseilles fell to a revolutionary army in August. Starving Lyons surrendered early in October after two months of bombardment and resistance. Since Lyons was France's second city after Paris and had defied the National

JUSTICE IN THE REIGN OF TERROR

THE REIGN OF TERROR CREATED A REPRESSIVE environment in which revolutionary courts often acted quickly to condemn traitors to the revolutionary cause. In this account, an English visitor describes the court, the procession to the scene of execution, and the final execution procedure.

J. G. Milligen, *The Revolutionary Tribunal* (Paris, October 1793)

In the center of the hall, under a statue of Justice, holding scales in one hand, and a sword in the other, sat Dumas, the President, with the other judges. . . . To the right were benches on which the accused were placed in several rows, and *gendarmes* with carbines and fixed bayonets by their sides. To the left was the jury.

Never can I forget the mournful appearance of these funereal processions to the place of execution. The march was opened by a detachment of mounted *gendarmes*—the carts followed; they were the same carts as those that are used in Paris for carrying wood; four boards were placed across them for seats, and on each board sat two, and sometimes three victims; their hands were tied behind their backs, and the constant jolting of the cart made them nod their heads up and down, to the great amusement of the spectators. On the front of the cart stood Samson, the executioner, or one of his sons or assistants; *gendarmes* on foot marched by the side; then followed a hackney, in which was the reporting clerk, whose duty it was to witness the execution, and then return to the public accuser's office to report the execution of what they called the law.

The process of execution was also a sad and heartrending spectacle. In the middle of the Place de la Revolution was erected a guillotine, in front of a colossal statue of Liberty, represented seated on a rock, a cap on her head, a spear in her hand, the other reposing on a shield. On one side of the scaffold were drawn out a sufficient number of carts, with large baskets painted red, to receive the heads and bodies of the victims. Those bearing the condemned moved on slowly to the foot of the guillotine; the culprits were led out in turn, and if necessary, supported by two of the executioner's assistants, but their assistance was rarely required. Most of these unfortunates ascended the scaffold with a determined step—many of them looked up firmly on the menacing instrument of death, beholding for the last time the rays of the glorious sun, beaming on the polished axe; and I have seen some young men actually dance a few steps before they went up to be strapped to the perpendicular plane, which was then tilted to a horizontal plane in a moment, and ran on the grooves until the neck was secured and closed in by a moving board, when the head passed through what was called, in derision, "the republican toilet seat"; the weighty knife was then dropped with a heavy fall; and, with incredible dexterity and rapidity, two executioners tossed the body into the basket, while another threw the head after it.

Q *How were the condemned taken to the executioner? How did this serve to inflame the crowds? How were people executed? Why?*

Source: J. M. Thompson, *English Witness of the French Revolution* (Oxford: Blackwell, 1938).

Convention during a time when the Republic was in peril, the Committee of Public Safety decided to make an example of it. By April 1794, some 1,880 citizens of Lyons had been executed. When guillotining proved too slow, cannon fire and grapeshot were used to blow condemned men into open graves. A German observed:

> Whole ranges of houses, always the most handsome, [were] burnt. The churches, convents, and all the dwellings of the former patricians were in ruins. When I came to the guillotine, the blood of those who had been executed a few hours beforehand was still running in the street. . . . I said to a group of sans-culottes that it would be decent to clear away all this human blood. Why should it be cleared? one of them said to me. It's the blood of aristocrats and rebels. The dogs should lick it up.[14]

In the Vendée, revolutionary armies were also brutal in defeating the rebel armies. After destroying one army on December 12, the commander of the revolutionary army ordered that no quarter be given: "The road to Laval is strewn with corpses. Women, priests, monks, children, all have been put to death. I have spared nobody." The Terror was at its most destructive in the Vendée. Forty-two percent of the death sentences during the Terror were passed in territories affected by the Vendée rebellion. Perhaps the most notorious act of violence occurred in Nantes, where victims were executed by sinking them in barges in the Loire River.

To a great extent, the Terror demonstrated little class prejudice. Estimates are that the nobles constituted 8 percent of its victims; the middle classes, 25; the clergy, 6; and the peasant and laboring classes, 60. To the Committee of Public Safety, this bloodletting was only a temporary expedient. Once the war and domestic emergency were over, "the republic of virtue" would ensue, and the Declaration of the Rights of Man and the Citizen would be fully established. Although theoretically a republic, the French government during the Terror was led by a group of twelve men who ordered the execution of people as national enemies. But how did they justify this? Louis Saint-Just (sanh-ZHOOST), one of the younger members of the Committee of Public Safety, explained their rationalization in a speech to the convention: "Since the French people has manifested its will, everything opposed to it is outside the sovereign.

ROBESPIERRE AND REVOLUTIONARY GOVERNMENT

IN ITS TIME OF TROUBLES, THE NATIONAL CONVENTION, under the direction of the Committee of Public Safety, instituted the Reign of Terror to preserve the Revolution from its internal enemies. In this selection, Maximilien Robespierre, one of the committee's leading members, tries to justify the violence to which these believers in republican liberty resorted.

Robespierre, Speech on Revolutionary Government

The theory of revolutionary government is as new as the Revolution that created it. . . . It behooves us to explain it to all in order that we may rally good citizens, at least, in support of the principles governing the public interest.

It is the function of government to guide the moral and physical energies of the nation toward the purposes for which it was established.

The object of constitutional government is to preserve the Republic; the object of the revolutionary government is to establish it.

Revolution is the war waged by liberty against its enemies; a constitution is that which crowns the edifice of freedom once victory has been won and the nation is at peace.

The revolutionary government has to summon extraordinary activity to its aid precisely because it is at war. It is subjected to less binding and less uniform regulations, because the circumstances in which it finds itself are tempestuous and shifting above all because it is compelled to deploy, swiftly and incessantly, new resources to meet new and pressing dangers.

The principal concern of constitutional government is civil liberty; that of revolutionary government, public liberty. Under a constitutional government little more is required than to protect the individual against abuses by the state, whereas revolutionary government is obliged to defend the state itself against the factions that assail it from every quarter.

To good citizens revolutionary government owes the full protection of the state; to the enemies of the people it owes only death.

Source: G. Rude, ed., *Robespierre* (Upper Saddle River, N.J.: Prentice Hall, 1967).

Q *How did Robespierre justify the violent activities of the French revolutionaries? In your opinion, do his explanations justify his actions? How does this document glorify the state and advance preservation of the state as the highest goal of modern politicians and policy makers?*

Whatever is outside the sovereign is an enemy."[15] Clearly, Saint-Just was referring to Rousseau's concept of the general will, but it is equally apparent that these twelve men, in the name of the Republic, had taken upon themselves the right to ascertain the sovereign will of the French people (see the box above) and to kill their enemies as "outside the sovereign."

THE "REPUBLIC OF VIRTUE" Along with the Terror, the Committee of Public Safety took other steps both to control France and to create a new republican order and new republican citizens. By spring 1793, the committee was sending "representatives on mission" as agents of the central government to all departments to explain the war emergency measures and to implement the laws dealing with the wartime emergency.

The committee also attempted to provide some economic controls, especially since members of the more radical working class were advocating them. It established a system of requisitioning food supplies for the cities enforced by the forays of revolutionary armies into the countryside. The Law of the General Maximum established price controls on goods declared of first necessity, ranging from food and drink to fuel and clothing. The controls failed to work very well because the government lacked the machinery to enforce them.

THE ROLE OF WOMEN Women continued to play an active role in this radical phase of the French Revolution. As spectators at sessions of revolutionary clubs and the National Convention, women made the members and deputies aware of their demands. When on Sunday, February 25, 1793, a group of women appealed formally to the National Convention for lower bread prices, the convention reacted by adjourning until Tuesday. The women responded bitterly by accosting the deputies: "We are adjourned until Tuesday; but as for us, we adjourn ourselves until Monday. When our children ask us for milk we don't adjourn them until the day after tomorrow."[16] In 1793, two women—an actress and a chocolate manufacturer—founded the Society for Revolutionary Republican Women. Composed largely of working-class women, this Parisian group viewed itself as a "family of sisters" and vowed "to rush to the defense of the Fatherland."

Despite the importance of women to the revolutionary cause, male revolutionaries reacted disdainfully to female participation in political activity. In the radical phase of the Revolution, the Paris Commune outlawed women's clubs and forbade women to be present at its meetings. One of its members explained why:

> It is horrible, it is contrary to all laws of nature for a woman to want to make herself a man. The Council must recall that some time ago these denatured women, these viragos, wandered through the markets with the red cap to sully that badge of liberty and wanted to force all women to take off the modest headdress that is appropriate for them [the bonnet]. . . . Is it the place of women to propose motions? Is it the place of women to place themselves at the head of our armies?[17]

Most men—radical or conservative—agreed that a woman's place was in the home and not in military or political affairs. As one man asked, "Since when is it considered normal for a

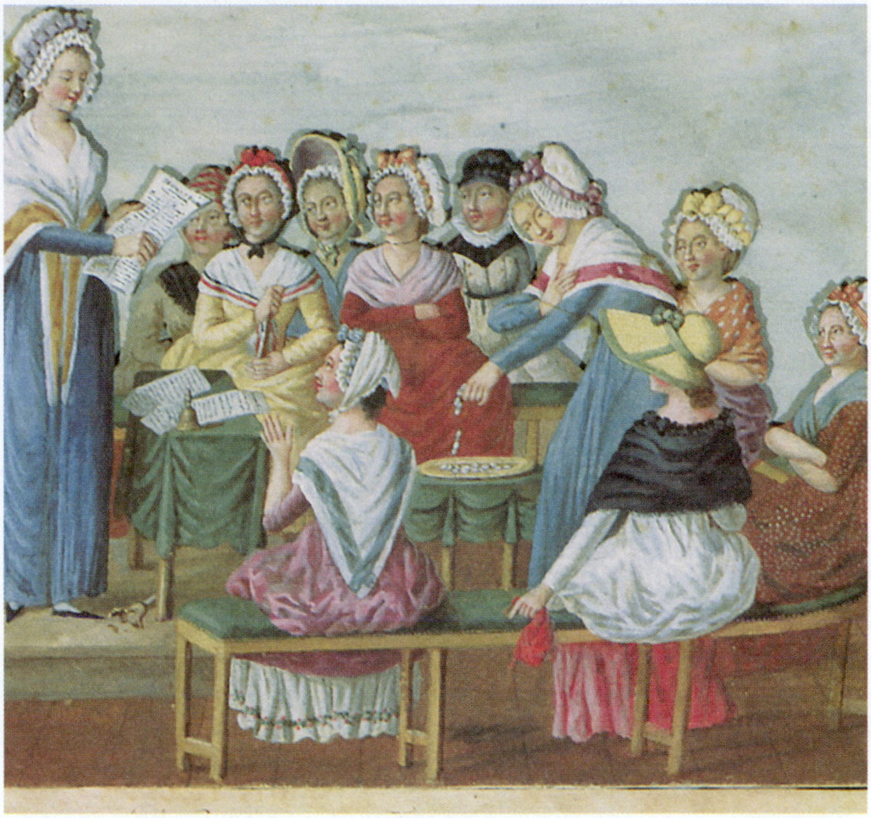

Musée de la Ville de Paris, Musée Carnavalet, Paris//Erich Lessing/Art Resource, NY

Women Patriots. Women played a variety of roles in the events of the French Revolution. This picture shows a middle-class women's patriotic club discussing the decrees of the National Convention, an indication that some women had become highly politicized by the upheavals of the Revolution. The women are also giving coins to create a fund for impoverished families.

woman to abandon the pious care of her home, the cradle of her children, to listen to speeches in the public forum?"[18]

DE-CHRISTIANIZATION AND THE NEW CALENDAR In its attempt to create a new order, the National Convention also pursued a policy of **de-Christianization**. The word *saint* was removed from street names, churches were pillaged and closed by revolutionary armies, and priests were encouraged to marry. In Paris, the cathedral of Notre Dame was designated the Temple of Reason (see the box on p. 580). In November 1793, a public ceremony dedicated to the worship of reason was held in the former cathedral; patriotic maidens adorned in white dresses paraded before a temple of reason where the high altar once stood. At the end of the ceremony, a female figure personifying Liberty rose out of the temple. As Robespierre came to realize, de-Christianization backfired because France was still overwhelmingly Catholic. In fact, de-Christianization created more enemies than friends.

Yet another manifestation of de-Christianization was the adoption of a new republican calendar on October 5, 1793. Years would no longer be numbered from the birth of Jesus but from September 22, 1792, the day the French Republic was proclaimed. Thus, at the time the calendar was adopted, the French were already living in year II. The calendar contained twelve months; each month consisted of three ten-day weeks called *décades* (day-KAD) with the tenth day of each week a rest day (*décadi*). This eliminated Sundays and Sunday worship services and put an end to the ordering of French lives by a Christian calendar that emphasized Sundays, saints' days, and church holidays and festivals. Religious celebrations were to be replaced by revolutionary festivals. Especially important were the five days (six in leap years) left over in the calendar at the end of the year. These days were to form a half-week of festivals to celebrate the revolutionary virtues—Virtue, Intelligence, Labor, Opinion, and Rewards. The sixth extra day in a leap year would be a special festival day when French citizens would "come from all parts of the Republic to celebrate liberty and equality, to cement by their embraces the national fraternity." Of course, ending church holidays also reduced the number of nonworking holidays from fifty-six to thirty-two, a goal long recommended by eighteenth-century economic theorists.

The calendar's anti-Christian purpose was also apparent in the renaming of the months of the year. The months received names that were supposed to evoke the seasons, the temperature, or the state of the vegetation: Véndemiaire (vahnh-duh-MYAYR) (harvest—the first month of thirty days beginning September 22), Brumaire (broo-MAYR) (mist), Frimaire (free-MAYR) (frost), Nivose (nee-VOHZ) (snow), Pluviôse (ploo-VYOHZ) (rain), Ventose (vahnh-TOHZ) (wind), Germinal (jayr-mee-NAHL) (seeding), Floréal (floh-ray-AHL) (flowering), Prairial (pray-RYAL) (meadows), Messidor (MESS-i-dor) (wheat harvest), Thermidor (TAYR-mi-dor) (heat), and Fructidor (FROOK-ti-dor) (ripening).

The new calendar faced intense popular opposition, and the revolutionary government relied primarily on coercion to win its acceptance. Journalists, for example, were commanded to use republican dates in their newspaper articles. But many people refused to give up the old calendar, as one official reported:

> Sundays and Catholic holidays, even if there are ten in a row, have for some time been celebrated with as much pomp and splendor as before. The same cannot be said of *décadi*, which

DE-CHRISTIANIZATION

THE PHENOMENON OF DE-CHRISTIANIZATION PRODUCED some unusual spectacles during the radical stage of the French Revolution. This selection from the minutes of the National Convention describes how the cathedral of Notre Dame was put to new use as the Temple of Reason.

The Temple of Reason

A member puts in the form of a motion the demand of the citizens of Paris that the metropolitan cathedral [Notre Dame] be henceforth the Temple of Reason.

A member requests that the goddess of Reason place herself at the side of the president.

The attorney of the Commune conducts her to the desk. The president and the secretaries give her the fraternal kiss in the midst of applause. . . .

A member demands that the National Convention march in a body, in the midst of the People, to the Temple of Reason to sing the hymn of Liberty there.

This proposal is passed.

The Convention marches with the People to the Temple of Reason in the midst of general enthusiasm and joyful acclamations.

Having entered the Temple of Reason, they sing the following hymn:

Descend, O Liberty, daughter of Nature:
The People have recaptured their immortal power;
Over the pompous remains of age-old imposture
Their hands raise thine altar.
Come, vanquisher of kings, Europe gazes upon you;
Come, vanquish the false gods.
Thou, holy Liberty, come dwell in this temple;
Be the goddess of the French. . . .
All kings make war on the sovereign People;
Let them henceforth fall at thy feet, O goddess;
Soon on the coffins of the world's tyrants
the world's peoples will swear peace.

Q *What was the purpose of de-Christianization? Based on the ceremony described here, how effective do you think it was?*

Source: P. H. Beik, *The French Revolution* (New York: Walker & Co., 1970).

> is observed by only a small handful of citizens. The first to disobey the law are the wives of public officials, who dress up on the holidays of the old calendar and abstain from work more religiously than anyone else.[19]

The government could hardly expect peasants to follow the new calendar when government officials were ignoring it. Napoleon later perceived that the revolutionary calendar was politically unpopular, and he simply abandoned it on January 1, 1806 (11 Nivôse XIV).

In addition to its anti-Christian function, the revolutionary calendar had also served to mark the Revolution as a new historical beginning, a radical break in time. Revolutionary upheavals often project millenarian expectations, the hope that a new age is dawning. The revolutionary dream of a new order presupposed the creation of a new human being freed from the old order and its symbols, a new citizen surrounded by a framework of new habits. Restructuring time itself offered the opportunity to forge new habits and create a lasting new order.

EQUALITY AND SLAVERY Early in the French Revolution, the desire for equality led to a discussion of what to do about slavery. A club called Friends of the Blacks advocated the abolition of slavery, which was achieved in France in September 1791. Nevertheless, French planters in the West Indies, who profited greatly from the use of slaves on their sugar plantations, opposed the abolition of slavery in the French colonies. When the National Convention came into power, the issue was revisited, and on February 4, 1794, guided by ideals of equality, the government abolished slavery in the colonies.

In one French colony, slaves had already rebelled for their freedom. In 1791, black slaves in the French sugar colony of Saint-Domingue (san doh-MAYNG) (the western third of the island of Hispaniola), inspired by the ideals of the revolution occurring in France, revolted against French plantation owners. Slaves attacked, killing plantation owners and their families and burning their buildings. White planters retaliated with equal brutality. One wealthy French settler reported, "How can we stay in a country where slaves have raised their hands against their masters?"

Eventually, leadership of the revolt was taken over by Toussaint L'Ouverture (too-SANH loo-vayr-TOOR) (1746–1803), a son of African slaves, who seized control of all of Hispaniola by 1801. Although Napoleon had accepted the revolutionary ideal of equality, he did not deny the reports of white planters that the massacres of white planters by slaves demonstrated the savage nature of blacks. In 1802, he reinstated slavery in the French West Indian colonies and sent an army that captured L'Ouverture, who died in a French dungeon within a year. But the French soldiers, weakened by

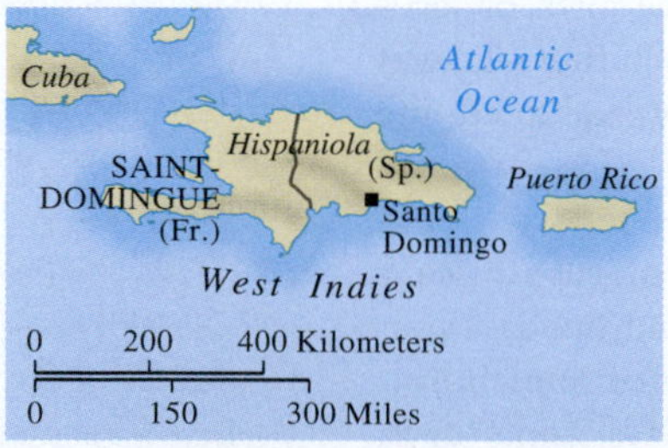

Revolt in Saint-Domingue (Haiti)

disease, soon succumbed to the slave forces. On January 1, 1804, the western part of Hispaniola, now called Haiti, announced its freedom and became the first independent state in Latin America. Despite Napoleon's efforts to the contrary, one of the French revolutionary ideals had triumphed abroad.

DECLINE OF THE COMMITTEE OF PUBLIC SAFETY Maintaining the revolutionary ideals in France proved not to be easy. By the Law of 14 Frimaire (passed on December 4, 1793), the Committee of Public Safety sought to centralize the administration of France more effectively and to exercise greater control in order to check the excesses of the Reign of Terror. The activities of both the representatives on mission and the revolutionary armies were scrutinized more carefully, and the campaign against Christianity was also dampened. Finally, in 1794, the Committee of Public Safety turned against its radical Parisian supporters, executed the leaders of the revolutionary Paris Commune, and turned it into a docile tool. This might have been a good idea for the sake of order, but in suppressing the people who had been its chief supporters, the National Convention alienated an important group. At the same time, the French had been successful against their foreign foes. The military successes meant that the Terror no longer served much purpose. But the Terror continued because Robespierre, now its dominant figure, had become obsessed with purifying the body politic of all the corrupt. Only then could the Republic of Virtue follow. Many deputies in the National Convention, however, feared that they were not safe while Robespierre was free to act. An anti-Robespierre coalition in the National Convention, eager now to destroy Robespierre before he destroyed them, gathered enough votes to condemn him. Robespierre was guillotined on July 28, 1794, beginning a reaction that brought an end to this radical stage of the French Revolution.

The National Convention and its Committee of Public Safety had accomplished a great deal. By creating a nation in arms, they preserved the French Revolution and prevented it from being destroyed by its foreign enemies, who, if they had succeeded, would have reestablished the old monarchical order. Domestically, the Revolution had also been saved from the forces of counterrevolution. The committee's tactics, however, provided an example for the use of violence in domestic politics that has continued to bedevil the Western world to this day.

DEA/G. DAGLI ORTI/De Agostini/Getty Images

Robespierre. Maximilien Robespierre, seen here in a portrait by an unknown artist, eventually became the dominant figure in the Committee of Public Safety. Fear of Robespierre, however, led many in the National Convention to condemn him, and on July 28, 1794, he was executed.

Reaction and the Directory

After the execution of Robespierre, revolutionary fervor began to give way to the Thermidorean Reaction, named after the month of Thermidor. The Terror began to abate. The National Convention curtailed the power of the Committee of Public Safety, shut down the Jacobin club, and attempted to provide better protection for its deputies against the Parisian mobs. Churches were allowed to reopen for public worship, and a decree of February 21, 1795, gave freedom of worship to all cults. Economic regulation was dropped in favor of *laissez-faire* policies, another clear indication that moderate forces were regaining control of the Revolution. In addition, a new constitution, written in August 1795, reflected this more conservative republicanism or a desire for a stability that did not sacrifice the ideals of 1789.

To avoid the dangers of another single legislative assembly, the Constitution of 1795 established a national legislative assembly consisting of two chambers: a lower house, known as the Council of 500, whose function was to initiate legislation, and an upper house of 250 members, the Council of Elders, composed of married or widowed members over age forty, which would accept or reject the proposed laws. The 750 members of the two legislative bodies were chosen by electors who had to be owners or renters of property worth between one hundred and two hundred days' labor, a requirement that limited their number to 30,000, an even smaller base than the Constitution of 1791 had provided. The electors were chosen by the active citizens, now defined as all male taxpayers over the age of twenty-one. The executive authority or Directory consisted of five directors elected by the Council of Elders from a list presented by the Council of 500. To ensure some continuity from the old order to the new, the members of the National Convention ruled that two-thirds of the new members of the National Assembly must be chosen from their ranks. This decision set off disturbances in Paris and an insurrection at the beginning of October that was dispersed after fierce combat by an army contingent under the artillery general Napoleon Bonaparte. This would be the last time in the great French Revolution that the city of Paris would attempt to impose its wishes on the central government. Even more significant and ominous was this use of the army, which made it clear that the Directory from the beginning had to rely on the military for survival.

The period of the Directory was an era of materialistic reaction to the suffering and sacrifices that had been demanded in the Reign of Terror and the Republic of Virtue. Speculators made fortunes in property by taking advantage of the government's severe monetary problems. Elaborate fashions, which had gone out of style because of their identification with the nobility, were worn again. Gambling and roulette became popular once more. Groups of "gilded youth"—sons of the wealthy, with long hair and rumpled clothes—took to the streets to insult former supporters of the Revolution.

The government of the Directory had to contend with political enemies from both ends of the political spectrum. On the right, royalists who dreamed of restoring the monarchy continued their agitation; some still toyed with violent means. On the left, Jacobin hopes of power were revived by continuing economic problems, especially the total collapse in the value of the assignats. Some radicals even went beyond earlier goals, especially Gracchus Babeuf (GRAK-uss bah-BUFF), who sneered, "What is the French Revolution? An open war between patricians and plebeians, between rich and poor." Babeuf, who was appalled at the misery of the common people, wanted to abolish private property and eliminate private enterprise. His Conspiracy of Equals was crushed in 1796, and he was executed in 1797.

New elections in 1797 created even more uncertainty and instability. Battered by the left and right, unable to find a definitive solution to the country's economic problems, and still carrying on the wars left from the Committee of Public Safety, the Directory increasingly relied on the military to maintain its power. This led to a coup d'etat in 1799 in which the successful and popular general Napoleon Bonaparte was able to seize power.

CHRONOLOGY	The French Revolution
Assembly of notables	1787
National Assembly (Constituent Assembly)	**1789–1791**
Meeting of Estates-General	May 5, 1789
Formation of National Assembly	June 17, 1789
Tennis Court Oath	June 20, 1789
Fall of the Bastille	July 14, 1789
Great Fear	Summer 1789
Declaration of the Rights of Man and the Citizen	August 26, 1789
Women's march to Versailles; king's return to Paris	October 5–6, 1789
Civil Constitution of the Clergy	July 12, 1790
Flight of the king	June 20–21, 1791
Legislative Assembly	**1791–1792**
France declares war on Austria	April 20, 1792
Attack on the royal palace	August 10, 1792
National Convention	**1792–1795**
Abolition of the monarchy	September 21, 1792
Execution of the king	January 21, 1793
Universal mobilization of the nation	August 23, 1793
Execution of Robespierre	July 28, 1794
Directory	**1795–1799**
Constitution of 1795 is adopted	August 22, 1795

The Age of Napoleon

Q **FOCUS QUESTION:** Which aspects of the French Revolution did Napoleon preserve, and which did he destroy?

Napoleon (1769–1821) dominated both French and European history from 1799 to 1815. The coup that brought him to power occurred exactly ten years after the outbreak of the French Revolution. In a sense, Napoleon brought the Revolution to an end, but he was also its child; he even called himself the Son of the Revolution. The French Revolution had made possible his rise first in the military and then to supreme power in France. Even beyond this, Napoleon had once said, "I am the Revolution," and he never ceased to remind the French that they owed to him the preservation of all that was beneficial in the revolutionary program.

The Rise of Napoleon

Napoleon was born in Corsica in 1769, only a few months after France had annexed the island. The son of an Italian lawyer whose family stemmed from the Florentine nobility, Napoleone Buonaparte (to use his birth name) grew up in the countryside of Corsica, a willful and demanding child who nevertheless developed discipline, thriftiness, and loyalty to his family. His father's connections in France enabled him to study first at a school in the French town of Autun, where he learned to speak French, and then to obtain a royal scholarship to study at a military school. At that time, he changed his first name to the more French-sounding Napoleon (he did not change his last name to Bonaparte until 1796).

Napoleon's military education led to his commission in 1785 as a lieutenant, although he was not well liked by his fellow officers because he was short, spoke with an Italian accent, and had little money. For the next seven years, Napoleon spent much of his time reading the works of the philosophes, especially Rousseau, and educating himself in military matters by studying the campaigns of great military leaders from the past, including Alexander the Great, Charlemagne, and Frederick the Great. The French Revolution and the European war that

RMN-Grand Palais/Art Resource, NY

Napoleon as a Young Officer. Napoleon rose quickly through the military ranks, being promoted to the rank of brigadier general at the age of twenty-five. This painting of Napoleon by the Romantic painter Baron Antoine-Jean Gros (GROH) presents an idealized, heroic image of the young leader.

followed broadened his sights and presented him with new opportunities.

NAPOLEON'S MILITARY CAREER Napoleon rose quickly through the ranks. In 1792, he became a captain and in the following year performed so well as an artillery commander in the capture of Toulon that he was promoted to the rank of brigadier general in 1794, when he was only twenty-five. In October 1795, he saved the National Convention from the Parisian mob, for which he was promoted to the rank of major general.

By this time, Napoleon had become a hero in some Parisian social circles, where he met Josephine de Beauharnais (zhoh-seff-FEEN duh boh-ar-NAY), widow of a guillotined general. Six years older than Napoleon, she lived a life of luxury, thanks to gifts from her influential male lovers. Napoleon fell deeply in love with her, married her in 1796, and remained committed to her for many years, despite her well-known affairs with other men.

Soon after his marriage, Napoleon was made commander of the French army in Italy (see the box on p. 584). There he turned a group of ill-disciplined soldiers into an effective fighting force and in a series of stunning victories defeated the Austrians and dictated peace to them in 1797.

Throughout his Italian campaign, Napoleon won the confidence of his men by his energy, charm, and ability to comprehend complex issues quickly and make decisions rapidly. He was tough with his officers and drove them relentlessly. With rank-and-file soldiers, he took a different approach. He ate with them, provided good food and clothing, and charmed them with his words. "They knew I was their patron," Napoleon once remarked. Throughout the rest of his life, these qualities, combined with his keen intelligence, ease with words, and supreme confidence in himself, enabled Napoleon to influence people and win their firm support. Napoleon liked to see himself as a man of destiny and a great man who mastered luck. He once said:

> A consecutive series of great actions never is the result of chance and luck, it always is the product of planning and genius. Great men are rarely known to fail in their most perilous enterprises. . . . Is it because they are lucky that they become great? No, but being great, they have been able to master luck.[20]

Napoleon also saw himself as a military genius who had a "touch for leading, which could not be learned from books, nor by practice."

In 1797, Napoleon returned to France as a conquering hero and was given command of an army training to invade England. Believing that the French were unready for such an invasion, he proposed instead to strike indirectly at Britain by taking Egypt and threatening India, a major source of British wealth. But the British controlled the seas and by 1799 had cut off supplies from Napoleon's army in Egypt. Seeing no future in certain defeat, Napoleon did not hesitate to abandon his army and return to Paris, where he participated in the coup d'état that ultimately led to his virtual dictatorship of France. He was only thirty years old at the time.

NAPOLEON IN CONTROL With the coup of 1799, a new form of the Republic was proclaimed with a constitution that established a bicameral legislative assembly elected indirectly to reduce the role of elections. Executive power in the new government was vested in the hands of three consuls, although, as Article 42 of the constitution said, "the decision of the First Consul shall suffice." As first consul, Napoleon directly controlled the entire executive authority of government. He had overwhelming influence over the legislature, appointed members of the bureaucracy, controlled the army, and conducted foreign affairs. In 1802, Napoleon was made consul for life, and in 1804 he returned France to monarchy when he crowned himself Emperor Napoleon I. This step undoubtedly satisfied his enormous ego but also stabilized the regime and provided a permanence not possible in the consulate. The revolutionary era that had begun with an attempt to limit arbitrary government had ended with a government far more autocratic than the monarchy of the old regime. As his reign progressed and the demands of war increased, Napoleon's regime became ever more dictatorial.

NAPOLEON AND PSYCHOLOGICAL WARFARE

IN 1796, AT THE AGE OF TWENTY-SEVEN, Napoleon Bonaparte was given command of the French army in Italy, where he won a series of stunning victories. His use of speed, deception, and surprise to overwhelm his opponents is well known. In this selection from a proclamation to his troops in Italy, Napoleon also appears to be a master of psychological warfare.

Napoleon Bonaparte, Proclamation to the French Troops in Italy (April 26, 1796)

Soldiers:

In a fortnight you have won six victories, taken twenty-one standards, fifty-five pieces of artillery, several strong positions, and conquered the richest part of Piedmont [in northern Italy]; you have captured 15,000 prisoners and killed or wounded more than 10,000 men. . . . You have won battles without cannon, crossed rivers without bridges, made forced marches without shoes, camped without brandy and often without bread. Soldiers of liberty, only republican troops could have endured what you have endured. Soldiers, you have our thanks! The grateful Patrie [nation] will owe its prosperity to you. . . .

The two armies which but recently attacked you with audacity are fleeing before you in terror; the wicked men who laughed at your misery and rejoiced at the thought of the triumphs of your enemies are confounded and trembling.

But, soldiers, as yet you have done nothing compared with what remains to be done. . . . Undoubtedly the greatest obstacles have been overcome; but you still have battles to fight, cities to capture, rivers to cross. Is there one among you whose courage is abating? No. . . . All of you are consumed with a desire to extend the glory of the French people; all of you long to humiliate those arrogant kings who dare to contemplate placing us in fetters; all of you desire to dictate a glorious peace, one which will indemnify the Patrie for the immense sacrifices it has made; all of you wish to be able to say with pride as you return to your villages, "I was with the victorious army of Italy!"

Q *What themes did Napoleon use to play on the emotions of his troops and inspire them to greater efforts? Do you think Napoleon believed these words? Why or why not?*

Source: J. H. Stewart, *A Documentary Survey of the French Revolution* (London: Macmillan, 1951).

The Domestic Policies of Emperor Napoleon

Napoleon often claimed that he had preserved the gains of the Revolution for the French people. The ideal of republican liberty had, of course, been destroyed by Napoleon's thinly disguised autocracy. But were revolutionary ideals maintained in other ways? An examination of his domestic policies will enable us to judge the truth or falsehood of Napoleon's assertion.

NAPOLEON AND THE CATHOLIC CHURCH In 1801, Napoleon made peace with the oldest and most implacable enemy of the Revolution, the Catholic Church. Napoleon himself was devoid of any personal faith; he was an eighteenth-century rationalist who regarded religion at most as a convenience. In Egypt, he called himself a Muslim; in France, a Catholic. But Napoleon saw the necessity to come to terms with the Catholic Church in order to stabilize his regime. In 1800, he had declared to the clergy of Milan: "It is my firm intention that the Christian, Catholic, and Roman religion shall be preserved in its entirety. . . . No society can exist without morality; there is no good morality without religion. It is religion alone, therefore, that gives to the State a firm and durable support."[21] Soon after making this statement, Napoleon opened negotiations with Pope Pius VII to reestablish the Catholic Church in France.

Both sides gained from the Concordat that Napoleon arranged with the pope in 1801. Although the pope gained the right to depose French bishops, this gave him little real control over the French Catholic Church, since the state retained the right to nominate bishops. The Catholic Church was also permitted to hold processions again and reopen the seminaries. But Napoleon gained more than the pope. Just by signing the Concordat, the pope acknowledged the accomplishments of the Revolution. Moreover, the pope agreed not to raise the question of the church lands confiscated during the Revolution. Contrary to the pope's wishes, Catholicism was not reestablished as the state religion; Napoleon was only willing to recognize Catholicism as the religion of a majority of the French people. The clergy would be paid by the state, but to avoid the appearance of a state church, Protestant ministers were also put on the state payroll. As a result of the Concordat, the Catholic Church was no longer an enemy of the French government. At the same time, the agreement reassured those who had acquired church property during the Revolution that they could keep it, an assurance that obviously made them supporters of the Napoleonic regime.

A NEW CODE OF LAWS Before the Revolution, France did not have a single set of laws but rather some three hundred different legal systems. Efforts were made during the Revolution to codify laws for the entire nation, but it remained for Napoleon to bring the work to completion in seven codes, the most important of which was the Civil Code (also known as the Code Napoleon). This preserved most of the revolutionary

Erich Lessing/Art Resource, NY

The Coronation of Napoleon. In 1804, Napoleon restored monarchy to France when he crowned himself emperor. In the coronation scene painted by Jacques-Louis David, Napoleon is shown crowning the empress Josephine while the pope looks on. Shown seated in the box in the background is Napoleon's mother, even though she was not at the ceremony.

gains by recognizing the principle of the equality of all citizens before the law, the right of individuals to choose their professions, religious toleration, and the abolition of serfdom and feudalism. Property rights continued to be carefully protected, while the interests of employers were safeguarded by outlawing trade unions and strikes. The Civil Code clearly reflected the revolutionary aspirations for a uniform legal system, legal equality, and protection of property and individuals. But the Civil Code strictly curtailed the rights of some people. During the radical phase of the French Revolution, new laws had made divorce an easy process for both husbands and wives, restricted the rights of fathers over their children (they could no longer have their children put in prison arbitrarily), and allowed all children (including daughters) to inherit property equally. Napoleon's Civil Code undid most of this legislation. The control of fathers over their families was restored. Divorce was still allowed but was made more difficult for women to obtain. A wife caught in adultery, for example, could be divorced by her husband and even imprisoned. A husband, however, could only be accused of adultery if he moved his mistress into his home. Women were now "less equal than men" in other ways as well. When they married, their property came under the control of their husbands. In lawsuits, they were treated as minors, and their testimony was regarded as less reliable than that of men.

THE FRENCH BUREAUCRACY Napoleon also worked on rationalizing the bureaucratic structure of France by developing a powerful centralized administrative machine. During the Revolution, the National Assembly had divided France into eighty-three departments and replaced the provincial estates, nobles, and *intendants* with self-governing assemblies. Napoleon kept the departments but eliminated the locally elected assemblies and instituted new officials, the most important of which were the **prefects**. As the central government's agents, appointed by the first consul (Napoleon), the prefects were responsible for supervising all aspects of local government. Yet they were not local men, and their careers depended on the central government.

As part of Napoleon's overhaul of the administrative system, tax collection became systematic and efficient (which it had never been under the old regime). Professional collectors employed by the state who dealt directly with each individual taxpayer now collected taxes. No tax exemptions due to birth, status, or special arrangement were granted. In principle, these changes had been introduced in 1789, but not until Napoleon did they actually work. In 1802, the first consul proclaimed a balanced budget.

Administrative centralization required a bureaucracy of capable officials, and Napoleon worked hard to develop one. Early on, the regime showed its preference for experts and cared little whether that expertise had been acquired in royal or revolutionary bureaucracies. Not rank or birth but only demonstrated abilities now determined promotion in civil or military offices. This was, of course, what many bourgeois had wanted before the Revolution. Napoleon, however, also created a new aristocracy based on merit in the state service. Napoleon created 3,263 nobles between 1808 and 1814; nearly 60 percent were military officers, while the remainder came from the upper ranks of the civil service or were other state and local officials. Socially, only 22 percent of Napoleon's aristocracy came from the nobility of the old regime; almost 60 percent were of bourgeois origin.

NAPOLEON'S GROWING DESPOTISM In his domestic policies, then, Napoleon both destroyed and preserved aspects of the Revolution. Although equality was preserved in the law code and the opening of careers to talent, the creation of a new aristocracy, the strong protection accorded to property rights, and the use of conscription for the military make it clear that much equality had been lost. Liberty had been replaced by an initially benevolent despotism that grew increasingly arbitrary. Napoleon shut down sixty of France's seventy-three newspapers and insisted that all manuscripts be subjected to government scrutiny before they were published. Government police even opened the mail.

One prominent writer, Germaine de Staël (zhayr-MEN duh STAHL) (1766–1817), refused to accept Napoleon's growing despotism. Educated in Enlightenment ideas, she set up a salon in Paris that was a prominent intellectual center by 1800. She wrote novels and political works that denounced Napoleon's rule as tyrannical. Napoleon banned her books in France and exiled her to the German states, where she continued to write, although not without considerable anguish at being absent from France. "The universe is in France," she once wrote; "outside it there is nothing." After the overthrow of Napoleon, Germaine de Staël returned to her beloved Paris, where she died two years later.

Napoleon's Empire and the European Response

When Napoleon became consul in 1799, France was at war with a second European coalition of Russia, Great Britain, and Austria. Napoleon realized the need for a pause. He remarked to a Prussian diplomat "that the French Revolution is not finished so long as the scourge of war lasts. . . . I want peace, as much to settle the present French government as to save the world from chaos."[22] The peace he sought was achieved at Amiens (AH-mee-en) in March 1802 and left France with new frontiers and a number of client territories from the North Sea to the Adriatic. But the peace did not last because the British and French both regarded it as temporary and had little intention of adhering to its terms.

In 1803, war was renewed with Britain, which was soon joined by Austria and Russia in the Third Coalition. At the Battle of Ulm in southern Germany in 1805, Napoleon surrounded an Austrian army, which quickly surrendered. Proceeding eastward from Ulm, Napoleon faced a large Russian army under Tsar Alexander I and some Austrian troops at Austerlitz (AWSS-tur-litz). The combined allied forces outnumbered Napoleon's forces, but the tsar chose poor terrain for the battle, and Napoleon devastated the allied forces. Austria sued for peace, and Tsar Alexander took his remaining forces back to Russia.

At first, Prussia had refused to join the Third Coalition, but after Napoleon began to reorganize the German states, Prussia reversed course. Acting quickly, Napoleon crushed the Prussian forces in two battles at Jena (YAY-nuh) and Auerstadt (AU-urr-shtaht) in October 1806 and then moved on to defeat the Russians, who had decided to reenter the fray, at Eylau (Y-lau) and Friedland (FREET-lahnt) in June 1807. The Treaties of Tilsit, signed by Napoleon and the rulers of Prussia and Austria at the beginning of July, ended the fighting and gave the French emperor the opportunity to create a new European order.

NAPOLEON'S GRAND EMPIRE The Grand Empire was composed of three major parts: the French empire, a series of dependent states, and allied states (see Map 19.3). The French empire, the inner core of the Grand Empire, consisted of an enlarged France extending to the Rhine in the east and including the western half of Italy north of Rome. Dependent states included Spain, the Netherlands, the kingdom of Italy, the Swiss Republic, the Grand Duchy of Warsaw, and the Confederation of the Rhine (a union of all German states except Austria and Prussia). Allied states were those defeated by Napoleon and forced to join his struggle against Britain; they included Prussia, Austria, and Russia. Although the internal structure of the Grand Empire varied outside its inner core, Napoleon considered himself the leader of the whole: "Europe cannot be at rest except under a single head who will have kings for his officers, who will distribute his kingdom to his lieutenants."

Within his empire, Napoleon demanded obedience, in part because he needed a common front against the British and in part because his growing egotism required obedience to his will. But as a child of the Enlightenment and the Revolution, Napoleon also sought acceptance everywhere of certain revolutionary principles, including legal equality, religious toleration, and economic freedom. As he explained to his brother Jerome, shortly after making him king of the new German state of Westphalia:

> What the peoples of Germany desire most impatiently is that talented commoners should have the same right to your esteem and to public employments as the nobles, that any trace of serfdom and of an intermediate hierarchy between the sovereign and the lowest class of the people should be completely abolished. The benefits of the Code Napoleon, the publicity of judicial procedure, the creation of juries must

MAP 19.3 Napoleon's Grand Empire in 1810. Napoleon's Grand Army won a series of victories against Austria, Prussia, and Russia that gave the French emperor full or partial control over much of Europe by 1807.

Q On the continent, what is the overall relationship between distance from France and degree of French control, and how can you account for this?

> be so many distinguishing marks of your monarchy. . . . What nation would wish to return under the arbitrary Prussian government once it had tasted the benefits of a wise and liberal administration? The peoples of Germany, the peoples of France, of Italy, of Spain all desire equality and liberal ideas. I have guided the affairs of Europe for many years now, and I have had occasion to convince myself that the buzzing of the privileged classes is contrary to the general opinion. Be a constitutional king.[23]

In the inner core and dependent states of his Grand Empire, Napoleon tried to destroy the old order. Nobility and clergy everywhere in these states lost their special privileges. He decreed equality of opportunity with offices open to talent, equality before the law, and religious toleration. This spread of French revolutionary principles was an important factor in the development of liberal traditions in these countries. These reforms have led some historians to view Napoleon as the last of the enlightened absolutists.

THE PROBLEM OF GREAT BRITAIN Like Hitler 130 years later, Napoleon hoped that his Grand Empire would last for centuries; like Hitler's empire, it collapsed almost as rapidly as it had been formed. Two major reasons help explain this: the survival of Great Britain and the force of nationalism. Britain's survival was due primarily to its sea power. As long as Britain ruled the waves, it was almost invulnerable to military attack. Although Napoleon contemplated an invasion of England and even collected ships for it, he could not overcome the British navy's decisive defeat of a combined French-Spanish fleet at Trafalgar (truh-FAL-ger) in 1805. Napoleon then turned

Museo del Prado, Madrid//Erich Lessing/Art Resource, NY

Francisco Goya, *The Third of May 1808*. After Napoleon imposed his brother Joseph on Spain as its king, the Spanish people revolted against his authority, and a series of riots broke out in Madrid. This painting by Francisco Goya shows the French response—a deliberate execution of Spanish citizens to frighten people into submission. Goya portrays the French troops as a firing squad, killing people (including a monk) reacting in terror. The peasant in the middle throws out his arms in a gesture reminiscent of crucifixion. Goya painted many scenes depicting the horrors of war in Napoleonic Spain.

to his **Continental System** to defeat Britain. Put into effect between 1806 and 1807, it attempted to prevent British goods from reaching the European continent in order to weaken Britain economically and destroy its capacity to wage war. But the Continental System failed. Allied states resented the ever-tightening French economic hegemony; some began to cheat and others to resist, thereby opening the door to British collaboration. New markets in the eastern Mediterranean and in Latin America also provided compensation for the British. Indeed, by 1810, British overseas exports were approaching record highs.

NATIONALISM A second important factor in the defeat of Napoleon was **nationalism**. This political creed had arisen during the French Revolution in the French people's emphasis on brotherhood (*fraternité*) and solidarity against other peoples. Nationalism involved the unique cultural identity of a people based on a common language, religion, and national symbols. The spirit of French nationalism had made possible the mass armies of the revolutionary and Napoleonic eras. But in spreading the principles of the French Revolution beyond France, Napoleon inadvertently brought about a spread of nationalism as well. The French aroused nationalism in two ways: by making themselves hated oppressors, and thus arousing the patriotism of others in opposition to French nationalism, and by showing the people of Europe what nationalism was and what a nation in arms could do. The lesson was not lost on other peoples and rulers. A Spanish uprising against Napoleon's rule, aided by British support, kept a French force of 200,000 pinned down for years.

Nationalist movements also arose in the German states, where a number of intellectuals advocated a cultural nationalism based on the unity of the German people. The philosopher Johann Gottlieb Fichte (yoh-HAHN got-LEEP FIKH-tuh) (1762–1814), who had at first welcomed the French Revolution for freeing the human spirit, soon became a proponent of a German national spirit radically different from that of France. Although philosophical voices like Fichte's did little to overthrow the French, they did awaken a dream of German nationalism that would bear fruit later in the nineteenth century.

In Prussia, feeling against Napoleon led to a serious reform of the old order that had been so easily crushed by the French emperor. As one Prussian officer put it, the Prussians must learn from the French example and "place their entire national energies in opposition to the enemy." Under the direction of Baron Heinrich von Stein (HYN-rikh fun SHYTN) and later Prince Karl von Hardenberg (KARL fun HAR-den-berk), Prussia embarked on a series of political and military reforms, including the abolition of serfdom, election of city councils, and creation of a larger standing army. Prussia's reforms, instituted as a response to Napoleon, enabled it to again play an important role in European affairs.

The Fall of Napoleon

Napoleon once said, "If I had experienced pleasure, I might have rested; but the peril was always in front of me, and the day's victory was always forgotten in the preoccupation with the necessity of winning a new victory on the morrow."[24] Never at rest, Napoleon decided in 1812 to invade Russia. It was the beginning of his downfall, but Russia's defection from the Continental System had left him with little choice. Although aware of the risks in invading such a large country, Napoleon also knew that if the Russians were allowed to challenge the Continental System unopposed, others would soon follow suit. In June 1812, Napoleon's Grand Army of more than 600,000 men entered Russia. Napoleon's hopes for victory depended on quickly meeting and defeating the Russian armies, but the Russian forces refused to give battle and retreated hundreds of miles while torching their own villages and countryside to prevent Napoleon's army from finding food and forage. Heat and disease also took their toll of the army, and the vast space of Russian territory led many troops to desert. When the Russians did stop to fight at Borodino (bor-uh-DEE-noh), Napoleon's forces won an indecisive and costly victory. Forty-five thousand Russian troops were killed; the French lost 30,000 men, but they had no replacements nearby. When the remaining troops of the Grand Army arrived in Moscow, they found the city ablaze. Lacking food and supplies, Napoleon abandoned Moscow late in October and made the "Great Retreat" across Russia in terrible winter conditions. Only 40,000 troops managed to straggle back to Poland in January 1813. This military disaster then led to a war of liberation all over Europe, culminating in Napoleon's defeat in April 1814.

The defeated emperor of the French was allowed to play ruler on the island of Elba, off the coast of Tuscany, while the Bourbon monarchy was restored to France in the person of Louis XVIII, brother of the executed king. But the new king had little support, and Napoleon, bored on Elba, slipped back into France. When troops were sent to capture him, Napoleon opened his coat and addressed them: "Soldiers of the fifth regiment, I am your Emperor. . . . If there is a man among you would kill his Emperor, here I am!" No one fired a shot. Shouting "Vive l'Empéreur! Vive l'Empéreur," the troops went over to his side, and Napoleon entered Paris in triumph on March 20, 1815.

The powers that had defeated him pledged once more to fight this person they called the "Enemy and Disturber of the Tranquillity of the World." Having decided to strike first at his enemies, Napoleon raised yet another army and moved to attack the nearest allied forces stationed in Belgium. At Waterloo on June 18, Napoleon met a combined British and Prussian army under the duke of Wellington and suffered a bloody defeat. This time, the victorious allies exiled him to Saint Helena, a small, forsaken island in the South Atlantic. Only Napoleon's memory would continue to haunt French political life.

CHRONOLOGY	The Napoleonic Era, 1799–1815
Napoleon as first consul	1799–1804
Concordat with Catholic Church	1801
Emperor Napoleon I	1804–1815
Battle of Ulm (defeat of Austria)	1805
Battle of Austerlitz (defeat of Russia)	1805
Battle of Trafalgar (naval defeat of Napoleon's forces)	1805
Battles of Jena and Auerstadt (defeat of Prussia)	1806
Continental System established	1806
Battles of Eylau and Friedland (defeat of Russia)	1807
Invasion of Russia	1812
War of liberation	1813–1814
Exile to Elba	1814
Battle of Waterloo; exile to Saint Helena	1815
Death of Napoleon	1821

CHAPTER SUMMARY

The late eighteenth century was a time of dramatic political transformation. Revolutionary upheavals, beginning in North America and continuing in France, produced movements for political liberty and equality. The documents created by these revolutions, the Declaration of Independence and the Declaration of the Rights of Man and the Citizen, embodied the fundamental ideas of the Enlightenment and set forth a liberal political agenda based on a belief in popular sovereignty—the people as the source of political power—and the principles of liberty and equality. Liberty meant, in theory, freedom from arbitrary power as well as the freedom to think, write, and worship as one chose. Equality meant equality in rights and equality of opportunity based on talent rather than birth. In practice, equality remained limited; men who owned property had great opportunities for voting and officeholding, and there was certainly no equality between men and women.

The leaders of France's liberal revolution during the National and Legislative Assemblies between 1789 and 1791 were men of property, both bourgeois and noble, but they were assisted by commoners, both sans-culottes and peasants. In this first phase

of the Revolution, the old order was demolished as a new constitution established a limited constitutional monarchy. Yet, despite the hopes of the men of property, the liberal revolution was not the end of the Revolution. The decision of the revolutionaries to go to war with European monarchs who opposed the Revolution "revolutionized the revolution," opening the door to a more radical, democratic, and violent stage between 1792 and 1795 under the National Convention led by the Committee of Public Safety. During this phase, revolutionary courts persecuted those not sufficiently supportive of the revolutionary cause, creating the infamous Reign of Terror. The excesses of the Reign of Terror, however, led to a reaction and a government headed by a five-member Directory, which governed from 1795 to 1799. But it satisfied neither the radicals nor the royalists. In 1799, Napoleon Bonaparte overthrew this government and established first the Consulate and then a new monarchy with himself as emperor. Napoleon, while diminishing freedom by establishing order and centralizing the government, shrewdly preserved equality of rights and the opening of careers to talent and integrated the bourgeoisie and old nobility into a new elite of property owners.

The French Revolution defined the modern revolutionary concept. No one had foreseen or consciously planned the upheaval that began in 1789, but after 1789, "revolutionaries" knew that mass uprisings could succeed in overthrowing unwanted governments. The French Revolution became the classic political and social model for revolution. At the same time, the liberal and national political ideals created by the Revolution and spread through Europe by Napoleon's conquests dominated the political landscape of the nineteenth and early twentieth centuries.

CHAPTER TIMELINE

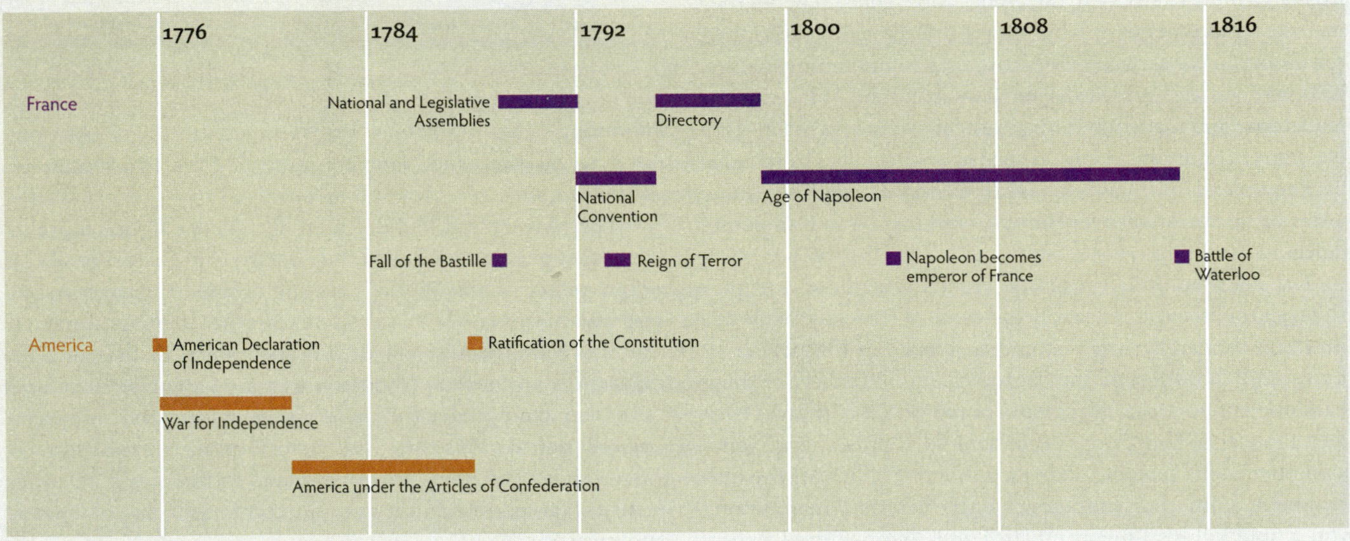

CHAPTER REVIEW

Upon Reflection

Q How was France changed by the revolutionary events of 1789 to 1792, and who benefited the most from these changes?

Q Why did the French Revolution enter a radical phase, and what did that radical phase accomplish?

Q In what ways did Napoleon's policies reject the accomplishments of the French Revolution? In what ways did his policies strengthen the Revolution's accomplishments?

Key Terms

revolution (p. 563)
old order (p. 565)
sans-culottes (p. 573)
Girondins (p. 573)
Mountain (p. 573)
nation in arms (p. 575)
de-Christianization (p. 579)
prefects (p. 585)
Continental System (p. 588)
nationalism (p. 588)

Suggestions for Further Reading

GENERAL WORKS A well-written introduction to the French Revolution can be found in **W. Doyle, *The Oxford History of the French Revolution***, 2nd ed. (Oxford, 2003). On the entire revolutionary and Napoleonic eras, see **O. Connelly, *The French Revolution and Napoleonic Era***, 3rd ed. (Fort Worth, Tex., 2000). A brief work is **J. D. Popkin et al., *A Short History of the French Revolution***, 4th ed. (Upper Saddle River, N.J., 2005). On the French Revolution in global perspective, see **S. Desan, L. Hunt, and W.M. Nelson, eds., *The French Revolution in Global Perspective*** (Ithaca, N.Y., 2013).

EARLY YEARS OF THE REVOLUTION The origins and early years of the French Revolution are examined in **W. Doyle, *Origins of the French Revolution***, 3rd ed. (Oxford, 1999), and **T. Tackett, *Becoming a Revolutionary*** (Princeton, N.J., 1996), on the deputies to the National Assembly. For an interesting insight into Louis XVI and French society, see **T. Tackett, *When the King Took Flight*** (Cambridge, Mass., 2003).

RADICAL REVOLUTION On the radical stage of the French Revolution, see **T. Tackett, *The Coming of the Terror in the French Revolution*** (Cambridge, Mass., 2015), and **D. Andress, *The Terror: The Merciless War for Freedom in Revolutionary France*** (New York, 2005). For a biography of Robespierre, one of the leading figures of this period, see **P. McPhee, *Robespierre: A Revolutionary Life*** (New Haven, Conn., 2013). The importance of the revolutionary wars in the radical stage of the Revolution is underscored in **T. C. W. Blanning, *The French Revolutionary Wars, 1787–1802*** (New York, 1996). On the republican calendar, see **M. Shaw, *Time and the French Revolution*** (Rochester, N.Y, 2011).

WOMEN On the role of women in revolutionary France, see **O. J. Hufton, *Women and the Limits of Citizenship in the French Revolution*** (Toronto, 1992), and **J. Landes, *Women and the Public Sphere in the Age of the French Revolution*** (Ithaca, N.Y., 1988).

NAPOLEON The best biography of Napoleon is **S. Englund, *Napoleon: A Political Life*** (New York, 2004). See also **D. Bell, *Napoleon: A Concise Biography*** (Oxford, 2015), and **A. I. Grab, *Napoleon and the Transformation of Europe*** (New York, 2003), on Napoleon's Grand Empire. On Napoleon's wars, see **O. Connelly, *Blundering to Glory: Napoleon's Military Campaigns***, 3rd ed. (Lanham, Md., 2006), and **D. A. Bell, *The First Total War: Napoleon's Europe and the Birth of Warfare as We Know It*** (Boston, 2007).

AMERICAN REVOLUTION A history of the revolutionary era in America can be found in **S. Conway, *The War of American Independence, 1775–1783*** (New York, 1995), and **C. Bonwick, *The American Revolution*** (Charlottesville, Va., 1991).

Notes

1. Quoted in R. R. Palmer, *The Age of the Democratic Revolutions* (Princeton, N.J., 1959), vol. 1, p. 239.
2. Quoted in ibid., p. 242.
3. Quoted in O. J. Hufton, "Toward an Understanding of the Poor of Eighteenth-Century France," in J. F. Bosher, ed., *French Government and Society, 1500–1850* (London, 1973), p. 152.
4. Arthur Young, *Travels in France During the Years 1787, 1788, and 1789* (Cambridge, 1929), p. 23.
5. Quoted in D. M. G. Sutherland, *France, 1789–1815: Revolution and Counter-Revolution* (New York, 1986), p. 74.
6. Quoted in W. Doyle, *The Oxford History of the French Revolution* (Oxford, 1989), p. 156.
7. Author's translation of *La Marseillaise.*
8. Quoted in W. Doyle, *The Oxford History of the French Revolution*, p. 184.
9. Quoted in J. Hardman, ed., *French Revolution Documents* (Oxford, 1973), vol. 2, p. 23.
10. Quoted in W. Scott, *Terror and Repression in Revolutionary Marseilles* (London, 1973), p. 84.
11. Quoted in H. M. Stephens, *The Principal Speeches of the Statesmen and Orators of the French Revolution* (Oxford, 1892), vol. 2, p. 189.
12. Quoted in L. Gershoy, *The Era of the French Revolution* (Princeton, N.J., 1957), p. 157.
13. Quoted in J. M. Thompson, ed., *French Revolution Documents* (Oxford, 1933), pp. 258–259.
14. Quoted in Doyle, *Oxford History of the French Revolution*, p. 254.
15. Quoted in R. R. Palmer, *Twelve Who Ruled* (New York, 1965), p. 75.
16. Quoted in D. G. Levy, H. B. Applewhite, and M. D. Johnson, eds., *Women in Revolutionary Paris, 1789–1795* (Urbana, Ill., 1979), p. 132.
17. Ibid., pp. 219–220.
18. Quoted in E. G. Sledziewski, "The French Revolution as the Turning Point," in G. Fraisse and M. Perrot, eds., *A History of Women in the West* (Cambridge, 1993), vol. 4, p. 39.
19. Quoted in F. Furet and M. Ozouf, *A Critical Dictionary of the French Revolution*, trans. A. Goldhammer (Cambridge, Mass., 1989), p. 545.
20. Quoted in J. C. Herold, ed., *The Mind of Napoleon* (New York, 1955), p. 43.
21. Quoted in F. Markham, *Napoleon* (New York, 1963), pp. 92–93.
22. Quoted in Doyle, *Oxford History of the French Revolution*, p. 381.
23. Quoted in Herold, ed., *The Mind of Napoleon*, pp. 74–75.
24. Quoted in S. Englund, *Napoleon: A Political Life* (New York, 2004), p. 285.

GLOSSARY

absolutism form of government in which the sovereign power or ultimate authority rested in the hands of a monarch who claimed to rule by divine right and was therefore responsible only to God.

Agricultural (Neolithic) Revolution *see* **Neolithic Revolution.**

agricultural revolution the application of new agricultural techniques that allowed for a large increase in productivity in the eighteenth century.

audiencias advisory groups to viceroys in Spanish America.

balance of power a distribution of power among several states such that no single nation can dominate or interfere with the interests of another.

Baroque an artistic movement of the seventeenth century in Europe that used dramatic effects to arouse the emotions and reflected the search for power that was a large part of the seventeenth-century ethos.

Black Death the outbreak of plague (mostly bubonic) in the mid-fourteenth century that killed from 25 to 50 percent of Europe's population.

boyars the Russian nobility.

Cartesian dualism Descartes's principle of the separation of mind and matter (and mind and body) that enabled scientists to view matter as something separate from themselves that could be investigated by reason.

Catholic Reformation the movement for the reform of the Catholic Church in the sixteenth century. It included a revived papacy; the regeneration of old religious orders and the founding of new ones, most notably the Jesuits; and the reaffirmation of traditional Catholic doctrine at the Council of Trent.

Christian (northern Renaissance) humanism an intellectual movement in northern Europe in the late fifteenth and early sixteenth centuries that combined the interest in the classics of the Italian Renaissance with an interest in the sources of early Christianity, including the New Testament and the writings of the church fathers.

civic humanism an intellectual movement of the Italian Renaissance that saw Cicero, who was both an intellectual and a statesman, as the ideal and held that humanists should be involved in government and use their rhetorical training in the service of the state.

Columbian Exchange the reciprocal importation and exportation of plants and animals between Europe and the Americas.

conciliarism a movement in fourteenth- and fifteenth-century Europe that held that final authority in spiritual matters resided with a general church council, not the pope. It emerged in response to the Avignon papacy and the Great Schism and was used to justify the summoning of the Council of Constance (1414–1418).

condottieri leaders of bands of mercenary soldiers in Renaissance Italy who sold their services to the highest bidder.

confession one of the seven sacraments of the Catholic Church. It provided for the forgiveness of one's sins.

conquistadors "conquerors." Leaders in the Spanish conquests in the Americas, especially Mexico and Peru, in the sixteenth century.

Continental System Napoleon's effort to bar British goods from the continent in the hope of weakening Britain's economy and destroying its capacity to wage war.

cosmopolitan the quality of being sophisticated and having wide international experience.

cottage industry a system of textile manufacturing in which spinners and weavers worked at home in their cottages using raw materials supplied to them by capitalist entrepreneurs.

cultural relativism the belief that no culture is superior to another because culture is a matter of custom, not reason, and derives its meaning from the group holding it.

de-Christianization a policy, adopted in the radical phase of the French Revolution, aimed at creating a secular society by eliminating Christian forms and institutions from French society.

deism belief in God as the creator of the universe who, after setting it in motion, ceased to have any direct involvement in it and allowed it to run according to its own natural laws.

divine-right monarchy a monarchy based on the belief that monarchs receive their power directly from God and are responsible to no one except God.

economic liberalism the idea that government should not interfere in the workings of the economy.

empiricism the practice of relying on observation and experiment.

enclosure acts laws enacted in eighteenth-century Britain that allowed large landowners to enclose the old open fields, thereby combining many small holdings into larger units and forcing many small farmers to become tenant farmers or wage laborers on the large estates.

encomienda in Spanish America, a form of economic and social organization in which a Spaniard was given a royal grant that enabled the holder of the grant to collect tribute from the Indians and use them as laborers.

enlightened absolutism an absolute monarchy in which the ruler followed the principles of the Enlightenment by introducing reforms for the improvement of society, allowing freedom of speech and the press, permitting religious toleration, expanding education, and ruling in accordance with the laws.

Enlightenment an eighteenth-century intellectual movement, led by the philosophes, that stressed the application of reason and the scientific method to all aspects of life.

estates the traditional tripartite division of European society based on heredity and quality rather than wealth or economic standing, first established in the Middle Ages and continuing into the eighteenth century; traditionally consisted of those who pray (the clergy), those who fight (the nobility), and those who work (all the rest).

feminism the belief in the social, political, and economic equality of the sexes; also, organized activity to advance women's rights.

gentry well-to-do English landowners below the level of the nobility. They played an important role in the English Civil War of the seventeenth century.

geocentric conception the belief that the earth was at the center of the universe and that the sun and other celestial objects revolved around the earth.

Girondins a faction in the National Convention during the French Revolution that favored keeping the king alive; so-called because their leaders came from the Gironde in southwestern France.

Great Schism the crisis in the late medieval church when there were first two and then three popes; ended by the Council of Constance (1414–1418).

heliocentric conception the belief that the sun, not the earth, is at the center of the universe.

Hermeticism an intellectual movement beginning in the fifteenth century that taught that divinity is embodied in all aspects of nature; included works on alchemy and magic as well as theology and philosophy. The tradition continued into the seventeenth century and influenced many of the leading figures of the Scientific Revolution.

high culture the literary and artistic culture of the educated and wealthy ruling classes.

Huguenots French Calvinists.

humanism an intellectual movement in Renaissance Italy based on the study of the Greek and Roman classics.

individualism emphasis on and interest in the unique traits of each person.

infanticide the practice of killing infants.

intendants royal officials in seventeenth-century France who were sent into the provinces to execute the orders of the central government.

Janissaries an elite core of eight thousand troops personally loyal to the sultan of the Ottoman Empire.

joint-stock company a company or association that raises capital by selling shares to individuals who receive dividends on their investment while a board of directors runs the company.

justification the primary doctrine of the Protestant Reformation, teaching that humans are saved not through good works but by the grace of God, bestowed freely through the sacrifice of Jesus.

laissez-faire "let (them) do (as they please)." An economic doctrine that holds that an economy is best served when the government does not interfere but allows the economy to self-regulate according to the forces of supply and demand.

Mannerism a sixteenth-century artistic movement in Europe that deliberately broke down the High Renaissance principles of balance, harmony, and moderation.

mercantilism an economic theory that held that a nation's prosperity depended on its supply of gold and silver and that the total volume of trade is unchangeable. Its adherents therefore advocated that the government play an active role in the economy by encouraging exports and discouraging imports, especially through the use of tariffs.

Middle Passage the journey of slaves from Africa to the Americas as the middle leg of the triangular trade.

millenarianism the belief that the end of the world is at hand and the kingdom of God is about to be established on earth.

Modern Devotion a movement founded by Gerard Groote in the fourteenth century, aimed at a practical mysticism based on leading lives serving the needs of fellow human beings.

Mountain a faction in the National Convention during the French Revolution that represented the interests of the city of Paris and favored the execution of the king.

mysticism the immediate experience of oneness with God.

nation in arms the people's army raised by universal mobilization to repel the foreign enemies of the French Revolution.

nationalism a sense of national consciousness based on awareness of being part of a community—a "nation"—that has common institutions, traditions, language, and customs and that becomes the focus of the individual's primary political loyalty.

natural laws a body of laws or specific principles held to be derived from nature and binding on all human societies even in the absence of written laws governing such matters.

natural rights certain inalienable rights to which all people are entitled, including the right to life, liberty, and property; freedom of speech and religion; and equality before the law.

neoclassicism a late-eighteenth-century artistic movement that emerged in France. It sought to recapture the dignity and simplicity of the classical style of ancient Greece and Rome.

Neoplatonism a revival of Platonic philosophy in the third century C.E., associated with Plotinus; a similar revival in the Italian Renaissance, associated with Marsilio Ficino, who attempted to synthesize Christianity and Platonism.

nepotism the appointment of family members to important political positions; derived from the regular appointment of nephews (Latin, *nepos*) by Renaissance popes.

new monarchies the governments of France, England, and Spain at the end of the fifteenth century, whose rulers succeeded in reestablishing or extending centralized royal authority, suppressing the nobility, controlling the church, and insisting on the loyalty of all peoples living in their territories.

old order the political and social system of France in the eighteenth century before the Revolution.

pantheism a doctrine that equates God with the universe and all that is in it.

parlements provincial law courts in France.

patronage the practice of awarding titles and making appointments to government and other positions to gain political support.

philosophes intellectuals of the eighteenth-century Enlightenment who believed in applying a spirit of rational criticism to all things, including religion and politics, and who focused on improving and enjoying this world, rather than on the afterlife.

Pietism a movement that arose in Germany in the seventeenth century whose goal was to foster a personal experience of God as the focus of true religious experience.

pluralism the practice of holding several church offices simultaneously; a problem of the late medieval church.

pogroms organized massacres of Jews.

politiques a group who emerged during the French Wars of Religion in the sixteenth century, placed politics above religion, and believed that no religious truth was worth the ravages of civil war.

popular culture as opposed to high culture, the unofficial written and unwritten culture of the masses, much of which was traditionally passed down orally and centered on public and group activities such as festivals. In the modern age, the term refers to the entertainment, recreation, and pleasures that people purchase as part of the mass consumer society.

portolani charts of landmasses and coastlines made by navigators and mathematicians in the thirteenth and fourteenth centuries.

predestination the belief, associated with Calvinism, that God, as a consequence of his foreknowledge of all events, has predetermined those who will be saved (the elect) and those who will be damned.

prefects officials appointed by the central government to oversee all aspects of a local government during the reign of Napoleon.

price revolution the dramatic rise in prices (inflation) that occurred throughout Europe in the sixteenth and early seventeenth centuries.

primogeniture an inheritance practice in which the eldest son receives all or the largest share of the parents' estate.

procurator the head of the Holy Synod, the chief decision-making body for the Russian Orthodox Church.

Puritans English Protestants inspired by Calvinist theology who wished to remove all traces of Catholicism from the Church of England.

querelles des femmes "arguments about women." A centuries-old debate about the nature of women that continued during the Scientific Revolution as those who argued for the inferiority of women found additional support in the new anatomy and medicine.

rationalism a system of thought based on the belief that human reason and experience are the chief sources of knowledge.

reason of state the principle that a nation should act on the basis of its long-term interests and not merely to further the dynastic interests of its ruling family.

Renaissance "the rebirth" of classical culture that occurred in Italy between ca. 1350 and ca. 1550; also, the earlier revivals of classical culture that occurred under Charlemagne and in the twelfth century.

revolution a fundamental change in the political and social organization of a state.

Rococo an eighteenth-century artistic movement that emphasized grace, gentility, lightness, and charm.

Romanticism a nineteenth-century intellectual and artistic movement that rejected the emphasis on reason of the Enlightenment. Instead, Romantics stressed the importance of intuition, feeling, emotion, and imagination as sources of knowing.

salons gatherings of philosophes and other notables to discuss the ideas of the Enlightenment; so called from the elegant drawing rooms (salons) where they met.

sans-culottes "without breeches." The common people, who did not wear the fine clothes of the upper classes and played an important role in the radical phase of the French Revolution.

scientific method a method of seeking knowledge through inductive principles, using experiments and observations to develop generalizations.

Scientific Revolution the transition from the medieval worldview to a largely secular, rational, and materialistic perspective that began in the seventeenth century and was popularized in the eighteenth.

scutage in the fourteenth century, a money payment for military service that replaced the obligation of military service in the lord-vassal relationship.

secularism the process of becoming more concerned with material, worldly, temporal things and less with spiritual and religious things; a characteristic of the Italian Renaissance.

separation of powers a doctrine enunciated by Montesquieu in the eighteenth century that separate executive, legislative, and judicial powers serve to limit and control each other.

skepticism a doubtful or questioning attitude, especially about religion.

Third Estate one of the traditional tripartite divisions (orders) of European society based on heredity and quality rather than wealth or economic standing, first established in the Middle Ages and continuing into the eighteenth century; consisted of all who were not members of the clergy or nobility (the first two estates).

tithe a portion of one's harvest or income, paid by medieval peasants to the village church.

transubstantiation a doctrine of the Roman Catholic Church that during the Eucharist, the substance of the bread and wine is miraculously transformed into the body and blood of Jesus.

triangular trade a pattern of trade in early modern Europe that connected Europe, Africa, and the Americas in an Atlantic economy.

viceroy the administrative head of the provinces of New Spain and Peru in the Americas.

world-machine Newton's conception of the universe as one huge, regulated, and uniform machine that operated according to natural laws in absolute time, space, and motion.

INDEX

Italicized page numbers show the locations of illustrations and maps.